CULTURE IN MIND

CULTURE IN MIND
Cognition, Culture, and the Problem of Meaning

Bradd Shore

OXFORD UNIVERSITY PRESS
New York   Oxford

"Thirteen Ways of Looking at a Blackbird" and the first four lines from "Anecdote of the Jar" by Wallace Stevens originally appeared in *The Collected Poems of Wallace Stevens* (Alfred A. Knopf, 1994) and are reprinted with the permission of the publisher.

The extensive quote from the journal of La Pérouse in Chapter 11 originally appeared in *The Voyages and Adventures of La Pérouse*, pp. 107–108 (University of Hawaii Press, 1969) and is reprinted with the permission of the publisher.

Figure 9.2 is based on a map appearing originally in Lloyd Warner's *A Black Civilization* (Harper and Row, 1937) and is reprinted with modifications by permission of the publisher.

A number of chapters contain material which I have published elsewhere. The publishers have kindly given permission for the reprinting of extensive passages from the following articles:

"Loading the Bases," *The Sciences*, pp. 10–18, May/June 1990.

"Human Ambivalence and the Structuring of Moral Values," *Ethos* 18:2, pp. 165–179, June 1990.

"Twice Born, Once Conceived: Meaning Construction and Cultural Cognition," *American Anthropologist* 93:1, pp. 10–27, March 1991.

"Marginal Play: Sport at the Borderlands of Time and Space," *International Journal of the Sociology of Sport 29*, pp. 349–366, 1994.

Oxford University Press

Oxford   New York
Athens Auckland Bangkok Bogotá Buenos Aires Calcutta
Cape Town Chennai Dar es Salaam Delhi Florence Hong Kong Istanbul
Karachi Kuala Lumpur Madrid Melbourne Mexico City Mumbai
Nairobi Paris São Paulo Singapore Taipei Tokyo Toronto Warsaw

and associated companies in
Berlin Ibadan

Copyright © 1996 by Oxford University Press

First published in 1996 by Oxford University Press, Inc.
198 Madison Avenue, New York, New York 10016

First issued as an Oxford University Press paperback, 1998.

Oxford is a registered trademark of Oxford University Press, Inc.

Library of Congress Cataloging-in-Publication Data
Shore, Bradd, 1945–
Culture in mind : cognition, culture, and the problem of meaning
Bradd Shore.
p.   cm. Includes bibliographical references.
ISBN 0–19–509597–9; ISBN 0–19–512662–9 (pbk.)
1. Ethnopsychology. 2. Cognition and culture. 3. Social
perception. 4. Symbolic anthropology. I. Title.
GN502.S49 1995 155.8—dc20 95-11828

1 3 5 7 9 8 6 4 2

Printed in the United States of America
on acid-free paper

For Florence Shore
and for
Linda, Emily, and Robert

Acknowledgments

I have been writing this book for six years and thinking about it for as long as I have been an anthropologist. My first contact with the world of cognitive science was as a participant at a 1980 conference on conceptual structures organized by Len Talmy and the Cognitive Science Department at the University of California at San Diego. I had the chance to spend several extraordinary days talking with and listening to George Lakoff, Eleanor Rosch, Len Talmy, Dedre Gentner, Marx Wartofsky, and many other stimulating colleagues from many different disciplines.

My assignment at the conference was to try to characterize the implicit theory of mind that anthropologists employed in their cultural analyses. In such heady company, it soon became clear to me that most of our work in symbolic anthropology proceeded innocent of any well-formed theory of mind whatsoever. It also became apparent from my initial discussions at that conference how important it was to begin to work out a conception of mental representations and processes that took culture seriously. What I did not appreciate then was that even this preliminary project on culture and mind would take up the next fifteen years of my life.

The book was conceived as such in 1988–89, during my residence at the Center for Advanced Study in the Behavioral Sciences in Palo Alto, California. The happy mix of intellectual stimulation and leisure that the center afforded made it possible for me to begin to transform numerous strands of my research and thinking into a coherent form that eventually (and slowly) became this book. My year at the center was made possible by generous grants from Emory University and from The National Science Foundation. Emory University supported the production of the book with a grant from the Graduate School of the Arts and Sciences.

Early versions of most chapters were circulated among friends and other scholars on whose advice I have long depended. Many were presented as seminars at various institutions in the United States and abroad. My students, both graduate and undergraduate, read a preliminary draft of the book in seminars on symbolic anthropology and psychological anthropology at Emory University. I particularly want to thank the students in my 1994 graduate seminar, "Culture and Mind," for their thoughtful reflections on an early manuscript of the book.

The book has benefited from many comments and suggestions from numerous friends, colleagues, and students over the years. Joan Bossert, Bob McCauley, Roy D'Andrade, Fredrik Barth, Alex Hinton, Donald Harper-Jones, Mary Murrell, Jerome Bruner, and George Lakoff, as well as several anonymous reviewers, read through an early draft of the book in its entirety. The final version, much altered and somewhat trimmed, has benefited greatly from their many comments and suggestions. Individual chapters were read by George Armelagos, Peter Brown, Jean Comaroff, James Clifford, Steven Cook, Alessandro Duranti, Shelly Errington, Richard Feinberg, Sir Raymond Firth, Alan Fiske, Irving Goldman, Roger Green, Stephen Harper, Cameron Hay, Allan Henderson, Alexander Hinton, Ian Keen, Janet Keller, Bruce Knauft, Howard Morphy, Kevin Morrison, Clara Mucci, Nancy Munn, Ulric Neisser, Charles Nuckolls, Robert Paul, Katrina Poetker, Elizabeth Povinelli, Mark Rijsford, Barbara Rogoff, Ann Salmond, Edward Schieffelin, David Schneider, Robert Scott, Ian Shapiro, Judith Shapiro, Warren Shapiro, Rima Shore, Daniel Smith, Richard Shweder, Michael Tomasello, Anna Tsing, Donald Verene, and Stanley Walens. I am grateful and indebted for all the help and advice offered over the years, though obviously I alone remain responsible for the use I have made of their counsel and for what finally came of it.

I owe a special debt of thanks to my student and friend Kevin Morrison for his critique of an early draft of Chapter 3. I was so impressed with his perceptive and eloquent reconstruction of my analysis of baseball through the eyes of a player that I asked him to contribute a chapter to this book. While ultimately space limitations forced the abridgement of this chapter into a small section of Chapter 3, our conversations about the game had a great influence on my own understanding, not just of baseball but of the whole notion of how cultural models are positioned.

Several of the chapters have appeared in one form or another in other publications. An abridged version of Chapter 2 appeared as "Loading the Bases" in *The Sciences* (May–June 1990). An earlier version of what became Chapter 4 was presented as a keynote address at the 1993 annual seminar of the International Committee of the Sociology of Sport in Vienna. It was published in the *International Journal of the Sociology of Sport* as "Marginal Play: Sport at the Borderlands of Time and Space." Much of the material from Chapters 7 and 8 originally appeared in a 1989 article titled "Totem as Practically Reason: Food for Thought," published in *Dialectical Anthropology* (vol. 14). The entire issue was part of a two-volume festschrift in honor of Irving Goldman, to whom my essay was dedicated. Chapter 12 contains material that, in quite different form, appeared in two published essays, a 1990 article "Human Ambivalence and the Structuring of Moral Values" (*Ethos*, vol. 18, no. 3) and an essay titled "The Absurd Side of Power in Samoa" to appear in a forthcoming volume, *Changing Patterns of Leadership in the Pacific*, edited by Richard Feinberg and Karen Watson-Gegeo. The seeds of Chapters 13 and 14 were planted in a 1990 article "Twice-Born, Once Conceived: Meaning Construction and Cultural Cognition," published in the *American Anthropologist* (vol. 94, no. 4).

A special note of thanks goes to Peggy Barlett, chair of the anthropology department at Emory University during 1993–94, who allowed me to juggle my teaching obligations to make possible a much-needed space to complete the manuscript. Walter Lippincott, director of the Princeton University Press, and Joan Bossert, my editor at Oxford, both took a keen interest in the book from the time they saw a few rough early chapters back in 1989. Their faith in the project and encouragement over the long period of writing and revising were critical factors in the book's completion. A special note of thanks is due to Joan Bossert, who, as the acquiring editor, was not obliged to do any copy editing at all but nevertheless undertook the arduous job of reading through the long mauscript with a careful eye for clarity and readability.

My wife, Linda, and my children, Emily and Robert, know all too well how many hundreds of hours this book has taken from my life with them. For their patience with my absurd hours and for keeping me whole and honest throughout the long gestation of this book, there really is no adequate thanks. In so many ways this book is theirs.

Contents

Foreword, Jerome Bruner, xiii

I THE PROBLEM OF CULTURE IN MIND

Introduction, 3

    1 The Psychic Unity Muddle, 15

    2 Rethinking Culture as Models, 42

II THE COGNITIVE LANDSCAPE OF MODERNITY

    3 Mind Games: Cognitive Baseball, 75

    4 Playing with Rules: Sport at the Borderlands of Time and Space, 101

    5 Interior Furnishings: Scenes from an American Foundational Schema, 116

    6 Technological Trends: The Neuromantic Frame of Mind, 136

III RETHINKING "PRIMITIVE CLASSIFICATION"

    7 Totem as Practically Reason: Rationality Reconsidered, 167

    8 Kwakiutl Animal Symbolism: Food for Thought, 188

IV DREAMTIME LEARNING

    9 Dreamtime Learning, Inside-Out: The Narrative of the Wawilak Sisters, 207

    10 Dreamtime Learning, Outside-In: Murngin Age-Grading Rites, 236

V THE PROBLEM OF MULTIPLE MODELS

    11 Tropic Landscapes: Alternative Spatial Models in Samoan Culture, 265

    12 When Models Collide: Cultural Origins of Ambivalence, 284

VI CULTURE IN MIND

    13 Culture and the Problem of Meaning, 311

    14 Analogical Transfer and the Work of Culture, 343

Epilogue: The Ethnographic Mind, 374

Bibliography, 383

Index, 413

Foreword

Jerome Bruner

The historical separation of anthropology and psychology, whatever may have caused it, must surely be counted as one of the most stunting developments in the history of the human sciences. It would be comforting to say that it is only in recent times that its baleful effects have been felt. But that it is not really so. We are probably more conscious of these affects now because the Cognitive Revolution has made us newly aware, on both sides of the divide, of what we had been missing. And this book, *Culture in Mind,* must be counted as a major event in the reopening of the frontier between the two disciplines. If it does not settle all the questions about culture and mind that have classically and famously troubled psychologists and anthropologists alike, at least it relocates them in a way that gives real promise of progress. And it does so powerfully and without recourse to any of the tiresome old clichés about "mind internalizing culture" or about the progression, so-called, from the "primitive" to the cultivated mind. And perhaps most important of all, it is a book that thrives on coexistence: Professor Shore makes plain that the study of man requires a division of labor between, indeed a consortium of, psychology and anthropology—not to mention computational scientists and neurophysiologists.

The separation of anthropology and psychology as two free-standing disciplines is full of historical ironies, and it is a story well told in the opening chapters of this book. In spite of their staking out separate territories of inquiry, the two disciplines were never able to ignore each other or, better, never able to resist raids into the other's territory. Just as anthropologists got repeatedly hung up in trying to define "the primitive mind" and the limits of rationality, so psychologists foundered in their efforts to "explain" culture by reference to the human impulse to conformity. But conformity to *what?* Given the individualistic ontology of psychology—witness the famously bitter rejection of the "group mind" in the early 1920s—it remained obscure what it was "out there" that individuals were conforming to. So increasingly, psychology took the low road of assuming that all things mental could be explained from the inside out, while anthropologists opted for the high road—that the life of mind could only be approached from the outside in. I still recall ruefully my colleague Clyde Kluckhohn shaking his finger at me and angrily spluttering, "You psychologists think there is no reality outside the skin."

In time, two philosophies of inquiry emerged, both of them defensive. The anthropological one was dedicated to interpreting field observations and the narratives of informants in a manner to capture their *local* generality and systematicity, the "-emic" view of the world seen from inside the culture. Context sensitivity was the paragon virtue. The psychologist, on the other hand, sought to explain isolated mental processes studied experimentally in the presumably context-free setting of the laboratory—or, as an anthropologist friend once put it, "in the culture of the dark room." So psychological theories of memory were devised to fit the canonized results that are obtained when you compel Western, literate undergraduates (at pain of not receiving credit in their introductory psychology course) to commit to memory nonsense syllables presented to them while seated alone in front of a memory drum that clicks out target syllables at, say, one each three seconds. The "culture free" claim, of course, is that this was memory-without-meaning. let it be said that thoughtful scholars on both sides of the divide despaired. The very founder of "experimental psychology," Wilhelm Wundt, eventually defected and spent his last years writing a multivolumed Völkerpsychologie in which he proclaimed the autonomous status of such cultural products as language, myths, and the like. Others—like Ignace Meyerson in France, F. C. Bartlett in Britain, and, of course, George Herbert Mead in America—sought ways of encompassing cultural product and individual psychological process in a common theory. And, in parallel, reflective anthropologists also tried to bridge the gap—Boas, Benedict, and most recently and importantly, Clifford Geertz. Not everybody was prepared to march to the music of Kroeber's claim that anthropology must exclusively concern itself with the "superorganic."

More deeply, alas, the divergence between the two disciplines obscured some profound philosophical issues that were, in fact, common to them both, issues inherent in the very study of man, where man perforce is both inquirer and subject of the inquiry. These are issues that have become particularly prominent in the last decade or two. Is an anthropologist's or psychologist's conception of mind or society ever independent of his or her own culture? Can a Western anthropologist, say Clifford Geertz in his *The Anthropologist as Author,* really do full meta-anthropological justice to his fellow Western anthropologists, given that they all swim in a common cultural stream? Can we stand as judges of the adequacy of prototype and feature theories of conceptualization without our own cultural linings showing? Does one (particularly in the human sciences) really set out innocently, as Newton put it, on a sea of ignorance in order to "discover" the islands of truth? Have we finally wakened from Newton's sleep? Perhaps the sea of ignorance is a product of our use of mind, and the islands of truth nothing more (or less) than recognizing what we already know or have come to expect.

But such postmodern conjectures may not be as dizzying as they seem. In certain ways, they yield to pragmatic steadfastness. There may be no universal, culture-free foundational truths about kinship or memory or concept formation, but at least we can know whether our versions of these matters are *right* for the purposes we have set for ourselves. That much self-consciousness, while it may not vault us beyond the limits imposed by perspective, at least can save us from false realism. But a pragmatic approach to truth and reality gets us into deep water in yet another sea of troubles.

For it runs counter to human intuition to hold that the truth about reality is only a matter of pragmatics, limited by the uses to which it is put. There is something irresistibly tempting about Newton's "islands of truth" just being there. People die and murder, nurture and protect, go to any extreme, in behalf of their conception of the real. More to the point, perhaps, they live out the details of their daily lives in terms of what they conceive to be real: not just rocks and mountains and storms at sea, but friendship, love, respect are known as false or real. Indeed, we *institute* such intersubjective realities, even give them embodiment in the layout of the village, in forms of address, in ritual and myth. This is the domain of meaning making, without which human beings in every culture fall into terror. The product of meaning making is Reality.

So how human beings construct their meanings needs necessarily to be at the center of the study of the human condition—whether in anthropology or psychology. That it has not often been so should be no surprise. For the so-called "problem of meaning" (as it is always referred to) is fraught with complexities. It has been famously resistant to analysis. And we are so immersed in it that it is hard to distance ourselves from it enough to reflect on it—like the fish who will be the last to discover water. Professor Shore recalls the stunning dialogue in which Meno answers Socrates' question about the nature of virtue by giving examples, while demurring on the general question. Socrates chides him: How could Meno choose examples if he did not know what virtue was in general? From which, of course, grew Meno's Paradox, what today we refer to as the *hermeneutic circle*. And so it is with inquiries into the nature of meaning itself. We can exemplify, abstract aspects of it (like literal and metaphoric meanings, or analogic and analytic meanings, and the rest) but are hard put to pose the issue of what meaning *is* and how we construct it (or them). But things are changing.

Meaning making is the leitmotif of this deeply moving yet often disturbing book—disturbing in reminding us of our past evasions and derelictions. The book is about the construction of meanings as products of individual human cognition and of human cultures. For meanings, to use Bradd Shore's challenging expression, are always "twice born." They are instituted in culture—the communal or canonical meaning *of* some thing or act or utterance, and the idiosyncratic meaning *for* some individual on some occasion. The challenge for the sciences of man, whether anthropology or psychology or, for that matter, linguistics and history, is to understand how these two aspects of meaning construction interact to ensure both a shared communal life and, at the same time, to permit the idiosyncratic play of individual imagination. This is the challenge at the focus of Professor Shore's inquiry.

He pursues it relentlessly over an astonishingly wide and sometimes exceedingly rough terrain, and does so with a firm tread. For he knows not only of anthropological matters, but of cognitive psychological ones as well. His discussions range from the systematicity of spatial meanings in Murngin "walkabouts" and Samoan village layouts, to the process of analogical thinking, in the course of which he may examine (knowledgeably) the promise of connectionist computational models for simulating analogical thought or the claims of neuroscientists to have a handle on the problem. Indeed, I found the discussion of some of the technical issues relating to the architec-

ture and functioning of individual human thought and culturally shared language so
lucid and suggestive that at one point I 'phoned Professor Shore to tease him about
crediting some writers with insights they should have had but didn't. This book
makes invigorating reading: tough, graceful, well informed, witty. I was struck, for
example, at Shore's forceful recounting of the contradiction between Saussure's insistent claim about the arbitrariness of semiotic signs when put against C. S. Peirce's
equally famous discussion of the threefold form of the *interpretant* in human sign
systems, at least two of which are nonarbitrary. But I must not tip the author's hand
any further.

The breadth and the timeliness of this excellent book, however radiantly they
may reflect the author's scholarship, cannot be attributed to his diligence and perspic-
uousness alone! As with most cultural matters—and scholarly books are cultural matters *par excellence*—*Culture in Mind* is very much a child of its time. The weather
has been breeding it. The last quarter century of primatological research, for example, has taught us that the evolution of the human mind is best conceived as a hominid adaptation of a cultural way of life, even more specifically, to a way of life
constrained by systems of culturally shared or *instituted* meanings. We know, too,
thanks to the work inspired by Piaget and his critics alike, that the ontogenesis of
meaning making involves a slow, orderly, highly systematic, but uneven development from, roughly, analogical to propositional thinking. And we now recognize,
though it eluded Piaget, that this uneven progression is powerfully shaped by the
demands of the culture in which we grow up—e.g., Western culture's requirement
that we always be able to "explain" ourselves to others probably accounting for why
we end up with such facility in propositional thinking, a facility by no means universal in all cultures. We also know that different domains of human experience are
privileged according to their place in the culture's instituted meaning system, and
that knowledge acquired in one domain does not automatically get "transferred" to
other domains. Propositional rationality, an idealized Enlightenment conception of
the powers of the human mind, is nowhere (save in such specialized pursuits as
mathematics) either the majoritarian fact or even the universal ideal of human
thought, whether looked at individually or as instituted in the culture. We make
human experiences meaningful by the narratives we bring to bear on them, and almost universally these narratives reflect (though they do not mirror) the "stored"
foundational narratives of the culture, altered imaginatively to fit the occasion and
its needs.

These are the kinds of findings and issues that preoccupy contemporary students
of the human sciences—be they neuroscientists concerned with modeling the myriad
analogical routes through which we recognize "similarities" in the world, behavioral
geneticists puzzled by the uniformities in human action left unexplained by current
genetic doctrines, or cognitive scientists trying to account for the alternation between
our holistic processing of perceptual Gestalten and our tendency to analyze the world
of experience into features so as to categorize it in a more rule-bound way. But it
hardly ends there, for I have hardly touched on the weather created by anthropologists. Thanks to their work, we begin to understand the seeming contradiction between claims for the "psychic unity of mankind" and for "cultural relativism." Given
a certain view of human mental function, they may be peas in the same pod. Even
Levy-Bruhl's conception of "participation" as an aspect of indigenous thinking merits

rethinking, despite our earlier embarrassment with its condescension when it was rendered rhetorically into the doctrine of "the primitive mind." A subway ride to a small claims court can get you into the vicinity of such thinking; you need not fly to the South Seas. We are even overcoming our hang-up on the issue of "rationality." Professor Shore suggests that anthropologists revisit the "ethnosciences" again, this time concentrating on "ethnopsychology"—for how a people believe the mind works will, we now know, have a profound effect on how in fact it is *compelled* to work if anybody is to get on in a culture. And that fact, ironically, may indeed turn out to be a robust cultural universal.

Indeed, Professor Shore does not evade the issue of universals, though he gives it a most original spin. I shall not try to condense his interesting argument, save to say that he sees deep significance in the interplay between implicit cultural foundations, patterned cultural practices, and the forming of personal concepts, an interplay mediated by cognitive processes that we now begin to understand. There is not only room for psychologists and anthropologists (and their close cousins—linguists, computer scientists, and neurophysiologists) in his vision of the human sciences. In his view, their collaboration is an essential part of the future. You may not agree with Bradd Shore's premises in detail, or even see their broad outlines somewhat differently. But what is plain as day is that our ways of life as students of humankind will be changed by what he has had to say.

I

THE PROBLEM OF CULTURE
IN MIND

Introduction

The implications are, quite literally, mind-bending. At birth, the human brain weighs a mere 25 percent of its eventual adult weight. This is a curious state of affairs for the brainiest of the primates. A macaque, by contrast, is born with a brain that is 60 percent of its adult weight. Its neural growth has already slowed dramatically while still in utero. Even our closest primate relation, the chimpanzee, is born with about 45 percent of its brain weight already developed, and its brain growth slows down shortly after birth. Chimps mature both physically and socially years ahead of their human cousins.[1]

Among primates, only the human brain continues to grow at fetal rates *after birth,* and the frantic pace of this postpartum neural building boom continues for the first two years of life before it begins to show any signs of abating. The cortex's natural insulation, the fatty myelin sheath that grows about the axons and permits efficient conduction of electrical impulses, is not completely formed until about the sixth year of life. Only at puberty is the physical maturation of the human brain complete. After that, neural development continues throughout life. But this is, strictly speaking, more a matter of "mind" than of brain.

This delayed maturation of the human nervous system is paralleled by a general developmental retardation of the human child compared with other primates. Humans also show a tendency to both physiological and behavioral neoteny, retaining juvenile traits in adult forms of both anatomy (i.e., head-body ratio) and behavior (i.e., playfulness).

This combination of premature birth and retarded development means that fully three-quarters of the human brain develops outside the womb, in direct relationship with an external environment. Evolution has equipped our species with an "ecological brain," dependent throughout its life on environmental input. This is a factor of extraordinary significance for cultural anthropology and cognitive psychology alike.

The human nervous system has presumably been preadapted by evolution for many perceptual skills. Take, for example, common human visual abilities like binocular vision, depth perception, back and forth translations between three-

3

dimensional visual images and two-dimensional representations, mental rotation of imagery, or perceptual coordination of sight, sound, and touch. Though the human sensorium seems to be genetically prepared for such visual acrobatics, actual feats of perception must be brought to life through an individual's concrete interactions with the world. People blind from birth who eventually gain vision through medical procedures can immediately "see" by means of their eyes but have to learn by practical experience to "perceive" actual forms and to coordinate perceptual relations between sight and other senses like touch.

The eco-logical brain does not develop simply in a natural environment. Our nervous system unfolds in relation to two quite different kinds of environment, the one more "natural" and the other more cultural. Basic cognitive skills like perception, classification, and inference have evolved in the species and develop in individuals as ways in which a particular kind of body (a human body) interacts with the contours of a particular kind of physical world.

Ecological psychology studies ways in which the human sensorium is pre-adapted to the "affordances" (i.e., the interactive possibilities and constraints) of such a generalized human life-space. Just as a toddler's foot and leg muscles must learn to balance and carry an upright body over a complex and ever-changing terrain, so the human sensorium has learned to "read" its physical environment in the (evolutionary) process of interacting with it.

At the same time, neural development also takes place within very particular and variable *sociocultural environments*. Cross-cultural psychologists have demonstrated that even basic aspects of perception are influenced by the way that experience is "modeled" by a particular sociocultural environment (Cole and Scribner, 1974). These "cultural models" might be usefully thought of as "cultural affordances," equivalent to the physical affordances of the natural environment.

For example, individuals growing up in cultures lacking two-dimensional realistic art must learn how to recognize images when presented with photographs. Similarly, there is evidence that people raised in "carpentered environments" (with lots of measured, regular angles and straight lines) tend to be fooled by certain optical illusions in a way that is not generally true for those raised in visually "natural" environments lacking artificial lines and angles and with no experience of two-dimensional representations. One cross-cultural psychologist who has studied cultural differences in numerous perceptual skills concluded that "ecological demands and cultural practices are significantly related to the development of perceptual skills. . . . In some sense, cultural and psychological development are congruent (Berry, 1967:228, quoted in Cole and Scribner, 1974:85).

So an important part of the evolutionary heritage of the sapient hominid is a nervous system that has evolved under the sway of culture (in general) and which develops in each individual under the sway of *a* culture (in particular). The human nervous system appears to be dependent on external models or programs for normal operation, and this notion of models has significant importance for anthropologists and psychologists alike.

Both cognitive psychology and cultural anthropology have employed the concepts of models and schemas. Since Bartlett's classic work on memory, psychologists have taken the Kantian notion of mental schemas or models as important components of any account of memory and learning. For their part, cultural anthropologists since

Benedict's early writings have employed a notion of "cultural patterns" (also called cultural templates, models, and schemas) to describe specific organizations of cultural artifacts (including symbolic artifacts) and the psychological patterns derived from them. While the anthropologist's uses of these concepts were derived from psychology, these terms came to represent *both* "external" institutions (culture-in-the-world) *and* "internal" mental representations (culture-in-the-mind). Little attention was given to the complexities of their relationship.

The idea of a "cultured brain" has some far-reaching implications not only for how anthropologists need to think about culture but also for how psychologists and philosophers need to think about the mind. This is not simply the problem of thinking about culture *and* mind but specifically the challenge of conceptualizing culture *in* mind. This is an ethnographic conception of the mind.

QUESTIONS ABOUT PSYCHIC UNITY

This book is the fruit of a very personal journey into this relationship between culture and mind. Long before I knew anything about anthropology, curiosity about cultural differences drew me far from home. Years later it was the question of "the psychic unity" of our species—the degree to which we could characterize human psyche as essentially the same despite the effects of cultural differences—that brought me to anthropology for answers. The original appeal of cultural differences for me was, to be sure, rooted in a romantic attachment to the exotic "other."

It was not until 1969, and my arrival in Western Samoa as a Peace Corps volunteer, that I had a serious encounter with a culture other than my own. Here I experienced not just *a* culture but the *idea of culture,* which I had only dimly understood. I had finally achieved what I had long wanted, to live among people very different from myself. But I was not at all prepared for the reality of cultural difference. What had seemed so appealing from afar was now incomprehensible and disturbing.

Early on I encountered the "psychic unity" puzzle. Back then, of course, I had no such label for what was troubling me. Were these people among whom I was to live for five years of the same "mind" as myself? Did they think like me and feel what I felt? Could I make sense of their reactions to things and predict what would happen next in any given situation? How were these differences related to those I had experienced between different individuals in my own culture? Back home, these issues had never really come up. Yet here the cultural framework of thought, feeling, and action suddenly seemed obvious. And it was everywhere. Having never before experienced such an apparent gap between my own reactions and expectations and those of the people around me, my first intuition was that these folks had a mind-set unlike any other I had ever encountered. I struggled for almost a year trying to make sense of a social and cultural world of which I had pitifully little understanding and even less control. The psyche, I concluded, was "cultured" all the way down and could never be adequately charactererized apart from the profound influences of culture.

But the questions about mind and culture were not to be so simply resolved. A year passed, then two. I went home to pursue graduate studies and returned to Samoa three years later armed with a little training in anthropology. Gradually my Samoan had improved and windows began to open for me onto a world I had not imagined existed. I paid more attention to patterns of thought and action that had begun to make themselves known to me. I began to sort things out and make sense of my surroundings. "The Samoan mind" was no longer such a practical problem for me. In fact, I began to notice how much Samoans differed among themselves in ways I could never have seen earlier on. I came to understand that Samoans often experienced the limits of their own culture, and that they sometimes felt great ambivalence about their own cultural forms. Great self-parodists, Samoans could make fun of themselves, as if they saw themselves from the outside. When we laughed together like this, I began to feel at home in Samoa.

The gradual blurring of the boundary between my mind and theirs meant that I was changing. I had begun to intuit the shape of complex cultural patterns—what I would someday call "cultural models"—patterns that governed conventional behavior and that Samoans largely took for granted. I began to understand how time and space were organized and what I had to do to move through them without making people laugh or squirm uncomfortably. I came to understand that, for Samoans, many emotional responses were orchestrated by local emotion models different from those I was used to. Samoans also had their own ways of explaining things, what we might call local "causal theories," that eventually began to make sense to me. A significant realization was that the ways Samoans talked about people suggested a conception of the person quite different from that which I was carrying around in my own head. I found myself walking differently and sitting differently as my body responded to new ways of understanding the "meaning" of posture. And so on.

What I learned in those first years abroad would radically alter my understanding of the psychic unity problem. The issues seemed far more complex and puzzling than I had assumed. I found myself constantly flip-flopping on the matter of psychic unity. Sometimes I was certain that Samoans had a mind of their own. At other times I was equally convinced that we were all of a common mind. I eventually came to realize that I was not really flip-flopping. I was just experiencing different aspects of the mind. The longer I lived in Samoa, the more I was able to use the Samoans' cultural resources to reconstruct my own mental models. As the months turned into years, the flow of my everyday experiences was increasingly filtered through Samoan models rather than those I had brought with me. Things gradually took on new meanings that they had not had for me in my first months in the Islands.

I was experiencing two quite different dimensions of mind. There were the exotic orchestrations of thought, feeling, and sensory experience that had initially separated me from those around me. These were Samoan cultural models and they came in many forms. During formal gatherings, I would sit cross-legged, rigidly upright for hours on end, inside a large, open meetinghouse. I could feel the rough weave of mats under me, and the coarse curve of my designated house post made a lasting impression on my back. I would fan away flies, and periodically I would stretch out my legs politely to one side, seeking relief from the pain and numbness. My senses swarmed with smells of coconut-oiled bodies and the acrid smoke from the cooking huts. The cadences of Samoan oratory coursed in and out of practical matters, always returning to the poetic forms that encapsulated all formal talk.

Though few recognized such ineffable patterns of experience as part of Samoan culture, these sensory gestalts were cultural models in their own right. They exercised a powerful influence over my own experience of being and place and to this day evoke memories of Samoa far more potent than those summoned up by many more obvious cultural models. None of these things were part of the usual anthropological account of culture. From this vantage point, there was no question of any simple psychic unity between cultures.

At the same time, I was discovering the importance of basic human processes of meaning construction and information processing. Without such shared cognitive processes, I could never have had access to a Samoan frame of mind. Just as I was gradually reconstructing my own mind-set "on the fly," so too were Samoans busy trying to make sense out of these new *pālagi* visitors who had fanned out all over their islands. We were all using our cultural and cognitive resources to construct meanings out of anomalous experiences, and it was here that we were all on common ground. Contrary to structuralist dogma, I discovered that meaning is not given to us ready-made, simply immanent either in cultural forms or in the mind. Meaning could be understood only as an ongoing process, an active construction by people, with the help of cultural resources. Viewed in this way, the study of cultural forms became for me not an end in itself but rather a necessary part of the study of the intentional process I call "meaning construction."

Anthropology's conventional wisdom understands our species' basic psychic unity as humanity's shared psychobiological endowment. According to this view, psychic diversity becomes the specific contents of the mind. This view is not exactly wrong. But the conventional Western metaphor, dividing the mind into container and contents, does not strike me as an adequate or illuminating account of culture's contribution to mind. Even at the level of cortical functioning, the metaphor will not (to exploit the image) hold water. The brain is not an inert lump of matter. Nor is it a passive recording device. And it is not a waiting shell into which specific contents are dumped. As Laughlin et al. have recently argued, "any view that construes learning as a process of pouring of information into a passive, 'floppy disk' brain, where it is then absorbed and stored in memory, is a totally outmoded and erroneous view" (1992:66). Far from a passive storage device, the living brain is a hierarchically organized, pattern-seeking, and pattern-generating organ ablaze with networks of electrochemical discharge. It is an adaptive and opportunistic information processor that transforms its data into meaningful patterns. To the extent that these patterned neural networks are altered through learning, it becomes difficult to clearly distinguish the container from the contents.

As for the mind, it is best understood as a relationship between the nervous system and a large set of models, both internal and external, on which it feeds (forward and back). This book takes the position that variations in cultural cognition can be traced to important local differences in the specific models and general schemas that constrain ordinary perception and understanding. In addition, I argue that there are cultural and historical differences in the distribution of analytic and nonanalytic modes of thought. These distributions are socially legitimated as an aspect of the sociology of knowledge in any community.

None of this evidence of psychic diversity throws into question the simplest meaning of "psychic unity"—that humans all share a common nervous system and that important cognitive entailments follow from this. Nor does it require us to resurrect outworn notions about cultural differences in cognitive capacity or totalizing "mentalities" (the vexing "primitive mentality" issue) that are held to distinguish different populations. What it does mean, however, is that the place of cultural models in mind can never be relegated to a kind of window-dressing over some primordial human hardware understood as the "real" meaning of mind.

Clifford Geertz was right when he insisted that we understand the mind as naturally located outside the head, in the midst of social life. But it is equally true that these culturally orchestrated landscapes are also to be found inscribed as dimensions of the mind. This is why cognitive science is unavoidably an ethnographic enterprise. It is also why the interpretation of cultures in particular has much to tell us about the character of the mind in general.

DEEP TROUBLE

This book's title is in part a plea to both cognitive scientists and anthropologists to keep culture in mind in the several senses of the phrase. It is telling that a cultural anthropologist should feel the need to defend, among his own colleagues, the significance of culture—a concept that has long been at the heart of anthropology. But the concept of culture, long the defining idea of our discipline, is in deep trouble. Over the last several decades, cultural anthropology has undergone several profound makeovers as it has made its way through some of the main intellectual and political currents of the late twentieth century.

Since the early 1980s, anthropologists have led the assault on their own scholarly traditions, attacking the ahistorical and apolitical representation of cultural forms that often characterized traditional ethnography. In part, the crisis has to do with the fact that our main unit of analysis has become harder to identify. So-called traditional cultures have transformed themselves before our eyes, so that historical analysis has supplanted synchronic cultural analysis as a privileged genre in our discipline. In the process, the presumed unity of culture has unraveled. Anthropologists have come to question the degree to which we can assume culture to be shared within a community in the face of competing interest groups and politically positioned individuals.

Our conception of culture as a master narrative has given way to a stress on competing voices or discourses. Attention has turned to the political processes whereby certain of these voices marginalize others as they achieve political and intellectual hegemony. Anthropology's postmodern identity crisis has been profoundly shaped by Michel Foucault's view of history as the flow of power mediated through competing "epistemes" understood as "discourses."

In its recent turbulent history, anthropology has simply mirrored the upheavals in the world at large. In the academy as in the world, forces of cultural and political homogenization from the center vie with the forces of differentiation coming from the periphery. Marginalized voices have forced their way to center stage not only in ethnography but in the world's political arena. Close to home, attention to issues of gender and ethnic diversity have profoundly changed how we understand our own world. At the same time as these concerns with "difference" have profoundly relativized our own knowledge frames, technological and economic trends have had the opposite effect of homogenizing knowledge. Differences come and just as quickly they seem to evaporate as rapidly proliferating information technologies promise to put everyone on the same wavelength, making all knowledge potentially simultaneous and available to all.

In terms of global politics, the decolonization process of the last forty years has entered a new phase in the 1990s, with a wave of often violent independence movements by marginalized groups from within the borders of political states. The world's cartographers have struggled to keep up with the shape of changing or contested political borders as differences come and go. The legitimacy of the basic units of international politics has come into question. Yet at the same moment as political distinctions proliferate, the concentration of capital strengthens the hold of the "world system." Processes of ethnic differentiation are paralleled by equally potent processes of economic homogenization and cultural globalization.

The ironies proliferate. Coke and Pepsi quickly make their way back into recently liberated South Africa. Knowing how the world works, the forces of liberation from the margins make way for the return of capital investment at the center. Just as technology, transportation, and the power of world capital conspire to overwhelm the world's cultural diversity, creating a global mass culture with Western commodities at its heart, a growing worldwide "fundamentalism" proclaims not only the legitimacy of sacred over secular authority but also the authority of "ethnic" claims of local groups over the "political" claims of modern states. Cultural differences dissolve on one stage only to reappear with vengeance on another. Both political liberation and ethnic genocide are the joint fruits of the new fundamentalism, and they are not always easy to tell apart.

To the extent that the field of anthropology has responded to these changes in the world it studies (and which also produces it), these theoretical shifts are constructive adaptations of a discipline to new challenges. The intense self-examination of anthropology has also made visible social voices and processes that earlier ethnographic practice had muted or left out altogether.

Yet in the process of exploring its margins, anthropology has come close to losing its center. The culture concept that has long been a rallying and organizing principle of the field has been deconstructed virtually beyond recognition. It has become something of a dirty word among many younger anthropologists who have come to equate culture with "essentialism" and with traditional centers of authority. Ironically, at the very moment that many ethnic groups have turned to identity politics and highly essentialist notions of culture as ideological supports for their own autonomy and authenticity, many anthropologists have abandoned the culture concept altogether as too essentialist, preferring the more politically and historically charged concepts of discourse, interest, and strategy.

But one of anthropology's main contributions to the human sciences has always been to foreground the significance of cultural variation in human life. Without a robust concept of culture, anthropology loses its distinctive analytical power, and a significant aspect of human life remains undertheorized and unexamined. The poststructural critique of traditional conceptions of culture is potentially of great importance for anthropology, but only if it is used to refine the notion of culture rather than to discard it.

THE COGNITIVE REVOLUTION

It is significant that as anthropology has become more closely allied to history and certain trends in philosophy, it has also become increasingly marginalized from the other great intellectual movement of the late twentieth century—the revolution in cognitive science. In recent years major streams of research from cognitive psychology, computer science, philosophy, linguistics, and neuroscience have converged in what Howard Gardner has called *The Mind's New Science* (Gardner, 1985). Yet since ethnoscience lost its hold on mainstream anthropology a generation ago, anthropologists (with a few notable exceptions) have not kept up with or contributed significantly to the cognitive revolution. This is a great pity. Many of cognitive science's approaches to the mind have important implications for how we might rethink the culture concept in light of the poststructuralist critique.

Conversely, the idea of culture as a component of the mind adds a critical and often underdeveloped middle level of analysis in cognitive science. Attention to cultural cognition has the potential for mediating the general studies of brain function from neuroscience and the more particular studies of individual mental representations found in cognitive psychology. At this crucial juncture in intellectual history, cultural anthropology and cognitive science need one another, though neither seems aware of the fact.

Of course not all anthropologists have resisted the cognitive revolution. A small but growing number of psychological anthropologists have been working to refine a cognitively nuanced conception of culture in line with some of the major insights of cognitive science.[2] Much of this research focuses on what has come to be known as "cultural models."[3] In a sense, the concept of culture as a collection of "models" is as old as Ruth Benedict's idea of "cultural patterns." But contemporary work on cultural models has benefitted from recent work on schema theory in psychology and also from the recent critique within anthropology of overly reified and rigid notions of shared culture (Strauss, 1992). Sensitive to the dual status of cultural knowledge as at once contingent personal knowledge and public models, research on cultural models points the way to an important revision of the culture concept with the unique potential to bridge the cognitive revolution and postmodern critical theory.

This book argues for the importance of a theory of "cultural models" in linking anthropology and cognitive science. It proposes an *ethnographic conception of mind*, a notion of a brain dependent for its functioning on a range of extrinsically derived models. Such a view of human cognition does not entail a tabula rasa approach to the mind or any other form of cultural determinism. Humans employ a spectrum of different kinds of mental models. Thus there are very "primitive" innate mental schemas, such as those that appear to regulate an infant's earliest attachments with caretakers or the perception of facial gestalts. These may be understood as forms of *species knowledge*, "learned" and transmitted biologically through Darwinian selection (Bateson, 1972).

At the other end of the spectrum are idiosyncratic schemas constructed opportunistically and ecologically by individuals as a way of negotiating novel environments. These are part of an individual's *personal knowledge*. Between the species and the individual lie prepackaged forms of knowledge that coordinate groups of individuals and are the property of communities. These socially mediated forms of knowledge are treated here as cultural models, aspects of *cultural knowledge*. *Culture in Mind* argues for the inclusion of these culturally derived models as an essential characteristic not only of human social life but also, as we shall see in Chapter 1, of human nervous system functioning (Changeux, 1986; Laughlin et al., 1992).

THE ORGANIZATION OF THE BOOK

The book is structured by the following set of questions:

1. *What is the history of anthropology's reluctance to pursue the culture and cognition question? How is this reluctance related to the troubling issue of the "psychic unity" of humankind?* Chapter 1 presents a historical overview of the psychic unity question within anthropology. The chapter traces the gradual disengagement of culture and mind in the thinking of leading figures in anthropology.

2. *What is a cultural model? How is cultural knowledge organized in time and space?* Chapter 2 is a discussion of the notion of cultural model and a detailed typology of the different kinds of cultural models that have been identified by anthropologists and psychologists.

3. *How is cultural knowledge organized cognitively? How are these structures related to other kinds of knowing in a "polyphonic" conception of mind?* This issue has been at the forefront of contemporary critiques of structuralism—critiques that have sought to replace "structure" with more fluid notions of discourse, practice, and strategy. These arguments have often proceeded by establishing false dichotomies in which structures have been consigned to a "straw man" role in relation to other kinds of knowing. Chapters 3 and 4 illustrate a complex polyphonic model of knowledge through an examination of the interplay of rule, strategy, and violation in modern sport.

4. *How is the culture concept related to the idea that there are there different modes of thought?* The book approaches these issues by returning to the classic issue of "primitive thought" and the long-standing "rationality debate" that this issue inspired among philosophers, anthropologists, and psychologists (Chapters 5 and 6). These problems are discussed in relation to the general problem of totemism (human/nonhuman symbolic identifications) and more specifically in relation to an analysis of Kwakiutl animal symbolism. A related issue is the modern counterpoint to the modes of thought issue: the relationship between industrial and electronic technologies and the postmodern cognition. The relationship between cognition and technical environments is taken up in Chapters 7 and 8, where I develop a conception of techno-totemism.

5. *How are public forms of knowledge transformed into personal forms of knowledge? How do cultural practices connect models in the world to those in the mind? What happens to this knowledge in the process?* These are issues about the role of social practices of knowledge transmission. I call the emergence of shared knowledge structures as aspects of personal experience *epistemogenesis*—the birth of

personal knowledge. In Chapters 9 and 10, epistemogenesis is be explored in a re-analysis of myth and ritual among the Murngin (Yolngu) of Arnhem Land in the Northern Territory of Australia.

6. *How do we understand the coexistence of multiple models for the same do-main of experience?* Chapters 11 and 12 address the problem of multiple models in relation to Samoan ethnography. In some cases, multiple models define alternate perspectives on experience. In other cases, they set the stage for conflicted perception and profound ambivalence. These chapters raise the fundamental question of the lim-its of cultural models in accounting for human experience.

7. *How does analogy formation figure in the way that cultural models under-write meaning construction for individuals?* Chapters 13 and 14 conclude the book by developing a theory of meaning construction intended to bridge the concepts of culture and mind. Chapter 13 deals with the problem of meaning in anthropology. It is a critique of several dominant approaches to meaning that have been influential in modern anthropology. The chapter outlines a concept of meaning construction as a kind of memory work employing analogy in the interest of incorporating novel expe-riences through older models.

The groundwork for this theory involves a rethinking of what linguists call "mo-tivation" in symbols and a reevaluation of the Saussurian arbitrariness principle that has been so influential in anthropological accounts of cultural symbolism. George Lakoff's theory of "experiential realism" is proposed as an alternative to Saussurian semiotics as a way of understanding the double life of cultural symbols as features of both the world and the mind.

Chapter 14 moves cultural forms from the world to the mind by considering analogy formation and analogical transfer as they figure in connectionism, cognitive psychology, and in cultural anthropology. The process by which cultural models become transformed into mental representations is termed *analogical schematization*. A review of some of the important research on analogy formation reveals that analog-ical schematization is a complex process that operates at various levels of abstraction. A theory of analogical schematization is proposed as a fundamental cognitive bridge between cultural models understood as social artifacts on the one hand and as mental representations on the other.

Viewing culture as a knowledge system helps to clarify the relationship between culture's two lives: its social life as a feature of public institutions and its cognitive life as a component of the mind. To link these two lives of culture, the book neces-sarily tacks back and forth between particular ethnographic studies (psychic diversity) and studies of general cognitive processes (psychic unity). Rather than presenting the general theory first, followed by illustrative case studies, I have opted to take the anthropologist's route, exploring the mind "outside-in" and placing the ethnography up front.

A more top-down approach to the subject, with case studies following theory, might well have rhetorical advantages in the short run. Yet I think that theorizing through ethnography is a far more effective and appropriate long-term strategy for a book of this sort. The theoretical discussions at the end of the book ultimately make more sense with the case studies already in mind. So the exploration of mind is a kind of outside-in journey, moving from ethnographic cases to psychological con-structs. In the interest of a unified argument, I have tried to suggest, in each of the case studies, the important theoretical issues at stake. In the same way, I return where relevant to the case studies in making the more general theoretical points at the end of the volume. Readers are free to read the chapters in any order they wish. Though the book has been written as a single coherent argument, it also has something of a modular structure, enabling readers profitably to read Chapters 13 and 14 first or to read through any of the book's ethnographic sections as self-contained arguments.

This volume has been written in the conviction that now is the time for anthropology to claim its rightful place in the cognitive revolution. To do so requires that we rethink what we mean by both "culture" and "mind." Conceptualizing *culture in mind* suggests both an ethnographic theory of mind and a cognitive theory of culture. Mind needs to be "denatured"—moved outdoors into the midway of social life. This is the ethnographic mind. The concepts that show the most promise for revealing this double-dealing aspect of culture are the related notions of "model" and "schema."

The cognitive view of culture proposed in this book is not a one-way translation of culture to either mentalistic or biological terms. It is intended as a bridge, both theoretical and empirical, between the cultural and the psychological understandings of how models work. A cognitive approach to culture is not a reduction of culture to psychology or to biology. It is the recognition of the role of cultural models as an integral component of nervous system functioning and the fact that cultural models are inevitably constrained by nervous system parameters. It is equally the recognition that cultural models, while not the same as mental models, have a very significant connection with them. It is in the hope of contributing to this kind of reciprocal view of the relations between mental and social life, and of inspiring others to take seriously the questions of culture in mind, that this book has been written.

Notes

1. On comparative rates of brain development, see Passingham, 1982:112. On the relative influences of genetic constraints and postpartum experience on brain development, see Konner, 1982:60 ff. On the neuro-biological implications of the evolution of culture, see Donald, 1991.

2. Among the leading contemporary figures in cognitive anthropology are Maurice Bloch, Pascal Boyer, Roy D'Andrade, Janet Dixon Keller, Sarah Harkness, Dorothy Holland, Edwin Hutchins, Tanya Luhrmann, Catherine Lutz, Charles Nuckolls, Gananath Obeyesekere, Naomi Quinn, Richard Shweder, Mel Spiro, and Claudia Strauss.

3. For important general works on cultural models, see Casson, 1983; D'Andrade, 1987a, 1987b, 1990, 1995; D'Andrade and Strauss, 1992; Holland and Quinn, 1987; Quinn and Strauss, 1993; Shore, 1990b.

1

The Psychic Unity Muddle

In early life we have been taught that human life is everywhere the same. . . . This error
we must replace by the truth that the laws of thought are everywhere the same.

—Herbert Spencer

How can you explain the workings of the human mind without a knowledge of the social
setting which must have played so great a part in determining the sentiments and opinions
of mankind?

—W. E. H. Rivers

[E]thnology is first of all psychology.
    —Claude Levi-Strauss

This is a book about anthropology's oldest and most vexing question: the psychic
unity of humankind. George Stocking has characterized this commitment to psychological universalism as "the major premise of the comparative method of ethnology"
and the cornerstone of "The Enlightenment view of man" (Stocking, 1968:115).
Grounded in eighteenth-century notions of rationality as a defining characteristic of
the human species, the psychic unity doctrine has appealed to social Darwinists and
cultural relativists alike.

Despite its status as the theoretical and moral bedrock of modern anthropology,
the idea of psychic unity has always had an uncomfortable relationship with the
idea of culture as a key element in human life. The philosophical commitments of
Enlightenment anthropology have had an uneasy relationship with the empirical evidence of human diversity—evidence amassed by generations of travelers, missionar-
ies, and professional ethnologists. Yet along with psychic unity, cultural anthropology has adopted cultural diversity as its defining issue. Anthropologists have
typically defended cultural difference as a defining human characteristic while repeatedly affirming their faith in humankind's psychic unity, usually without noting the
apparent tensions between these two views.

The contradictions inherent in such a project have proven theoretically troublesome. The problem is how to reconcile faith in a single human nature with the
reported variations among communities—variations not only in physical characteristics but also in matters of custom, belief, and temperament. For the cultural anthro-

pologist, the challenge has been to square psychic unity with cultural diversity. Many of the recurring anxieties of contemporary anthropology can be traced directly to the contradictions implicit in this attempt to ground anthropology in both a powerful conception of cultural relativity and a procrustean faith in humankind's psychic unity.

This volume is intended as a rethinking and qualification of the psychic unity doctrine, a doctrine that is virtually an article of faith among modern anthropologists. Its perspective is that of cognitive anthropology, understood broadly as the study of the relationship between "cultural models" and "mind." Once cultural models are recognized as a dimension of mind, the issue of psychic unity versus psychic diversity becomes much more problematical and theoretically complex than is commonly acknowledged by anthropologists. No modern anthropologist seriously questions that all humans share the same basic nervous system and a common range of *potential* cognitive processes. This idea of shared hardware is what is commonly meant by "psychic unity." Yet such a shared neurological endowment alone does not make the case that all humans, irrespective of culture, can be said to be of the same psyche or mind.

PSYCHIC UNITY AND THE HUMAN BRAIN

Any case for human psychic unity or diversity will inevitably rest on how the psyche is conceived. It is easy enough to defend a simplistic notion of psychic unity by emphasizing the common design features of the human nervous system. This approach effectively reduces the psyche to structures of the brain and stresses very general species-defining characteristics like tool use, language, or symbol use. Lists of such species characteristics can be found in any introductory anthropology textbook.

But attention to the biological and evolutionary basis of cognition does not really support any significant notion of psychic unity. Modern neurobiology does not paint an essentialist picture of the human nervous system. Our mental hardware turns out not to be as "hard" as we had presumed. Many neurobiologists view the human nervous system as the biological basis of an "adaptive intelligence" (Changeux, 1986; Laughlin et al., 1992; Piaget, 1971). The nervous system is highly programmable within the limits of what Changeux terms its "genetic envelope" (Changeux, 1983:468; see also Laughlin et al., 1992:53–54).

The flexibility of the human brain, its openness to the world around it, is suggested by the fact that much of its development and all of the myelinization of the cortex take place outside the womb in the first five years of life. Attempting to move beyond the relatively simplistic oppositions between the competing characterizations of brain functioning as either totally plastic or hard-wired, Changeux proposes a developmental theory of brain functioning that stresses a "selective stabilization" of neural networks during an early "labile" phase of brain development (Changeux, 1983). Laughlin et al. provide the following summary of Changeux's theory:

> Changeux begins from the position that there is too small an evolutionary increment
> in genetic material to account for the remarkable increase in complexity of human neural

organization over that of, say, the chimpanzee. A solution to this apparent paradox is to be found in a process by which patterns of synaptic innervation are stabilized out of a field of potential synapses. Processes develop and synapses are tentatively established during an early "labile" phase of neural development. During the labile phase, the developmental processes have a high redundancy factor and are largely determined by the genetic labeling producing the generalized cell type of which any particular neuron is a member. A period of selection follows the laying down of the field of synapses, during which some synapses are reinforced through activity *at both pre- and post-synaptic sites on the membranes of the cell and its target,* and many other synapses are eliminated by irreversible regression and cell death due to inactivity. [Laughlin et al., 1992:41; emphasis in original]

This view of brain development distinguishes various levels of environmental responsiveness in different kinds of neural networks (Rosenzweig et al., 1962, 1972). Some networks are relatively hard-wired and constrained by a tight genetic envelope. Laughlin et al. refer to such hard-wired neural associations as "highly prepared associations" (Laughlin et al., 1992:63). Others are subject to selective stabilization early in life during the labile phase of brain development. And still other neural networks remain subject to reprogramming throughout an individual's life and account for the neural basis of lifelong learning.

It is thus clear that the active human psyche cannot be reduced to its common biological substrate, abstracted from the conditions of its development and the particular environment within which it is functioning at any given time. While certain neurological features may be characterized as intrinsic to the normal development of any human brain, others are more flexible and inscribe in the form of particular neural networks the particular environment in which the brain has been developed.

Viewing the mind in this way—as dependent on a variety of neurologically grounded models of different degrees of flexibility—we can see how it is possible for anthropologists to justify either the psychic diversity of the species or its essential psychic unity. We can also understand the sense in which the unity/diversity debate is based on a false dichotomy. In the face of the complex and equivocal character of the human brain, the immediate question becomes why, for so many years, anthropologists have chosen largely to ignore the implications of culture for understanding the important degree of psychic diversity characteristic of our species.

Given the cultural anthropologist's penchant for particularistic rather than universalistic accounts of human experience, this history of support for the psychic unity doctrine and its implicit essentialism may seem puzzling. In its rush to clear up any doubts about the species' psychic unity, anthropology inevitably drove a theoretical wedge between the ideas of culture and mind. The modern legacy of this move was the marginalization of anthropology from the deepest currents of the cognitive revolution.

How and why did culture and mind come to be separated in this way? This split is the legacy of Victorian anthropology and its commitment to understanding difference exclusively in terms of a notion of general evolution. The psychic unity doctrine became entangled in complex ways with the discredited ideas of racial character and "progressive" cultural evolution. Until the issue of cultural diversity could be unhooked from its evolutionary (and racial) moorings, modern anthropologists were not free to contemplate the implications of cultural difference for an understanding of mind. In the rest of this chapter, we consider the troubled roots of the culture/mind divide in the complex intellectual currents of Victorian anthropology.

EARLY SPECULATIONS ON PSYCHIC UNITY

For Victorian anthropology, the idea of general evolution resolved the apparent contradiction between cultural variability and psychic unity. The belief that cultures progressed through a fixed sequence of historical phases led anthropologists to understand cultural difference as *stages* of evolution (Sahlins et al., 1960). So long as evolution was understood as *general* (i.e., unilinear) and *progressive* (i.e., directed), it was possible to reconcile an essentialist view of human nature with the cultural variability of the species.

The evolutionism of Tylor, Morgan, and Spencer preserved the Enlightenment faith in psychic unity, but only by ignoring the kind of opportunistic variability implicit in Darwin's theory of natural selection and adaptive radiation. Whether in culture or biology, specific evolution (speciation) is always a problem for those proposing a unilinear conception of evolution. The idea of general cultural evolution made possible a comparative ethnology by providing anthropologists with a single evolutionary track and an associated taxonomy of historical types for classifying human variability.

Evolution was anthropology's early solution to the psychic unity problem. In Spencer's terms, the cultural diversity in human life could be acknowledged, while the "laws of thought" remained common human property, albeit unfolding over evolutionary time. The human mind was assumed to operate on laws that were independent of a particular culture, even though specific cognitive abilities were closely tied to the group's level of social evolution. The mind, unified in its essence, was pluralized in its temporal existence. Mental evolution was treated as an "orthogenesis," a directed linear development linked to the orderly unfolding of cultural stages. For evolutionists like Spencer, the human mind might be fixed and universal but, as Stocking suggests, "mentality" was contingent and plural:

> For Spencer, the crucial factor in the formation of primitive mentality was the closeness of the primitive mind to its external environment. The sensory perceptions of the savage were notoriously acute, but as a result of the antagonism between "perceptive" and "reflective" activity, his mental processes rarely rose above the level of sensation and the "simple representative feelings directly associated with them." Improvident, credulous, incapable of abstraction, his behavior was primarily a matter of reflexive or imitative response to environmental stimuli; though fundamentally impulsive and indeed antisocial, he was paradoxically subject to the most extreme fixity of habit and rule of unthinking custom, since his "simpler nervous system, sooner losing its plasticity" was unable to take on a modified mode of action." Inherent savage mentality produced a certain type of social life; but savage social life, by a circular Lamarckian process, also produced the hereditary savage mentality. [Stocking, 1960:117–118]

This implicit distinction between a fixed "mind" and a fluid, environmentally conditioned "mentality" became an article of faith among Victorian anthropologists. Yet, as I have suggested, this complex position on the psychic unity of humankind was disturbingly ambiguous at best and, at worst, self-contradictory. It was just these troublesome issues about the psychic unity doctrine that impelled the first generation of anthropological fieldworkers to set out from the academy for distant lands, natural laboratories where they might have a first-hand look for themselves.

AMERICA: BOAS AND THE MIND OF PRIMITIVE MAN

In 1883, Franz Boas, then a young student of physics, left Germany for Baffinland, in northern Canada. His primary intent was to study how Eskimos perceived the color of ice and seawater in their natural setting. This research was to be an extension of his dissertation research in the psychophysics of vision. But even before he left Germany, Boas's intellectual agenda was complex and in transition.

During his year-long arctic sojourn, Boas endured considerable physical hardship and found himself painfully isolated intellectually. Yet as he overcame the strangeness of his new surroundings, Boas found himself quite charmed by what he saw as the essential humanity of his Eskimo hosts. "[A]fter a long and intimate intercourse with the Eskimo," Boas wrote in 1887, "it was with feelings of sorrow and regret that I parted from my arctic friends." He continues:

> I had seen that they enjoyed life, and a hard life, as we do; that nature is also beautiful to them; that feelings of friendship also root in the Eskimo heart; that, although the character of their life is so rude as compared to civilized life, the Eskimo is a man as we are; that his feelings, his virtues, and his shortcomings are based in human nature, like ours. [Boas, 1887a:402]

To occupy himself during the long and frigid arctic nights, Boas had brought with him a copy of Kant's *Critique of Pure Reason*. Boas's developing interest in ethnology emerged under the unlikely joint influence of Eskimo hospitality and Kantian philosophy. Kant directed Boas's attention to questions of the mind's reliance on categories and the resulting complex relations between the objective world and mental representations (Stocking, 1960:143–144).[1] As he became increasingly absorbed in the lives of his Eskimo hosts, Boas's interest in the effects of seawater on the perception of light began to give way to a new set of questions: issues of human value and meaning.

During his laboratory experiments attempting to measure the absorption of light by different samples of water, Boas had begun to realize the importance, even in scientific measurement, of what he termed "situational factors," by which he meant the psychological predispositions of the observer (Stocking, 1960:142 ff.) "I learned to recognize," Boas wrote in 1938, "that there are domains of experience in which the concepts of quantity, of measures which can be added and subtracted like those with which I was accustomed to operate, are not applicable" (Boas, 1938, cited in Stocking, 1974:42). Turning from psychophysics, Boas took up as his life's work the question of "the relation between the objective and the subjective worlds . . . the reaction of the human mind to the natural environment" (Boas, 1938, cited in Stocking, 1974:42).

Boas's early field studies, really the cornerstones of modern anthropology, were driven by issues of cross-cultural psychology and questions about the flexibility and variability of human psychological processes. From the outset, however, the cross-cultural study of psychological processes was beset by theoretical problems. Mostly the problems stemmed from a tradition of treating group differences in terms of evolutionary stages. While he initially shared the Victorian assumptions about cultural evolution, Boas gradually changed his views, increasingly directing his theorizing against the notion of evolutionary hierarchies of cultural and psychological characteristics.

Boas sought to replace evolutionary taxonomy with detailed descriptions of individual cultures understood as integrated isolates. In interpreting cultural artifacts, for instance, Boas invoked a contextualist relativism that made cross-context comparisons virtually meaningless:

> We have to study each ethnological specimen individually in its history and in its medium. . . . By regarding a simple implement outside of its surroundings, outside of other inventions of the people to whom it belongs, and outside of other phenomena affecting that people and its productions, we cannot understand its meaning. [Boas, 1887b, cited in Stocking, 1974:62]

"In ethnology," Boas asserted, "all is individuality" (Stocking, 1974:66). By "individual," Boas meant individual culture.

In a 1909 address at Clark University, Boas underscored the centrality of the psychic unity issue for anthropology. "The fundamental problem on which all anthropological inquiry must be founded," he said "relates to the mental equipment of the various races of man" (Boas, 1910a:371). Boas had not broken completely with the prevailing evolutionary assumptions of his day, and his subsequent comments suggest the degree to which his conception of mind was grounded in biological essentialism:

> Are all races of mankind mentally equally endowed or do material differences exist? The final answer to this question has not been given, but anatomical observations on the various races suggest that differences in the form of the nervous system are presumably accompanied by differences in function, or, psychologically speaking, that the mental traits which characterize different individuals are distributed in varying manner among different races; so that the composite picture of the mental characteristics of one race would presumably not coincide with the composite picture of the mental characteristics of another race. [Boas, 1910a:371]

Boas qualified this conception of racial variation in mentality with the assertion that such difference does not necessarily imply that one group is more advanced than another. "It would seem," he went on, "that the weight of evidence is, on the whole, in favor of an essential similarity in mental endowment in different races, with the probability of variation in the type of mental characteristics" (p. 372).

This discrimination between a common mental "endowment" and racial variation in mental "characteristics" echoes the distinction made by Boas's old mentor Adolph Bastian between *Elementargedanke* (primal/basic thought) and *Völksgedanke* (local "folk" thought). But already Boas was moving away from this distinction toward another. The term "endowment" suggests an inherited characteristic and anticipates the distinction that Boas was later to make between race and culture. Boas was trying to draw a line between mental characteristics based on race and those based on membership in social groups. He attributed the latter characteristics not to racial influences but to "the habitual reactions of the society to which the individual in question belongs" (Boas, 1910a:372).

In his extraordinary essay "Psychological Problems in Anthropology," one senses Boas's struggle to forge a set of crucial distinctions: between race and ethnicity, between mental "endowment" and mental "characteristics," and between racial differentiation and evolutionary advancement. Yet in 1910 Boas had not freed himself of the notion of general evolution as a framework for understanding group differences. Distinctions between racial groups and ethnic groups were still linked in his mind with differences in evolutionary advancement.

The nature of "primitive thought" was still at the heart of Boas's view of psychological anthropology. Thus Boas claimed that the "primary object of [anthropological] researches would be the determination of the fundamental categories under which phenomena are classified by man in various stages of culture" (Boas, 1910a:377). Boas proposed the importance of investigations into the "domain of certain simple sense perceptions" such as color, noting that color terminologies in some languages make finer discriminations than in others. He favored rigorous comparative investigation of such differences in the classification of sensory phenomena.

Boas appears to be uncomfortably straddling a thoroughgoing cultural relativism and an older evolutionism. Difference has not yet emerged simply as difference but rather as developmental level. On the one hand, Boas's view anticipates by half a century the research project of ethnoscience. On the other hand, it clearly resonates with Spencerian assumptions about the failure of the "primitive mind" to make fine sensory discriminations. Though he comes close, Boas has not quite untangled the psychic unity conundrum.

Boas's most famous statement on the issue of psychic unity is his 1911 volume *The Mind of Primitive Man* (Boas, 1911/1938). Though the book jacket of a 1963 printing highlights Boas's affirmation of the psychic unity of mankind and his rejection of the racial mentality notion, the book is in fact considerably more equivocal on these issues.[2] The crux of Boas's actual position on these matters is found in Chapter 11. Here Boas clearly repudiates the notion of unilinear evolution from simple to complex cultural forms, at least in relation to what he terms "particular cultural phenomena" (Boas, 1911/1938:180). On the other hand, Boas acknowledges that "increasing intellectual achievements" have produced clear advantages for human communities in security and food production. This change, in turn, leads to "new approaches to truth, and a more systematic development of knowledge" (p. 184). These changes also represent to Boas clear cultural advances.

In terms of cognitive characteristics, Boas still believes in evolutionary developments in sense perception. Classifications in different cultures are "founded on fundamentally distinct principles" (p. 190), principles echoing Spencer's evolutionary sequence. Primitive thought is linked, in Boas's view, with anthropomorphism, concreteness, difficulty in forming abstractions, and a tendency to reify abstract phenomena into agents or objects (as in theories of illness). But though he seems to confirm the classic evolutionist's view of primitive mentality, Boas is, in fact, attempting to make a crucial distinction—not between primitive and civilized mind but rather between the "traditional ideas" that their respective cultures provide. There is, Boas concludes, no reason to attribute differences in thinking to "any fundamental peculiarity of the mind of primitive man" (p.199). In his words, "The difference in the mode of thought of primitive man and that of civilized man seems to consist largely in the *difference of character of the traditional material with which the new perception associated itself"* (p. 199, emphasis added).

Boas preserved the psychic unity of humankind while freeing himself of the racial assumptions of the evolutionist position. He achieved this freedom by distinguishing between *cultural traditions* and *mental endowment* as the basis for differences in mental life.

By focusing on the cultural sources of different mentalities among human groups, Boas moved closer to making sense of the psychic unity problem. But the Boasian solution to the problem of psychic unity had a serious cost, one that has continued to trouble modern anthropology. General evolution is overcome by clearly disengaging culture from mind. With the "fundamental" unity of the mind assured, ethnologists are free to document in great detail the variety of cultural traditions. These traditions may legitimately be held to shape a people's "mode of thought," their "style of thinking," and their "beliefs." Yet in no sense may we conclude that there is any fundamental difference between "minds." The human mind, Boas concludes, is *essentially* free of cultural effects.

This intellectual sleight of hand is reinforced by an implicit metaphor of mind-as-container. Culture is conceived as one of the *contents* of mind rather than as a defining *attribute* of mind. Thus anthropology achieved an independence from psychology. The study of culture could be dissociated from the study of mind.

BRITAIN: RIVERS AND THE UNITY OF SOCIETY AND MIND

Fifteen years after Boas's first encounter with the Eskimos, a group of British scientists from Cambridge University traveled to the South Pacific to collect information on exotic life forms in Melanesia. The 1898 Torres Strait expedition was led by Cambridge marine biologist Alfred C. Haddon. Accompanying Haddon was a team of psychologists made up of William Rivers and two of his Cambridge students, Charles Meyers and William McDougall (Stocking, 1968:216).

Rivers left England for the South Pacific armed with the latest psychometric tests of the day. Like Boas before him, Rivers planned to study the effects of environmental differences on human sensory perception. Though experiments were conducted on a wide range of sensory reactions, the team was particularly interested in visual perception. Rivers administered the famous Müller-Lyer illusion to natives of Murray Island and discovered that they appeared to be somewhat less susceptible to the visual illusion than European populations. Rivers's findings were early evidence for what would eventually come to be called the "carpentered environment hypothesis." The exposure to the precise and regular angles of so-called carpentered environments was thought to affect human spatial perception. It was this effect which was tapped by the Müller-Lyer illusion.

On the general issue of human psychic unity, the team's experiments were inconclusive and inconsistent. McDougall reported that his Papuan subjects were twice as sensitive to tactile stimuli as Europeans but half as sensitive to pain. Myers, whose test results on reaction time were hardly conclusive, nonetheless concluded that any recorded differences in reaction time were the "expression of racial differences in temperament" (quoted in Stocking, 1968:216). McDougall would later become a believer in the racial determination of temperament and an advocate of a doctrine of racial inequality (p. 217).

As for Rivers, he returned from Melanesia somewhat confused about the psychic unity issue. Though his field research had inspired in him a serious interest in ethnology, Rivers tended to keep his psychological and ethnological interests separate. Whenever he did attempt to bring these interests together, the result was ambiguous at best.

Though his early writings were on the borderline between psychology and neurology, Rivers gradually became interested in the connections between psychology and social life and more particularly the influence of social and physical environment on perception and thought. Despite his psychoanalytic orientation, Rivers was drawn to a highly relativistic view of the human psyche. Sixteen years after his Melanesian research, Rivers wrote: "The two kinds of process, social and mental, are so closely connected that there must be relations between the two throughout. The two paths will have interconnections even while they are parallel to one another, and these interconnections will become still more numerous as the paths converge" (Rivers, 1916/1926a).

By psychology, Rivers apparently meant the understanding of human motivation. His own fieldwork in both Melanesia and India as well as his wide reading in ethnology convinced him of the strong influence of local tradition on what psychologists had assumed was basic human motivation. In the 1916 essay, the chief example he used was revenge. Rivers succinctly summed up his objections to the assumption of psychic unity of motivation: "In place of asking 'How can you explain the blood feud without revenge?' I would rather ask, 'How can you explain revenge without a knowledge of the blood feud?' " (p. 11).

Early on, Rivers developed a set of contradictory views on the psychic unity issue. In his 1906 ethnography *The Todas,* Rivers writes of "the extraordinary similarity of custom throughout the world" and affirms the importance of the independent invention of widely distributed cultural traits (quoted in Smith, 1926:217). Here Rivers reflects the influence of Adolph Bastian. Eventually Rivers's attempt to interpret his Melanesian materials led him to renounce Bastian's notion of psychic unity as implicit in the conception of *Elementargedanke.* In an essay "Convergence in Culture," Rivers argues for a pluralistic view of human psychology. "[I]n the study of human culture," he writes,

> the nature of a practice is not to be explained by the working of motives which move ourselves, nor is it even to be explained fully by the immediate motives of those who now put the custom into practice. It is only by historical inquiry, by finding the social concomitants and antecedents of the custom, that we can hope to understand its nature. [Rivers, 1916/1926b:146]

By 1911, just five years after the publication of *The Todas,* Rivers had all but abandoned the assumptions of psychic unity in favor of a notion of socially shaped motivation. But there was still the issue of accounting for cultural similarities between widely separated populations. Rivers turned to diffusionism—the borrowing of traits between cultural groups—as a way of explaining cultural parallelism. Diffusionism did for Rivers what cultural particularism did for Boas. It allowed him to evade the troubling aspects of the psychic unity question by disconnecting cultural from evolutionary questions.

To what extent was Rivers actually able to overcome the contradictions about the psychic unity of mankind that beset the thinkers of his time? For Boas, the contextualism of his idiographic approach to cultural description was seen as an alternative to both evolutionism and to diffusionism. For Rivers, however, diffusionist explanations of cultural similarity were presumed to be consistent with the perspective of general evolution. The evolutionary conception of mind, with its notions of advanced versus primitive thinking, go unchallenged by Rivers. He turns to diffusionism because it seems to him empirically preferable to evolutionary accounts.

In both Boas's and Rivers's pioneering work, an early interest in the relationship between culture and mind was gradually replaced by a theoretical split between culture and mind. Once this break was made, the evolutionary issues were put to rest, but at a price. The relationship of culture to individual motivation and cognition became problematical. Rendered as "spirit," culture lost its body. The culture-mind split was simply another version of the Cartesian mind-body dualism, but with an ironic twist. In affirming psychic unity in the face of cultural diversity, mind became roughly equated with brain and thus with body, a position with which many contemporary neuroscientists would concur. But culture (understood as mentality or mental characteristics) was conceived in a disembodied fashion as *Geist* (or spirit) and therefore not understandable in the same terms as organic evolution.

THE FRENCH CONNECTION: RATIONALITY AS ROMANCE

By the end of the nineteenth century, leading French social thinkers were wrestling with the same questions about human psychic unity that were troubling their English and American counterparts. The terms of the French debate were set out by Émile Durkheim and his followers and by the philosopher-ethnologist Lucien Lévy-Bruhl. These leading French figures shared with Boas and Rivers a focus on the relationship between cultural differences and mind. Yet from the outset French social thought had a distinctively Gallic flavor, a pervasive intellectual tension between cognitive romanticism and classical rationalism.

Durkheim and Lévy-Bruhl shared the Spencerian vision of social evolution that was the received wisdom of their day. General evolution presumed the gradual replacement of simpler and undifferentiated social forms with complex and differentiated ones. For Émile Durkheim and his nephew Marcel Mauss, the evolution of both social and mental forms involved a gradual increase in both complexity and "differentiation" out of what they termed a primitive "state of indistinction" (Durkheim and Mauss, 1963:5). The classic case of the Bororo Amazonian tribesman literally identifying himself and his clan with the totemic *arara* parakeet is marshaled by Durkheim and Mauss as an example of the sort of mental confusion that represents at once the earliest stages of human evolution and the earliest phases of the development of the individual mind.[3] This passing reference in *Primitive Classification* to the presumed parallelism between individual and phylogenetic development was characteristic of the social thought of the time. Yet it does seem odd to find such a claim in the work of writers who devoted so much effort to arguing for the dissociation of social facts from those of individual psychology.

Despite Durkheim's apparent embrace of evolutionism, the romantic strain in French anthropology provided a fascinating countercurrent to the straightforward evolutionary thinking in his work. For French thinkers, primitivism was more than mental confusions and undifferentiated social forms. The primitive suggested for these writers a romance of meaning, a vision of a prelapsarian world as an uninterrupted chain of signification.

For Durkheim, the romance took the form of the idea of "collective representations" that defined the solidarity of the "archaic societies." In his *Division of Labor in Society,* Durkheim contrasted the "organic solidarity" underlying complex societies with the "mechanical solidarity" of simpler societies. But in moving from simple to complex society, the very meaning of "solidarity" undergoes a telling shift. Mechanical solidarity is a function of religious belief and practice and constitutes a unity of minds—a shared system of common representations. Organic solidarity, however, unites needs rather than minds in a shared-in system of diverse economic specializations. In short, primitive society was distinguished by its proliferation of shared meanings, while so-called civilized society traded off such common meanings for economic interdependence.

Though he clearly distinguished primitive from civilized social forms, Durkheim shared with the English evolutionists a strong commitment to the psychic unity doctrine. In fact he and Mauss wrote *Primitive Classification* as a vigorous defense of the idea of psychic unity. And while evolution produced changes from simple to complex and undifferentiated to differentiated social forms, they claimed that the character of the human mind had remained essentially unchanged from the beginning. That character is to be found in the fundamental rationality of human classification. "Primitive classification" is seen as an early form of the basic human mind:

> Primitive classifications are not . . . singular or exceptional, having no analogy with those employed by more civilized peoples; on the contrary, they seem to be connected with no break in continuity, to the first scientific classifications. In fact, however different they may be in certain respects from the latter, they nevertheless have all their essential characteristics. [Durkheim and Mauss, 1963:81]

For Durkheim, psychic unity is not based directly on the common nature of mind but on the commonality of human social processes. Classificatory logic, the capacity to oppose and to order concepts hierarchically, is derived from the processes of group formation, group hierarchy, and social opposition. Mystical identifications and confusions in "primitive" thought were treated as a psychic residue of an earlier, undifferentiated social state. For Durkheim, this residue had the positive effect of promoting the unity of the clan. In stressing connection over differentiation—the *solidarity* of clan members—their identification with each other and with their totemic species are for Durkheim and Mauss relatively "primitive" human traits. Social identification is conceived of as a kind of evolutionary residue left over from "the state of the initial confusion from which the human mind has developed" (Durkheim and Mauss, 1963:81). By contrast, the logic of social *distinctions,* such as those defining traditional divisions of the tribe into increasingly smaller "nested" groups (moiety, phratry, and clan) suggests for Durkheim and Mauss the more highly evolved classifying and differentiating phase of social/psychic development (p. 81). The startling implication is that, for Durkheim, the "mechanical solidarity" of simpler societies—defined by shared representations, similarity of worldview, and a lack of economic differentiation—is linked to residues of mental confusion. It is here that Durkheim's evolutionism and the French romance with meaning come together. Though Durkheim dissociated his views from Lévy-Bruhl's radical opposition of scientific and prelogical thought, Durkheim's association of primitive society with undifferentiated mechanical solidarity bore a striking similarity to Lévy-Bruhl's brand of primitivism, with its stress on prelogical "participations" and identifications between heterogeneous species.

Durkheim's social determinism of thought has been subject to many critiques. Yet it is important to remember that Durkheim was arguing for an understanding of mind as dependent on cultural models. Like Rivers, Durkheim argued against the explanation of social phenomena in terms of psychological characteristics. Durkheim and Mauss proposed instead that properties of mind be derived from aspects of social experience. In a famous passage he states:

> Far from it being the case, as Frazer seems to think, that the social relations of men are based on logical relations between things, in reality it is the former which have provided the prototype for the latter. According to him, men were divided into clans by a pre-existing classification of things; but on the contrary, they classified things because they were divided by clans. [Durkheim and Mauss, 1963:82]

Durkheim's conception of a "social mind" whose functioning is grounded in external models is surprisingly modern in its anticipation of cognitive anthropology. In fact, Durkheim and Mauss articulated an early version of what has become known as "prototype theory" in cognitive psychology, whereby basic-level categories may be derived from key cultural exemplars.

Yet while Durkheim proposed an enlightened view of the cultural basis of classification, he was also anxious to distinguish sociology (social facts) from psychology, which he viewed as the study of purely individual experience. In his preface to *Suicide,* Durkheim stressed that social facts were "realities external to the individual" (Durkheim, 1951:37–38).[4] Durkheim left unresolved and problematical the relations between social forces and individual motivation. Like Boas, Durkheim constituted culture ("social representations") as a distinct domain for inquiry. But he accomplished this by splitting culture off from the psyche and simply asserting a relation of difference or opposition. The result was that the role of culture *in mind* as a source of personal as well as social motivation became something of a black box.

LÉVY-BRUHL'S "PARTICIPATION"

Durkheim presumed a link between the psychic unity implied by classification and the social basis of mental representations. Lévy-Bruhl took a different path. His project was to play out the romance with meaning to its "prelogical" conclusions.[5] This entailed for Lévy-Bruhl a decisive break with the psychic unity doctrine. Lévy-Bruhl became increasingly fascinated with cultural difference and struggled, without complete success, to characterize cultural difference in a nonevolutionary way.

Lévy-Bruhl's most influential ideas about the psychic unity of humankind are contained in his 1910 book *Les fonctions mentales dans les sociétés inférieures,* which was misrendered in English as *How Natives Think.* Through the linked concepts of "prelogical mentality" and its "principle of participation," Lévy-Bruhl tied the romance of meaning to cultural evolution. Lévy-Bruhl chose the unfortunate term "prelogical" to describe the quality of mysticism that he attributed to primitive religious thought. By "prelogical," Lévy-Bruhl meant that many religious beliefs and practices violated Aristotle's principle of "noncontradiction." Conceptions proposing the coexistence of apparent mutually exclusive states (e.g., life in death, unity and multiplicity of being, the identity of distinct forms of life or distinct species) were logical and categorical anomalies. "Primitive thought" simply ignored the apparent logical anomalies in such conceptions.

Lévy-Bruhl insists that the failure to note contradictions is not due to the lack of any cognitive capacity for logic but rather a lack of interest in the logical consistency of a set of relations. The difference in mentality is traced to differences in "social milieu" (p. 43). For Lévy-Bruhl, prelogical and logical modes of thought are derived from a common brain but different *collective representations,* or what we would now call distinct cultural models. Logical and prelogical thought are matters of cultural value rather than cognitive capacity. "Undoubtedly," Lévy-Bruhl affirmed, "they have the same senses as ours . . . and their cerebral structure is like our own. But we have to bear in mind that which their collective representations instill into all their perceptions" (p. 43).

The social value that underlies the disregard of logical consistency is positively defined in terms of "the law of participation," which proposes correspondences or relationships where logical thought proposes differences and oppositions. The law of participation accounts for mystical thought and its identification of things which, in everyday life, appear to be separate:

> For instance, "the Trumai (a tribe of Northern Brazil) say that they are aquatic animals.—The Bororo (a neighboring tribe) boast that they are red araras (parakeets)." This does not merely signify that after their death they become araras, nor that araras are metamorphosed Bororos, and must be treated as such. It is something entirely different. . . . It is not a name they give themselves, nor a relationship that they claim. What they desire to express by it is actual identity. That they can be both the human beings they are and the birds of scarlet plumage at the same time, Von den Steinem regards as inconceivable, but to the mentality that is governed by the law of participation there is no difficulty in the matter. [Lévy-Bruhl, 1910:43]

The other important characteristic of "participation" is the fact that concepts are sensuous, colored by feeling and by bodily activity, and are not apprehended as pure ideas: "In its purest form, primitive mentality implied a participation which was felt and lived, both by individuals with the social group, and by the social group with the surrounding ones" (p. 366). Lévy-Bruhl asserts that only with the emergence of "individual consciousness" do such sensuous concepts take on an abstracted and ideological quality. Ultimately, participation gives way to abstract relations of symbolic identification, of similarity and of metaphor.

I have dwelt at length on Lévy-Bruhl's conception of primitive mentality because I think that his important insights into human thought have been lost to modern anthropology. This has been due in part to the long history of misunderstanding of what Lévy-Bruhl was getting at.[6] Lévy-Bruhl's work has been sidelined from the canon of social theory because of the residual and patronizing evolutionism in his discussions of the "primitive."

At the end of his life, Lévy-Bruhl finally gave in to his increasingly vociferous critics who sought to defend the psychic unity doctrine against what they saw as Lévy-Bruhl's insupportable challenge. In his *Notebooks,* Lévy-Bruhl asserted that he had erred in characterizing so-called primitives in terms of a single prelogical mentality. Yet even in his early work, Lévy-Bruhl had never claimed that prelogical thought was the exclusive province of one sort of human being. What he had asserted was that the collective representations of some groups legitimized mystical thinking in a far greater number of contexts than other groups did.

Lévy-Bruhl came the closest of any early writer to recognizing the serious problems faced by a field that insisted on foregrounding cultural diversity while clinging to an unrefined notion of psychic unity. Alone among the major thinkers of his time, Lévy-Bruhl openly questioned the idea of psychic unity. In recognizing that "mentality" lay at the intersection of a common human sensorium and a variable set of cultural representations (models), Lévy-Bruhl might well have laid the foundation for a cognitively grounded conception of culture and an intellectually vigorous vision of the psychic diversity of humanity. But his critics never permitted this to happen.

In reevaluating Lévy-Bruhl, there are also issues of the substance of his thinking about mind. What is a modern anthropologist to make of Lévy-Bruhl's notion of prelogical mentality? It is a safe bet that the vast majority of modern anthropologists would have little positive to say about Lévy-Bruhl, and most would probably admit to never having had extensive contact with his writings. Yet I have long found his discussions of participation and contradiction quite compelling, even if they are derived from romanticized readings of the ethnography. What Lévy-Bruhl has identified is not, of course, a mentality that could be exclusively associated with any single human group or type. Nor could it be seen as a "lower" form of human cognition than any other. But he has identified in somewhat vague terms a particular "mode of thought" that is found to one degree or another in all human communities and has strong empirical validation in relation to key life experiences (see Chapters 5 and 6 of the present volume). In Chapter 14, we revisit the notion of "participation" that Lévy-Bruhl was getting at and discover that it is closely connected to the process of analogical schematization that underlies meaning construction for all humans.

Stripped of its evolutionary framework, Lévy-Bruhl's questioning of human psychic unity no longer looks as threatening as it once did, since it conceives of the mind as an emergent phenomenon at the nexus of the nervous system and a variable field of social values. His emphasis on the sensuous and nonrational component of mind finds renewed significance in light of recent work on the embodiment of human understanding.[7] Though the jargon has changed and few would recognize their kinship to Lévy-Bruhl, the concept of participation is, in fact, a live issue in modern anthropological research.

RECENT ANTHROPOLOGY AND THE PSYCHIC UNITY QUESTION

In the last quarter century, cultural anthropology has fragmented into numerous theoretical camps with widely divergent and sometimes mutually hostile research agendas (Shore, 1988b). Despite this fragmentation, the doctrine of psychic unity has gone largely unchallenged by the mainstream of anthropologists. The notion of general evolution of culture and the social Darwinism that supported it have been either eliminated in modern anthropological discourse or self-consciously purged of their racialism and ethnocentrism. Yet the legacy of Victorian anthropology looms large in the conscience of the field. Though Boas, by clearly distinguishing among the concepts of race, culture, and language, should have cleared the way for a reevaluation of the psychic unity doctrine, modern anthropologists tend to retain an unexamined version of the doctrine as a matter of faith.

LEVI-STRAUSS AND THE RATIONALITY OF THE SAVAGE MIND

Without question, Claude Levi-Strauss must be considered the most influential thinker in anthropology in the last half of the twentieth century. Though his work spans the full range of ethnological concerns (social organization, myth, ritual, language, and history), the problem of culture and mind is at the heart of his thinking, much as it had been for Durkheim, Mauss, and Lévy-Bruhl. Even Levi-Strauss's early work on social organization focused less on behavior than on the implications of norms and rules for an understanding of human nature. Gradually, the focus of his work shifted to a more direct confrontation with the problem of mind as revealed by myth and art.

Levi-Strauss's writing betrays a deep ambivalence about the question of psychic unity, an ambivalence reflecting the characteristic French tension between rationality (and its attraction to universality) and romanticism (and its passion for diversity). The French tradition of philosophical anthropology, stemming from Rousseau, Durkheim, and Lévy-Bruhl, bequeathed to Levi-Strauss the romance of the "primitive" or "savage," terms which he never abandoned despite their disreputable associations.

Levi-Strauss's influential work *The Savage Mind* is a complex argument, part science, part poetry, for psychic unity defined in terms of a human desire for order through systematic classification. The so-called savage mind is, in Levi-Strauss's magisterial treatment, a subspecies of Linnaean rationality, a different machine compelled to impose categorical order on the world. In an interview for Canadian radio, Levi-Strauss discussed his lifelong struggle against irrationality: "Since I was a child,

I have been bothered by, let's call it the irrational, and have been trying to find an order behind what is given to us as disorder" (Levi-Strauss, 1979:11).

Yet Levi-Strauss's work does not simply affirm the common rationality of all human thought; rather, it adopts an implicit evolutionism and splits the mind into two forms of rationality—one primitive, one modern. The modern scientific mind, like the mind of the engineer, operates through the rationality implicit in hypothesis testing and the manipulation of abstract concepts (Levi-Strauss, 1966:19). In contrast, "mythical thought" employs "the science of the concrete," interrogating nature indirectly by means of concrete signs and symbols rather than directly through abstract concepts.

Myth may be a species of scientific thought, but it is one that operates according to a distinct epistemology which Levi-Strauss calls "bricolage." Both the scientist and the bricoleur are empiricists. But the scientist's propositions are presumed to be open to the disconfirmation of contrary experience (or experiments). The bricoleur, by contrast, betrays what Levi-Strauss has termed a "totalitarian ambition" (Levi-Strauss, 1979:17). Mythic thought exploits the expressive possibilities of the finest details of nature and of the play of human events in a poetic reaffirmation of an all-encompassing world view that is beyond disconfirmation.

Mythic thought may share with modern science a disinterested passion for explanation and order. But it is not completely disinterested, and the two species of thought are not quite the same. At the same time as Levi-Strauss affirms psychic unity, he points to the profound gulf that he believes separates these two frames of mind:

> To say that a way of thinking is disinterested and that it is an intellectual way of thinking does not mean that it is equal to scientific thinking. Of course it remains different in a way, and inferior in another way. It remains different because its aim is to reach by the shortest possible means a general understanding of the universe—and not only a general but a total understanding. That is, it is a way of thinking which must imply that if you don't understand everything, you don't explain anything. This is entirely in contradistinction to what scientific thinking does, which is to proceed step by step, trying to give explanations for very limited phenomena, and then going on to other kinds of phenomena. [Levi-Strauss, 1979:17]

The Savage Mind and *Totemism* were both written in refutation of Lévy-Bruhl's "false antinomy between logical and prelogical mentality" (Levi-Strauss, 1966:268, 1979:16). Levi-Strauss attempted to demonstrate alternate forms of rationality that defined, in one puzzling package, the common mental capacities of humankind and the split between primitive and modern science. His project was in part motivated by his joint commitment to the psychic unity doctrine and the importance of cultural differences in the definition of mind.

The ambivalence about difference at the heart of Levi-Strauss's work is reflected in the following comments he made during a radio interview:

> Today we use less and we use more of our mental capacity than we did in the past. *And it is not exactly the same kind of mental capacity as it was either.* For example we use considerably less of our sensory perceptions. . . . You cannot develop all the mental capacities belonging to mankind at once. You can use only a small sector and this sector is not the same according to the culture. [Levi-Strauss, 1979:19; emphasis added]

Levi-Strauss uses a radical statement of the cultural variability of mind to support the psychic unity doctrine. For he concludes his comments with the extraordinary claim: "It is probably one of the many conclusions of anthropological research that, not withstanding the cultural differences between the several parts of mankind, the human mind is everywhere one and the same and that it has the same capacities. I think this is accepted everywhere" (Levi-Strauss, 1979:19).

As is customary in anthropology, the human mind is held to be unitary, whatever the local differences in its productions, so long as one can maintain that *its capacities* are everywhere the same. But as readers will quickly note from the apparent contradiction between the two passages (from the same page of *Myth and Meaning*), the definitions of both "mind" and "capacities" are left crucially ambiguous. Dan Sperber is one of the few anthropologists to have noted this fascinating tension in Levi-Strauss's work: "Levi-Strauss' originality, . . . which has often gone unnoticed or been misunderstood, is to have developed this notion of psychic unity of humankind while, at the same time, putting forward new arguments to show that ethnography has a true, indeed unique psychological relevance" (Sperber, 1985:71).

Levi-Strauss is, quite literally, of two "minds." In one frame of mind, both reductive and materialistic, Levi-Strauss seems to equate mind with its organic substrate in the brain or nervous system.[8] Any presumption of difference would then have unfortunate racial implications, so he is forced to affirm the psychic unity doctrine. Yet in quite another frame of mind, Levi-Strauss goes so far as to claim that even mental capacities can be understood as distinct under different historical and cultural conditions. In this view, Levi-Strauss adopts an implicit conception of mind as an emergent property of the interaction of brain and organized experience. This is a radically different position from the materialistic conception of mind that underlies Levi-Strauss's understanding of psychic unity. Far from justifying the psychic unity doctrine, this latter view of mind is actually consistent with a radically pluralistic vision of psychic diversity.

Levi-Strauss often dissociated his own views from those of Lévy-Bruhl. His main objections are to Lévy-Bruhl's categorical distinction between mentalities and to the characterizations of mythic thought as emotional and participatory rather than logical or conceptual. While these are genuine enough differences, I think that the two writers are actually somewhat closer in conception than Levi-Strauss allows. Both affirm an important conception of psychic diversity, and for both, this diversity is clearly attributed to the influence of distinct social experiences on mind. Moreover, Levi-Strauss's conception of a distinct species of mind called "savage" recalls Lévy-Bruhl's primitivism, the romance with meaning: ˴

> The exceptional features of this mind which we call savage and which Comte described as spontaneous relates principally to the extensive nature of the ends it assigns itself. It claims at once to analyze and to synthesize, to go to the furthest limits in both directions, while at the same time remaining capable of mediating between the two poles. [Levi-Strauss, 1966:219]

The synthetic aspect of "savage thought" is the meaning-constructing impulse of mind, an impulse that Levi-Strauss attributes to the primitive bricoleur but which is more accurately identified with religious thought in general. What Levi-Strauss identifies as synthesis, Lévy-Bruhl characterized as participation. While there are distinctions between these concepts, I think they both reflect the same romance with meaning and the misleading overidentification of meaning-constructing cognitive processes with "primitive people."

In both visions, the diversity of mind is understood as a response to variable social representations. A range of different modes of thought, though held in common by all humans as cognitive potentialities, is in fact characterized as subject to differential social distribution. Though both Lévy-Bruhl and Levi-Strauss were quick to defend the doctrine of human psychic unity, they did so only in terms of *a common organic substrate of mind*. As they wrestled with exotic cultural texts, both writers were led to theoretical positions that viewed the mind as an emergent and contingent property of social experience. From the postulated psychic unity, both writers were led by the evidence to a potentially radical position of human psychic diversity.

CLIFFORD GEERTZ: BRINGING CULTURE TO MIND

While structuralism dominated the intellectual life of cultural anthropology through the early 1980s, Boasian cultural particularism was experiencing a sophisticated revival in the United States starting in the late 1960s. The new cultural relativism became known variously as "interpretive" or "symbolic" anthropology. Its emergence as a dominant paradigm in cultural analysis is associated with the Department of Anthropology at the University of Chicago and most particularly with the work of David Schneider and Clifford Geertz, both products of Harvard's Department of Social Relations and students of Talcott Parsons. Though Geertz and Schneider shared an early interest in culture and personality, both would later renounce psychologism in culture theory as they sought to carve out a distinctive niche for cultural analysis.

Geertz's early essays on culture theory are particularly interesting in the context of the psychic unity issue. In two brilliant early essays, "The Impact of the Concept of Culture on the Concept of Man" and "The Growth of Culture and the Evolution of Mind," Geertz laid the foundations for a conception of mind as an emergent phenomenon at the crossroads of brain and extrinsic programs—what he termed cultural "templates." That vision should have provided the underpinning for a cognitively grounded conception of culture and a culturally grounded conception of mind, but it did not. Why it did not is a telling commentary on the staying power of the psychic unity doctrine.

Geertz looked to the implications of hominid evolution to provide a biological basis for the importance of culture in human life. For Geertz the human capacity rests on the extensive symbolic mediation of behavior. He stresses the human need for symbolic models of and for reality. Cultural templates are at once public (i.e., socially accessible to a community) and conventional (i.e., historically and locally contingent). For Geertz, culture is a semiotic system, an ensemble of "structures of signification" (Geertz, 1973c:9) which function as an external control system for human action:

> The "control mechanism" view of culture begins with the assumption that human thought is basically both social and public—that its natural habitat is the house yard, the marketplace, and the town square. Thinking consists not of "happenings in the head"

(though, happenings there and elsewhere are necessary for it to occur) but of a traffic in . . . significant symbols. [Geertz, 1973d:45]

This human reliance on what Geertz calls "symbolic sources of illumination" derives from our species' behavioral and semantic plasticity and the relative incompleteness of the human neonate:

> The behavior patterns of lower animals are, at least to a much greater extent, given to them with their physical structure; genetic sources of information order their actions within much narrower ranges of variation, the narrower and more thoroughgoing, the lower the animal. For man, what are innately given are extremely general response capacities, which although they make possible far greater plasticity, complexity, and, on the scattered occasions when everything works as it should, effectiveness of behavior, leave it much less precisely regulated. . . . Undirected by cultural patterns—organized systems of significant symbols—man's behavior would be virtually ungovernable, a mere chaos of pointless acts and exploding emotions, his experience virtually shapeless. Culture, the accumulated totality of such patterns, is not just an ornament of human existence but—the principal basis for its specificity—an essential condition for it. [Geertz, 1973d:45–46]

The human dependence on culture affects not only how we understand contemporary human nature but also has significant implications for our conception of the selective forces in evolution which shaped that nature. Geertz's arguments are directed against what he views as common fallacies about hominid evolution and human nature. One such fallacy he terms the "critical point" theory of evolution, which mistakenly postulates a biologically complete hominid suddenly inventing culture after having reached the critical point of evolution. Geertz's point is that symbolically mediated adaptations exerted selective pressures on evolving hominid lines, and thus that culture was an intrinsic selective factor in the evolutionary process and not simply its end product.

The other view of human nature Geertz seeks to dispel is what he terms "the Enlightenment view of man." This was the view that underlay the psychic unity doctrine in its Spencerian version. Human nature, having been laid down once and for all through evolution, is invariant and regular. As we have seen, this view was reconciled with the obvious diversity of physical and cultural types in two ways. First, variations were treated as relatively superficial phenomena in contrast to the deep inner human constancies. Second, variations were understood in relation to orthogenetic principles of development. In other words, difference was translated into evolutionary/developmental stages.

Geertz's profound but elementary insight is that in view of the plasticity and social dependence of the human sensorium, human variation must be viewed as a constituting feature of the human rather than a superficial addition to it. Culture moves from the peripheries of human life into its very center as a postnatal completion of human development. The study of human nature minus culture does not produce a more basic understanding of the human but an understanding of a protohuman, a creature that is all bioessence but lacking recognizable qualities of human existence. In Geertz's estimation, time and space, history and culture are as central to the definition of the human as is the stuff of genetics.

Better than anyone before him, Geertz laid out the implications of cultural evolution for a theory of mind. Geertz explicitly rejected the reduction of mind to its organic basis, arguing instead for a view of mind as a relationship between a nervous system and its extrinsic sources of activation. In reviewing developments in neurobiology, Geertz notes, however, the "apparent paradox" in brain evolution of increasing centralization, autonomy, and hierarchical complexity of the nervous system which together produce a brain increasingly dependent for its functioning on external sources of patterning and activation. The implications for culture theory are profound:

> [T]he accepted view that mental functioning is essentially an intracerebral process, which can only be secondarily assisted or amplified by the various artificial devices which that process has enabled man to invent, appears to be quite wrong. On the contrary, a fully specified, adaptively sufficient definition of regnant neural processes in terms of intrinsic parameters being impossible, *the human brain is thoroughly dependent upon cultural resources for its very operation;* and those resources are, consequently, not adjuncts to, but constituents of, mental activity. [Geertz, 1973b:76; italics in original]

Having thus proposed a conception of mind with psychic diversity at its heart, Geertz takes the remarkable step of using this view of mind as a justification for the psychic unity doctrine. He does this by ignoring his own insights about the emergent character of mind. In an argument that has become all too familiar in anthropology, Geertz ignores the cognitive implications of his own insights by equating psychic unity with an bioessentialist view of the mind:

> [A] denial of the simple independence of sociocultural and biological processes in pre-*Homo* sapiens man does not imply a rejection of psychic unity, because phyletic differentiation within the hominid line effectively ceased with the terminal Pleistocene spread of *Homo* sapiens over nearly the whole world and the extinction of whatever other *Homo* species may have been in existence at that time. [Geertz, 1973b:69]

The fact that this phyletic differentiation has equipped humans with an ecological brain seems not to trouble Geertz's thinking about psychic unity. For Geertz, the denial of psychic unity would appear to imply an evolutionary hierarchy of mentalities. "The doctrine of psychic unity of mankind," he proclaims, "which, so far as I am aware, is today not seriously questioned by any reputable anthropologist, is but the direct contradictory of the primitive mentality argument; it asserts that there are no essential differences in the fundamental nature of thought processes among the various living races of men" (Geertz, 1973b:69).

It is not clear what Geertz means here by "the fundamental nature of thought processes." Yet one can hardly imagine a more fundamental sort of variability in mind than the kind of brain-culture interactionism that Geertz outlined in the very same article.

Like Boas before him, Geertz struggled with anthropology's fundamental contradiction. With characteristic eloquence and erudition, he tries to write his way out of it. Yet the result is an obscure vision of culture in its relation to mind. Like Levi-Strauss, Geertz wavers uncomfortably between two incompatible models of mind. ✳The one, essentially organic and fixed, justifies psychic unity; the other, emergent and contingent, justifies cultural diversity.

Geertz's insistence on the external and public nature of cultural texts was in part motivated by a kind of deep antipathy to what he called "psychologizing." For those, like Ward Goodenough, who took a cognitive view of culture as a system of knowledge, Geertz reserves his most strident scorn. In an eloquent if completely misguided series of passages in his famous essay "Thick Description: Toward an Interpretive Theory of Culture," Geertz compares the cognitive theory of culture to a confusion between a musical performance and the score. Culture, in Geertz's view, must be limited to the "text" and not to the "reading." No reason for this limitation is ever adduced by Geertz, other than a dismissive reference to culture-in-mind as one of "the privacy theories of meaning" (Geertz, 1973c:12). Yet if Geertz's own conception of mind is right, and thought is public to its very core, then there is no way in which culture-in-mind could be construed as "a privacy theory of meaning." For ideological reasons, Geertz has not followed out the implications of his own argument. The echo of Durkheim's distinction between social and individual facts resounds in Geertz's categorical split between culture and mind.

Having culturalized the mind, Geertz resisted a cognitively nuanced apprehension of culture. This resistance to a cognitive conception of culture as knowledge may well be due to the dominance, at the time of Geertz's writing, of what has variously been called ethnoscience or componential analysis. Ethnoscience viewed the mind as a kind of sorting device for generating taxonomic order in various delimited domains like kinship, disease, color terms, and the like. The cognitivist's quest for methodological rigor was successful in demonstrating a limited range of variability in cultural classifications. Most important, ethnoscience gradually helped clarify the nature of basic-level categorization, a development that revolutionized our understanding of thinking (see Chapter 13). Unfortunately, ethnoscience also tended to squeeze the life out of culture by limiting cultural knowledge to abstract classificatory schemata divorced from human action.

The arid formalism of ethnoscience was a far cry from the thick description of enacted texts that Geertz saw as the goal of cultural analysis. Geertz called for a kind of literary, "experience-near" rendering of culture, evoking the textures and tonalities of everyday life. Having identified cognition with a purely taxonomic view of the mind, it is little wonder that Geertz was so anxious to draw the line between culture and mind. Yet he himself had laid out a vision of mind in which there was scope for a wide variety of cultural models of a nontaxonomic sort: in kinesthetic image schemas, iconic models localized in house structures, "ludic" (play/performance) models like cockfights, calendrical systems, scripts, and systems of personal names.

Geertz's work had opened a window onto a world of tropes not reducible to taxonomies—tropes that were as much a matter of mind as they were of social order. But the complex relations between culture's two lives, as social text and as mental model, could never be worked out so long as culture and mind were presumed to have no articulate joint life. Culture had been brought to mind. What remained was to bring mind back to culture, viewed as a knowledge system.

CULTURAL PSYCHOLOGY: SHWEDER'S "ROMANTIC REBELLION"

In recent years a new sort of cognitive anthropology, a kind of cognitive romanticism, has begun to crystallize. Its roots may be traced to a number of intellectual wellsprings: to Lévy-Bruhl's notion of a plurality of human mentalities; to the old configurationist school of culture and personality studies associated with Margaret Mead, Gregory Bateson, and Ruth Benedict; to the linguistic relativity of Sapir and Whorf; to Saussure's conception of the arbitrariness of linguistic signs; to Schneider's and Geertz's interpretive anthropology; to Victor Turner's brilliant eclecticism in symbolic studies; to Obeyesekere's powerful accounts the complex relations between conventional and personal symbols; and to contemporary developments in "schema theory" from cognitive psychology and metaphor theory from linguistics and philosophy.

Cognitive romanticism is a cognitively nuanced version of the sort of cultural relativism that Geertz and Schneider had long been advocating as an alternative to psychologism. One of its leading proponents is Richard Shweder. Shweder shares with Schneider and Geertz common institutional roots in Harvard's Department of Social Relations. But his explicitly psychological and hypothesis-testing orientation to the study of mind landed him at Chicago's Committee on Human Development rather than its Department of Anthropology.

From his home in human development, Shweder straddles the worlds of psychology and anthropology and has embarked on an ambitious project of synthesis. In a seminal essay on the fate of the concept of mind in anthropology, Shweder contrasts the Enlightenment view of psychic unity and its uniformitarian vision of human nature with what he terms "anthropology's romantic rebellion" (Shweder, 1984). This recurrent tension between anthropology's two faces pits the general study of "culture" against the more particularistic interpretation of "cultures."

In an afterword to this essay, Shweder attempts a formidable taxonomy of anthropological theories of the mind. Enlightenment approaches are distinguished into rational and irrational, while the romantic vision of mind is set aside as simply "nonrational." The other axis of his typology distinguishes the sort of "universalism" associated with structuralism or transformational grammar from a "developmentalist" stress that links evolutionists like Tylor and Horton with developmental psychologists like Piaget or Heinz Werner. Relativism differs from universalism and developmentalism in its emphasis on simple and noncomparable diversity. Yet it shares with developmentalism an interest in human variation.

Shweder's main purpose in this essay is to clarify the underlying premises of anthropology's perennial and seemingly irresolvable debate on the nature of culture and mind. However, in a 1990 essay introducing a paradigm-defining volume of essays by psychologists and anthropologists, Shweder takes a strong stand in favor of the romantic view of mind. His aim is to distinguish what he terms "cultural psychology" as an interpretive discipline from other ways of studying culture and mind:

> Cultural psychology offers an alternative discipline of interpretation of the fundamentals of mind. The mind, according to cultural psychology, is content-driven, domain specific, and constructively stimulus bound; and it cannot be extricated from the historically variable and cross-culturally diverse intentional worlds in which it plays a constitutive part. [Shweder, 1989:13]

Cultural psychology cannot embrace general psychology's search for what Shweder calls a "central processing unit." Instead, its object is the "intentional worlds" within which human action takes place, a view which defines mind as an emergent and contingent relationship between brain and social context. The search for inherent properties is replaced by "descriptions of local response patterns contingent on context, resources, instructional sets, authority relations, framing devices and modes of construal" (p. 13). In other words, Shweder is outlining the possibility of a cognitively oriented *ethnography of mind.*

Shweder's "cultural psychology" comes close to a constructive transcendence of the dilemma that has haunted anthropology since its inception: the problem of how to reconcile a pluralistic conception of culture with a uniformitarian conception of mind. In the face of the powerful but unwarranted grip that the psychic unity dogma has had on modern anthropology, Shweder has been an exuberant advocate for the study of psychic diversity.

Nonetheless, Shweder's promising view of a truly cultural psychology does pose a few conceptual problems. Shweder's critique has the virtue of drawing a number of bold distinctions between competing approaches to the cross-cultural study of mind and clarifying their implications. In two important contexts, however, he misrepresents or overstates his case for culture in mind. The first problem has to do with his emphasis on the "arbitrariness" of cultural systems viewed from the romantic perspective. The second problem is his assumption that cultural psychology is somehow irreconcilable with a view of mind as a central processor.

In his defense of cognitive romanticism, Shweder characterizes the romantic view of mind in terms of nonrationality and arbitrariness (Shweder, 1984:47ff).

> A good deal follows from the idea of the "arbitrary" or "non-rational." To be a romantic is to be anti-normative. It is to be suspicious of the concept of "progress." That's not to say the romantic is an anarchist—clearly there are rules to any game, and any "frame" has its own internal standards. . . . The romantic's anti-normative point is that there are no standards worthy of universal respect dictating what to think or how to act. [Shweder, 1984:47]
>
> The whole thrust of romantic thinking is to defend the coequality of fundamentally different "frames" of understanding. The concept of nonrationality, the idea of the "arbitrary" frees some portion of man's mind from the universal dictates of logic and science, permitting diversity while leaving man free to choose among irreconcilable presuppositions, schemes of classification, and ideas of worth. [p. 48]

Shweder subscribes to a very common false dichotomy in anthropology. If cultural practices or beliefs are not fully determined or universally shared, the fallacy goes, then they must be arbitrary and thus infinitely variable. But in assuming that arbitrariness is the only alternative to a reductive and deterministic understanding of cultural practices, Shweder has overlooked a third possibility, a view of cultural institutions that stresses their conventional character as human creations without confusing the conventional with the purely arbitrary. In this alternative view, cultural phenomena are better characterized as conventional arrangements that may or may not be arbitrary. A familiar example will make this distinction between the conventional and the arbitrary clear: the cough or sneeze. In their most common forms, neither is generally considered a cultural convention but rather a physiological reflex. But a particular style of "handling" coughing or sneezing, or of holding back a sneeze in certain contexts, or of using a specifically stylized cough-analogue as a polite social warning—all are examples of "conventional" institutions based on and thereby constrained by biological processes but not reducible to them.

Conventions are human creations. Their forms and social distribution show a certain degree of free play and indeterminacy. This is one of the reasons human cultures are so diverse and ultimately not reducible to their encompassing material constraints. To call cultural facts matters of convention is to recognize their inherent indeterminacy. But it also recognizes the possibility that their range of variability may not be absolute, arbitrary, or unmotivated. Many cultural practices are constrained but not determined by other factors (Shore, 1988b). They vary within the limits of their constraints (like Changeux's "genetic envelope"), but within those limits their status is indeterminate.[9]

The confusion of the arbitrary with the conventional in human affairs is admittedly a subtle mistake. But it is an error that has had serious implications for any theory of culture. For to characterize cultural life as arbitrary is tantamount to arguing that there is no significant relationship between cultural practices and anything else. The analysis of a collection of practices that were genuinely arbitrary would be, quite literally, cultural non-sense. This is denied not only by the logic of the case but also by the very practice of anthropology. For devoting one's life to the study of endless arbitrary beliefs and practices could be neither edifying nor very engaging for an outsider.

Such a cultural solipsism invites a justified incredulity from many corners, not the least of which is from the people whose lives are thus characterized. The assertion of unmotivated arbitrariness in human affairs where what is meant is actually the indeterminacy of conventional arrangements invites all sorts of misguided attacks on the nihilism implicit in "cultural relativism." I shall return throughout this book to the unfortunate implications of the confusion between arbitrariness and conventionality, for it has a profound bearing on a fundamental problem of culture—the problem of intentionality and meaning construction.

The second problem I have with Shweder's view is his presumption that a commitment to the cognitive relativity of cultural psychology necessitates the rejection of the "central processor" view of mind. The view Shweder is attacking is a kind of high-tech version of the Enlightenment faith in universal rationality. It is the common view from experts in artificial intelligence that the essential human mind is a kind of computational machine.

Now I am unsure whether this is an appropriate metaphor for some aspects of the mind, though I think it is likely that computation of some sort is involved in many aspects of nervous system functioning (see Chapters 13 and 14). Yet in fact Shweder's conception of culture and mind is fully compatible with modern connectionist models of mind (see Chapter 14). And while these models are quite different from those that Shweder seems to have in mind, they do suggest some viable conception of central processing. As we have seen in Geertz's early attempt to define central nervous system processes in relation to culture, there is no inherent incompatibility between a central processor and an emergent conception of a culture-dependent mind. A more defensible position might be that taking culture seriously as a dimension of mind implies that a central processor can never be a *sufficient definition of mind*.

To exploit the computer metaphor, the reduction of mind to a central processor would be like reducing the functioning of a digital computer to its hardware, ignoring the emergent properties of both the general operating system and particular programs. While it would be fair to say that the character of any application is *constrained* by the characteristics of its operating system and that the operating system is *constrained* (but not determined) by hardware design, in both cases no sufficient account of the operation of a computer could be given based solely on an understanding of its hardware. But any adequate account of the functioning of such a machine would have to take into account the constraints imposed by hardware architecture.

CONCLUSION: MOVING BEYOND THE MUDDLE

*Being anti racist-
An important
feature of us.*

The repeated insistence that cultural variability in no way compromised the anthropological doctrine of human psychic unity grew out of the discomfort of anthropologists with the evolutionism implicit in cognitive accounts of cultural difference. It is easy to understand the well-intentioned motives of this resistance to any perceived reference to mental evolution and its usual racist entailments. Yet the unfortunate result of this desire to bury our past has been to drive a wedge between culture and mind, explaining each according to its own properties and principles and avoiding serious discussions of their connections.

In consequence, anthropology has inherited a conception of culture that is alienated from some of the deepest sources of human motivation. This alienation is the legacy of a conception of culture as exclusively arbitrary symbolic forms, where meaning is understood solely in terms of the internal relations of signs.[10] It is hardly surprising that, having inherited these assumptions about culture and mind, anthropologists have come to think of culture in two radically opposed visions. One vision equates culture with external power, largely external to the realities and motivations of the self. The other sees culture as purely private experience, disconnected from shared realities. Culture becomes either the exclusive property of public, political life or it is thoroughly privatized as personal experience. What is lost is an appreciation of the life of cultural forms at the *juncture* of the public and private. This requires a cognitive view of culture and a cultural view of mind.

Meanwhile, cognitive psychologists and neurobiologists have begun to make some headway in understanding the nature of mental representations. The cognitive revolution has gathered steam from work in artificial intelligence as well as from linguistics, experimental psychology, and neurobiology. But the notable successes of the artificial intelligence approach to mind have exacted a cost on our understanding of mental representations. By stressing computational models of thought based on information sorting processes, meaning construction and cultural cognition have been seriously marginalized from the cognitive revolution.

The argument of this chapter has been that the marginal role played by anthropology in the cognitive revolution results in great part from a long-standing set of misconceptions about psychic unity. The muddle in the psychic unity argument emerges from the very structure of the debate. To propose that the mind is *essentially* uniform or that it is *essentially* variable phrases the relationship between culture and mind in terms of a false and irresolvable dichotomy. The question cannot be phrased as psychic unity *versus* diversity. If mind exists at the intersection of brain and extrinsic models, we need to model brain-culture interactions so that they reveal at one and the same time the general cognitive processes of information processing and meaning construction as well as the culturally diverse manifestations of those processes in action. Neither dimension is more basic or more important than the other.

Put in this way, addressing the psychic unity question seriously becomes a matter of characterizing the role of cultural models in the functioning of the human nervous system. This is a tall order. Cognitive scientists have only just begun to understand brain functioning. And we anthropologists have only recently begun to pay close attention to the cognitive properties of cultural models. Before considering the relations between culture and mind, it is important to begin to develop a robust conception of models, one that will illuminate the links between anthropological and psychological versions of what models are and how they work. But the literature in both psychology and anthropology is notoriously imprecise on the matter of models. In the following chapter I argue for the usefulness of the "models" approach to cognition. But approaching the problem of culture in mind through the concept of models requires a far more refined theory of cultural models than we have had up until now. Chapter 2 attempts to refine our understanding of models by clarifying a number of important distinctions—distinctions that should permit us to both differentiate and relate cognitive and cultural models.

Notes

1. In Boas's most famous work on the psychic unity question, *The Mind of Primitive Man*, his Kantian view of reason is clear:

> Since the foundation of human thought lies in the rise into consciousness of the categories in which our experience is classified, the principal difference between the mental processes of primitives and ourselves lies in the fact that we have succeeded by reasoning to develop from the crude, automatically developed categories a better system of the whole field of knowledge, a step which primitives have not made. [Boas, 1911–1938:198]

Boas's emerging interest in the relativity of the mental categories on the basis of which even simple discriminations are made is evident in his 1888 essay "On Alternating Sounds," in which he anticipates the discovery of the phoneme as the psychologically relevant basic unit of language (Stocking, 1974:72–77; Stocking, 1960:157ff., see also Boas 1911/1938, chap. 11)

2. The book jacket in the 1963 Free Press edition of *The Mind of Primitive Man* cites the following quote from the text:

> [T]here is no fundamental difference in the ways of thinking of primitive and civilized man. A close connection between race and personality has never been established. The concept of racial type as commonly used even in the scientific literature is misleading as a logical as well as a biological redefinition.

3. For a recent discussion of this classic Bororo parakeet metaphor see Turner, 1991.

4. This attempt to separate social facts as autonomous sources of motivation was most elaborately worked out in *The Rules of the Sociological Method*.

5. Shweder calls Lévy-Bruhl anthropology's "romantic founding figure" (Shweder, 1984:30).

6. For an excellent discussion of the long history of misreadings of Lévy-Bruhl in anthropology, see Littleton, 1985.

7. Lakoff and Johnson, 1980; Johnson, 1987; Lakoff, 1987a, Leder, 1990; Stoller, 1989; Shore, 1988b, 1990b; Csordas, 1994a, 1994b.

8. In a remarkable statement in the chapter "History and Dialectic" from *The Savage Mind*, Levi-Strauss anticipates the eventual triumph of natural science: "the reintegration of culture in nature and finally of life within the whole of its physico-chemical conditions" (Levi-Strauss, 1966:247).

9. The notion of constraint on symbolic representation is treated in later chapters in terms of a theory of *symbolic motivation*. Understanding cultural symbols as *constrained* points to a way out of the dilemma posed by competing theories which treat cultural symbolism as either fully *determined* or completely *arbitrary*. While framed here in relation to "realist" versus "nominalist" versions of semiotic theory, these distinctions also have great significance in debates in Marxist theory about "materialist" and "idealist" understandings of value. The concern with symbolic motivation is implicit, for instance, in Sut Jhally's defense of Marx's conception of use value (Sahlins, 1976; Baudrillard, 1981). Both Sahlins and Baudrillard criticize Marx for his tendency to "naturalize" the use-value of goods as opposed to stressing "use" as a culturally constituted value and a symbolic construct. Jhally quotes the following passage from *Capital* in refutation of this claim: "The usefulness of a thing makes it a use-value. But this usefulness does not dangle in mid-air. It is *conditioned* by the physical properties of the commodity, and has no existence apart from the latter" (Marx, *Capital,* quoted in Jhally, 1987:43; emphasis added by Jhally).

Jhally notes that the Moscow English translation of *Capital* translated "conditioned" as "constrained" and concludes:

> Thus the meanings of a particular product are not open-ended and infinite, but neither are they unique, and I believe that Marx would not have claimed that they were so. But this does not mean that they are not determined, not objectively given, for if they are not infinite, then there is some boundary to the range of meanings available in any contextual setting. [Jhally, 1987:43]

Jhally is right to suggest in the same passage that *constraint* on meaning points to some kind of materialist theory of meaning as what he terms a "partial necessity" (Jhally, 1987:43). Still, I do not agree with Jhally's use of "determined" as the appropriate alternative to "infinite" in characterizing meaning. The recognition of an inherent "range of meanings" for any product also suggests that some part of meaning will remain contingent, hence the inappropriateness of the term "determined." These issues are taken up in considerable detail in the last two chapters of the book in relation to the cognitive processes involved in the translation of social symbols into forms of personal knowledge.

10. These issues are taken up in much more detail in Chapter 13.

2

Rethinking Culture as Models

I know noble accents
And lucid, inescapable rhythms;
But I know, too, that the blackbird is involved
In what I know.
                              —Wallace Stevens

You go to my head
And you linger like a haunting refrain.
                              —Gillespie and Coots

Over twenty years ago, just before undertaking my first fieldwork, I was hired by the Peace Corps Office in Western Samoa to work with their cross-cultural training of a new group of volunteers. My job was to speak to the newly arrived volunteers about Samoan culture. During the initial phase of training in the town of Apia, I lectured to these newcomers about Samoan history, food customs, the complex system of political titles, kinship obligations, and matters of local ettiquette. I found myself frequently referring to Samoan "culture" in my accounts, and when one of the volunteers asked me what anthropologists meant by "culture," I was surprised to find myself at a loss for a simple answer. I struggled to articulate for the trainees some kind of all-purpose unit of culture that would clarify just what we were getting at. I do not remember what I said, but it presumably was neither very definitive nor especially convincing. Here, in a country that prided itself on being the last holdout of traditional Polynesian culture, culture seemed to be everywhere. But for that very reason it seemed to elude simple definition.

Several days later, my confidence in the culture concept was further shaken when the local Peace Corps director, a young and aggressive lawyer without much patience for anthropology, challenged me to locate Samoan "culture" for him. "I don't know what you anthropologists think you have to research so hard," he quipped. "It's just people figuring out how to deal with each other," he said. "I can't see any basic difference between what we have to do back home in the States when we walk into a store and want to buy something, and when we walk into a village shop here in Samoa to pick up a box of mosquito coils. Only here they speak Samoan instead of English." He suggested that we anthropologists made too much of the idea of culture. Most human behavior, he insisted, could be explained in terms of an intuitive practical logic—commonsense strategies of people simply trying to get on with one another.

He was wrong, of course. And although he took obvious delight in goading an inexperienced scholar, I think he knew he was wrong. Yet he had a point. Aside from the obvious exotic Samoan artifacts, like fine mats or kava bowls that museums use to represent Samoan culture, it was not easy for me to point my finger at something in everyday village life and say "there's culture." But this was not because of the absence of culture, rather the opposite. Culture seemed to be everywhere and in everything. It was not easily pried free from the flow of life, so that one could isolate a moment of experience and say that there, at last, was a unit of culture for inspection.

Within a month, the trainees were taken to a Samoan village to continue their language training in a more traditional setting than the town of Apia provided. Language lessons consisted of "dialogues" of typical interactions within a village that the students memorized and used with each other. One such dialogue was an "invitation-to-eat-and-polite-response" script that had the trainees pretending to walk through a village while people called out to them from their open houses to come in and join them for a meal. Trainees learned two versions of this invitation dialogue. One ("Please come in for a meal") suggested that there was indeed food ready and that they could accept the invitation. The other was phrased negatively ("Won't you come in for some food"). It called for a polite refusal.

One day, after the trainees had gone through their language drills, we sent them out for a walk through the village for some real-world experience with the language. Within twenty minutes, some of the trainees returned from their walk. I remember the look of bemused surprise from one trainee as she approached me. "I can't believe it!" she said. "These villagers must have read our language text. They knew the dialogue word for word. It was amazing!"

Here at last, I thought, was a concrete instance of culture at work, one that I could draw attention to and say, "There you have it. Samoan culture in a nutshell!" Years later, of course, after having read through Shank and Abelson's treatise on restaurant scripts, I came to realize that the writers of the Samoan language text had simply recorded a canonical form of a cultural script for the trainees to learn. This one was quite useful for beginners, since Samoan etiquette frequently takes the form of highly codified and predictable exchanges with only minor individual variations. They were more rigid in form than many of our own cultural scripts, so they made a strong impression on those volunteers that maybe there was something to this notion of culture after all. And, as with many cultural forms, most Samoans did not think of their invitations as any kind of performance of a "script." They were simply asking, out of their genuine compassion for visitors and their love of entertaining, an appropriate question. From the outsider's perspective, these scripts appeared to be kinds of objects—predictable social artifacts, like a dialogue from a textbook. But to the people who used them, the scripts felt more like spontaneous speech, part of a taken-for-granted world of normal human intentions and feelings.

APPROACHING CULTURE THROUGH MODELS

Obviously, this invitation script was not anything close to Samoan culture in a nutshell. Whatever cultures are, they do not fit inside nutshells. But while is relatively easy to say what culture is *not,* it is much more difficult to describe what culture *is.* Anthropologists have conceptualized culture and its constitutent units in many ways: as a patchwork of traits, integrated configurations, constellations of symbols and meanings, symbolic templates, a web of meanings, taxonomic trees, measurable units of behavior, a collection of material artifacts, systems of knowledge, sets of values and beliefs, sets of characteristic strategies for accomplishing a desired goal, and, more recently, a field on which a cacophonous cluster of diverse voices or "discourses" plays itself out. But the relatively simple notion of script I came upon in those early years in Samoa points to a particularly powerful way of thinking about culture: as an extensive and heterogeneous collection of "models," models that exist both as public artifacts "in the world" and as cognitive constructs "in the mind" of members of a community.

This book adopts the view that a culture is best conceived as a very large and heterogeneous collection of *models* or what psychologists sometimes call *schemas.* Conceiving culture as a stock of models has much to recommend it for anthropology. To the extent that they are public artifacts, cultural models are out in the world, to be observed by outsiders as well as experienced by locals. In this sense, cultural models are empirical analogues of culture understood as knowledge. As we shall see, they are not analogues in any simple sense, since public models are not exactly the same thing as mental models. But approaching culture as a collection of models has the advantage of showing that making sense of culture as an aspect of mind requires that we both distinguish and relate these two notions of model.

As external and public forms, cultural models point to a great variety of human institutions that are the projections of conventional understandings of reality set in time and space, for all to experience as artifacts of a community's life. Houses, pottery, tools, paintings, songs, dances, types of clothing—all are examples of such public models. Because they are projected into material form, we often call them examples of "material culture." But cultural models can take less palpable forms, such as conventional styles of movement, speech, or social interaction. And they differ from one another in their degree of formalization. Some cultural models are highly formalized and given explicit labels, as part of a stock of self-conscious cultural forms. Samoans do this with kava ceremonies, fine mats, and certain styles of dancing, while Americans might point to the Thanksgiving dinner or to the Super Bowl as characteristic models in their own culture. As we shall see, other cultural models are less conscious and more tacitly known.

The other important advantage of conceiving of culture as a stock of conventional models is that the very notion of model provides a bridge between the empiricist concept of culture as "objects" and the cognitive concept of culture as forms of knowledge (or, more pretentiously, as mental representations). Anthropologists have borrowed this notion of model from both philosophy and psychology. Plato, and in a quite different way Kant, developed the notion of general forms (Kant called them "schemas") which were believed to underlie or guide human understanding of particular experiences. Early in this century, F. C. Bartlett suggested that cognitive schemas structure memory processes. The best known of the schema theorists is probably the Swiss psychologist Jean Piaget, who employed schema theory as the basis for a developmental view of human intelligence. Even in anthropology, the idea that knowledge comes to us prepackaged rather than piecemeal is an old one, dating back to the Ruth Benedict's notion of culture as variable patterns or configurations.

In recent years, a new cognitive version of this old view of culture as templates or patterns has emerged. Just as Benedict borrowed her vision of cultural organization from the gestalt psychology of her day, modern cognitive anthropologists have adapted the notion of "model" or "schema" from cognitive psychology as a way of representing the structured nature of cultural knowledge. Through the notion of *cultural models,* the culture concept has taken on new life as an aspect of mind. Each of the case studies in this book approaches the relationship between culture and experience through this idea of cultural models.

WHAT IS A CULTURAL MODEL?

The idea of cultural models is a useful alternative to dissolving the concept of culture altogether into vague notions of power or discourse. Yet the idea of a cultural model is also imprecise, serving as a catchall phrase for many different kinds of cultural knowledge. So long as the notion of cultural models remains undertheorized and vague in this way, its potential to provide a long overdue bridge between anthropology and cognitive science will be seriously hampered. The aim of this chapter is to develop a useful set of distinctions—to clarify what cultural models are and how they work. While several important general accounts of cultural models have appeared, no attempt has yet been made to characterize in a thoroughgoing fashion the functional and structural diversity of cultural models.[1]

In an important survey of the field, Roy D'Andrade defines a cultural model as "a cognitive schema that is intersubjectively shared by a cultural group" (D'Andrade, 1990:809). This handy and concise definition is still somewhat too vague for our purposes. For example, it does not distinguish between "special-purpose models" of relatively limited application and "foundational schemas" that structure a large number of apparently diverse models. Thus, in Samoa, the invitation script is a special-purpose model. By contrast, the center-periphery model, described in Chapter 11, is really a foundational schema of far more global application that structures a whole cluster of special-purpose models.

Another limitation of D'Andrade's definition is that it suggests an unproblematical "intersubjective sharing" of cultural models within cultural communities. But the claim that models are shared is one that deserves careful consideration. How shared must a cultural model be in order to qualify as a true cultural model rather than a personal construct? What are the relationships between cultural models and personal or idiosyncratic knowledge? These are some of the issues I take up in this book.

Perhaps most important, D'Andrade's general definition of cultural model does not distinguish between models as publicly available forms (what I call "instituted models") and models understood as mental constructs. Culture on the ground and culture in the mind must be carefully distinguished before they can be usefully related. Clearly, the notion of cultural models needs a lot of work. Even at the expense of rendering the idea of cultural model less intuitive and more complex, I want to propose a set of distinctions aimed at making the models approach to culture serviceable as a foundation for bridging cultural anthropology and cognitive science.

The human brain has often been characterized as an information processor, but its equally crucial role as a model generator is as important, though often overlooked. Human beings are opportunistic and creative model builders and model readers of great virtuosity. So it should come as no surprise that no one has tried to document the full range of possible or even existing cultural models. There is presumably no end to the variety of cultural models human communities could come up with. Furthermore, the attempt to classify cultural models into distinct genres is hampered by the fact that special-purpose models are often nested into more general and abstract schemas. It is sometimes difficult to know when we have two distinct models as opposed to different instances of the same genre. Thus, the general "restaurant script" in the United States is linked to the more specific "fast-food restaurant script." Are these two different models or two versions of the same model? Clear categorization of even this one genre of script-model is therefore very difficult.

MENTAL MODELS: PERSONAL AND CONVENTIONAL

The human ability to create mental models as ways of dealing with reality has two distinct dimensions: personal and cultural. Important as culture is for humans, our experiences are never exhaustively accounted for by a cultural analysis. Even in terms of the mental models we use to explain, predict, or justify our experiences, culture is not the only resource we have for making sense of things. While one might argue that any individual's life-world is inevitable orchestrated by culture, this assertion is somewhat misleading. Not all experience is culturally modeled to the same degree. And cultures differ in the extent to which certain classes of experience are modeled for individuals.[2]

At the personal level, each of us is adept at constructing idiosyncratic models of experience on the fly, as a basic meaning-making strategy. Common examples of such idiosyncratic model making are the mnemonic strategies we use for remembering things such as personal names or lists of vocabulary terms in a foreign language by creating very idiosyncratic associations for the new words. I have also created several mental maps of my neighborhood and my city, each of which bears only a very schematic relation to its actual layout. Each map employs landmarks of special interest to me, such as the houses of neighbors I know or the highway exits relevant for my habitual journeys. My children, who do not drive, clearly have their own mental maps of this same terrain that are quite different from mine. And their maps will have to change once they start driving. My wife's mental maps tend to be specific tracks defined by concrete landmarks. Mine tend to be more schematic, bird's-eye representations of space, though for some purposes I switch to point-to-point maps. These various maps are all mental models that have been personally constructed or "schematized" by myself and my family as a normal part of our negotiation of our physical and social world. For the most part, these *personal mental models* are idiosyncratic in that they are not shared in their details by others in my community.

In addition to these personal mental models, I have a set of concepts that I have internalized from conventional models, models that are part of the stock of shared cognitive resources of my own community. I hear "The Star Spangled Banner" being sung at a baseball game and I know I am to stand up and take off my hat. If I am watching the game on television, however, I neither stand nor remove my hat (if I am wearing one) unless the screen happens to be in the ballpark. In driving down the street, I tend to keep to the right and pass on the left unless I am driving in Britain. At home, I know I must stand if a visitor enters, while in Samoa I know that the visitor must quickly sit upon entering someone's house.

These special-purpose programs are not of my own making but are conventional models I have internalized as part of my own stock of ready-made responses. They are *conventional mental models*. Their creation is more complex than that of personal models, since they have been externalized as shared institutions as well as internalized by individuals. Conventional gestural models, such as an American handshake or a Japanese bow, emerged gradually as social institutions. Their origins are part of the largely unrecorded history of cultural conventions. Cultural models are born, transformed through use, and eventually die out. Their continued existence is contingent, negotiated through endless social exchanges. Such shared models are a community's conventional resources for meaning making. To gain motivational force in a community, these models must be reinscribed each generation in the minds of its members. In this way conventional models become a personal cognitive resource for individuals.

Both personal and conventional cognitive models are kinds of "mental models," what cognitive scientists like to call mental representations.[3] In many ways, the cognitive processes that underlie the creation and use of such conventional models are basically the same processes that are involved in the formation of any "mental models."[4] Mental models, such as my mental maps for driving to work or picking up the kids from school, are creative and adaptive simplifications of reality. Thus they do not contain many colors or sounds. And they delete the vast amount of visual detail that is actually available along these routes, retaining only abstracted, schematic information relevant to my purposes. Details are reduced in complexity and at times eliminated altogether, while salient features of an environment are selected and sometimes exaggerated or otherwise transformed by a process of formalization and simplification—a process I call "schematization." In this sense, every mental model is part memory, part invention. But there is an important difference between personal models and cultural models. Cultural models are constructed as mental representations in the same way as any mental models with the important exception that the internalization of cultural models is based on more socially constrained experiences than is the case for idiosyncratic models. Cultural practices that constrain attention and guide what is perceived as salient are not left open to much personal choice but are closely guided by social norms.

Take the case of rites of passage, which mark important status transitions for individuals. To the extent that the experiences of puberty or marriage are purely personal experiences, individuals will come to understand them through more or less personal memories. But when these life changes are marked by highly conventional ritual forms, as they are in so many societies, people's personal models of their life changes will tend to share a great many features, with overlapping salience structures. Such "shared" cultural models will not produce total cognitive homogeneity among individuals within a community but rather a tendency for personal models to overlap far more than they would if left to purely individual experience. This is the conventionalization of memory through ritual that Paul Connerton has emphasized (Connerton, 1989). Chapters 9 and 10 will explore this conventionalization of personal experience in the lives of young Murngin boys from Arnhem Land in Northern Australia, a case where the initiation rites appear to have a powerful effect in shaping how these young boys will understand and experience the general process of knowledge acquisition itself.

So conventional models are schematized by people, just as personal models are. But the processes by which they are schematized are socially constrained and reinforced by both positive and negative social feedback. Try not standing to acknowledge "The Star Spangled Banner" next time you attend a baseball game, or try crossing a busy intersection in a German city when the facing traffic light is red. You will quickly understand the power of negative social feedback.

Because it may approximate conventional models to many different degrees, the status of any "mental model" is inherently ambiguous. In some cases, an individual's mental models may be derived directly from a public (i.e., instituted) model, in which case it is a highly conventional mental model. But in other instances the mental model may diverge sharply or even be completely independent of any conventional representation, in which case it is a highly personal model. And there are all sorts of intermediate cases. One would expect, for instance, that the mental models that Catholic nuns of the same order would have of their relation to Christ would be far more conventionalized than would the models of this relationship for a Christian who attended no particular church and whose relation to Christ was markedly less mediated by conventional ritual. This is not to say that the nuns' models would all be identical but rather that their deeply personal and perhaps idiosyncratic motivations for their faith would rest on a similar experiential framework of great evocative power.[5]

Psychologists have documented the individual variability of mental models. Gentner and her associates have for years studied a kind of "naive physics," the conceptual models of the physical world that individuals construct as explanatory frameworks for how things work (Gentner, 1983). The thrust of this research is to understand the difference between expert knowledge and nonexpert knowledge in technical domains.[6]

Other research documents how individual experience transforms more general conventional cognitive models into highly personal forms. In a delightfully playful account of his experiences eating out around the world, Roger Schank has described how people construct idiosyncratic versions of restaurant scripts based upon salient personal experiences.[7] In this case a conventional model (a restaurant script) plus personal experience produce personal models. The utility of this slippery distinction is that it allows us to characterize the processes that govern the variability of mental models along a continuum, from the idiosyncratic to the conventional.

Not infrequently, individuals have conflicting personal and conventional models for a given domain of experience. In Thailand, for instance, it is expected that young men will be initiated early into sexual relations by visiting prostitutes, often with friends. The conventional model of such relations is that casual extramarital sex is a male prerogative and a natural and pleasurable part of life. In the case of a young man trying desperately to mask or deny his homosexual urges or afraid of contracting AIDS, however, there would be considerable discrepancy between the conventional attitudes he might struggle to adopt and his personal model of the encounter. Such discrepancies can produce considerable anxiety for individuals.

These situations, in which a conventional model conflicts with a personal model are not to be confused with cases in which an individual subscribes to conflicting cultural models. Chapter 12 examines a series of Samoan case studies of conflicting cultural models. Sometimes it is difficult to decide whether a widely shared alternative to a dominant cultural model represents another (counterhegemonic) cultural model or a convergence of personal models. For example, Unni Wikan's account of one Balinese woman's struggle to maintain a "bright face" in the midst of personal turmoil is described by Wikan as both personal experience (in opposition to a cultural model) and as an alternative (but less obvious) cultural model of personhood for the Balinese (Wikan, 1991; see also Abu-Lughod, 1986).

Since cultural models can have significant psychic costs for individuals, it is reasonable to suppose that dominant cultural models are often accompanied by widely shared but not highly cognized or publicly symbolized alternative models. It is hard to say whether such alternative models qualify as cultural or personal models. As Obeyesekere has shown in his ethnographic portraits of Sri Lankan ecstatic worshipers, such countermodels may, under special circumstances, actually become the basis of the creation of novel cultural models (Obeyesekere, 1981).

So far, I have stressed the importance of a distinction between personal mental models and those that are culturally mediated. The mainstream of research in cognitive psychology has studied personal mental models, while anthropologists have tended to assume that most mental models were cultural models. The assumptions of each discipline are quite different. Cognitive psychologists treat mental models largely as subjective representations constructed by individuals in a relatively direct relationship with a physical environment. By contrast, cultural anthropologists assume that cultural models are intersubjective representations, constructed by individuals in relation to a social environment. The distinction is subtle but important. Cognitive psychologists interested in mental models often base their research on the following general model:

$$\text{Individual} \rightarrow (\text{mental model}) \rightarrow \text{physical environment}$$

in which the construction of mental models mediates an individual's encounter with a particular physical world.

By contrast, research on cultural models uses a somewhat different general model:

$$\text{Individual} \rightarrow [(\text{Cultural model}) \rightarrow \text{social environment}] \rightarrow$$
$$\text{physical environment}$$

The introduction of a social environment changes the way in which anthropologists conceive of mental models. The social environment includes a stock of shared social models that constrain and motivate the construction of cognitive models. By contrast, mental models research is based on a kind of methodological individualism. The individual's cognitive orientation and adaptation become the paramount question, to which mental models are the answer. By introducing a social environment into the equation, the anthropologist transforms the problem of models into one involving intersubjective communication and not just adaptation. There is some truth to each of these representations, since, as I have argued, some but not all mental models are culturally mediated.

Research focusing on conventional models presumes that individuals adapt to the world in large part through shared resources. Many of these resources come "preconstructed" for individuals in the form of what I call instituted models. For the anthropologist, the cognitive issues become questions of (1) how external, publicly available instituted models are reconstructed as cognitive models (the two-births issue; see Shore, 1990b, and Chapter 14) and (2) the relations between relatively conventional and relatively personal mental models for any individual (Obeyesekere, 1981, 1990; D'Andrade and Strauss, 1992).

INSTITUTED MODELS

Twenty years ago, Clifford Geertz reopened Durkheim's case against psychologism in culture theory. In an influential essay, "Thick Description: Towards an Interpretive Theory of Culture" (Geertz 1973c), Geertz attacked what he termed "a theoretical muddlement in contemporary anthropology." The general criticism was aimed at what Geertz called "privacy theories of meaning" (p. 12) in cognitive anthropology. More specifically, Geertz objected to the view that "culture is composed of psychological structures by means of which individuals or groups of individuals guide their behavior" (p.11). His specific target was Ward Goodenough's cognitive characterization of culture as "whatever it is one has to know or believe in order to operate in a manner acceptable to its members" (cited in Geertz, 1973c:11). Culture, Geertz argued, was properly located in the byways of public life rather than in anyone's mind. Culture was, in his words, "an acted document."

Geertz's argument against psychologism in culture theory invoked a now famous example of how to understand a musical score. His example was a Beethoven quartet:

> [N]o one would, I think, identify it with its score, with the skills and knowledge needed to play it, with the understanding of it possessed by its performers or auditors, nor . . . with a particular performance of it or with some mysterious entity transcending material existence. . . . But that a Beethoven quartet is a temporally developed tonal structure, a coherent sequence of modeled sound—in a word, music—and not anybody's knowledge or belief about anything, including how to play it, is a proposition to which most people are, upon reflection, likely to assent. [pp. 11–12]

Yet to claim to know a Beethoven quartet as disembodied form is, like Yeats's famous conundrum, to vainly attempt to "know the dancer from the dance." There is a sense in which the quartet is, as Geertz claims, not reducible to any of its local manifestations either in performance or in the minds of its performers. Yet, ironically, unknown and unperformed, a piece of music has no real existence either. For

Geertz to acknowledge that the quartet is "a temporally developed tonal structure" and a "sequence of modeled sound" is to invoke an absent agent, the necessary agent of the embodiment of the music as an event rather than as pure potentiality. As lived experience, a musical composition, like any social institution, takes its life through its performances and as forms of knowledge by its devotees. Moreover, a composition may be understood as a "document" (to use Geertz's own metaphor) only in a tradition that includes written conventions of notation. In a purely oral tradition, Geertz's document metaphor would not appear so apt and musical compositions would be more easily understood to have their only life in their enactments as knowledge and performance. Thus, by means of a misleading analogy, Geertz made the case for understanding culture and meaning as public artifacts *rather than* as forms of personal knowledge.[8]

Geertz's influential formulation has since come under considerable criticism in anthropology.[9] Yet for all the limitations in his constriction of the culture concept, Geertz's reaffirmation of the classic Durkheimian distinction between individual and social facts was a brilliantly effective rhetorical stroke. For like Durkheim, Geertz was not wrong in his insistence on viewing culture as a public rather than a private phenomenon. But he was surely guilty of what Donald Donham (personal communication) has aptly termed "strategic overstatement," a rather effective vice not unknown elsewhere in cultural anthropology. Geertz's argument proceeds from a false dichotomy between culture-in-the-world and culture-in-the-mind.

The upshot of Geertz's overstatement was to shift the attention of a generation of talented scholars to the character of cultural symbolism. In much the same way as Boas had earlier argued for the relative autonomy of culture from biology, Geertz claimed for cultural symbols a terrain all their own. Yet what both Geertz and Goodenough failed to emphasize was that the locus of culture was inherently ambiguous and could not be adequately characterized in exclusively psychological or social terms. By their very nature, cultural models have two quite different lives: as social artifacts and as cognitive representations. The enforced distinction between these two dimensions of cultural models allowed each to thrive in its own domain (anthropology and psychology), each relatively innocent of an understanding of the other. Serious attention to the crucial question of the relationship between culture's two lives awaited a more ecumenical intellectual environment.

What Geertz called "templates" I call *instituted models*. Instituted models are social institutions—conventional, patterned public forms such as greetings, calendars, cockfights, discourse genres, houses, public spaces, chants, conventional body postures, and even deliberately orchestrated aromas. In what sense can we consider such conventional shared arrangements to be "models"? After all, models imply not simply that something exists but that something exists *for someone*. Instituted models always lead a double life, as part of an external social world and as products of intentional behavior. They are models in two different senses. First, instituted models are human inventions, the product of the continual social production of publicly available forms. Instituted models are the externalization in the social world of particular *models of* experience. Second, to the extent to which these instituted models govern concept formation of newly socialized individuals, they are also *models from* which individuals construct more or less conventional mental models.

While the distinction between instituted models and conventional mental models is of great theoretical importance, it is not always easy to separate the two. The sorts of models privileged by Geertz's analysis (i.e., cockfights, calendars, time reckoning, personal names) all have the advantage that they are relatively easy to observe empirically, independent of their existence as cognitive representations. Geertz's conception of culture as acted public documents rests on a careful selection of examples, those that intuitively seem firmly rooted as public artifacts of social life. For other models, the distinction between social and cognitive representations is more problematic. The difference lies in how "institutionalized" the models are.

Models become "institutionalized" when they are objectified as publicly available forms (Berger and Luckmann, 1966). The most obvious examples of highly institutionalized cultural models are performance genres like rituals, carnival, dance genres, or games. The status of such cultural performances as expressive cultural artifacts is underscored by performance frame markers—the physical stage, the raising and lowering of curtains, costumes, the dimming of the houselights, and so on—and highly formalized behavior, setting them off from the flow of normal life. Highly objectified verbal conventions like proverbs and myths are also easily detachable from the contexts of their ongoing creation and production in the flow of discourse. Wherever such forms are detachable in this way and become objectified for people as relatively stable cultural institutions "in the world," it is relatively easy to distinguish them from their instantiations as conventional mental models "in the mind."

Other kinds of cultural models, like scripts or taxonomies, are also modeled in social discourse. Like those just discussed, they are social models, public artifacts of culture. But often these more implicit models are embedded in the flow of discourse and are not marked as performance frames in the same way as rituals or games. Whereas people are usually aware of highly institutionalized models in their culture, they are rarely cognizant of the existence of implicit cultural models.

Terms like "ritual," "performance," or "script" have a literal quality when applied to institutionalized performance frames like religious ritual or theatrical drama. But they take on a more figurative sense when applied by scholars like Victor Turner, Erving Goffman, or Schank and Abelson to more implicit models like restaurant scripts, conflict-resolution strategies, or patterns of elevator behavior.

The reason for stressing the distinction between conventional mental models and instituted models is that there is not a simple one-to-one correspondence between a social model and its cognitive analogue. It is conceivable, for example, that under certain conditions, members of a community will fail to fully internalize a cultural model because their personal experiences are incompatible with the conventional model. For these people the cultural models have become "dead models." These individuals may well have alternative mental models, models that may be highly idiosyncratic or socially manifested as marginal cultural representations or as cultural innovations.

The second kind of disparity between instituted and conventional mental models derives from the cognitive processes by which social models are given their second life as mental representations. I call these processes "meaning construction." Meaning construction is quite different from what Strauss (1992) calls "the fax view" of internalization, where cultural models are seen as copied directly as mental analogues in the mind. The contingencies of meaning construction are complex and suggest that public cultural models undergo a variety of transformations as they are brought to mind. Meaning construction is discussed at length in Chapters 13 and 14.

FOUNDATIONAL SCHEMAS

There is some confusion in the literature on mental and cultural models about what constitutes a model. The terms "model" and "schema" are often used interchangeably to refer to organizations at different levels of abstraction. Thus, for instance, Quinn argues that the metaphors people use for talking about marriage in the United States can only be understood in relation to the "American cultural model" of marriage (Quinn, 1991). She seems to imply here that (as opposed to Lakoff and Johnson, 1980) the metaphors *refer to* cultural models and that a cultural model for marriage exists at a higher degree of abstraction and generality than the metaphors that organize people's talk about marriage. The analysis does make clear what such a general cultural model of marriage looks like and how it is different from a metaphor model.

For both mental and instituted models, we need to distinguish between abstract global models and more concrete and particular instantiations of those models. I call the more general and abstract forms *foundational schemas,* reserving the term "model" for the particular and more concrete instantiations of those schemas.[10]

Foundational schemas organize or link up a "family" of related models. Obviously, the difference between a model and a foundational schema is relative rather than intrinsic or absolute. The distinction between a foundational schema and a model becomes useful mainly when a set of specific cultural models shares a common general schema. The distinction is really a matter of context. Take, for example, the general hub-and-spoke spatial plan we see in airports, school buildings, and shopping malls. As a general spatial organization, the hub-and-spoke layout could be considered a foundational schema in relation to any of its specific architectural genres, which I would call models. On the other hand, the hub-and-spoke building plan might be treated as a model based on an even more general radial schema that informs a variety of related arrangements, such as route scheduling for airlines or trains or the relationship between home office and regional managers or between central administration and teaching staff.

Lakoff (1987a) and Johnson (1987) both use the term "schema" to refer to abstract cognitive forms in their discussion of the "image schemas" that inform many particular metaphors. Image schemas, like the "center-periphery schema" so common in Samoa (Shore, 1982; and Chapter 11) or the "container" or "journey" schemas central to the Murngin worldview (Chapters 9 and 10), are inherently abstract and perceptually uncommitted forms. Such abstract schemas are commonly (though not inevitably) derived from concrete bodily experience (Johnson, 1987; Lakoff, 1987a; Lakoff and Johnson, 1980).[11] Yet as foundational schemas, what they lose in specific sensory reference they gain in their ability to organize a wide diversity of particular models. As such, they underwrite the possibility of meaning construction in a variety of contexts.

Not all cultural models have an encompassing foundational schema. Many cultural models are special-purpose models with no family resemblance to other models. On the other hand, those models linked through foundational schemas have a special status in any community, contributing to the sense that its members live in a world populated by culturally typical practices and a common worldview. The extent to which communities will differ from one another in the degree to which cultural mod-

els are linked by foundational schemas has never to my knowledge been systematically studied by anthropologists. Yet certain societies appear to exploit a relatively
small number of foundational schemas to structure many of their specific cultural
models. Perhaps the best-documented example of a culture whose institutuons are an
extreme elaboration of a few foundational schemas are the Australian aboriginal
groups, for whom the Dreamtime journey schema seems to have special significance
(see Chapters 9 and 10).

The importance of such foundational schemas will be evident in all of the case
studies we look at in this book. In Samoa, for instance, the center-periphery schema
is instantiated in numerous cultural models, ranging from dance styles to the organization of village space. The common foundational schema that appears to connect
these diverse cultural models motivates, for Samoans, a high degree of coherence in
what appears to be a complex social system. The same is true of the "inside-outside"
container schema central to Murngin cosmology (Chapters 9 and 10; also Morphy,
1991, especially chapter 5). Chapters 5 and 6 describe a very general "modularity
schema" that is a powerful organizing principle of many American institutions.

Typically, people are more likely to be aware of the organization of specific
cultural models than they are of the existence of the common underlying schema. To
the extent that individuals are aware of schematic knowledge at all, it is usually tacit
knowledge. For example, in the next chapter we find that baseball fans are often
quite conscious of the special character of baseball space. They are aware of the
particular charm of the traditional baseball park compared with the modern domes.
Baseball writers were eloquent about the significance of the return to traditional baseball space in the building of Baltimore's Camden Yards. The same kind of awareness
by fans characterizes their appreciation of the special character of baseball's orchestration of time (the celebration of baseball's glorification of inning time over clock
time). But rarely are these same "experts" aware that these specific models of time
and of space have a common underlying (asymmetrical) schema.[12]

A MATTER OF PERSPECTIVE: ACTORS' MODELS AND
OBSERVERS' MODELS

In the 1960s and 1970s three of the most influential approaches to the study of culture
were structuralism (dominated by Levi-Strauss), the Chicago school of symbolic anthropology (dominated by Geertz, Turner, and Schneider), and ethnoscience (whose
many champions included Frake, Goodenough, Sturdevant, Lounesbury, and Conklin). In its own way, each of these schools of thought claimed to be dealing with
the relationship between culture and mind. Yet in each the concrete subject of culture
was hard to find. These versions of culture theory tended to give us disembodied
systems, structures, or programs—knowledge without any particular knower in mind
and structures of thought that lacked any flesh-and-blood thinkers.[13] Real people
were replaced by hypothetical entities—"the savage mind," the "typical" or "average" members of a community. People appeared more as the passive sites of cultural
programming than as purposeful agents, strategists, and meaning makers. Despite
these serious shortcomings, these midcentury approaches to culture did have a significant virtue. The culture concept was given very powerful theoretical articulation

in the form of structures, taxonomic programs, and systems of symbols and meanings. Yet the culture concept gained in clarity at the expense of its concrete agents. We came to know more about cultural systems in general than we did about people in particular.

Over the past two decades, anthropologists have sought to redress the omission of the concrete subject in culture theory by reconstituting the field of culture as a complex arena with many voices, often discordant. In this poststructuralist version, the agents of culture are no longer hypothetical or average natives but look like real individuals with specific histories, particular interests, and concrete strategies. Rather than as members of homogeneous cultures, we now are more likely to conceive of our natives as enmeshed in complex power relations. As a remedial strategy, this reconstitution of the living subject of culture has been an important corrective to the excesses of earlier theories of culture. Yet it is hard to miss the irony. As the concrete person has been given new life in anthropology, the very concept of culture that has been at the heart of the discipline has receded from view and is all but lost to us. Anthropologists no longer have what might be termed a "cultural imagination." We now know much more about particular people within the cultures we study than we do about the cultures themselves.

While many have greeted these developments as wholly salutary, I think that our newfound insight into the contingencies and loose ends of culture as lived come at a serious cost: a lamentable loss of focus on the notion of culture itself. When the very notion of culture becomes equated with bloodless structures and disembodied programs, anthropologists trained in the new poststructuralism flee from the concept that once defined their field, finding their legs in the more hospitable fields of history and identity politics.

I suspect that the very idea of cultural models has, in the minds of many anthropologists, become synonymous with these presumably outmoded structuralist approaches to culture theory. Particularly in the area of the cultural construction of emotion, some anthropologists have managed rather successfully to reconcile the idea cultural models with an agent-centered poststructuralist vision of culture. In particular, Catherine Lutz and Lila Abu-Lughod have used cultural models in this way. But they have done so largely by defining cultural models as matters of speech rather than in the more cognitive idiom of mental models (Abu-Lughod, 1986; Lutz, 1988; Lutz and Abu-Lughod, 1990). Reconstituted as discourse, cultural models have quite literally "surfaced" in a retreat from any kind of rigorously cognitive characterization of culture. More than anything else, it is probably this retreat from any sort of depth psychology into the surfaces of cultural life that has driven a wedge between cultural anthropology and cognitive science.

This rejection of cognitive models as an approach to culture is unfortunate and misguided. I am very sympathetic with the anthropologist's shift of attention to human agency and contingency in cultural life. Yet properly conceived, this focus should lead us further *into* the issues of the relations among culture, mind, and models rather than signal a retreat from the cognitivist paradigm.

What has been missing in cognitive anthropology is careful attention to the distinction between actors' and observers' models. In fact, the difference between actors' and observers' models is hardly acknowledged in anthropology and so has not been well studied by anthropologists. It is well recognized, however, by psychologists interested in visual processing, spatial representation, and cognitive maps. In the analysis of Samoan spatial models in Chapter 11, this distinction in how cultural models are positioned suggests not only alternative ethnographic strategies for anthropologists but also the significance of alternatively positioned native models. The Samoan case suggests that subtle but significant differences between actors' and observers' models may exist for many domains of experience.

In general, actors' models employ symbolic forms that are dynamic and graded, permitting the representation of an individual's changing relationships to any phenomenon. They are dynamic ecological models that govern the negotiation of a changing landscape. By contrast, observers' models are adapted for the representation and social coordination of abstract general perspectives. Thus observers' models tend to be organized more in terms of categories, permitting mutual rather than just personal orientation. Structuralism, with its attention to culture as categories, was enamored of observers' models and failed to acknowledge that the flow of attention and action was also subject to modeling of a quite different kind. A kind of objectivist knowledge was unfortunately put forward as a sufficient account of the whole of culture. In Chapter 11, I argue that the proper remedy for this error is not to abandon the idea of cultural models but rather to use what we know about various kinds of mental maps of spatial relations to rethink the issue of perspective in approaching culture through the concept of models.

MODEL GENRES

Cultural models fall into a large number of general genre forms. These genres have been the most important way that cognitive anthropologists have distinguished different cultural models from one another. Because a single genre of cultural model may serve several different functions, it is useful to treat the structural variations in models separately from the question of function. Probably the most basic structural distinction in any typology of cultural models is that between *linguistic* and *nonlinguistic models*. Linguistic models have been studied far more thoroughly by anthropologists than have nonlinguistic models (D'Andrade, 1990:795).

Linguistic Models

Linguistically coded models exhibit a great diversity and complexity in human life. To exhaust the description of linguistic models would be to rehearse virtually the whole of linguistics. Here I deal with linguistic models at a relatively high level of organization (as opposed to micromodels of phonological, morphological, and syntactic patterns in language). I consider the following genres of linguistic models:

- Scripts
- Propositional models
- Sound symbolic models
- Lexical models
- Grammatical models
- Verbal formulas
- Trope models

Scripts are standardized conversation templates for organizing interactions in well-defined, goal-oriented situations. A more elaborate discussion of script models is presented below in the section on functional dimensions of cultural models (task models). Scripts are really ritualized conversations and are pervasive in discourse. The basic unit of any script is a conversational unit which linguists sometimes call "a turn." Turn-taking is often a highly scripted activity in conversations, and is modeled for children in a variety of conventional verbal games and routines (Garvey, 1977).

Propositional models are cultural models in the form of linguistic propositions. In logic, propositions are statements asserting or proposing a state of affairs. For Susanne Langer, propositional symbolic forms are characterized by discursiveness. They move around things rather than presenting them directly. Langer suggests that such discursive symbolisms as ordinary language or mathematics have a high degree of abstractness from which they derive their power to re-present experience rather than iconically modeling it (Langer, 1957).[14] D'Andrade echoes Langer when he defines propositional schemas as "abstract, language-based representations" (D'Andrade, 1990:810).[15]

The Ten Commandments are an important propositional model in the Judeo-Christian tradition. When the police read a criminal suspect his rights, the information is encoded in a propositional model. Western legal codes tend to be formalized as propositional models, though legal decisions based on "precedent" may actually use nonpropositional models as the basis for deciding cases.

Sound symbolic models are important features of all languages but have been relatively ignored by linguistics.[16] Sound symbolic models convey important information through conventional phonological patterns. *Phonesthemes* are forms of buried onomatopoeia that unite whole classes of terms (e.g., glitter, glow, glisten, glimmer). Phonesthemes are discussed in more detail in Chapter 13. *Phonological speech registers* are pronunciation styles that index different contexts in a language. In Chapter 11, the cognitive implications of Samoan phonological speech registers are considered in detail.

Lexical models use sets of related terms to model forms of experience. Examples of different sorts of lexical models are *taxonomies, lists* of names or other linked items, *dictionaries,* and clearly defined subsets of *vocabularies,* such as honorifics or curse words. Thanks to the work of linguistic anthropologists and the tradition of ethnoscience, we know far more about taxonomies than we do about most other kinds of cultural models. For instance, Berlin et al., in a set of classic papers on folk taxonomies, have proposed that folk taxonomies are rarely if ever more than five levels deep. Moreover, there appear to be limits on how many classificatory terms will appear under any single node. The upward limit is fifty (Berlin et al., 1966, 1973; D'Andrade, 1990:797). While memory and other processing limitations appear to place universal constraints on taxonomies, the degree of elaboration of any domain and the salience of different taxonomic levels are culturally quite variable (Dougherty, 1978).

Grammatical models are highly abstract models of time, space, movement, and causality that are encoded by grammatical forms such as noun classes, verb aspect, tense structures, and agent markers. An early analysis of the cultural implications of such grammatical models was contained in classic papers by Edward Sapir and particularly by his student Benjamin Whorf (Sapir, 1921/1949; Whorf, 1956). More recent analyses of "cognitive grammar" can be found in the work of Jakobson (1971), Lakoff (1987a), Langacker (1987), Talmy (1978, 1983), and Hanks (1990).

Verbal formulas encode traditional wisdom, specialized knowledge, or techniques in highly conventional forms of speech. Examples of verbal formulas are proverbs, sayings, traditional narratives, prayers, spells, and nursery rhymes.[17] Clichés are highly conventional phrases that come ready-made for certain occasions; they are important (if annoying) linguistic resources that all speakers have, which serve to lubricate conversations by providing a degree of automatism in response patterns. In this sense, clichés are closely related to script models, though they are generally limited to phrases rather than comprising whole conversations.

Narrative is one of the more complex and important kinds of cultural model. It has a uniquely ambiguous status among verbal formulas. On the one hand, the term "narrative" refers to the activity of adjusting and creating reality through talking it out. In narrative, people continually make sense of their worlds "on the fly." Through narrative, the flow of events is given an articulate form, made into a kind of model. Experience is literally talked into meaningfulness. In this sense of narrative, cultural models orchestrate the rules of conversation—such as turn-taking, topic control, and speech styles—but not necessarily the content of the narrative.

On the other hand, narrative also refers to the instituted result of this structuring process.[18] Formalized narratives range from rumor and gossip through everyday recountings of ordinary events, to just-so stories, and ultimately to sacred myth narratives. Such formalized narratives are the negotiated end product of the narrative process.[19] And, of course, the creative relationship between narrating as activity and narrative as product is mutual. Any formalized narrative is subject to renegotiation through further talk, as are the very norms of conversation.

The role of narrative in meaning construction becomes especially clear following anomalous or otherwise disturbing events. An earthquake strikes, a group of people witness a shooting, a baseball player makes an "impossible" catch to save a game, or an umpire makes an incomprehensible call to lose one. Any such unexpected event is, for normal people, relatively indigestible until it is processed by talk into a palatable form. Following such disturbing events, people generally become talkative. They tell and retell the story until the events are gradually domesticated into one or more coherent and shared narratives that circulate among the community of sufferers. The meanings are emergent in the narrative process.

Through narrative, the strange and the familiar achieve a working relationship. Narratives like this provide comfort in the familiarity of their sedimented forms, just as they provide excitement in the novelty and contingencies of their contents. Jerome Bruner sees narrative as among culture's main resources for handling what he calls "an exception to the ordinary":

> All such stories seem to be designed to give the exceptional behavior meaning in a manner that implicates an intentional state in the protagonist (a, belief or desire) and some canonical element in the culture (national holiday, fund-raiser, fringe nationalism). The function of the story is to find an intentional state that mitigates or at least makes comprehensible a deviation from a canonical cultural pattern. [Bruner, 1990:49–50]

In this way, we can see the connection between the kinds of homespun narratives created on the fly to make sense of anomalous situations and the work of traditional narrative forms like fairy tales and children's bedtime stories (Bettelheim, 1976). Both narrative genres provide a comforting framework within which to relate often discomforting events.

Tropes are important linguistic models that permit language to transcend literal reference. Tropes alter our understanding of things. *Metaphor models* are, with the exception of taxonomies, probably the best-studied cultural models.[20] Recently, anthropologists have begun to pay more attention to the importance of *metonym models,* an important kind of trope that establishes a part-for-whole relation between two things. Smoke has a metonymic relation to fire, a flushed face has a metonymic relation to anger, a sickle (as in the Soviet flag) has a metonymic relation to the domain of horticulture and labor more generally. Because they define what Peirce called indexical relations, metonym models are particularly important in diagnostic procedures. Because speech is so thoroughly saturated with linguistic tropes, it is easy to overlook them in any account of cultural models. The complex relationship between metonymic and metaphoric models is explored in detail in Chapters 7 and 8 in reference to the problem of totemic classification. Chapters 13 and 14 deal with the connection between these tropes and the cognitive processes involved with meaning construction.

Nonlinguistic Models

As the name suggests, nonlinguistic models are a heterogeneous collection of models that exploit a great diversity of sensory modes and representational forms. I divide nonlinguistic models into the following genres:

- Image schemas
- Action sets
- Olfactory models
- Sound image models
- Visual image models

Image schemas are highly abstract schemas that organize and relate a wide variety of different cultural models. Lakoff calls these "image schematic models" (Lakoff, 1987a:118) and defines them as "schematic images, such as trajectories or long, thin shapes, or containers" (pp. 113–114). George Lakoff and Mark Johnson (Lakoff and Johnson, 1980; Johnson, 1987; Lakoff, 1987a) have both argued that most of these schemas are derived from somatic experience (up-down schemas, center-periphery schemas, container schemas, movement schemas, and so on) and are commonly grounded in relation to bodily experience. While I generally agree with this understanding of the embodied character of image schematic knowledge, it is useful to distinguish these general spatial schemas from those that have a direct and explicit link with the body and its changing states, which I call *kinesthetic schemas.* Kinesthetic schemas model an individual's relationship to the immediate environment through conventions affecting posture, interpersonal space, and muscle tone. Bowing, sitting, walking, and even sleeping are often highly stylized through kinesthetic cultural models and convey important cultural information about status, mood, and relationship.

Emotion models have been generally studied as linguistic models (Lakoff, 1987a; Lutz, 1988; Lutz and Abu-Lughod, 1990); the dynamic feeling states associated with conventional emotions have not received the same kind of attention (though see Langer, 1967). These bodily states are also subject to cultural modeling and would fall under the general rubric of "kinesthetic schemas." The most elaborated and self-conscious kinesthetic schemas are associated with dance.

Action sets are gestural models that have a structure much like a conversation. Simple, stylized body movements can become integrated into a coordinated interchange. Children sometimes spontaneously invent or improvise on conventional action sets in the form of games that require reciprocal actions and movements. When action sets become institutionalized, they become cultural models. Action-coordination play sets appear to be a very basic way in which individuals coordinate relationships. The most primitive action-coordination play set is undoubtedly the peek-a-boo game between infants and their caregivers. Hand-shaking, clapping games among children, mutual bowing, and embracing are other examples of culturally salient action sets that are usefully thought of as gestural conversation scripts. Other common cultural genres employing action sets are conventional greetings and threat displays. Highly complex action sets often in conjunction with other kinds of models are what we normally refer to as *ritual performances*.

Smells are sometimes orchestrated as *ofactory models*. Because of their special relation to long-term memory, olfactory models are often used to mark special occasions, individuals, or relationships. The use of incense or perfumes to create a powerful atmosphere for a special occasion is very common but has hardly been studied by anthropologists. Despite their importance as cultural models, we seem to lack an adequate vocabulary or set of concepts for analyzing smells. It is likely that smell has a distinct status as a model because of its relatively inarticulate nature and its special relation to memory (Sperber, 1975).

Sound image models, because of their interest to linguists and ethnomusicologists, have been better studied than olfactory models. Many rituals use sounds as an important component. Obviously, the most important sound image models are musical forms that figure prominently in many areas of life. (For ethnographies that stress the cultural significance of sounds image models, see Basso, 1985; Feld, 1982; and Schieffelin, 1976.)

Visual image models have been well documented by anthropologists and art historians. These include *iconographic models*—culturally salient paintings and decorative motifs (Morphy, 1991; Munn, 1966, 1973; Reichard, 1974)—and *color symbolism* (Reichard 1974; Turner 1967a). Though there is nothing especially new about the study of sound or visual image models, much less is known about the cognitive implications of the stress on one sensory modality over another. The Kaluli of New Guinea, for example, seem to privilege sound image models in meaning construction, living as they do in a tropical forest where much is accessible only through sound and not visually. Polynesians, by contrast, seem to stress visual models—bright colors and large forms (as in houses or bodies), reflecting the presence of spiritual power *(mana);* (see Koskinnen, 1968; Shore, 1989).

FUNCTIONAL DISTINCTION AMONG MODELS

While function is sometimes closely tied to form, a functional typology of cultural models actually looks quite different from an analysis of structural types. Because cultural models are symbolic representations of reality, it does not often occur to anyone to ask what different kinds of work models do. Representation sometimes seems to be a self-evident function that requires no further comment. Yet cultural models actually have a wide variety of functions. Up to this point, no attempt has been made in the cultural models literature to outline in detail the major functions of cultural models. This section deals with pragmatic aspects of cultural models, classifying them in functional terms.

These functional classifications are orthogonal to the structural classification of models, viewing many of the same models from a different vantage point. Thus a particular genre of cultural model might serve several different functions. Or several distinct genres might all serve a similar function. Because there is no simple one-to-one mapping of functions to structures for cultural models, it is important to make both kinds of distinction.

From a functional perspective, it is useful to divide models into three general classes:

- Orientational models
- Expressive/conceptual models
- Task models

Orientational Models

Orientational models provide members of a community with a common framework for orienting individuals to one another and to what Hallowell called their behavioral environment (Hallowell, 1955). There are several important kinds of orientational models:

- Spatial models
- Temporal models
- Social orientation models
- Diagnostic models

Spatial Models

Spatial models orient people to the physical environment. There are many kinds of models that function for spatial orientation. Important examples include the following:

- *Area maps* of all kinds of geographic entities
- *Navigational models* such as Micronesian star charts (Hutchins, 1991); verbal formats for giving traveling directions
- *Route maps* realized in propositional form, pictorial form, or (as is common among Australian aborigines) in song lyrics
- *Models of interpersonal space,* which code for aspects of power and intimacy

- *Context markers,* which frame spaces as distinctive behavioral contexts (sports fields, play frames, and performance frames are all examples of spatial context markers)

Temporal Models

Temporal models orchestrate culturally specific time frames. Important kinds of temporal model include the following:

Incremental models, which show the progress of time, sometimes as measured from a beginning point. All manner of watches, stopwatches, some calendars, and oral counting schemes model the forward movement of time. A special kind of incremental temporal model measures the passage of time either from a significant past event or in relation to a significant future event. These temporal schemes often model time in religious traditions by providing mythical orientational points toward which or away from which time is understood to flow.

Decremental models structure the counting-down of time. Many games are temporally organized by decremental models. The count-down NASA uses for its space launches is a familiar decremental model of time. As with incremental models, decremental models may use digital or analog coding (such as an hourglass or, in basketball, a shot-clock). Radioactive dating techniques in paleoanthropology employ decremental time models based on the half-lives of particular radioactive elements.

Cyclical models provide a punctuated view of time viewed as cycles. Javanese and Balinese gamelan music employs a complex cyclical framework of sound (McPhee 1966), which has its analogues in Balinese calendars, kin terms, and cycles of personal names (Geertz, 1973e). Like the walkabout schema of the Murngin, these complex cultural models all function to shape the perception of various spans of time as cycles.

Rhythmic models break up the flow of time into rhythmic segments for the purpose of framing musical or verbal expression. Metronomes, baton movements, clapping, body movements, and percussion instruments all aid in the conventional keeping of time.

Biographical models are conventional models for conceptualizing people's life cycles. Our biographical models tend to be incremental, focusing on aging or getting older. In some cultures, however, biographical models stress the cyclical nature of the human life cycle or the replacement of one personality by another.

Context-framing devices mark off special time frames in the same sense as spatial models frame places. Time is segmented into special spaces, such as sacred time, secular time, or game time.

Social Orientational Models

Social orientation models orient individuals and groups to one another and to a socially differentiated environment.

Models of social relations have been well studied by several generations of social anthropologists. Social relations are modeled in a great variety of ways. Best studied, no doubt, are the *lexical models* that map kin terminologies. Anthropologists have traditionally ordered these into taxonomies, most commonly semantic trees, using conventions for representing kin relations. *Personal names and titles* are other kinds of lexical models that organize social relations in complex ways.

Kin relations may also be modeled in numerous other ways. *Metaphorical models* for mapping kin relations are common. Evans-Prichard made famous the complex metaphoric mappings between kin types and cattle types made by the Nuer (Evans-Prichard, 1940). Australian aboriginal groups and some groups from Papua New Guinea model kin relations through analogical mappings of kin onto human body parts (Schieffelin, 1976; Shapiro, 1981).

Significant social relations are commonly modeled through *verbal formulas* such as chants, songs, proverbs, and narratives. Among many Australian aboriginal groups, *iconic representations* in the form of diagrams and track maps (now a popular form of tourist art) model mythically grounded kinship and marriage relations among groups (Morphy, 1991; Munn, 1973).

Social coordination is promoted through a number of different kinds of cultural models. Among the most important are *rituals,* highly scripted and formalized action sets that provide a shared behavioral framework for coordinating social relations. The coordinating function of ritual is particularly evident in greeting rituals and rites of solidarity, like cheers, huddles, and group dancing. Rituals involving songs and action sets are also common ways of coordinating group work activities.

Social role sets model the division of labor. In modern industrial organizations, work roles are modeled by taxonomic trees called organizational charts, which model functional and authority relations. The most famous non-Western cultural model of social roles is the Varna system of India and its elaboration into the various localized subcaste role-set models collectively known as the *jajmani* system. Here the division of labor is conceptualized through several kinds of cultural models, including metaphor models, narrative models, and elaborate ritual models.

Emotion models are an important kind of cultural model that has been extensively studied in recent years by anthropologists.[21] I include them here as a form of orientational model to stress the orienting and communicative function of emotion models. As Levy has argued, emotions index fundamental qualities of relationships, and cultural models of emotion provide a degree of standardization in emotional response within a community (Levy, 1984).

Diagnostic Models

Diagnostic models provide conventional means of taking "readings" of important phenomena. In semiotic terms, they are conventional indexical models, readings of signs as indices of underlying states, causes, or conditions.

Medical diagnostic models include taxonomies and divination rites as well as metonymic and metaphoric models that read somatic symptoms in relation to classifications of disease types.

Checklists are models for taking inventory of complex procedures or collections of objects or people.

Divinatory models are strategies for uncovering hidden causes for a community's problems.

Meteorological models are models by which communities read the state of the natural world. They include all sorts of models for weather forecasting but also models for interpreting the relationships between natural events (seasons, floods, eclipses, volcanoes, storms, tides, etc.) and their social, moral and supernatural correlates.

Intention displays are cultural models by which members of a community read each others' intentions.

Expressive/Conceptual Models

Expressive and *conceptual models* crystallize for communities important but otherwise unspoken understandings and experiences. They are an important means by which shared personal experiences become objectified, conventionalized, and thereby transformed into cultural artifacts. I divide expressive/conceptual models into four subtypes:

- Classificatory models
- Ludic models
- Ritual and dramatic models
- Theories

Classificatory models were the bread and butter of ethnoscience in the 1960s and 1970s. Most of these models were predominantly lexical taxonomies of distinct domains like kinship, color, fauna, flora, disease, and foods. Early studies focused on classical models of classification (what anthropologists called componential analysis). Classification was assumed to be based on well-formed categories, defined in terms of the intersection of more primitive semantic components or attributes.

For Johnson-Laird, the classical approach to category formation is distinguished by its reliance on concepts such as "Boolean functions—negation, conjunction, disjunction, and their combinations—of simple concepts" (Johnson-Laird, 1983:186).[22]

In the mid-1970s, the pathbreaking work of Eleanor Rosch and her associates shifted the focus away from the classical model of category formation to the role of "prototype effects" as manifested in exemplars, best cases, metonymy, typicality, and basic-level categories.[23] Basic-level categories tend to be at a level of specificity intermediate between global inclusiveness and perceptual particularity. Basic-level objects are easily rendered as simple gestalts, making them easy to identify and use as perceptual templates. Children generally learn basic-level terms before they master more general or specific levels of categorization. Basic-level categorization employs part-to-whole associations (synecdoche). They serve as *exemplar models* for the identification of related objects, both more general and more specific (Lakoff, 1987a:47).

Classificatory models may have a number of different functions, including diagnosis and orientation. Yet I have distinguished classification as a distinct function of cultural models. This is because, whatever else classificatory models may accomplish for people, the clarification of experience through classificatory models seems to be an irreducible end in itself.[24]

Exemplars are culturally salient instances of objects, people, or events. Exemplars typify experiences for us in that they represent a best case or ideal version and become the model against which other similar experiences are matched. Exemplars account for many of the *prototype effects* in human categorization where not all examples are considered equally good instances of a category.

Exemplars come in many forms. *Object exemplars* are often the basis on which people classify objects. *Person exemplars* underlie the classification of significant others and are frequently modeled in stories, drama, pictorial forms, or through verbal tropes like metaphor or synecdoche ("He's a Don Juan!"). *Person exemplars* define heros, villains, and personality types on the basis of which people make sense of their social worlds. *Event exemplars* are a way in which people classify events in relation to typicality or predictability. *Narrative exemplars* are found in myth, story, and verse. They set out foundational scenarios and event structures that provide the basis for comparing and clarifying other events and situations. Exemplary narratives figure importantly in most religious traditions.

Ludic models include games, sports, and other playful genres like joke telling. While numerous functions have been suggested for ludic genres, they share with other kinds of cultural performances the power to crystallize, in a discrete performative frame, key cultural problematics. Chapters 3 and 4 deal with the importance of ludic models in modern life.[25]

Ritual and dramatic models include all forms of dramatic performances. Like ludic models, ritual and drama are important ways that communities externalize and objectify otherwise inchoate or inarticulate experiences. Whatever purely personal functions such performances have, they have the social function of constituting experiences as public artifacts.[26]

Theories are important cultural models that provide communities with a conceptual picture of a complex state of affairs. *Scientific theories* are a special kind of highly explicit theory model. Their creation and maintenance are constrained by the norms of the "scientific method." Folk theories are the cultural equivalent of mental models of naive physics. Like scientific theories, folk theories are always empirically based in that they are motivated by complex human experiences.[27] Unlike scientific theories, folk theories are often forms of tacit knowledge. They are also far more conservative than scientific theories and are more resistant (though not completely resistant) to empirical disconfirmation. Under the rubric "bricolage," Levi-Strauss has studied some of the important symbolic strategies used in many cultures for maintaining these theories (Levi-Strauss, 1966).

One of the best-studied genres of folk theories is what has come to be called *ethnopsychology*—local theories of the person. *Scholarly theories* such as those put forward in treatises in the humanities and social sciences are like scientific theories in that they are self-conscious creations, subject to discussion and critical review. Unlike scientific theories, however, they are not usually subject to strict criteria of verification and falsification. Most theories are realized by propositional models, though theoretical knowledge is also commonly modeled nonpropositionally in diagrams, pictures, and action sets.

Task Models

These are culturally modeled strategies or programs for getting practical things done. Most of the pragmatic tasks humans do are aided by conventional models, models that facilitate (1) the memorability of complex procedures, (2) the predictability of results, and (3) the social coordination of complex tasks. I distinguish five basic genres of task models:

- Scripts
- Recipes
- Checklists
- Mnemonic models
- Persuasion models

Scripts are general performance models that include both verbal and nonverbal dimensions. They have a general form that can be adapted to a great variety of specific cases by slight modifications. The best-studied cultural script is the American restaurant script (Schank 1991; Schank and Abelson, 1977), though script models underlie a wide range of human interactions. The basic script for most ordinary (as opposed to highly formalized) scenarios is a kind of foundational schema that can be realized with many variations and has room for spontaneous individual variation as well.[28] Sacred scripts, often associated with ritual models, tend to be far more constrained and (at least in theory) less open to this sort of variation.

Recipes are conventional task models for performing complex routines like dancing, making tools, preparing food, or harvesting crops. Many of these tasks can be performed through trial and error, without the aid of recipes. Whenever complex tasks are standardized and broken down into smaller segments embodied in a standardized form, we can speak of recipe models. While we normally associate recipes with language models (spoken or written), nonverbal kinesthetic or pictorial recipes are also possible, where techniques are modeled by picture or gesture. In dance, for instance, Laban Notation has been developed as a way of encoding discursively complex kinesthetic patterns, so that whole ballets may be presented in a highly analytic model as a kind of recipe.

Where techniques are modeled directly for imitation, we have *mimetic models,* which are quite different from the abstract discursive models we normally associate with the term "recipe." Mimetic models often involve the close interaction of teacher and learner, such that the learner is taught by a combination of repeated observation and "guided participation," where the teacher verbally and physically moves the student through the motions of the target activity (Lave, 1990; Rogoff, 1990). Here an abstract set of procedures is modeled for a learner as a set of guided practices rather than a set of analytic propositions.

Checklists are standardized inventories of functionally related objects or persons. Most written cooking recipes in the West begin with a checklist of ingredients. While the term "checklist" suggests a written model, inventories are commonly taken orally. To aid in memory, oral checklists like roll calls or pilots' preflight checklist routines tend to be rhythmically chanted or even sung, as in the U.S. Military.

Mnemonic models are used to promote the memorability of important and frequently used information. In oral traditions, prosodic devices like rhythm, rhyme, alliteration, and melody are commonly used as mnemonic aids. We all have a fairly rich stock of mnemonic models, most of them learned while we were quite young. Familiar examples are times tables, the calendrical rhyme "Thirty Days Hath September . . . ," and the spelling aid that begins "i before e except after c. . . ." Recent studies of epic forms of poetry have suggested that these long narrative forms embodied many formal characteristics whose function was to aid memorability (Havelock, 1982).

Persuasion models are conventional ways in which people seek to influence the hearts and minds of others. Persuasion models include a wide variety of specific conventions like prayer, sacrifice, begging, debate, sorcery, love magic, rational argument, sympathetic or contagious magic, apology, commands, and promising. From these examples it is clear that many, but certainly not all, persuasion models are verbal models. Conventionalized kinesthetic models also serve as persuasion models, as when beggars adopt a conventionalized begging posture as part of their plea.

DIVERSE SENSORY MODALITIES

In concluding this typology of cultural models, I should note that models differ significantly in their primary sensory modality. Visual models are different in their formal and cognitive properties from verbal models, written models, or kinesthetic models. This implies that what may abstractly seem like a single model (say, a ritual) is actually two quite different models, depending on whether one is observing the ritual or participating in it. In the latter case the ritual schema is realized as a predominantly kinesthetic model and only secondarily as a visual experience. For observers, the ritual schema is realized as a model heavily (though not exclusively) dependent on visual imagery.

Until the advent of photography, performers had little opportunity to see themselves perform, so that a performer's experience of virtually any cultural performance was experienced largely kinesthetically and aurally. Attending to sensory modalities as a central dimension of models has the added virtue of reintroducing the subject's own experience as a central aspect of the study of cultural models.

The relationship between the dominant sensory modality of cultural models and human experience has been well studied from the point of view of the cognitive implications of literate as opposed to oral transmission of knowledge. This topic has been the subject of much research in psychology, history, and anthropology[29] and is taken up in some detail in Chapter 6.

Relatively little is known about the cognitive implications of other distinctions in sensory modality among cultural models. For instance, are models encoded in non-propositional forms more tacitly known than propositional models? What is the general role of kinesthetic models in socialization, and how are they related to linguistically coded models? What are the experiential implications of modeling social relations through metaphor rather than through taxonomic trees? To what extent do anthropological conventions of genealogical representation which stresses taxonomies and abstract diagrams misrepresent the actual models that people use in representing their social world to themselves and one another? These fascinating questions open up a host of important research possibilities, but they are all dependent on the kind of detailed classification of cultural models that has been outlined in this chapter.

CONCLUSION: THE CULTURAL MODELING
OF HUMAN EXPERIENCE

This chapter has introduced the concept of cultural models in considerable detail. In the face of the anthropologist's current interest in how cultural forms are used creatively and strategically by people, the models approach to culture has considerable explanatory power. But to exploit the power of this idea, it was necessary to clarify a number of important distinctions. First, I distinguished between two kinds of mental models, personal and conventional. While the relationship between them is inevitably fuzzy, it is important to recognize that conventional models studied by anthropologists do not exhaust the model-making capacity of the human mind.

I also stressed the crucial distinction between two kinds of cultural models, instituted and mental ones. Instituted models are the public life of culture, empirically observable social institutions that are available as resources for a community. Mental models, by contrast, are cognitive representations of these instituted models but are not simply direct mental mappings of social institutions. The complex relationship between mental and instituted models defines what I have termed the "twice-born character" of cultural forms.

A third distinction among kinds of cultural models sets off special-purpose models from more abstract and encompassing foundational schemas. While this distinction is inevitably fuzzy, cultural models differ quite dramatically in their schematizing power. Foundational models are distinctive in their capacity to organize a superficially diverse set of special-purpose models with a common form. Though natives are often unaware of foundational models, they provide much of the coherence that anthropologists have traditionally attributed to cultures. Many of the case studies that follow employ the notion of foundational model.

The fourth distinction I made had to do with the perspective implied by different kinds of cultural models. Specifically, I distinguished between observers' models, which convey an abstract and categorical view of an experience, and the more dynamic actors' models. Actors' models organize experience from the viewpoint of engaged action, whereas observers' models convey a kind of neutral structure.

Finally, I was at some pains to suggest, even if provisionally, the extraordinary range of structural and functional genres in which cultural models can be found. Clearly, the elaborate typology of cultural models presented in this chapter does not exhaust every possible kind of model. Yet the extraordinary elaboration of cultural models in even this preliminary attempt at a taxonomy should suggest just how important the cultural modeling of experience is for humans and how multifaceted is the work of culture. Cultural models are a stock of tools, at once external and internal, social and cognitive. Models aid in the processing of information and in people's active construction of meanings out of the complex, diverse, and partial information they gather.

From a structural perspective alone, it may be hard to understand why cultural evolution produced such a prolific and varied stock of conventional models. But when this diversity is understood functionally, the multiplicity and abundance of cultural models become easier to understand. As Roy D'Andrade has reminded us, human beings are opportunistic information processors "who in constructing systems of symbols will make use of any kind of structure that will help to communicate information of interest" (D'Andrade, 1990:804). Different kinds of models are appropriate for processing distinct sorts of information.

There is also another reason for the diversity of cultural models. In addition to the well-studied role of cultural models in information processing, they have an equally important but little understood role in underwriting meaning construction. The issue of meaning construction occupies the last two chapters of this book. There, we consider in detail the complex relationship between social models (in the world) and cognitive models (in the mind). Culture's second birth, as mental representations, will be explored in relation to the cognitive processes involved in the ongoing construction of meaning that characterizes human intelligence.

Before we turn to these important general issues, we need to take these models out of doors and explore their complex life as they figure in a variety of cultural settings. The ethnographic heart of the book, which occupies the next ten chapters, will explore a great many of the cultural models and schemas described in this chapter with the intent of illuminating the social life of the mind. It is to this outside-in vision of human cognition that we now turn.

Notes

1. For general accounts of cultural models, see Lakoff, 1987a; Casson, 1983; Spradley, 1972; D'Andrade and Strauss, 1992; Strauss and Quinn, 1994; Holland and Quinn, 1987; D'Andrade, 1987a, 1990, 1995; Shore, 1990b, 1994.

2. The recognition that experiential domains may be subject to different degrees as well different kinds of cultural modeling makes it possible to understand the powerful effect on individuals of immersion in a new culture. Long cross-cultural experience can profoundly alter individuals' consciousness and provide them with new insights. These transformations take place by giving people access to models for experiences that were not represented or were underrepresented in their native cultures. Cultural models or their absence can account for what Levy has termed "hypo-cognized" and "hyper-cognized" experiences (Levy, 1973).

3. Strauss defines these mental models (she calls them "cognitive schemas") as "learned, internalized patterns of thought-feeling that mediate both the interpretation of ongoing experience and the reconstruction of memories" (Strauss, 1992:3). She distinguishes cultural models as "culturally formed cognitive schemas" (1992:3).

4. On mental models, see Johnson-Laird, 1983, 1990; Gentner and Stevens, 1983; and Norman, 1988.

5. The best anthropological account of the relationship between personal knowledge and conventional symbolism (albeit one not in the cultural models tradition) is Obeyesekere's Sri Lankan work (Obeyesekere, 1981, 1990).

6. See Gentner, 1983, 1989; Gentner and Stevens, 1989; Gick and Holyoak, 1983; Johnson-Laird, 1983; Haskell, 1987b; Sternberg, 1977.

7. Schank, 1991. See also Schank and Abelson, 1977, for a more detailed discussion of restaurant scripts.

8. See Strauss, 1992, for an interesting critique of Geertz's analogy.

9. See Walters, 1980; Asad, 1983; Roseberry, 1982; Wikan, 1991; Shankman, 1984; Crapanzano, 1986; Keesing, 1987; Gulick, 1988; Segal, 1988; Shore, 1988a.

10. Johnson-Laird defines a model in terms of its specificity. Failing to make the distinction between model and schema, he is forced to characterize models simultaneously in terms of both specificity and generality: "Although a model must be specific, it does not follow that it cannot be used to represent a general class of entities. The interpretation of a specific model depends upon a variety of interpretive processes, and they may treat the model as no more than a representative sample from a larger set" (Johnson-Laird, 1983:157–158).

11. Lakoff is actually somewhat inconsistent in his use of the terms "models" and "schemas." Thus, while he uses the term "schema" for such abstract entities as "kinaesthetic image schemas," he calls the encompassing set of general mental structures idealized cognitive models (ICMs) (1987a:68). This would seem to reverse the more common usage of schemas for the more abstract mental structures. In any case it is not consistent with the usage in this book.

12. The fact that foundational schemas are rarely the subject of consciousness awareness creates a particularly thorny methodological problem. There may be no foolproof way to distinguish such general schemas, inferred by an outside observer from a collection of potentially

specific models having no cognitive reality for a native, from a schema that is actually a mental representation for the members of a community. The fact that an outside observer may infer a general schema common to a set of models does not in itself mean that this schema has any reality as a cognitive construct for the members of that society. The general schema may be the ingenious construction of the observer.

Even the acknowledgement by natives of analogies between cultural models does not argue for the psychological reality of foundational schemas. In a given family of related models (A, B, and C) C might have been produced by analogy from B and B might have been produced by analogy from A with no general master schema necessary. Thus the great variety of modular institutions that are discussed in Chapter 5 might produce the illusion of a common foundational schema but might equally well be accounted for by the fact that any one modular institution was directly modeled on any other. The pattern thus would be a function of a chain of reasoning from existing specific models rather than the product of the induction of or from a common foundational schema. This is, of course, the common objection to structural analysis, which appears to suggest that because a common general structure can be inferred by an outside observer from a collection of "texts," it must have a psychological reality for those who produced those texts.

While this critique surely undermines the certainty that any particular foundational schema has psychological reality for natives, we know that reasoning analogically from particular cases is often done by a process of schema induction, in which a general schema is induced from the particular cases, which is then applied to other cases (see Gick and Holyoak 1983; also Chapter 14 of this volume). It is unlikely, I think, that people could reason successively from a salient case to construct analogical cases without some degree of general schema induction occurring in the process. I also think that the familiar ethos of a community, and the sense that individuals live in a world with a common horizon of expectations, is the result not simply of a collection of similar models but of a tacit sense of the general forms that those models share. Nonetheless, the epistemological criticism of the foundational schema notion must be acknowledged as serious. I am grateful to my colleagues Robert McCauley and Ulric Neisser for pointing it out to me.

13. In many ways Victor Turner must be acknowledged as a significant exception here. While no anthropologist has been more significant in characterizing the structural properties of cultural symbols, Turner was notable among his peers in his attention to the complex relations between symbols as cultural artifacts and as lived experience.

14. The term "propositional model" has been used in various senses by linguists and philosophers. Kearney distinguishes between propositional models, which he identified with anthropologists' models, and images which are the natural form for a people's worldview (Kearney, 1984:48). This formulation is overly dichotomized, though there is an important way in which Kearney is right. Still, propositional models are not the exclusive province of the scientist-observer.

15. Johnson-Laird specifies propositional representations as one of the three kinds of mental representations, the other two being images and mental models (Johnson-Laird, 1983:146) Here he uses the term "model" in a much more restricted sense than I do. A mental model in his view is restricted to an analogical representation that plays a direct representational role, since it is analogous to the structure of the corresponding state of affairs of the world—as we perceive or conceive it (p. 156). For Lakoff, propositional models are one of five kinds of idealized cultural models, the other four being image schematic models, symbolic models, metaphoric models, and metonymic models (Lakoff, 1987a:113–114). What Lakoff calls propositional model I call analytic models (see Chapter 16). My typology is in some ways more elaborated than Lakoff's, and I have restricted the term "propositional models" to a single type of linguistic model.

16. There are exceptions. On the importance of sound symbolism see Jakobson, 1971;

Sapir, 1921/1949; Benveniste, 1966; Friedrich, 1979; Bolinger, 1980, 1986, 1989; Nuckolls, 1994; and Shore, 1990b.

17. For an interesting study of proverbs as cognitive schemas, see Honeck et al., 1987.

18. On the process by which traditions "sediment" out of human interaction, see Berger and Luckmann, 1966.

19. Young children's narratives show a developmental shift from specific event-based accounts to generalized scripts employing a "timeless" present tense. According to Bruner, the relative frequency of these generalized scripts in the speech of young children doubles between the ages of twenty-two and thirty-three months. Here we can see ontogenetically the process of sedimentation of narrative scripts out of descriptions of actual events. Bruner sees this process as the emergence for children of an important distinction between the canonical forms in culture and exceptional experiences (Bruner, 1990:91ff.).

20. Important works on metaphor are Black 1962, 1977; Johnson, 1987; Lakoff, 1987a; Lakoff and Johnson, 1980; Haskell, 1987; Marks et al., 1987; Fernandez, 1974, 1991; Ortony, 1979; Crocker and Sapir, 1977; Turner, 1974; Urton, 1985.

21. Briggs, 1966; Rosaldo M., 1984; Rosaldo R., 1980; Geertz, 1973c; Schieffelin, 1976; Lutz, 1988; Lutz and Abu-Lughod, 1990; Levy, 1984; Gerber, 1985; Shore and Worthman, in preparation.

22. On classical categorization, see Lounesbury, 1964; Schneider, 1969b; Smith and Medin, 1981; D'Andrade, 1990.

23. On the role of basic level categories and prototype effects, see Rosch and Mervis, 1975; Rosch et al., 1976; Rosch and Lloyd, 1978; Rosch, 1978; Smith, 1990; Sweetser, 1987; Tversky and Gati, 1978; Barsalou, 1987; Garner, 1978; Harnad, 1987; Keil, 1987; Keil and Kelly, 1987; Lakoff, 1987a, 1987b; Medin and Barsalou, 1987; Medin and Wattinmaker, 1987; Mervis, 1987; Neisser, 1987; Newport and Bellugi, 1978; Berlin et al., 1966, 1973; and Lakoff, 1987a.

24. On the human need for classification, see Durkheim and Mauss, 1963; Levi-Strauss, 1963, 1966; Douglas, 1966.

25. On children's play see Piaget, 1932, 1962; Huizinga, 1938; Bateson, 1955; Caillois, 1958; Erikson, 1977; Garvey, 1977; Gluckman and Gluckman, 1983; Harris and Park, 1983; Turner, 1983. On sports as cultural performances, see Gardner, 1975 Goldstein, 1979; Harris and Park, 1983; Guttman, 1978; Harris, 1983; Hart, 1972; Lipsky, 1983; Lowe, 1977; Mac-Aloon, 1984; Novack, 1976; Slusher, 1967; Voigt, 1974, 1983; Weiss, 1969; Whiting, 1977; Calhoun, 1987; Candelaria, 1976; Gruneau, 1982; Coffin, 1971; Edwards, 1973.

26. On the cultural-expressive functions of ritual and drama, see D'Aquili et al., 1979; Kluckhohn, 1942; Geertz, 1965, 1980; Gluckman, 1954, 1962; Goffman, 1967; Grimes, 1976, 1982, 1985, 1990; Handelman and Kapferer, 1980, 1975, 1984; Leroy Ladurie 1979; Levi-Strauss, 1967c, 1967d; MacAloon (ed.), 1984; MacAloon, 1984; Morgan, 1984; Munn, 1969; Obeyesekere, 1981; Rappaport, 1979; Salter, 1983; Schechner, 1977, 1985; Schechner et al., 1990; Schieffelin, 1976; Stoeltje, 1978; Turner 1967, 1967a, 1969, 1972/1983, 1984; Turner and Schechner, 1986.

27. On scientific theories see Kuhn, 1970; Polanyi, 1966. On folk models and mental models of the physical world, see Pepper, 1942; Radin, 1927; Gentner and Stevens, 1983; D'Andrade, 1987a; Berlin et al., 1966, 1973; and Norman, 1988.

28. For a cognitive study of scripts and related genres, see Mangler, 1984.

29. See Heim, 1987; Ong, 1967, 1971, 1977, 1982; Goody, 1977, 1986.

II

THE COGNITIVE LANDSCAPE OF MODERNITY

3

Mind Games:
Cognitive Baseball

> I placed a jar in Tennessee
> And round it was, upon a hill.
> It made the slovenly wilderness
> Surround that hill.
> —Wallace Stevens

WHAT'S IN A GAME?

An ethnographic conception of mind suggests an outside-in view of thinking. Though most of us consider thinking something that happens in the head, private and out of sight, social psychologists like Vygotsky and anthropologists like Geertz have stressed the public and social nature of thought. For Vygotskians, thinking is understood to be a form of "inner speech" derived from a conversational environment (Vygotsky, 1962). From this perspective, thinking is thoroughly social in nature—no matter how private it may seem. For Geertz, much of human thinking and feeling is modeled for individuals through public "templates" that are part of the everyday social landscape (Geertz, 1973b). Geertz's most famous example of a social template is the Balinese cockfight, which he interpreted as a way in which Balinese model for themselves important aspects of (male) status rivalry in a format that is socially safe because it is considered merely a kind of play, albeit a particularly "deep" and psychologically engaging sort of play (Geertz, 1973f).

Games and sporting events are examples of what in the previous chapter I called "ludic models." Ludic models take the form of performances or contests whose functions seem to be more matters of fun—physical or esthetic pleasure rather than serious or practical business. In addition to sports, ludic models include a wide range of cultural performance genres like games, contests, and spectacles.[1] In this chapter and the next, I look at sporting events as important kinds of ludic models that engage serious cultural issues in the very rules and structures constituting the field of play. Such a serious look at culture at play will enable us to explore more than just a few examples of ludic models. By looking at sports in this way several very basic questions about the nature of cultural knowledge are addressed:

- To what extent is cultural knowledge accounted for by models comprising relatively static rules and structures?
- How do these structures relate to the apparent dynamism and freedom of human action as they are experienced by individuals?
- How do ludic models crystallize in a powerful and accessible public form far more abstract social experiences?
- How do these models, in turn, structure other domains of thought and experience?
- How do cultural models build in "perspective," such as the perspective of an observer as opposed to an actor?

In later chapters, we return to a number of these questions in relation to several classic debates in the history of anthropology. In the process, we will be dealing with ethnographic material from a number of exotic cultures. But to begin to make the case for culture-in-the-mind, we begin closer to home with cultural forms that will be familiar to most readers.

Our first ethnographic view of mind takes us just down the street to the local ballpark. The premise of this chapter is that baseball, as our most venerable national sport, has something to tell us about the American mind. More specifically, in its complex representations of time, space, and action, baseball models important tensions in mainstream American culture between communitarian and individualistic values. And, in turn, baseball provides a source domain for modeling other areas of life where analogous tensions are experienced.

Though baseball is not America's only national sport and though it has been eclipsed by football as the nation's favorite spectator sport, there remains a special relationship between baseball and the American imagination. Yet the nature of this special tie is elusive. To understand America's way with baseball, we need to get under its skin and gain some distance from the familiar sights and sounds of the ballpark. This perspective on the game places us at an "experience-distant" vantage point and affords an odd and potentially disconcerting view. But it does make possible an appreciation of the "ritual" elements of baseball, a view of the game as a cultural performance. "Ritual baseball" differs from the usual experience of the game-in-play by stressing the cultural meanings that have been derived from its characteristic forms rather than emphasizing its unique and contingent events.

Like all performance genres, sporting events are model worlds of human action. In games, time, space, and action are framed in ways that are distinct from everyday experience but reflect back on that experience. To see baseball in this way is to treat the sport more as a civic ritual than as a game in motion. More to the point, it is to see the experiences of (watching or playing) baseball as involving two different kinds of knowing, the knowing that goes into the understanding of the game in play and (at the same time) a different sort of knowing involved in experiencing baseball as a cultural performance.

In viewing baseball with an anthropologist's eye, I was struck by how consistently *asymmetrical* the game's structure is compared with our other field sports.

Everywhere we look in the game, there is an endearing oddness rather than the balance of basketball, football, or hockey. There is barely an even number associated with baseball. Nine players, nine innings, three strikes, three outs, and a seventh-inning stretch. A full count in baseball is a five—three balls and two strikes. Even the apparent symmetry of the diamond is broken by its division into three bases and a home plate. Three bases are square, but home plate is always a lopsided pentagon. Charmingly out of balance, baseball gives us no quarters and no halftimes.

BASEBALL TIME

This asymmetry shapes the odd sense of time made possible by the game. As has often been noted, baseball is unique among American field sports in having no clock time. Baseball is controlled by inning time, which means by the contingencies of events. The game is over only when the losing team has had at least nine at-bats *and when a difference between the teams has been generated*.[2] The only exception is when a game is called for bad weather. The fearful symmetry of a tie score is normally not allowed. Unless a difference is produced, a baseball game can go on forever, and the record books delight in reporting contests that stretched endlessly into the night.

The open-endedness of baseball, its subordination of the logic of the clock to the contingency of its own events, is underwritten by baseball's theoretically endless moments. A batter could hypothetically foul away an unlimited number of pitches into the stands and thus never end his at-bat. Or a team could begin an interminable hitting streak, so the side would never retire. The game might go into an infinity of extra innings, where the needed winner never emerged to end the game. These "record-breaking" possibilities of the game are not lost on the more philosophical baseball writers. Joel Oppenheimer has written:

> The dream is of a game that goes on and on, the last out never being made—or a batter fouling, fouling, fouling, so that no ball is ever fair again and the game goes on. Thus time and space, so carefully denoted, are forever destroyed, or at least put on the shelf. I'm talking about that sag of spirit when you realize in the top of the ninth that you're five runs ahead and that unless the other team scores five the game will be over and you won't go to bat again; it happens to me whether I'm playing or watching. *I want the game to go on*. That's an unrealistic view of the universe. [Gordon, 1987:148]

Baseball's detractors are fond of pointing to baseball's slow pace as the game's most glaring defect. Interestingly, aficionados rarely deny the charge but instead locate much of the game's genius in its alternation of long periods of inactivity with sudden bursts of action. The notorious slowness of baseball is governed by a kind of wave motion. Baseball action comes in surges. Baseball's ability to arrest the flow of time is not just a spectator's eye view of the sport. Players themselves experience the game through alternations between surges of intense action and a kind of slow motion. Keith Hernandez, a former Mets star first baseman, has vividly described how the eye of an especially "sharp" batter can slow down the perception of a blazing fastball:

You've heard many times that the pitch takes about one and a half seconds to reach the plate and less than that, usually. That seems like an impossibly short time in which to make any kind of decision at all. You'd think it would just come down to reflexes. And when you're slumping, that's about right. You don't feel like you have any time at all. But when you're sharp and seeing the ball well, you actually feel that you have all the time in the world. The one and a half seconds seem like . . . I don't know, three or four seconds, plenty of time to identify the pitch and make the decision almost methodically about when and where to swing. That's when hitting is really fun. [Hernandez, and Bryan 1994:7]

For fans, baseball's wave motion affords a kind of oscillating engagement, an alternation between attention to the public spectacle at hand and the withdrawing of attention into more private or domestic pursuits, such as small talk or buying hot dogs while the game is going on. Because the public/private switching occurs within the framework of the game, there is no need in baseball for the half-time break that characterizes other field sports. In a two-hour game, there is perhaps fifteen minutes of action. The rest of the game is a mix of staring, discussing the game, anticipating what is to come, eating, drinking, or just chatting.

For the uninitiated, these long breaks in the action account for baseball's tedium. But for the real fans, this pace seems to promote a kind of imaginative engagement with baseball, an engagement lacking in fast-paced games like soccer or basketball. In a famous essay on baseball and intellectuals, Roger Kahn suggested that watching baseball has a particular appeal to imaginative individuals (Kahn, 1957:347).

Baseball's ability to pull fans in through "empathic engagement" is different from the immediate kinesthetic connection that spectators feel when they throw themselves, body and soul, into a 100-yard dash or a furious volley of punches in a boxing match. Baseball makes possible a rhythmic alteration of attention from the field of action to what Roger Angell once called baseball's "inner game—baseball in the mind" (Angell, 1972:292). Mental baseball involves a mix of strategizing, telling anecdotes, and maintaining the scorecard and getting the stats realigned.

Baseball's romance with time, its genius for overcoming the clock, is equally apparent in its capacity to subdue the flow of history. Baseball has a way of resurrecting an agrarian past downtown. Sports writer Donald Hall has argued that: "It is by baseball, and not by other sports, that our memories bronze themselves. Other sports change too fast, rise with the highrise, mutate for mutability, modify to modernize. By baseball we join hands with a long line of forefathers and with the dead" (Gordon, 1987:8–9).

For many men, baseball encapsulates their personal histories through a chain of teams that propels the ambitions of youth into age and projects age back to reclaim, momentarily, its lost vitality. From Tee-Ball to Little League, Babe Ruth League, Senior League, high school, college, the minor leagues and the majors, baseball is an idiom by which the dream of the endless summer becomes tied up with an individual biography. It is baseball that most old-timers seem to think of when they imagine they can recapture their youth through one last swing of the bat.

Herb Caen once wrote: "Whereas we cannot imagine ourselves executing a two-handed slam-dunk or a 50-yard field goal, we are still certain we have one base hit left in us."[3] Old-Timer's Day in football or basketball could never have the same significance for us that it does in baseball. Roger Angell, one of our best baseball writers, admitted that "Part of me, much of the fan in me, is attracted to baseball games because they connect me on a long straight line to my own boyhood" (Angell, 1977:312). Where else do you see the old men of the sport, the coaches and managers, dressed up in playing gear as if they were about to take the field?

Baseball's nostalgic quality is partly an accident of our history. One nation has attached its identity to a single sport. But part of baseball's way with time is built into its very rhythms.

> Within the ballpark, time moves differently, marked by no clock except the events of the game. This is the unique, unchangeable feature of baseball, and perhaps explains why this sport, for all the enormous changes it has undergone in the last decade or two, remains somehow a primitive pastime, unviolent, and introspective. Baseball's time is seamless and invisible, a bubble within which players move at exactly the same pace and rhythm as their predecessors. . . . Since baseball time is measured only in outs, all you have to do is succeed utterly; keep hitting, keep the rally alive, and you have defeated time. You remain forever young. [Angell, 1972:303]

The notion that baseball can surmount time is built into both the game's specific history and its general form. Its special way with time underlies the nostalgia baseball evokes and the sport's mythic innocence, a game of boys and not of men, of summer and not of autumn. We can understand the durability of the historically inaccurate perception that players come "up" to the cities from the farms and towns of America, rural hayseeds, always white young men, usually freckled, with straw between their teeth, just in from the farm, or the farm team, or the bush league.[4] Baseball's mythic hero is the rustic, "the natural."[5]

Of our major sports, only baseball has sustained the false impression that big-league players come right from their small towns rather than from colleges. Though many players in fact are scouted from colleges, college baseball has simply never captured the popular imagination. I think this is because college is too slick for baseball's image and suggests a severing of the links between home and the field.

If baseball summons up a keen nostalgia for past times and lost places, it does so in two quite different senses. For those whose childhood and youth were spent playing ball, the chain of seasons and teams gone by is an idiom by which an actual life may be mapped by a sport. This is nostalgia as a memory of things past. But the nostalgia of baseball seems to have a powerful effect even on those who never played the sport as kids. This sort of nostalgia is like a memory of times absent, a recollection of something that never was.[6] In this way, baseball is indeed a "field of dreams"—an urbanite's "memory" of a rural time and place never actually experienced. This sort of pseudomemory is created by the myth model, the rural park carved into the face of the urban landscape.

FIXED BEGINNINGS

If baseball as cultural model proposes an open-ended conception of time, it nonetheless maintains its characteristic asymmetry by insistently fixing its beginnings. If a game's ending is contingent, its start is always ritually precise: the national anthem and the cry "Play ball!" set it in motion. As for the baseball season, it may end with a contingent series rather than a set game, but it begins with a single sacred act: the presidential toss on opening day. For fans, in the annual rebirth of baseball, the world returns to its beginning in a rite of renewal and the winter is overcome. As in all such renewal rites, the flow of time is at once acknowledged and denied.

A tradition of the Cincinnati Reds opening the season echoes the start of professional baseball itself, where the Cincinnati Red Stockings are annually honored for being the first professional (i.e., salaried) team. Tom Wolfe, claiming that baseball is "a part of the whole weather of our lives," echoed an often expressed sentiment of players and fans when he associated the first real spring day each year with the crack of a ball against a bat, the smell of flowers, the smack of horsehide against the pocket of a mitt, the first maple leaf, and the smell of the bleachers, "that resinous, sultry, and exciting smell of old dry wood" (Wolfe, cited in Gardner, 1975:64). It is in this spirit, one imagines, that noted baseball writer Tom Boswell chose to name one of his books *Why Time Begins on Opening Day*.

This need to demarcate its beginnings was behind the creation of a mythical starting point for baseball. In 1903, the Englishman Henry Chadwick, the premier authority on baseball of his day, testified in his *Baseball Guide* that the American game had sprung from the English school game of rounders that he had played in his youth (Gardner, 1975:66). This claim was so disturbing to sports magnate and former player Albert Spalding that he called for the establishment of a fact-finding committee to determine baseball's true pedigree. In 1907, Spalding's commission issued a report certifying that in spite of Chadwick's compelling evidence, baseball was in fact a deliberate and authentic American invention.

The myth of the American origins of baseball grew out of reminiscences of Abner Graves, a war buddy of General Abner Doubleday. Doubleday, whose certifiable field of action was a Civil War battlefield, happened also to be a friend of the commission's chairman, Abraham Mills. Graves's evidence comprised memories half-a-century old. He recalled how in 1839 his old friend Doubleday had set right a scruffy local game of town ball, played by a bunch of local boys in Cooperstown, New York. By mapping out an orderly field onto a cow pasture and codifying the game's loose rules, Doubleday was said to have single-handedly given America its national game.

Like our Constitution, baseball could now lay claim to a fixed domestic origin, a certifiable beginning in an act of deliberate reason. So, we now hold to the improbable myth that baseball actually began on a summer day in 1839 through the marking out of a diamond in a cow pasture.[7] Baseball was thus given in one generative act both a mythic time and space.[8]

BASEBALL SPACE

Baseball models time as the juxtaposition of a fixed beginning and an open end, the determinate and the contingent, in a characteristic asymmetrical tension. This pattern might be dismissed as coincidental or trivial if it were not so closely paralleled by the game's orchestration of space.

Though the first real team, the New York Knickerbockers, was an urban phe-nomenon, baseball is still symbolically the country reclaiming the streets of the city. But it is, in fact, a thoroughly modern pastoral. The game's authentic home is the "park" or the "field." Only in 1923, in the Bronx, did we witness the birth of the urban "stadium," home of the Yankees (Angell, 1977:34). Whereas all other Ameri-can field sports use a symmetrical field, defined by sides and ends, the baseball park is asymmetrical. It defines a tension between an ever-narrowing inner point, called "home," and an ever-receding and widening outer "field." The home area, which includes the "diamond," is marked out with great precision and is the same in every park. In 1877, home plate was moved from just outside the inner apex of the dia-mond, beyond the limits of the infield, to just inside the magic square (Frommer, 1988:62).

While the infield area is precisely and uniformly measured, there are no rules fixing the size or the boundaries of the outfield. Outfield distances are governed by minimum, not maximum dimensions. From home plate to the outfield fence, as mea-sured along the foul lines, a professional field must measure at least 250 feet (325 feet for parks built after 1958). And from home plate to the center-field fence, on a line drawn through second base, the field must stretch *at least* 400 feet. As with time in baseball, there are no outer limits in the constitutive rules governing baseball space.

Home may be precisely demarcated, but the outfield is open, and its dimensions are contingent. Like great batters, classic baseball parks like Wrigley Field, Com-iskey Park, Yankee Stadium, Ebbets Field, and Fenway Park have distinctive individ-ual identities (see Boswell, 1984, chapter 1). The indeterminacy of the outfield also means that the field and hence the game are subject to historical revision. Only in baseball can the outfield be reshaped to accommodate new configurations of talent, changing the odds, altering the possibilities (Hollander, 1967:61).

When, in 1983, in preparation for the Gold Anniversary All-Star Game, the White Sox's new owners refurbished Comiskey Park, they shortened the outfield fence a mere eight feet to reshape the field to the particular configuration of pitching and hitting talents of the White Sox of the 1980s. Tom Boswell referred to this as "marrying your park to your team" (Boswell:1984; see also p. 65). Fences can also be adjusted in other ways. Perhaps the most notorious example of such boundary manipulation was owner Bill Veeck's adjustable-height fence. In the early 1950s, Veeck's St. Louis Browns were so inept that Veeck had to resort to unheard of marketing gimmicks like bat day and car giveaways to entice fans into the park. To enhance his team's home-field advantage, Veeck installed an outfield fence that could be raised or lowered depending on who was at bat, thereby giving the owner an edge in shaping the odds of anyone hitting a home run (Gardner 1975:40–41).[9]

Whereas other field sports present focal goals for the object in play at both ends of the field, the baseball field actually extends beyond the park into the community.[10] The batter's goal is actually beyond the park itself to the city streets, though precious few can achieve this distinction. Players sometimes talk of their intentions to "hit the ball downtown" (Frank, 1983:94).

Technically, it is a human event rather than a fixed boundary that determines whether a ball is foul or fair. It is not where the ball is hit that decides whether it is in play or out of play, but whether it is caught. In theory, a fielder who could propel himself high enough to intercept a ball headed out of the park or into foul territory would retire the batter, robbing him of a home run or another chance at the ball.

In no other field sport are the performance boundaries between player and spectator so blurred as in baseball. Though the infield boundaries are scrupulously observed, the limits of the game are nowhere near as clear in relation to the outfield. From the field, the game extends itself naturally into the stands, where the U.S. president makes the first throw of the season and where the "grandstand fielders" try to catch fly balls or to forestall an unwelcome home run by knocking a ball heading over the fence back onto the field.

The field's open-endedness narrows the perceptual gap between player and audience, encouraging the imaginative engagement of the fans discussed above. For safety's sake, fans just behind the plate are blocked from the field of play by a net or screen. But no clear boundary separates the grandstand from play. Just scan the attire of any of the fans in any ballpark, and it immediately becomes apparent that the baseball uniform, the cap, the shirt, and even the shoes and the mitt are as appropriate in the stands as on the field.

This contrast between the enclosed and fixed "home" and the open and contingent social "field" informs the lopsided and open-ended shape of the baseball field. This is very different from the "bowls" associated with football, arenas that totally surround the players, cutting the game space off completely from the surrounding community. The introduction of hybrid bowls suitable for both baseball and football is for most baseball fans a very unfortunate recent development in baseball. If, traditionally, baseball parks were endearingly idiosyncratic, the modern era has surely encouraged a standardization that was alien to baseball's authentic locale.[11]

A LONE BATTER

The asymmetries in the way baseball orders time and space are tied to the game's central asymmetry: its lopsided social organization. *Of all American field sports, only baseball never directly confronts a team against a team.* The game pits a team (in the field) against a lone batter (at home plate). The fact that a team may never be seen facing another team directly is underscored by the absence of the team at bat from sight in an underground bunker called a dugout.[12] Thus, the focus at home is on individual batters and runners and not on a team.

With the notable exception of the pitcher, each player has two personas, a defensive identity in which he plays a part in a highly coordinated communal enterprise on the field, and an offensive persona in which he faces the crowd and the opposing team as an individual batter. The implications of this asymmetry are embedded in the linguistic conventions whereby those "out" in the field "play" positions, while the batter "is" at bat. A runner who *is* on first is distinguished from the fielder who *plays* first. The only fielder who completely shares the status of the batter is the pitcher. Consider the awkwardness of the phrases: "Lenny Dykstra is playing the batter" or "Whitey Ford played pitcher for the Yankees in their heyday."

Baseball's essential moment, revealed in the language of "being," is linked not just to the batter but to the ideas of player as agent and of space as domestic. Pitchers and batters *are* what they do. More passive and defensive roles *play* positions. Essential baseball is also keyed to the symbolic geography of the field, where "being" rather than "playing" is associated with something called "home" and a "plate." While "playing" left field and "being" the pitcher sit comfortably on the tongue, "playing" catcher sounds slightly awkward, reflecting the catcher's ambiguous status as a fielder who plays at home, a receiver who often calls the pitches.

Thus, essentialist language attaches comfortably to those fielders who work at or near home and whose relation to the action is more active than reactive. So the pitcher is rarely conceived of as "playing" pitcher. The catcher's status is more ambiguous. Subtle differences in a player's status shape how we can talk about him. "Playing catcher" is only a mildly awkward usage, "playing pitcher" sounds even stranger, while "playing batter" is a completely unacceptable usage. The only player who might conceivably be said to be "playing" batter is the pitcher, whose authenticity is linked to the mound rather than the plate. This unique status of the pitcher underlies the common assumption that a good pitcher and a good batter are mutually exclusive. Only a pitcher distinguishes his career statistically in the field rather than at the plate. Moreover, the designated hitter in the American League reflects the notion that since pitchers are only playing at batting, they might as well be replaced by authentic batsmen.

These linguistic conventions model a worldview in which authentic being is linked to an "inner space" of individuated activity in a domestic or home environment. Conversely, the language of social life, what we sometimes think of as role-playing, is linked to an "outer" field. In the field, players constantly modulate their actions to suit the changing conditions of interaction. They play their roles. What makes fielding so difficult and elegant in baseball is the speed with which the situation changes, requiring instantaneous recoordination among players. Despite the high level of social and technical skill needed for good fielding, the defensive status of fielders means that they play relatively passive or reactive roles in the game and thereby have a compromised status.[13] Whether as a fielder or a runner, to be a success is to come home "safe"; to fail is to be "out," whether "out" in the field or "out" at the plate.

Field sports like soccer, basketball, hockey, or football all share a common symmetrical action plan. One team tries to move an object from one end of a field, through a hostile set of defenders, to a goal at the opposite end. In these field games, it is not the player but rather the object (usually a ball) that scores; it must be placed in the goal. Only baseball has a completely different action plan. In baseball the runner scores, not the ball. In fact, the ball and the batter have a peculiar inverse relationship. The batter is successful to the degree that his own trajectory is different from that of the ball. The ball (which belongs to the defensive team) is largely under the control of the fielders, whose ability to move it around the field works against the runner's interest. The batter thus opposes the ball, facing it down at the plate. Most heroically, he tries to get it out of the park, free of the control of the field. When he fails and the ball returns to confront the runner, he risks being "out."

WALKABOUT

In baseball, individuals attempt to leave home and make a circuit through a dangerous social field. But it is not getting to the field that scores in baseball. A score is
recorded only when a runner returns safely home. Baseball is an American enactment
of a mythic journey. A lone hero sets out on a perilous adventure, with the hope of
returning home with newfound wealth or wisdom. Baseball is our version of what
Australian aborigines call a "walkabout," a circular journey into alien territory, with
the aim of returning home having made contact with sacred landmarks and overcome
obstacles along the way (see Chapters 9 and 10). Michael Novack has commented
on the mythical quality of baseball's circular journey. " 'Around the world' is the
myth: batter after batter trying to nudge forward his predecessor in this most American of games, until the whole universe is circled, base by base, and the runners can
come 'home' " (Novack, 1976:57).

The commercially successful baseball film *Field of Dreams* captured this mythic
structure of the game within the very shape of its plot and in the textures of its
theme. No film has so vividly brought home baseball's special way with history and
its ability to raise the dead. Like the game itself, *Field of Dreams* is structured as a
series of walkabouts, visionary journeys whose ultimate destination is home—in its
several senses. And in a parallel with Australian aboriginal cosmology, the film's
hero discovers that his journey finally brings him back to his origins, to play one last
game of catch with his own dead father, and to connect his father with his own child.
Baseball in this vision becomes a bridge through which a man becomes whole by
linking his father's generation with the generation of his own child, thereby bending
time right back upon itself.

What, then, do all of baseball's asymmetries model for Americans? In its handling of time, space, and play, baseball models for Americans the cultural problem
of how to reconcile communitarian and social values with a tradition of heroic individualism, privatism, and social atomism.[14] By symbolically privileging heroic individualism over social subordination, baseball can be viewed, as Michael Novack has
suggested, as "a Lockean game, a kind of contract theory in ritual form, where a set
of atomic individuals assent to patterns of limited cooperation in their mutual interest" (Novack, 1976:59).

A QUANTIFIED PASTORAL

Allen Guttman sees in baseball a "quantified pastoral," a peculiar reconciliation of
arcadian myth and technological precision (Guttman, 1978:95). The lure of the
"stats" has been perhaps the most commonly noted distinctive aspect of baseball.
Every player is trailed by an aura, visible to only the initiated. A host of statistics
"swarm and hover above the head of every pitcher, every fielder, every batter, every
team, recording every play with an accompanying silent shift of digits" (Angell,
1977:149).

Baseball's romance with numbers has often been linked to the game's very

American obsession with mechanistic precision (Frank, 1983:111). Baseball is structurally predisposed to quantification by its spatial separation of players and by the relative separation of the pitcher-batter duel from the rest of the game, facilitating the collection of individual as well as team tallies.

Batting averages known by fans down to the thousandth decimal place, RBIs, earned run averages, all contribute not only to baseball's concern with precision but to a qualified egalitarian ethos, a social leveling that stresses equality of opportunity if not equality at the finish line. Through statistics, players who do different jobs in the field can be compared with everyone else at bat or on the mound. Players are, through numbers, distinguished in the only way an individualist knows—quantitatively rather than by distinctions of kind.

Such an obsession with statistics is a characteristic strategy of a society at once democratic and individualistic, both egalitarian and deeply competitive, a nation preoccupied with enforcing a vision of community upon a heterogeneous population. Differences are admired once they can be rendered comparable, rankable, and thus potentially interchangeable. What "stats" do for baseball, polls, elections, and surveys do for the society at large. The "will of the people" gains a quantifiable shape.[15]

It is fitting that stats are one of the most important ways by which fans participate in the professionals' game, bridging the distance between the professional player and the average spectator. Through the meticulous cultivation of a knowledge of baseball statistics, fans can "master" and thus mimic the skills of the players. If differences in players' skills can be translated through statistics into a quantitative hierarchy of value, so differences in skill and devotion among fans can be ranked through a contest that engages their knowledge of the numbers. This is metabaseball. One can be bored with the sluggishness of an actual game yet nonetheless relish the ongoing Pythagorean drama of numbers piling up against numbers in the mind's own ballpark.[16]

Kids enter early into this cosmic baseball game, through a simplified and vivid version of the record books called baseball cards. These cards do not commonly depict baseball teams but rather individual players. Team or group pictures are never as valued as individual player cards. Through cards, players can be lifted out of their local team contexts and placed into the wider marketplace of historical baseball, their stats compared and their value determined. Kids can even enter the world of high-stakes baseball capitalism in which communitarian interests give way completely to a more atomized market mentality. Through deals and purchases, trades and exchanges, children mimic the owners, collecting and swapping players, assessing and reassessing their market value. Here in baseball's most atomistic rendering, the team disappears altogether (baseball cards rarely highlight entire teams), replaced by a world of free agents.

The quest for individual records, so important to both a player's ego and his market value, has sometimes overshadowed the concern for the team's own standing. In 1941, for example, as Joe DiMaggio's hitting streak approached a new record, opposing pitchers deliberately avoided walking him, conspiring, in a sense, with their opponent in the interest of the record book rather than the immediate game.

RULES

As in all games, the competitive relationships among players in baseball are mediated by rules. Like rituals, games usually symbolize the ultimate subordination of contingent action to conventional regulation. But because baseball is a game that throws into question the relationship between individual freedom and social regulation, rules themselves have a distinctive place in the sport. The pace of baseball, the long contemplative stretches punctuated by bursts of action, suggests the game's ambivalence toward the very rules that make it possible. At the apex of the infield, behind home plate, where it all starts and ends, stands an umpire, an authority whose judgments put the rule book into practice and whose word represents the final authority in matters of balls and strikes.

Baseball is about fair play and foul and negotiating one's way through a field filled with obstacles and rules. Not surprisingly, the attitudes toward rules in baseball are ambivalent. Though the umpires control the game and wield absolute power over play, coaches and players regularly treat the decisions as if they were open to protracted and sometimes violent negotiation.[17] One writer has gone so far as to suggest that disputing the rules and the umpires' decisions should be considered as an essential part of any "properly played" baseball game (Gardner, 1975:62, 78).[18] This venerable tradition of challenging authority continues even though umpires never change a decision, certainly not in response to the threats of a player or coach. The arguments are more likely to symbolize the negotiability of authority rather than the bootless aim of effecting a real change of heart in the umpire.[19]

While the umpire's authority seems to symbolize the sacredness of the rulebook, the actual status of rules in baseball is ambiguous. The umpire's calls are as likely to underscore the arbitrariness of power as its sacredness. Bad calls are as much a part of the mystique of good baseball as are rules well kept. Just as the owners have the right to tamper with the dimensions of their home-field boundaries, so also do umpires have the power to mess with the strike zone at home plate. One umpire's strike zone is not another's, and any player knows that the strike zone is subject to rapid revision depending on the particular situation of the game. With two outs, for instance, a batter knows better than to count on a narrow strike zone and an easy walk.

The proper attitude of the fans and players alike toward the umpire models disdain for authority. In fact, in no other sport is there traditionally a call to kill the umpire. Ritual baseball enacts rebellion not only against a particular call but against the very notion of social regulation.[20] Nineteenth-century owners actually encouraged the fans' humiliation of the umpires, recognizing in it an authentic American passion, to say nothing of burgeoning box office profits from increased attendance. As Albert Spalding once put it, "Fans who despise umpires are simply showing their democratic right to protest against tyranny" (cited in Frommer, 1988:121). Thus, though fair play may be the dominant theme of the game, minor rebellion, whether in the field or the stands, is its undercurrent.[21]

Baseball fans can be notoriously rowdy, though they are rarely riotous in the manner of European soccer crowds. Some home-team crowds, like the latter-day Yankee rooters, can inspire genuine fear in the hearts of visiting teams.[22] In the nineteenth century, fans were called "cranks," an appropriate title given their predilection for razzing players, heckling umpires, and even rioting (Frommer, 1988:8). But the same reckless spirit can be found within the game itself. Stealing bases, getting off spitballs, and threatening to hit a batter with a pitch are all little moments of insurrection that have a revered place in the sport.[23] This delight in petty villainy is wonderfully evoked by the writer Michael Blumenthal:

> I remember how once, sliding into second during a steal, I watched the sun rest like a diadem against the head of some spectator, and thought to myself in the neat preutterance of all true feeling, how even our thieveries, well-done, are blessed with a certain luminousness, how a man rising from a pilfered sanctity might still upright himself and return, like Odysseus, to some plenitude of feast and fidelity. It is why, even then, I loved baseball: the fierce legitimacy of the neatly stolen, the calm and illicit recklessness of the coaches with their wet palms and arcane tongues of mimicry and motion. It is why, even now, I steal away from my wife's warm arms to watch the moon sail like a well-hit fly over the stadium, then hump my back over the pitcher's mound and throw that old curve of memory toward the plate where I run for a swing at it—the moon and the stars approving my middle-aged bravado, that boy still rising from his theft to find the light. [Gordon, 1987:42]

Though baseball models cynicism toward authority, its challenge to social order has always had an endearing tameness about it. It is the schoolboy playing hookey, or the pilfering of penny candy from the glass jar at the sweet shop, rather than the darker, more serious insurrections of elders. The authentic hero of American baseball is not the rapacious soldier but the errant knight. It is the reckless heroics not of the man but of the babe. Thus Babe Ruth was the perfect embodiment of baseball's ambiguous relationship with the ideal of order:

> For Ruth was the embodiment of many of the dreams and values that Americans cherished. He had come up the hard way, he had reached the top without special training, without a college education; he was a graduate of "the school of hard knocks." He was a big man, with big appetites. He was irreverent and scornful of authority. He liked kids. And he made a lot of money. . . . The man was irrepressible. He drove his huge car like a maniac and he gave talks on road safety. He drank and ate enough for two men, ignored training rules and curfews, yet he played baseball better than anyone else around. . . . Ruth, it seemed, could get away with anything, while Americans chuckled and muttered in envious admiration, "That Babe . . ." [Gardner, 1975: 85–86, 87]

This devil-may-care reputation has been with baseball from the start. Thus, the first salaried baseball team in America, the Cincinnati Red Stockings, were loved in the 1860s not just for their adventures on field but for their "[e]xcessive alcohol consumption, a penchant for skipping practices and missing trains, and an eccentric and individualistic attitude" (Frommer, 1988:14).

THE HOME RUN

The pervasive asymmetries of baseball model a kind of conversation. The determinate and closed are set against the contingent and free in a dialogue that engages both our communitarian and individualistic visions of our selves. The expressive power of baseball cannot lie, as some have claimed, only in the affirmation of the order of the game, the elegant unfolding of an intricate web of ties that bind player to player, team to team and individual to rules. It is also the celebration of the possibility of heroic action momentarily overcoming the game itself.

This is, I think, the meaning of the home run. Not your everyday homer that merely drops into the stands, but the legendary smash that sails clear of the park, beyond the reach of the fielders, beyond the fans, beyond the boundaries of the game itself.

BASEBALL AS A SOURCE FOR MODELING OTHER SOCIAL RELATIONS

Konrad Lorenz once pointed out that animal behavior often becomes subject to ritualization when it involves significant ambivalence or contradiction. This is also the case for human rituals, both religious and secular. Rather than cleanly resolving contradictions, many of which are irresolvable anyway, rituals serve to crystallize the contradictions. Objectified through ritual performance, tensions that are normally understood only diffusely may be experienced in an articulate and communal form. Baseball provides a cultural model of the tensions between the domestic, the private, and the individual on the one hand and the social, the public, and the communitarian on the other. In action, baseball proposes not the simple dominance of the one over the other but various renderings of their possible relations. In addition to its status as a general model *of* social relations for Americans, baseball also serves as a model *for* conceptualizing a specific domain of social relations where the tension between the private and public aspects of human relations is prominent. This is the domain of "dating." By a kind of analogical transfer, the structure of baseball play is mapped onto a new model for social relations, providing a charming and familiar way for Americans to think about the complex relations between love and marriage. Specifically, this transfer is done through an extensive set of metaphors. Consider the following expressions:

- I can't get to first base.
- I made a big hit with him.
- He struck out with the girl.
- He made a play for me.
- He really knows how to make a pitch.
- I scored last night.
- She wouldn't go all the way with me.

For schoolboys, sexual conquests are often talked about as a kind of base running, where physical intimacy with a girl involves progressing around the bases and, with luck, "going all the way" and "scoring" (Fine, 1987:107).

At first glance, these baseball phrases seem to model attitudes about sexual conquest. But consider the following inappropriate sentences.

- My wife and I went all the way last night.
- I couldn't get to first base with the prostitute.
- I made a play for my surrogate sexual partner.

- Finally, on his honeymoon, Dan scored with his new bride, Ellen, who had insisted on remaining a virgin until her wedding night.

The last statement would be acceptable if Dan had managed to sleep with his reluctant fiancée the night *before* their wedding. The baseball metaphor does not seem to apply to sex when it is either (1) fully domesticated and private or (2) a fully public and commercial transaction. Baseball idioms have been adopted to model a sexual problematic that suits the American interpretation of the game. It refers to sexual adventurism in dating behavior, where a male must negotiate a dangerous social field of play with at least the possibility of bringing his "catch" back home.

This mapping from baseball to dating behavior involves considerable subtlety. If the social foreplay of the dating game employs the *fielding metaphor* from baseball, the closer the drama gets to sexual intimacy, the more likely it is to shift to the perspective of the plate. The more social aspects of a date involve "playing the field"—making a pitch or a play for an especially good catch. But in the classic scenario, the ultimate aim is always that of the batter: first making a hit, then getting to first base, and finally going all the way. Failure is never a fielding "error" but a strikeout. The aim of dating is conceptualized as moving from "playing the field" to "making a hit" and finally "to scoring." Baseball language has been deployed to model our understanding of an activity which, like the game itself, puts into play the problematical relationship of self-interest to social responsibility.

It is evident that these associations between domesticated love and baseball go deeper in American thought than just a set of verbal clichés. It is not uncommon, for instance, to find a newly married couple, sometimes still in their wedding clothes, seated just behind home plate at a game. Moreover, proposals of marriage are often made publicly at games by an announcement flashed on the electronic screen, to the cheers of fans.

GAMES AND RITUALS

In treating baseball as a cultural model and thus focusing on the meanings that have been constructed from its forms, we have viewed baseball more as a ritual than as a game. To many fans, treating baseball as a kind of ritual may seem strange and even somewhat irritating. Normally, we think of ritual as religion in motion, practices directed toward the sacred. Baseball, on the other hand, is only a game. Yet in *The Savage Mind,* the French anthropologist Claude Levi-Strauss provokes us to rethink the relation between games and rituals. "All games," writes Levi-Strauss,

> are defined by a set of rules which in practice allow the playing of any number of matches. Ritual, which is also "played," is on the other hand, like a favored instance of a game, remembered from among the possible ones because it is the only one which results in a particular type of equilibrium. The transposition is readily seen in the case of the Gahuku-Gama of New Guinea who have learnt football but who will play several days running, as many matches as are necessary for both sides to reach the same score. . . . This is treating a game as a ritual.
>
> Games thus appear to have a *disjunctive* effect: they end in the establishment of a difference between individual players or teams where originally there was no indication of inequality. And at the end of the game, they are distinguished into winners and

losers. Ritual, on the other hand, is the exact inverse; it *conjoins,* for it brings about a union (one might even say communion in this context) . . . between two initially separate groups.

[T]he game produces events by means of a structure; and we can therefore understand why competitive games should flourish in our industrial societies. Rites and myths, on the other hand . . . take to pieces and reconstruct sets of events . . . and use them as so many indestructible pieces for structural patterns in which they serve alternately as ends and means. [Levi-Strauss, 1966:31–33; emphasis in original]

For Levi-Strauss the difference between games and rituals hinges on the relationship between the fixed rules or structural forms and the unforeseeable events they occasion. In games, the structure of play is taken for granted, receding into the background. Play lets us concentrate on the ephemeral electricity of a game in motion. The openness of the game mind-set to chance is why we call games, but not rituals, "play." Games use the rules to generate small histories, events that create a disequilibrium between players or teams that had started out as equals.[24]

On the other hand, rituals bring forward into consciousness the shared framework of forms and rules within which participants enact their histories. Ritual sometimes serves as a kind of publicly available social memory. It is a community's recollection in action, an enactment of shared experience, reminding us that our private moments and often conflicted actions unfold within shared worlds. This experiencing through ritual of a transcendent form and collective memory is why rites have been universally appropriated for expressing and experiencing the sacred.

In another sense games and rituals are both forms of play in that they are variations of ludic models. Not surprisingly, play seems a lot more "playful" than ritual. As writers on play have often noted, play can vary and even change while under way. Play can transform itself from the loosest of improvisations to highly scripted behavior.[25] In fact, there is an interesting continuum evident from (free) *play* to (rule-governed) *games* to (sacred) *ritual.* In this view, ritual is simply the most formalized kind of play.

Ritual promotes a high degree of social coordination, whether in human or other animals. In ritualized play, forms that are repeated frequently enough take on a kind of automaticity that we ascribe to "habits" when they are singular and "institutions" when they engage whole communities. For humans, rituals become experienced as external "objects" or institutions with a life of their own rather than as momentary human creations or unique events.[26]

Highly formalized games like baseball have an interesting intermediate position in this continuum, reflecting both the openness of free play and the fixity of ritual. This ambiguity of sports is what makes them so fascinating to anthropologists and fans alike, a fact we explore further in the following chapter.

FRAMING REALITY

The other often noted distinctive characteristic of games is that they are not "for real." As we say, they are "just play." Gregory Bateson has pointed out that play always takes place within a "play frame" that suspends to some extent the seriousness of ordinary activity. Even for some animals, Bateson argued, nips are one thing—a kind of play attack, while bites are something else. Bateson suggests that this distinction is as apparent to a dog as to its owner and that the ability to distinguish play from nonplay is a big step in the evolution of intelligence (Bateson, 1972).

The play frame is defined by both time and space, so that the suspension of ordinary reality is understood to be in effect only within the confines of the "park" or the "game space" and only for as long as the game is "on." Sometimes we talk of life as a kind of game, a figure of speech taken quite literally by game theorists. But if life is a game, it is a high-stakes game played for keeps. This lack of the play frame against which games are understood as "just" games is quite foreign to the normal sensibility of play.

This bracketing of "seriousness" is an interesting aspect of many games precisely because it flies in the face of the apparent seriousness with which players and fans alike often engage in the play. As any sports fan knows, play is often far from "playful." The play frame may require the game events to be seen as not "for real." But the peculiar power of games is that they can also inspire a suspension of this disbelief, so that participants come to treat the events of the game *as if* they had life-and-death consequences. That sports now and then do indeed have life-and-death consequences, for players and for fans, gives this kind of double suspension of disbelief empirical support.

Ritual shares with games this framing of reality. Often, however, ritual is assumed to be more important than everyday behavior rather than less so. If games seem to operate just below ordinary reality, rituals operate just above it, in a transcendent mode. This is because ritual, particularly religious ritual, is frequently believed to be the repetition of sacred primal events. To a religious person, ritual may be fairly characterized as more real than reality. This is not normally the case for games.

Though Levi-Strauss seems to confirm our intuition that rituals and games are two different things, they are better understood as alternative perspectives on the same thing. Whether we call a sporting event a ritual or a game is often merely a matter of emphasis on what is brought forward to consciousness: the structural patterns or the events they make possible.

In games, the "ritual" framework is experienced like the bass line in a piece of music: a barely perceptible but deeply resonant structural grounding on which the melody dances with illusory freedom. But our enjoyment of the game really depends as much on our subliminal grasp of the repeated forms as it does on the free play of the action. In ritual, this relation is inverted. The bass chords that hold the piece together come forward into consciousness. Free play takes a rear seat but still lurks in the background as a persistent possibility. Ritual draws its power from the interplay between the surety of its forms and the ever-present possibility that a real event might chance upon the scene.[27]

Without this tension, rituals are dead—"mere rituals," we call them. Efficacious rituals always flirt with actuality at the edge of performance, throwing into doubt their predictability at the moment they realize it. Thus rites of passage are, for the participants, often on the border between the scripted and the real. Symbolic pain or ritual death can come frighteningly close to the bodily experience, whether for novices in New Guinea or fraternity initiates on college campuses. Real pain, authentic danger, and not infrequently bodily mutilation figure prominently in such rites, throwing into doubt their status as mere performance.

We can see these tensions between ritual and game in the spectrum of different enactments of Christ's death and rebirth: the communion, the passion play, and the actual ten-minute crucifixions that some penitents undergo in Good Friday rites in the Philippines. The closer the reenactment of Christ's passion comes to an actual crucifixion, to what Richard Schechner calls "restored behavior" (Schechner, 1978), without actually destroying the performance effect, the greater the ritual's evocative power for the celebrant.

Many ritual performances move the audience alternately through moments of distance, where they achieve an unusual degree of self-awareness, to moments of intense engagement, in which performance distance is lost (Kapferer, 1984). If rituals risk spilling over into actual events, games always chance losing their playfulness and revealing themselves as "fixed" productions. For instance, professional wrestling gains its peculiar popularity from the ability of the actors in the ring to enforce a willing suspension of disbelief on the spectators, who treat the show as if genuine contests and authentic hostilities were in play. They will themselves to see the competitors hurled brutally to the ground rather than bounced skillfully onto a taut trampoline.

In this light, we can understand the sense of betrayal of sports fans who discover that their beloved game has been "fixed"—frozen by artifice, fed by greed, into pure ritual performance.[28] This is why spectators, who themselves may enjoy participating vicariously in a game through wagers, are so disturbed by the implications of teams or players betting on their own games.

If this complex relationship between games and rituals sounds familiar, it may be because the duet between free play and rule-governed activity has frequently been identified as central to the development of social life in children. Piaget, Erikson, and Garvey have all stressed the transition from free play to games with rules as a central aspect of child development (Piaget, 1962; Erikson, 1977; Garvey, 1977). For Garvey, ritualized play, where children develop stylized interaction sequences in play, is a crucial feature of the transition from autonomous play to coordinated social interaction. Piaget once compared the emergence of rules from free play as a primitive enactment of the social contract (Piaget, 1932). Underlying this capacity for fixing our actions into shared norms, reifying our creations as sacred public objects, is the process of "objectification," by which society as we know it becomes possible (Berger and Luckmann, 1966).

Viewing games through the lens of ritual raises some interesting questions. Does the meaning of a game like baseball lie within its general forms or in its immediate enactments? Do we locate the analysis of the game in its given design of rules and relationships, as if the game created our consciousness by virtue of its intrinsic patterns? Or do we look, rather, to the game as a field on which we negotiate historically contingent meanings and imbue the game forms with new life as we play them out?

The first approach is what we might call the "structuralist view," since it emphasizes the stable and often unconscious structures that underlie ordinary human action. The second approach is what has become known in trendy circles as "poststructuralist" or "praxis" theory. This view stresses the active role of people in creating the forms within which they live through practical action.

In fact, however, baseball provides a nice example of how these two views of human action actually depend on one another. In baseball, we can see how abstract cultural structures and concrete practices create each other over time. For instance, baseball itself is a historical product, evolving out of the imposition of American forms on what had been a British public school game of rounders and cricket. But once instituted, the game turned back on its creators as a powerful socializing agent, perpetuating its messages through its routines and practices.[29] And finally, the game itself has continually undergone a historical evolution in its very execution, reflecting changes in time and space. Japanese baseball is not exactly American baseball, revealing how the drama of the game can flourish in quite different cultural keys (Whiting, 1977).

Baseball in the 1990s—with its free agents, designated hitters, and big-business mentality—is not quite the same game it was in the forties or fifties. Indeed, baseball's more atomistic tendencies, as a kind of contract theory in play, have become highly developed in the modern era. It is true that television and the big-business mentality have changed the popular perception of the game, though not its individualistic spirit, which has been there from the start.[30] Hence the dialogue of ritual and game plays itself out more generally as a conversation between the shaping of our behavior through cultural structures and the reciprocal fashioning of those same structures through concrete human acts.

ANOTHER VOICE

Cultural models like baseball suggest that cultural knowledge is comprehended in several different ways at the same time. Our experience tends to have a complexity and depth that is not explainable by reference to any one kind of knowing. In this view, human consciousness might be referred to, using a musical metaphor, as "polyphonic." A thick and complex texture of conscious experience is made possible by the simultaneous interactions of several "layers" of different sorts of knowledge.

The experience of watching or playing baseball demands no choice between encountering the sport as a game or as a ritual. Baseball is both at once, and its power as an experience is tied to this polyphony. The observer's perspective on the game takes its place as one of several ways in which baseball can be known.

Kevin Morrison, an avid student of baseball and a long-time player, has suggested to me that the model of baseball I have presented is largely an observer's model and does not quite capture the way time and space are experienced by players. His own very perceptive view of the game, drawn from a lifetime of diverse experiences with baseball, refracts the action of the game into three distinct angles: those of the player, the fan in the park, and the television viewer. Morrison's multiple attachments to the sport allow him to do what anthropologists can only rarely do: reflect on the game at once from within it and as an observer. His focus on the multiplicity of perspectives baseball affords is an important reminder that, even from the standpoint of cultural models, there is no one privileged perspective from which cultural knowledge can be viewed. Since I want to stress the importance that perspective plays in cultural models, it is appropriate to let Morrison make his argument in his own words, which I have excerpted from a longer unpublished essay he has written in response to my analysis (Morrison, n.d.).

> The most distinctive characteristic of the player's perspective in baseball is the bifurcation of experience into two different kinds of time. The time between when the ball is pitched and returned to the pitcher can be called "active time," while the time between pitches is a kind of "passive time." Baseball has a slow, rhythmic, silent "pulse," the understanding and appreciation of which, however tacit, is necessary for successful play. The pulse's beat is each pitch, and its relaxation is the time between pitches. In understanding the rhythm, a player can fill up the time between beats with examining and solving the endless permutations of events possible with the inevitable next pitch.
>
> What takes place in those seconds when the baseball is in play is not driven by conscious thought. It is driven by a player's tacit connection to the structures of the game and the objective that has been driven into him by everyone around him, including his teammates, his manager, the press, and others: to win. Baseball team practices consist of many drills, most of them aimed at improving the "fundamentals" of the game. These fundamentals consist of knowing to which base to throw in any given situation, of knowing how to bunt effectively, of knowing where to hit the ball in any given situation and being reasonably able to do so, of generally understanding the "mental aspect" of the game.
>
> The reason coaches and managers spend so much time on fundamentals is that in those brief moments between when a ball is pitched and the time it gets to a player, there is simply not enough time to think about what must be done. Players need to be able to react appropriately and automatically to a situation. The correct strategies must be so well drilled into them that it becomes almost instinctual for them to throw the ball to the right place or to do whatever else is necessary. Paradoxically, in a game in which there are no time limits, there is not enough time in any given moment after the ball is pitched to do anything but react.
>
> However, between pitches there is plenty of time to think. During this "down" time, which is the cause for many people calling baseball "slow," players must consciously avoid letting their minds wander from the game. The game's deceptive pace can finally catch up with even the best player. To avoid such mental lapses, signs are given by coaches and players to remind players of their duties. In between pitches, coaches in the dugout give signs to their fielders about where they should be positioned, catchers give signs to their pitchers about which pitch to throw, coaches next to the bases give their hitters and runners signs about what to do on the next pitch, players exchange signs about who's covering which base if the ball is hit in a certain place or if a runner is stealing. And all of these signs may change on the very next pitch, depending on whether a ball or a strike is thrown, on whether there are one or two outs, on whether there is someone on base, or on any other situation. Within its structures, the game is always changing .
>
> What about the experience television viewers have of the game? There are two relevant characteristics of the television perspective: instant replay and the proliferation and emphasis on statistics. The availability of instant replay drastically distinguishes the viewer's perspective from the player's. Simply put, there is no instant replay for a player, for what he is experiencing and interested in is not visual images but action. If a television viewer misses a play because she has gone to get something to eat, she can return quickly to see an instant replay of anything important. If a player's concentration momentarily lapses and he misses a play, he can't do it over again .
>
> The result of the availability of instant replay is a drastic shift in the way moments

are perceived. A player experiences any given moment of play as both fleeting and unrepeatable. A television viewer sees an event in a game as a capturable image, something which can be viewed over and over again with the same delight, minus only the initial pleasure of surprise. Realizing this, television producers are wise enough to show interesting images over and over again, sometimes with analysis, in the down times between pitches. This repetition can transform the flow of play into a series of repeated frames, something like ritual.

From their perspectives from the stands, the fans' view of a game is greatly influenced by the ballpark itself, by whom they attend the game with, by particular sensory associations like the smell and the feel of the park. The experience is even shaped by the weather on a certain day or evening. All of these characteristics are essential to a ballpark. But overall, the ballpark is unique because of its mixing of the physical with the visual, of the game with the seeing of the game.

The fans at a baseball game are physically part of the game. As Shore's analysis suggests, they can catch foul balls and home runs. They cheer to encourage their team on. They even run onto the field if they want to (and perhaps get arrested). There is no consequential spatial barrier between spectators and players. And in addition to being part of the action, they also watch the game. For this reason, in every Major League stadium, there is a giant television screen in center field which replays important or exciting events in the game taking place on the field directly below it. It is also on this screen that every important statistic about the current batter is often shown, in addition to periodical updates on other games being played on the same day. In fact, stadium builders often think enough of other scores to construct permanent scoreboards in the park, either digital or hand-operated.

While the perspective of a fan in the ballpark shares many of the same characteristics with those of the player and the television viewer, it is also missing some. The essential difference between the spectator and the player is the spectator's exclusion from that essential active moment, the kinesthetic dimension of play, around which a player structures his game. In those moments, the fan has little or no control over what takes place on the field, while the player does. So while a spectator is physically present, his "play" is all vicarious. He is rarely physically consequential to the proceedings of the game.

Comparing the perspectives of spectator and viewer further illuminates the kinds of perceptual and experiential tradeoffs that any perspective requires. As the spectator both loses and gains something by not being physically consequential to the game, so does he both lose and gain something by viewing the game in the ballpark. By being in the ballpark, he is privileged to his particular sensory experiences, such as being part of the crowd and scrambling for foul balls, all of which draw spectators to the ballpark in the first place. However, for these experiences, the spectator sacrifices a certain visual flexibility by not watching the game on television. He only has one view of the game, that from his seat, while the viewer has access to a view from any place in the park (or above it) equipped with a television camera (which is probably why more and more people these days are bringing pocket televisions with them into the upper decks of stadiums).

The game is given form by the combination of its internal essential bonds (its rules), its contingent events and the "position" from which it is experienced. What we observe is inevitably affected by the structures of our position in time and space in relation to the game taking place, a position greatly affected by our role in the game, by our location in the proverbial "ballpark." In this light, it is important not to impose a single privileged perspective as the real "meaning" of baseball. There is no single essential account of a game, as there is not for any human institution. Once we bring it out of the rule books, it takes its life from the perspectives of those who are engaged with it.

CONCLUSIONS: SHIFTING LAYERS

As Morrison suggests, the dominant perspective informing this account of baseball as a cultural model has been distant from the experience of baseball play. It is what might be termed an "observer's model" of baseball—representing a very different perspective than any player is likely to have of the game. As with any cultural model, there is no natural or privileged version of a baseball game other than that which powerful accounts or representations of the game manage to impose on our perception of the sport. The total experience of any culturally organized institution is always multivocal, so that any particular representation is inevitably partial and implicitly positioned as someone's view.

Moreover, the experience of a game, from whatever perspective, is inevitably layered, revealing the polyphonic structure of knowledge. In baseball, as in other culturally organized activities, our immediate attention is normally taken up in the flow of the game's events and uncertainties. But the total experience of the game also includes the tacit awareness of the game's recurrent "structures," which have a resonance of their own. Rather than as opposed forms of knowing, ritual and game normally form a unity in experience. The taken-for-granted rhythms of the ritual make possible our attending to the immediacy of play. The layering of one sort of knowing atop another means that there are many things we know only tacitly. This is why a description of our own cultural forms cast as an observer's model may strike us at once as surprising and familiar.

It takes an unusual event to make us aware of the normally tacit dimensions of play frames. One way to bring tacit knowledge to the surface is through this kind of experience-distant analysis. But earth-shattering natural events in the midst of play can also have the effects of shifting levels of awareness. It was in this way that the complex polyphony of baseball, ritual and game, was driven home for every fan in the autumn of 1989, when San Francisco was rocked by a major earthquake just as the third game of the World Series between the Giants and the Oakland A's was about to get under way. It was as if the San Andreas Fault, in a cruel parody of the contest being waged between the two sides of the Bay, had split the Bay Area apart. When the earth started shaking at Candlestick Park, the delicate threads that normally bind game, ritual, and reality into a seamless whole suddenly unraveled before the uncomprehending eyes of the world. The apparent unity of structure and event was ruptured along with the earth's surface. Television viewers found themselves jolted and confused by the sight of uniformed players huddled with wives and children, humbled before the terrible power beneath their feet, a power that had broken through from somewhere beyond the game space of the field.

In the face of the grim reality of cars crushed beneath tons of cement, of fractured bridges and flattened buildings, of square blocks of city set afire, baseball, even at World Series time, was suddenly rendered insignificant. Yet something odd happened in San Francisco. As bodies were being pulled from the twisted wreckage of the collapsed Oakland Freeway, the series surfaced again in conversation. People began to debate when or if it should be resumed. The significance of baseball had shifted, as concern focused not so much on who would win but on how a sense of normalcy might be reclaimed for shaken fans by the simple restoration of the series. And when, after what was deemed a respectable interlude, the Giants and the Athletics once more took the field at Candlestick, the rebirth of baseball, game and ritual, was for many like waking from a nightmare to look again on the real world.

Notes

1. For a discussion and classification of different genres of cultural performance, see MacAloon (ed.), 1984.

2. In Alexander Cartwright's revised baseball rules of 1846, a game was declared over when one team scored 21 runs or "aces" (Frommer, 1988:4).

3. Herb Caen, "Big Wide Wonderful World," April 3, 1983. "Sunday Punch," p.1, *San Francisco Chronicle,* cited in Frank, 1983:111.

4. On the myth of the agrarian origins of players, see Crepeau, 1980:54–55. The truth seems to be that baseball's American origins were neither rural nor democratic. The earliest baseball teams drew their players from the upper classes of New York City. While, by the turn of the century, baseball had become a realistic ambition for youth coming from the poorer segments of society, the players remained by and large city boys. In 1897, nearly a third of all National League players came from Pennsylvania or Massachusetts, while just ten came from the South or West. The only aspect of the myth that was accurate and was to remain so for nearly half of the twentieth century was the fact that all the "boys of summer," at least in the major leagues, were, with a short-lived exception or two, white males. Though "softball" is a popular sport among women as well as older men, only men are supposed to play "hardball." This gendered distinction between "hard" and "soft" forms of the game reproduces American metaphor models of maleness and femaleness that link baseball to such domains as emotions (hard = logical, soft = emotional) and professions ("hard" sciences = male, "soft" sciences = female). It is thus hardly ironic that the relative absence of women from baseball lore should confirm rather than undercut baseball's status as a American cultural performance. For an account of baseball's earliest roots, see Frommer, 1988. For the history of blacks in baseball and sports more generally, see Gardner, 1975, chap. 7; Voigt, 1976, chap. 8; Olsen, 1969; Edwards, 1969.

5. See Mark Harris's *Bang the Drum Slowly* (1984) for an evocation of this mythic hayseed player in the person of Bruce Pearson.

6. It is interesting that the word "nostalgia" covers both a longing for a cherished past life and the longing for something that has never been experienced. Thus, as an urbanite, I sometimes feel profound nostalgia when I drive through the beautiful small towns of the rural South. Though the feeling is of remembering something dear, long gone, I have never in fact lived in such a place. In this case I would seem to be "remembering" through a model rather than through a direct memory.

7. The Doubleday myth was decisively refuted by Robert Henderson, a librarian from the New York Public Library, who had spent years researching baseball's evolution, tracing its development through numerous literary references (Gardner, 1975:68). Historians appear to concur that the game was a refinement of various New England bat-and-ball games like "baste ball," "goal ball," and "town ball," all tracing their genealogies from the British games of cricket and rounders. Most likely, the game was given its modern American form in 1842, when its rules were first formalized by Alexander J. Cartwright, Jr., son of an English ship's captain. Baseball was historically an urban enterprise. The first baseball games were sandlot affairs played on a vacant lot on 27th Street and Fourth Avenue in Manhattan. It is interesting

to note that Cartwright's original teammates, far from being rural hayseeds, were drawn from among his colleagues who worked in New York's financial district (Frommer, 1988:3).

8. Cooperstown has, of course, been consecrated as a shrine to the game. Since shrines tend to produce relics, it is not surprising that in 1935 a descendant of Abner Graves produced an old baseball that he claimed to have found in a local attic and which was, one could not doubt, the very ball Doubleday had used in his first game (Gardner, 1975:68).

9. Veeck was also famous for hiring a midget to play for his team. The idea was to hire a player whose strike zone was so small that no pitcher could ever strike him out.

10. Actually, the relationship has gone in both directions. Until the turn of the century, it was not uncommon for cars and carriages to be parked in the outfield of the ballpark (Frommer, 1988:114).

11. "Fires and progress would make steel and concrete replace the wood and timbers of the nineteenth-century ballparks. The idiosyncratic dimensions of stadiums, the marching bands, even the real grass in many instances—all of these would ultimately become footnotes to baseball history" (Frommer, 1988:118).

12. At home, baseball language employs "above" and "below" metaphors that seem to invoke the image of a ship. Thus, the batter is "up" at plate, while his successor is "on deck." Whether this imagery is related to the "dugout" conceptualized as a kind of canoe I am not sure, though the connection strikes me as farfetched.

13. "The fielders perform only defensive functions. They are, in a sense, always in a submissive position in which they have to receive the attacks of the opposition unless they can defend themselves by relying on their agility and dexterity. Consequently, the taunts directed toward the fielders, often portray them as being clumsy and imply a sexual inferiority in those who cannot control their bodies" (Frank, 1983:79).

14. On baseball's role in mediating the tension between the ideals of team play and individualism, see Reiss, 1980:26; Frank, 1983:11, 111; Crepeau, 1980:125.

15. Rousseau noted long ago in *The Social Contract* that, in a democracy, there is inevitably a difference between the general will and the will of all. Though it must appear conceptually indivisible, the general will can never really be truly general; it can only be manifest in the vote, through the assertion of numerical superiority.

16. "Not the actual game so much—to tell the truth, real baseball bored him—but rather the records, the statistics, the peculiar balances between individual and team, offense and defense, strategy and luck, accident and pattern, power and intelligence" (*The Universal Baseball Association, Inc., J. Henry Waugh, Prop.,* by Robert Coover).

17. The negotiation of the rules by coaches is characteristic of Little League baseball. Because Little League umpires are themselves not always aware of the subtleties of the rule book, coaches frequently appeal—with success—to precedent in arguing the umpire's calls (see Fine, 1987:22–23).

18. "The author once sat in a New York park and watched as five young boys arrived with bat, ball and gloves to play baseball. They argued who was on whose side, which side should bat first, in which order the players should bat, where home plate should be placed, where the other bases ought to be, which fielder should wear which glove, and where the foul lines were. It was nearly ten minutes before the first pitch was thrown. The batter hit it, and the ball bounced off a tree, causing another lengthy dispute about whether the tree was in fair or foul territory" (Gardner, 1975:65 fn.).

19. In terms of the negotiability of rules, the front office was not any different from the field. The early history of baseball was marked by incessant bickering among owners, who were always seeking to tinker with the rules of the game to the advantage of their teams (Frommer, 1988:61).

20. Frommer (1988:118–119) provides the following verse, which seems to question the authority of only one of the lawgivers associated with "home."

Mother, may I slug the umpire,
   May I slug him right away?
So he cannot be here, Mother,
   When the clubs begin to play?

Let me clasp his throat, dear Mother,
   In a dear, delightful grip,
With one hand and with the other
   Bat him several in the lip.

Let me climb his frame, dear Mother,
   While the happy people shout:
I'll not kill him, dearest Mother,
   I will only knock him out.

Let me mop the ground up, Mother,
   With his person, dearest, do;
If the ground can stand it, Mother,
   I don't see why you can't too.

21. A Marxist reading of baseball's significance as a proletarian sport emphasizes the role of the sport in inculcating an acceptance of authority and an emphasis on the subordination of the individual to the requirements of team play. But if baseball is to be thus understood, we are forced to underplay the degree to which the game throws such subordination into question. Another possible argument would be to stress the degree to which baseball's rebelliousness is ritualized. Like all ritual rebellion, it both valorizes rebellion *within* the play frame and tacitly supports the status quo in the "real world" beyond the game. In either case, baseball cannot be understood as *simply* reinforcing values of obedience and subordination.

22. The exuberance of baseball fans is a highly idiosyncratic and individualistic affair. Organized cheering, though promoted by team organists, is relatively muted in baseball. While Japanese teams have organized cheerleaders and cheering sections, such cheerleading has never been part of American baseball and seems strangely alien to the game as we play it.

23. When first introduced to Japan, baseball was viewed with considerable suspicion by some Japanese, who recognized its ambiguous relationship with the concept of "fair play." Thus one critic, Inazo Itobe, a teacher who was later to become an official of the League of Nations, called baseball "A pickpocket's sport . . . in which the players are intensely on the lookout to swindle their opponents, to lay an ambush, to steal a base. It is therefore suited to Americans, but it does not please Englishmen or Germans" (cited in Whiting, 1977:3).

24. Like Huizinga (1938), Levi-Strauss seems to assume that games are inherently competitive contests, so he does not consider as "games" activities like "playing house" or other nonagonistic forms of make-believe that involve no winners and losers. From the perspective of this essay, the agonistic element is not an essential feature of games. Rather, the notion of degree of contingency or "free play" is more central to my analysis than the existence of a contest.

25. For important works on play that take the relation between freedom and rules as a central issue, see Caillois, 1958; Huizinga, 1938; Piaget, 1962; Erikson, 1977; Garvey, 1977.

26. Some writers have referred to this process by which human creations detach themselves from the conditions of their creation and take on a kind of externality and permanence as "reification" or "objectification" central to the evolution of culture (see Berger and Luckmann, 1966).

27. Robert Scott (personal communication) tells of a baseball game he witnessed in which a fight broke out between the teams and fans came rushing onto the field to join in the melee. Uniformed policemen joined the crowd on the field to break up the fight, when the game's

umpire took control of the situation and successfully ordered both the fans and the police to clear the field. Here, the order and disorder of the play frame momentarily threatened to give way to real violence, and "real" police saw this contest as their domain. What appears to have transpired, however, was the successful claim by the umpire that game reality (in which he has the final authority) rather than external reality (in which the police enforce the rules) was still in play.

28. The most famous example of game fixing in baseball is the Black Sox scandal of 1919, in which eight Chicago White Sox players were accused of throwing the World Series in exchange for cash payoffs from gambling interests. Though legally exonerated of conspiracy charges by a jury, the eight White Sox players were assumed to be guilty by Baseball Commissioner Judge Kennesaw Mountain Landis and barred from the game for life (see Gardner, 1975, chap. 9; Asinof, 1963).

29. See Reiss, 1980, for baseball's role as an agent of socialization and enculturation during the first two decades of this century.

30. Though it is a commonplace of baseball nostalgia to mourn the loss of the game's innocence to late capitalism and its market mentality, it is important to note that baseball was relatively atomistic from the beginning. Free agency was part of the game's authentic American soul. Thus, in the 1860s, baseball players drew fire from newspapers for their predilection for "revolving," by which was meant moving from team to team, at the call of the highest bidder (Frommer, 1988:10).

4

Playing with Rules:
Sport at the Borderlands of Time
and Space

[T]he unceasing vigilance one needs to exert so as to be "carried along" by the game, without being "carried away" *beyond* the game, as happens when a mock fight gets the better of the fighters, is evidence that practices as visibly constrained as these rest on the same principle as conduct more likely to give an equally misleading impression of free improvisation, such as *bluff* or *seduction,* which play on the equivocations, innuendos, and unspoken implications of verbal or gestural symbolism to produce ambiguous conduct that can be disowned at the slightest withdrawal or refusal, and to maintain uncertainty about intentions that always hesitate between playfulness and seriousness, abandon and reserve, eagerness and indifference.

—Pierre Bourdieu

It ain't over 'til it's over.
        —Yogi Berra

Performances like drama and games have always been useful models for thinking about everyday life. Most of us realize that "playing" at life on the stage or athletic field is inevitably simpler than real-life dramas. Like all models, a game's power to reveal the character of social life has something to do with its ability to conceal some of the contingencies and complexities of that life. But this simplicity of models also has its advantages, helping us to clarify some of the important features of the more complex dramas that make up everyday life.

In the last chapter we saw how baseball serves Americans as a cultural model of social relations, simplifying the understanding of complex tensions between communitarian and individualistic aspects of our lives. We also saw how the baseball model has been appropriated by contemporary Americans for modeling one particular domain of those social relations—dating—by metaphorical transfer from baseball to the language of love. This is the creative dimension of cultural models that Lakoff and Johnson have stressed in their understanding of the uses of metaphor in extending understandings from one domain of experience into another (Lakoff and Johnson, 1980).

Looking at baseball as a form of knowledge (a conventional cognitive model) has suggested a polyphonic conception of mind. Knowledge structures are layered such that deeper layers are less flexible and less conscious than structures closer to the surface of awareness. The relatively fixed and stable rules of the game that govern time, space, and the social relations of play are deeper forms of knowledge than are the rhythms of play in motion and thus less accessible to conscious awareness. Similarly, people are generally more focused on the strategies of play than they are on the rules and more conscious of the contingencies of a game's events than of the strategies.

In this chapter, I take up the complex relations among these different levels of organization in the experience of sports. This chapter argues that much of the excitement of watching and playing sport has to do with the complex relations among these different levels of structure that provide the texture of our knowledge of a game. The best vantage point for examining these relations is from the margins of play, the areas of a game where these layers of knowledge come into problematical contact. When this happens in sport, we have a phenomenon I call "marginal play."

Marginal play engages issues of how rules and structures relate to more dynamic and contingent properties of games, like strategies and unpredictable events. For this reason, the study of marginal play in sport provides an excellent way to conceptualize these problematic relations between rules, strategies, and events as they figure in other domains of social life. The best way to understand what I mean by marginal play is by example, and for one of the best examples I know, we return to baseball, a sport that is particularly at home with marginal play.

GRANDSTAND FIELDING

"I am sure there are several things we don't understand," conceded Yankee manager Buck Showalter. "But in my job, I can't get involved in fate and destiny." The occasion for Showalter's flirtation with fate and destiny was the Bronx Bombers' bizarre reversal of fortunes late in the '93 season. It was September 21, and the Yankees were in hot pursuit of the Toronto Blue Jays for the American League East division title. It was the bottom of the ninth inning at Yankee Stadium, in a crucial game against the Red Sox. The Yanks were trailing Boston 3–1. With two down and no one on base, Mike Gallego was hit by a pitch and took first. The tying run in the person of pinch hitter Mike Stanley came to the plate. Stanley hit an easy fly ball right to the left fielder. To no one's surprise, it was caught. By all rights, the game was over.

But just as the ball soared skyward, a lone figure emerged from the box seats and ran out onto the field. A teenage fan had entered the game space unannounced. And before the left fielder had the ball safely in his mitt, umpire Tim Welke was frantically waving his arms and calling "time out." The ball looped dead into the fielder's glove. Despite the loud protests of Red Sox General Manager Lou Gorman, the out was canceled and the Yanks were still alive. The batter got an unexpected new lease on life at the plate, and the Yankees went on to rally for two runs at the very bottom of the ninth inning, robbing the Red Sox of what had seemed a sure victory.

Actually, it was not the Yankees who had won the game at all but rather the errant fan, who, by entering game space illegally at just the right moment, had won the game on behalf of his team. "The game," lamented Gorman, "should have been over." But instead, it was won, and not so much at home plate as at the margins of time, space, and play.

This is a particularly exciting example of "marginal play," a phenomenon found in all sports but with a special affinity for baseball. In sport as in the rest of life, there is much to be learned from things that do not go quite right. Erving Goffman showed us how the normal contours of human institutions and human behavior might be illuminated by paying attention to the minor pathologies of everyday social interaction (Goffman, 1959, 1967). The study of marginal play is, in a sense, the use of petty pathologies of play to tell us something important about ourselves.

Much has been written about the role of time and space as constituting frames for sports and games more generally. Yet much less attention has been paid to the implications of those moments when play overflows its constituting framework of rules and boundaries. In Chapter 3, I used baseball to develop a polyphonic view of mind. We have seen how cultural knowledge can be understood as being stratified into layers of different kinds of knowing. A layered view of knowing makes it possible to reconcile views of culture as more or less stable structures with those views stressing choice, contingency, and culture as an emergent property of human action. In this chapter, the ludic model is used to refine our understanding of the stratified nature of cultural knowledge.

We can understand these paradoxes of play in relation to three different levels at which action is regulated in sport. By distinguishing between (1) *constitutive rules,* (2) *procedural rules,* and (3) *strategies,* we can see how marginal play sheds light not only on the character of sport but on the polyphonic orchestration of cultural norms more generally.

MORE EXAMPLES

Two further examples will serve to introduce the phenomenon of marginal play. The first story takes us to the Arbor Day Golf Open (Wertz, 1981:29–30). Lon Hinkle was about to tee off on the long and winding eighth hole. Rather than playing it the usual way, Hinkle adopted an odd strategy to get an advantage on his competitors. Instead of driving the ball down the main path of the fairway, Hinkle turned sideways and teed off straight down the adjacent seventeenth fairway. From the seventeenth, he hit a couple of low iron shots back onto the green of the eighth hole, which curved back around the seventeenth. With this odd approach, Hinkle shortened the hole by 75 yards. Was this simply clever golf strategy or had Hinkle cheated? Since Hinkle had broken no actual rules of play, he was not technically guilty of cheating. But his strategizing came very close to violating the integrity of the game and surely must have enraged his rivals in the Open.

I witnessed the second incident in 1989. My young children were involved in a Tee-ball league. Tee-ball is a kind of beginner's baseball for very young children. Rather than pitching the ball to the kids, the coaches place the baseball on a stand or "tee" and help the kids to hit it. One five-year-old managed to get to second base on a string of the usual fielding errors. The next batter also connected with the ball. To everyone's surprise, it sailed over the head of the shortstop and dropped into left center field.

Instantly, the excited coaches and parents were on their feet roaring their support for the bewildered base runner. "Go home! Head for home!" everyone screamed, hoping that the child would score a much-needed run. The confused runner looked terrified as he raced to third base. But instead of running around third base and heading into home plate, the terrified child—hearing the cries "Run home! Go home!"—bolted straight off the field and toward the parking lot. Heeding the cries of the crowd, he had decided to head for home.

Like the Yankees' triumphant tale of last-second victory, both of these amusing stories point to those moments of marginal play when the game suddenly spills over the boundaries that frame it. In addition to being games played for the fun of it, athletic competitions are also cultural performances. To view sport as a cultural performance is to study what Lipsky calls "an analogic world that dramatizes the domain of values in an arena that excludes much that is problematic in real life" (Lipsky, 1983:83). Performance theory in anthropology examines the relations among a variety of different cultural performance genres—specifically, games, sports, drama, and ritual.[1] As a form of play, sport may well exclude many of life's real problems. Yet sports are also serious business. Part of what makes sports serious business is that they have the power to dramatize key cultural themes and distinctive cultural contradictions.

TIME AND SPACE IN SPORT

Dutch historian Johan Huizinga once pointed out that all forms of human play operate within distinctive time and space frames—frames that define a play world set apart from normal life. Howard Slusher has written: "Although sport operates within a framework of meaning, it can be determined that within this framework is a structure of reality which is centered in real time and space. It is not the same time and space of the outside world, but it is real nonetheless" (Slusher, 1967:14). The sportsman, Slusher continues, "uses the matrix of time, force and space to order his world."

The field of play is, in Eliade's terms, a kind of sacred space. "For religious man, space is not homogeneous; he experiences interruptions, breaks in it; some parts of space are qualitatively different from others. . . . For religious man, this spatial nonhomogeneity finds expression in the experience of an opposition between space that is sacred—the only *real* and *real-ly* existing space—and all other space" (Eliade, 1965:20). In the same way, the time frame of games is carved out of the flow of time, a kind of sacred period set apart for play. Within game time, spectators and players alike are bound to the rules of play. As in baseball, game time is not always clock time. Similarly, game space is not always measured by artificial units.

Often, game time is framed simply by the duration of events, as in races, golf, tennis, or baseball. Still, it is customary to ritually mark the beginning and the end of play in both time and space. The markers can be painted lines or bells, whistles or flags. They can be calls or distinctive acts like the opening pitch or serve, the lighting of the Olympic Flame, or the planting of a flag at the summit of a newly conquered mountain peak.

Game space can be demarcated by lines, or it can use natural features of the landscape as boundary markers. Whatever the convention for spatial demarcation, the laying out of a playing field is a kind of cosmogony. In Eliade's words ". . . the religious experience of the nonhomogeneity of space is a primordial experience, [comparable] to the founding of the world" (Eliade, 1965:20–21).

CONSTITUTIVE RULES, PROCEDURAL RULES AND STRATEGIES

These spatial and temporal boundaries of sport are an aspect of the structure of governance in games. Such rules distinguish organized games from what Roger Caillois calls *paidiá*—free play (Caillois, 1958). But the organization of regulations is hierarchical, with three distinct levels of control: constitutive rules, procedural rules, and strategies.

Constitutive rules establish the basic framework of any game. They include conventions of personnel, action, time, and space. In part, games are constituted by assembling temporary communities and marking out artificial boundaries in time and space. Often these boundaries have names: halves, innings, quarters, periods, zones, bases, or penalty boxes. Along with the game's personnel, they make up the skeletal framework of play.

Whereas constitutive rules define the shape of a game as a whole, *procedural rules* govern the action of play in motion. Always contingent on specific circumstances, procedural rules nonetheless apply to all players. Examples of procedural rules are offsides rules in soccer, the infield-fly rule in baseball, and the shot clock or rules governing fouling in basketball. Such rules are usually enforced by game officials such as referees and are the frequent subject of dispute. Violations of constitutive rules annul the game, but violations of procedural rules do not. In fact, such violations are an expected part of the game. Fouling in basketball is an interesting example of a procedural violation that is often adopted as a strategy in a well-played game. Procedural violations are intrinsic to the enjoyment of a game and deliberate infractions often become part of a well-thought-out game plan.

Strategy is the third regulatory dimension in sport. Strategies involve flexible and inventive configurations of time, space, and action. Unlike the other two kinds of rules, strategies do not come as part of the rule book. They are devised by players and coaches to maximize successful play under changing circumstances. In their critique of structuralism and its vision of action proceeding mechanically from transcendent or immanent structures, praxis theorists like Bourdieu have stressed the importance of strategizing in even the most apparently rule-bound human activities. In my view, strategies emerge in human play as an entailment of constitutive and procedural rules in any institutional framework of human activity. Bourdieu, however, appears to characterize strategizing as a kind of alternative to rules, a momentary liberation from regulation, filling the gaps between rule-governed moments of social play:

> But even the most strictly ritualized exchanges, in which all the moments of the action, and their unfolding, are rigorously foreseen, have room for strategies: the agents remain in command of the *interval* between the obligatory moments and can therefore act on their opponents by playing with the *tempo* of the exchange. [Bourdieu, 1977:15]

Like procedural rules, strategies can be violated or broken. Far from occupying the gaps that are left unfilled by rules, strategies are best understood as a distinct level of regulation governing play.[2] Nonetheless, as Bourdieu implies, strategies are different from other kinds of regulations. Strategies regulate not the game itself but only a certain optional approach to playing the game. They are enforced by coaches rather than by referees, and violations are private matters between player and coach. A football player fails to follow the game plan in the coach's playbook. A runner ignores her trainer's plan for pacing a long-distance race, surging to the front too early. A tennis player volleys consistently to his opponent's backhand when that is the opponent's greatest strength. In each of these cases, players violate strategic plans. But the games themselves are not spoiled. No constitutive or procedural rules have been broken. No referee will ever intervene on behalf of a broken strategy.

As we saw with Lon Hinkle's unusual approach to golfing, strategies of play are ambiguous in relation to other game rules. Theoretically, strategies operate within the framework of constitutive and regulative rules of a sport. But they can also work to undermine those rules and become the source of innovation in sport, or undermine altogether the integrity of the game. Midway between external constraint and playful impulse, strategies are one of the borderline phenomena characteristic of play.

A LIMINAL ZONE

This conception of borderline phenomena brings us once again to marginal play, where a game overflows its own constituting boundaries entering a space and time frame somewhere between that of the game proper and the world of nongame. Anthropologists, inspired by Victor Turner's seminal work on ritual, call such an ambiguous situation a *liminal* (derived from the Latin word for margin or border) zone of time and space. Liminal phenomena are what Turner often called betwixt-and-between things. Violating neat categories, the liminal is neither inside nor outside, neither here nor there. Partaking of two discrete worlds, liminal entities belong properly within neither.

In studying ritual, Turner focused attention on a liminal phase of most rites of passage. This is a phase of social transition for novices during which they are considered symbolically dead as they pass from one stage of life to another. Anthropologists have examined many kinds of liminal phenomena.

Approaching baseball with the idea of liminality, we noted in Chapter 3 ambiguities of time and space boundaries that were part of baseball's constitutive rules. In this chapter, we take a broader look at the importance of boundary violations in a variety of sports. Focusing on marginal play illuminates not just the special structure of each game but helps to explain some of the curious paradoxes that are part of all genres of cultural performance.

As in the case of the overenthusiastic Yankee fan, play may spill over from the official players to encompass pseudoplayers like spectators, managers, players on the bench, or a technical support team. Play can become spatially marginal when the playing field's boundaries are temporarily breached to include the spectator stands or other peripheral areas as part of the play. In relation to time, play becomes marginal when it flows into periods before or after official play or when time-out periods become an important part of the play itself. Finally, play becomes marginal when strategies of play push against the constitutive boundaries of the game itself and create significant paradoxes of play. In looking at marginal play, we enter a liminal world, unsure of our footing, unclear as to whether we are located within a game world or in the "real" world beyond the play.

Though it has, to my knowledge, never been subject of detailed study, marginal play is clearly a significant part of sport and beyond that of many other performance frames. So it is important to understand what produces these anomalies of play. This is a complicated matter, since not all instances of marginal play have the same explanation. This chapter proposes three related explanations for marginal play: the first is *normative liminality*, the second *empathic engagement*, the third *frame violations*.

NORMATIVE LIMINALITY

When boundary violations are built into the constitutive rules of the game, we have normative liminality. Here broken time or space is a normal part of the game and paradoxes of time and space are central to the basic organization of the sport. They are part of its governing framework and reflect in part the cultural meaning of the sport as a performance.

Normative liminality characterizes some marginal institutions like communes or monasteries where expected norms of social relations in the "outside world" are sometimes deliberately violated as a defining feature of life within the community. It is also the spirit of carnival.[3] Rules for breaking normal rules are central to all rites of reversal and symbolic inversions (Babcock, 1978). Thus, when an Australian aborigine sings and dances out dreamtime myths, or a Huichol Indian from Mexico goes on a yearly peyote hunt and engages in elaborate symbolic reversals in speech and action, they are employing normative liminality. They are deliberately using various boundary violations as an implicit commentary on the normal boundaries that are being violated.

All sports reveal some degree of normative liminality. People may touch each other in ways that would be unacceptable outside the game (just think of wrestling). And forms of violence are encouraged that might be considered illegal assaults in another setting. But some games employ extraordinary forms of spatial and temporal boundary violation as a notable part of their constitutive rules.

As discussed in Chapter 3, baseball has a special affinity for normative liminality, particularly in terms of spatial and temporal regulation. In baseball, the constitutive rules simultaneously create and deny the boundaries of time and space governing play. Baseball time is structured much like baseball space. Beginnings are always ritually fixed, while endings are always open and conditional. These asymmetries are part of the charm of the sport, but normally fans are not really conscious of the relationship between their love of the game and its structural asymmetry.

Periodically, however, something happens that brings the shape of baseball front and center into consciousness. A recent example was the opening of Oriole Park at Camden Yards, the Orioles' new ballpark in Baltimore. In an age dominated by symmetrical domed stadiums, Oriole Park was a self-conscious throwback to the traditional ball fields that have long defined the canonical form of game space in baseball. The park was greeted by fans all over the country with a mixture of nostalgia and euphoria. Once again, baseball had overcome time to reclaim its lost history. It was as if Shoeless Joe Jackson really had come back from the dead for one last game. Typical of fan reactions was the following article which appeared in a local newspaper in Atlanta:

> I have seen heaven, and it's a baseball park: Oriel Park at Camden Yards, a joyous amalgam of architecture, restoration, and urban planning. Its location and ambience are utterly right. . . . Camden Yards complex transforms what was once a decaying neighborhood into the star of Baltimore's City Center.
>
> The edifice itself is not so much physically stunning as it is evocative. Architectural details along with the structure's asymmetrically shaped exterior and the corresponding configuration of the playing field, deliberately invoke such beloved 1900's baseball palaces as Forbes Field, Pittsburgh (brick outfield wall); Shibe Park, Philadelphia (sun deck); and Ebbets Field, Brooklyn (canted right field fence). . . .
>
> The nostalgia for these old ball parks exists not because they were particularly beautiful or comfortable, but because they were personal. . . .
>
> The west side [of an old warehouse] defines Oriel Park's outer perimeter, an extension of the outfield. The portion of Eutaw Street running between it and the park's right field has been transformed into a lively pedestrian promenade that's busy all day, every day, game or no game.
>
> Inside the park . . . there's the incomparable vista of Baltimore's varied architecture, symbolic of its rich history—on continuous display behind the ballpark fence. And a glorious, deep green color flows uninterrupted from the thick grass of the playing surface to the top of the stands. (The single thing that contributes most to an intimate, old-time feeling in a ballpark is dark green seats. . . .). [Jinkner-Lloyd, 1993:28, 31]

This review captures the powerful symbolism of baseball space for Americans discussed in the last chapter. It makes a clear set of connections among four aspects of game space. First is the asymmetry of the field. Second is the importance of the individual character of ballparks. Third is baseball's ability to evoke the past and overcome the flow of clock time. The fourth aspect is the openness of the outfield and the extension of baseball game space into the spectator stands and beyond into the community. We also see here the world-creating ability of a playing field, its capacity for transforming and ordering a decaying urban environment.

Asymmetries of time and space are part of baseball's constitutive rules. They establish the game's basic rhythms as well as its governing structure. These rhythms are part of the unconscious attraction of the game for its fans and its players. For the anthropologist interested in cultural symbolism, the temporal and spatial framework of the sport can provide important clues to its cultural meaning as a performance.

The normative opening up of the boundaries of time or space in sport is inherent in all sports whose aim is to extend temporal or spatial records. Thus races other than sheer endurance contests usually fix distance in order to make possible increasingly short time periods within which the course is traversed. Field events—like shot put, discus, high jump, and long jump—and even mountain climbing aim at unlimited spatial extension. Extending space or contracting time replaces the stress on fixed boundaries. The only time constraint on mountain climbing is set by the technological limits of provisions of food, water, or even air for the climbers. Thus a key factor in the first successful ascent of Mt. Everest was how long the oxygen supply would hold out. In this sense the ascent of Everest was a race against "air time," understood as oxygen flow (Hillary, 1966). However, these temporal limits were set by strategic rather than constitutive limitations. It is the breaking of records rather than the fidelity to boundaries that characterizes record-extending sports. That is why we do not normally call foot races or mountain climbing "games."

Such open-ended sporting activities model a linear conception of human historical activity. These performances put on display miniature dramas of human rationality and technology overcoming external physical limitations. Record keeping reinforces a view of history as progress. The absence of intrinsic spatial or temporal limitations on play is itself a constitutive feature of these activities. This is normative liminality. Here, spatial and temporal openness projects a local vision of the human condition and a historically distinctive understanding of human relations with the natural world.

EMPATHIC ENGAGEMENT

The second type of marginal play is empathic engagement between spectators and players. The term "empathic" suggests sport's tendency to arouse powerful identifications in spectators. Spectators not only "engage" as loyal fans, but can also experience powerful physical empathy, a kinesthetic resonance with the play itself.

Empathic engagement is a feature of all spectator sports. Spectator sports always establish a constitutive boundary between players and spectators. This boundary is marked spatially by a kind of magic circle or square, which only players and referees may normally enter. Spectators are confined to marginal areas in the arena, a distance that shapes their relatively experience-distant perspective on play compared to that of the players. This distance affords spectators reflexive self-awareness or, at worst, boredom.

In contrast, we assume that players are caught up in the psychic "flow" of play, a kind of kinesthetic engagement where all awareness of the passage of time is muted and the players' skills are engaged in a kind of autopilot mode. Despite these conventional distinctions between players' and spectators' perspectives, the actual relations between the reflexive frame of mind and the flow of pure engagement are unstable and variable. In fact, spectators commonly find themselves caught up in game play.

With strong kinesthetic involvement, they can easily forget that they are merely viewers. This is empathic engagement.

Researchers have documented the powerful effect that such empathic engagement can have on fans. Spectators come to experience a kind of flow with the game that is quite far from the reflexivity normally associated with spectatorship. Such cathartic engagement of spectators is like Durkheim's notion of collective effervescence, which he associated with religious rites. It is the psychological underpinning of the power of spectator sports to crystallize potent group loyalties and to trigger equally potent rivalries between opposing groups.

Empathic engagement is behind the periodic blurring of the boundaries of play, where spectators become players in a game of their own making. Spectator activity is an important feature of all spectator sports. Much of the "play" in the stands is in the form of organized cheering and other group displays in support of one of the teams.

One "sport" where empathic engagement figures in an important way is professional wrestling. Empathic engagement is deliberately scripted into professional wrestling by its producers, for whom it is a kind of theatrical performance masquerading as sport. Wrestling deliberately inspires empathic violence on the part of the audience. Professional wrestling engages the audience by deliberately channeling the violence of the match beyond the boundaries of the ring and beyond the limits of the bell.

Much of the most exciting action in wrestling deliberately violates the constitutive framework of the sport. Sidelined wrestlers or managers jump into the ring. Or wrestlers engage one another just outside the ring, after the round or even the match has been ended by the referee. Promoters in professional wrestling obviously understand the peculiar power of marginal play for the fans and regularly stage such frame violations to ignite spectators. In the process, they enact a kind of ritual drama by which heroic evil or heroic virtue overcomes the petty limits of the rules themselves. No figure appears less important in sport than the referee in professional wrestling, whose calls and authority are always being upstaged by both wrestlers and fans.

SOCCER HOOLIGANISM

Probably the most dramatic and sociologically significant example of empathic engagement in organized sport is what has become known in Britain as "soccer hooliganism." Soccer has been notorious among spectator sports for inciting violent displays of empathic engagement. The term "hooliganism" was applied to soccer only in 1961. The occasion was the actual invasion of a playing pitch by inflamed spectators at Sunderland. The invasion came when the home team scored a tying point in the quarter final of a championship match against the first division's ranking team, Tottenham Hotspur. In a 1982 article on soccer violence, Taylor describes the emergence of soccer hooliganism in relation to a mythic orderly past in which spectators knew how to keep their place:

> Popular folklore . . . insists that the pitch was always understood in the 1950s as
> sacred, an area reserved for the club's players only: in effect the *stage* on which the

people's game was to be regularly played. In the early to middle 1960s the pitch invasions escalated, on occasion, into attempts to force postponement of the games, when the supporters' teams were threatened with defeat. There were also new attempts by the crowd to distract the attention of the goal-keepers whilst they took goal kicks, as well as of players taking penalties (interventions which would not have been thought of by spectators prior to the 1960s). [Taylor, 1971/1979:41]

In effect, the spectators assumed the right to impose their own strategies of play on the game. Such practices threatened not only the safety of all present but also the constitutive rules of the game itself.

By the 1968–1969 season, skinhead violence had become a common feature of British football matches. What is so interesting about this apparent disruption of play was its gamelike and rule-bound character, mimicking the very game it sought to disrupt. The goal of rival gangs of youths was to "take the ends" of the fields, chanting taunts at their rivals. The ends are the areas of terrace behind each goal. These marginal zones were favorite vantage points for fans who wanted to be close to the goal-mouth action. In this spectator-driven parody of football, rival gangs of supporters did physical battle before, after, and even during the match. The contest was one to control territory (Gaskell and Pearton, 1979:284 ff.).

What I have called empathic engagement is an important aspect of the power of all performance genres to pull an audience into the performance. As Gregory Bateson argued, all forms of play—including theater, ritual, and sport—have a paradoxical message, at once asserting and denying their status as genuine events (Bateson, 1972). Empathic engagement takes its character from this paradox. Competitive sports are at once violent martial encounters and harmless play. But to be effective, play must never be simply make-believe.[4] The spectator needs to feel that if the match is not really war, it nevertheless comes very close to war. As Bateson would put it, sporting competition is not war but it is also *not* not war. It hangs at the very edge of its performance frame.

Periodic moments of real violence overflow the constraints of the game. Such eruptions of violence into the game provide for spectators an affirmation of the authenticity of the contest. If viewed from a purely game perspective, the context would appear to be a harmless diversion. For example, consider a recent fight that broke out between two American baseball teams during a game. Not only did the players fight, but the police struggled with the game umpires over who had the authority to control the violence. The umpires won out, affirming an interpretation of the fight that the violence was taking place within the frame of the game and was therefore the province of the umpire's authority. It was by legal standards not a real fight. But it was not quite fake either. It was a kind of marginal play: play-fighting, or fighting-play.

While authentic violence erupts in all spectator sports, it has become a norm in certain sporting contests. Hockey is one example where spectator violence has become almost a norm. In hockey, it is team members who are expected to fight. For hockey officials, violent intrusions from the margins of play onto the ice are merely part of the game of hockey. They are not only tolerated but constrained by their own norms, distinguishing between acceptable and unacceptable forms of fighting. Occasionally, however, police will decide that hockey fights have moved beyond the game, and they will treat the fight as a violation of law. In soccer and hockey, empathic engagement from spectators or sidelined players has entered into the regulative rules of the game itself, as marginal play.

FRAME VIOLATIONS

The transformation of spectator into player brings us to the third source of marginal play: frame violations. As cultural performances, sporting events enter into complex relations with other behavioral frames. Games are not simply performance "stages" in contrast to the "offstage" of real life. Observers of the human scene from Shakespeare to scholars like Kenneth Burke and Erving Goffman have argued the case for viewing human life as theater, with no offstage. It is performance all the way around. What appears like an offstage event turns out, on closer inspection, to be just another stage. Apparently offstage areas in sports—such as the grandstands, the dugout, or the locker room—all have their own performance rules. So what we call games are just performance frames that enter into complex relations with other frames. Therefore it is hardly surprising that offstage and onstage sometimes become confused, their boundaries blurred. This is frame violation.

An example of a frame confusion is the relation between racing time and "downtime" in the pit during Formula I races (Lowe, 1977:210). While pit stops are normally considered outside the frame of the race proper, it is in fact the speed and skill of the pit crews that often decide the race. A 500-mile car race can be won by a single car length. So reducing pit time by even a second can often make the difference between winning and losing a race. In this frame violation, an "outside" spatial and temporal frame turns out to be a decisive part of the main event. The same goes for the strategic use of time-outs in basketball. A good coach will use such time-outs as an important part of game strategy. What appears to be a moment beyond the game is actually a key part of play strategy.

A particularly amusing and illuminating example of a frame violation occurred at Wimbledon during the 1935 men's championship match (Laney, 1966:607 ff.). American Don Budge was pitted against Baron Gottfried von Cramm, the German national champion. Von Cramm was not only a seasoned champion but also a sophisticated aristocrat. His elegant and controlled manner provided a vivid counterpoint to the American's boyish if disingenuous charm. The two were volleying during the second set.

Suddenly, Queen Mary entered the royal box. Wimbledon etiquette is very precise on the matter of royalty entering center court. Forgetting the volley in progress, Cramm snapped smartly to attention just beneath the royal box. In deference to the Queen, he clicked his heels together. Eighteen thousand spectators were instantly on their feet at stiff attention. The only figures moving in the entire arena were the Queen and Don Budge. The American seemed oddly unaware of the ritual occasion that had momentarily upstaged the tennis match. One performance frame had, without warning, upstaged another.

After an awkward pause, the crowd seated itself again and play resumed. Budge and Cramm exchanged courts for the next game. At the end of the game the two players exchanged some words. Cramm flushed in anger at his American competitor.

Budge walked slowly toward the near end of the court to take service, placing himself right beneath Queen Mary. Suddenly, Budge cast a glance up at the Queen. With a boyish grin, he raised his right arm above his head and tossed off a little wave of greeting. The crowed gasped at the American's breach of etiquette. Queen Mary was clearly bewildered as well. She sat rigidly upright, unsure how to respond. Then, to the relief and amazement of all present, Queen Mary smiled back at Budge and gave him a little wave in return. From the stands there arose a chorus that all could hear: "God bless the Queen." The thousands of spectators broke spontaneously into wild cheers for both their Queen and for Budge. In the end, Budge emerged as an unlikely hero (or antihero) in a contest between radically opposed cultural styles and political ideologies.

Even under normal circumstances, Wimbledon is an excellent example of multiple performance frames. The play on center court is embedded in a broader framework of ritual, involving not only players but spectator behavior as well (Laney, 1966). The arrival of the Queen set in motion another set of performance norms. The embedded or alternative norms were shared by all present except for Budge, who improvised his own idiosyncratic response to the Queen's entrance.

In the complex set of relations involving Budge, Cramm, the spectators, and the Queen, several levels of ritual and several kinds of contest crowded onto the same performance field. The frame violations of this scenario produced a level of tension that engaged the passions of all present in ways that were clearly only dimly understood at the time. From one contest, another was born.

CHEATING

In a sense, all instances of playing strategies that encroach on the constitutive and regulative framework of sports play are frame violations. Games are organized in hierarchies of rules, from the most basic and fixed constitutive rules through procedural rules to more flexible strategies. In this way, games provide an excellent model for thinking about the complex polyphonies of cultural knowledge more generally. In games as elsewhere in human life, strategies can come to undermine the very integrity of a game, as they push at the constitutive boundaries that define the game's special universe.

When this kind of pushing is done deliberately we call it cheating. Yet there are degrees of cheating and important variations in what sorts of boundary pushing will be permitted. Sometimes players adopt their own rules of play, which come into conflict with the rules of the game. In such cases, the private framework can supersede the official rules, if only in the mind of the player.

Chess masters sometimes make private deals with opponents who are friends or who hail from the same country. Such secret agreements fix matches so they will end in a draw. The morality governing friendship or national honor sometimes conflicts with the rules of normal play. Thus, in 1975, Grandmaster Samuel Reshevsky had the nerve to complain to the tournament director that his adversary Paul Benko had broken a pregame agreement to fix a draw. Reshevsky complained that Benko had violated the embedded "rules" of their private deal (play to a draw) by following a basic constitutive rule of tournament chess (play to win). Benko played to win in the final round of the U.S. Chess Championship. In effect, he "cheated" by refusing to cheat (Hearst and Wierzbicki, 1979:60 ff.).

In a similar vein, there is the case of the private game plan of pitching great Don Drysdale. Drysdale had a 2-for-1 rule. Whenever he knew that one of his teammates had been deliberately hit by a pitch, he would hit twice as many of the opposing team's players. In a game where deliberately hitting a batter is illegal, Drysdale's private game was a clear case of frame violation. Personal morality overrode the game's own rules.

CONCLUSION: PLAY AS PARADOX

In this chapter we have extended our analysis of ludic models by examining some marginal areas of sporting life. We have spent time in the liminal zones of sport, just out of bounds of normal play, watching how sporting events tend to spill beyond the temporal and spatial borders that normally define them. Marginal play was explained in terms of three concepts. First was normative liminality, where violations of spatial and temporal boundaries are built into the constitutive framework of play. Normative liminality often serves to symbolize important cultural and historical problematics, so that it becomes part of the ritual significance of the sport.

The second concept was the empathic engagement of spectators. Empathic engagement pulls spectators into the play and blurs the boundaries between the viewer and the player. Spectators lose their distance and identify powerfully with the players, sometimes taking over the game itself and creating a game of their own. The third explanation for marginal play was frame violation. This is the confusion of embedded performance frames that surround any sporting event. Frames are violated when the game itself is penetrated by any of these other performance frames. Frame violations occur within a game when a player plays by his own private rules, which violate the normal rules of play. Frame violations can also involve conflicts among several conventional performance frames. This was the case with Queen Mary's entrance into the center-court stadium at Wimbledon.

This notion of frame violation brings us to the heart of the matter—the connection between play and paradox. As Gregory Bateson has taught us, paradox is the mother of all play. All boundary-breaking play shares some sort of structural paradox. Sport may be understood as a kind of compromise formation between two necessary but incompatible human impulses: playfulness and gamesmanship, both of which are essential to the creation and institutionalization of cultural forms. The play impulse is by nature hostile to boundaries. Caillois and Piaget identified this spontaneous, open, and boundary-breaking turbulence with the play of young children. Caillois called it *paidiá*. He contrasted this kind of free play with *ludus,* the rule-governed quality of organized games. Games are oriented toward formal control and the subordination of personal energies to social constraints.

So sport is an inherently borderline phenomenon at the crossroads of *ludus* and *paidiá*. Sports engage a fundamental human conflict. On the one hand, sport evokes the impulse for creating order and setting boundaries. At the same time, it arouses the equally powerful human flair for play, the impulse to break free of the boundaries of the game itself. It is no accident, I think, that among adult primates only humans retain the child's capacity for play and sport. And it is no accident that organized sport inevitably engages the paradox of play. For the dialectic of play—the endless point-counterpoint of making rules and breaking records, of imposing boundaries in order to challenge limits—is inherently, inevitably human.

The sapient primate is also the playful primate—*Homo ludens*—and not just during leisure hours. And I suppose it is no coincidence that the playful primate, the master of games, is also the primate who had to face the great evolutionary paradox of having constantly to invent a life world while attributing to that world the character of both structural and moral necessity. The human love of play and sport is in part an acknowledgment of this paradox. Piaget recognized the great paradox of human play when he titled a discussion of children playing marbles: "Children Invent the Social Contract" (Piaget 1932). If we look closely at sporting events, this paradoxical stance uniting *ludus* and *paidiá*—the most conservative and most creative parts of our nature—reveals itself not just at center stage. It also accounts for the tendency of games to overcome themselves periodically by violating their own constitutive framework while at the same time reaffirming that framework. This is why marginal play resides at once on the fringes and at the center of any performance frame.

Notes

1. For important works on performance theory, see Ashley, 1990; Babcock, 1978; Bakhtin, 1981; Barth, 1975; Bateson, 1955; Benamou and Carnello, 1977; D'Aquili et al. (eds.), 1979; MacAloon (ed.), 1984; Geertz, 1973f; Geertz, 1980; Gluckman, 1954; Gluckman, 1962; Grimes, 1982, 1985, 1990; Guttman, 1978; Hymes, 1975; Le Roy Ladurie, 1979; Schechner, 1977, 1985; Schechner et al., 1990; Stoeltje, 1978; Turner, 1967, 1969, 1974, 1983; Turner and Schechner, 1986.

2. While the anthropologist as outsider may be predisposed to view a game in terms of its constitutive rules, for the player, the "purest" level of regulated play is experienced as an unfolding of mutual strategy. Here strategy does not occupy the "free" interstices between regulated play but defines the structure of the game itself. For a brilliant evocation of "pure baseball" understood as strategic play, see Hernandez and Bryan, 1994.

3. For studies of the ritual elements in carnival, see DaMatta, 1984; Flanigan, 1990; Abrahams and Bauman, 1978; and Le Roy Ladurie, 1979.

4. Note how children commonly recount tales of roller coaster accidents just before taking a ride on one. In the same way, sport competition must periodically deny its status as play to really engage the spectator.

5

Interior Furnishings:
Scenes from an American
Foundational Schema

It is the mode of handling problems, rather than what they are about, that assigns them to an age. Their subject-matter may be fortuitous, and depends on conquests, discoveries, plagues, or governments; their treatment derives from a steadier source.

—Susanne Langer

At the moment when the natural environment was altered beyond the point that it could be personally observed, the definitions of knowledge itself began to change. No longer based on direct experience, knowledge began to depend upon scientific, technological, industrial proof.

—Jerry Mander

Chapter 3 offered us a close look at a single American cultural model, the game of baseball. We saw how, in addition to its obvious role as pure entertainment, baseball models the problematical relationship between individualistic and communitarian values, enduring issues in American culture and history. The analysis also showed how this baseball model contributes to the structure of the American cultural model of love and marriage.[1] This kind of cross-mapping between models is not uncommon. Models enter into complex relations with other cultural models. In some cases, (sub)-models are parts of larger encompassing models (D'Andrade, 1992:30 ff.). In other cases, as in the baseball example just cited, one model serves as a source for structuring a second model through a kind of analogical transfer. The transfer from baseball to dating is accomplished largely through language and involves the metaphorical mapping of baseball jargon onto important aspects of dating behavior. This cross-mapping between these two cultural domains is also accomplished in other ways. Marriage can become an actual part of a baseball game, creating a kind of metonymic transfer rather than metaphor. This happens when marriage proposals are flashed on the electronic board in ballparks or when newlyweds still in their wedding garb seat themselves behind home plate.

This "leakiness" of cultural models, and the resulting relations between cultural models in any community, are among the most important sources of creativity and continuity in cultural life. The many cross-mappings among different cultural models guarantee a flow of meaning between discrete domains and contribute to what Peirce called a continual process of "semiosis." This flow of meaning between models not only contributes to the creativity of culture but also accounts in part for a degree of semantic coherence that characterizes the cultural life of even the most complex societies.

There is also another important source of continuity in cultural life: *foundational schemas* (see Chapter 2). A foundational schema is a high-level model of great generality and abstractness. Generally, foundational schemas are not dedicated to a single domain of social life but organize and underlie a large number of specific cultural models whose forms are roughly analogous to one another.

THE MODULARITY SCHEMA

This chapter and the one that follows will make the case for the usefulness of the distinction between foundational schema and cultural model. The case will be made in culturally familiar terms by exploring one of the most pervasive and powerful foundational schemas in modern American life: the *modularity schema*. This modularity schema, through its power to structure a very large number of specific cultural models, virtually defines the cognitive landscape of modernity and has a lot to do with the emergence of a recognizably postmodern mentality. What I call the modularity schema is also understandable as a kind of high-tech cognitive style, a machine-driven logic that has powerfully affected the way in which much of our knowledge of the world has been coded.

Though Chapter 6 proceeds through some fairly esoteric terrain, the present chapter begins deliberately in a more homely fashion with a personal reminiscence about familiar styles of furniture. I choose to begin in this way because it was through such a set of reminiscences that I first began to understand that even the apparent decomposition of coherent experience in the postmodern world could be traced (ironically) to an unanalyzed master model that envisions reality as modular. As it unfolds, the chapter turns from personal thoughts on furniture styles to consider more global design and organizational trends by which modernity and its industrial infrastructure have furnished the postmodern mind with its set of recognizable and distinct forms of knowledge.

The case is made for the modularity schema by navigating a broad and apparently heterogeneous landscape of diverse cultural models that share a family resemblance. This resemblance suggests the generative role of the encompassing modularity schema. A foundational schema functions as a kind of template, a common underlying form that links superficially diverse cultural models and contributes to the sometimes ineffable sense of "style" or "ethos" characteristeric of a culture. In more technical language, we can say that the foundation schema provides a "source domain" for the creation of a family of related cultural models. Moreover, the idea of foundational schema presumes that these models have evolved by means of a usually unconscious "schematizing process," a kind of analogical transfer that underlies the creative life of cultural models. The nature of this schematizing process will be the subject of Chapter 14.

"America," Baudrillard wrote, "is the original version of modernity" (Baudrillard, 1988:76). What Baudrillard terms "the myths of modernity" (p. 81) have a distinctly American accent, yet it would be misleading to assign their power exclusively to the character of a single nation. Modernism can lay claim to no single home but has taken hold wherever its technological and economic roots have dug in. Still, as Baudrillard suggests, modernity is, in an important sense, an American invention, one that has alternately enthralled and appalled European intellectuals since De-Tocqueville. While there is no single definition of modernity, I have isolated one feature of modern thought, an orientation to modularity, as a good candidate for an important American foundational schema. Modularity is a design strategy that breaks complex wholes into elementary units that are understood to be recombinable into a variety of different patterns. A modular orientation to reality views a wide range of phenomena as assemblages, subject to decomposition and recombination. It values qualities such as flexibility, efficiency, and control. By exploring the modular organization of many American institutions, I hope to show that this modular frame of mind is America's legacy to the modern world—a technologically driven foundational schema exported from America's factories and laboratories.

SCENE 1: MODULAR FURNITURE

The story begins comfortably, with furniture. I have always loved furniture, particularly trying out easy chairs and sofas. Perhaps this is because some of my earliest pleasant recollections are of big, soft, and overstuffed pieces in whose surrogate laps I spent so many hours as a kid. This was a time in modernity's infancy when sofas and chairs had but a single purpose. Their physical contours had about them the recollection of a seated human form. As psychologists would say, they *afforded* the human body quite nicely. A chair was for sitting and nothing else. There were also stretched-out chairs—sofas or couches—which had the same virtues and defects as chairs, only they were longer, designed out of an image of several seated bodies rather than just one.

These chairs and sofas were essential seating objects and could not easily be used for anything other than that for which they had originally been designed. They were not especially portable. Once set in a room, they tended to put down roots and their placement defined the room's shape and atmosphere. Such rooted furniture fostered a sense of place and defined spaces. Beds also tended to be just beds. Bulky, not easily moved or dismantled, beds were pretty comfortable for sleeping but not for much else. Beds quite literally defined fixed sleeping spaces known as bedrooms.

In the 1960s we got our first sofa bed and with that single purchase became modern. A sofa bed was an odd piece of furniture, for it had the body of a couch but the heart of a bed. It was, my back recalls, a pretty fair couch but an awful bed. Sofa beds were "convertibles," furniture designed with transformations in mind: images of sleeping-sitting bodies. A twist, a tug, a lift, and a little luck transformed one structural arrangement into another. A sense of fixed form gave way to a momentary arrangement. This was provisional furniture, and times were changing.

The sofa bed went downstairs into a room that had been called the cellar but was fast becoming a "family room," or "den," or "playroom." Most of the time, it was an informal living room and the sofa was for sitting. But occasionally an overnight guest could be accommodated and the room would be transformed into a kind of bedroom. It was a bedroom in the same contingent sense that the sofa both was and was not a bed. The room had become the product of a transient structural arrangement.

It was around this time that our local elementary schools began to be built with something called a "multipurpose room," a great hall with movable walls and reconfigurable attachments that made possible a variety of structural arrangements. The multipurpose room was equally suitable (or unsuitable) as a gym, lunchroom, or assembly hall. Modular architectural design has been around since the Bauhaus movement of the 1930s. But it came of age in the 1960s. By the 1950s, American living spaces were already beginning to change. In my grandparents' house, rooms had for the most part single-purpose personalities: bedrooms for sleeping, sitting rooms for sitting, kitchens for cooking, and dining rooms for eating. Then rooms that had been designed with fixed functions began to open up. They were shedding their "roomly" qualities and becoming "spaces" or "areas." Living areas could become sleeping rooms. More commonly, the living room and the dining room fused into two areas of common space.

The dining "area" might be separated from the living space by an L-shaped turn or by an archway gently suggesting a change of function. In smaller homes, the dining area was often informal, borrowing its space from the kitchen rather than the living room. We called these eating areas *dinettes,* a term that was also applied to the new kind of vinyl-and-metal furniture that was scaled to these informal eating spaces.

VINYL CAUSE, EFFICIENT CAUSE

Plastic was beginning to make itself at home throughout the American domestic environment. The virtue of plastic was its easy transformability. Its particular genius was general: it could become (virtually) anything. Plastic was our first step toward virtualizing reality, since its nature was to have no particular form or function. The plastic revolution gave birth to a new surfacing material called Formica. Initially, the use of these new materials combined with the loosening up of rooms into multipurpose spaces, which were most pronounced in what we called "ultramodern" houses. In its flexibility, plastic was an extraordinarily efficient material. It could mimic wood, glass, cotton fabric, or even leather. Plastic, a word which itself implies flexibility, made possible modernity's first virtual environment.

The first truly modern house I ever saw was in Radburn, a new suburban "development" in Fair Lawn, New Jersey, where I grew up. Radburn was one of the first planned communities in the United States and we all marveled at our friend's gleaming "ranch" house. The house had lots of subtle levels, but you could not easily name them. What seemed like acres of glass brought the outside into the house, blurring the boundaries between inside and out. One space slipped into another so that you almost flowed through the house without any sense of rooms at all. When I arrived in California in the mid-1960s, I saw other striking examples of these new houses with innovative living spaces like "conversation pits" or "lofts." Rather than being divided by walls, these living spaces were defined by "levels," so that a step up or down brought one into a new kind of space.

In the fifties we had "modernized," lowering the ceilings of rooms, often with lime-green acoustic tile. Clean lines replaced fussy architectural detail like moldings, decorative "gingerbread," or ceiling decoration. Rooms took on a crisp, cubic starkness. By the sixties and seventies, the most up-to-date houses no longer suggested the idea of a house as comprising a stable collection of distinctive rooms. Instead, we had all-purpose spaces that could be configured and reconfigured according to changing needs and different inhabitants.

I bought my first modular furniture as an undergraduate in California in the mid-sixties. Modular furniture was something new back then, at least to me. And it was perfect for a nomadic student life. Modular furniture was not designed with a human form in mind. What it did keep in view was maximum flexibility of use. A fixed shape was replaced by regular geometric surfaces and angles. Such modular units could be linked mechanically in various configurations, depending on need.

At the extreme end of the design spectrum, modular furniture was nothing but soft building blocks: analytical, elementary furniture units. With such furniture, it was hard to speak of chairs or sofas or beds per se, since these were now mere surface arrangements of a more or less temporary nature. They lacked essential "bedness" or "chairness." They had quantity (mass, dimensions) but no intrinsic furniture *qualities*. One form could easily be reconfigured into another as fast as the blocks could be reassembled. Existentialism had arrived at the furniture store. We could now equip our homes with furniture which, like the spaces it occupied, had only particular existence but no discernible essence.

Of course, modularity of this kind never did come close to overtaking our furniture. Most chairs and sofas retained some degree of traditional shaping. But the modular design concept opened up furniture in ways that continue to influence modern furnishings. From sectionals to configurable wall units to office plans, modularity has left its mark on our interiors. But it is such a familiar part of the landscape that we hardly notice how modularization has come to shape our experiences.

SCENE 2: THE MALL

Before the 1950s one usually shopped at a particular kind of store for a particular kind of product. There were shoe stores for shoes, grocery stores for groceries, bookshops for books, and milliners for hats. Each was distinctive in function and most had individual identities because they were one-of-a-kind establishments, taking on the local character of their owners and their surrounding environments. In 1974, when I lived for six months in New Zealand, I experienced this kind of quaint shopping environment in the city of Auckland. I was delighted to discover there a world of particular shops: greengrocers, butchers, fishmongers, and dry-goods merchants rather than malls or discount chains.

Gradually, in the sixties and seventies, this intimate shopping landscape began to change. Partly, this was a function of a change in scale, as large corporations took over the retailing of items that had once been sold by small mom-and-pop enterprises. Chain stores became familiar places to shop—stores that cloned themselves around the country guaranteeing instant familiarity to a shopper regardless of the location. Even department stores sprouted branches, usually down-scaled suburban versions of the urban parent store. Names like Macy's, which once referred to a unique New York retail institution on 34th Street, would eventually come to mean any one of dozens of interchangeable department stores scattered throughout the country.

In modern society, the mass reproduction of cultural forms has been paralleled by the transformability and transience of people, places, and things in particular. Too much attachment to specific, concrete places becomes a significant cognitive and social liability. In the movie *Rainman,* Raymond, an autistic idiot savant, is incapable of recognizing the interchangeability of chain stores. Obsessed with acquiring a new pair of boxer briefs, he keeps insisting that they must be bought at K-Mart in Cincinnati, where he had previously shopped for underwear. K-Mart for Raymond refers to a concrete place rather than a general type of store. His exasperated brother tries in vain to convince him that a K-Mart is a K-Mart no matter where it is, and one pair of boxer briefs is the same as any other. Raymond's extreme attachment to particulars leaves him with virtually no flexibility in relation to his environment. This kind of autism exemplifies an extreme form of what might be termed "amodularity."

With the growth of the suburbs and the proliferation of the "chain" concept in retailing, the full implications of modularization began to be felt. Commercial enterprises became less identifiable with specific products or services and more generalized and abstract in function. Markets became supermarkets and stores became chains.

Then came the mall, the everything/anywhere place—a superconstellation of stores, a virtual shopping environment. In the mall, stores were themselves modular units that could be reproduced anywhere in the country. They were interchangeable spaces on huge reconfigurable floor plans. One could wander from area to area and even from mall to mall hardly aware that the location had changed. Even traditional department stores opened branches at the mall. Their floor plans underwent modularization. What once had been fairly fixed and predictable "departments" lost their firm contours. Instead, we had selling areas, with fake or temporary walls at best, whose virtue was that they could be reconfigured at will. If clothing styles changed from year to year, why not the stores themselves?

It was exciting for shoppers, who could be guaranteed a virtually limitless supply of novel sensory stimulation by the ever-shifting environment. In fact, the malls were designed to provide a kind of perpetual buzz of bright sound and sight for the stimulus-hungry consumer. While it was a little disconcerting not to be able to find your way in the same store from year to year, there was the compensating comfort of entering a mall in a strange part of the country and immediately feeling at home.

Department stores have tried, with varying degrees of success, to counteract the homogeneity and abstractness of such modularized environments. One relatively recent strategy has been to create, within department stores, microstores—modular boutique environments, which are sometimes associated with specific designers and at other times with functionally specific product lines. This boutique phenomenon has reproduced a structural nesting of modules, a mall-within-a-mall. While the boutique strategy can successfully address the diversity-within-unity goals of a modern mall, it can also leave us strangely disconcerted. This is because we gradually come to perceive these environments as pure surface arrangements lacking the depth of authentic places with histories.

Malls are a triumph of configural illusions, modular design environments orchestrating well assembled surfaces. They are more like "stage sets" than what we used to think of as shops. What mall architecture, even at its best, cannot convey is the store as an authentic place with a local history. I suspect that the most powerful but unconscious experience of this loss is the absence, in mall shops, of authentic smells of the kind that permeate traditional grocery stores, outdoor markets, old-fashioned five-and-tens, and even older clothing stores. The smells of these stores are the smells of social history, and they have been neutralized at the modern mall or supermarket. The people who sell us things appear to have undergone a similar neutralization becoming increasingly interchangeable. We hardly ever know them personally. More peculiar yet, it is hard to tell one kind of seller from another. Once there were jewelers, furriers, clothiers, but now there are retailers or salesmen, salespersons, or even interchangeable "sales personnel" who are a multipurpose sales force.

SCENE 3: HAMBURGER TECHNOLOGY

Modularity revised our experience not only of where we shopped but also of what we bought. Perhaps the most famous example of the modularized commodity is one that proliferated in the late fifties and early sixties: fast food. The extraordinary success of McDonald's points to the power of modularization in transforming our basic subsistence activities. The Golden Arches reproduced themselves on what seemed to be every commercial thoroughfare. The hamburger itself became a modular entity, a variable configuration of edible components. The appeal of this new sort of food was that it might serve individual needs through mass-production techniques. McDonald's success in mass-producing these elementary American food units was proclaimed from the top of each Golden Arch, where the number of units sold nationwide was constantly updated. What these elementary patties lacked in quality or in size they made up for in numbers. The virtue of a hamburger lay in its endless reproducibility. Like digits, hamburgers multiplied seemingly without end.

This transformed hamburger had become an edible module, subject to reconfiguration. It was no longer food to be made but a constructed food "item." Hamburgers could be assembled their way ("we do it all for you") or our way ("we do it your way"). Interestingly, a precursor to the McDonald's hamburger was a more modest chain operation called White Castle, whose little square hamburgers were virtual icons of modularization: mass-produced beef building blocks. We could get single, doubles, or whatever we wished. Like edible skyscrapers, the patties could be stacked to any reasonable height and then configured in any one of numerous combinations.[2]

SCENE 4: CORPORATE MODULES

Modularization permits a high degree of flexibility and expandability in whatever it organizes. The postindustrial phase of capitalist "flow" created a new kind of business entity—a modular transnational corporate enterprise that could transform itself into anything the market demanded. Under the banner of diversification, many corporations adopted modular growth strategies. On the heels of World War II, these multinational "conglomerates" saw a dramatic expansion. These were companies whose roots lay in specific product or service lines and whose names traditionally described their products: General Electric, General Motors, R. J. Reynolds Tobacco Company, National Biscuit Company. But as they expanded, they often acquired diversified business holdings whose concrete connections were hard to imagine. Holding companies managed collections of diverse businesses of sometimes astonishing variety.

The new conglomerates presented novel marketing and public relations challenges. What sort of concrete identity could they be given? What kind of name could adequately summarize their identities to the public? Corporate names became referentially empty and highly abstract. Names like The Transamerica Corporation, "A Company called TRW," AMR Corporation, or Gulf & Western bore only the faintest hints of what they did in their names. Sometimes too concrete a reference was deemed too limiting and inaccurate. National Biscuit Company became Nabisco, Standard Oil of New Jersey became Esso ("S.O.") and then Exxon. United Airlines became a subsidiary of the more abstract holding company UAL Inc.

One solution to the problem of vacant reference is the logo, an easily remembered icon that can stand for and literally incorporate whatever diverse products are associated with the company. The advantage of such abstract images is that they make possible conceptual linkage among the various products and services produced by the company that may have nothing else in common. Another strategy has been to conceive of corporate names using sound symbolism to convey to the public a general sense of corporate orientation. This strategy has been adopted by many high-tech companies like Textron, Syntex, and Exxon, where the name employs sound combinations that have come to suggest science in action.[3] A corporate name can sometimes mimic the very modularity that has brought it about. Thus the name Genentech, derived presumably from "genetic engineering technology," employs morphemes in a modular manner that suggests recombinant genetics, which is the company's primary business. The firm's name is modeled in the very form of its business.

SCENE 5: CHANNEL SURFING

Television did not need to become modularized. It was born that way: a cathode-ray tube sprayed with 300,000 phosphorescent dots creates distinct images by breaking up and recombining fast enough to maintain the illusion of form. While the brain can translate the retinal information into imagery about ten times each second, television tricks the mind by broadcasting its information at three times that rate (Mander, 1978:194). The box before us presents visual forms so engaging that we literally cannot keep our eyes from the screen when it is in close proximity.

The experience of TV watching is a disturbing kind of everything-and-nothing experience, full and empty at the same time. Television is a completely compelling perceptual (if not intellectual) experience, but only while it is on. Turn it off and the presence is completely gone, instantly. We are freed from its pull, as if it were never there, without the buzz or halo effect one sometimes gets in a movie theater or from a good book.

Television allows channel-flipping (called "roaming" or "surfing" within the industry). Instant reconfigurations of the screen permit viewers to wander, often aimlessly, amid totally disconnected stimuli. Virtual worlds with no bridges between them instantly assemble and evaporate before our eyes. Television is the agent of what Kroker and Cook (1986) have termed the "hypersimulation" of reality. Even within the confines of a single channel, television's authentic mode is modular and atomistic. Todd Gitlin has characterized commercial television as a form of "recombinant culture" where a limited number of visual and sound elements are endlessly juggled (Gitlin, 1980; see also Jhally, 1987:105).

This modularity characterizes all levels of television viewing down to television's most primitive perceptual experiences. Turn off the sound and you see a rapid-fire sequence of crisp image pulses. In expensive ads, upwards of forty distinct image "set-ups" per minute can flash by in a visual staccato, each a self-contained sensory unit with its own message. Unlike film, television does not use "shaped" transitions like fadeouts nearly as much as simple atomic image blocks. On commercial television, commercial modules ("ads") are assembled in endless combinations, breaking up any continuity of the already fragmented shows. The commercial segments break up the show; the show segments break up the commercials. The distinction fades. We have come to accept this television choplogic as a kind of natural perception in which sequential images pile up with no necessary connection to one another. In television, time is money, lots of it. Appropriately, television time has been reified as an abstract product. Segmented into modular chunks called "dayparts," commercial television time is as much a commodity to be bought and sold as are the goods it is designed to peddle (Jhally, 1987:79 ff.; Twitchell, 1992:220).

The atomization of the television image at virtually every level of representation is the sensory analogue of this commodification of time. So familiar has this experience become for most of us that we hardly notice how unnatural are the perceptual habits required to make sense of television watching. Imagine how odd it would be for someone with no prior experience of television to encounter this kind of sensory fragmentation.

In his early account of American national character, Geoffrey Gorer noted the characteristic modularity of television programs as far back as the late forties:

> The atomic aspect of American TV is most striking in those programs whose noncommercial portions contain material of potential civic importance, but it is not confined to these. The most popular entertainment programs consist of a series of amusing nonsequiturs uttered by a small group of stereotyped characters. . . . The greater number of scripts could be cut up and reassembled in any other order without losing comprehensibility or laughs. [Gorer, 1948/1964:149]

Though intrinsically atomistic, television has in recent years become increasingly modular in its handling of programming. When I was growing up, certain television shows defined the days of the week for me. My favorite was always Friday nights, when *I Remember Mama* predictably marked the start of the weekend. Saturday mornings were *Rin Tin Tin* and *Andy's Gang*. Shows tended to stay put in one time and place long enough for us to maintain the illusion that they were really ours.

But over the years, something seems to have happened to television. Shows are now apparently conceived of as entertainment modules. "Segments" are fitted into "time slots" and positioned in a modular configuration with other blocks and against competing shows. These shows, particularly the modularly named "sitcoms," are structured to attract the widest range of "market segments" and "audience shares." Their casts are assembled with particular age, regional, and ethnic markets in view. Since television slots are generally in thirty-minute increments, shows can be treated as elementary entertainment units and slotted into many combinations to suit viewer habits and preferences.

Shows come and go, appearing and slipping away with a disturbing casualness. Even when they do not disappear, shows tend to roam from slot to slot, from night to night, and even from channel to channel, making it difficult for people to attach themselves to any given configuration of time and show. New sitcoms, with totally unfamiliar characters, are sometimes presented to us with a fake familiarity, as if we had known them all along. Television "personalities" or characters are often gone before any kind of real acquaintance can be established with an audience. More successful characters sometimes slide from one show to another, visiting other sitcoms in "guest appearances" or even "spinning off" into a linked series. This combination of flexibility, rapid reconfiguration, and superficiality is characteristic of modular organization.

Television shows are interchangeable in content as well as form. In part, this homogenization of television shows is inherent in all modular organizations, where interchangeability of modules enhances flexibility. There are also powerful economic incentives for replicating successful programming formulas. The inexorable tendency for programmers endlessly to clone tried-and-true formats and themes is partly due to the economic pressures on networks to maximize audience share as determined by the ratings. Truly novel or subtle experiences take time for audiences to adjust to, but the short-term pressures of the ratings on advertising revenues do not usually allow the programmers to indulge in the longer-term project of reeducating viewers' sensibilities.

There are other, perhaps less obvious sources of television's often noted homogeneity of content. The perceptual basis of TV watching encourages a tendency toward replication of predictable images. The potential educational benefits of television have often been noted, most recently in relation to the instant worldwide communication of news that CNN has made possible. Less appreciated, however, is the use of television not for stimulation but as a kind of electronic meditation, equivalent to staring at a fireplace.

The best published account of the power of the television medium over the mind of the viewer is Jerry Mander's book *Four Arguments for the Elimination of Television* (Mander, 1978). As a highly successful advertising and public relations executive from San Francisco, Mander became disenchanted with the very medium of television with which he had had so much professional success. He decided to research the effectiveness of television advertising, not so much from a content perspective as from the point of view of the cognitive power of television as a physical medium. The general effect of television watching, according to Mander, is what he terms a "dimming out of the human" (p.164), a flattening out of sensory stimulation affecting both physical and mental functioning. Part of this dimming effect is related to the unique viewing conditions of television, which is normally a fixed point of light in a partially darkened room. Television viewing requires a virtually fixed focus for long periods of time. The effect of long periods of immobilized staring at the rapidly flickering light source of the TV screen (a result of the rapid "refresh" rate of the screen) has been likened to that of trance induction (Mander, 1978:197).

The "pull" of television thus may be less its entertainment value than its pervasive trance-inducing qualities, which provide for a kind of electronic stress reduction. This might explain why travelers often put on the television immediately after entering a new hotel room. The combination of the familiar programming content and the regularity of its electronic rhythms may act to reduce the stress of being in an unfamiliar environment. If this is the case, then television programmers may have unwittingly recognized the true function of television in their strategy of providing highly predictable and stereotypic content to their already modularized programming format.

Modularization has not only shaped our most powerful entertainment medium but has also contributed to a loosening up of distinctions among the different entertainment genres. Movies become television shows, books become movies, and we have such peculiar hybrids as "electronic magazines" or "TV novels." Reciprocally, newspapers like *U.S.A. Today* look like printed color television programs, and indeed this paper has recently cloned itself into an electronic TV newsmagazine. The media are becoming increasingly interchangeable, which always means that their forms are becoming more homogeneous.

SCENE 6: EDUCATIONAL REFORM

Educational institutions are among the prime ways in which a society explicitly tries to reproduce its worldview. It is hardly surprising that modularization has profoundly influenced American education. In a fascinating historical analysis of the emergence of modular institutions in America, John Blair traces a fundamental change in the basic conception of higher education curricula in nineteenth-century America (Blair, 1988; Chap. 2). He singles out the work of two prominent educational reformers, the Rev. Francis Wayland, President of Brown University throughout the mid-nineteenth century, and Harvard's Charles William Eliot, who in the last quarter of the century oversaw the Americanization of Harvard's educational scheme.

Wayland replaced the European fixed curriculum with the notion of a set of electives among which students might choose in assembling a more individually tailored curriculum. He sought to place other subject areas on an equal footing with the classics by proposing that they be viewed as alternatives in a "system of equivalents" (Blair, 1988:16). The more rigid and holistic European model of higher education retained considerable prestige in nineteenth-century America, and Wayland's reforms did not long outlast his tenure at Brown. It took Eliot's Harvard reforms toward the end of the century to transform American higher education into its current distinctive forms.

Whereas a European conceived of a "course" as a hierarchically integrated and coherent body of skills and knowledge, the American reforms redefined a course as a single specialized unit of learning. A "major" would then comprise an assemblage of distinct courses. Examinations would be understood to "cover" only the specific material dealt with in one unit of education rather than a general body of traditional works and knowledge in a discipline. Eliot's goal was to break down the educational process into recombinable units which, being selected by the individual student, would allow both greater flexibility in content and stronger motivation on the part of the student.

These nineteenth-century reforms have continued to provide the basic template for contemporary American education. The breaking down of knowledge into alternative blocks has given us such educational staples as "credits" or "units," "electives," and "requirements" (a term which takes on significance only in relation to a system marked by a high degree of individual choice). The traditional European model of a curriculum as an integrated and organic system of knowledge organized around traditional subjects (the *trivium* or the *quadrivium* of the medieval university), or around an established canon of great works to be mastered, was replaced by a more atomistic vision of a curriculum as a collection of equivalent subjects among which students might choose in constructing a particular education.

An echo of the older, more holistic sense of curriculum was retained through sets of core requirements. In a few cases, the European model has transplanted itself at philosophically conservative institutions. St. John's of Annapolis and its sister school in Santa Fe have retained the classic model of a fixed curriculum, while at the University of Chicago, Robert M. Hutchins put in place a modified European curriculum based on the "Great Books" idea and its commitment to education as the transmission of a canonical body of essential learning.

Though educators have endlessly debated the relative merits of fixed and open curricula, many American college students appear to see their curricular choices more in terms of convenient practical arrangements rather than of intrinsic intellectual coherence or value. At least this is the impression one gets from Michael Moffatt's analysis of Rutgers University students:

> How did the students make their choices? Educational planners sometimes assumed they did so on purely pedagogical grounds, but the students' decisions were actually based on intricate calculations and tradeoffs of necessity, convenience, availability and difficulty. First you took care of requirements in your major. . . . Then you started thinking about your minor and your mini; what did you find interesting? Alternatively, what possibly complemented your major and made you vocationally more attractive? Economics and English, for instance. Then, what fit your preferred hours and days for classes? What, on the other hand, was impossible? Did you have to make a campus bus connection between back-to-back classes. . . . You also wanted a balanced schedule— one that was not too difficult in any particular semester, one that perhaps combined boring requirements with more interesting electives. Some students signed up for their electives blind, but more experienced students asked around. [Moffatt, 1989:285]

This passage highlights a number of key values that are consistent with the modular organization of American curricula. First is the stress on pragmatic flexibility. Students value being able to "arrange their schedules" for convenience. Second, the orientation is toward self-satisfaction or enhancement rather than mastery of a body of knowledge or skills. Third is the emphasis on voluntarism. Electives are often assumed by students to be intrinsically more interesting than requirements, which are presumed to be boring. The fact of choice itself seems to make the course more attractive. Finally, there is the stress on curriculum as process rather than content. Educational goals tend to lie beyond the courses themselves, in immediate or long-range pragmatic considerations.

The dominant metaphor for modern American undergraduate education is a market and not predominantly a market of ideas. Educational strategies in America tend to be framed in quantitative terms. Students shop around for courses, which are often known by number. Even majors may be mixed and matched through double majors or major-minor combinations. Some institutions even allow for individual majors, assembled by students presumably in consultation with an advisor. Courses are often conceived of as atomic commodities "offered" for variable "credits" or "units."

In such a setting, students are encouraged to see themselves as consumers. They can "weight" course preferences with the help of precise quantitative ratings of potential courses and teachers, available through printed consumer guides that use student evaluations to rank competing choices. The atomization and quantification of education permit virtually limitless course combinations. They also promote a notion of education as homogenized learning understood in terms of units that can be compared and averaged. Letter grades are thus readily translatable into numerical equivalents. The final outcome of a college career is summed up in a "cumulative grade point average" which is known commonly as G.P.A. or "cume."

EDUCATIONAL EXPERIMENTS

The 1960s was the heyday of the educational "experiments" carried out at colleges like Bard, Livingston College at Rutgers University, Hampshire College, Antioch, Bennington, Sarah Lawrence, and the Santa Cruz Campus of the University of California. Most of these experimental schools are still around, though some, like Santa Cruz, have repackaged themselves somewhat for a more conservative and career-oriented constituency. These innovative schools took the American notion of modularized education even further than more "traditional" institutions were ready to do.

Interestingly, several of these institutions superficially mimicked England's Oxford and Cambridge models. Santa Cruz conceived itself as a collection of individual residential colleges with central "university" facilities like libraries and laboratories. Students were encouraged to develop a close identification with their residential college (Reisman et al., 1970:93). Sarah Lawrence adopted an Oxbridge-based tutorial system, complete with academic advisors called "dons."

But the European touches were relatively superficial compared with the thoroughly American orchestration of education that these institutions achieved. In some ways they sought to minimize the atomization and "quantification" of higher education by providing individualized and more flexible curricula. Though these institutions often prided themselves on being well out of the American educational mainstream, in some important ways they simply extended creatively the American predilection for modular institutions.

Each of these experimental schools opened up the educational process in its own way.[4] Traditional units like departments or divisions were broken down. Hierarchy, whether in the organization of subjects or in social relations, was replaced by an emphasis on equality and equivalence. Requirements were usually reduced to a minimum, and individual choice was encouraged at all levels. Majors were loosened up or abandoned completely in favor of double majors or even individualized curricula. Faculty ranking was often minimized or (rarely) eliminated completely. Students and faculty were encouraged to see themselves as part of a community of learning rather than a stratified society teachers and students. Traditional departmental and divisional structures were weakened to encourage fresh cross-disciplinary combinations.

Modular orientation was also evident in a set of proposals for educational reform made in the late 1960s by Axelrod and his colleagues in a book which, like many reformist documents, grew directly out of the campus unrest of the sixties (Axelrod et al., 1969). The authors set out four alternative models for college reform that might be combined in various ways at any given institution. This strategy is itself a modular approach to the question of academic reform. One model, envisioned as a cluster college at a large urban university, organizes students into primary groups of about seventy-five members. From there, the organizational principles are highly flexible:

> The seventy-five students in the primary group sometimes meet together as a full group. . . but more typically the student group is divided into three subgroups of twenty-five students each. However the number and constituency of the subgroups are flexible and may change from hour to hour and from day to day, depending upon the particular needs that must be met. [Axelrod, et al., 1969:128]

A second proposed model, "A B.A. Program in Future Studies," is designed for future leaders in law or any of the other professions. The description of this "Model P" curriculum is interesting in that it highlights the emphasis on open-endedness and on the conception of the world as rationally constructed or assembled. "Model P's basic premise is that the future leaders of the human race must learn to 'invent' the future—must learn how to make it different by planned intervention. The entire design is built with that concept at its center" (p.138).

Since modularity as an organizing principle is inherently dynamic and open-ended, it is not surprising that American educational experiments focused more on process than content. "The emphasis seems to be on the process of learning in each discipline, with the objective that the student will master the structural principles in a variety of subjects and then be capable of making an infinite number of applications" (Charles, 1965, cited in Axelrod et al., 1969:64).

Such structural innovations are based on the values of diversity, mobility, and novelty (usually called "creativity"). They are often neutral in regard to any of the debates about the content of education, such as the importance of the humanities versus the sciences, the significance of historical studies, the place of non-Western studies in a curriculum, or the relative merits of idealist and materialist theories in the social sciences. Modular organization can always evade such issues of content or value, because it places all alternatives on an equal footing. Since any such commitment is just one possible configuration, students have only themselves to blame for an unsatisfying education.

THE ORIGINS OF MODULARIZATION

The nineteenth-century origin of the modularized American curriculum is significant because it suggests that the roots of the postmodernist frame of mind reach deeper into the American soil than is usually reflected in accounts stressing the recent emergence of postindustrial technology and the thorough penetration of world markets by late-twentieth-century capitalism. The argument here is that the specific technological underpinnings of the postmodern mind were themselves prefigured by a confluence of early industrial production strategies and eighteenth-century political ideology. Nowhere was this convergence more apparent than in the newly independent United States.

While there is ample evidence that the modularity schema has penetrated deep into American institutions and American thought, it is important to remember that the patterns I have described have not operated uniformly in American life. And they have not been accepted by everyone to the same degree. Moreover, many of these design strategies have taken root well beyond the United States. But modularity does seem to speak to us in an American accent.

What is it about American culture that promoted the extraordinary effusion of modular institutions? There are several possible answers to this question. One response is to deny that modularity has any privileged claim on American culture. The most extreme rejection of the Americanist argument would be the assertion that modularity is a design principle of nature rather than a particular cultural or historical phenomenon. Certainly, modular forms can be found throughout nature as well as in human cultures. Philip Morrison, a physicist, has argued that what he calls "the modularity of knowing" is merely a reflex of a modularly structured universe:

> The world is atomic, which is to say modular; our knowledge is modular as well. All can be counted and listed; our very analysis implies atoms of knowing, as the material itself is atomic. The prodigality of the world is only a prodigality of combinations, a richness beyond human grasp contained in the interacting multiplicity of a few modules, but modules which nature has made in very hosts. [Morrison, 1966:1]

In an apparent challenge to the association of modularity with modern and postmodern cultural forms, Lawrence Anderson finds modularity to be the basis of many of the great Old-World architectural masterpieces (Anderson, 1966). And if linguists like Charles Hockett are right, modularity is an intrinsic "design feature" of human communication and underlies the expressive power of language (Hockett, 1960). If this is the case, then the model of DNA proposed by Watson and Crick would suggest that recombinant modularity has been selected for in the evolution of human communication systems, whether genetic or cultural. In this spirit, linguist Jerry Fodor has proposed that the mind itself has a modular design (Fodor, 1983; Donald, 1991). This view of the mind resurrects a kind of faculty psychology that treats the mind as an assembly of different cognitive "organs," each with specific functions, rather than as an all-purpose neural net.

Modularity may well be a basic organizational principle of nature. But this does not mean that its structural and epistemological implications have everywhere been exploited to the same degree. The universalist argument cannot account for historical and cultural differences in the extension of this principle into human institutions. A more historically and economically oriented perspective links modularity with the rise of industrial technology and mass production. In this view, the efficiency and flexibility inherent in modular organization led inevitably to the standardization of production and the growth of recombinant technology. But such a transformation in industrial production required a receptive environment for it to take hold and proliferate beyond its technological roots.

While Walter Ong has noted that interchangeable type was actually the first truly modular mass-production technique, Blair has argued that it was only in nineteenth-century America, and particularly in musket manufacture, that the modularization of industrial production was fully worked out (Blair, 1988). Thus the explanation for the rise of modular production techniques involves the interaction of a set of efficient technical practices inherent in modular organization and a specific cultural environment hospitable to these techniques. This brings us back to the question of America and its special affinity for modular social arrangements.

As a cultural trend, there is ample evidence that modularization does indeed have an American accent and was evident in the United States as far back as the mid-nineteenth century (Blair, 1988). In his influential 1948 study of American national character, British anthropologist Geoffrey Gorer included a remarkable chapter called "Man as Machine?" in which he traced the pervasive influence of what I have called modularity throughout American life. Gorer's book anticipated by some three decades the social critique of postmodernists like Baudrillard.

Noting the pervasive atomism in American institutions, Gorer related these trends to the great success of the production line as the foundation of American industry. The logic of the production line became the foundation for a distinctively American approach to social relations. The American industrial genius was for breaking down production processes into their primitive constituents and then maximally rationalizing production by conceiving of labor and time as modular entities subject to manipulation.

> Americans first of all imported the finished articles and subsequently the craftsmen who had learned their trades in Europe. They then proceeded to analyze systematically the finished article, the implements used for making it, and the gestures which the skilled craftsmen employed; they questioned the necessity, the validity of each implement, of each gesture, and they then devised machines to do as much of the work as possible, and reduced the gestures to a series of controlled and analyzed movements which could often be learned in fewer hours than the original craftsmen took months to learn their skills. In some cases, of course, the final products had less individuality, less finish, fewer lasting qualities than the original craftsmen's creations, but they were produced in millions instead of hundreds. [Gorer, 1948/1964:139–140]

The industrial metaphors, Gorer claims, became the basis of a distinctive American vision of human activity. The human was understood as an extension of the mechanical, rather than the other way around. Thus the characteristic American approach to social relations has been various kinds of "social engineering" programs, of which charm schools for women and image-management courses for men were the most common (p.136).

The argument for the special historical links between modularity and America has been most vigorously advanced by Blair (1988), who adopts a historical and comparative view of modularization in American culture. He argues that American modularity is distinctively different from a European holism and organicism and examines a wide variety of institutions like education, religion, and architecture for evidence of a culturally distinctive mind-set. What is most compelling about this argument is that Blair's evidence comes not from modern industrial America but from the mid-nineteenth century.

SOCIAL ATOMISM

In the last chapter, we saw how the prevailing social atomism of American culture is reflected in baseball viewed as a cultural model—in its rules, its language, its way of handling social relations, and its orchestrations of time and space. What I have called modular thinking is consistent with those same individualistic and egalitarian values that have been part of American experience since the earliest English colonies were established. Gorer saw a direct link between the atomism of the American political ideal, based as it was on the notion of the free citizen, and the mechanistic attitude of Americans toward social relations. In Chapter 3 we saw how these attitudes about social relations are reflected in the baseball idioms adapted to describe dating behavior. American social ties, according to Gorer, were characterized by an "emotional egalitarianism" in which all relations had to resemble those of love and intimacy (Gorer, 1948/1964:133). Political loyalties were thus modeled on personal relations, and the job of political candidates was to be likable.

The art of the American politician was more the art of making friends than legislative competence or statecraft. The personality in its American version becomes the raw material for social manipulation—what Erving Goffman called "impression management." Under the influence of late capitalism, this notion of personality as a commodity would resurface as the concept of "lifestyle," which is treated in the next chapter.

If the Americanist argument is right, America's affinity for modular design forms has its roots in both American economic history and the Enlightenment political philosophy that underwrote America's distinctive political institutions. The twin sacred charters of the American polity—the Declaration of Independence and the Constitution—both stress autonomy and equality as foundational values. The Declaration of Independence is a justification for replacing an organic and hierarchical conception of colonial relations with an egalitarian view of contingent relations among equals. The basis of this claim is an assertion of inalienable rights, not of classes or communities but of individuals.

The social atomism implicit in this formulation was worked out in great detail in *The Federalist Papers* and the Constitution. The attempt to limit the concentration of power in the hands of any group or individual led to an elaborately worked out "separation of powers." The ingenious solution was a thoroughgoing federalism, a modular conception of the union of states as semiautonomous bodies and of its governing institutions as three separate, equal, and interdependent "branches." Each government branch was assigned functions, most of them complementary and some overlapping. Each served to "check and balance" the powers of the others.

This model was a radical departure from the Old World political models it was intended to replace: the French notion of "estates" or the feudal class system based on a medieval notion of an organic hierarchy, with God at the top. These visions of society were dramatically less "modular" in nature than the American paradigm.

The Constitution proper is followed by the Bill of Rights, which does for individual citizens what the Constitution does for government entities. It defines an intricate set of protections or entitlements for individuals against the encroachment of government or of other individuals. The Bill of Rights implies that society can only be a kind of residual association of individuals with strictly delimited powers over them. Social holism is replaced by political atomism. The key idea is the notion of natural rights and liberty. A political union is thus conceived as a rational contract among individuals, who trade their natural and authentic freedom for the benefits and protection of political association.

The distinctiveness of the American pattern emerges even more convincingly when compared with non-Western political systems based on what Marshall Sahlins has called "hierarchical solidarity" (Sahlins, 1983). Though we often associate class and status lines with social divisions and oppositions, there are many societies in which hierarchy is believed to underlie the ultimate unity of society.

In places like traditional Polynesia, Japan, the Indic States of Insular Southeast Asia (Bali, Java, etc.), or India, the traditional political order was, at least by those in power, represented as a kind of organic holism closer to medieval conceptions of society in the West. Social caste or rank differences were conceived as a natural order of inequality.[5] In such settings, society is not understood as a voluntary association of individuals who bring with them inalienable rights and presocial identities. Nor is the individual thought of as having the same rights and potentials as any other individual. Rather than embodying in miniature the whole of humanity, the person speaks to the greater community through what sociologists call ascribed roles, as a part to the whole. Neither self-sufficiency nor personal choice are stressed in such societies. Human relations are considered part of the nature of things rather than contingent human choices. In other words, such societies are not conceived as modular organizations, where autonomous individuals voluntarily enter into a contract for form a society.

French anthropologist Louis Dumont distinguished these organic and holistic models of society as based on what he termed a *communitas* conception of human relations (Dumont, 1965). The more atomistic and voluntaristic associations that emerged in the West along with the notion of social contract Dumont calls *societas* models. Properly speaking, he argues, the modern conception of the individual is found only in societies organized along the *societas* model, of which the American experiment is the most highly developed example.

If this analysis is right, then the American romance with modular design is hardly an arbitrary cultural pattern. It possesses the intrinsic advantages of flexibility and organizational efficiency that modularity always has. Presumably, these structural properties proved advantageous in the evolution of many natural modular forms and have something to do with the durability of the American polity. But obviously an appeal to a universal advantage cannot account for the dramatic extension of modularity throughout American culture. Here we need a historically based argument. Though modular design forms are found throughout human history and in a great variety of human cultures, they were elaborated with special verve during the industrial revolution, when mass production led to a need for interchangeable parts and rational assembly techniques. And they have further extended their reach into everyday thought and experience through the dramatic expansion of information processing technologies since the 1960s. Most particularly, the atomistic logic of industrial production took hold in America, where it met little resistance from older, more holistic habits of thought. For in nineteenth-century America, the path to industrial modularization was paved by a tradition of political atomism and voluntaristic association that made modular technology seem right at home.

Cultural patterns do not occur in a vacuum and rarely are they ever arbitrary. As we have seen, to understand a complex cultural pattern like modulariity requires a multifaceted approach in which specfic political, economic, and technological factors are considered in addition to the inherent advantages of modular organization. To the extent that we can recognize modularity as a foundational schema for Americans, a feature of both the American landscape and the American mind, we recognize that mind to be both cultural and historical in nature. What we discover as cultural patterns in a local setting are in fact a kind of "snapshot mode" for historically rooted forms of consciousness.

Having traced the early modern roots of the postmodern frame of mind, we will rejoin the search for the modern technological foundations of that framing in the next chapter. There the focus is on the more direct cognitive implications of electronically mediated modularity in its postmodern moment. We will take a look at some of the significant transformations in our understanding of language, and communication more generally, that bring modularity directly to mind in some unsettling ways.

Notes

1. On love as an American cultural model, see Quinn, 1987, 1992; Lakoff and Johnson, 1980; Holland 1992.

2. It is one of the great ironies of modern marketing that the term "Mac"/"Mc" has become the verbal icon of both a computer and a fast-food chain. In both cases, the term has been used (modularly) to suggest variable components of a larger configurable product line. We have such modules as the Big Mac, the Mac II, Chicken McNuggets, MacDraw, MacPaint, and Egg McMuffins. This felicitous "synergy" between two modularized product lines has probably affected our perception of both, suggesting the seductive accessibility of a computer as a mass-consumption item and the high-tech character of modularized hamburger production.

3. Ironically, science and precision technology have come to be iconically represented by the "x" or "ex," which is mathematics' classic empty sign, whose virtue was supposed to be its arbitrariness of reference.

4. In the 1960s many public schools took the notion of "open" education quite literally. Schools without walls were built, in which classes occupied "spaces" on an open floor plan rather than rooms. From speaking with teachers who have taught in such "learning environ-

ments," I have the impression that they were very difficult to work in. Many students had problems connected with their inability to concentrate.

5. On Japan, see Nakane, 1970, and Doi, 1974. On India, see Dumont's seminal work on the cultural underpinnings of Indian caste relations (Dumont, 1965, 1970). On Insular Southeast Asia, see Geertz, 1980, and Errington, 1989. For analyses of Polynesian conceptions of hierarchy, see Goldman, 1970; Sahlins, 1963, 1983; Valeri, 1985; Marcus 1989; and Shore, 1982, 1989.

6

Technological Trends:
The Neuromantic Frame of Mind

[T]he computer represents the possibility of modelling everything that exists in the phenomenal world, the breaking down into information and then simulating perfectly in infinitely replicable form those processes that precybernetic humanity had held to be inklings of transcendence. With the computer, the problem of identity is moot, and the idea of reflection is transformed into the algorithm of replication.

—Istvan Csicery-Ronay, Jr.

Diet Pepsi technicians have now successfully demythicized the romantic mumbo-jumbo of the human brain, which fundamentally is no more than a binary system of on-off switches, and employing immaculate logic, the Pepsi team has isolated the consumer principle in a "computer generated" image, which replicates tone without temperament, which is at once the consummate image and the consummate reproduction of images, and which, despite its "marginal humanness," is sexy.

—Harold Jaffe

[T]he inspiration for our theories and our understanding of abstract phenomena is always based on our experience with the technology of the time.

—David Rumelhart

MODULAR LANGUAGE

The 1960s saw the emergence of a scientific study of language suited for the information age. Linguistics became a high-prestige science. I remember the excitement that overtook the English Department at Berkeley in the 1967 when the famous MIT linguist Noam Chomsky arrived in town to deliver the Beckman Lectures.[1] I arrived early for every lecture and sat transfixed, with my notebook, near the front of the lecture hall, trying to understand what all the excitement was about. It was all a bit hard to follow at first. I was in my senior year at Berkeley and my knowledge of linguistics at that point amounted to a single introductory linguistics course. But that course had not treated language in anything like the fashion that Chomsky did. It was clear to me then that something big was happening to the study of language, and everyone seemed to think that it mattered a lot.

I was struck by Chomsky's elegant and logical mind as he set out for us the philosophical assumptions behind his notions of "transformational grammar" and "generative syntax." What was happening in fact was a revolution in the way that language was being conceived. Chomsky's work at MIT was funded by the Navy, which was interested in developing the capability for "machine translation" of natural language. It resulted in a new high-tech and high-status discourse about language, a discourse that indeed succeeded in bringing speech into an intimate relationship with information machines.

The sort of talk that we produced all the time was now thought of as "surface structure" in language, something Chomsky referred to as "performance," which was not really the proper object of linguistic analysis.[2] The real aim of linguistics, according to Chomsky, was to discover the language module of mind—linguistic "competence"—in the form of an innate and universal grammar that inhabited the human mind (Chomsky, 1957, 1965, 1968). The Saussurian distinction between *langue* (language proper) and *parole* (speech) had been reworked in terms of a new sort of faculty psychology.

The key was to understand how surface talk (utterances they were called then; today we call it discourse) was "generated" from underlying "deep structures" by transformation rules such as "deletion" or "inversion." Base structures were thought of as "nodes" or slots defined by traditional grammarian's terms like "noun phrase" or "verb phrase." Though there were said to be relatively few of these base structures in any language, syntactic rules of transformation and recombination gave language its most important characteristic—generative creativity, by which an unlimited set of utterances could be produced from a limited number of operations performed on a relatively small set of basic units.

Chomsky spoke of replacing outdated approaches to grammar (so-called finite-state grammars and phrase-structure grammars) with transformational grammars that would, for the first time, make clear how language could produce a virtually limitless array of utterances from a relatively limited collection of language resources. His examples demonstrating the necessity for the dichotomy between deep and surface structures were often amusingly ambiguous. His most famous such example is "Flying airplanes can be dangerous." His point was to demonstrate that grammars that focused only on the surface combinations of units, the phrase structures, could never account for the ambiguities of such double-dealing sentences. Only by distinguishing between the superficial "surface" structure and the underlying "deep structures" that generated it could we begin to account for the productive capacity of a language system.

This was also the heyday of structuralism in anthropology, and Chomsky's distinctions between levels of language were quite familiar to anyone who had read Levi-Strauss's cultural analyses. Though the Chomskian revolution was carried out in relation to syntax, similar structural approaches had long been in vogue in phonology, the study of the organization of sound in language. These approaches had profoundly influenced both linguistics proper and, through Levi-Strauss and the Russian linguist Roman Jakobson, had revolutionized the study of all cultural forms. Most influential were what was called "Prague school" linguists like Trubetzkoy, Halle,

and Jakobson (Trubetzkoy, 1969; Jakobson and Halle, 1956). The ingenious contribution of structural phonologists was to break language down into its most elementary sound units and show how complex and subtle were the rules of combination by
which intelligible utterances were assembled. First, there was the phoneme, an abstract unit on the basis of which speakers classified different sounds as different
versions of the same sound (such as in the "p" in spit, pat, problem). Later, phonologists would further decompose the phoneme into even more basic units called distinctive features, much as physicists sought to break down the atom into increasingly
elementary particles.

The logic of this reductive effort was essentially modular:

- Language was modular in structure.
- Large units like phrases or words could be shown to be composed of combinations of more basic units.
- Forms of speech emerged from the relations among these linked units rather
  than from the units themselves.
- Linguistic meaning was therefore *relational* rather than *intrinsic* to the units,
  depending on principles of selection, combination, and context.
- Meaning in language was disconnected from the forms of language and attributed to conventional assignment.

Naturalistic theories of meaning—which focused on sound symbolism or on
analogies between language forms and external reality (like Rousseau's famous attempt to derive the origin of language from the imitation of animal calls)—were
generally ignored, dismissed as relatively unimportant aspects of language, or consigned to the implicitly degraded status of resources for "oral cultures."[3] These influential structuralist views of the nature of language are sophisticated applications of
the same modular logic that has been so influential in shaping our everyday lives.
They view language not so much as an extension of creative and expressive impulses,
or the human drive toward meaning, or, in Langer's genial phrase "significant form,"
but rather as a set of logical tools, a kind of symbolic technology for the manipulation
of reality.

This account of the human language faculty represents a strong endorsement
of a particular vision of the human mind, a hyperrationalism stressing the kind of
"productivity" that endless recombination of basic elements makes possible. But the
price of this focus on the modularity of language is a semantic vacuum, or at least a
semantics of noncommitment. Where atomism and recombination thrive as the basis
of a theory of knowledge, meaning inevitably emerges as a problem. For since Saussure, structuralists have assumed that linguistic meaning is "contextual" and "relational," the effect of structural arrangements rather than of intrinsic connections between forms of life and signs. In relation to the world, however, the linguistic sign
was assumed to be arbitrary. Meaning became something of a black box.

In fact, the whole issue of how meaning happened for people (in language or in
culture more generally) tended to be dismissed from consideration altogether. Thus
Chomsky argued for the separation of the study of syntax from the study of semantics, to which, it was argued, syntactic analysis could provide little insight. Thus
modern structural linguistics provided the first glimmer of a kind of high-tech vision
of language, where hyperrational means led straight to a semantic dead end.

MODULAR DISCOURSE

Though these rarified issues in scientific linguistics appear to have little to do with our everyday life, it is interesting how the modular view of language on which they are based has filtered into our ordinary language. Instead of concrete words with specific references, we see more and more terms that are abstract and modular.[4] "School" becomes "instructional facility," "prison" becomes "correctional facility," and "garbage dump" is transformed into "waste-management facility." Rather than teachers, we have "instructional facilitators." Job counselors are converted into "human resource management specialists." Though this kind of language can be seen merely as the legacy of a highly bureaucratized and rationalized society, it is equally the exploitation of the plastic qualities of language viewed as a modular communication system.

Words that are too content-specific and too evocative of specific experiences are replaced by semantically more abstract and empty units whose generality makes them multipurpose terms. Sentences, like mathematical algorithms, can be flexibly configured to suit a variety of purposes. Modularized discourse has been encouraged not ony by the proliferation of technical specialities and the proliferation of large bureaucracies but also by changing political sensibilities. In the effort not to "discriminate," politically aware language (i.e., "persons with disabilities," "young female person") often replaces concrete and specific reference with more abstracted and noncommittal terms.

The atmospheric impact of modularized discourse can be felt with special force in the newly proliferated synthesized-speech technologies. Computer-generated voices may be heard with increasing frequency in telephone communications, at airports, and in other public places. These voices produce a chilling effect—the concatenation of phonemes by which words are composed reverberate, minimizing the prosodic flow of natural speech by removing normal intonational contours and all emotion.

With the proliferation of increasingly elaborate automated telephone answering systems, humans find themselves communicating more and more with machine-mediated voices. Speech is reduced to information by its conversion into a format of modular conversation frames where our "turn" consists of pressing number keys. More and more our responses are simply digits. Automated answering systems use hierarchically organized digital pathways to allow customers to access a large variety of prerecorded messages. From an information perspective, each of these messages becomes a discrete module that only superficially resembles the open-endedness of natural speech. The most fine-grained use of such modularized speech is the recent introduction of computerized telephone number information, in which a real human voice mimics a synthesized one by concatenating any sequence of numbers in a poor imitation of normal human speech.

TYPOGRAPHIC CONSCIOUSNESS

In recent years, a lot of attention has been paid to the effects of writing systems on previously oral traditions (Goody, 1977, 1986; Havelock, 1982; Heim, 1987; Ong

1967). The invention of writing appears to have been far more than a simple extension of speech into a written medium. Writing has transformed what Ong calls the "noetic field," the interface between the human mind and its enabling environment of known objects (see, also Heim 1987:109).

The loss of an exclusively acoustic relationship with language has had far-ranging cognitive consequences. Most obvious, of course, is the inception through written signs of relatively "nonvolatile" information storage, replacing the less reliable individual memory capacities of humans. The whole world of verifiable "facts" and listings, procedures and regulations eventually replaced the ongoing reinvention of reality that was encouraged by orally transmitted traditions. Conventional oral genres were finely tuned to the cognitive requirements of retention and transmission.

Havelock (1982; see also Heim, 1984:50 ff) has documented how Homeric verse forms and narrative conventions were in fact elaborately adapted to the constraints of oral transmission and human memory. While all speech is necessarily linear and sequential, it was writing—and most especially alphabetic writing—that most powerfully exploited language's linear character. The invention of a true alphabet was an early recognition of the modularity of word formation. Discrete sounds rather than whole concepts could now be represented in atomic fashion. Anyone equipped with a relatively small repertory of written letters could read and write an unlimited variety of different words, something not possible in idiographic writing systems like Chinese. Even unfamiliar words could be transcribed by mapping sound to letter.

Alphabetic writing made writing and reading available for the first time to a mass audience. With writing, language became fixed in space and lost the characteristic of speech that Charles Hockett has called "rapid fading" (Hockett, 1960). Our spoken words die away as we speak them, but writing (as with sound recording of any kind) freezes the utterances of the moment, sometimes to our dismay.

The notion of words taking up space, or extending in a line, would be unthinkable in a purely oral tradition. The linearity of written speech permitted the development of such cultural forms as formal logic, lists, and records as well as notions of prose style, plot, and character development in literary forms. Yet profound as these cognitive transformations were, the world of handwriting, what Ong terms "chirographic culture" (*cheiros* is Greek for hand), is still at a great remove from modern textual consciousness. Chirographic culture retains a close kinship to the world of speech. Handwriting still bears the "embodied" character of personal speech. A hand-written message always bears the personal imprint of its scribe, an imprint every bit as idiosyncratic as the voice. The resistance of the pen on paper is also the precondition for the inscription of the personality into the message. This is why to this day a hand-written note is always seen as the most appropriate form for the most intimate communications. Thank-you notes, sympathy messages, apologies, love letters, party invitations, and all signatures are still normally handwritten, in deference to the personal imprimatur of the individual in the act of writing.

Hand inscription of speech—whether through pen, brush, or blade—has the quasimystical character of the mimetic arts, and scribes have often been credited with an almost priestly sanctity (Heim, 1987:62). Calligraphy remains an art form even today, particularly in those Asian traditions like the Chinese and (in part) Japanese. It was the so-called Guttenburg revolution, the invention of movable type in the fifteenth century, that transformed words into fully abstract commodities, removing them forever from their original conditions of personal articulation.[5] Alphabetic letterpress printing, in which each letter was cast on a separate piece of metal or type, marked a psychological breakthrough of the first order. It embedded the word itself deeply in the manufacturing process and made it into a kind of commodity. The first assembly line, a technique of manufacturing in which series of set steps produced identical complex objects, was not one that produced cars, stoves, shoes or weaponry. The first mass-produced commodity was the printed book (Ong, 1982:118).

As printing technology proliferated text to a degree unheard of in an age of hand transcription, it rendered text relatively uniform, creating objective or neutral discourse, divorced from its authenticating origins in the language of particular individuals. Henceforth, one's personal mark on a text would be viewed as a distinctive literary "style," but never in its original physical inscription. The sacredness of the word, easy to imagine when words were carved in stone, is harder to maintain when the word is realized as movable and interchangeable type.

WORD PROCESSING: FROM MODERN
TO POSTMODERN CONSCIOUSNESS

The emergence in the 1960s of the concept of "word processing" takes the modular characteristics of language implicit in movable type to a totally new frontier.[6] The impact of word processing on our apprehension of language forms and on cognition more generally is only beginning to be studied.[7] The truth is that no one can be sure of the long-term implications of word-processing technology, if for no other reason than that the software and hardware technology that support word processing are evolving so rapidly.

On the face of it, the effects of word-processing technology on writing are obvious and exhilarating for most writers. These advantages can be summed up by two words: "fluidity" and "flexibility." In both cases, word processing manages to overcome the most obvious limitations of writing, its obstinate attachment to the page and its relentlessly linear character. In their spatial mobility, electronic words have a kind of atavistic character, more closely linked with words in their older forms as spoken language or as thought than with typographic or chirographic text.

The natural units of word-processed text are modular. Words are chunked into "blocks," "pages," "screens," or "windows." The notion of a "block move" or a "block delete" is completely natural for a word processor but would be an ungainly concept at best in any earlier form of writing ("cut-and-paste" is a particularly messy metaphor) and unthinkable in oral traditions. Spoken words cannot be unsaid. Any text chunks may be moved about in electronic "cyberspace." Text modules may be combined, reconfigured, reduced, expanded, appended, or deleted from other units at the touch of a finger or the click of a "mouse." Thus while text units ultimately have the linear character of all written text, their processing manages to overcome these spatial limitations.

Many word processors contain their own outlining programs, though "stand alone" outliners or "idea processors" may be used as modules in their own right in conjunction with standard word processors. I use one such outline processor, which "pops up" at my fingertip's command over my word processor and may "import" or "export" text to and from the word processor. Such idea processors permit "chunks" of ideas to be entered in any given order or no order at all. Then these chunks may be manipulated in various ways to link them up with each other in some form of outline. Moving idea chunks about in this way overcomes the normal linear nature of prose composition and allows for the possibility of viewing these chunks in many combinations.

HYPERTEXT AND INTERACTIVE FICTION

Hypertext is a relatively recent extension of word-processing software.[8] The intention of hypertext is to free word processing completely from the linear straitjacket of normal written speech. Whereas normal written text is controlled by a narrator, in that the flow of the text moves in the direction preordained by the original writer, hypertext is, at least in theory, controlled by the reader. It is organized as a collection of central concept nodes, each of which branches off into a series of linked concepts, themselves nodes around which other concepts or topics cluster.

The aim of hypertext programs like Apple Computer's Hypercard is to deconstruct knowledge into elementary units, each of which may be linked by a user to any number of other units. The programs are designed to avoid imposing upon knowledge a preconceived hierarchy or set of links. They offer the reader or writer no point of view of their own. Readers "navigate" using their own resources, constructing their own pathways "on the fly."

One recent book about hypertext applications noted the complete absence in Hypertext of a fixed sense of space, asserting instead that

> information space" has no natural topology. It is true that there is a "high level/low level" view that can be mapped onto a hierarchy but this is relevant for probably only a small minority of knowledge domains. Are there as many structures as there are domains? Or can all knowledge be organized along a few relatively straightforward dimensions? For the building of intelligent tutoring systems, where the system must in some sense "know" about its subject matter, then it is crucial to have an answer. In the context of exploratory learning, however, we can make a virtue of giving the learner no "view" at all of overall structure. [Mays, et al. 1990]

Hypertext employs "chunks" of information but is really a kind of high-level programming language that encourages users to "program" the raw information into any combinations they find useful.

The loss of the master narrative or of a narrative center of a text is a much noted feature of postmodern culture. This decentering of perspective is built into the modular organization of all word processing and has been best exploited by the newer hypertext programs. It is thus not surprising that the word processor has given rise to a new breed of fiction, called "interactive fiction," in which the reader engages with the original program writer as a coagent of the story's creation rather than as a passive receiver of a ready-made tale.

Interactive fiction had its early start in relatively simple programs like Zork, which allowed the user to choose among many possible "tracks" through a narrative, with a limited number of variant endings. The program set out a series of problems for the "reader" and was able to recognize a limited range of input responses. The more sophisticated the program, the more complex its interactions with the reader and the greater the freedom of the reader to transform the story "on the fly." Again, the original programmer is successful to the extent that the end user is empowered to create a piece of fiction in tandem with the computer. The program must offer no fixed perspective on plot or character development.

Another natural development of hypertext is called hypermedia. Since the computer is really not limited to any single medium, but can engage a variety of different media, from music, to sounds, to pictures (still and moving), it is hardly surprising that hypertext has spawned a multimedia offspring. In hypermedia, only now coming into fairly wide use among computer enthusiasts, the chunked information can be packaged in virtually any sensory form. Users can then explore any topic, navigating among a host of sensory modules, to savor the sights and sounds (and perhaps eventually the tastes and smells) of any topic.

THE WINDOWED ENVIRONMENT

It is not possible today to consider the impact of word processing on cognitive processes in isolation from the larger software environment of the modern personal computer. The modularization of knowledge into information chunks has shaped the organization of the computer screen at every conceivable level. Word processing is itself only one of many possible modules (or programs) that can be "layered" upon a screen. So-called shell programs, of which Microsoft Windows for MS DOS is now the most famous, permit users to shuffle among a large number of different programs, each a microworld of its own. Spreadsheet programs, database programs, financial programs, writers' tools like the thesaurus or spell checker, outliners, and a host of so-called desktop accessories like a phone book, a calendar, and a calculator are all waiting to "pop up" at the click of the mouse. So complex has the "housekeeping" become on today's computer screen that unwary users can spend as much of their work time configuring their hardware and software options as they do running their applications. The result of this dramatic expansion in the complexity of the modern personal computer is a sense of simultaneity, omnipresence, and the desirability of having total control over computing resources.

THE NEUROMANTIC FRAME OF MIND

It was Heidegger who, at the very dawn of the computer age, noted this modern impulse toward what Heim has called "the all-at-once simultaneity of totalizing presentness" [Heim, 1987:85]. Because of the passions that this cybernetic view of mind generate among computer enthusiasts, I refer to this Heideggerian vision as the "neuromantic frame of mind."[9] The sense of mastery over language resources that word processing bestows on the experienced user is intimately related to Heidegger's notion of enframing *(Bestellen),* a subjection of the world to human will that Heidegger saw as a characteristic of all modern technology (Heidegger, 1977).

For Heidegger, enframing is not merely a set of techniques aimed at control. It is an attitude of modern humankind toward their world which treats the phenomena of the world as what Heidegger calls "standing reserves," resources to be harnessed and manipulated for human ends. Where the whole world becomes thus totally transparent to human manipulation, Heidegger believes, it darkens, losing something of the poetic "indwelling" which should mark what Heidegger likes to call the "coming into being with the world."

What is particularly disconcerting about this enframing of the world-as-resource-base (or, in its late capitalist version, world-as-market-segments), which is the hallmark of the technological attitude, is that we rarely perceive what has happened to us in the process. For most of us, the exuberant sense of power and freedom with language made possible by the word processor, the new romance/neuromance of cybertech, masks from us the true nature of the enframing that has accompanied it, the utter transformation of our experience of language and of the world glimpsed through that language. It is the loss of the poiesis of creation, a loss upon which this new technology of the word is founded. The essence of enframing," Heidegger warns, in his characteristically cryptic voice, "is that setting-upon gathered into itself which entraps the truth of its own coming to presence with oblivion. This entrapping disguises itself, in that it develops into the setting in order of everything that presences as standing-reserve, and rules as the standing-reserve" (Heidegger, 1977: 36–37).

WORLD PROCESSING

Technology has granted us an extraordinary power to synthetically reconfigure our experience of the world by altering our "picture" of the world. In computer circles, this ultimate enframing activity goes by the name "virtual reality." It is the logical if extreme extension of the frame of mind implicit in the trend to extend word processing into a kind of "world processing." What technophiles call VR (virtual reality) is housed in "cyberspace," a kind of electronic everywhere/nowhere that is at least superficially reminiscent of the dreamtime concept of Australian aborigines (see Chapters 9 and 10). It is the place behind the television screen, the place from which cash comes in the ATM, or the electronic bulletin board where virtual communities around the world gather to exchange messages. Just as the new iconically oriented software borrows the visual language of three-dimensional objects to represent electronic realities, so VR appropriates the language of space to represent realities that are in fact placeless.

To Ann Balsano, a student of this new technology,

> The metaphor of Cyberspace is very evocative to describe as a new space for social interaction, a space that already exists with people plugging into networks and bulletin boards and news groups. To me that space you're communicating in electronically is Cyberspace. It's a space of exchange—exchange of information, of data, of identities,

of subjectivities and so on . . . a new space that's not materially grounded in any place—it's spread out. [Quoted in Huff, 1992:13]

Narrowly defined, virtual reality is a kind of total immersion in computer-simulated time and space made possible by highly sophisticated hypermedia that place an individual "inside" of a computer-generated world. Flight simulators used to train pilots are the best-known and most sophisticated form of the current virtual reality technology. The National Aeronautics and Space Administration (NASA) has collaborated with Ames Research in developing the Virtual Interface Environment Workstation (VIEW) for planning (or virtualizing) future space missions (Huff, 1992:17). Even surgery can now be done virtually through a kind of simulation called laparoscopy that requires almost no "hands-on" body contact by the surgeon.

In the most recent incarnation of virtual reality, special helmets provide a three-dimensional visual experience of a digitally generated world. Special suits adjust the dimensions of this world to our physical movements so that we seem to be moving within this world. Virtual reality simulates the embodiment of experience, the corporeal "indwelling" by which we orient ourselves to our ordinary worlds. Yet, paradoxically, it does so in such a way as to totally "disembody" experience, freeing the user from the sort of fixed point of view to which physical mass, gravity, and Newtonian physics condemn all normal human activity. Virtual reality achieves its embodiment/disembodiment trick by its thoroughgoing control of the sensations that anchor our everyday links to reality:

> Interaction with a computer-generated "multi-sensory representation" provides the feeling of total "immersion" through 3D imagery, sound and tactile sensation. The ability to manipulate objects in the virtual reality environment, change view and interaction (such as float above the floor, and move through objects) provides the sensation of total autonomy. [Huff, 1992:13]

Early 3D movies like *The Wax Museum* were primitive attempts at creating virtual realities by overcoming the flatness of the screen and bringing the audience into the movie or, more accurately, pulling the movie out of the screen into the theater. But modern information technology has dramatically extended the possibilities of this sort of sensory manipulation.

The closest that a traditional society could come to the creation of such a virtual reality might be a parallel reality to which a shaman might have access by means of a hallucinogen.[10] But the worldview within which shamanic excursions take place is completely different from that which makes virtual reality possible. Virtual reality is the creation of a modular view of reality, in which the world-as-construct is deliberately altered by a digitally masterminded reconfiguration of the senses.

Some champions of virtual reality technology contend that all the computer has done is to heighten our awareness of the degree to which all reality is necessarily a construction. In this view the term "virtual reality" is a kind of tautology. Robert Anton Wilson, one of the more famous enthusiasts of VR, has argued that there is no alternative to understanding reality as virtual. "I have long believed," Wilson is quoted as saying, that ". . . the study of neurology and general semantics more and more show that all realities are virtual realities. . . .Everyone lives in a reality created by their parents and teachers . . . we all live in a reality manufactured by our brain and we believe that to be the only reality" (Quoted in Huff, 1992:17).

Wilson misses the point here. Whether or not all reality is a virtual construct *in fact*, it does matter a great deal if one conceives of reality in this way. And surely most people in the world would agree that reality is *not* virtual. This notion that reality is always and everywhere a human construction is, of course, a central tenet of modern phenomenologically oriented social science and has been attacked in recent years by religious fundamentalists as a central dogma of "secular humanism." It is significant, in this context, to note that this constructivist assumption about reality is implicit in the nineteenth-century German idealist notion of worldview *(Weltanschauung)*. This conception of the world as picture or the world as construct is, according to Heidegger, directly related to the enframing mentality induced by the conditions of industrial technology: "The fundamental event of the modern age," Heidegger wrote

> is the conquest of the world as picture. The word "picture" *[Bild]* now means the structured image *[Gebild]* that is the creature of man's producing which represents and sets before. In such producing, man contends for the position in which he can be that particular being who gives the measure and draws up the guidelines for everything that is. [Heidegger, 1977:134]

VIRTUAL VIOLENCE

One of the most disturbing aspects of the electronic simulation of reality has been the proliferation of virtual violence. The virtualization of physical violence began with the introduction of the first weapon that allowed violence between individuals without any direct physical contact. The spear and the bow and arrow increased the physical distance between antagonists, while the gun dramatically increased the anonymity of an attack. Modern electronic warfare has created virtual military communities whose violent activities are mediated by layers of electronic gadgetry and communications. Meanwhile, electronic mediation permits apparently harmless violence to be simulated on computer screens as video games, most of which employ war narrative as their organizing principle.

A convergence of the video game and electronic warfare is apparent in the notion of war games, serious computer simulations of warfare used by military strategists, but with deadly real-world possibilities. The 1983 movie *War Games* brought together the worlds of the video enthusiast, the hacker, and the military strategist. It is the story of how a teenage hacker manages to break into a North American air defense computer and wreak havoc on military security. So convincing was the movie that the scenario of *War Games* was taken by Pentagon officials as a serious threat to national security (Haffner and Markoff, 1991:115).

Because electronic warfare, whether in the video parlor or in the Pentagon's strategy rooms, is an interactive game, it inevitably blurs the distinction between viewer and participant. While television violence distinguishes viewer and actor, its video-game counterpart does not. From the military end, the rocket launcher and the gunner on a modern bomber now become "viewers" as well as fighters, viewing their targets through electronically mediated scopes and video screens.

Commentators have noted the distinctive status of the recent war in Iraq as the first fully virtualized war. For the millions of viewers of CNN, their first image of the war was through the window of their TV screen, itself an imaging of a flak-filled Baghdad sky as seen through the hotel windows of the CNN reporters. In the later days of the Gulf War, viewers were treated to a startling view of how the new generation of "smart bombs" were guided by lasers to their Iraqi targets. The smart bomb had turned the war into a "viewing" game for the pilots as well as for the audience. The tragic consequences for the lives of millions of victims of these bombs were masked from viewers and soldiers alike by their electronic domestication as little more than a familiar computer game.

No one knows for certain the psychological effects of the virtualization of violence, but there are some disturbing signs that these effects may not be trivial. The emergence in Hollywood's own backyard of the phenomenon of the "drive-by shooting" may well be linked to the distancing effects of virtualized violence. Drive-by shooting is a kind of fast-food brutality, a takeout violence of the MTV generation. When murder is committed through the window of a moving car, the perception of the consequences of physical violence may approach the experience of the TV screen. At once real and illusory, the consequence of violence can be annulled by a flip of the switch. The scene of the crime vaporizes on the screen, while it whizzes out of sight for the occupants of a speeding car.

AIR TRAVEL: VIRTUAL GEOGRAPHY

Virtual reality is central to postmodern ontology. While its ubiquitous presence is intimately linked to the rapid growth and increased accessibility of computing power, the presuppositions underlying the VR ideology have their roots in the more general modular orientation that has long been an intimate part of modern industrial life. Thus it is not surprising that our sensibilities have long been prepared for the coming of VR by a set of far more mundane experiences that have gone relatively unnoticed as precursors of virtual reality.

For example, most of us have participated in another kind of virtual reality which is far more common than that generated by computer. This is the experience of air travel. The modern jet has made possible an experience of placelessness that would be impossible to achieve without its technological base. Most modern air travel has "shrunk" the world in such a way that the body no longer experiences any sense of significant transition from place to place. At one with modern telecommunications, modern air travel conveys a sense of total geographic simultaneity, of everywhere as nowhere special, of anyplace as everyplace.

This odd experience of the interchangeability of place is a result of the travel industry's transformation of places into commodities, interchangeable tour stops, or trip segments. Even when the stops bear strong marks of geographical and cultural difference, the effect is less one of travel than of a real life carousel slide projector, with mechanical and transitionless shifts from one world into another. I once took an around-the-world flight and, in a matter of days, had touched down on four continents and perhaps a dozen different countries. But the overwhelming experience was less one of motion or transition than it was of simultaneity. I remember a sequence of discrete worlds, with no transition between them, other than my time in the nul place and nul time of the plane or waiting rooms at anonymous airports. It was as if I kept awakening from a dream into a new world, only to have that world disappear as suddenly as it had appeared.

The experience of this sort of travel is actually closer to changing channels than it is to any physical sense of traveling in the preindustrial sense of the word. Except when air turbulence intrudes to remind the passengers that air travel is in fact physical motion, modern jet travel has a disengaged and disembodied quality. The traveling body is, for the most part, cut off from the normal sensory cues that signal motion from one place to another. The body is moved, but does not itself move from place to place. "The body," notes Baudrillard, of life within the metallic vectors of air transport, "wearies of not knowing where it is, whilst the mind is excited by that absence, as if by a lively, subtle quality that is its own" (Baudrillard, 1990:119).[11]

This literal disembodiment of motion and the loss of a sense of spatial transition is intensified by modern airplane design. The airplane provides its own relatively homogeneous and neutral internal environment, so that there is no gradual change of air, smell, or temperature or any sort of sensory indication of moving from one environment into another.[12]

Jerry Mander has noted the pervasiveness of such "sensory-deprivation environments" in the modern landscape (Mander, 1978:61ff). The modern office building is prototypical: "The air is processed, the temperature regulated. It is always the same. The body's largest sense organ, the skin, feels no wind, no changes in temperature, and is dulled" (p. 61). Noting the powerful interrelationships between our mental life and our most basic physical experiences, Mander remarks that the effect of the modern modular office environment, what he calls "sensory reduction chambers," has been to increase the focus of workers on the immediate task at hand by reducing sensory awareness of a wider, more complex environment (p. 64). Modern airports into which passengers are deposited are a good example of such modularized and homogenized environments. Coming off a plane into such a neutral and predictable environment reduces the awareness of physical transit and promotes the sense of placelessness, or what Baudrillard calls "deterritorialization" (Baudrillard, 1990:119), that characterizes modern air travel.

LIFESTYLE: THE SELF AS MODULAR COMMODITY

Of all the effects of modularization on the modern mind, none has been more far-reaching than its impact on our conceptions of what constitutes a person. The logic of recombinant technology has produced a conception of identity engineering that seeks to reconfigure both the psyche and one's social identity. This transformation of the very idea of what constitutes a "person" is not a totally new phenomenon. It has emerged gradually with the extension of the modularity schema into every facet of modern life. Take the notion of "personality." The term has long been used in a variety of ways by psychologists. But on the whole, "personality" usually implies for psychologists a relatively stable set of behavioral dispositions that characterizes an individual. One's personality is assumed to be largely beyond personal choice, and personality may differ significantly between individuals. Personality was a psychologist's version of the "soul," an enduring essence at the center of a person's being.[13] Like most concepts from academic psychology, personality became part of an American folk psychology and for a long time retained its associations with a personal inner core of mental dispositions.

But over the last several decades, "personality" has come to be used in new ways in popular psychology, ways that reflect the impact of modular technology on how we think of ourselves. In contemporary usage, the personality concept has surfaced and gradually come to refer not to the inner core of a person but to the successful management of social impressions about the self. This is closer to what we usually mean by "self-image" than to traditional notions of personality. The observation that someone has a "lot of personality" or is a "winning personality" is a statement about social effectiveness rather than about personal essence. Personality in these usages deals with social effects rather than causes of behavior. Similarly, remarks about a "television personality" or "stage personality" do not refer to mental dispositions conducive to success in entertainment careers. These phrases are used to describe individuals who have been successful at creating a winning impression on audiences.

In this usage, "personality" has come to mean success at what Erving Goffman called "impression management" (Goffman, 1959) through the mobilization of memorable images. Goffman's work is interesting in this context, because his conception of self, derived from George Herbert Mead's notion of a "social self," is at the crossroads of academic and popular discourse. His work has not only had a major impact on social psychology but has also helped shape and validate popular notions of personality as equivalent to impression management.

This idea that the self can be configured to a variety of practical ends has spawned an entire industry in the United States. The technology of "personal growth" or "self-help" specializes in personality engineering. It ranges from venerable self-improvement guides like *How to Win Friends and Influence People* to dozens of pop psychology manuals providing advice and programs for changing basic orientations in life to elaborately packaged personality-transforming technologies like EST or Alcoholics Anonymous.[14]

The general appeal is to increase control over one's life by the use of personality enhancement techniques. Here is an excerpt from an ad for the Dale Carnegie course, one of the most successful of these self-help programs:

> The Dale Carnegie Course is designed to help men and women discover, develop and use more of their untapped inner resources. It helps them to build on these innate human talents and capabilities and draw upon them every day to meet the challenges in their work, in their lives. . . .
>
> In the Dale Carnegie Course. . . [y]ou learn how to determine what motivates people, what makes them think and act as they do. And you become better able to interact with others with greater harmony and cooperation.
>
> Participants soon feel a positive difference in themselves. Their self-image is enhanced, their self-confidence grows. They become more enthusiastic, more alert, more energetic and self-reliant. Their personalities become more vibrant, more interesting and attractive to others. . . . They discover a new vitality, a new excitement as they begin

to use their newly developed skills and abilities to reach the goals they set for themselves.

The ad appeals to more effective exploitation of an inner self, but the language
is mechanistic. Such programs teach the "building" of confidence out of psychic raw
materials. Personality-enhancement techniques are aimed not so much at one's own
character development as at the successful organization of others in line with one's
own goals. Though the ad promises increased ability to work harmoniously with
others, the emphasis is still on success through increased autonomy and control.

Diet guides and fitness plans are other kinds of self-improvement technology
that orchestrate the physical transformations which are an essential part of making
over the self. Just as we can "build self-esteem" through manipulations of the psyche,
bodies can be built through manipulations of diet or exercise. Thighs are trimmed,
waistlines reduced, breasts enlarged, stomachs flattened. In its most extreme form,
reconfiguring of the body is done through sophisticated medical procedures like plastic surgery and the implantation of prosthetic devices like artificial hips or breast im-
plants.

These technologies of identity engineering do not treat the body as an organic
whole with a natural shape that grows in relation to its own laws and to stages of
maturation. It is viewed as assemblage of modules, each of which can be remade to
suit the desires of the individual. Hair color, nose shape, body size, eye color, breast
shape, and even internal organs all become technologically negotiable.[15] In this context, the new popularity of drugs like Prozac and Thorazine to treat specific mental
illnesses is really an extension of the idea of technological makeovers of the self,
understood as a configurable entity. Moreover, this kind of symptom-specific modification of the personality through chemical manipulation is in many ways more consistent with the modularity schema than are the more traditional "talking therapies"
and the psychoanalytic model on which they are based.

People sometimes say of therapeutic and technological interventions that they
have made possible "a whole new self," a basic change in identity or a total transformation of their lives. Personal identity seems to be linked not to notions of character
or essential personality but to "a life." More to the point, the creation of identity has
become associated with life viewed as a configurable entity, what in the 1970s came
to be called "lifestyle."

In America, notes Baudrillard, "[t]he charm to be found in social graces and in
the theatre of social relations is all transferred outward into the advertising of life
and lifestyles" (Baudrillard, 1988:85). Lifestyle is an identity constructed through a
particular orchestration of surfaces: dress, activities, companions, and material extensions of the self, like houses and cars. The key element of the lifestyle notion is
flexibility and mobility. The lifestyle concept is also a potent marketing tool for
commercial interests anxious to cash in on the desire of people to have access to
means of creating and displaying their new selves. To write a book about someone's
life would be to stress the people and events that gradually shaped their character.
But to write a book about someone's *lifestyle* would be to stress a particular configuration of surface features and commodities that define a temporary persona subject to
voluntary change.[16]

THE FEATURES OF MODULAR ORGANIZATION

The diverse cultural arrangements discussed in this chapter and the last have all been called modular. What is it that they all share? Certain general features are common to all the examples we have considered.

- A limited number of standardized units are employed as the building blocks of more complex organizations.
- Differences between patterns are derived from variations in and combinations of these primitive units. They are properties of organization rather than essential differences. Moreover, these differences are linked to quantitative rather than qualitative variations. Strictly speaking, there are no irreducible "types" or "kinds" of modular entities, only various arrangements. In this sense, modular structures are atomistic rather than holistic in character (cf. Blair, 1988).
- Modular systems encourage experimentation and change. They are dynamic in that they permit numerous recombinations. Because they are open-ended, they encourage a future orientation.
- Modular constructions have no well-formed "interiors." Our attention is directed to surfaces, and especially to surface arrangements.
- Modular structures encourage individual variation of expression. From children's Legos to adult Scrabble, even to the geneticist's passion for the recombinant engineering of DNA, modular structures promote a playful response and an interest in producing variation.
- There is an egalitarian bias in modular systems, since there is no intrinsic basis for valuing one configuration over another.

Other characteristics are linked to some kinds of modularity, but not all. For instance, some modular systems, like automobile manufacture, require highly specialized units. No part can be interchanged for any other. Such specialization of parts was the hallmark of the industrial revolution [Blair, 1988]. Fodor has used the term "modular" to describe the mind understood as an assemblage of relatively discrete cognitive faculties, each having a high degree of functional specialization (Fodor, 1983).

From a design perspective, the functional specialization of modular entities is not intrinsic to modularity. Instead, the isolation of discrete and replaceable parts from the functioning whole was the advantage modularity bestowed on industrial production. This interchangeability of parts was taken a step further when such systems' components could be further reduced to different combinations of homogeneous elementary units. The functionally distinct units could be conceived as distinct organizations of a few basic design elements. Thus, the logic of modularization encourages a homogenization of component units, a kind of "minimalism" in design. For instance, the more extreme forms of modular furniture employed fairly standardized basic design units. The fewer the design elements and the greater their combinatorial potential, the more elegant the design concept.

ANALOG AND DIGITAL CODING

Perhaps the ultimate form of standardization in modular systems is the design of the "difference machine," the digital processor, where extraordinarily complex instruction sequences are generated from combinations of simple on-off switches. The modularization of knowledge as information has made possible a radical qualitative reduction in knowledge forms and an accompanying convertibility of all knowledge as digital data. David Mindell has noted this qualitative reduction in our symbolic media:

> Society's signals are becoming digitalized: Letters become Faxes, records become CDs; speech is compressed and sent as mail. Even telephone conversations, paradigms of analog communications, are being transmitted through fibre-optic networks in digital form. But digital storage forces a kind of equivalence on various signals, removing them from their "real world" analog contexts.
>
> In fact, digital signal processing is so broadly applicable only because, once inside a computer, "signals" are essentially all the same. Music, speech, codes and even images can be converted to strings of numbers containing a given quantity of "information" to be distinguished and extracted from noise. [Mindell, 1989:256]

As a cultural schema, modularity proposes that reality is atomic. Ontological atomism is a kind of radical reductionism that seeks to decompose experience into its elementary building blocks. Since more complex experiences are understood only as quantitative increments of the more basic ones, understanding is equivalent to isolating the most primitive unit that can be discovered and specifying its combinatorial possibilities.

This replacement of irreducible forms or shapes of life with bits of knowledge can also be detected in the proliferation of a binary logic that we associate with digital computers. Binary systems are made up of combinations of two-value units, simple on-off switches. They represent a kind of limiting case of modularization. Binary codes are inherently quantitative in that they construct complex messages by combinations and accretions of primitive units. They are poor at *directly* presenting "qualities" and do so only by approximation. For example, a digital image system, like an image-scanning digitizer, creates an illusion of shape by fine-grained construction of elementary units.

Similarly, digital sound systems do the same thing with bits of sound.[17] The fact that we may perceive these sound or visual images as irreducible patterns with distinct qualities is a tribute to modern technology and to the power of perceptual illusion. In their cruder forms, we have an awareness of experiences that are poorly shaped and inauthentic. When the illusion does not work, our experiences become what we sometimes call "synthetic."

Analog phenomena are created by a continuous mapping of contours and a direct translation by analogical transfer between one medium and another. When light is transformed through exposure to sensitive film, a series of (negative) analog images of the initial stimulus is created, and we have the basis for traditional photography. Similarly, analog sound production is accomplished by the action of sound waves on continuously variable diaphragms or other resonating surfaces, such as the human ear or a record player. Analog coding differs from digital coding in that its variables are continuous rather than bounded and discrete. Moreover, they are formed by projections of whole patterns from one medium to another rather than by approximations of forms through the assembly of regular building blocks.

A good everyday example of the distinction between analog and digital coding is in how we represent time. Each mode of time measurement reflects what Heim calls "a different atmosphere in the apprehension of time" (Heim, 1987:119). A sundial, a rather direct analogic encoding of time, marks the passage of hours by the direct projection of the sun's movement across the sky (really the earth's rotation on its axis) on a horizontal table. An analog watch or clock projects this movement on a set of pointers (or hands) that rotate on a circular plane surface. Though more abstract than the sundial, these clocks still bear a perceptual link with the movement of the sun across the sky.

Digital timepieces are another story. They reckon time not by continuous mappings of movement positions but by what Michael Heim calls a "discrete information interface" (Heim, 1987:119). Time becomes a kind of information unit. Discrete digits represent time abstractly by changing combinations that in no way mimic the solar movements by which time is experienced naturally. No longer is there any echo of the sun's passage across the sky. Yet what digital timepieces lose in their intuitive linkage with the passage of time they gain in their direct readability and their accessibility to manipulative calculations.

"Time management" is enhanced by this transformation of the flow of time into static digital units.[18] Our sense of what Walter Ong calls "abstract computed time" (Ong, 1982:97), was alien to the consciousness of medieval or early Renaissance Europe. Computed time in this modern sense was technologically conditioned, Ong suggests, by the abstraction of experience made possible by the interiorization of speech as writing.

Imagine trying to describe or even calculate the "length" of time between two events on a sundial. One might indeed come up with a spatial representation of a length of time, but a precise calculation of a unit of duration would be much harder. Even on an analog watch, this is only made possible by digitalizing the sweep of the hands with precise markings. But only the use of digitalized time reckoning allows for direct addition and subtraction of time units.

So digital coding has a great advantage in being free from fidelity to preexisting forms. Digits can orchestrate an infinite number of patterns, including totally novel forms. These units are open to considerable manipulation. In computer jargon, this organizational freedom is expressed by the term "programmable." This programmability of digital codes is behind what linguists call the "productivity" or "generativity" of language (Chomsky, 1957; Hockett, 1960; Donald, 1991), by which a limited set of sound units can combine into endless sentences. It is also behind the fun kids have with modular toys, ranging from simple blocks through more complex construction sets like the old Erector sets or the more up-to-date Legos.[19]

The limits of digital coding are obvious to anyone who has tried to draw on a computer screen. Digitalized constructs are relatively poor at representing contours, so that natural shapes that the hand can draw are crudely rendered by blocks of light on the screen. Even the best high-resolution screens have difficulty imaging curves perfectly. On the other hand, digital technologies are quickly advancing in both audio and video representation. The programmability of digital sound or images means that the signals can be reworked (synthesized) to maximize clarity or color or reduce static. So long as digital approximations can trick our senses into detecting continuous variation, digital representations can have significant advantages over analog in sound and image processing.

The jury is still out on the relative quality of analog versus digital recreations of human experiences. Some audiophiles (though the number seems to be decreasing) continue to reject digital recording techniques because of what they claim are its synthetic results. What they seem to miss is an acoustic version of what Walter Benjamin once called the "aura" that distinguishes hand-made from mass-produced objects (Benjamin, 1968).

ORIGINAL SYN: THE KNOCKOFF AS REALITY

Digitalization lies behind the proliferation of what Baudrillard (borrowing from Plato) called the "simulacra" of postmodernity—the synthesis of endless copies that have no original. Simulacra bear no traces of the direct physical presence that always marks analog production. The information age represents the apotheosis of the "knockoff" and the consequent change in the conception of value. The ease and effectiveness with which modern technology can reproduce virtually anything has created something of a legal and moral challenge to conventional notions of property and value.

Traditionally, the valuation of property has been dependent on the assumption that value is related to inherent qualities that define the distinction between an original and a copy. But modular technologies do not recognize the distinction between original and copy in this way. Modularity transforms copying into cloning. The ability to clone endlessly cheap copies of valuable commodities like watches, perfumes, handbags, or designer clothes has shifted the marketing emphasis away from the intrinsic quality of an item to the "designer" name that is attached to it. The designer name or its readily identifiable icon moves from the inside of the item to the outside and becomes the source of value to the commodity.

Digital information is subject to easy and cheap replication. This has generated a moral and legal crisis in property and copyright law. While publishers (of music, books, or software) are desperate to instill in consumers a sense of both fear and guilt about illegal copying, the public has been slow to accept their arguments about the inviolability of such intellectual property. Theft, like value, has always been associated with the assumption of the inherent limits of physical property: if I take something from you, then you no longer have it. But with the diffusion of the technologies of simulation, digital information becomes an endlessly shareable good, and its dissemination seems to be morally closer to the ethic of sharing than to theft. John Markoff of the *New York Times* notes the "widespread attitude that electronic information is, in effect, in the public domain and should not be protected as private property" (Markoff, 1992).

Traditional conceptions of property value (and, by implication, notions of theft) presume the importance of the distinction between an original and a copy. For instance, it is only in terms of this distinction between original and copy that forgery can be construed as a form of theft. But these understandings of property value are based on the constraints of the physical world and its reliance on analogic reproduction. In a physical world, replication comes inevitably at the cost of some kind of real-world distance from an original. So analogic reproduction is inherently *historical* in that the distinction between the original and the copy always bears the mark of time. The original is older, the copy newer. Alternatively, copying may involve a fading from old to new, with the copy losing something in the reproduction. In either case, the process of replication embodies the passage of time.

Digital replication evades these physical constraints inherent to analog reproduction. This is why digital reproduction undercuts the traditional basis of value in scarcity. Digital reproduction is inherently *ahistorical* in that there is usually no perceptible gap between original and clone that is directly related to time. Or it is *antihistorical* in that when there is a gap, the copy turns out to be more "real" than the original, which may have suffered structural decay (as in old data). Digital information does not fade in time. It mutates or becomes defective.

Baudrillard has suggested that digital reproduction produces "simulacra" rather than copies. Simulacra are reproductions that lack a true original. They constitute a class of reflexive signs, signifiers without external referents, ostensive symbols that point only to themselves. A true software copy is never considered a fake; it is just another copy. "Faking" software would require simulating the look or feel or functionality of an original program but using different code. The notion of "faking" presumes the notion of "the original." For any digital information, the copy is not a diminished version of an original but an exact clone, a reproduction that bears no trace of time or of the effects of the hand of the copyist. Under such circumstances, the concept of copy becomes meaningless, and with it the notion of originality.

The closest that software comes to an authentic original is the "source code" written in high-level programming language in which the programs are initially composed. By the time these programs reach end users, they have been translated by compilers into machine-readable digital form (coded as strings of ones and zeros that digital computers can digest). The "original" source code is carefully guarded by software companies. But here "original" refers to a representation and not to the authenticity of the program as material object. Any good "copy" of the source code would be exactly the same as the original electronic inscription.

These peculiar features of digital reproduction have clearly affected notions of property valuation and are an important aspect of the counterculture morality of the world of the computer hacker (see Haffner and Markoff, 1991). Mitchell D. Kapor, Lotus Development Corporation's founder, sees the proliferation of digital technology as posing a grave crisis for current property law: "Our current intellectual property laws are in danger of breaking down completely in the face of this digital revolution. . . . And big publishers are hesitant to move forward without more of a feeling of comfort that they have copyright protection in the new digital world" (Quoted in Markoff, 1992:C4).

Whatever the distinctive character of digital transcription, digital technology has nonetheless become rather adept at "virtualizing" more direct experience and thereby reconciling the flexibility of digital coding with the real-world comforts of analog representation. Digital recording of music or of visual images is being refined to a state where the atomic organization that makes it work is effectively invisible to the human senses. Even in computer software, vastly increased processor speeds and chip memory have made possible graphic iconic interfaces that have transformed the computer screen from an array of numbers and letters into a sensuous and colorful array of "virtual objects" that may be handled in a manner approximating real-world object manipulation.

The relations between analog and digital coding, whether in artificial or natural intelligence, are complex and not yet completely understood. Analog and digital processing seem to be complementary rather than alternative strategies. For instance, information may be digitally stored but reproduced for consumption in at least partially analog fashion. Such is the case with digital sound production, which involves several translations back and forth between digital processing and analog transmission.[20]

Thus the chain of sound transmission includes both digital filters, for sampling sound streams and transforming them into sequences of discrete values, and analog transmitters, like speaker cones and the human eardrum, which transmit continuously variable (and thus truly shaped) signals. In relation to natural intelligence, it appears likely that the human central nervous system uses somewhat similar combinations of digital and analog coding. Thus, while the firing of individual neurons seems to be a digital phenomenon, controlled by chemical neurotransmitters that have discrete activation levels, the far more complex patterns of brain activity involving neural networks and what is now called distributed parallel processing seem to behave more like analog phenomena (Changeux, 1986; also, see Chapter 14).

For computers, at least, digital processing does appear to have an advantage when problems have clear-cut variables and involve arithmetic calculation. But where pattern recognition and "intuitive" intelligence are involved, under circumstances requiring so-called "fuzzy logic," a new generation of computer chips based on analog processing shows greater promise.

COGNITIVE CONSEQUENCES

To the extent that modular strategies in design show characteristics of digital coding, we can only wonder what sort of effect a modularized cultural style may have on human perception and cognition more generally. The difficulty of digital codes in directly representing shape, contour, or image may have an important bearing on the limits of modular structures as codes for human experience.

At normal levels of awareness, many of our most basic perceptions occur in irreducible patterns or what psychologists call *gestalts*. Complex gestalts that are sometimes called schemas mediate our perceptions. Though some psychologists have argued for an essentially quantitative and modular theory of image perception (Pylyshyn, 1981), the consensus in both psychology and philosophy is that perception is not atomic and there are no elementary building blocks that combine to generate our images of the world (Kossylyn, 1978, 1980; Langer, 1957). It seems that we do not assemble our perceptions by mechanically sticking together pieces of light or sound.

Recognition of a few of the most basic patterns, such as the human face, appears to be under fairly tight genetic control. Faces are a good example of perceptual holism, since most of us can recognize a face without being able to analyze why or describe it in terms of its parts.

Most of these orienting patterns are probably not innate, however, but are experientially derived. They are prepackaged for us in the form of cultural models and become the basis of a distinctive view of the world, the foundation of a worldview. The implications of these ideas are worked out in greater detail in Chapters 13 and 14 of this book. Suffice it to say at this point that to the extent that our everyday experiences are encoded in predominantly modular models, they would seem to present an unparalleled challenge to the meaningful integration of experience.

The extent to which digital coding can successfully virtualize stable human environments in the way that analog models have traditionally done is, as we have seen, an open question. On the skeptical side are Walter Benjamin's warnings about the loss of "aura" that accompanies mechanical reproduction and synthesis of real-world objects. And Benjamin's misgivings are echoed by Heidegger's bleak vision of the enframing mentality, which is at once the agent and the product of a technologically mediated environment. Futurists, on the other hand, are more likely to express a heady optimism about the unlimited potentials of the digital remapping of our everyday world.

It would appear beyond question that the rapid proliferation of modular design strategies and their associated technologies have had a powerful and ubiquitous effect on human perception and the psychic environment within which we operate. As Heidegger suggests, part of the difficulty in specifying the nature of these cognitive effects is their very pervasiveness. Since the modularity schema has come to shape our very approach to the analysis itself (I am writing this chapter in a "window" of my computer!), grasping their overall potency may prove quite difficult.

In Chapter 13, I propose the importance of a distinction between "information processing" and "meaning construction" as dimensions of cognition. "Meaning construction" requires relatively stable mental models or schemas by means of which people can maintain a sense of fundamental stability in their apprehension of reality, even as they navigate in a world of unpredictable and sometimes novel experiences. Such mental models—whether in the form of image schemas, body habits, linguistic metaphors, category structures, scripts, or any number of other models—are the source of human creativity as well as the basis of cognitive stability (Lakoff, 1987a).

Humans need general models *of* experience which become orienting models *for* making sense of future experience. Some of these general models are explicit. Religion in particular provides in word and action vivid general orientational models, and their foundational status is marked through what we call their sacredness. In Chapter 3, we looked at one such general model embedded in a baseball game.

Life, death, evil, virtue, love, sexuality, gender, power, hierarchy—these are some of the main ingredients of a worldview, what Husserl and Schutz called a "lifeworld." The very vague and diffuse character of these themes suggests the need for vivid embodiments in persons, acts, and objects. These are the themes of great artistic productions and the basic nourishment of sacred education in most societies. The emphasis of sacred education is most commonly on the potential unity of experience, not on its atomization or negotiability. Without such integrating models and their embodiment in relatively direct experience, perception becomes fragmented and orientation becomes difficult and fraught with anxiety.

When digital coding and modularity emerge as the fundamental organizational principles for social institutions, the experience of the resulting orientational models is surely transformed. For example, pattern stability gives way to an apprehension of flexibility and of contingent and transient possibility. Patterns come to be comprehended as negotiable surface arrangements, perceptions that would not appear to be appropriate as life-affirming orientational models. How far can the stability of such orienting models be compromised before experience loses its integration? Ironically, the modularity schema has produced a whole landscape of modular-based cultural models, such that modularity has become an important resource for meaning making in the modern world. So meaning construction seems to be alive, if not completely well, in the postmodern world. Yet the proliferation of modular conceptions of reality almost certainly has had profound consequences on how effectively we construct stable meanings for ourselves. I suspect there are distinct cognitive limits for humans in how well modular models of reality can serve as resources for successful meaning construction. But the truth is that no one really knows for sure.

CYBERPUNK AND THE BORDERLANDS
OF MEANING CONSTRUCTION

Some of the more disconcerting possibilities come from the imaginations of contemporary science fiction writers. One conception of how perceptual integration can break down is seen in the replacement of what some call "master narratives" or foundational schemas with negotiable and contingent collections of atomic "facts," bits of knowledge with no grounding contexts in relation to which they can be rendered meaningful. The brutal textures of this atomic world have become the hallmark of the postmodern esthetic, most exuberantly proclaimed in the genre of science fiction writings and films that have come to be known as "cyberpunk."

Here the lifeworld has been replaced by the deathworld. Cyberpunk worlds, vividly portrayed in Anthony Burgess's early masterpiece *A Clockwork Orange,* Ridley Scott's *Bladerunner* and *Alien* series, Paul Verhoeven's *Robocop,* or James Cameron's *The Terminator* are violated landscapes that have been reconstructed technologically without organic shape or vegetable presence. Their heros and heroines are cyborgs or quasicyborgs, often disturbing amalgams of human and machine, and the enemy is some sort of anonymous corporate entity run amok.

Even the human heros of these worlds, like *Alien's* Sigourney Weaver, have a tooled, surgically mediated look, glorifying the possibilities of the marriage of (wo)man and machine. Their representation of technology weds visions of hyperrationality and control to anarchy and madness. At its best, cyberpunk sci fi manages to capture the ultimate paradox of machine-generated worlds, in which the arbitrariness of the digital emerges as the end of logic. This is the tech(no)logical paradox in which total control and total anarchy become indistinguishable.

TECHNO-TOTEMISM

These postmodern myths are steeped in what I call *techno-totemism*. Techno-totemism, prefigured by Mary Shelley's *Frankenstein*, is the industrial and postindustrial version of human-nonhuman hybrids that are so common in the art forms of pre-industrial cultures. Both traditional totemism and techno-totemism are vivid representations of the problematic limits of what it means to be human. Traditional totemic imagery explores human-animal mixtures (see Chapters 7, 8, and 9). Techno-totemism, however, substitutes combinations of machines and humans. An attenuated form of techno-totemism has consumers identifying intimately with a world of manufactured commodities or (as in the fetishizing of designer labels) with their manufacturers (Jhally, 1987:202). Such "status symbols" are all forms of machine- or commodity-mediated human identity that have replaced older identifications mediated by natural species.

Another vivid example of techno-totemism is Michael Jackson's video pavilion at Disneyland. In Jackson's 3D video, he plays the part of a kind of quasicyborg hero, a space captain who liberates humans and other creatures who have become literally absorbed into the metalwork of a totally machined environment. The electronic projection of the film into the audience draws the audience into the film in much the same ways that its protagonists are encompassed by the machine.

In a parody of the "good conquers evil" narrative, Jackson defeats the enemy through the violence of his music. But this is not the victory of the human over the machine so much as it is the victory of the human who controls the machine by embodying it. From his surgically mediated facial features to the staccato violence (he's *BAAAD!*) of Jackson's singing and dancing, he is the coming-into-body of the cyberpunk esthetic. Androgyny and the glorification of human autonomy herald the end of a sexually mediated world. Ever menacing, ever protected, Jackson proclaims the eroticism of postsexuality. Jackson's heat is that of the machine. In his carefully orchestrated fusion of innocence and menace, Michael Jackson has become a kind of cultural icon of techno-totemism, a true cyberpop villain/hero.

Cyberpunk represents worlds that have no organic contexts for meaning integration, worlds at the borderlands of recognizable culture and humanity. While cyberpunk visions are darkly fanciful images, their hold on the postmodern consciousness of the MTV generation suggests the degree to which the loss of integrating contexts for experience has characterized much of modern life and underlies the distinctively postmodern form of cognitive stress that Alvin Toffler popularized as "future shock."

Among the themes that predominate in cyberpunk literature is that of madness born of technological insult. Istivan Csicsery-Ronay, an editor of *Science Fiction Studies,* characterizes the "horrifying element" in cyberpunk science fiction as "the disruption of knowledge in its most tangible form":

> Cyberpunk is part of a trend in science fiction dealing increasingly with madness, more precisely with the most philosophically interesting problem of madness: hallucination (derangement). Tales are constructed around the literal/physical exteriorization of images representing the breakdown of stable, standard-giving rational, perceptual, and

conceptual categories. So the most important sense is not fear but *dread*. [Csicsery-Ronay 1991:189]

This vision of madness as category-disrupting imagery conveys the sense in which the electronic virtualization of reality has coopted and compromised the traditional cognitive work of cultural models.

Though the popular media, like television, may be the most potent source of cultural models for contemporary Americans, it is a mistake to characterize such models as simply the modern equivalent of traditional cultural models. These electronically mediated models are schemas, of course, as this analysis has made clear. They are open to the same kind of hermeneutic unpacking as any other cultural models. In this sense, postmodern cultural criticism is simply an extension of older cultural hermeneutics.

But these similarities mask a deeper gulf. While electronic images and traditional narratives share the same status as models subject to interpretation, they have radically different semiotic characteristics and therefore distinct cognitive characteristics. Highly modular electronic images are totally different from other sorts of models. Though they mimic cultural models, such cybermodels are not actual cultural models. They are *virtual* cultural models, more like metamodels (representations of a modeling process) than stable models themselves.

The digital form of such virtual models impairs their effectiveness as foundational models at the very moment of their creation. Compared with the traditional analogically grounded media of culture transmission, digitally constituted culture models reality as fractal. The best examples of the medium can be found in expensive television ads or, even more dramatically, on MTV. The typical MTV show serves up a dizzying series of rapid-fire images, changing as much as every second and often betraying little sequential coherence. The experience of perpetual motion results from a combination of frequent setup changes, constant zooming, and a tendency to use tilted camera angles or a visibly unsteady camera. As Twitchell has pointed out, the resulting experience of rapid-fire visual change has replaced, for many viewers, the need to "surf" among the channels with the channel changer (Twitchell, 1992). Televised information thus tends to come packaged in a form that makes concentration and reflection on stable images virtually impossible. The sensorium is fed stimuli faster than the mind can rationally process them and becomes largely a passive receiver, a "viewer" rather than an audience (Mander, 1978).

Through television, culture becomes lifestyle, a theater of pseudoculture that is more a commodity than a form of life. Under the sway of such virtualized pseudoculture, Toffler's information explosion is inevitably accompanied by a general implosion of meaning, as meaning-constructing cognitive processes are impeded by the lack or the breakdown of orientational models that can be grasped experientially.[21] The proliferation of modular institutions and design strategies is at the heart of the so-called information revolution. The benefits and transformative power of this revolution have received much notice. Yet the present analysis confirms Heidegger's own suspicions that this technological triumph has also exacted a significant price—the loss in human life of a what he poetically calls a gentler "revealing which . . . lets what presences come forth into appearance" (Heidegger, 1977:27).[22] In the terms set out in this book, Heidegger's technologically inspired crisis may be understood as the loss of analogically grounded and organically mediated cultural models that can serve as sources for meaning construction. The loss of such models amounts to what Heidegger called "the darkening of the world." The loss of the narrative center is the fruit of a technologic trend that employs rational means for semantically vacant ends. It is at once the birth and the fabrication of the postmodern mind.

Notes

1. These lectures were published the following year as *Language and Mind* (Chomsky, 1968).

2. Today, "performance" studies have enjoyed great popularity in linguistics and other disciplines. Under the sway of a confluence of intellectual currents ranging from practice theory in sociology and anthropology to discourse analysis in linguistics to ethnomusicology to Jacques Lacan's interest in the ongoing play of signification through speech in psychoanalytic discourse to, finally, Foucault's revisionist histories of power understood as cultural "discourses," Chomsky's interests in "deep structure" have been replaced in much of social science by a fascination with the play of surfaces that has come to be known as "discursive practices"—discourses in motion.

3. Exceptions to this dismissal of naturalistic or imitative theories of language may be found in Jakobson, 1971; Benveniste, 1966; Sapir, 1921/1949; Friedrich, 1979; and Shore, 1987; 1990b.

4. All languages "build" higher-level units (like words or phrases) from lower-level units (like morphemes) using modular strategies of one sort or another. Yet Sapir long ago recognized that language families differ widely in the specific strategies employed to generate higher-level units. Languages like German, which make extensive use of modular constructions of polysyllabic words composed of simpler words strung together, Sapir called "agglutinating" languages. "Polysynthetic" languages, among which were many of the Amerindian languages Sapir studied, employ complex suffixes, prefixes, and infixes, with much internal modification of word forms in the construction of one-word complex propositions. "Isolating" language like Chinese built up complex concepts by concatenating simple words, each of which was a single-concept isolate (Sapir, 1949).

5. It is interesting to consider the popularity, among computer enthusiasts, of the rapidly proliferating font technology that puts an elaborate variety of infinitely scalable fonts at almost anyone's fingertips. I suspect that this has something to do with a desire to recover something of the idiosyncratic iconicity of handwriting in modern computerized output.

6. The term "word processing" was coined by IBM in 1964 in conjunction with its newly developed electronic typewriters called M.T.S.T. (Magnetic Tape Selectric Typewriters). These first word processors (really transitional machines between typewriters and modern word processors) incorporated magnetic text storage and retrieval into the typing process.

7. See Michael Heim's *Electric Language* (Heim, 1987) for a provocative if preliminary assessment of the philosophical and psychological implications of word processing technology.

8. For some recent discussions of hypertext and its applications, see Schneiderman and Kearsley, 1989; McKnight et al., 1991; and Jonassen and Mandl, 1990.

9. The marvelous double entendre is William Gibson's, whose novel *Neuromancer* is generally considered the finest example of cyberpunk literature.

10. It is hardly coincidental that one of the leading "gurus" of the VR movement is none other than Timothy Leary, whose earlier interest in consciousness expansion focused on chemical rather than electronic manipulations of experience.

11. Baudrillard refers to this decoupling of body and mind in flight as "the anamorphosis of travel" (1990:19).

12. "At 30,000 feet and 600 miles per hour, I have beneath me the ice-flows of Green-

land, the Indes Galantes in my earphones, Catherine Deneuve on the screen, and an old man—a Jew or an Armenian—asleep on my lap" (Baudrillard, 1988:24).

The "virtuality" of air travel is imminent in the effects of in-flight entertainment. Movies and music are piped into the interior of a modern jet, inserting themselves between the passengers and their apprehension of physical motion. Piped-in sound and sight transport the traveler into the virtual reality of the headset and the screen at the very moment that the jet is "in fact" transporting him or her over a terrain that is largely unavailable to the senses. The consciousness of the passenger is thus at least twice removed from the physical activity of spatial travel.

13. Social learning theorists, like Bandura (1974) or Mischel (1968), whose work stresses the contextuality and mobility of personality, would not be comfortable with such essentialist definitions of personality as "soul" "inner core."

14. See Gorer, 1948/1964, for an early discussion of these technologies of personality management. On EST training techniques, see Mander, 1978, pp. 100ff.

15. Such body-manipulating technologies perform on the phenotype what recombinant genetic engineering performs on the genotype. Both strategies are the natural application to human biology of modular thinking.

16. The heightened sense of reality as a contingency is reflected in the rhetorical uses of "post" in hip writing. To characterize one's own epoch as poststructuralist, postmodern, postindustrial or even postcyberpunk is to locate it on a moving trajectory, in time, but not in space. The effect is to foster a sense of reality as characterized by a kind of dynamic absence and an inarticulate presence. The self-consciously hip language of cyberpunk fiction is intended to knock us off our feet: "The oxymoronic conceit in 'cyberpunk' is so slick and global it fuses the high and the low, the complex and the simple, the governor and the savage. The only thing left out is a place to stand. So one must move, always move" (Csicsery-Ronay Jr., 1991).

17. In computer science, analog signals, which are continuous-time contours, are converted into digitalized states, which are discrete-time representation, by digital filters. Digital filters are devices for converting continuous to discontinuous signals by sampling analog inputs and generating a string of discrete values to approximate them (Mindell, 1989).

18. The transition between these two experiences of time is apparent in the change in analog timepieces from a so-called "sweep" second hand with continuous flow to one that marks seconds in discrete segments of second-hand movement.

19. A "user-friendly" form of modular programmability has recently emerged as a new goal of software design under the banner of "object-oriented programming," or OOP. Software companies like Borland have devoted considerable resources to developing this OOP technology for software design (Fisher, 1992). The idea is to chunk complex software programs into discrete modules or "objects," which can be manipulated easily by end users in constructing a wide variety of higher-level programs. This approach to high-level programming is being implemented in many commercial programs, allowing users to treat any part of a document (a cell, a word, a character) as a module that can be manipulated or edited independently. The OOP technology also allows end users to develop their own applications programs by assembling premade packages of code, using logical operators. The following description, taken from the user's manual for Novel Corporation's *Perfect Office* (3.0), makes clear the modular design of their AppWare program:

> To create an application using AppWare, drag and drop appropriate icons from the Object & Function palette into the subject worksheet. You can then set values and link icons using lines that represent the flow of the application process. The icons represent self-contained, reusable blocks of code, called AppWare Loadable Modules (ALMs).
>
> AppWare Loadable modules contain two components: an *object* and one or more *functions*. An *object* is a programming module that contains data and the code needed to maintain that data. Objects can act upon or be acted upon by a function. Functions

are operations performed by or on an object, such as opening a file or building a spread-sheet. Functions control the processes and logic of an application. (p. 42)

It is interesting to consider how the modularity schema shapes not only the product being described but also the language used to describe it. The name AppWare is itself a modular concatenation of word chunks. The use of highly generalized words (objects, functions, data, modules, and so forth) along with the use of acronyms (ALMs) highlight the modular potential of language and give the description a distinctly high-tech flavor that iconically models the program under discussion itself.

Object-oriented programming is simply an extension of the user-configurable software environment that has emerged as a concomitant of the personal computer. Individual programs have not only become very flexible but they have also grown by the addition of functionally specific modules that can be activated at any time by the user. Programs that were once discrete have increasingly been brought into communication with one another, through "shell" programs like Windows, emulation environments like Softwindows for Macintosh computers, or through totally modular operating environments like UNIX or Appledos or OS2. In these cases, whole programs become high-level "objects" or modules in an ever-expanding, inte-grated digital world.

20. I am thankful to Allan Henderson of IBM for clarifying this distinction between storage and reproduction.

21. In "The Implosion of Meaning in the Media" Baudrillard employs this same image of meaning imploding in the face of an information explosion, though he is concerned with information in the more usual sense of media reporting (Baudrillard, 1983).

22. Heidegger notes that the Greek term *technē,* from which our own term "technology" and its variants derive, meant something like "the bringing forth of the true into the beautiful" and was closely allied with the notion of poiesis (poetry):

> In Greece, at the outset of the destining of the West, the arts soared to the supreme height of the revealing granted them. They brought the presence *[Gegenwart]* of the gods, brought the dialogue of divine and human destinings, to radiance. And art was simply called techne. And the poiēsis of fine arts was also called techne. It was a single manifold revealing. It was pious, promos, i.e., yielding to the holding sway and the safekeeping of truth. [Heidegger, 1977:34]

III

RETHINKING "PRIMITIVE CLASSIFICATION"

7

Totem as Practically Reason:
Revisiting the Rationality Debate

A symbol which interests us also as an object is distracting. It does not convey its meaning without obstruction. For instance, if the word "plenty" were replaced by a succulent, real, ripe peach, few people could attend to the mere content . . . when confronted with such a symbol. The more barren and indifferent the symbol, the greater its semantic power. Peaches are too good to act as words; we're too much interested in peaches themselves.

—Susanne Langer

Despite all our efforts, we do not understand how things which are distinct and separate from each other nevertheless participate with one another, sometimes to the point that they form only one (bi-presence, duality-unity, consubstantiation).

—Lucien Lévy-Bruhl

AN ODD COUPLING

Chapters 5 and 6 explored some of the cognitive implications of a thoroughly machine-mediated environment and the modularity schema it has produced. Perhaps the most striking thing about the modularity schema is that it has led to an odd coupling: a highly developed notion of rationality wed to an impoverished notion of meaning. The hyperrational orientation is inherent in the very notion of modularity, with its tendency to analyze reality into elementary units that are subject to rule-governed recombination and substitution. This technological frame of mind represents a convergence of the logics inherent in industrial production, in the capitalist commoditization of all forms of experience, and in the methodology of empirical science.

This kind of technologically driven thought makes a strong claim for the naturalness of categorical knowledge. Human understanding becomes equated with taxonomic knowledge, which, in turn, is equated with classical categories. Classical categories are neat rather than fuzzy. A classical category is taken to be the conceptual nexus of all the necessary and sufficient semantic features that constitute any class of experience.[1] So the category "dog" is understood as the intersection of all of the essential attributes of the animal ("animal," "four legs," "bark," "tail," etc.). The mainstream of cognitive science has extended this crisp approach to knowledge and has tended to produce computational models of human thought, models that treat understanding as a kind of propositional logic where "programs" in the form of strings of manipulable symbols can be run on a computer.

I have noted the irony in the fact that such logical means have led to significant semantic dead ends. This semantic crisis is suggested by the extreme fragmentation of reality as depicted in postmodern and cyberpunk esthetics. It also has to do with the apparent failure of certain dominant schools of structural linguistics and analytic philosophy to account for certain basic aspects of meaning (see Chapter 13). This marriage of hyperrational means and semantically empty ends is one of the great paradoxes of "modernism." Neither logic nor information could alone guarantee meaning.

By contrast, the paradox of anthropological "primitivism"—the search for the distinctive features of "the mind of primitive man"—has been its association of irrational or prelogical thought processes with a surfeit of meaning. What was once called "primitive thought" seemed to underwrite a perpetual semiosis, the unceasing production of meaning. With little room for accident or coincidence, and with theories about the world that seemed immune to disconfirmation, the "savage mind" seemed to overdetermine the meaningfulness of things.

In this light it is hardly surprising that the Western encounter with exotic systems of thought and practice should have produced a century-long debate among scholars about the rationality of "primitive thought."[2] It was just these implications of cultural difference for human rationality that produced anthropology's "psychic unity muddle," discussed in Chapter 1. The question of the relation between cultural models and human rationality is an old one in anthropology. In the next four chapters, we turn away from familiar landscapes of thought to take another look at some of the classic issues that occupied an older anthropology in its attempt to come to terms with the issue of "primitive thought" and its implications for sustaining the psychic unity doctrine.

The psychic unity problem produced what came to be known as "the rationality debate." The rationality debate is really a series of extended conversations over the last century between philosophers and anthropologists, conversations about the cognitive implications of exotic systems of thought and practice reported by generations of ethnologists. Many of these exotic "mentalities" appeared to violate strict canons of logic, a state of affairs that was certain to produce considerable anxiety among the defenders of the psychic unity doctrine. Among the most influential chapters in this prolonged debate have been the following:

- Freud's equating of primitive thought with primary process, with dreaming, and with the mental life of psychotics (Freud, 1950)
- Lévy-Bruhl's assertion (and then recanting) of the doctrine of prelogical mentality, and its "law of participation" (Lévy-Bruhl, 1926, 1975)
- Frazer's influential distinctions between the logics implied by sympathetic and contagious magic, a distinction which prefigured the theory of tropes and its basic distinction between metonymy and metaphor (Frazer, 1935)
- Malinowski's distinctions between religion on the one hand and science and magic on the other (Malinowski, 1954)

- Durkheim and Mauss's affirmation of the social origins of categorical logic, which was understood to be based on models of tribe, moiety, clan, and so on (Durkheim and Mauss, 1963)
- Evans-Prichard's attempt to rationalize Azande magical beliefs and the heated debate his account inspired among English philosophers and social scientists (Evans-Prichard, 1937; Wilson, 1970)[3]
- Levi-Strauss's equivocal attempt to affirm the fundamental rationality of human thought (understood as categorization) while nonetheless distinguishing primitive "bricolage" from modern science (Levi-Strauss, 1966)

MANY KINDS OF RATIONALITY

While I make no attempt here to provide a detailed summary of the complex course of the rationality debate, it is fair to say that many of the arguments as to the rationality or irrationality of magical practices or totemic beliefs hinge on unanalyzed assumptions about the meaning of "rationality." It is instructive, in considering the durability of the rationality debate, to consider just how ambiguous and slippery the whole idea of rationality is.[4] It is possible to conceive of at least nine distinct kinds of rationality. Many of the following types of rationality have been invoked in the rationality debate, but often with no acknowledgment of their unstated assumptions or even that rationality was subject to multiple definitions.

- *Logical rationality* assumes that beliefs follow canons of formal logic, such as consistency (defined as in terms of the Aristotelian law of noncontradiction) and specific forms of syllogistic logic, such as *modus ponens* or *modus tolens.*
- *Contemplative reason* assumes that beliefs or acts are based on clearly thought out principles rather than on emotion or desire. Irrational acts in this view imply that passion rather than reason holds sway.
- *Conscious reason* assumes that actions are subject to conscious (as opposed to unconscious or nonconscious) awareness. This sense of rationality is commonly tied to the Freudian belief in levels of the psyche, where the unconscious is assumed to be the source of the most irrational behaviors.
- *Causal reason* assumes that actions or statements can be understood as being coherently caused or motivated rather than unmotivated. In this view, an event whose cause cannot be accounted for is irrational in that it "doesn't make any sense."
- *Calculating rationality* assumes that means are "realistically" adjusted to one's goals or interests. This is the sort of rationality implied by the role of ego functions in Freudian theory, as they mediate between desire and reality. Calculating rationality drives several influential theories in behavioral science, such as marginal utility theory in economics, optimal foraging theory in behavioral ecology, and kin selection theory in sociobiology.
- *Functional rationality* assumes that a set of beliefs or acts is (consciously or unconsciously) adaptive for an individual or group. This is closely related to calculating rationality, though functional adaptation may be predicated on

unconscious processes or even on notions of undirected survival rather than rational calculation. In this limited sense, cultural ecology is a *rational* approach to explaining the distribution of cultural institutions.

- *Communicative rationality* assumes that behavior is adjusted to demands of social communication (rather than, say, truth or abstract logic). Grice's maxims of communication presume this kind of communicative rationality at work in everyday discourse (Grice, 1989).
- *Empirical rationality* assumes that statements or behaviors are consistent with an accurate perception of reality. Nonrational behavior in this context is assumed to be delusional or based on misapprehension.
- *Contextual rationality* assumes that acts or statements are "logical" in terms of an often hidden context of supporting beliefs or acts with which they are functionally integrated. For instance, acts or statements are understood as reasonable entailments of an unstated principle. In such accounts, the empirical rationality of these principles is often not questioned. Evans-Prichard attributed such contextual rationality to many Azande practices that appeared at face value to be irrational. Many religious practices (e.g., "I never eat milk and meat together") can be shown to be rational in that they are consistent with a set of unstated premises. Contextual rationality is the most common relativistic account of the reasonableness of apparently incomprehensible actions and beliefs. Many paradoxes of religion (e.g., "Christ is both man and God") may be illogical and even empirically irrational, but they are rational in light of the context of their belief systems and people's professed experience.

TOTEMISM

In this chapter and the three that follow it, I hope to shed new light on the rationality debate by returning to the old problem of *totemism*. The problem of totemism, the apparently literal identifications that many cultures appear to make between human and animal or plant species, became one of the most important battlegrounds in the rationality debate. Admittedly, there is something antiquarian about dredging up this subject in a modern text on culture and mind. In fact I would guess that most anthropologists today would assume that the meaning of totemism was no longer at issue in anthropology, having been settled once and for all by Levi-Strauss in his classic monographs on classification (Levi-Strauss, 1966, 1967a).

Yet totemism has been something of a phoenix among anthropological concepts, emerging repeatedly from the ashes of its own deconstruction. Totemism has been the subject of numerous classic analyses in early ethnology.[5] Yet totemic classification has also been dismissed by important writers, who declared totemism to be a nonproblem and a pseudoconcept.[6] Other accounts have sought to dissolve totemism into something more basic. For Lévy-Bruhl, it was the emotions that underlay the primitive identifications with totemic species (Lévy-Bruhl, 1926). For Freud, it was the primal crime, an echo of an original act that linked cannibalism, incest, and the foundations of the social order (Freud, 1950). Durkheim and Mauss reduced totemism to the self-representation of the clan, and this to the social component of human identity (Durkheim, 1915; Durkheim and Mauss, 1963).[7]

Levi-Strauss argued for the fundamental rationality of human thought. In this context the problem of totemism was at once resolved and dissolved into primitive "science"—the classifying faculty of the human mind. In this view, the particular symbols used for the classification are relatively unimportant, bearing little intrinsic interest of their own. As Levi-Strauss put it, "That the system should have recourse to animal and vegetable names is a particular case *of a method of differential designation,* the nature of which remains the same whatever the type of denotation employed" (Levi-Strauss, 1967a:12; emphasis added).

Yet even after emerging from an encounter with Levi-Strauss's savaging of the "totemic illusion," one cannot help feeling that, far from doing away with totemism as a problem, he has actually resurrected the issue (Levi-Strauss, 1963, 1966). His remarkable analyses inspire a fresh look at the special significance of the complex interspecies associations we once called totemic.[8]

FAMILY RESEMBLANCE

As numerous anthropologists have observed, totemism has no simple definition. But totemism is neither an illusion nor simply an anthropologist's category (Boas, 1916:321). In light of current understandings of human cognition and how humans actually use categories, we now know better than to expect all concepts to fit the classical model of well-formed categories. "Totemism" refers to a significant group of associated ideas that are found in a many societies.[9] Totemism points to a set of important connections made by many groups, connections that include the following features:

- Cultural classificatory schemes, sometimes elaborate, that employ relations among nonhuman forms as models for human social relations
- The recognition of complex identifications and exchanges between humans and the associated species (beliefs about common origins, exchanges, transmutability, and consubstantiality)
- The use of these identifications to define and regulate significant social boundaries, as in the regulation of sexual relations and eating practices

TWO APPROACHES TO TOTEMIC SYMBOLISM

Like linguistic signs, totemic signs have both a synthetic function of identifying discrete entities and an analytical function of separating related phenomena. For instance, to name a social group "The Elks" suggests (1) that a social group might be identified with the animal species we call "elks"; (2) that The Elks is, in some sense, not the same as the natural species "elks" (but only in a special, out of the ordinary way); and (3) that this group is a member of a paradigmatic set of groups (e.g., lions, moose, cubs) whose names form alternative possibilities and distinctive oppositions.

Totemic signs always identify and differentiate simultaneously. But the sorting and merging potentials of totemic signs are not equally stressed in ethnographic examples of totemism—sometimes the one, sometimes the other is emphasized.[10]

Most of the well-known attempts to interpret totemistic symbolism deprive totemism of its essential and generative ambiguity. In societies where subsistence depends largely or exclusively upon hunting and gathering, any identification of fauna and flora with human groups inevitably engages interests both intellectual and practical. So the classificatory power of species is never fully separable from their inherent interest as objects of consumption and regeneration. Their practical roles can be said to "motivate" in part their meaning as classifiers. In the terms set out by Susanne Langer in the epigraph to this chapter, such symbols are peculiarly compromised as classifying markers because they are also of consuming practical interest in their own right. So we can rightly ask why, given the human capacity for a high degree of arbitrariness and abstractness in symbolic activity, classification should make use of such a distracting set of signs.

As emblematic signs, animals bear necessarily abstract and metaphorical relations to humans. They point to the importance of the natural world as a conceptual model. As Goldenweiser noted long ago, plants and animals "are beautifully adjusted to the function of classifiers . . . for they contain many individuals belonging to the same or to several wide categories, they are familiar and congenial to man, yet outside the circle of specifically human things and activities, thus not being subject to the disturbing agencies that abound within that realm" (Goldenweiser, 1918:293).

And in a passage that both prefigures Levi-Strauss's transcendence of the totemic "illusion" and turns Durkheim and Mauss on their heads, Goldenweiser added:

> Moreover, to the eyes of men organized into internally disparate and internally homogeneous units, the kingdom of animals and only to a less degree that of plants present a spectacle of strange congeniality: for just as in their own social system, these kingdoms embrace beings or things that belong to the same general kind, but are subdivided into categories that are disparate while internally homogeneous. [Goldenweiser, 1918:293]

But as objects of human desire, as intrinsic values in a chain of organic transformations linked with subsistence, animals also have concrete relations to humans. Despite Levi-Strauss's rejection of totemism as an instance of practical reason, totemic species and humans are sometimes understood to "participate" materially and spiritually, each in the regeneration of the other. So plants and animals bear concrete metonymic as well as abstract metaphorical relations to people. As links in a food chain, totemic species point to the importance of direct, material exchange and incorporation between the human and nonhuman as a precondition of regeneration.

This inherent ambiguity in the relationship that obtains between humans and animal and plant species has produced two quite different approaches to interpreting totemic symbolism. One approach might be called "metaphorical totemism" and is associated with Levi-Strauss. Metaphorical totemism stresses the metaphorical relationships evident in animal-human relations, understood as analogies. Metaphorical totemism stresses the intrinsic rationality and categorical nature of human thought. In this understanding of totemism, the logic of the system is that "natural" categories such as the difference between bear and elk are used to model the categorical opposition between human groups such as clans or teams.

In contrast to this "logical" character of metaphorical totemism is the apparently irrational character of "metonymic totemism." Metonymic totemism stresses the literal identification of the species from which a name is taken and the named individual or group. In this case, there is held to be something significantly bearlike about individuals or groups named Bear, while the designation Elk describes a privileged relation between elks and a certain group or individual. Metonymic totemism conceives of direct spiritual or physical "participations," incorporative relations between animals or plants, on the one hand, and humans on the other hand. These direct identification reflect both a mystical bond between human and totem and sometimes consuming practical interest in a species as a source of food necessary for the continuity of human life.

Unfortunately, this idea of a direct relationship between totem and human became associated by way of Lévy-Bruhl's early writing with the notion of a primitive or prelogical mentality (Lévy-Bruhl, 1926). For example, Franz Boas criticized the stress of Durkheim, Wundt, and others on the identification of humans and animals in their treatment of totemism.[11] While admitting that such identifications are an important issue, Boas argued that they have "little bearing upon the question of totemism as a social institution" (Boas, 1916:323).

AN UNEASY MIX

The enduring fascination that totemism holds for anthropology is linked to this uneasy mix of "logic" and "participation" that totemism has suggested. Both views of totemic symbolism—metaphorical and metonymic—may be understood as complementary modes of propagation. Metaphorical totemism suggests that naming is understood as a kind of symbolic propagation. Chapter 11 describes how, for the Murngin of northern Australia, the act of naming is often understood as a form of creation, and the transmission of names is a kind of reproduction. On the other hand, metonymic totemism celebrates the propagation of a group through physical and spiritual incorporations of animal and human, with sexual or eating relations the most frequent mediators. This generative ambiguity in totemism is not surprising, since both classification (differentiated relations) and incorporation and transformation (identity relations) are basic processes in human life and in human thought. Natural species are well suited to bridge these functions, since humans partake in a double relationship with "nature," both participating in the natural order as part to whole (i.e., metonymy) and categorically distinguishing themselves from nature as distinct but parallel forms of life (i.e., metaphor).[12]

Since these ambiguities are, for human populations, real problems, neither the classifying nor incorporating aspects of totemic beliefs challenge in any way the rationality or competence of the mind that produces them. Darwin's vision of the connectedness of species is no less rational than Linnaean conceptions of their division. Nor does totemism force us, as Levi-Strauss lamented, to arbitrarily draw a

line between "primitive" and "scientific" mentalities, relegating the presumed to-
temizers to the status of *Naturvölker* (Levi-Strauss, 1967a:2).

In the following chapter we explore this ambiguity more concretely in relation
to the animal symbolism of the Kwakiutl of Vancouver Island on Canada's far west
coast. For the Kwakiutl, the richness of their religious symbolism involves precisely
the dual significance of totemic species proposed above—as both abstract labels for
social groups and the material content of transformative relations. There is an inevitable tension in any totemic system between the tidy job of classification and the mess-
ier implications of concrete interchanges between natural species and humans.[13] In
the Kwakiutl case, we shall see how the very attractiveness and utility of animals for
representing transformative relations (metonymic totemism) contributes to their relative weakness for the Kwakiutl as pure social classifiers (metaphoric totemism).

The "problem" of totemism is that it seems to point to a practice that is at once
highly logical and (by scientific standards) deeply irrational. Since, prior to Levi-
Strauss's reanalysis of totemic classifications, totemism was typically associated with
an early stage of cultural evolution, the whole issue of psychic unity rested on how
totemic symbolism was understood by anthropologists. The characteristic strategy for
dealing with the ambiguity of totemism has been reductive. Totemism has been deprived of one or another pole of its inevitable ambiguity and explained away as the
manifestation of either pure mysticism or as pure logic. This strategy has, I think,
left the totemic problem unresolved. It has also produced serious discontinuities between theories that account for totemism and ethnographic materials, such as those
on the Kwakiutl, which those theories are supposed to illuminate.

THE "DEMYSTIFICATION" OF TOTEMISM

While many of the early classic accounts of totemism emphasized the spiritual or
generative relationship between humans and natural species, it is fair to say that the
characteristic modern solution to the problem of totemism has been one of demystify-
ing the institution. By reconstituting totemism as a particular type of classification,
Durkheim, Mauss, and Levi-Strauss sought (in different ways) to purify totemism of
its traces of "mysticism" and demonstrate the ultimate rationality of human thought.

It may seem inappropriate to conflate the work of Durkheim and Mauss with
that of Levi-Strauss, since Levi-Strauss singles out Durkheim as one his main targets
in *Totemism*. While Durkheim and Mauss (Durkheim and Mauss, 1963) looked to
society as the source for the mind's categories, Levi-Strauss was more faithful to
Kant, deriving social categories (including "totemic" ones) from the intrinsic character of the human mind. The mind was presented as if it were a category generator
and mediator. Still, both of these French traditions share a strongly rationalist bias.
In both, the issue of "participation" between humans and nonhuman beings is effectively factored out of the totemic equation. Because their solutions to the totemic
problem are widely accepted as popular wisdom in modern anthropology and because
of the difficulties with which they present us in understanding the Kwakiutl use of
animal symbolism, it is important to look carefully at the fate of the "participation"

problem in the hands of Levi-Strauss and the Durkheimians. Only then can we turn, in the next chapter, to a closer look at Kwakiutl totemism.

DISTINCTIVE CREATURES: LEVI-STRAUSS AND THE LOGIC OF THE CONCRETE

Levi-Strauss's solution to the totemism problem is actually more consistent and straightforward than Durkheim's. It is therefore, in some ways, less interesting. In his two most famous works on classification, *Totemism* and *The Savage Mind,* Levi-Strauss sought to discredit the distinction between primitive and scientific mentalities—made famous by Lévy-Bruhl's notorious formulation—by demonstrating the preeminence of logical classification in all human thought.

At first glance *The Savage Mind* seems to uphold the distinction between the primitive "them" and the civilized "us." In a limited way, primitive thought still figures as a viable concept for Levi-Strauss. The "concrete logic" of bricolage employs the left-over materials of historical events in constructing systematic reaffirmations of a priori structures. True scientific thought, however, seeks experimentally to affirm or disconfirm hypotheses that are assumed to be contingent rather than eternal. But what all humans share, according to Levi-Strauss, is more basic: an irreducible taxonomic sensibility. Considering this rationalist emphasis in Levi-Strauss's affirmation of human psychic unity, totemism in its classic formulation presented a serious challenge. Though he objected to the integrity of the totemism concept on the usual empirical grounds (the phenomena classed as totemic were too diverse to represent a single institution), his real targets were (1) the linkage between totemism and practical interests in plants and animals and (2) the concept of identification or participation between humans and totemic species.

If the totemic identification across species was an accurate account of totemism, if certain Bororo did indeed believe they really were arara parrots, then clearly the classic Aristotelian logic of noncontradiction could not be said to characterize all human thinking.[14] Thus even as Levi-Strauss is forced by the weight of ethnographic evidence to recognize the intimate intercourse between animal and human suggested so frequently in myth, he attributes such ethnobiology to sentiment rather than to any rational faculties:

> This disinterested, attentive, fond and affectionate lore acquired and transmitted through the attachments of marriage and upbringing is here described with such noble simplicity that it seems superfluous to conjure up the bizarre hypotheses suggested to philosophers by too theoretical a view of the development of human knowledge. Nothing here calls for the intervention of a so-called "principle of participation" or even for a mysticism embedded in metaphysics which we now perceive only through the distorting lens of established religions. [Levi-Strauss, 1966:37–38]

In diverting attention from the "determinate content" of the totemic relation (1966:76), Levi-Strauss shifts his focus to the most basic aspect of classification, the establishment of systems of difference and the creation of classificatory templates. In this view, natural taxonomies are used as a model for speciating human groups into cultural classes. The only relevant relations in this view are relations of opposition within levels, rather than relations of identification or even similarity between levels. For Levi-Strauss, the analogy that totemism establishes is not really between actual social groups and specific natural species but rather "between the differences which manifest themselves on the level of groups on the one hand and that of species on the other. They are thus based on the postulate of a homology between two systems of difference, one which occurs in nature, and the other in culture" (Levi-Strauss, 1966:114).

In several schematic diagrams, Levi-Strauss distinguished his own stress on *relations of opposition within levels* (Model B) from the older (and allegedly incorrect) emphasis on *content relations between levels* (Model A). These diagrams are reproduced in Figure 7.1.

Were totemism to suggest direct homologies between the concrete terms (as in Model A) rather than indirect homologies between their relations (i.e., oppositions) as in Model B, Levi-Strauss assures us that "[t]his structure would be fundamentally impaired" (1966:115).

Totemism, denied its content, is given new life by Levi-Strauss as a manifestation of a more general information-generating process:

> [T]he operative value of the system of naming and classifying commonly called totemic derives from their formal character: they are codes suitable for conveying messages which can be transposed into other codes, and for expressing messages received by means of different codes in terms of their own system. The mistake of classical ethnologists was to try to reify this form and tie it to a determinate content. Far from being an autonomous institution definable by its intrinsic characteristics, totemism, or what is referred to as such, corresponds to certain modalities arbitrarily isolated from a formal system, the function of which is to guarantee the convertibility of ideas between different levels of social reality. [Levi-Strauss, 1966:75–76]

This well-known resolution of the totemic problem has several interesting implications. Totemic symbolism becomes in no significant way different from linguistic symbolism as conceived by phonologists (Jakobson and Halle, 1956; Trubetzkoy 1969; Saussure, 1959). Meaning is construed as an informational process, guaranteed by "syntagmatic relations," relations of difference or opposition between signs whose relation to their referents is largely arbitrary. Totemic symbols become distinctive features whose main character is that they are handy markers of difference.

Now if we look more carefully at the two diagrams of Levi-Strauss in Figure 7.1, this conception of totemism raises some interesting problems. Levi-Strauss is proposing that totemic operations work through analogy. But analogy is used in a special and limited way. Conventionally, the "totemic" analogy of the sort

$$\text{Elks : Group A :: Lions : Group B}$$

is in reality a double analogy, implying also:

$$\text{Elks : Lions :: Group A : Group B}$$

Each analogy presupposes the possibility of the other. The equations suggest both the possibility of (1) some sort of analogy between Elk and Group A and Lion and Group B (a *content analogy*) and (2) an analogy between the *opposition* of elk and

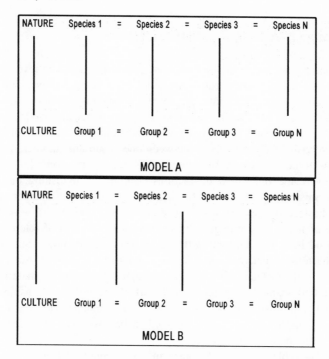

Figure 7.1. Two Versions of the Totemic Relationship (after Levi-Strauss, 1966)

lion and Group A and Group B (a *formal analogy*). Note that the latter kind of analogy is not necessarily one of simple opposition. It is a "relationship" before it is an "opposition" and may suggest a wide variety of connections. Not only differences but also positive features of the specific animals may come into play.

Thus the Lion/Elk relation, as used for American male societies, would have very different implications if it were, say, Lion/Rat or Lion/Cockroach. In using phonology as his model for totemistic classification, Levi-Strauss has employed the level of language analysis most removed from meaning. This choice had significant implications. By insisting on understanding totemic markers as purely oppositional and formal, Levi-Strauss has deprived the analogical operation of one of its critical dimensions: *the dimension of concrete meaning.*

More generally, this understanding of symbolism lacks any important role for "motivation" in symbolic analysis, either in language or especially in more empirically committed codes like totemism. The idea of motivation, a nonarbitrary relationship between symbolic form and content or reference, was most fully developed in the work of Ullman (1957), and has been given significant consideration by Benveniste (1966), Jakobson (1971), Friedrich (1979), Sperber (1975), Lakoff (1987a), and Shore (1987, 1990b). Totemic symbolism, in Levi-Strauss's treatment, has the power to impose a common, if arbitrary, formal representation on different domains of human life. But in the process, totemism loses its capacity to state anything in particular about the concrete relation of the symbolizers to that world from which they borrow their symbols.[15]

DURKHEIM AND THE DENATURED EMBLEM

If Levi-Strauss's approach to the totemism problem was to relieve totemic belief and practice of its distinctive religious foundations (Levi-Strauss, 1963:103–104), Durkheim's moved totemism into the center of primitive religion. In the process, however, something peculiar happened to religion: it became wedded to a kind of sociological reductionism. The totem was understood as the soul of the clan and therefore the basis of the distinction between one group and another. In merging the individual with the social unit, the totemic relation required some kind of "participation" that overcame individual distinctions. But in distinguishing one group from another, totemism was also linked to classificatory logic in a manner not dissimilar to that emphasized by Levi-Strauss a generation later.

In and of itself, this ambiguity in Durkheim's treatment of totemism has much to recommend it. It is consistent with the inherently ambiguous character of totemism. Yet the tension between classification and identification in Australian thought does not sit easily in Durkheim's work. Though the Australian materials on which Durkheim relied seemed to suggest some sort of concrete relationship between totemic species and those who bore their names and emblems, Durkheim seemed uneasy with the implications of what seemed to be excessive mysticism and mental confusion on the part of the Aranda.

In a remarkable series of passages in his *Elementary Forms of the Religious Life* (1915), Durkheim gradually abandoned the "participatory" aspects of totemism, replacing them by a view of totems exclusively as arbitrary labels for groups. This "de-natured" conception of totemism is not far from the highly rationalistic view Levi-Strauss would adopt a generation later.

Early in the book, Durkheim stresses the literal identifications between species that totems seems to convey:

> Every member of a clan is invested with a sacred character which is not materially inferior to that which we just observed in the animal. This personal sacredness is due to the fact that while the man believes that while he is a man in the usual sense of the word, he is also an animal or plant of the totemic species. . . . So each individual has a double nature: two beings coexist within him, a man and an animal. [p.134]

The relations implied are not just of similarity, analogy, or comparison but of essential identity. Durkheim leaves no doubt about how we are to understand the Australian equations:

> When an Australian of the Port Mackay tribe says that the sun, snakes, etc., are of the Yungaroo phratry [social group], he does not mean to apply a common, but nonetheless purely conventional nomenclature to these different things: the word has an objective signification for him. He believes that "alligators" really are Yungaroo and that Kangaroos are Wootaroo. . . . An internal bond attaches them to the group in which they are placed; they are regular members of it. . . . Thus a bond of mystic sympathy unites each individual to those beings, whether living or not, which are associated with him. [pp. 148–149]

This sounds like a passage straight out of Lévy-Bruhl.

Early in *The Elementary Forms of the Religious Life,* Durkheim makes an interesting observation that will provide him with the means for unraveling the "mystical" bonds that appear to exist between human and totemic species:

> Since the number and importance of the interdictions which isolate a sacred thing, and keep it apart, correspond to the degree of sacredness with which it is invested, we arrive at the remarkable conclusion that the images of totemic beings are more sacred than the beings themselves. . . . The representations of the totem are . . . more actively powerful than the totem itself. [p. 133]

To overcome the vulgar identification of human and totem, and its logical problems, Durkheim begins to reformulate the relationship.

> We are now in a better condition for understanding what the native means when he says that the men of the Crow phratry, for example, are crows. He does not exactly mean to say that they are crows *in the vulgar and empirical sense of the term,* but that the same principle is found in all of them, which is their most essential characteristic, which they have in common with the animals of the same name and which is thought of under the external form of a crow. [p. 189; emphasis added]

This common essence or spirit is, for Durkheim, social identity, the common identification of a group of individuals by which they feel and think of themselves as one. Taxonomic and social identity, the one logical the other moral, have a common origin: "It is along with the feeling of tribal unity that the feeling of the substantial unity of the world awakens" (p. 196).

At this point, the totemic relationship, once characterized by Durkheim as total identification between totemic species and human group, has been loosened up considerably. It is more like a comparison or analogy. The aborigine becomes a symbolist and the totemic relationship has become emblematic. Durkheim tells us early on in the book that actual physical resemblances between humans and animals could not have any more than an occasional and minor part in motivating totemic identifications. But unlike Levi-Strauss, Durkheim does not simply dismiss the troubling problem of the apparently illogical "participation" between human and animal or plant that totemism implies. In fact, he sees the issue as the crux of the totemism problem:

> [B]efore all else, men resemble their relatives and companions, and not plants and animals. Such rare and questionable analogies could not overcome such ambiguous proofs, nor could they lead a man and his forefathers in forms contradicted by daily experience. So this question remains untouched, and as long as it is not answered, we cannot say that totemism is explained. [p. 170]

Durkheim's solution is ingenious. However illogical it might seem for aborigines to posit identities between humans and kangaroos or lizards, such "participations" do not actually violate logic. Durkheim wants to show us that the global identification of distinct things is actually the most primitive basis for all logical classification.

> It has been said that the participations . . . implied by the mythologies violate the principle of contradiction, and that they are opposed to those implied by scientific explanations. Is not the statement that the man is a kangaroo or the sun a bird, equal to identifying the two with each other? But our manner of thought is not different when we say of heat that it is a movement, or of light that it is a vibration of the ether, etc.

Every time that we unite heterogeneous terms by an internal bond, we forcibly identify contraries. [p. 238]

"Participation" is the soul of all categorization, precisely because it allows us to transcend perception as the basis for forming concepts or classes. In particular, to-temic identifications must, in this account, have a source other than direct experi-ence since

[t]here is nothing in experience which could suggest these connections and confusions. As far as the observation of the senses is able to go, everything is different and discon-nected. Nowhere do we really see beings mixing their natures and metamorphosing themselves into each other. It is therefore necessary that some exceptionally powerful cause should have intervened to transfigure reality in such a way as to make it appear under an aspect that is not really its own. It was religion that was the agent of this transformation. [pp. 235–236]

Mysticism is made to serve rational ends. Religion has as its true object not the transcendence of the secular but its justification. A half-century later, Victor Turner would oppose structure and communitas (or antistructure) and identify religious expe-rience with communitas (Turner, 1967, 1969). But Durkheim has collapsed these distinctions, so that totemism and its participations are seen as underlying the rational ordering of social units, and by Durkheim's famous socio-logic, totemism underlies logical thought itself.

It is puzzling that Durkheim, like Levi-Strauss after him, could recognize in totemic identifications no empirical confirmation. For in his contention that transfor-mations and participations among distinct kinds of beings had no basis in experience, Durkheim was obviously wrong. One need not invoke evolutionary processes, too slow to be accessible to our experience, to show Durkheim's mistake. We can all see and experience these "confusions" in life's most basic processes of regeneration.

In sexual congress, two become one (if for a moment) and the male-female distinction is both psychologically and biologically overcome. In birth, one gradually becomes two (or more), and in the case of male offspring, gender distinction as well as individual identity is implicated. And in the ingestion of plants and animals, di-verse species are incorporated and transformed. Biologists call this kind of "participa-tion" the food chain. Is it not precisely these regenerative processes that are the subject of so much myth and ritual, most notoriously among the very aboriginal populations Durkheim was trying to understand?[16] And are they not authentic human mysteries, the subjects of deep speculation, both scientific and religious?

We have seen how Durkheim gradually denatured totemism by transforming what had been an intrinsic relationship between human and totem into a symbolic tie, in which the emblems came to be more sacred than the totemic species itself. Durkheim is right, but only partly right. Surely his understanding of the priority of the symbolic over the material in totemism has ample ethnographic support, from Australia and beyond. But is this logocentric transcendence of the physical in totem-ism the deepest sort of understanding we can have of totemism?

Totemism will not be simply dismissed as a crucial problem for anthropologists to puzzle over. The attempt to reduce those peculiar and fascinating symbolic associ-ations between humans and other forms of life that we call totemic to a logical operation devoid of practical interest will not survive close ethnographic study. This is because "totemic operators," as Levi-Strauss called them, are not about logic alone. Totemic signs are nonarbitrary classifiers whose character as pure signs is always compromised by an intrinsic interest in the symbols as objects of literal identification. They are, in part, categorical designators, and thus almost conform to a model of rationality as categorical logic. Totemic plants and animals are also objects of practical interest, such as food sources or images of animal ancestry. Bringing together the logical and pragmatic aspects of such symbolism, we recognize in totemism a form of thought that is *practically logical,* in both senses of the phrase.

The literal identifications between human and animal or plant have been seen as proof of the illogical or prelogical qualities of "primitive" thought. Lévy-Bruhl was much maligned for his conception of such prelogical thought as based on such mystical identifications between subjects and objects and between subjects and signs. The assumption has always been that to conceive of something "participating in" something else of a different nature or kind was fundamentally illogical. However much "participation" may violate *logical rationality,* it can easily be shown to be rational in both the *empirical* and *contextual* senses of the term, discussed at the beginning of this chapter. The cross-species identifications suggested by totemism can be shown to have significant empirical validity. And in the context of conceptual systems concerned with issues of organic generation and transformation, Lévy-Bruhl's notion of participation makes logical as well as emotional "sense."

Not only is totemism not to be equated with a single mode of thought, but it is profoundly misleading to associate totemism with certain kinds (or, even worse, stages) of culture. Though its forms have been transformed in relation to changes in the forms of social and physical reproduction, totemism is very much alive in the postindustrial world.

TECHNO-TOTEMISM: CROSS-SPECIES "PARTICIPATION" IN THE AGE OF TECHNOLOGY

In Chapter 6, a concept of human-machine hybrids was examined that represent a sort of "techno-totemism" common to postindustrial cultural representations. The ambiguities in what is human and what is not have always been a subject of human speculation and figure prominently in religious representations of all sorts. Where the culturally salient forms of reproduction are organic, we get classical organic totemism. Where mechanical and electronic reproduction become dominant, the totemic problem will reappear in the form of compromised relations between humans and the inert world of tools or electronic virtual entities.

This new world of technologically mediated humanity is brilliantly invoked in the opening passage from William Gibson's influential "cyberpunk" novel *Neuromancer.* Part I of the novel is called "Chiba City Blues," which turns out to be a reference not so much to the world of direct human feeling but to a world whose intimate perceptual contours have been thoroughly infiltrated by technology:

> The sky above the port was the color of television, tuned to a dead channel,
> "It's not like I'm using," Case heard someone say, as he shouldered his way
> through the crowd around the door of the Chat. "It's like my body's developed this

massive drug deficiency." It was a Sprawl voice and a Sprawl joke. The Chatsubo was a bar for professional expatriates; you could drink there for a week and never hear two words of Japanese.

Ratz was tending bar, his prosthetic arm jerking monotonously as he filled a tray of glasses with draft Kirin. He saw Case and smiled, his teeth a webwork of East European steel and brown decay. Case found a place at the bar, between the unlikely tan on one of Lonny Zone's whores and the crisp naval uniform of a tall African whose cheekbones were ridged with precise rows of tribal scars. . . .

The bartender's smile widened. His ugliness was the stuff of legend. In an age of affordable beauty, there was something heraldic about his lack of it. The antique arm whined as he reached for another mug. It was a Russian military prosthesis, a seven-function force-feeder manipulator, cased in grubby pink plastic. "You are too much the artiste, Herr Case," Ratz grunted; the sound served him as laughter. He scratched his overhang of white-shirted belly with the pink claw. "You are the artiste of the slightly funny deal." [Gibson 1984:3–4]

Techno-totemism is nothing new, of course, and has been a form of totemism for as long as humans have created tools as extensions of their own bodies. A familiar if somewhat homely example is the tale *Pinocchio,* in which a solitary woodcarver creates a child through technological rather than organic reproduction. Gepetto then vainly seeks to transform the ambiguously alive puppet into a "real boy," but can only do so after the intervention of a woman in the form of a fairy godmother.

In modern postindustrial society, the compromised autonomy of the human in relation to the machine is a pervasive problem that is reflected in the popular arts as well as in more abstruse forums like medical ethics and property law. While the most dramatic form that techo-totemism takes is the cyborg-type human-machine hybrid *(The Six Million Dollar Man, Robocop,* or, less obviously, the car-as-best-friend as in the TV series *Knight Rider),* techno-totemism is revealed in a wide variety of technologically mediated human conditions. Mechanical "participations" in human physical existence—such as prostheses, mechanical organs, in-vitro fertilization, plastic surgery, and gene splicing—are all increasingly common forms of virtual organicism that have begun to radically alter the conception of what it means to be human.

This sort of techno-totemism is a historically specific form of totemism, responding, as do all forms of totemism, to particular lifeworlds within which human reproduction and subsistence are carried on. In Chapters 5 and 6, the case was made for a radical transformation of thought under the influence of the modularity schema. Totemism's recent incarnation as techno-totemism is not simply the introduction of new content in a traditional symbolic format. Techno-totemism celebrates not just novel cross-species mixtures but literally a new way of thinking about them—the elaboration of digital coding in the formulation of a postmodern worldview.

CONCLUSION

The totemic "problem" that dominated the early years of anthropology has not really gone away. It is, in fact, the most elaborate version of the classic psychic unity problem. Part of the difficulty anthropologists have had in interpreting totemism has been a failure to take the natives seriously in their accounts of totemism and to consider totemic thought to be a kind of serious philosophical speculation on certain real-world problems. Paying serious attention to what the people whom we study have to tell us can prove quite enlightening, not simply as data for our theories but as a genuine contribution to our own theoretical speculations.

In attempting to rescue the notion of psychic unity from the implicit evolutionism of Lévy-Bruhl's prelogical mentality, Levi-Strauss and others have overstated the case for the arbitrariness of the signs by which people classify their worlds. These same theorists have also overstated the categorical nature of human thought. Lévy-Bruhl's principle of "participation" will not be so easily dismissed. But the mode of thought which recognizes the limits of everyday categorization cannot be called "irrational" (or "prelogical") except in relation to the very limited notion of logical rationality implicit in Aristotle's concept of noncontradiction. And it does not reflect any sort of mental confusion.

Though human communication requires the use of categories for relatively unambiguous classification, such categories will never exhaust a people's experience of their world. Though cultural orders may well proliferate well-formed categories, life "in the world" does not always provide a good "fit" with these categories. Marginal play (Chapter 4) is not only a condition of games but an inevitable part of the human condition. The transformations and exchanges of organic life will always tend to violate categorical logic. Like other creatures, humans survive and reproduce only by engaging in substantial interchanges with other forms of life or with artifacts whose substance and identity will inevitably compromise the autonomy of the individual person, group, or species. Hunting, eating, sexual intercourse, marriage, gestation, and tool use are all areas where conceptual and existential autonomy are inevitably breached.

All human cultures have recognized in their totemic formulations the inherent tensions between conceiving of particular forms of life and the transformative processes of living. In the context of life, a machine "logic" exclusively attuned to the production of crisp categories would be "irrational" in the sense that they would be maladaptive and empirically false. To make sense of totemism, logical rationality, in its strictest sense, must give way to empirical and contextual rationality.

Human thought has several distinct modalities, only one of which has been traditionally accorded the status of logical. It was to Lévy-Bruhl's credit that he attempted to draw attention to another mode of thought. In characterizing that mode as "participation," Lévy-Bruhl put his finger on a key aspect of meaning-construction which in more recent writing has been called "embodiment." Lévy-Bruhl's error, of course, was in characterizing this mode of thought as both prelogical and as associated with only one sort of human being.

Classic totemism, the "participations" of humans with the world of plants and animals, is not, to be sure, evenly distributed among human communities. For those of us whose worldviews have been shaped by industrial technology, Australian aboriginal beliefs about such interdependencies do seem like the product of an exotic mind. Yet this has nothing to do with the evolution of mind and everything to do with differences in real-world subsistence practices and techniques of social reproduction. In a world in which gathering and hunting have been replaced by the manufacturing and commoditization of food products, the empirical power of the organic totem as a fact of life is all but invisible and appears irrational.

In our world, however, the problem of organic totemism reappears in a new, historically determinate form. Organic totemism has resurfaced in debates about evolution and the Darwinian denial of the categorical distinction between species that underlies the creationist's creed. The irony is that the modern version of organic totemism comes from science and finds its deepest foes in fundamentalist religion. What to aborigines is sacred reality (animals and humans are all one) becomes scientific doctrine in the West. On the other hand, the Australian view of secular life (everything outside of the Dreamtime is separated) becomes a modern religiously grounded ontology. "Participation" does not disappear from postindustrial thought, however, but sneaks in the back door, unannounced, as techno-totemism.

Totemism, in the expanded sense proposed in these pages, is not a relic from a lost phase of human evolution. Neither is it, however, rationalized away as the expression of a one-dimensional categorizing impulse of the human mind. Totemism is a complex reflection of the tensions between the human need for categories and the human recognition that all life is an exchange between heterogeneous forms. It draws upon several modes of human thought (classificatory/metaphorical, participatory/metonymic) and mobilizes these modes of thought differently under different conditions of subsistence and social reproduction. Thus, while we can recognize these complex formulations as employing human cognitive resources in response to human experiences, the cognitive models employed will be historically and culturally diverse, reflecting different ideologies and distinct modes of production and social reproduction.

In Chapters 6 and 7 we have seen that a high-tech version of totemism is alive and well in contemporary popular culture. To appreciate the diversity of such classificatory cultural models, it is important to juxtapose these contemporary Western models with several exotic and more traditional examples of cultural systems in which complex kinds of identification between humans and other natural species figured prominently in religious thought and practice. Chapters 9 and 10 will take up the classic case of Australian aboriginal totemic classifications through a reexamination of one of the best-studied aboriginal groups, the Murngin (or Yolngu) of Arnhem Land. But first we turn to a less typical case study of totemism, drawn from the extensive anthropological literature on the Kwakiutl from the northwest coast of North America.

Notes

1. For critical discussions of the classical notion of category, see Rosch and Lloyd, 1978; Lakoff, 1987a; Smith and Medin, 1981; Smith, 1990:502–503. See also below, Chapter 14.

2. On the concept of the "primitive" in Western thought, see Stocking, 1968; Torgovnik, 1990.

3. For a brilliant account of these issues about rationality and culture in relation to contemporary cults of witchcraft in Britain, see Luhrmann, 1989.

4. Dan Sperber also attempts to distinguish different sorts of rationality, though ultimately in defense of a nonrelativistic view of cognition. His approach is to distinguish propositional and semipropositional representations, which he terms "a half-understood idea" (Sperber, 1985:51). He also distinguishes representations from explanations, noting that "a semi-

propositional representation can be given as many *propositional interpretations* as there are ways of specifying the conceptual content of its elements (a half-understood idea can be made more precise in many ways)" (p. 51, emphasis in original). He also distinguishes *factual beliefs* from *representational beliefs,* which he describes as "a fuzzy set of related mental attitudes few of which seem to be universal" (p. 56). These distinctions allow Sperber to classify beliefs on a four-way matrix of possibilities which serves not so much to distinguish different *kinds* of rationality as different *degrees* of rationality.

In his critique of symbolic anthropology, Sperber has made the radical proposal that symbolism (which he distinguishes from language) does not communicate *meaning* at all (Sperber, 1975, 1985). This odd statement derives from his very narrow view of what constitutes "meaning." For Sperber, meaning is "sentence meaning," tied to the classical models of categorization and to logical criteria of noncontradiction. While natural language for Sperber clearly exhibits the logical characteristics of analyticity and paraphrase, cultural symbols, as embodied in myth and ritual, do not (Sperber, 1975).

Most intriguing for our purposes is Sperber's argument that symbolism be understood as a distinct kind of code from language, a code that is cognitive rather than semiological and primarily individual rather than collective. In Sperber's highly dichotomous view, when rational means (i.e., language) fail, irrational ones (i.e., symbolism) take over. Symbolism, he says, is the product of an innate symbolic mechanism which "kicks in" when the more conventional resources for meaning making are overwhelmed or inadequate. Cultural symbolism is seen here not as a way of communicating meaning but rather as a shared "evocative field" that focuses attention and permits members of a community to have parallel symbolic evocations.

I think that Sperber's conception of meaning is far too narrow even to make sense of meaning in language. Sperber's work takes for granted a theory of language that has been challenged by a whole school of linguists disenchanted with symbolic (logic-driven) models of language. These new conceptions of language no longer rely on purely analytic models of meaning and classical notions of category recognition. The new field of cognitive grammar has demonstrated the role of prototype effects, basic-level categorization, analogy, and metaphor in accounting for the meaningfulness of both words and syntax (Lakoff, 1987a; Johnson, 1987; Langacker, 1987; Talmy, 1978, 1983). These studies would not support Sperber's rigid dichotomy between linguistic meaning and symbolic evocation.

Still, I find Sperber's distinctions between analytic "meaning" (which I call information processing) and nonanalytic "evocation" to be quite intriguing. But rather than exclude these latter processes from the notion of meaning, I would like to take the opposite tack and suggest that it is precisely to the evocative work of symbolism that we need to turn if we want to understand "meaning construction" as a cognitive phenomenon and how instituted models are transformed into mental representations.

5. McLennan, 1869–1870; Elkin, 1933–1934; Goldenweiser, 1910; Van Gennap, 1920; Frazer, 1910; Roheim, 1945.

6. For a brief history of the deconstruction of the once influential problem of totemism, see Levi-Strauss, 1963, especially pp. 1–14. See also Boas, 1916.

7. "If the totemic principle is nothing else than the clan, it is the clan thought of under the material form of the totemic emblem; now this form is also that of the concrete being whose name the clan bears. Owing to this resemblance, they could not fail to evoke sentiments analogous to those aroused by the emblem itself" (Durkheim, 1915:222).

8. Levi-Strauss himself foresaw this possibility, which he noted as an undesirable possible consequence of his publishing a book on totemism. The first chapter of *Totemism* opens with the remark:

> To accept as a theme for discussion a category that one believes to be false always entails the risk, simply by the attention that is paid to it, of entertaining some illusion

about its reality. . . . The phantom which is imprudently summoned up, in the hope of exorcising it for good, vanishes only to reappear, and closer than one imagines, to the place where is was at first. [Levi-Strauss, 1963:15]

9. Goldenweiser used the term "totemic complex" as a summary term for the group of associated cultural traits that make up the institution of totemism. While the specific content of totemic beliefs differs from clan to clan, Goldenweiser argued for the universality of the form the features take, by which he means their functional link to the clans (Goldenweiser, 1918:282).

10. Sexual symbolism is open to the same kind of divergence that, as we have seen, characterizes animal symbolism. An interesting example of the different fates for sexual symbolism is found in Polynesia. Traditional gender concepts in Eastern Polynesia (Tahitians, Maoris, Hawaiians, etc.) emphasized husband-wife as the prototypical male-female bond. Images of sexual conjunction were tied to conceptions of *mana* (power). It is from Eastern Polynesia that the popular conceptions of Polynesian eroticism are derived. In Western Polynesia (Tonga, Samoa) the prototypical gender dyad was commonly brother-sister, and the dominant symbolic modality was avoidance rather than conjunction. Power was associated with sisters, virgins, and the withholding of reproductive sexuality in the interest of cosmic regeneration. In these societies, the brother-sister bond, predicated on perpetual opposition, generated pervasive dualism in social organization, political organization, and in cosmology. Where conjunctive "sexual" relations were stressed, monolithic theories of power predominated, culminating in the ideal of incestuous brother-sister marriage among the highest Hawaiian chiefs. Where disjunctive "avoidance" relations were stressed, dualistic theories of power and elaborate dual organization were found (Shore, 1978, 1989).

11. Durkheim's own view of these relations was, at best, equivocal.

12. In a somewhat different formulation, Levi-Strauss appears to have recognized the ambiguity inherent in totemism even as he sought to dismantle the concept. "[o]ne might almost say," he suggested, "that metonymy corresponds to the order of events, metaphor to the order of structure" (Levi-Strauss, 1963:27). See also Tambiah, 1969, pp. 454–455.

13. Compare Tambiah's analysis of animal symbolism in a Thai village (Tambiah, 1969). Recognizing the tensions between practical (participatory) and intellectual (classificatory) interests in local fauna, Tambiah concludes:

> I submit that the Thai villagers' relation to the animal world shows a similar complexity which expresses neither a sense of affinity with animals alone nor a clear-cut distinction and separation from them, but rather coexistence of both attitudes in varying intensities which creates a perpetual tension. And I submit that dietary regulations are intrinsic to this relationship. They provide a clue to the ritual attitude toward animals, to linking eating rules to sex rules, to man on the one hand drawing nature into a single moral universe, and also at the same time vigorously separating nature from culture. [Tambiah, 1969:455]

14. The Bororo belief that men were red parrots (arara) is the locus classicus of the totemism problem and has a long history in anthropology. It was first reported by Van den Steinen in 1894 as an instance of primitive thinking from the Amazon. Since then it has been repeatedly invoked as a central problem of primitive classification (Durkheim, 1915; Durkheim and Mauss, 1963; Karsten, 1926; Levi-Strauss, 1966, 1967b) and more recently as a key problem for a theory of metaphor and other tropes (Crocker, 1985; Urton, 1985; Van Baaren, 1969; Smith, 1972; Turner, 1991). While recent analyses of the famous classificatory paradox focused on metaphoric thinking, Terence Turner's analysis demonstrates convincingly that, for the Bororo, their relations with red parrots (araras) can only be understood through complex combinations of metaphorical and metonymic relations that define human-bird relations in Bororo thought.

15. His extended treatment of caste relations derives castes from precisely an overvaluation of the relation between totemic marker and human group, creating within humanity pseudospecies: "The more each group tries to define itself by the image which it draws from the natural model, the more difficult it will become for it to maintain its links with other social groups, and in particular to exchange its sisters and daughters with them *since it will tend to think of them as being of a particular 'species'* " (Levi-Strauss, 1966:116–117; emphasis added).

In a peculiarly defensive footnote to this analysis, Levi-Strauss seems to hastily, and unconvincingly, retreat from the implications of this passage for his dismissal of the totemic illusion:

> It will perhaps be objected that . . . I denied that totemism can be interpreted on the basis of a direct analogy between human groups and natural species. But this criticism was directed against a theory put forward by ethnologists and what is in question here is an—implicit or explicit—native theory which indeed corresponds to institutions that ethnologists would refuse to classify as totemic. [Levi-Strauss, 1966:116–117]

This is an odd claim. One might have thought that what was at issue was a general conception of human classification, one which denied a significant place for the kind of "irrational" identifications that have been resurrected by Levi-Strauss to account for the transformation from totemic to caste systems.

16. For the Yolngu (Murngin) of Arnhemland, in northern Australia, the categorical ordering of experience, represented in myth by the separation of distinct species from a primal unity, is ritually and mythically linked to the separations of son from mother in birth and later in ritual. Duality—the basis of Murngin social organization and classificatory logic—is thus linked to fundamental generative processes. Interestingly, it is the *overcoming of such oppositions* (ritual identifications of men with totemic ancestors, and in death, when the original unity of living things is reclaimed) that the Murngin associate with the sacred (Warner, 1936/1958). For a detailed analysis of the Yolngu material see Chapters 9 and 10.

8

Kwakiutl Animal Symbolism: Food for Thought

> [A] concept is not an isolated, ossified, changeless formation but an active part of the intellectual process, constantly engaged in serving communication, understanding, and problem-solving.
>
> —Lev Vygotsky

It is no coincidence that the problem of totemism engaged so many important thinkers for so many years. Nor is it surprising that noted psychologists and philosophers joined anthropologists in trying to understand what totemistic classifications were all about. As we saw in the previous chapter, the interpretation of totemism depends inevitably on a stated or unstated theory of human classification and symbolization. And to theorize about symbols and classification is to propose a theory of mind. Important matters were at stake in how totemism was accounted for.

For generations of theorists, totemism was the battleground on which theories about the relation between culture and mind were waged. Totemism provided ample food for the most diverse thoughts about the mind. To some, the mystical totemic identifications between species suggested the workings of "prelogical" mental processes. To others, they represented repressed memories of a primal scene at the dawn of humanity. More recently, rationalists like Levi-Strauss found comfort in the universal taxonomic sensibility to which such classifications seemed to point.

To understand how totemism could have produced such a wealth of contrary views on the mind, it is helpful to examine in detail ethnographic cases of symbolic systems employing identifications between species of a totemic type. In this chapter, we will take a fresh look at a less typical case of totemism among the Kwakiutl of Vancouver Island, with a view toward refining our understanding of the role of classification in a theory of mind. Then in Chapter 9 we turn to a classic instance of totemism among an aboriginal group from northern Australia.

KWAKIUTL TOTEMS

Magnificent totem poles were part of the astonishing artistic production of the great chiefdoms of the North American coastal northwest. So it is odd that these societies never figured prominently in discussions of totemism. The use of natural species names for classifying descent groups was practiced by the Tlingit, Tsimshian, Heiltsuq, and Haida but not by the Kwakiutl, who, according to Boas, lacked totems "in the proper sense of the term" (Boas, 1897:323; Frazer, 1910:319).

The Kwakiutl did lack the clearly bounded, exogamous descent groups named after ancestral nonhuman species, the classic example of "totemic" social organization. Kwakiutl residential units, or *numayma,* were not, strictly speaking, descent groups at all.[1] Their names, while occasionally poetic, did not normally identify them with animals, plants, or other natural phenomena. In his nearly exhaustive compilation of clan names of those groups speaking Kwakiutl dialect (i.e., Koskimo and Kwakiutl), Boas lists eighty-six clan names, most of them glossed with what one assumes are literal translations (Boas, 1897:329–333). The vast majority of these names refer to social prerogatives or status characteristics such as "the chiefs," "whom no one dares to look at," "those who receive first," "the supporters," "the rich ones," and "people from the head waters of the river." Only two of the names bear any totemic associations, "crabs" and "thunderbirds." This is in sharp contrast to the thoroughly totemic clan names Boas provides for the Tlingit (1897:324).

Moreover, a closer look at the presumed totemism of some of the northern tribes does nothing to clarify the matter. In none of the groups of the northwest coast are the animals that figure in local art and myth held to be ancestors of the clan members in a strict genealogical sense (Boas, 1897:324). Durkheim attributed this apparent absence of a notion of descent from animal ancestors among the Haida, Tlingit, and Tsimshian to "a more highly developed mentality" in the Americas. The American groups did not appear to manifest the "confusions so troubling to the mind" that such totemistic beliefs, common in Australia, seemed to imply (Durkheim, 1915:135).

Yet Durkheim recognized that something like classic totemism was clearly evident in the northwest coast populations:

> It is true that there are societies (the Haida, Tlingit, Tsimshian) where it is no longer admitted that a man was born of an animal or plant; but the idea of an affinity between the animals of the totemic species and the members of the clan has survived there nonetheless, and expresses itself in myths which, though differing from the preceding, still retain all that is essential in them. [Durkheim, 1915:135]

Even the southern Kwakiutl tribes placed considerable emphasis on special relationships between social groups and totemlike figures. Especially prominent are mythical, ancestral animals whose features were inscribed on Kwakiutl house posts, cannibal poles, house carvings, and feast dishes. These animal representations or "crests" were not necessarily the exclusive property of *numayma.* Nor was each descent group associated with only a single figure. Instead, these animal crests symbolized complex relationships between a *numayma* and what we call the natural world. These relationships involved not only concerns with social classification but also an interest in human origins, reproduction, and regeneration. Totemic emblems embodied Kwakiutl understandings about the physical and spiritual interconnectedness of the human, natural, and spiritual domains.

CONSUMING INTEREST: KWAKIUTL ANIMAL SYMBOLISM

Though the Kwakiutl did not possess the classic form of totemism, multiplex relationships between animals and humans dominated their religious beliefs and practices and figured prominently in their artistic productions. Kwakiutl myth and ritual were populated by a variety of creatures that were either animal or animal-like humanoid spirits. ravens, wolves, grizzly bears, thunderbirds, salmon, seals, sparrows, beavers, Sisiutl (the double-headed serpent), and Hozhoq (the great brain-devouring crane) are all animal figures with human qualities. On the other hand, Dzonoqwa (wild woman), Hamatsa and Hamshamtses (cannibal spirits), Baxbakualanuxsiwae (the chief cannibal, whose body is covered with snapping mouths), Winalagilis (making-war-all-over-the-Earth) are all examples of more humanoid figures who manifest destructive powers associated with animals. This compromised status, between animal and human, has something to do with the issue of whether "cannibal" or "man eater" is an appropriate translation for Baxbakualanuxsiwae (Goldman, 1975:10).

The Kwakiutl entered into several kinds of relationships with the numerous animal species around them. They hunted and fished them for flesh and for fur. The bulk of their meat diet was from the abundant resources of the sea and the rivers: whales, seals, sea lions, codfish, halibut, herring, oulachon, and, of course, salmon (Boas, 1897:318). In the summer, the fish was baked over hot coals, or it might be dried—either in the sun or over fires—for use in the winter. Bears, elk, birds, and, in the winter, deer provided supplementary protein (p. 319). Smaller animals like beaver, mink, otter, martin, and fur seals "donated" their skins for clothing and blankets, so that these animals circulated in cycles of human marital exchange and ritual initiation of chiefs' sons.

The Kwakiutl viewed their subsistence relationships with animals as a form of exchange rather than as predatory. Animals were believed to confer their flesh and skins on humans in the fulfillment of a covenant by which each species agreed to contribute to the regeneration of the other (Boas, 1930:133). Goldman described this as a pact "for reciprocal benefits, which would sustain the permanent circulation of life: The animals sustain mankind, mankind would sustain them" (Goldman, 1975:124). This can only mean that the ritual activities of the Winter Ceremonial must be understood as form of repayment by the Kwakiutl to the animals who, having given life for human renewal in the hunt, are ritually revitalized. "The encounter between the chiefly hunter and his prey seems to involve a vital interchange. The animal yields its life for the welfare of the community. The hunter dedicates himself in turn to the rituals of maintaining the continuity of the life cycle for all" (Goldman, 1975:53).

Goldman characterizes the Kwakiutl view of the animal-human relationship in an apt genetic metaphor:

> The relations between men and animals may be visualized as two strands, coiled helix-wise around each other, touching at some points, separating at others, but always

symmetrically positioned. When they touch, they exchange powers; when they are separate, they reflect each other—humans appear as animals, and animals as humans.
[p.185]

The double-helix image nicely suggests the involvement of animals and humans
in each other's regeneration and also that these processes involve both metaphorical
relations (of distance and symbolic reference) and metonymic relations (of proximity
and incorporation).

Stanley Walens suggests this tension in the way the Kwakiutl conceived of animal-human relations. He proposes for the Kwakiutl a conception of metaphor that
transcends its usual paradoxical status as proposing at once that two propositions are
the same and that they are not the same. Resemblance for the Kwakiutl, Walens
argues, was understood as both transformation and identification.

> [F]or the Kwakiutl metaphors express not merely likeness, not merely similes, but
> equivalences, and . . . the central importance of transformation in Kwakiutl ontology
> is a statement not of how one thing is like another (and, therefore not the same as the
> other) but of how one thing is another, of how it becomes another by being eaten by it.
> [Walens, 1981:18]

Walens emphasizes the connections between (1) imitation, (2) metaphor, and (3)
procreation through the assimilation and transformation of food. His analysis sheds
light on why the Kwakiutl characterized their ceremonial life as "fraud" or "simulation" (Boas, 1966:172ff; Goldman, 1975:104; Levi-Strauss, 1967b). The idea that
animal-human metaphors could become vehicles for transformative relations between
humans and animals, with eating as the transforming operator, provides a fascinating
literal rendering of Max Black's interaction theory of metaphor. Black, in a famous
formulation, proposed that metaphor works by an "interaction" between the literal
and figurative meaning of a metaphorical proposition, transforming both in the process (Black, 1962, 1977).[2] For the Kwakiutl, ritual, which is to say symbolic representation, is a kind of creation, linked to the "taming" of destructive powers of
the world (cf. Boas, 1966:260).[3]

TWO SEASONS

The Kwakiutl understood their relations with animals both through metaphorical comparison and metonymic conjunction. But the dominant symbolic modality of this
connection shifted seasonally. During the summer season, the Kwakiutl held that
baxus, or secular life, "was on top," while *tsetseqa,* or spiritual existence, was "on
the bottom" (Boas, 1897:418; Goldman, 1975:103, 180). Biologically generative
processes predominated during the summer. Spiritual propagation, in the form of
ritual artifice, became the dominant reproductive mode of the winter season, when
the natural generative processes were dormant. As a form of sustenance, ritual commemoration is analogous to dried fish—both provided sustenance in the winter season.[4] Both were means of preserving forms of life in the interest of overcoming death
in winter.

Walens argues that the differences between secular and sacred seasons was linked to changes in how the Kwakiutl conceived of their relations to the world of spirits.

> Sacred and secular behavior are conceived as two totally different states of existence. In a secular state, the relationships called to the fore are human/human relationships, involving individuals only as individuals. In a state of sacredness, however, analogies are created that abrogate or de-emphasize ties between humans and replace them with ties that unite individual humans with individual spirits. [Walens, 1981:41]

Walens then provides a diagrammatic representation (Figure 8.1) of this seasonal shift in the animal/human relationship (1981:42).

Though Walens makes no reference to Levi-Strauss, his diagrams closely approximate Levi-Strauss's representations in *The Savage Mind* of true and false conceptions of the totemic relationship (Levi-Strauss, 1969:115), reproduced as Figure 7.1 in the previous chapter. In Levi-Strauss' s view, anthropologists have long been misled by the assumption that totemism proposed actual identifications between a human group (often an exogamous descent group) and a species held to be ancestral to that group. Levi-Strauss's correction of the totemic "illusion" was to argue that totemic emblems were logical "operators" that proposed analogies between two sets of oppositions, a natural set drawn from an inventory of natural species and a cultural set of allied but opposed social groups.

In light of the Kwakiutl case, Levi-Strauss appears to be only partly right. For Levi-Strauss, the "correct" understanding of totemism is what Walens identifies for the Kwakiutl as *secular* relations. What the Kwakiutl understand as the sacred union achieved between the spirit world and the human becomes in Levi-Strauss's formulation the classic *misreading* of totemism. Yet it would appear that, at least for the Kwakiutl case, Levi-Strauss's intellectualist solution to the totemic "problem" has been at the expense of totemism's sacred dimension.[5]

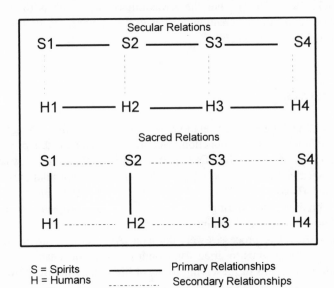

Figure 8.1. Kwakiutl Human-Spirit Relations: Secular and Sacred Versions

The dialectic for the Kwakiutl is between animal signs used for metaphorical ends in establishing differences and animals signs as mediators used to enact participation (metonymies) between distinct realms. This dialectical view of the unstable status of totemic symbolism requires a more complex understanding of analogy than we are accustomed to. In Waléns's view, Kwakiutl analogies continually undo their own status as signs:

> [A]nalogies collapse connections of one kind precisely so that others can be constructed. In the Kwakiutl case the homologic, syntagmatic connections between humans are collapsed so that the analogic connections between humans and spirits can be erected. . . . Yet, since there are situations in which these syntagmatic relations between humans need to be reestablished, the structure of analogies must also permit the deconstruction of the analogy itself. An analogy joins a thing and its symbol, but it can do so only because the distinction between it and its symbol is always implicit and emergent. The structure of an analogy must permit both the power of the analogy to encompass, and the realization that an analogy is only an artificial construct. [Walens, 1981:67]

Kwakiutl animal symbols had a clearly classificatory function. In the summer season, the emphasis was on parallelism and on formal analogies of the kind Levi-Strauss understood as central to totemism. Human ranking was echoed in the natural world by orders of precedence among animals. The eagle was believed to eat first, and wolf, deer and mink were other chiefs of the forest creatures. The vegetable realm had similar hierarchy (Goldman, 1975:179).

Lineage and tribal histories are represented iconically through ensembles of carved totemic figures that make up the totem and cannibal poles decorating both the exterior and the inside of Kwakiutl houses. These and other carved animal images decorating feast dishes and wooden treasure boxes constituted emblems or "crests" of creatures with special mythical relations to the group.

As we have seen, *numayma* names were not normally totemic for the Kwakiutl. On the other hand, the secret societies of the winter season tended to utilize animal species for naming. Most important were the Seal and Sparrow societies, which figured prominently in the staging of the Winter Ceremonial. But other societies also bore animal names (Boas, 1966:180). Thus, during the summer season, the relations between animals and humans remained largely metaphorical in the usual sense. But during the winter season, the analogies literally consumed themselves. What was metaphorical became metonymic. Humans and animals encountered each other through relations of assimilation, incorporation, and mutual transformation. Rather than the sexual symbolism that pervades Australian concepts of totem-human interdependence, the Kwakiutl conceived of their relations with their spirit ancestors through images of eating.

ORAL TRADITIONS: SWALLOWING TRIBES

In Kwakiutl thought, sexual reproduction was at once revealed and concealed through oral imagery. Walens's account of the Kwakiutl worldview documents in detail the pervasiveness of oral symbolism (Walens, 1981):

' The Kwakiutl world is predicated on a single fundamental assumption: that the universe is a place where some beings are eaten by other beings and where it is the role of some beings to die so that other beings may feed on them and live. Theirs is a world where the act of eating becomes the single metaphor by which the rest of their lives is interpreted. Food provides for them a model of the nature of life; the act of eating provides a model of assimilation that recurs throughout every aspect of their culture: and the food chain itself provides the link between one human and another and between humans and the rest of the world. Metaphors of eating and assimilation provide the model by which the Kwakiutl can encompass items within a particular single rubric by which they can differentiate between items. Metaphors of assimilation and eating provide the cognitive model by which the Kwakiutl predicate the structure and process of their universe. [1981:12]

Totemic animals were classified in large part through specific oral characteristics: shape of mouth, eating habits, preferred foods, and so on (Walens, 1981:98–99). Through vivid associations with swallowing and biting, the mouth was represented as a seat of aggression and death. Man-Eater-at-the-North-End-of-the-World is portrayed in myth and ritual as a grotesque carnivore, whose body is covered with snapping mouths, ready to swallow all he encounters. Status competition between tribes during the winter season was conceived through the idiom of one tribe attempting to swallow the other.

But the Kwakiutl symbolic mode is clearly dialectical, and the same images that proposed death also proposed its transcendence: "For Kwakiutl, all metaphysical issues of antagonism are resolved simply and neatly by the Hegelian trick of transformation into opposites: death turns to life, life to death. As the *hamatsa* dancer sings: 'I do not destroy life. I am the life maker' " (Goldman, 1975:104).

In this way, the mouth became a source of both destruction and regeneration for the Kwakiutl. This was accomplished in several ways. First, the destructive imagery of swallowing is reversed and overcome by the creative act of vomiting. Thus, in some of the cannibal poles, animals are portrayed hanging out of the mouths of other animals: a food chain. What is so startling about the effect of this imagery is that it is impossible to tell if they are being swallowed or regurgitated. The dialectic of destruction and regeneration that we know as the food chain is given a strikingly literal form.

Second, the balance of life and death, by which one creature dies so another can live, is commemorated in Kwakiutl beliefs about hunting. The generative power of hunting is also suggested by the myths that relate the initial encounters between the original animal spirits and the lineages with which they come to have a privileged relation (Boas, 1966:304ff).

Third, the ritualization of aggression is itself the most basic level at which destructive forces are converted into generative ones. The Kwakiutl were aware that replacing war with ritual was a life-enhancing activity. This is the secret of the power Kwakiutl attributed to sham or fraud over life itself. Through the powers of artifice, winter's death-dealing forces could be tamed. Not only did the rituals dramatize the taming of death figures but the very enactment of the drama itself becomes part of the "taming" process. As the dancers tamed the Hamatsa, so the dancing tamed the dancers. Boas records, for instance, the repeated claim during a Winter Ceremonial performance that in the old days crests and privileges were passed down directly from the animal spirits from which the beneficiaries were descended. No ritual was available (Boas, 1966:258). But the old days, before ritual controlled human relations with the spirits, were not understood as a golden age. Boas recorded the following potlatch speech, expressing a belief in the life-giving power of ceremony: "In former times I and my people have suffered at your hands, Kwa'g.ul. We used to fight with bows and arrows, with spears and guns. We robbed each other's blood. But now we fight with this here [pointing at the copper which he was holding in his hand] and if we have no coppers, we fight with canoes or blankets. That is all" (Boas, 1966:206).

Finally, while the explicit theme of the Winter Ceremonial and the potlatch feasts was linked with death and loss, the implicit theme was always regeneration and excess. Every loss would result in increase. Some came to call it "profit." Thus, to be feasted by a Kwakiutl tribe meant to be ritually swallowed, but it also meant to receive vast quantities of food and wealth. To win was to lose; to lose was to win. This is the great dialectic that dominated the dramas of the Winter Ceremonial (Boas, 1966, chap. 8; Goldman, 1975; chaps. 5 and 6). Thus, Kwakiutl myths and ritual drama frequently enacted the depletion of the tribe through sudden and inexplicable death, specifically through the mock loss of a chief's son. But the subtext was always the son's return and his succeeding to his father's office.

Metaphors of destruction are assimilated by images of generation and abundance. The very act of swallowing another tribe or *numayma* in a potlatch was often intended to celebrate not war or destruction but fruitful marriage between the rivals. The "swallowing" thus entailed the transfer of powers, ceremonial prerogatives, and wealth from the bride's father to the groom's family on behalf of the offspring of the marriage. Bride-wealth payments by the groom's family were no match for the ongoing plenitude that flowed from the bride's family (Boas, 1966:311; Goldman, 1975:77–78). This is not only a political or economic statement about status rivalry but a vivid representation of the increase that was associated with the bride's fertility properly channeled through ritual.

ALIMENTARY STRUCTURES OF KINSHIP

One of the most peculiar aspects of Kwakiutl symbolism is the relative paucity of explicitly sexual symbols in a culture obsessed with issues of regeneration. The pattern is set out at the beginning in the myths that detail the relationships between the tribes and their ancestral spirit animals. These origin myths are not about ancestral progenitors. For the Kwakiutl, sexuality does not seem to be the primary way in which totemic origins are to be conceived. Instead, their myths tell of the "coming down to the beach" of the ancestral animal spirits who removed their animal skins and became men. These foundational acts, commemorated in the Winter Ceremonial in the donning and removing of costumes, suggest a theatrical idiom for creation. Human and spirit made a covenant that would forever implicate each in the regeneration of the other (Boas, 1966:258, 304–305). Genesis is not directly about sex, eros, or death but about the relationship between hunting and ritual commemoration. Animals would, through the donation of their flesh in the hunt, continue to provide for the life of the Kwakiutl. For their part, the Kwakiutl would ritually perpetuate the spirit ancestors by periodically assuming animal form in the winter dances (Boas, 1930:144; Goldman, 1975:53).

The totemic "line," as represented by the totem poles, suggests that the generations were conceived of as a food chain rather than more directly through birth imagery. A powerful conflation of oral and genital symbolism is apparent. A number of observers of Kwakiutl art have noted the not infrequent substitution in Kwakiutl animal art of mouths for genitalia (Boas, 1897:377, 395; Fowler, 1972:125; Walens, 1981:145).[6]

An alimentary theory of reproduction is the most obvious meaning of this symbolism. It is also conceivable that the oral symbolism represents a kind of logocentric vision of genesis, with words and other ritual forms replacing organic generation. This second interpretation is consistent with Goldman's contention that the Kwakiutl notion of asexual reproduction implies a kind of ritual transmission of life along a male line. This masculine form of ritual propagation of life both parallels and seeks to encompass sexual reproduction through women:

> The confinement of all principal exchanges to men and among men implies a concept of asexual propagation of vital entities. We may go so far as to say that the incarnation involved in the assumption of a new name is like a birth. . . . This analogue of birth is, however, postulated as a spiritualized and desexualized process, one that is the primary prerogative of men. The process takes a parallel asexual form in the primary exchange when a male ancestor sheds his animal form soul, thereby propagating the propatrilineal transmission of the crest. [Goldman, 1975:140]

Though the co-optation by males of feminine generative symbolism is a common form of symbolic domination, the Kwakiutl go one step further. Sexual imagery is pushed offstage completely and is replaced by a novel and male-dominated idiom for reproduction. One entire metaphorical universe is masked by another, deriving its very power from the sexual meanings it has consumed. Kwakiutl conception beliefs stress various notions of oral conception of life (Walens, 1981:104). Pregnancy is attributed, in part, to the power of reptiles, especially frogs. In the hope of conceiving, women squat over a place where a frog had been sitting or eat a potion containing lizards' heads (Walens, 1981:117). Walens proposes for the Kwakiutl a notion of reproduction by direct transformation. Notably, beliefs about the regeneration of salmon conceptualized the spawn of salmon not as eggs, which would grow into fry, but as a kind of excrescence of old salmon that would directly and magically regenerate into new salmon (Walens, 1981:106). The image is closer to vomiting than it is to sexual genesis.

In terms of marriage, ritual exchange rather than female fecundity was stressed as the way in which tribal alliances overcame death. The fecundity that was emphasized was not that of the bride directly but rather a kind of indirect transmission by her father who, through marriage, transmitted wealth and ritual privileges down to his son-in-law (Boas, 1966:311). Among the most valuable of these marriage treasures passed between tribes to sons-in-law were feast dishes in the form of ancestral animals (Boas, 1897:390–394). Goldman describes these dishes as "symbolizing a range of life-conserving powers, from the elementary act of eating to the metaphysical issues of death and resurrection" (Goldman, 1975:77). Once again, sexual metaphors are consumed by alimentary ones.

A TOTAL REGENERATIVE ARTIFACT

For the Kwakiutl, the totemic animal was the single most important guarantee that Man-Eater would not finally win out in the struggle to perpetuate life. The totemic animal participated in regenerative cycles in three distinct ways. To appreciate how the animal functioned as a kind of total regenerative artifact, we need to examine the triple fate of the animal in Kwakiutl hands.

First, by donating its flesh to the hunter, the animal participated in the regeneration of the human body. For the Kwakiutl, to live off of animal flesh was to participate in the physical life of the donor. Humans could be said to be human on the outside but animal within, just as ancestral animals were human on the inside but animal without. Animals take off their skins to become human, but humans don those very skins as clothes for survival and, in the winter, as costumes for spiritual renewal. Human and animal formed a single thread of life, a continuous chain of participations, perpetually exchanging insides and outsides.

This layering of animal on human on animal is vividly apparent in many of the Kwakiutl masks, in which animal faces open to reveal an inner mask that is more human (see Boas, 1897:464, 470). One only need add to the effect the next two layers, the human face under the mask and the animal-generated flesh beyond the human skin, to appreciate the power of the Kwakiutl imagery.

The flesh consumed, the Kwakiutl utilized the animal skins for the second great chain of life: marriage. Before they were replaced by Hudson Bay blankets, animal skins were the primary media of marriage exchange. In this way animals participated in the regeneration of the human species. The recognition of the original significance of animal skins in Kwakiutl thought, and their eventual transformation into the Hudson Bay blankets used in potlatches, is one of the most significant contributions of Goldman's reanalysis of the Kwakiutl (Goldman, 1975:60–61, 227–228).

The third way in which the animal contributed to human propagation was through its form, or outer shape. This shape was considered a kind of soul and its reproduction in works of art and in costume was one of the ways in which humans propagated their spiritual ancestors. This propagation of form was mutual, however, since these forms became the basis of sacred crests which, transmitted lineally within the chiefly *numayma,* guaranteed the conceptual continuity of the chiefly line. Crests—embodied on posts, houses, feast dishes, boxes, masks, and costumes—were the animals' gifts of their intelligible forms. What this gift made possible was symbolic reproduction of the *numayma* itself, through its sacred emblems. The feast dishes were made in such a way that in eating from them, one reenacted the incorporation of the animal's flesh and the transformation of the outer form into an distinct artifact.

Here, at last, we recognize the missing classificatory function of the totemic species. Up to now the metaphorical function of the Kwakiutl totem had been lost in the complex of unstable incorporative relations that defined the totemic animal as both eater and eaten in the alimentary chain of life. As crests, however, animals took on the emblematic function to which anthropologists have reduced the totemic operator. Goldman distinguishes between the exchange modalities that involved animal skins and those that involves crests:

> Crests are individual, and have epithetic names; animal skins are generalized and are namelessly generic. Crests move down precise channels of patrilineal and matrilineal kinship, animal skins circulate ceaselessly within the tribes. The crest is the form soul of an ancestor who was dual (animal, or other, and human). But the skins of hunted animals are those of ordinary and unitary beasts, and therefore. . . belong exclusively to the animal world. [Goldman, 1975:125]

The triple status of the animal in Kwakiutl religious thought (Figure.8.2) suggests the full complexity and ambiguity of the totemic relationship.[7]

PURITY AS DANGER

It is clear from this analysis of Kwakiutl totemic symbolism how much is lost by reducing totemism to its classificatory function. Because the totemic species often bear multiple relations to a group's conception of itself, it is much more useful to retain rather than purge the ambiguities that have characterized classical accounts of totemism. For the Kwakiutl, animals were not thought of exclusively or even primarily as a classificatory code for ordering human relations taxonomically. Animals were total regenerative artifacts, participating with humans in cycles of reproduction— physical, spiritual, and intellectual. As food, the dominant symbolic modality was incorporative and participatory. However "illogical" such participations may sound to us, they were empirically rational, based on impeccable facts about eating, assimilation, and the interdependence of a chain of life that linked animals with humans and one tribe with another. As skins, the emphasis was on symbolic mediation between human groups and the momentary transformability of tribal opposition into unity through marriage. And as crests, animals entered into metaphorical relationships with humans and came closest to serving a genuine classificatory function.

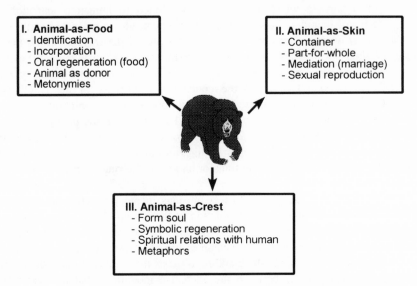

Figure 8.2. The Triple Fate of the Kwakiutl Totemic Animal

These three distinct symbolic modalities were never fully separable. Classification (or separation) always implied for the Kwakiutl the overcoming and incorporation of the other. For the Kwakiutl, their consuming interest in symbolic incorporation and transformation meant that classification could never exhaust the functions of a symbolic model. Goldman put it succinctly: "In the Kwakiutl scheme, categorical purity is a defect" (Goldman, 1975:189). From a semiotic perspective, animals functioned for the Kwakiutl as multivocal "polytropes" rather than as pure metaphors (Friedrich, 1991; Turner, 1991).

TOTEMISM AND SYMBOLIC MOTIVATION

The ability of symbolic analysis to illuminate *what* things mean requires that we understand *how things come to have meaning.* We need an adequate conception of the various ways in which the world takes on symbolic form for people. This issue has been approached in two ways. The first way in which semiotic theories have tried to classify symbols is in terms of the different possible types of symbolic vehicles. These typologies have focused on how signifier and signified are linked. Most famous, perhaps, is Peirce's elaborate typology of signs (Peirce, 1932). Of the numerous subtle distinctions made by Peirce, three have become relatively influential in anthropology. The distinction between iconic, indexical, and conventional signs (legisigns) has proven useful in characterizing different kinds of cultural symbols (Daniel, 1984). Other significant distinctions include analog versus digital codes (Bateson, 1972; Shore, 1990b; Wilden, 1972), signs versus symbols (Langer, 1957), and physiognomic versus arbitrary signs (Werner and Kaplan, 1963).

The second major way in which symbolic forms have been approached has been to focus on what people can do with signs—in other words, how signs work in specific contexts. This "pragmatic" approach to symbolic analysis has used Austin's notion of performatives in language use to distinguish the work done by linguistic signs in different sorts of discourse (Austin, 1962; Murray 1977). Pragmatic approaches to signs are important because they draw our attention to the intentions of people as they use or interpret signs.

These theoretical approaches in semiotics vary in terms of whether they emphasize the *logical* characteristics of the sign or the *psychological* relation of a sign user to the sign.[8] Thus, for instance, it is commonly (but wrongly) assumed that the iconic or indexical qualities of a sign can be determined without reference to the intentions of any subject. On the other hand, Werner and Kaplan's notion of the *physiognomic* apprehension of signs emphasizes the psychological qualities of the apprehension of signs by users rather than the formal character of the sign itself (Werner and Kaplan, 1963). Performatives go one step further than considering how signs are apprehended. They are based on a typology of intentions by users that distinguishes proposing, persuading, and enacting as alternative uses for language signs.

The analysis of totemic symbolism in this chapter suggests a need to formulate a more coherent conception of signs that takes into account their degree and type of motivation (Ullman, 1957).[9] The notion of *symbolic motivation* implies some kind of nonarbitrary relationship between a signifier and its referent. In Peirce's terms, iconic and indexical signs are both highly motivated—the former by relations of formal analogy, the latter by concrete metonymy (or participation). Purely conventional or arbitrary signs, on the other hand, are usually held to be unmotivated, though they are better thought of as socially or conventionally motivated. Some writers have distinguished such arbitrary signs as "symbols," though this usage is notoriously inconsistent and confusing (Finegan and Besnier, 1989; Langer, 1957:58–61; Saussure, 1959; Sperber, 1975). The less motivated the sign, the greater is its referential freedom. Linguistic symbols (signs, in the Saussurian tradition) have often been characterized as largely arbitrary (Finegan and Besnier, 1989:3; Saussure, 1959; Shore, 1987).

All signs, but especially arbitrary ones, are potential means of taxonomic classification. Arbitrary signs classify largely through the enforcement of categorical distinction and conventional assignment. Iconic signs classify on the basis of analogies that rely both on preexisting similarities and on subjective constructions of similarity. Metonymic signs, or what Langer calls "symptoms" (Langer, 1957:57), are especially interesting in the totemic context, because they are inherently compromised as classifiers. In their freedom of representation, metonymic signs are part way between arbitrary symbols and icons. Freed from the constraints of iconic fidelity, metonymic classifiers are nonetheless not fully free, always restrained by functional and practical relations to their referent. Metonymic signs (like smoke, blood, food, droppings, or pheromones) are "participatory" symbols, never quite achieving a full detachment of the signifier and signified. What metonymic signs lack in their ability to establish arbitrary differences they make up for in their ability to model concrete transformative processes.

Symbolic motivation is always both a logical and a psychological fact. This means that no matter how much "natural" resemblance a signifier bears to its referent, the analogy must be perceived as such in order to be effective. The first life of any sign lies in the *empirical nature* of the relation a signifier bears to a referent. Signs have different sorts of *affordances* for producing psychological meaning. The sign's second life is in the establishment of a *psychological relationship* between signifier and referent in someone's mind. This "double birth" of signs is the subject of the final two chapters of this book.

Any iconicity of signs is in some part a psychological construct. But clearly, some signs appear to be *empirically motivated* more than others. Idiographic writing systems employ abstract signs, but they are generally more empirically motivated than alphabetic systems. On the other hand, it is clear that even in the absence of much empirical correlation between sign and referent, humans tend to perceive even abstract signs—like words, personal names, or inkblots—as if they were motivated and bore an internal correspondence to their referents. I call this kind of purely subjective motivation of signs *psychogenic motivation* and distinguish it from *empirical motivation.*[10]

Psychogenic motivation has been most commonly noted in relation to sound symbolisms and synesthesia, processes that will be discussed in some detail in Chapter 14. Werner and Kaplan have used something like this concept in discussing the earliest basis of all symbol perception (Werner and Kaplan, 1966). In their view, the arbitrariness of symbols is "achieved" by subjects only gradually and partially by overcoming an initial "physiognomic" apprehension of symbols that ties them to bodily experience.[11]

Psychogenic motivation points to the active role of the subject in constructing analogies between signs and their referents. Werner and Kaplan refer to this process as the "inner structuralization" of a sign by the subject. Such analogic constructions motivate to some degree even the most apparently abstract and arbitrary symbols. Psychogenic motivation appears to be a central process in all metaphorical production and is probably tied to meaning-making processes central to human cognition. This means that all signs in human use are motivated to some extent, since analogic construction requires some perception of empirically available properties of both sign and referent. But clearly there are differences between signs in the degree of empirical versus psychogenic motivation (see Figure 8.3).

For conventional signs, the work of psychogenic motivation increases in proportion to the arbitrariness of the sign. But for natural symbols—signs drawn more directly from human encounters with the world—the notion of motivation becomes more complex and problematic. Natural signs tend to fall on the empirical end of the spectrum, though, as Levi-Strauss has shown, animal signs can in some contexts approach a heavily arbitrary status as a code.

Langer has suggested that natural signs tend to have distinctive characteristics: "A natural sign is a part of a greater event, or of a complex condition, and to an experienced observer, it signifies the rest of that situation of which it is a notable feature. It is a *symptom* of a state of affairs" (Langer, 1957:57, emphasis in original).

Langer is suggesting that natural signs tend to be grasped indexically by subjects, because such signs participate materially in the larger context of which they are a part. In the case of animal symbolism, however, this indexicality entails a more intimate form of metonymy, in which the relation moves between representation and actual assimilation. Thus we have, among empirically motivated signs, a secondary distinction between those whose motivation is metaphorical and conceptual and those whose motivation is metonymic, and functional (Figure 8.4).

The ambiguities of totemic symbols can be understood in light of the status of animals as signs. Totemic signs may occupy various positions along the metaphor-metonym scale, as illustrated in Figure 8.4. These variations constitute the crux of the totemic "problem" that has occupied anthropologists for a century. Levi-Strauss has brilliantly demonstrated the degree to which animals suggest metaphorical humans and has thereby grounded totemism in a theory of classification. But Levi-

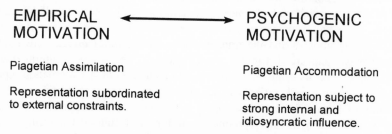

Figure 8.3. Two Types of Symbolic Motivation

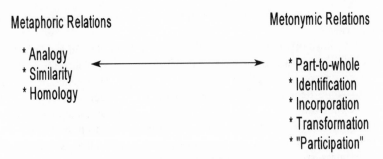

Figure 8.4. Dimensions of Variation among Empirically Motivated Signs

Strauss's view of totemic symbols defined such metaphorical relations largely in formal terms as systems of opposition, and therefore his account lacked any significant theory of motivation.

But, as the Kwakiutl case illustrates, animals can also easily be understood as metonymic humans, through images of eating and assimilation.[12] As incorporative signs, totemic animals are empirically motivated by the activities of hunting and eating. They constitute metonymic signs for humans, and thereby provided a way for the Kwakiutl to conceptualize the chain of life and death that links the human and animal worlds in concrete ties of regeneration. For the Kwakiutl, the value of totems as metaphors tended to be assimilated and overshadowed by their metonymic value, their literal "participations" with animals as concrete relations. The Kwakiutl seem less interested in animals as classifiers than as material and spiritual participants in human life. So we do not find, in this part of the world, elaborate totemic taxonomies of the sort so well documented for Australian aboriginal totemism.

In light of the power and truth value of such symbolism, we need to reconsider just what Lévy-Bruhl's concept of "participation" might really mean.[13] The mysteries of organic transformation and interdependence are fundamentally different from the questions of classification and logic that have dominated anthropological discussions of totemism. And so the question of the "rationality" of totemic beliefs and practices cannot be considered exclusively in terms of their adherence to principles of categorical logic. As Vygotsky reminds us in the epigraph at the head of this chapter, concepts as embodied in human intentional worlds are living entities, not ossified museum pieces. They serve human ends—ends that may be practical, intellectual, or esthetic or any combination of the three. It profits us little simply to assume that cultural forms as rich and complex as totemic symbols speak to all humans with a single voice and a unique function. The divergences between the classificatory (metaphorical) impulse and the transformative (metonymic) impulse are matters of local emphasis and are distributed quite differently in different cultural traditions. The use of animals as symbolic classifiers and as images of transformation represents different moments, each rational in its way, in the general dialectic by which the continuity of forms of life is linked both to the physical transformation of those life forms and to their symbolic reproduction as forms of cultural knowledge. To arbitrarily declare only one of these moments to be the essence of totemism is to take arbitrariness one step too far.

Notes

1. The Kwakiutl *numayma* (meaning "one kind") has proven relatively recalcitrant to definition in conventional anthropological terms. Boas both stressed the importance of patrilineal descent ideology in matters of succession and inheritance (Boas, 1966:52, 53) and denied that the *numayma* was either strictly patrilineal or matrilineal (1966:51). Though the chiefly core of the *numayma* was a true patrilineage, not all members traced common descent, which means that the *numayma* was a "descent group" only in a very loose sense. Commoner members of the group were often related to the chief by a variety of nongenealogical ties (Goldman, 1975:36–37, Boas, 1966:43–44). The aristocratic lineage provided basis for both patrilineal ideology and authority, while the structural continuity of the unit stressed not so much a succession of leaders linked through patrifiliation as a more abstract set of names, titles, and privileges—a bequest by ancestral spirits to the *numayma* (Boas, 1966:50; Goldman, 1975:37). For Levi-Strauss, the *numayma* was an example of a nonunilineal descent group of a kind more commonly found in Polynesia. Because coresidence rather than common descent underlay its coherence as a unit, Levi-Strauss termed the Kwakiutl a "house society" (Levi-Strauss, 1982), employing the Kwakiutl's own stress on the house as the unifying image for conceptualizing the *numayma*.

2. For a psychological treatment of metaphor using this same notion, see Ortony, 1979.

3. This Kwakiutl association of symbolism and metaphor with "taming" of death and with regeneration is probably more widespread. Specifically, a similar set of associations may underlie Durkheim's claim that, for the Arunta, the symbolic representations of the totemic beings were more sacred than the beings themselves (Durkheim, 1915:133).

4. The connection between dried fish and ritual is more than simply metaphorical. Dried fish appear as an actual element in the Winter Ceremonial itself (Boas, 1966:233).

5. For the Yolngu (Murngin) of northern Australia, the symbolic relations between dancers and totemic animals are understood as the "outside" meaning, masking a deeper "inside" set of identifications between creatures who are outwardly distinct. See Chapter 9.

6. Walens notes with interest the role of the frog in Kwakiutl fertility ritual: "Frogs play a particularly large part in impregnation ritual perhaps because, with their large mouths and long tongues with bulbous tips, they reproduce both phallic and vaginal images" (Walens, 1981:117).

What is also obvious in this description is the equally important conflating of oral and genital penetration.

7. Compare Levi-Strauss 1966:106–108. Levi-Strauss's quite similar analysis of the symbolism of food divisions among the Elema of New Guinea is intended, however, to underscore the ideological distinction of human and animal forms for this group, rather than their consubstantiality. Yet, as the Kwakiutl case reveals, so-called totemic beliefs and practices often betray a more equivocal attitude toward human-animal identifications, affirming them on one level as they are undercut on another.

8. Langer calls this distinction the difference between the "logical" and the "psychological" aspects of signs (Langer, 1957:53).

9. The discussion of symbolic motivation is complicated by a lack of agreement on basic terminology. Sometimes, in the literature on semiotics, *symbols* are distinguished from *signs* by the fact that the former are motivated while the latter are not (i.e., are arbitrary). As Sperber has noted, however, these distinctions are often hard to maintain (Sperber, 1975:23 ff). Moreover Peirce, whose theory of motivation has been particularly influential, defined different kinds of motivation in terms of a typology of *signs*.

10. Obeyesekere (1981) uses the concept of "psychogenic" symbols to refer to symbols that have their origin in a general human psyche. He contrasts such symbols with "personal"

symbols, whose explanation requires a more localized understanding of individual biography. This is, obviously, a different kind of distinction from the one made here.

11. Similar ideas have been developed in relation to the role of metaphor in thought. See Lakoff and Johnson, 1980; Lakoff, 1987a; Johnson, 1987. See Chapter 14 for a more complete discussion of this issue.

12. In his provocative analysis of animal naming, Levi-Strauss does indeed consider the implications of name sets for animal species which have a metonymic relation to human society (Levi-Strauss, 1966:204–207; see also Tambiah, 1969). But his notion of metonymic relations between human and animal is highly abstracted and far removed from the sort of consubstantiality that fascinated the Kwakiutl. Thus, though he recognized, for cattle, a status of "metonymical inhuman beings" (p. 207), the metonymy proposed is that cattle "form part of our technical and economic system" (p. 205). The issue of empirical participation between cattle and humans is neatly avoided. Levi-Strauss's appears to be a vegetarian's sensibility.

13. Paul Rozin and Carol Nemeroff at the University of Pennsylvania have carried out a series of fascinating experiments using college students to demonstrate the pervasiveness of the principle of "contagion" in human thought. They discovered that students were very reluctant to ingest anything that had either a formal resemblance to or had come into physical contact with an insect such as a cockroach. This was true even when it was clear that the food was perfectly sterile. Rozin and Nemeroff demonstrated that something very much like "participation" was operative in a wide number of contexts in which exuviae of animals or other individuals was at issue (Rozin and Nemeroff, 1989).

IV
DREAMTIME LEARNING

9

Dreamtime Learning, Inside-Out:
The Narrative of
the Wawilak Sisters

> There is . . . a sort of fundamental antipathy between history and systems of classification.
> —Claude Levi-Strauss

THE TOTEMIC ILLUSION

The "illusion" of totemism was not to be found in the mystical "participation" Lévy-Bruhl recognized in the totemic equations between humans and animals. What was illusory were the false dichotomies perpetuated by generations of observers, dichotomies that artificially distinguished the mystical principles of "primitive thought" from those informing Western logic. These principles were used to construct our own classifications, dividing "primitive" from "civilized" forms of humanity.

Totemic beliefs and practices model in various ways the complex relations and exchanges between human groups and other forms on which humans depend for their continuity and regeneration. Traditionally, those other life forms have been plant and animal species that figured as alimentary and generative images of continuity. In industrial societies, however, the same problems cluster around machine-human relations, producing a distinctive techno-totemism.

By attempting to reduce totemism to either the mystical participations between species or the logical categorizations mapped by totemic emblems, anthropologists have often bypassed the real richness and complexity of totemism. Close analyses of Kwakiutl animal symbolism as well as cyborg images from contemporary science fiction suggest a far more interesting set of models, models that represent a wide range of relations linking animals, machines, humans, and spirits.

From a semiotic perspective, the totemistic complex is not reducible to a single symbolic or cognitive modality. In fact, totemism derives much of its philosophical and symbolic power from its capacity to model the multiple relations humans bear with other forms of life, *and the transformations of those relationships over time.*

207

Not surprisingly, these multiple representations exploit several distinct semiotic and cognitive modes.

The reason that different observers were able to find the essence of totemism in both rationalism and mysticism is that totemism always implies a complex relation between classification and participation. To the extent that human life depends materially on various kinds of exchange with other forms of life (or technology), humans tend to reflect these "participations" symbolically in complex metonymies that model (sometimes "mystically") hybrid forms of life. These metonymies model humanity compromised in its categorical purity by its necessary intercourse with the non-human.

Such is the power of these material connections among forms of life that they may also serve metaphorically as classifiers of difference. As metaphors, animal, plant, or machine emblems propose parallel worlds to humans and engage the human as symbols of classification, modeling difference rather than participation between forms of life. This is what I called totemism's *classificatory moment,* a manifestation of what we identify as the classifying function of mind. But totemism can be reduced to this function only by abstracting it from its rich and complex unity. In its wholeness, totemism proposes a dialectical relationship between the physical reproduction of life through participation and the intellectual regeneration of life forms through categorization.

AUSTRALIAN TOTEMISM

Chapters 9 and 10 are grouped together under the title "Dreamtime Learning." The complex Australian ethnography has been organized here to explore an important problem in cognitive anthropology: the "outside-in" fate of cultural models—the way in which cultural "texts" or "practices" become internalized as experiences. A central problem for cognitive anthropology is how to connect the two lives of any cultural model. All human institutions are necessarily human creations, the projection of someone's feelings and thoughts into publicly accessible forms (Obeyesekere 1981, especially part 5). So from the perspective of objectivist history, human culture might be said to be produced inside-out—from the mind into the world. Yet for any individual born into a community, cultural forms have their first life as instituted models. These external models become experiences only to the extent that they can be translated "outside-in" into mental models—from the social world to the mind.

These "two births" of culture, inside-out and outside-in, present a serious challenge to an adequate cognitive theory of culture. This analysis of Dreamtime learning in an aboriginal setting will provide one ethnographic answer to the question of how culture is brought from the world to the mind. But we will first examine, by way of an astonishingly subtle and rich origin myth, how a group of aborigines conceive of the origin of their cultural forms. The myth recounts a set of primal beings whose actions establish a set of foundational patterns, or models, that comprise what modern Murngin consider their "law." So while Chapter 10 deals with the question of the second birth of culture—outside-in, as mind—this chapter considers how these people represent culture's first birth—inside-out, as external institutions.

A DISTRIBUTIVE VIEW OF CULTURAL KNOWLEDGE

As anthropologists have come to better understand the social life of everyday knowledge, they have increasingly adopted a "distributive" view of culture. Culture is not accurately conceived of as a neat packaging of traditions possessed equally by all members of a community. A distributive view of culture sees culture as a complex knowledge system unevenly appropriated in social and political time and space. The clearest statement of this distributive view of cultural knowledge has come from Fredrik Barth. In a recent work on New Guinea, Barth refers to his object of analysis not as a culture or even a culture area but rather as an "aggregate tradition of knowledge." His goal, he says, is to examine "the (variety of) ideas it contains, and how they are expressed, the pattern of their distribution, within communities and between communities; the processes of (re)production in this tradition of knowledge, and how they may explain its content and pattern of distribution; thus the processes of creativity, transmission and change" (Barth, 1987:1).[1]

Distributive studies of cultural knowledge often stress the "sociology of knowledge," an observer's account of the functional implications of the social allocation of knowledge. The present analysis is a little different. It emphasizes the "culture of knowledge" and its acquisition over time by Murngin youth. The "culture of knowledge" implies a sort of "ethno-epistemology," the folk theory and social practice of knowledge acquisition of a particular community.

THE MURNGIN

Arnhem Land is a vast territory on the northern coast of Australia, bordered by the Arafura Sea to the north and west and the Gulf of Carpentaria to the east. This sprawling coastal region of northern Australia is tropical in climate, with marked alternation between wet and dry seasons. Acacia, ti, and eucalyptus trees provide green respite in an otherwise barren landscape. The vegetation is largely of the savannah variety, and during the rainy season spear grass covers much of the otherwise arid plains. With the coming of the rains, the land is dotted with temporary lakes. Numerous bays and tidal rivers punctuate the coastal regions. The coastal waters abound in edible sea life. Scattered along coastal sites and along the numerous islands lying just offshore is dense mangrove jungle.

The northeast and central regions of Arnhem Land are home to approximately four thousand aborigines who are well known to anthropologists as the Murngin and now tend to be called Yolngu.[2] It is hardly surprising that the problem of the discreteness of cultural units should become apparent in Arnhem Land. Here are populations that until the 1960s wandered their vast and relatively bountiful savannah in "bands" of flexible size, gathering plant foods, hunting small land animals (marsupials and lizards), and fishing the tidal rivers and the sea.

Traditionally the societies of aboriginal Australia were made up of patrilocal bands of foragers lacking clear political or ethnic borders. Australian social organization comprises fission-fusion societies where the size of foraging groups swells or contracts from season to season. Before their total resettlement in government and mission camps, local groups varied from tiny foraging units of up to ten individuals to larger aggregates of a hundred or more for religious celebrations. Typically, these variations were seasonal and depended on the availability of food. Warner's 1936 account underscores the significance of these seasonal changes in rainfall:

> In the rainy season great torrents of tropical rain fall daily, making large portions of the mainland south of the Arafura Sea, for weeks and sometimes months at a time, a series of islands in a shallow sea of mud and water. Then, with rare interruptions there is continuous drought for six or seven months. . . . The water recedes, the water holes become drier and drier, and a large number disappear entirely; birds and fish are gone and the many varieties of lilies and yams disappear. It is then that the native appreciates the value of water, just as before he realized the harm it could do him. . . . It is small wonder that with the food and drink of life dependent on the water holes, and possible death resulting from the great floods, the native has made water his chief symbol of the clan's spiritual life. [Warner, 1936/1958:20]

Starting with European penetration into the northern territories of the subcontinent in the 1920s, the aborigines of Arnhem Land were gradually settled into several mission stations. But since the 1970s, many groups have once again dispersed to their traditional homelands, living at what are now called "outstations," where they feel less vulnerable to European intrusion.

While Murngin elders serve as local leaders and wield an often considerable degree of ritual and political authority, there are no specialized political institutions above the local group, though Murngin elders have since the 1960s effectively lobbied the Australian government on behalf of their land claims (Williams, 1986).[3] Kinship and marriage relations, and the complex obligations they entail among individuals and groups, are the basis of Murngin "politics."

In this kind of setting, local groups, moieties, clans, clan aggregates, dialect groups, and traditional networks through marriage ties all define a complex skein of related groups and categories, with many variations in language and tradition. Here the local "culture" can only be accurately described in Barth's terms as an "aggregate tradition," differentially distributed among numerous groups and individuals. Nonetheless, many of the local groups in northeast Arnhem Land appear to share several important cultural schemas that give them a degree of cultural unity despite this diversity. Still, variations in virtually every important cultural practice are not merely recognized by local groups but are prized as markers of ethnic distinctiveness.

The uneven diffusion of cultural knowledge in this region is not limited to regional variations in understandings. Even within any local group there is a deliberate segregation of men's and women's knowledge traditions. The most sacred rituals and beliefs are largely controlled by men and are (at least in theory) withheld from women. In recent years, however, many of the "inside" or sacred forms of knowledge have been opened up both to Murngin women and to Europeans through the commercialization of Murngin culture. Morphy, however, suggests that what has really happened has been merely the intensification of processes that have always characterized Murngin knowledge creation. Formerly sacred (inside) knowledge has been selectively released, while new forms of inside knowledge have been created to take their place (Morphy, 1991, chap. 5; especially pp. 78 ff).

The distinctions between knowledge appropriate for initiated men and that appropriate for all others remains a powerful force in contemporary Murngin life. The origins and significance of the separation of men's and women's knowledge are important subjects of Murngin ritual and myth. There is also an important allocation of knowledge over social time. Murngin initiation practices control the transmission of knowledge from (certain) elders to (certain) youths at privileged moments. Murngin "religion"[4] is a complex of beliefs and practices that regulates and directs the reproduction of cultural knowledge in such a way as to maximize the power inequalities between men and women and between old and young.

AN ECONOMY OF RELIGIOUS KNOWLEDGE

Keen has written of "an economy of religious knowledge" among the Murngin, through which Murngin men maintain control over vital resources, not the least of which is Murngin women (Keen, 1978:2). These same practices also underwrite the domination of the old over the young. In this context, religion becomes an economy of vital knowledge focusing on the control of reproduction and the regeneration of all forms of life. For the Murngin, as for the Kwakiutl, "reproduction" refers to interrelated processes that are at once physiological, psychological, social, ecological, and cosmic. This concern with reproduction as a total social and cosmic issue is expressed in sacred rites and narratives as well as in an elaborate set of social categories and processes that anthropologists term "social structure."

While anthropologists usually distinguish the study of religion from that of social structure, this distinction is not viable in every society. There appears to be no clear distinction between social structure and religion for the Murngin. Moreover, separating the study of social organization from that of religion and cosmology has unnecessarily encumbered our insight into these people.

AN EPISTEMOLOGY EMBEDDED IN SOCIAL PRACTICE

What interests me about the Murngin is the the centrality of processes of knowledge acquisition to their conception of social and biological reproduction. Murngin social organization and religion comprise a set of intricate models of how the emergence of knowledge is connected to the regeneration of people, plants, animals, society, and the cosmos itself. From a cognitive perspective, it is notable is that in their rituals and stories the Murngin simultaneously *propose* a theory about knowledge and *enact* that theory in the ritual transmission of knowledge from elders to the young. *What* the young men learn in the initiation rituals is intimately linked with *how* it is learned. An epistemology is embedded and transmitted in social practice. The Murngin vision of how an initiate's understanding unfolds in a sacred education is linked to their vision of creation as a dialectic integrating what philosophers would call analytic and synthetic modes of knowledge.

Each Murngin clan derives its identity, its own particular law *(rom)*, from its local stories (Keen, 1978:41). These narrative models link a clan with a collection of particular songs, designs, dances, and power beings. These are their *madayin*, their "religious law" (Keen, 1978:41; Morphy, 1991:48–49). The Murngin landscape, which may appear rather empty and even forbidding to outsiders, is filled with objects and places of great significance for the Murngin. To the Murngin clans whose "countries" these are, these sacred places and objects are *mali* (shadows or emblems) of the power beings who left them behind. A group's *ranga*, its totemic sacra, are the emblems of its specific ancestral power beings. A clan's sacred *ranga*, which include a wide variety of objects—ranging from rocks, feather strings, and particular animal species to constructed ritual artifacts—all are signs of the continued efficacy of the ancestors' original creative acts, acts that took place in the *bamun* or primal creative epoch.[5]

In addition to the numerous local tales, the Murngin also have several key narratives that serve as foundational schemas for the entire northeast region of Arnhem Land. The events revealed in these narratives underlie important regional rituals. Two of them, the chronicle of the wanderings of the Wawilak sisters and the Djunkgao sisters' journey, belong jointly to all the clans of the Dua moiety, though the associated rituals necessarily involve the Yiritja moiety as well.[6] A third narrative, the Laindjung story, is the Yiritja clan's equivalent of the Djunkgao narrative. It deals with a male stranger, Laindjung, who visits the Yiritja clans and brings them their religious "law" (Allen, 1975:59 ff).

The two Dua moiety narratives are creation stories and share a similar structure. Both recount how women (two sisters, ancestral power beings) originally possessed all the creative potency needed by their people but came to lose part of their power to the men through a series of misfortunes. The narratives are charters that underwrite the current unequal distribution of knowledge, and the transfer of ritual power and know-how from women to men.

Each of these narratives is linked with a complex set of rites. The Djunkgao[7] narrative provides the imagery for Murngin Narra ceremonies, in which clans reveal their most sacred *ranga* to young men who are deemed ready to see them and understand their significance.[8] The Wawilak narrative is linked with the most important rites of male initiation in the region. Marndiella and Djungguan are important rites commonly associated with circumcision. Gunabibi[9] celebrates fertility, marriage, and the interdependence of moieties. Ulmark is a dry-season ceremony in which, according to Warner's somewhat vague description, "a boy . . . is placed definitely in the men's age grade" (Warner, 1936/1958:301).[10]

While the Djunkgao and the Wawilak tales are important throughout much of northeast and central Arnhem Land, there is considerable local variation in the details of both narratives. This is because all sacred narratives involve clan claims of rights over certain land and associated resources. Thus the specific "map" defining the narrative journey as well as which events will be highlighted will vary depending upon which clan is telling the story. Clans tend to place the central episode of a story in their own clan country, since the telling of the story is always a claim of ownership to both countries and associated ceremonies (Keen, 1978:75).

Different clans also tend to substitute their own totemic snakes as the central figures in the Wawilak story, thereby focusing the story on their own country and its *ranga*. These local recreations of the foundational tale are especially useful when one clan is in the process of taking over the country of another (Keen, 1978:75–76). Local variations in the narratives will be emphasized when claims are being pressed or when clans with competing versions are not present. However, Keen suggests that the Murngin also have rhetorical strategies for suppressing the perception of incongruity among variations of a story when the appearance of consensus and harmony is important. Individuals will generally not challenge a "foreign" version of a story unless it is taken as a direct challenge to their own clan's specific claims. Even the fact that some clans stress the Djunkgao version of creation while others stress the Wawilak version can be rhetorically masked, if necessary, by the allusion to the story of "those two sisters," a reference that encompasses both narratives.

The Wawilak story provides a narrative foundation for Murngin age grading. Its central focus is the distribution and reproduction of sacred cultural knowledge. The Wawilak narrative and its associated rites deal directly with epistemological issues and so will provide the ethnographic focus for Chapters 9 and 10.

WHAT KIND OF NARRATIVE IS WARNER'S WAWILAK MYTH?

Because the Wawilak narrative is crucial to an understanding of knowledge emergence in initiation, I will paraphrase Warner's version at length.[11] The matter of which version of the story is used is far from trivial. Catherine Berndt has written on the great range of variation in any such narrative between different regions, between men's and women's versions, and between different individuals' renderings of the myth. Variations include not only specifics of content but also amount and complexity of detail and the sequencing and ordering of the elements of the story (Berndt and Berndt, 1970:13–17). Nonetheless the story has the same basic form throughout the region.

Warner's text version of the story is probably a fairly faithful translation of a narrative told to him by an informant at Milingimbi.[12] It is important to remember that a story of this sort would only rarely have been related as a coherent oral text. The Wawilak narrative is among the most sacred ("inside") of all Murngin stories. As such, it would hardly ever be presented to anyone in the fashion in which Warner has recorded it. First of all, only a few senior men would know the myth well enough to recite it in detail (Jeffrey Heath, personal communication). It is not even clear that the story has any reality as a "text" except in the publications of anthropologists. Howard Morphy, who studied Murngin paintings at Yirrkala, claims:

> Neither I nor any anthropologist I know has heard the Wawilag myth told as an oral story in any indigenous contexts, though I have seen it painted, danced and sung— or rather paintings, dances and songs performed that are part of its presentation. Yolngu certainly do have formal story-myth telling speech forms. . . . *But* the Wawilag myth would not be told in this way. [Morphy, personal communication]

In Chapter 10, we will take up the important question of how a narrative model such as the Wawilak story is "known" to initiates when its reality is not a narrated text but rather an emergent product of various configurations of dances, songs, and painting performed at different points in an individual's ritual life cycle.

In this chapter we begin with Warner's text and leave to Chapter 10 the questions of the actual form in which the narrative is transmitted from old men to young men during initiation.

THE NARRATIVE

The story takes place in the *Bamun* (mythological) period, a time of *Wongar* (mythological) power beings, when, according to Warner's informant, "everything was different" and "animals were like men" (Warner, 1936/1958:240). The informant begins by announcing that two Wawilak sisters had walked from the "far interior" of Wawilak Kardao Kardao country to the Arafura Sea. One of the sisters carried her infant son in a paper-bark cradle, while the other was pregnant with her first child.

The sisters also carried bush cotton, hawks' down, and stone spears. On the way, they killed various food animals, and gathered bush yams. As they killed each food species, they gave it the name it currently bears. To each species they killed and named, the sisters said "You will be *maraiin* [sacred] by and by" (p. 241).[13] They moved on in their journey, naming all the countries through which they passed. They also moved from language to language, clan to clan. They spoke Djaun, Rainbarngo, Djimba, Wawilak, and finally Liaalaomir, a language of the northern part of Arnhem Land.

In Wawilak country the sisters had cohabited with their own clan brothers, who, like them, belonged to the Dua moiety. "This was very wrong and asocial." Feeling her baby starting to move within her, the younger sister stopped to rest. Labor began. Soon her child was born. Before this birth there was only the Dua moiety. But now, the mother being Dua, the child belonged to the Yiritja moiety. In this first birth, social difference is created.

The older sister gathered more bush food. Then both sisters and their children resumed their journey toward the sea. Passing through all the territories of the Dua clans, the sisters continued to name the lands and all the localities within them. But in all their travels, they never left Dua country. They did not stop until they arrived at the great Mirrirmina ("rock python's back") water hole in the country of the Liaalaomir clan, on the upper Woolen River. At the bottom of this well lived Yurlunggur, the great copper snake and python totem of the Dua moiety. For the first time they called the name of the country Mirrirmina.

The elder sister made a fire and began to cook the animals, yams, and other bush foods they had brought with them. After each plant and animal was cooked, it came back to life. Leaping from the fire, each species jumped into the Mirrirmina water hole:

> They all went into this Djungguan and Gunabibi well. The crab ran in first. When he did this, the two women talked Liaalaomir for the first time; before this they had talked Wawilak. The other plants and animals followed the crab. The yams ran like men, as did the iguanas, frilled-neck lizard, darpa, ovarku snake, rock python, sea gull, sea eagles, native companions and crocodiles. Each ran and dived into the clans' totemic well and disappeared from sight. [p. 242]

The older sister made a paper-bark bed for her sister's new baby. Turning to her sister, she proposed that they soon circumcise their two sons. As the elder sister walked near the water hole to gather bark for the cradle, some of her menstrual blood spilled accidentally into the well where Yurlunggur, "the Big Father," lives.

Yurlunggur, asleep on the bottom of the pool, smelled the blood in the water and raised his head several times to trace the scent. Throwing a stone which covered the well's bottom onto the land (where it can be seen today), Yurlunggur opened the well and crawled out slowly "like a snake does." Emerging from the well to see who had dripped blood into his well water, Yurlunggur produced a flood of well water which began to inundate the land.

A black cloud swelled overhead. The rain began to fall. Unaware of where the rains had come from, the sisters quickly built a small house and hurried in for shelter. Confused by the lone black cloud in an otherwise cloudless sky, the sisters feared that something terrible was about to happen. The younger sister stayed in the house and sang. The older sister went outside and beat the ground with her yam stick. "[S]he knew now that Yurlunggur was going to swallow her, and she wanted to stop the rain." She sang and danced around the house, and uttered the taboo names of the Mirrirmina well, hoping that Yurlunggur would spare them. But the singing was for nought. Soon the sisters found themselves surrounded by all the Dua totem snakes in the land, who had heard the call of their father Yurlunggur.

The older sister tried to sing away the snakes and the rain. She began by singing all the "outside" songs that are now sung in the general camp (i.e., the less secret songs). When that did not work, she sang the less powerful general camp songs of the Gunabibi rites. But that too was futile. "She was afraid of this rain, for it came out of a cloud she could not understand, because this cloud had come from nowhere" (pp. 244–245). In desperation, she began singing the sacred "inside" songs of the Djungguan ceremony, singing first the Dua subsection songs, then the Yiritja subsection songs. The younger sister led the singing, much as the male ritual leader does today. But the deluge only intensified.

When the women started to sing of Yurlunggur and of menstrual blood, the great python heard the songs. He rose from out of the well. He found the women and their sons asleep. He licked them, bit their noses to make blood come. Then he swallowed all four of them in order of age. The old sister went first. At dawn, Yurlunggur lifted himself skyward, standing straight like a tree. "His head reached as high as a cloud. When he raised himself to the sky, the flood waters came up as he did. They flooded and covered the entire earth" (p. 244). While thus erect, and with the sisters and their sons inside him, Yurlunggur proceeded to sing all the songs of the Marndiella, Djungguan, Ulmark, and Gunabibi ceremonies, thus completing what the sisters had started.

The Dua moiety totemic snakes gathered together to talk. They discovered that they all spoke different languages. Lamenting that they did not speak one tongue, the totemic snakes agreed that they would hold their ceremonies together. After all, they shared the same totemic emblems. They then sang together, their voices echoing throughout the skies, like thunder.

Yurlunggur inquired of various Dua snakes what they had eaten. The snakes replied that they had consumed various fish and animals. But the Wessel Island snake was reluctant to admit that he had eaten the wrong kind of food—a blue parrot fish with white teeth. Yurlunggur berated his *yukiyuko* (younger brother), the Wessel Island snake, for having eaten the wrong sort of food. But when the Wessel Island snake turned to Yurlunggur and inquired what sort of food *he* had eaten, the great rock python was ashamed to admit the truth. After much prodding from the angry Wessel Island snake, Yurlunggur admitted that he had ingested two sisters and a small boy and girl.[14]

Once Yurlunggur confessed to eating the sisters and their children, the winds began to roar and the southeastern monsoon started blowing from off of the land. The Wessel Island snake withdrew into his own well. Yurlunggur let out a roar, and at the same moment fell to the ground with a thud. The impact split open the earth, creating the present dance ground at the Liaalaomir ceremonial place. Sure that his fall had killed the women and children inside him, he spit, regurgitating the two women and their children into an ant nest.[15] The Wessel Island snake, Yurlunggur's younger brother, was disgusted when he realized that Yurlunggur had eaten his own sisters *(yeppas)* and his sisters' children *(wakus)*.

Yurlunggur slowly made his way back into his water hole. Without warning, the Yurlunggur totemic trumpet suddenly appeared next to the python. It sang out on its own, blowing over the two women and their sons, all of whom appeared to be dead. Green ants came and bit them, and the sisters and their children suddenly jumped up. Surprised to see that the sisters and their babies weren't dead after all, Yurlunggur picked up two sticks. He called his sons—snakes, lizards, snails—and draped them all on his head. Then Yurlunggur proceeded to beat the sisters and their sons on the head with the two sticks. Then, once again, he swallowed all four of them. But realizing that he had again swallowed his own Dua people, Yurlunggur felt sick.

Mandelpui snake asked him what he had eaten, but Yurlunggur lied that he had eaten bandicoot. Not believing him, Mandelpui snake insisted that Yurlunggur confess the truth. When he did, admitting that he had eaten "two Dua women and two Yiritja boys," Yurlunggur fell once again, and the impact of his body created the Gunabibi and Ulmark dancing grounds.

Yurlunggur returned to the deep subterranean waters of the Liaalaomir well, placed a stone over its entrance, and stopped the water which had been flooding the land. He then swam underground to the Wawilak country. He wanted to take the two women and their sons back to their own country. Arriving in Wawilak country, Yurlunggur spat out his sisters one last time. The two sisters turned to stone, and can be seen as such in Wawilak country today. But the women's sons, Yurlunggur's own *wakus*, he kept inside of him "for they were Yiritja and he was Dua. The two women did not circumcise their sons as they intended because Yurlunggur had interfered before they were ready. It was because they so intended, and said for other people to perform this act, that people cut their sons today" (p. 248).

While these great events were taking place, two Wawilak *wongar* men had seen the sky filled with lightning and had heard the thunder voice of the great python. Realizing that something was amiss, they followed the sisters' tracks for many days until they came upon the tracks of the great snake. Immediately, one of the men guessed that the sisters had fallen prey to something terrible, like a python. When they arrived at Mirrirmina well, and saw the ants all over the place, and saw the well water shining like a rainbow, they knew there was a great snake below in the waters of the well.

Then they discovered the dancing grounds that Yurlunggur had made in his falls to the earth. The men realized that a *wongar* python had been there. They also found the blood of the women and the boys on some stones. The *wongar* men made a basket of paper bark and collected two baskets full of blood. At the dance ground the men erected a bush house on the part of the ground that was made by the snake's tail.

One man took hawk feathers and bush cotton and stuck them onto his body with the blood from the sisters. The other made a Yurlunggur trumpet out of a hollow log. The men then fell into a deep sleep, and while asleep they dreamed what the two sisters saw and sang and danced while they were trying to stop the rain. The Wawilak sisters came to the men in their dreams. They taught them all the ceremonies they knew, all the songs and all the dances, both general and "inside." The sisters warned the men that they were to use this knowledge every year, painting their bodies with the blood feathers, and dancing out the things that the women saw and named on their journey. "After the men danced the new dances and ceremonies for the first time, they went back to their own country. "We dance these things now because our Wongar ancestors learned them from the two Wawilak sisters" (p. 249).

EPISTEMOGENESIS: CREATION AS EXTERNALIZATION [16]

This extraordinary narrative is an odd kind of creation story. It is not clear what sort of creation the two sisters achieve. In the biblical Genesis, God creates the world ex nihilo and then proceeds to order his creation by separating out the basic elements of the cosmos. By naming the animals, Adam continues this act of creation through a generative logos. The Wawilak sisters possess no powers of primal creation. Their story begins at a time and place when everything already exists, albeit in a kind of indistinct wholeness. As Stanner has argued, "Nowhere in the [aboriginal] myths was there a suggestion of that extraordinary idea of creation ex nihilo. To Aborigines, something always was" (Stanner, 1976:24). The role of creation in these myths is that of reordering and structuring that which was already present. What the sisters actually accomplish is much like Adam's creative work of naming the animals. This kind of creative activity is the creation of a knowable world by imposing form and difference on a primal undifferentiated wholeness. The primary act of knowledge creation is to give things names and thus distinct identities. Categories are created by drawing boundaries.

The sisters' generative acts involve them in many kinds of *separation*. In the narrative, this separation is represented as what we might call *externalization*.[17] The sisters' initial journey moves them from "deep" inside Wawilak country outward toward the shore. At the same time the younger sister gives birth, her child moving from within her womb out into the world. The two sisters taken together (as two images superimposed) suggest the sequence or process of giving birth, the elder sister having recently given birth, the younger just about to.

They move from possessing what Murngin call "inside" or "deep" knowledge of creation to having merely "outside" camp knowledge, which is what contemporary

Murngin women are supposed to know of sacred matters. This transformation in the sisters' knowledge of the world is linked with a kind of externalization of their knowledge onto the surfaces of things. They lose their grasp of "inner" or "deep" understandings, understandings that we would term symbolic or metaphorical.

This externalization of women's knowledge is marked by the sisters being spit out from the belly of the python totem. In an inversion of their own birthing of their sons, the sisters are expelled from the totemic womb. At the same time their sons are retained within Yurlunggur. In this inverted birth, the women's children are separated from their mothers, both physically and as types. In the case of any wrong marriages, Murngin always calculate a child's identity in (negative) relation to its mother rather than its father. A child's initial social identity is achieved by a separation from its mother(s) rather than by identification with its father(s). For example, membership in social categories that organize marriage relations among local groups, categories that anthropologists call subsections, is always calculated by *opposing* a child to its mother. This is merely a more elaborate version of discovering a child's moiety membership in (negative) relation to its mother's.

Up to now everything has been classified as Dua, of the same nature. But now the sons are understood to be Other in relation to their mothers. They introduce the category of Yiritja into a Dua world. This initial separateness is won out of primal identification. Separation is the initial phase of knowledge creation, or what I call *epistemogenesis*. Just as the organization of professional baseball in America is based on the fundamental sorting of teams into National and American Leagues, everything in the Murngin world takes on its fundamental meaning in relation to the division of Dua and Yiritja moieties. Not only people but land, objects, and sacred symbols are, according to their natures, either Dua or Yiritja.

We have already noted the ambiguity over the sex of the sisters' offspring that Warner and others have reported for this narrative. Some accounts relate that both children were sons, others that they were a son and a daughter, and still others seem to move between the two alternatives. This ambiguity is not a "flaw" in the narration or even a matter of local variation. It is a crucial part of the story. The gender ambiguity derives from the fact that the sons have not yet been circumcised. During the Djungguan ceremony, which is linked to Murngin rites of circumcision, the boys are initially identified with the two sisters as females rather than males. Dressed in feather-string breast girdles, the initiates are closely identified with the Wawilak sisters rather than with any of the male figures in the story. Moreover, the sacred posts erected during the rites represent both the sisters and their sons (Morphy, 1991:91, 130). Since the initiates' foreskins, what Murngin consider the female part of male infants, have not yet been separated from the infants, they are, strictly speaking, not yet fully male but still retain part of their original female identity (see Warner, 1936/ 1958:120). The sisters' offspring, when taken together (as images superimposed), represent maleness as a process of transformation rather than a biological fact.

Creation is initially portrayed as externalization. The sisters produce from themselves not just children but children who gradually become thoroughly "Other" to the sisters. While their "brothers" and their "father" (Yurlunggur) were males, they were Dua males, at once different and the same as the sisters. Only in their sons do mothers create a being that becomes so completely Other in relation to her. Females create males; Dua produces Yiritja. This externalization is gradual. To bring it about requires not simply biological transformation but ritual work as well. Little wonder that the offspring of the sisters are said sometimes to be two males and sometimes a male and a female. Within the limits of the story, this transformation of the offspring into the sisters' Other remains incomplete. The sisters never do circumcise their sons as they had planned.

The sisters externalize a male from out of their own bodies. They also come to externalize male forms of work from out of their own labors. Initially, the sisters hunt *and* gather food. They perform all the work that is now divided between men and women. Similarly, they attempt to control both physical birth and ritual rebirth. Not only do the sisters bear their sons, but they carry with them the hawk's down and bush cotton that will come to be used for the initiation ritual. Just as the sisters externalize male offspring from a female body, they eventually externalize certain parts of their labor to men.

There is another form of externalization evident in the myth. This is what becomes socially correct marriage. The sisters learn that they must separate from their clan brothers and have relations with men who are outside their own moiety and thus "other" than themselves. This prohibition of incest is another form of externalization. The sorting out of right relations dominates not only the sisters' sexual relations but the "eating" relations of the Dua totemic snakes. You do not, they learn, eat your own.

Initially, the sisters appear as self-sufficient.[18] In fact, it is not at all clear whether they need men at all.[19] The narrative reveals them to be pregnant even before it reveals that they sleep with their own moiety brothers. Eventually, they copulate, but with Wongar Dua men, their own brothers. But it remains unclear who the fathers of these children are. This incestuous mating is a kind of half step to recognition of interdependence, and otherness. Once kinship is gradually established by the snakes, the sisters recognize that they must unite with "other" men in order to give birth to "other" children. Cycles of externalization and identification are established, and society as we know it commences.

BLOOD BONDS

In the Wawilak story as in life, men never overcome their reliance on women to reproduce themselves. The narrative suggests that men must forever wrest their sons from their wives and complete their birth by forms of symbolic creation. Symbolic transformation upstages organic transformation but never really overcomes it. The very forms of men's rituals call to mind physiological processes at the same moment as they seek to deny them. Male symbols of ritual potency are transformations of female symbols of fecundity. As such, they point to the centrality of women's physiological processes at the same time as they attempt to cancel them.

The key symbol of such a compromised transformation in the Wawilak story is blood. For the Murngin, blood is a potent symbol of life (Berndt, 1976:28). As Morphy suggests, blood is a multivocal symbol that proposes the transformational relations between death and life (Morphy, 1991:281 ff). The other life-giving liquid is water, often associated by Murngin with semen. The Murngin recognize four stages in the conception of a child (Keen, 1978:304–305): (1) menstruation begins with an act of intercourse, which opens up the vagina and allows the menstrual blood to flow out; (2) repeated entry of the penis into the vagina blocks up the flow of blood, forcing it back up to the uterus and causing it to clot (Berndt, 1953:271; Keen, 1978:304–305; Munn, 1969:184–185); (3) while clotted menstrual blood makes up the fetus's blood and soft parts, deposits of semen are responsible for the bone, the body, and especially the limbs; (4) but a child is not formed until a "spirit child," often in the form of a freshwater fish or an animal, enters the women and makes the connection between her uterus and her heart (Keen, 1978:304).

Spirit children (or conception totems) are often said to live in fresh water and are commonly linked with seafood. Often the spirit child is first glimpsed in a dream by the child's father (pater). It may enter the woman through her vagina. Women are particularly likely to conceive spirit children when they are washing near wells or near water associated with wells. Morphy describes spirit conception in terms of a kind of water cycle, in which the spirits of the dead rise skyward as clouds and fall again to earth in the form of rain, where they enter the wells and thence into women as regenerated humans (Morphy, 1991:255). Alternately, a spirit gains entry orally, through certain "strong" foods, particularly honey and fish, given to a woman by her husband (Munn, 1969:184–185).

The Wawilak narrative is full of indirect symbolic allusions to conception. In the narrative, the sister's menstrual blood falls from the sister's body and accidentally enters the watery pool of her "brother" Yurlunggur. The image employs many of the elements of conception but inverts them (Munn, 1969:185). Blood flows freely into the snake's water. It forces the snake to the surface. This is an inverted image of a phallus entering a vagina, depositing semen, and forcing the menstrual blood up into the uterus to clot (see Morphy, 1991:255 ff).[20]

Later in the narrative, the Dua snakes discuss how they have eaten and spewed up various freshwater fish and game animals. Again, an inverted image of conception is proposed whereby the phallic snakes ingest the "strong" foods and thus the spirit children. But Yurlunggur's ingested spirit children are his two nephews *(waku)*. The image is complex and subject to numerous readings. In one reading, that exploited by the Djungguan ceremony, this image of a gestating male constitutes a grotesque inversion of normal conception. It is part of what Munn calls "a distorted sexual cycle" (Munn 1969:185) and symbolically recapitulates the sisters' incestuous copulation with their clan brother.

When the Wongar Wawilak men retrace the sisters' steps and immediately recognize what has happened, they mimic their sister's childbirth by making a bark cradle and gathering up the blood left behind from the heads of their sisters and their sons. In the narrative, the Wongar men collect two baskets of blood which they use to perform their rituals. Note their use of the blood. The men allow the blood to coagulate overnight. When it is sticky, it is used to attach the hawks' down and cotton to their bodies, implicitly transforming them into totemic ancestors and thereby reclaiming the wholeness that was left behind in the initial stages of creation.[21]

For women, the act of gashing the head is a form of ritual mourning, so the blood associated specifically with the head is linked to mortuary rites. (Morphy, 1991, Chap. 12). The complex symbol of blood in this story thus calls upon understandings of the various symbolic associations of head blood, menstrual blood, and the men's arm blood used in ritual body painting and decoration. The narrative, like conception beliefs, suggests that coagulated blood is life-producing. Without the work of men in reproduction, menstrual blood spills freely from the body and produces no life. The Murngin at Yirrkala, studied by Berndt, call a menstruating woman a "spring woman." They explicitly compared menstrual flow to the flowing waters of the spring (Berndt, 1951:26; Munn, 1969:185). The unstoppable flow of blood calls forth an unstoppable flow of water. The image of the uncontrolled flow of vital fluid bringing destruction rather than life is one of the central images of the Wawilak story. It is in this context that coagulated blood takes on such significance as an image of transformation.

For the Murngin, it is the role of men to transform the flow of blood into a coagulated form that can be channeled into the production of life. In physical birth, male penetration forces menstrual blood into the uterus, where it can clot and form a fetus. In the second birth, initiation, men's own "arm blood" is allowed to coagulate and is then stuck back on novices to transform them into totemic Wongar creatures. Such ritually "bound" blood is held to be especially potent and especially dangerous to women (Warner, 1936/1958:237).

As with blood, so with knowledge. The outflow of blood from the women is paralleled by their uncontrolled loss of knowledge. With both of these losses, the women are deprived of self-sufficiency in reproduction. Ritual "stops up" the flow of knowledge in forms that are contained and controllable. The Wongar men, in discovering the powers of coagulated blood, simultaneously find a way to "memorialize" the transient events of the narrative and transform them into permanent forms of ritual reproduction (Munn, 1969:182–183).

SACRED DIALECTIC: CREATION AS KILLING

Initially, the sisters carry out two kinds of creation. They bear children and bestow names and languages on the world. They also intend to circumcise their children but never accomplish that act. With each generative act, an individual is separated and externalized by degrees from a prior wholeness. In giving birth, women give physical life and autonomy to their sons. In giving names, they bring forth types and individuals, making things knowable and communicable. Williams has argued that, for the Murngin, words, and especially names, constitute the most important noncorporeal property for any group (Williams, 1986:42). Naming is essentially an act of asserting ownership. For men, the correct knowledge and use of the "power names" for ritual dances and songs is a kind of identification with the spirit creatures associated with the rituals (Williams, 1986:44).

But though naming, especially in ritual contexts, appears to have deeply religious associations for the Murngin, in the myth the significance of naming is far more complex. For as the sisters name the animals and plants, giving them life as knowable life forms, they also kill them. The plants and animals achieve articulateness but at the cost of their lives.

Each life form is killed repeatedly, with the name, with the spear, with the fire, and finally by jumping into the totemic well. The final "death" (in the well) appears to transcend the other forms of destruction and shows them to have been false deaths. As they name and kill each creature, the sisters assure it that it will be *maraain* (sacred/powerful) "by and by." In one hand, the sisters carry a spear, the instrument of the totemic animals' death. Yet in the other hand they carry bush cotton and hawks' down—the (ritual) instruments of the resurrection of the totemic species in the dances of the initiation ceremonies and in the paintings that will cover their bodies.

With the aid of coagulated blood, the down and cotton will effect an identification between people and totems, transforming dancers back into Wongar forms. Separation is overcome by identification. The distinction between animals and humans is bridged. Once again, human and animal and plant are indistinguishable, as in the Bamun.

This is a remarkable formulation. The Murngin seem to refute the Durkheimian (and the Jewish) equation of the sacred as separate (that which is set apart). As with the Kwakiutl, distinctness is not the soul of the sacred. The kind of distinctness suggested by name giving and all other forms of externalization is presented as a kind of death, a loss of an original wholeness. This "death" is a limited form of life. It is *life-in-the-world* and defines the logic of "outside" existence. So it approximates what we usually mean by secular existence rather than sacredness. Sacredness in this view comes eventually ("by and by"). But it is achieved only when the life forms reenter the well and thereby return to the "Dreamtime" or *Bamun* state.[22] Here separation is overcome and the lost wholeness is recovered.

The process traces out a general foundational schema for the Murngin. The schema proposes that separation is overcome by a reunion of divided parts after a journey through a complex landscape of organized categories. It is a kind of "walkabout," a dialectical model of social process (Figure 9.1). The walkabout schema is a particularly good example of what, in Chapter 2, I termed a foundational schema. In itself it is very abstract, but it serves as a common organizing template for a large number of specific Murngin cultural models.

The myth enacts this foundational schema in four ways:

- The food species are named, killed, and cooked. Then they are "reborn" twice, once as they leap out of the fire, and again as they return to the *Bamun* or *Wongar* state by jumping into the totemic well. In their final destruction they overcome the opposition between life and death.
- The children are separated from their mothers in birth only to be swallowed up again by Yurlunggur. To the boys, the python is both a father *(bapa)* and a maternal uncle *(gawel* or *ngapipi)*. This act of incorporation generates several distinct images that will be exploited in initiation ceremonies.
- The ambiguously male infant sons will be ritually killed and cooked (steamed) before they are reborn as males to their clan fathers in both Djungguan or Marndiella circumcision rituals and in Ulmark.
- Even the separation of the Dua moiety into distinct clans with distinct names and countries is overcome by the Dua Wawilak myth itself and its associated age-grading rites. The myth recounts the necessity to order the cosmos by

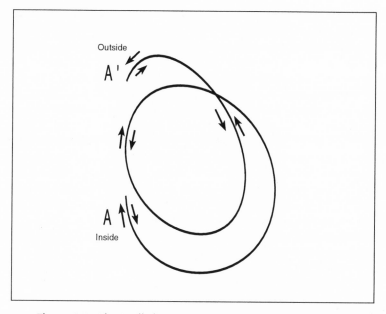

Figure 9.1. The Walkabout: A Murngin Foundational Schema

making distinctions and getting the relations right among the parts. But it also celebrates the ultimate ("inside") unity of all that had been externalized and rendered distinct.

The two visions are mediated by the ambiguous status of Yurlunggur. He is not just a multivocal symbol but a true polytrope, suggesting in a single ambiguous image various kinds of relationship. The python is presented as at once a symbol of the separateness of clans, the unity of the moiety, and the interdependence of opposing moieties.[23] As "older brother" *(wawa)* to the other snakes, Yurlunggur is an emblem of clan distinctness (as the central totem of the Liaalaomir clan). As "father" *(bapa)* of all Dua snakes, Yurlunggur embodies their unity and identification. As moiety emblem, Yurlunggur is the image of the great python with all his "sons" draped around his neck. And as *gawel*[24] (mother's brother/wife's father) to the boys within his belly, Yurlunggur proposes the interdependence and reunification of opposites (Dua and Yiritja) through marriage. He also reconciles the opposition between male and female, not simply in being a male representative of a maternal line but also in the image of a phallic womb.

The swallowing/spitting action is at once a phallic, ejaculatory image and a uterine birth image. As with the Kwakiutl cannibal poles, the images of ingestion and expulsion are inextricably linked in a kind of visual and generative oxymoron. Just as the sisters' offspring are ambiguously male, their maternal uncle, Yurlunggur, merges male and female roles in conception. Berndt's informants at Yirrkala often referred to the snake as female but nonetheless as explicitly phallic (Berndt, 1951:21, 25; Munn, 1969:181). As a totalizing social model, a reconciliation of normally distinct kinship and gender statuses, Yurlunggur represents at once the social distinctions between brother and father, father and maternal uncle, female and male, and also the possibility of overcoming these distinctions by being all at once. The key emblem of difference is also the key to the transcendence of difference.

In their rituals, the Murngin seek to overcome the separation of the distinct languages and dialects in the region. As the Wawilak narrative illustrates, clan groups and moiety differences are often associated with distinct *matha* (languages or tongues) (Warner, 1936/1958:16, 36–39; Williams, 1986:40). Murngin theorize that the distinction between Dua and Yiritja is, at heart, linguistic (Keen, 1978:30, Warner, 1936/1958:38.) Keen reports that the songs of the Gunabibi rite are sung in a special ritual language. "Songs are in no Yolngu [Murngin] language, indeed they are in no language at all. Some song-words resemble Yolngu words, some are names of objects used in ceremony whose meaning varies in any case. The songs are all capable of a multiplicity of interpretations" (Keen, 1978:168).

Warner also refers to the use during the Ulmark ceremony of Ki-jin, a kind of pidgin, a composite of languages like Millikin, Djaun, and other tongues from the south of Arnhem Land (Warner, 1936/1958:312). His informants told him that Ki-jin was the "language" used by the Wawilak sisters when they sang to try and stop the rain (p. 313). While secular language creates social divisions and semantic distinctions, sacred language transcends such divisions. It unites distinct groups through a composite "language" and unites disparate referents through semantic ambiguity and polysemy.

THE EMERGENCE OF SYMBOLISM: FROM *"INSIDE"* TO *"OUTSIDE"* KNOWLEDGE

The Wawilak sisters and their generative powers dominate the first part of the myth. Then, one of the sisters accidentally lets some of her menstrual blood drip into a sacred totem well. At the bottom of the well sleeps the great python Yurlunggur. He is their own brother, and also their father. The blood mingles with the water of the well. The snake is aroused. The sisters' understanding of their world, as well as their power to create with words, begin to wane. As the great carpet snake emerges from the well to see where the blood came from, he floods the world with well water and a great rainstorm ensues.[25] Here is (with emphases added) how Warner's informant described this episode.

> When he came out he sucked some of the well water *into his mouth. He spat* it into the sky. Soon a cloud about the *size of a man's hand* appeared from nowhere in the center of the sky. As Yurlunggur slowly rose from out of the bottom of the pool the *totemic well-water rose* too and flooded the earth. He pulled himself up on the stone which he had thrown, and laid his head there. *He saw* the women and their babies. . . .
>
> Yurlunggur continued to look at them. *He hissed. This was to call out for rain.* There was no cloud in the sky until then, but soon the two sisters saw a small, a very small black cloud appear in the heavens. *They did not see* the great python lying there watching them. [Warner, 1936/1958:242–243]

In this complex narrative Yurlunggur's emergence from the well is described not once but several times. Each retelling of the event involves a subtle change in the "interpretation" of the event. This transformation in knowledge is signaled in the narrative by a gradual shift in how the rainfall is understood. Several times the action seems to be stopped and replayed.

- Initially, the flooding is described as Yurlunggur spitting into the sky.
- Then the physical act of producing the water is repeated, but as the splash resulting from Yurlunggur's physical emergence from the well.
- In the third version, Yurlunggur only hisses, halfway between spitting and speaking.
- Then, fully articulate, he calls for rain.
- And finally, the great python's role is completely obscured by a small cloud "the size of a man's hand" that seems to come from nowhere.

The sisters can see only the cloud-darkened sky. Clouds for Murngin symbolize death. With their knowledge thus "clouded over," the sisters have no further understanding of the true source of the flooding. The passage seems to be an account of the "inside" (or underlying) meaning behind the annual rains that flood Arnhem Land. It is also the pivotal moment in the myth, the appropriation of some of the sisters' generative powers by the men.

Like the heavens, the sisters' understanding of their world becomes clouded, as the python emerges from his rest. The cause of the rain shifts from direct and physical to indirect and symbolic. More specifically, the change is from efficient cause (the python's body, or spitting), to metonymy (clouds), to metaphor (rain as a symbolic evocation of the mythic event).

But to the sisters, this shift in causality is experienced as a beclouding of their understanding. In the end, the material source of the rain (Yurlunggur) becomes unknowable to the sisters. This inside knowledge has now become abstracted, mediated by all sorts of symbols. The sisters' literal vision cannot penetrate the cloud or the emergent symbolism that it precipitates.[26] With Yurlunggur's emergence, the inner cause of the rain (the python) is now understandable only through interpretation. Physical causality does not disappear. But now it is mediated by a world of abstract signs.

The "inside" meaning of the rain remains the python and its semantic chain of associated meanings. But to the sisters, the meaning of the rain is limited to the cloud which Yurlunggur precipitated. What the sisters perceive as the real causes of the rain are merely indications of something deeper, but something to which they have no interpretive access. The sisters' knowledge has been fully externalized. Inside meanings have been replaced by outside ones. But these meanings are viewed as literal facts of nature rather than as an index of deeper meanings.

As the women's understanding becomes externalized and impoverished, the men seem to gain in insight. The Wongar men know intuitively what has happened to the sisters. They can read the signs left behind. Only those with powers over symbols can achieve an inside understanding. Those who have left the Bamun behind, and thus are deprived of initiation, have no access to symbolic knowledge. They are equipped to know the world in a limited and literal way. In a world now mediated by symbols, the second creation of humans through ritual requires men's (interpretive) power rather than women's (procreative) power.

Initially, the sisters' own relation to life processes was both material and symbolic. They created by naming species as they journeyed outward from their home country. And at the same time, they gave birth to sons. But with the python's emergence, they lose access to symbolic (ritual) potency, which becomes the prerogative of the men. The myth represents this transfer of powers, *both* as the men (through Yurlunggur) appropriate it *and* as the women voluntarily pass on their secrets. Though the sisters bear their sons, it remains for the men to complete the creation of the boys through ritual initiation.

NARRATIVE ANOMALIES

The Wawilak story unfolds in space and action, but it does so in a peculiar way. Two alternative models of space and action appear to be superimposed upon one another, giving the narrative an "illogical" spatial and temporal framework. The narrative recounts the sisters' journey as a linear track from inside (south) to outside (north), "from the far interior to the Arafura Sea" (Warner, 1936/1958:240). Specifically, this outbound journey ends at the Mirrirmina well, near the Woolen River in Liaalaomir country.

Yet when the narrative specifies the languages the sisters spoke, presumably an indication of the countries through which they traveled, it does not suggest a linear track at all, but rather a kind of circle—a walkabout. In fact, the narrative insists that the sisters began their trip in Wawilak country. If we equate language with country, then they spoke in sequence the following "languages": Wawilak, Djaun, Rainbarngo, Djimba, Wawilak, and Liaalaomir. I have reproduced this journey on a map taken from Warner's book (Figure 9.2). There is no reference on Warner's map to Djaun country, but Murphy (personal communication) identifies it as Djawany. One can see that the trip described is no simple south-north journey, but rather something more circular.[27]

Particularly strange is the reference to the sisters speaking Wawilak just before they spoke the language of Liaalaomir. This apparent return to their own home language underscores the circularity of their journey. At a later point in the narrative, the sisters cook a crab they caught, and he jumps into the well. The narrator comments, "When he did this, the two women talked Liaalaomir for the first time; before this they had talked Wawilak." Again, the sisters are said to move on from speaking Wawilak, but at the same time they never seem to really move beyond their first language. As with their incestuous intercourse, they seem to recognize social differentiation at the same moment as they deny it. In the end, Yurlunggur does take the sisters on the return track back to their own home country, where they are immobilized as stone. The sense of the sisters making a linear journey is canceled. Only their son(s) end up continuing the journey, but this time through ritual.

The journey of the Wawilak sisters moves simultaneously forward and back upon itself. The same structural paradox characterizes the narrative, which proposes a set of primal events that turn out (on second thought) not to have been events at

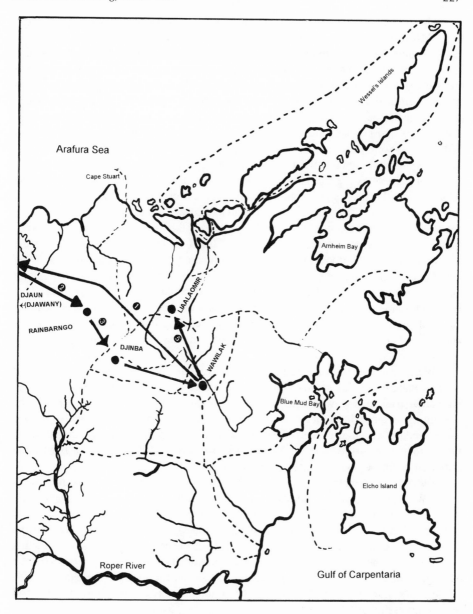

Figure 9.2. The Wawilak Sisters' Track (after Warner 1936/1958)

all. Every creative act of the sisters—whether the individuating of the plants and animals, the birth of their sons, or the separating of Dua languages and territories— is also *undone* in the course of the story. Animals are made separate, only to return to a primal wholeness. Sons are externalized into the world from a maternal womb, only to be reincorporated into an avuncular one. The snakes sort out their separate Dua identities, only to be reincorporated in the head of their father Yurlunggur.

The point is *not* that Murngin myth proposes an absence of change or linear time. Much has been written about the presumed circularity of aboriginal time concepts (Stanner, 1966; Williams, 1986). Yet Eliade's notion of the *eternal return,* a denial of historical change (Eliade, 1965), is somewhat misleading in reference to the Murngin. The Murngin view superimposes such a return upon a linear change. It suggests *transformation within repetition.* Von Sturmer put it well when he characterized the aboriginal conception of time as "Still and moving all at once—like days and seasons in a regular sequence, a sequence (or a change) of sameness" (quoted in Williams, 1986:35, fn. 16).[28]

Morphy has written, "Because of the nature of the Yolngu conception of time, mythological events are not simply located in the distant past but are also in some sense seen to be part of the continuous present" (Morphy, 1991:45). This view of time is dialectical. Time is at once acknowledged and transcended. This transcendence evokes Hegel's notion of *Aufhebung.* This is the idea that what is canceled in a dialectic is also encompassed in (literally "lifted up into") the return. But in the Murngin schema the process is a kind of downward penetration rather than a lifting up. *Aufheben* combines the sense of canceling or erasing something with the notion of incorporating it at a higher (or, in Murngin conception, more inside) level. This Hegelian notion of "transcendence" approximates the Murngin view of time and action.[29] Time and events may be overcome by a cycling back, but they are also acknowledged and incorporated. The traveler bears the marks of the journey taken (see Figure 9.1).

While the Murngin suggest that the individual emerges from a dreamtime *Wongar* state into a differentiated world, the course of life will ultimately return that individual back to the well, the source of all that is sacred. But a *return* to the Dreamtime is quite different from the condition of never having left. Time is at once acknowledged and transcended. The fate of humans is to journey, whether through the reproductive history that marks Murngin women's status throughout life or the initiation history by which males are socially marked.[29]

As with the totemic plants and animals that eventually return to the well, sacredness for humans is achieved not by *being* a Dreamtime creature but by *becoming* one again, through a return. In terms of the life cycle, Murngin mortuary rites aim at reincorporating one of the two spirits of the deceased back into the ancestral well so it can be recycled back into life as a new cycle of generation. From the individual's perspective in the course of initiation, what is gained on the journey—both for the Murngin males who are allowed to undergo the sacred rites and for the older females who may be shown the most sacred objects in the *narra* rites—is self-knowledge and consciousness of one's true identity.

In the Wawilak narrative these paradoxes of temporal and spatial representation are repeated in relation to action. While it appears to be a creation tale, it is far from clear whether the sisters actually create anything de novo. To name animals, to speak languages, to label countries is not the same thing as creating them. The narrative suggests that the sisters simply give voice to names, languages, and labels that had always been there. This is also true of the songs and dances the sisters perform for the first time. They do not compose these songs, they appropriate them, singing them as if they had always been there for the performing.

So just as the narrative proposes an outward journey that in the end goes nowhere at the same time as it proceeds on its outward track, it also describes a set of primal events that are also nonevents or preexisting facts. They are foundational models of reality that have no origin in the external world but do have a history in the consciousness of each initiate. These anomalies which appear in the narrative structure of the myth are thus central to the theory of knowledge that the story is proposing. They suggest that this narrative presents a story simultaneously from two perspectives: an "outer" perspective of a fixed and timeless set of laws and an "inner" perspective of a young boy's coming into awareness of those laws. The Murngin have, in a most remarkable way, represented in a single complex narrative form the two births of culture.

TRANSFORMATION OF KNOWLEDGE: MURNGIN THEORY AND PRACTICE

These narrative anomalies suggest that the Wawilak tale is not a straightforward creation story. The cosmogony of the Wawilak narrative is logocentric. It operates through language: through naming, language differentiation, and sung narrative. The notion that the origin of the cosmos involves the imposition of linguistic form on an otherwise undifferentiated world is a common feature of creation stories. This logo-centric conception of creation conforms to the general emphasis of the Murngin on the importance of controlling names and sacred words as powerful identifications both with land and with spiritual entities.

In the Wawilak narrative, the first stage of creation is analytical and logical, the drawing of boundaries and the creation of difference where there was indistinction. Creatures are given names and groups are given distinct languages and territorial boundaries.

The second stage involves the establishment of relations between the differenti-ated parts. Once categories are demarcated, then orderly relations of exchange among them can be constituted. The sisters together with the totemic snakes authorize an ordered universe in which words and categories enter into complex relations of ex-change and avoidance. Kinship, the syntax of social reproduction, is established.

Yet we might also ask what the *experiential basis* of such a logocentric view of creation might be. In everyday experience, we know of no physical world that is created simply by speech. The logocentric view of creation appears irrational in that it is empirically false. Yet there *is* one kind of world creation that is, in fact, always mediated by language. This is the origin of one's *consciousness of the world*. The Wawilak story, like our own Genesis, embeds its ontology in the ontogeny of con-sciousness, collapsing the origin of the world into the origin of the world's *knowabil-ity*.[30] This is genesis as epistemogenesis.

The emergence of a child into a self-conscious and world-conscious adult is a kind of creation that has some of the peculiar narrative anomalies we have seen in the Wawilak tale. The emerging consciousness of the child is the preexisting world of the adult. It is a journey which is at once linear and static, in which everything that is being "created" also already exists. It is simultaneously a becoming and a being.

The Wawilak narrative is not just a creation story. It is specifically the narrative that is used to "structure" the age-grading rites of Murngin boys. It employs the imagery of world creation to shape the course of consciousness creation for Murngin males. While Murngin myth surely proposes an ontology of the world, the Wawilak narrative is more clearly about the origin of knowledge than it is about the physical world per se. These epistemological biases are evident *both* in the myth's content and in its very narrative structure.

In its content, the Wawilak myth recounts the transfer of sacred knowledge from the hands of women into the hands of men. It also proposes a general dialectical schema for the creation of knowledge. At first things are all one, but they are indistinct and inaccessible to humans. Then knowledge unfolds by distinctions of all kinds: things get distinct names, groups distinct languages and countries, and individuals distinct kinship statuses and relations. Once things are distinct, they can be reconnected. But the first kind of connectedness is not through relations of identity but through syntactic relations of difference—relations of rule-governed exchange. These are the very relations that so absorbed generations of anthropologists who called them "social structure" and at times despaired of ever figuring them out. The myth proposes that such complex exchange relations tend toward both organic increase and systemic complexity. The notorious complexity of Murngin social arrangements is not simply a peripheral characteristic of their social life. It represents at the level of mind and of abstract system the same increase and vitality that progeny represent at the level of organic life.

"ONE SMALL DOT, TOO MANY MEANINGS"

To conclude our characterization in terms of such syntactic complexity would be to miss the significance of the Murngin dialectic. Such complexity represents for the Murngin a transitional kind of understanding, knowledge-in-the world, a knowing that is essential for being a member of a human society. The myth also proposes that all such analytical knowledge is also a kind of death, for it gains knowledge of the parts by sacrificing a direct apprehension of the wholeness of things.

So in the end, the Wawilak story proposes an ultimate transcendence of this kind of partialness by suggesting that what was known through externalization and relations of exchange may eventually be "re-cognized" as unification, a return to the wholeness of things, a jumping back into the well. In terms of Murngin symbology, it proposes that the extraordinary fan of meanings of any given symbol or symbol complex in myth, painting, or song will eventually be understood to be a coherent and unitary picture of reality. As the Murngin say "It's all the same . . ." even when things sometimes appear to be a profusion of disparate images.[31]

Morphy's informant, himself a distinguished Murngin artist, commented, while trying to explicate the multiple meanings of his red dots: "One small dot, too many meanings." (Morphy, 1991:143). Yet, ultimately, the meanings converge. This kind of knowledge, the return to a former wholeness, is the "sacred" *(maraiin)* quality that the totemic animals and plants have when they are killed, cooked, and returned to the well. And it is equally the sacred character of humans who are permitted to take the parallel journey from undifferentiated fetus to differentiated adult to sacred elder. For the totemic species, the journey is mediated by myth; for the humans, it is mediated by initiation rites.

The Murngin theory of knowledge is thus built into both the myth's content and its narrative textures. The narrative is recounted in this manner to propose that in its very forms a kind of knowledge is mirrored that proceeds by differentiation and forward movement but which simultaneously overcomes that differentiation by turning back upon itself, turning a trip outward bound into a kind of walkabout.

The rhetorical power of this narrative does not reside so much in its status as text as in its narrative structure, which replicates the life course through which initiates must pass. The myth comes to be known only through its diverse instantiations in ritual acts and representations. The theory of knowledge as creation contained in the Wawilak myth, what Morphy calls "a continual process of semiosis" (Morphy, 1991:144), is never simply proposed to Murngin youth directly. Instead, the myth itself is deconstructed by Murngin elders and revealed to the novices piecemeal, in conjunction with the central age-grading rites of Murngin society. It is to the practices of knowledge creation, the outside-in perspective on Dreamtime learning, that we turn in the following chapter.

Notes

1. This change from viewing cultures as bounded entities within which knowledge is fully shared to a view of cultures as open and dynamic knowledge systems in which competence is distributed unevenly parallels the biologist's change from the taxonomic approach to viewing "races" as discrete biological populations to a more "populational approach" in which distributions of gene frequencies define populations only in terms of statistical frequencies of traits within a gene pool. Yet it is interesting that in both cases, the ideologies of ethnicity continue to insist on viewing populations both as bounded "races" and as discrete "cultures."

2. There is no agreed upon collective name for the aborigines living on the northeast coast of Arnhem Land and the islands between Arnhem Bay (to the east) and Cape Steward to the west. This is mainly due to the fact that, lacking a sense of themselves as a distinct political unit, the four thousand or so "Murngin" that were the basis of Warner's ethnography have no collective name for themselves. The name Murngin has become famous in anthropology because it is the name that W. Lloyd Warner used for the population around Milingimbi, a Methodist mission station in central Arnhem Land, which was the basis of his 1936 classic ethnography *A Black Civilization*.

There has never been any agreement among anthropologists about the appropriate collective name for the people of northeast and central Arnhem Land or even about the significance of the name Murngin. Warner himself claimed that the name Murngin actually referred to the largest of the eight local groups he called "tribes," which were the basis of his ethnography (Warner, 1936/1958:15). Warner claimed that Murngin (meaning "fire sparks") was the name of the tribe whose country bordered Arnhem Bay.

Yet the issue remains in doubt. Ian Keen, whose fieldwork in the region was carried out in the 1970s, identifies the "Murrungun" as a "semi-moiety name" from the Roper River area (Keen, 1977:22). Berndt, however, suggests that "Murungun," meaning "red ochre," is the name of "a small *dua* moiety clan . . . associated with two or more dialect units" (Berndt, 1976:19). The name Murngin became something of a household name among anthropologists because of the famous "Murngin problem" (the problem of sorting out the relations between the subsection terminology and the Murngin marriage norms), which generated an entire literature of its own in anthropology.

More recent ethnographies have coined a variety of new collective names for these people, further confusing the issue. Shapiro calls them Miwuyt (Shapiro, 1981). Berndt, whose fieldwork was centered at the mission station of Yirrkala on the northeast coast of Arnhem Land, referred to the people collectively as Wulamba in his early work [Berndt, 1955]. More recently he has suggested the term Malag, the term used for these people by their neighbors in western Arnhem Land, or else Miwoidj, that which refers to the different dialects linked with the clan (Berndt, 1976:19–20). Most recently, the name Yolngu has become a popular collective appellation for these people (Keen, 1978; Williams, 1986). Yolngu means "human being" or "black person," as opposed to Europeans or Asians.

Were this book intended for mainly specialists on Australia, I would probably follow the current practice of using the term Yolngu for this population. However, at the risk of anachronism and continuing to perpetrate a kind of part-for-whole error, I have decided to use Warner's term Murngin because it is by far the most widely recognized name among anthropologists at large. The same goes for spellings, which have never been standardized and therefore are slightly different in virtually every publication on the Murngin. Though they are probably not quite as phonetically accurate as some of the more recent transcriptions, I shall stick with Warner's spellings.

3. The issue of verb tense is important and problematical in this context. For some thirty years now, no aboriginal populations have lived an exclusively nomadic life as foragers. All have been settled into government and mission camps and reservations, though many have moved in recent years to more isolated and dispersed outstations. In many ways all references to "traditional" subsistence belong in the past tense and not in any misleading "ethnographic present." On the other hand, from all published reports, social organization and religious practices remain largely in place for these populations, though how much longer the traditional sacred knowledge will be passed onto succeeding generations is clearly in question. Because these traditions and social practices are still vital for the Murngin population, I shall use the present tense when writing about them and the past tense when writing about events and practices that are clearly defunct.

4. The term "religion" is somewhat misleading for the Murngin, since they appear to recognize no clear boundaries between religious and secular matters. Their "religious" beliefs and practices pervade almost every important aspect of their lives.

5. The Murngin terms *"Bamun"* and *"Wongar"* suggest a common aboriginal concept of a foundational set of events and power beings who once and for all laid down the patterns for all life, and whose work is carried on by contemporary aborigines through stories, and ritual. This notion has frequently been translated as The Dreamtime or The Dreaming (but see Williams, 1986; appendix I).

6. A moiety system is a kind of dual organization in which any social group or unit is divided into two halves, which are then related to each other by some sort of exchange relationship. British "house" systems in public schools or the National and American Leagues in North American baseball are familiar examples of moiety organization. Moieties are a common features of Australian aboriginal social organization. Their significance for the Murngin will be discussed further on in this chapter.

7. Berndt calls this myth and its associated song cycle and *Narra rites* Djanggawul (Berndt, 1953).

8. Detailed accounts of the Djunkgao story may be found in Allen, 1975:43–58; Berndt, 1953; Warner, 1936/1958, chap. 10; and Keen, 1978: chap. 4. For analyses of the associated Narra rites, see Warner, 1936/1958, chap. 10; and Keen, 1978, chap. 6. Berndt, whose ethnography comes from Yirrkala and Milingimbi mission settlements, claims that the Djunkgao "cult" is really the oldest and most sacred of the religious cults on northeastern Arnhem Land. The Djunkgao myth is centrally concerned with origins, while the Wawilak complex focuses more on the ordering of social relations and the transmission of sacred knowledge by daughters of the original Djunkgao sisters (Berndt, 1953:14).

9. Compare Berndt's *kunapipi* (Berndt, 1951).

10. Warner (Warner, 1936/1958:301) reported that Ulmark was a fairly recent innovation in central Arnhem Land and had not yet been fully learned by all the old men at Milingimbi. Yet Keen (1978:156) reports that Ulmark appears to be no longer practiced in the Woolen River area, which suggests that it never was fully incorporated into the Murngin age-grading complex.

11. Warner calls his version of the narrative "The Myth of the Wawilak Women" (Warner, 1936/1958:240 ff). Other published versions of this myth are found in Allen, 1975, and Berndt, 1951.

12. Milingimbi, where Warner collected most of his ethnographic material, was the earliest Murngin settlement, founded in 1922. The other two settlements are Yirrkala (1935) and the Elcho Island settlement (1942). Some of the variations among ethnographic reports of Murngin culture stem from local variations from settlement to settlement.

13. The term *maraiin* comes from *mar,* a Murngin term for spiritual power.

14. Warner notes that his informants could not agree whether the Wawilak sisters had two sons or a son and a daughter. We shall discuss this ambiguity, which I suspect is not coincidental, below.

15. For an analysis of the significance of ants in the narrative and in the Djungguan ceremony, see Munn, 1969.

16. This analysis has benefited from Nancy Munn's profoundly insightful analysis of the sources of the psychological effectiveness of the symbols of the Wawilak myth and the associated age-grading rites (Munn, 1969).

17. Munn refers to these processes as "memorialization" and "symbolic objectifications" (Munn, 1969:183).

18. This same suggestion of a primal reproductive self-sufficiency is also present in the story of the two Nyapililingu from Djarrakpi analyzed by Morphy, 1991 (see especially chap. 12).

19. In Berndt's analysis of the Djunkgao (Djangguwul) sisters myth, the two creator sisters and their brother are described as having abnormally long genitalia. One of Berndt's informants suggested that the women's long clitorises meant that they were hermaphroditic possessing both male and female reproductive organs. By way of clarification, the informant told Berndt of a man who had been born in historic times who had the sexual attributes of both male and female and was thus able to reproduce by self-impregnation (Berndt, 1953:11).

20. Morphy recounts another Murngin narrative from Yirrkala dealing with the Nyapililngu woman (or women) from Djarrakpi, whose menstrual blood creates an entire lake. The image, suggests Morphy, is linked to the idea of women's menstrual blood being the medium of regenerating human spirits. Thus it is clear that for Murngin, menstrual blood is a multivalent symbol which, in different contexts, conveys images of creation, destruction, and their mutual transformations (Morphy, 1991:282–283).

21. Nancy Munn has analyzed the transformations in blood symbolism within the myth as it relates to the sisters and then to their male counterparts:

> [t]he women's blood is detached from their bodies and painted on the bodies of the men in order to "play back" the original events. Although ostensibly this blood is from the snake's bites . . . it is also identified with the women's menstrual blood. The blood is thus translated from the interior of the women's bodies to the external world, where, separated from its biological matrix, it enters the realm of the symbolic, social things. [Munn, 1969:183–184]

22. While Warner uses the term "Bamun," other works on the Murngin/Yolngu suggest the more common term of "Wangarr" or (in Warner) "Wongar" for the mythological period. See Williams, 1986:28. Williams discusses at length the somewhat misleading use of the

English words "dreaming" or "dreamtime" as a translation for the aboriginal concept of a mythological period (Williams, 1986:234 ff).

23. On the importance of the multivocality of Murngin symbols and the continuous process of interpretation by which symbolic forms are renewed, see Morphy, 1991.

24. Keen (1978) and Shapiro (1981) use the term *ngapipi* for mother's brother/wife's father, a term which seems to be in more common usage than *gawel*.

25. Warner interprets this pivotal episode as suggesting the Murngin belief that women are profane and particularly so when they are menstruating (Warner, 1936/1958:65). Both Berndt and Keen attempt to refute this assertion. Keen argues that while women are not made sacred *(duyu)* in ceremonies, as men are, they are not considered ordinary or profane. "On the contrary," Keen argues, "men are inclined to say that 'women are the real bosses' (Keen, 1978:370; see also Berndt, 1953:14). Berndt goes even further. He argues that women actually have a sacred status, and that this is enhanced during their menstrual periods (Berndt, 1976:28). This is because all blood is assumed to have life-enhancing powers:

> [T]here is . . . positive value accorded to blood (whether menstrual or afterbirth, or from ritual defloration, or from penis incision). Not only is blood sacred, symbolizing as it does life-giving attributes; it also has a sexual connotation, which in turn emphasizes the social significance of coitus. Contrary to Warner's view . . . women's physiological functions were not regarded as "unclean" or as profaning sacred ritual. . . .
>
> Also, while a menstruating woman was subject to certain tabus and ideally should not have intercourse at that time, there is evidence to suggest that this physical condition was seen as enhancing her sexual attractiveness.

Berndt's refutation of Warner's claims about female pollution are remarkably similar to an argument proposed by Hanson on the status of Maori women in relation to menstruation (Hanson, 1982).

Morphy also stresses the centrality of female powers at the heart of all Murngin ideas of power. Morphy's informant, Narritjin, frequently told him that in relation to all generative power, "really, women are the inside" (Morphy, 1991:97). As for the distribution of ritual knowledge, Morphy argues that women actually know much of what goes on in the most sacred rites, and this fact is central to the power of the ideology of secrecy of Murngin epistemology (Morphy, 1991).

26. The narrative transformation in the Wawilak story of literal action into abstract symbol has its parallel in the Murngin conception of the gradual penetration of symbols involved in understanding the meaning of paintings. In his fascinating study of Yolngu art and knowledge, Howard Morphy describes an interpretive system whereby the relatively figurative and literal "outside" representations in art are gradually transformed into "inside" forms that are more general, abstract, and comprise geometrical motifs rather than directly iconic figures. This "movement" from specific figurative forms to more general geometric representations distinguishes more open and outside paintings from more restricted and inside ones. The same semiotic shift also characterizes an individual's changing understanding of a sacred painting through sacred education (Morphy, 1991, especially chap. 10).

27. On page 241 the narrative makes additional references to numerous place names where the sisters stopped, but since these localities are not included on any maps of Arnhem Land I could find, there is no way for me to check whether this section of the narrative reproduces the same anomaly as the one just discussed.

28. I am grateful to Professors Donald Verene and Rudolph Makreel of Emory University's philosophy department for clarifying the Hegelian notion of *Aufhebung*.

29. Murngin girls and women are generally known by terms that indicate their reproductive status, while boys and men are classified by their state of ritual knowledge as indicated by the sequence of initiation rites.

30. On Genesis as a story of the emergence of consciousness, see Paul, 1977.

31. It is important to note that the same walkabout schema that governs Murngin notions of knowledge creation and transmission also structures many of the extraordinarily complex models governing kinship and marriage relations. The Murngin have numerous cultural models governing marriage. They are alternate phrasings of a single general schema. Marriage models range from simple moiety exogamy, to "Mother's Brother's Daughter's" marriage, to subsection rules, to very complex long cycles of exchange between alternate generations and distant lines. These latter attenuated models include a form of mother-in-law bestowal, where a man and his sister arrange for his daughter to produce a wife for their own kutara "Mother's Mother's Brother's Daughter's Son". The common schema for all of these models is one proposing that one must separate in order eventually to overcome the separation and reunite. This is true not only for marriage but also for kinship personalities as manifested in kin terms. Kin terms tend to disappear, only to cycle back again in extraordinarily complex but persistent patterns (Morphy, 1991; Keen, 1978; Warner, 1936/1958). These kin models are linked by a "walkabout" schema, proposing that one leaves home only to effect an eventual return, having been transformed by the journey.

10

Dreamtime Learning, Outside-In: Murngin Age-Grading Rites

The same symbol may be reckoned to have different senses at different phases in a ritual performance, or rather, different senses become paramount at different times. Which sense shall become paramount is determined by the ostensible purpose of the phase of the ritual in which it appears. For a ritual, like a space rocket, is phased, and each phase is directed towards a limited end which itself becomes a means to the ultimate end of the total performance.

—Victor Turner

LEARNING CULTURE

The case for culture in mind rests on an understanding of how public models—what I call instituted models—are internalized by members of a community and born again as mental models—the cultural dimensions of personal experience. The study of cultural learning was pioneered by Margaret Mead and Gregory Bateson. In New Guinea and in Bali, they used photography to document the cultural messages embedded in the culturally patterned behavior between caretakers and children. This "cultural communication" was assumed to shape the children's perception of fundamental aspects of experience (Bateson and Mead, 1942). Mead and Bateson studied what they called "Balinese character" outside-in. Their primary data were not psychometric tests, life histories, or psychodynamic interviews but rather photos of a large number of standardized behavioral patterns that were assumed to model for children basic orientations to the world. Issues such as deference and respect, balance, sharing, narcissism, body imagery, and shame are treated as learned through culturally orchestrated practices, petty ritual models that structure parent-child interactions.

The culture-as-message approach to socialization understands cultural models as an information system. Conventionally coded information is passed among individuals and especially between generations. This approach usually distinguishes the *primary socialization* of basic orientations very early in life from *secondary socialization* of individuals later in life. Secondary socialization (often called "education") is commonly a matter of domain-specific skills and knowledge. In contrast to "education," primary socialization often involves covert messages that get built into the patterning of very basic human experiences like language learning, body posture, eating behavior, and personal hygiene. In this way, cultural models come to be deeply embedded in early experience, so that they appear to be natural to members of a community rather than matters of convention.[1]

Not surprisingly, language learning turns out to be one of the most important arenas of primary socialization, where important cultural schemas are embedded into social practices. In a series of important comparative studies in the Pacific, Bambi Schieffelin and Elinor Ochs have documented how language learning involves the communication of significant metamessages about the local character of social relations (Ochs, 1988; Ochs and Schieffelin, eds., 1979; Ochs and Schieffelin, 1984; Scheiffelin, 1990; Schieffelin and Ochs, 1986). This embeddedness of cultural models *in the very forms* that frame basic social institutions accounts for the depth and tacitness of foundational knowledge.

Another important influence on the study of cultural learning is the work of the great Russian psychologist Lev Vygotsky. Vygotsky's approach to cognitive development has influenced a number of distinguished cross-cultural psychologists who have explored in great detail how particular cultural models are learned by children and how cultural learning shapes cognitive development more generally.[2] Vygotsky turned the enterprise of developmental psychology inside out, stressing the social and cultural origins of even the most intimate and private aspects of thinking. For Vygotsky, the social context within which cognitive development takes place is not just the local cultural setting but the entire historical context within which social relations are embedded.

Rather than viewing the child as passively developing or simply responding to its surroundings, Vygotsky stressed the active participation of a child in helping to shape his or her cognitive development. Vygotskians emphasize the primary socialization of higher mental functions in the context of a child's primary social relationships. Especially important are the child's experiences with caregivers in what he termed the "zone of proximal development," which Barbara Rogoff defines as "the region of sensitivity to social guidance where the child is not quite able to manage the problem independently" (Rogoff, 1990:36).

Of course this zone of proximal development will itself vary from culture to culture. Rogoff's seminal research on cognitive development among American and Guatemalan children focused on a domestic zone defined by parents and other primary caregivers. But in societies with elaborate rites of passage for children, the zone of proximal development can be decisively shifted at different stages of life. In Murngin society, foundational schemas are learned by novices in a highly ritualized proximal zone in which parents are replaced by senior males of the group. Murngin epistemogenesis is achieved for the young male initiates by a series of ritually guided experiences that serve to translate the narrative model described in the last chapter into more intimate kinds of personal experience. In this chapter we complete our Australian walkabout by returning to the Wawilak narrative. This time around, the analysis focuses on how the public narrative model, explicated in the previous chapter, is translated into mental models for Murngin youth through a set of age-grading rites that define the conventional life course of Murngin men.

Murngin appear to make no clear distinction between social structure and religion. What unites these domains is a common concern with regeneration. Regeneration is related to knowledge in three different senses. First, the diverse models of regeneration share a common underlying cultural schema that links them as forms of cultural knowledge. Second, the subject matter of both the sacred narratives and the rites that instantiate them for novices concerns epistemogenesis—the origin of the known world conceived of as the birth of its knowability. And finally, this local epistemology is put into practice through the translation of the narrative into rites of passage for the young. This third dimension of social reproduction is the subject of this chapter.

RELATING MYTH AND RITUAL

The Wawilak myth is the narrative foundation for men taking young boys from their mothers and remaking them into men. The narrative is a charter for these initiation rites in four different senses: (1) The story justifies the men taking charge of the boys, transferring the work of reproduction from women to men. (2) The narrative is completed by the ritual work, since the myth ends where the age-grading begins. (3) The age-grading rites derive their imagery and story line from the content of the myth narrative. In a sense, the different initiation rites constitute distinct retellings of the myth, framed in different "keys." (4) In its narrative structure, the story of the Wawilak sisters sets out a general schema for the acquisition of knowledge. It is this schema that is enacted in the subsequent age-grading rites and in many forms of Murngin social reproduction (i.e., kinship and marriage).

There is no way that a thorough analysis of even one of the ceremonies can be undertaken within the limits of a chapter like this.[3] Each is a cycle of dozens of songs and dances, which Warner compares in scale and complexity to a Wagnerian opera. The intention here is (1) to clarify the thematic relations among each of the major age-grading ceremonies and the Wawilak narrative and (2), to suggest how the rites transform the *narrative model* of knowledge transfer into the *experience* of knowledge transfer for the initiates.

THE CEREMONIES

Warner focuses on four ceremonies that his informants recognized as closely linked to the Wawilak narrative. Two of the ceremonies, Djungguan and Marndiella, are rites frequently associated with circumcision. In the words of one of Keen's informants, these ceremonies are "for foreskins" (Keen, 1978:148). Keen's informants suggested that Djungguan and Marndiella are also about death. Morphy calls Djungguan a "regional fertility ceremony." Performed by clans of both moieties who assemble from a wide area, "its successful performance is thought to enhance the fertility of the land and its people and to create a feeling of well-being in the participants" (Morphy, 1991:85). We will focus on the Djungguan ceremony, which is the main

Murngin ritual setting for circumcision and, according to Keen, the most important of all Murngin age-grading ceremonies.

Berndt termed Kunapipi (Gunabibi) "a fertility cult" (Berndt, 1951). Keen's informants characterized it as playful, a kind of game that makes people happy (Keen, 1978:148). It appears to be aimed at the initiation of circumcised youths. Gunabibi is associated with sexuality, procreation, and marriage.

According to Warner, Ulmark is a more recent introduction into northeast Arnhem Land than the other ceremonies and was not as well understood by the old men. At the time of Warner's fieldwork, Ulmark was not seen as a mandatory part of initiation. More recent observers in Arnhem Land have noted that Ulmark does not seem to be performed any more. Ulmark appears to have marked the entrance of young men into the center of the men's ceremonial ground and into a deeper understanding of the meanings of their clan identity. In this sense it comes closest of the age-grading rites to the Narra Ceremony, in which sacred totemic emblems are shown to clan members. Ulmark introduced novices to some of the more secret terms and clan emblems. They were also taught a special language called *ki-jin,* a kind of pidgin that combined words from a number of different local languages.

In the normal course of things, the life history of a Murngin male would likely be marked by passing through, in sequence, Djungguan (or Marndiella), then Gunabibi, and finally (and optionally) Ulmark. I have not been able to discern from the literature whether this sequence was invariable. Warner suggests that the age-grading ceremonies form a sequence that is linked with changes in an individual's familial status (Warner, 1936/1958:134). By means of these graded rites, he moves from the junior generation to senior generation status. These changes are paralleled by changes in his spatial position in the campground. Gradually, the rites transfer him from the outside camp, where women and children stay, to the men's ceremonial ground, and ultimately to the "inside" triangular dance ground and totem house where the most sacred totemic emblems are kept. Warner's diagram suggests that the spatial and sociological transformations in a male's status are conceived as parallel journeys.

What follows is a summary of each of the three major ceremonies, as described in Warner's account.[4] Each summary is divided into the following sections: (A) action sequences, (B) key symbols, and (C) relation to the Wawilak narrative. Every part of the ceremony involves songs and dances that commemorate particular totemic species and relevant moments from the Wawilak narrative.

Djungguan
A. *Action Sequences*
   1. A trumpet is made and blown to announce the start of Djungguan.
   2. Novices, usually in pairs, are forcibly taken from their mothers and sent on a "walkabout" accompanied by a close male relative.
   3. Novices return to the general camp, where their mothers wail over them while dancing around the two *warngaitja* poles.[5] The men then repeat the abduction of the boys from their mothers, taking them for the first time into the men's ceremonial ground.
   4. A fire is made in the men's ground, and the novices are placed near it.
   5. The old men sing of Yurlunggur and his well, and the great Yurlunggur trumpet is blown over the novices.

6. The novices are taken to the triangular dance ground, where a fire is made. The boys watch the old men dance numerous animal dances, with Dua and Yiritja men alternating as presenters.

7. The night before the actual circumcision, the older men bleed themselves and collect the blood, allowing it to coagulate somewhat. This blood is used to paint the Yurlunggur trumpet. This ritually induced and coagulated blood is said to be powerful, like a totemic emblem (Warner, 1936/1958:271).

8. The morning of the circumcision, men paint themselves with this blood and dance a series of dances on the triangular dance ground.

9. Boys are painted with totemic emblems, but with the juice of an orchid bulb. Blood is considered too potent an adhesive for the boys.

10. Men take the uncircumcised boys (usually in pairs) into the general camp where the women are. The women have prepared by painting themselves (though not with blood). The men form a tight circle around the novices, who are given a drink of water, which will be their last chance to have water for the next 24 hours. The boys are told that a great flood has come over the earth, and the water has become too salty too drink. Then, using a spearhead tipped with blood, the men circumcise the boys. The foreskins are placed into a basket of water for safekeeping.

11. A fire is built in the men's ground. The newly circumcised novices are placed near the fire where they are "steamed." At the same time, they are given advice by their elders on how young men should act. They are taught the sacred totemic names of every kind of food that is in the camp, and, as they utter the names, they swallow the food.

12. The boys are kept apart from the women until their wounds heal.

13. The Yurlunggur trumpet is buried in the mud, out of sight of the women. The Murngin say that it is returning to its well.

B. *Key Symbols of Djungguan*

1. Two *warngaitja* poles, erected in the general camp. These multivocal symbols represent the two sisters, the novices being taken from their mothers (p. 256), as well as the two sons in the Wawilak narrative who Yurlunggur separated from their mothers.

2. The trumpet. This is Yurlunggur, emerging from the well and calling for the boys' foreskins.

3. Triangular dance ground *(molk)*. It was made by Yurlunggur when he fell in the Wawilak narrative.

4. Men's arm blood, made potent by controlled bleeding and drying. Having the power of a totemic emblem, it is put back on the men's bodies, and on the Yurlunggur trumpet in the form of such emblems, transforming them into *Wongar* beings.

5. Separation. Boys are separated from women, blood from the body of men, and the foreskins are taken from the boys' penises.

6. Fire. The boys are "cooked" after they have been ritually killed. Only then is the secret knowledge of totemic emblems revealed to them.

7. Water. The men's ritual acts result in the boys' being deprived of water. The foreskin is placed in a container of water.

8. Swallowing. The snake swallows the boys' foreskin. The boys swallow the foods, after they learn their names. The men "swallow" the boys by incorporating them into their camp.

C. *Djungguan's Link with the Wawilak Narrative*

The Djungguan replays the Wawilak myth in a specific symbolic key, focusing on (1) the emergence of Yurlunggur from the well, (2) the swallowing of the boys, and (3) the spitting out of the mothers. Swallowing is symbolically linked with the violent separations the novices undergo, being torn from their mothers, at the same time as the "female" part of their anatomy is cut away.

Gunabibi

A. *Action Sequences*

The Gunbabibi is very long and complex in structure. Here is a summary of the main events that Warner witnessed in a performance of Gunabibi at Milingimbi, as set out in *A Black Civilization.*

1. The bull-roarer *(Mandelprindi)* is made. It is covered with human blood or red ocher and has a snake design painted on it.
2. Elders of the Liaalaomir clan and other clan elders confer and decide which boys are old enough to go through Gunabibi.
3. All members of participating clans form a large group in outside camp.
4. A Dua man, hidden in the bush, whirls Mandelprindi and makes a humming sound.
5. Yiritja men enter the men's ceremonial ground, to act as go-betweens and guardians for the novices.
6. The next day, men enter the ceremonial ground and, undecorated, begin singing and dancing animals in the song cycle, starting with seagull dance. Women in the general camp respond with a shrill sound. The seagull dancer is covered with blood and wears a tall "dunce cap" hat. Men surround the dancer and call out "Gunabibi!"
7. A long cycle of songs commemorates totemic animal species. Each species has three songs, which celebrate the male, female, and eggs. The cycle ends with songs to Muit (Python totem) and Four Muits.
8. On subsequent days, several totemic animals will be commemorated in song and dance. First, the males are commemorated, then the females, and finally the union of males and females.
9. Men carrying lighted torches enter the general camp and surround the women. Two older women beat the ground with yam sticks or clubs.
10. Two Yiritja men dressed as Yiritja water snakes appear before the women, calling out to them. Women respond in the same shrill tones used to respond to the bullroarer. The women give presents to the Yiritja men who are said to "swallow" the women's gifts.
11. The two old women beat the ground and cry out to Muit not to swallow them any more since they are now clean.
12. A hole is dug, representing the Mirrirmina well and the dancers enter the well hole.
13. Two Yiritja messengers make a circuit and invite other clans to visit the Gunabibi. They may journey a month or more before returning. With the arrival of outside visitors, the most important part of the ceremony begins.
14. Two Yiritja messenger "snakes" and an initiated Dua son of the ceremonial leader announce to the gathered clans that the initiation is about to begin.
15. Before the messengers return, the well-hole is abandoned and the men dig a crescent-shaped trench *(kartdjur)* 5 to 6 feet in depth and 10 feet long, with earth piled up along its rim on both sides.
16. A dance is done representing a single man filled with sexual desire, seeking a mate. Then a man impersonates a woman seeking a mate. Finally, the two dance together, simulating intercourse at the entrance to the trench.
17. The Muit snake dancers enter the trench and dance. No one else may enter.
18. The Yiritja "helpers" make Yermerlindi, two poles representing a palm tree and a python.
19. In the Yiritja campground where the Yermerlindi are constructed, no Dua men may enter. But Dua men send presents to this ground to thank their Yiritja kin for making the poles.

20. Novices are placed on raised ground on the concave side of the *kartdjur* trench.
21. From one side of the trench, a long narrow extension about 50 feet long is dug.
22. The novices have bushes placed under their armpits and their eyes are rubbed with the sweat of the Yiritja snakes and the Dua ritual leaders.
23. Many men dance around the trench. They are covered with white clay and represent opossums. As the opossum dancers dance, they start filling up the trench with loose dirt.
24. Two dancers perform the dance of the Wawilak sisters as they carried paper bark cradles. They squat inside the trench and imitate the whining of babies, to the hilarity of the amused onlookers.
25. Yermerlindi is sung, a fire is built, and men cry that Muit is emerging from the water. Two Muit emblems are introduced, and the novices are assured that these are genuine snakes, having the spirit of Muit inside them.
26. Two men carry in a pole, which they hold parallel to the ground several feet above the trench. The Yermerlindi posts are brought to the edge of the trench and allowed to fall down, hitting the horizontal pole. This is repeated many times, to the shrill cries of all present.
27. The Yermerlindi poles are brought into the *kartdjur* trench, while the older men cover themselves with arm blood and kangaroo fat.
28. Visitors and hosts spend much time discussing their relations and sorting out how they are related. Warner reports this involves considerable intellectual effort and is enjoyed by many of the men (Warner, 1978:296). During these discussions, men agree to exchange wives for the evening, for ceremonial intercourse. Ritual preparations are made so that these participants in ritual promiscuity will not become ill. Ritual intercourse is believed to be an obligation of all married participants in Gunabibi.
29. The morning following the ritual intercourse, two forked poles are erected along the boundary between the men's ceremonial camp and the general camp. A connecting pole is placed inside the forks, so that the whole structure resembles a house frame. Branches are placed over the top so the whole structure is enclosed on all sides.
30. Two Yiritja messenger snakes sit at either end of the structure and in a shrill voice call out to the women of the camp who come to see who is calling. The novices are seated beneath the branch that hangs from the ridgepole. The women, smeared with red ocher, sit down about 10 yards away from the structure from which the shrill cries are emanating.
31. The Dua men enter the dance ground and surround the women and the house structure. The Yiritja snakes call out, and the Dua women respond. Then the women return to their own camp.
32. The Dua men sit in a line and the novices are taken to the head of this line. The men extend their left arms and one by one the initiates crawl under the men's arms. They emerge by one of the forked poles, where a Yiritja snake gives them food to eat. The novice spits out the food.
33. In the evening, Mandelprindi sounds one last time. The men gather the initiates in a group, and dance around the youths. The boys' forehead bands are then removed, marking the end of the Gunabibi.

B. *Key Symbols of Gunabibi*
   1. Mandelprindi, the bull roarer, is the voice of the great python.
   2. The well hole represents the Mirrirmina water hole from which the python emerged in the Wawilak narrative. When outsiders arrive at the ceremonial ground, it is replaced by the *kartdjur* trench.

3. Muit is the Gunabibi name for Yurlunggur, the "great father" rock python of the Dua clans studied by Warner.

4. *Kartdjur* represents a vagina, and at the same time its curved shape commemorates the two Wawilak sisters as they lay down to sleep.

5. Totemic songs all stress the sequence of male, then female, then their union or offspring.

6. The complementarity and interdependence of Dua and Yiritja is stressed. The role of the Yiritja snakes as helpers, messengers, and go-betweens is a central theme of the ritual.

7. The two Yermerlindi poles represent both a palm tree and the snake.

8. The ceremonial exchange of wives celebrates the attraction of men and women to one another.

9. The forked poles represent the Wawilak sisters' house in which they tried to take refuge from the rain.

C. *Gunabibi's Link with the Wawilak narrative*

In Gunabibi, the images of swallowing and incorporation, central to the Wawilak story, are replayed as images of sexual conjugation. The stress is on the reunion of Dua and Yiritja and their interdependence, not only conceptually but also practically in the enactment of the ceremony. Yiritja "helpers" unite with Dua "owners" to make the ceremony come off.

This interdependence of Dua and Yiritja is also equated with the natural attraction of male and female. The well as paternal source is transformed into the vaginal image of the trench. The playfulness and vitality of carnal sexuality is celebrated with abandon, especially in the exchange of wives that is the climax of the rite.

In Djungguan, Yurlunggur's expulsion of the sisters and his incorporation of their sons stressed the separation of men from women and of Dua men from Dua women (incest prohibition). In Gunabibi, however, this same act is redefined as an enactment of the marriage—that is, as the interdependence of male and female, and of the moieties. Yurlunggur as Muit is not father so much as father-in-law or mother's brother. The ceremony celebrates fertility and fecundity through songs which suggest that $1 + 1 = 3$, the union of male and female producing offspring. This transforms images of loss and separation into images of enlargement and multiplication.

Ulmark

A. *Action Sequences*

Ulmark as witnessed by Warner was very long, lasting up to two full years. Like Gunabibi, it is a very elaborate series of rites.

1. Older men cut down a tree, making it into a log. The log is used to mark the separation of the main camp from the men's ceremonial ground.

2. In the morning, two Dua men representing the stone kangaroo and two Yiritja men representing the large gray kangaroo sit on the log. Other initiated men sit in a line facing these four.

3. The women are brought near the log, where they carry yam sticks and sing *"kait-ba! kait-ba!"* The four kangaroo men run away into the men's ceremonial ground, followed by the other initiated men. The singing women follow the retreating men.

4. Entering the men's ceremonial ground, the kangaroo men strip completely and cut their hair. After this, in the morning and evening, the men take up singing and dancing. Each man dances while the others sing as a chorus.

5. While this dancing continues, several senior men cut down a tree and make it into a

drum 4 to 5 feet long, called *uvar*, representing the great python. The *uvar* is painted with snake figures, emus, and other totemic species and placed in a small house in the men's ceremonial camp.

6. Ulmark begins when the drum is beaten with a pandanus drum stick, and the women respond with *"kait-ba! kait-ba!"*

7. The kangaroo men, carrying, respectively, emblems representing the tail of a large gray kangaroo and that of a stone kangaroo, undertake a journey to inform surrounding clans of the ceremony that has begun and inviting them to attend. Upon nearing an encampment, they hit a tree with a stick to signal their arrival and announce their invitation.

8. Arriving visitors decorate their bodies with red ocher and signal their arrival by singing *"kait-ba! kait-ba!"*

9. Back at the ceremonial ground, the older men make a triangular dance ground very similar to that used during the Djungguan. It is called *barn-ga-ga* (python's body).

10. The novices remain in the ceremonial ground until the ritual is completed. The women remain in the general camp. The women sing *"kait ba!"* while men of various clans sing songs evoking various totemic creatures sacred to the particular clans for whom the ceremony is performed, in this case honeybees and various grubs.

11. The Torres Strait pigeon dance is performed.

12. The kangaroo men do a stone spear-head dance.

13. A series of tree grub dances and songs are performed, whereby men, holding feather headdresses, imitate bees, kangaroos, and various grubs. The dancers move on the dance ground from the snake's tail to its head and back to the tail.

14. Large representations of *Dua* and *Yiritja* kangaroo tails are constructed. Dua and Yiritja kangaroo dancers "leapfrog" over one another, Dua over Yiritja, Yiritja over Dua.

15. The first part of the Ulmark ceremonial is over. Some performances of the Ulmark ceremonial are carried out over two years, in which case the visitors now disperse to their own camps.

16. When it is decided to finish the Ulmark in the course of a single season, Dua and Yiritja kangaroo men dig a triangular pit in the center of the ceremonial ground. This triangular pit is excavated as deep as a man's shoulders. Similar in shape to the triangular "snake" dance grounds in Djungguan and Ulmark, this dance pit has a path leading out to one side of the triangle.

17. While this pit is being dug, women are clearing a meandering path that snakes around the whole of the men's ceremonial ground.

18. Men make snail-shell rattles.

19. A rainy-season type of bark house is built on the ceremonial ground. Pictures illustrating scenes from the Wawilak myth are painted on the inside walls of the structure.

20. A snail-shell rattle dance is done by a line of men facing the women in the camp. The men offer the women presents.

21. Messengers are dispatched to announce the concluding events of Ulmark to nearby clans.

22. Initiated men do a number of animal dances of *Wongar* ancestors for the novices who are told to watch carefully.

23. Numerous grubs and honeybees are danced over for a period of a month to six weeks.

24. Any old feuds among clans are settled. The leaders of the ceremony begin to use *ki-jin* language, which is a kind of pidgin incorporating words from a number of different local languages. "Clowns" take the role of peacemakers, attempting to convert anger to laughter.

25. The Torres Strait pigeon dance is performed.

26. Initiates lie down in two lines, while the kangaroo messengers sing in *ki-jin* language.

27. Men and women of the same clan face each other at the boundary between the ceremonial ground and the general camp. The men and women throw a snail-shell rattle back and forth from one line to the other. The women keep it, finally.

28. Two men make paper-bark cylinders about 12 inches in diameter and about 20 feet in length. A fire is made, and one end of this cylinder is placed near the fire. Yams are placed at the fire end of the cylinder, while spears are placed at the other end. The bark is lit, and men dance over the burning bark, singeing their leg hairs. The paper-bark cylinders are burned up in the process.

29. Two men dance a frill-neck lizard dance and jump into the fire.

30. Two by two, men perform dancing commemorating flying foxes, kangaroos, and tiger snakes entering the triangular pit.

31. The initiates are prevented from witnessing this next event. All the older men run into the path leading into the triangular pit, and they enter the hole in the ground.

32. Men do a series of snake and kangaroo dances. The men then leave the dance ground and return to the general camp.

33. A large forked pole is erected, similar to one of the poles used in Gunabibi. The women gather around this pole and two older women climb up and sit atop its forked branches.

34. The women make a fire that follows the path made by them earlier in the ceremony. The fire surrounds the men's camp and moves from the women's camp toward the men's camp.

35. Men paint themselves with red ocher and give themselves a totally new appearance. They shave themselves and cut their hair. The women wash themselves and then repaint themselves and all their possessions to make themselves look new.

36. The men leave the dance ground and surround the women sitting on the forked post. The men roar like thunder. The two women jump down off the pole, and their places are taken by two men. These men jump down off the forked pole into the chorus of men who surround them, and they all return to the men's ceremonial ground.

37. Men paint their spear throwers with red ocher and dance the spear-thrower feather-headpiece dance. The novices are not permitted to see these spear throwers and head-pieces.

38. Two lines of gray kangaroo dancers form, one on each side of the triangular pit. Inside are sitting three groups of men wearing their feather headpieces. On both sides of the dance pit, right next to the kangaroos, two lines of fire are made.

39. The men spend the night singing the songs of the stars, moon, sun, evening star, and morning star. At dawn, the men pick up a lighted torch, and a group of flying fox dancers gathers near the bush. Crying out like flying foxes, the flying fox dancers run one-by-one up to the triangular pit and hurl themselves in.

40. The forked pole sequence (described in number 36 above) is repeated.

41. Old men build numerous stone fires in the general camp. All the men divide into groups and surround these fires. They inhale the smoke and squat over the fires to allow smoke to enter their anuses.

42. A week or so later, women bake a large palm nut bread, which is divided and consumed by the men participating in the Ulmark.

43. A huge fire is made.

44. Each man dons new body ornaments. Each mature male holds a green bush.

45. Men dance around the fire, and the women dance around the men. All the participants (male and female) are "smoked" over by a smoldering branch.

46. Wet leaves are placed over the fire to create steam. The novices are then placed over this fire so that they are "steamed" both anally and orally. The novices may now eat large game that had been previously taboo for them.

B. *Key Symbols of Ulmark*

1. The great python Yurlunggur is represented repeatedly through a wide variety of different images. His emblem is present in (1) the triangular dance ground, (2) the triangular pit, (3) the burning bark cylinders, (4) the snaking path dug by the women surrounding the men's ground, (5) the log separating the men's from the women's camps, and (6) the two men sitting on the forked pole, who are said to be the snake's head.

2. Both the forked pole (in which the two women sit) and the bark house represent the house in which the two Wawilak sisters took refuge from the rain.

3. Men and women of the same clan exchange songs and gifts.

4. Fire and smoke are dominant symbols throughout the ceremony.

5. Kangaroos, snakes, and other totemic animals are swallowed up by the fire.

6. Fire is also used to cook and to purify people.

7. Transformation and renewal of the participants are major recurring themes in the ritual. Images of renewal and transformation include making peace between feuding groups, stripping off old ornaments, adorning oneself with new ornaments, shaving, cutting hair, painting the body with ocher or kangaroo grease, and (for women) washing the body.

8. Images of union among disparate elements are symbolized through *ki-jin* language, sharing of bread, settling of feuds, and the general mingling of people from different clans and moieties.

9. Paths are forged, linking up disparate groups. The triangular dance pit has a path leading from one of its sides. The women make a path from their camp to that of the men.

10. Blood as body decoration is replaced by kangaroo grease. The key symbols of sexual reproduction disappear.

C. *Ulmark's Link with the Wawilak Narrative*

Once again the ritual enacts episodes from the Wawilak narrative. The two sisters' attempts to hide from the rain are replayed, as are images of the snake swallowing them. There is no direct reference in Ulmark to their sons, though the novices are identified with the cooked totemic animals. It is the sisters who are swallowed up, and it is they who are returned to their homes via the snake and fire imagery.

In Ulmark, the Wawilak narrative is reconstituted around the early episodes where the sisters kill the totemic animals, name them, cook them, and then look on as the animals are brought back to life only to jump out of the cooking fire and back into the well. The images of swallowing and incorporation are prominent in Ulmark, as they are in the other ceremonies. But here swallowing is not represented as separation, destruction, or marriage. In Ulmark they become images of purification and renewal by fire. An act of incineration that would seem at first glance to suggest destruction turns out to bring on new life.

The schema of separation-death-fire-reconstitution that patterns the fate of the totemic species in the narrative is played back in the ritual through the metaphor of the snake swallowing the women and returning them "home." The fire-smoke-steam-cooking imagery whose "outside" meaning in the narrative is destruction is replayed in Ulmark to reveal a new significance. The "inside meaning" of these acts is revealed as cleansing and rejuvenation. An "outside" death turns out be an "inside" rebirth.

Such inversions of meaning are an important part of the effectiveness of Murngin symbolism and point to developmentally layered understandings. Interpretations at an early level of understanding are deepened and often reversed at a later stage of knowledge. Morphy describes with great insight this layered conception of knowledge (see Morphy, 1991:77).

The inversion in the significance of key symbols appears to be a structural feature of Murngin sacred education. Munn (1969) made this sort of inversion in the meaning of bloodletting a central feature of her analysis of the psychological effectiveness of the Murngin rites. Morphy shows the same kind of inversion in blood symbolism from death-dealing (outside meaning) to life-promoting (inside meaning) in his analysis of the Nyapilingu story and associated paintings (Morphy, 1991: chap. 12, especially p. 285). In the age-grading rites, this layered conception of knowledge is realized in the gradual transformation of the initiate's experience of key symbols as he moves from outside to inside understandings.

RITUAL TRANSFORMATIONS OF INITIATES' KNOWLEDGE

Each of the three age-grading rites dramatizes key moments from the Wawilak narrative. But none of the rites is a full enactment of the myth itself. The story line of the myth is alluded to in both the ritual songs and dances and in the informants' exegesis of the rites provided by Warner. But the narrative quality of the story line is replaced by a kind of flashbulb effect. Key moments of the myth are frozen, taken out of context, and represented as archetypes—separable submodels, with variable meanings. The most important of these archetypes are the following:

- Two sisters with their digging sticks
- Uncontrolled flows (water and blood)
- The two children (sons) of the sisters
- Sexual reproduction (intercourse, pregnancy, birth)
- The great python (Yurlunggur, Muit, Bapa Indi)
- The house in which the sisters tried to hide from the rain
- The flood caused by the emergence of Yurlunggur from the well
- The well itself
- The swallowing of the sisters and their sons by the snake
- The *Wongar* creatures named by the sisters on their journey, in this instance grubs, honeybees, kangaroos, lizards, snakes
- The fire in which the sisters cooked the creatures they named
- The jumping of the animals into the fire

The Wawilak narrative may be thought of as being refracted through each of the ceremonies into a series of abstract themes. These themes are dislocated from the flow of the story and realized with diverse images and with varying semantic emphases throughout the series of initiation rituals. This is puzzling. One might expect that the ceremonies would reinforce rather than mask the narrative unity of the story on which they depend and to which they point.

In this context, it is important to remember that from the perspective of the novices, *the rites produce the narrative* and not the other way around. The myth narrative is only very rarely told as such and never to uninitiated Murngin. It is among the most secret and sacred of Murngin stories. The complete narrative is supposed to be known only to the most senior Murngin men. From the point of view of these senior ritual leaders, the rites may well be interpreted through their understanding of the implied narrative. But from the perspective of the novices, the rites and the associated songs and paintings constitute, in their fractured way, their only detailed knowledge of the Wawilak story. What kind of understanding of the narrative is possible when it is transmitted in such a form?

THE NOVICE'S POINT OF VIEW

In his analysis of initiation rites among the Baktaman of New Guinea, Fredrik Barth proposes that we need to focus not so much on the abstract cosmology that is being passed on to the novices but on the ways in which the tradition is encoded for the novices (Barth, 1975). He argues that the gradual disclosure of mysteries to the novices by their elders is done in such a way as to lead them to a sort of layered understanding of the world, by which truths are partial and emergent. What is understood at any one point in the initiation is both transcended and deepened by subsequent revelations.

While the Baktaman conception of knowledge is somewhat different from that of the Murngin,[6] Barth's insight into the relationship between the mode of transmission of knowledge and the experience of that knowledge by the initiates is relevant to the Murngin case. Specifically, we need to examine the connection between the specific way in which the Wawilak narrative is ritually disclosed to the Murngin novices and the kind of understanding this sort of transmission makes possible. Of course, it is virtually impossible to know what the inner experience of any of these novices would actually be. But we can assume from the available evidence that what they experience of the narrative at any given moment in their initiation is puzzling and disjointed at best.

The conditions of transmission and the inherent ambiguity of many of the ritual images would also permit each of the novices to construct idiosyncratic "readings" of the ceremonies, in addition to whatever orthodox interpretation is eventually promoted.[7] The repeated ritual images and their various permutations point to an emergent narrative. This emerging narrative is probably inferred only very gradually by the boys and young men and initially comprehended not in a general form but only in terms of its different emphases in each of the different ceremonies.

This partial and emerging character of the knowledge conveyed to the boys in the initiation rites is not a peripheral issue. For the narrative is a story of epistemogenesis. Its theme is the emergence of knowledge and the role of the two women in the creation of a world that is open to human comprehension. This is why their role in creation initially involved both giving birth and giving names. And it is why the second function was taken from them by the men, who assumed control over the ritual second birth of boys. The explicit narrative journey of the sisters is partially masked to the novices in the ritual versions of the narrative they witness. But the theme of the emergence of a knowable world out of a total primary order is reproduced in the experience of the novices through their diffracted experience of the ceremonies.

From the perspective of the old men, the myth narrative is *reproduced* through the ceremonies. But from the perspective of the novices, the myth model is *produced* out of the rites. From an outside observer's perspective, a public cultural model is gradually transformed by way of the experience of rites into a partial and emergent mental model. But the repetition is not through a direct reproduction of the story line in the rituals. Rather, the narrative "plot" is reproduced indirectly in the rites, *by the orchestration of the novices' experience of the myth through the rites.* The story is lost to the boys as narrative, only to be recovered as experience. Only from their vantage points as adults, I suppose, is the experiential coherence of the rites linked up with the narrative coherence of the myth, understood now as a narrative with fairly standardized form.

THE SEQUENCING OF RITUAL DISCLOSURE

The Wawilak narrative is initially disclosed to novices in two ways. First, the Wawilak myth underlies a series of enacted images, images that point to an implicit but undisclosed narrative. Second, the sisters' journey that is the core of the myth is "repeated" by the novices as a set of personal experiences of progressive transformation of their understanding as they go through the sequence of ceremonies. These transformations in the novices' consciousness are motivated by the variations in how each ceremony "reads" the myth. This technique of modeling transformations in consciousness by a repetition of the same narrative in a sequence of different versions was used in the Wawilak narrative itself in the account of Yurlunggur's flooding the world. It is a way of representing a transformative process as a series of snapshots. It also has the effect of transforming the flow of an event into a sequence of memorable, frozen archetypes. This narrative technique is similar to that made famous by Alfred Hitchcock, of momentarily "freezing" a key scene in a film so that it would be imprinted in the viewer's memory.

The strategy of indirectly recreating the sisters' journey in the novices' own experience of changing knowledge makes sense of the fragmented character of the ritual imagery. It sets into motion for novices the gradual emergence of understanding from what must be considerable anxiety and confusion.

The novice's epistemogenesis, the birth of a new understanding of things, is structured by the sequencing of the initiation ceremonies. Each of the three ceremonies is a distinctive reading of the narrative. Taken as a series, the three readings of the Wawilak narrative realized in Djungguan, Gunabibi, and Ulmark form a "narrative" sequence. These ritual rereadings of the myth, enacted for males over many years of their early manhood, gradually transform a novice's understanding of the underlying myth narrative as well as his understanding of his own emerging life course. The implicit narrative sequence of these three readings is represented in Figure 10.1.

In their rituals, the Murngin exploit both the multiple associations and the semantic stratification (outside-to-inside) of many of the narrative's key symbols—the snake, wells, rain, swallowing, emergence, and sexuality. Each ceremony's reading of the symbols transforms the metaphors to bring out new layers of signification for the novices. Moreover, the revelations are sequenced for the Murngin in terms of their general knowledge-acquisition schema, which moves understanding from "outside" *(djinawa)* to progressively "inside" *(warrangul)* meanings, recovering the old understandings in new ways.

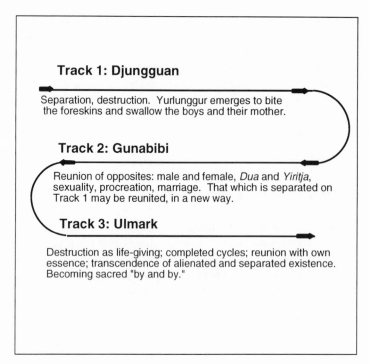

Figure 10.1. The Narrative Structure of Three Age-Grading Rites

This means that meanings at earlier levels are not lost but rather transcended and deepened. Symbols take on a multivocal depth that they did not have in the beginning. In keeping with the Murngin path metaphor, Figure 10.1 models the sequence of ritual readings of the myth as a "track" leading downward from outside to inside knowledge. This inside-outside model has the advantage of bringing together in a useful way the Murngin perspective on epistemogenesis and the conception of culture being developed in this book. In the terms of Murngin cosmology, the outside-in movement suggests the increasing access of the novices to sacred knowledge and hidden meanings. In terms of the two births model of culture proposed in this book, the outside-in movement suggests the internalization of the walkabout schema as a mental model for Murngin initiates.

Djungguan is a ritual occasion during which the youths are forcibly separated from their mothers and circumcised. It is also a particular "reading" of the Wawilak narrative. The Djungguan reading interprets Yurlunggur as generic male and as a lethal "separator" who spits out the sisters and retains the sons, who smells foreskins and seeks to sever the female part of the boys. From every angle, this reading stresses separation, distinguishing, splitting, and difference.

It reproduces not only certain episodes from the narrative but also the first stage of knowledge creation that the sisters undertake. At this stage, knowledge creation is the act of separating distinct species from a primal wholeness (as in naming and speaking distinct languages). This phase of epistemogenesis deals inevitably with relationships between death and destruction on the one hand and with orderliness and distinction on the other. For the animals are killed-to-be-reborn at the very moment they are created-to-be-killed. This is why, I think, Murngin say that Djungguan is both about foreskins and about death.

The Gunabibi reading of the narrative reverses the emphases of the Djungguan. What was separated in Djungguan is reunited in Gunabibi, though on a higher plane. If Djungguan celebrates a boy's separation from his *arndi* (mothers), Gunabibi celebrates the reunion of a boy with his *galle* (wives). Gunabibi is a celebration of licit procreation, sexuality, sensuality, and their lifegiving powers. These are all the fruits of the proper working out of a complex system of social relations. The imagery of Gunabibi reveals the complementarity and mutual attraction between male and female, Dua and Yiritja. Yurlunggur's well becomes transformed into a vaginal trench *(kartdjur)* into which the men descend in a direct enactment of sexual intercourse. The phallic aspects of the snake, here called Muit, are stressed with the erection of the two *yermerlindi* poles.

This lifegiving theme recalls the totemic species coming back to life after having been killed by the sisters. It is about the fruitful conjunction of things which are initially separated. And it is about the generative mathematics of procreation whereby $1 + 1 = 3$ (male + female + offspring). What was set apart is now shown to be reunited in a series of displays underscoring the attraction of opposites and the triumph of ordered relations.

To any novice, Gunabibi is obviously a revelation about the role of marriage in the continuity of life. While Yurlunggur was symbolically father, Muit becomes more like Gawel (mother's brother/wife's father) to the boys. Being Dua, Muit may indeed incorporate the Yiritja boys but not their Dua mothers, who are his own sisters. This incorporation becomes more clearly an image of marriage than of destruction, so that Muit becomes a Gunabibi reading of Yurlunggur consistent with the rest of the ceremony.

Finally, the Ulmark reading of the Wawilak narrative is associated with the young men being shown their own highest totems and understanding another kind of incorporation. If Gunabibi celebrates the union of opposites, Ulmark commemorates the ultimate union of an individual with his own kind, transcending all oppositions and distinctions while also encompassing them. Of course, this is precisely the kind of union that was precluded in the early Djungguan reading of the myth. But what was incestuous in this early reading becomes the highest form of identity in this later reading: all the same but different.

Ulmark celebrates the incorporation of a young man into the innermost part of the men's camp and into a deeper understanding of his own nature. The ritual's reading of the myth exploits the swallowing motif once more, but this time employing the repeated images of the animals being cooked and then jumping back into the well. This was, in fact, the fulfillment of the sisters' promise that these creatures would be sacred *(maraiin)* "by and by." Blood as a symbol and the role of women in reproduction are completely transcended in this reading of the myth, and kangaroo grease becomes the rite's dominant body fluid.

Ulmark proposes a kind of knowing, where the distinctions made at other levels of knowledge are no longer needed. A former wholeness is recovered, but recovered only through having passed through earlier kinds of understanding. It is about self-knowledge as well as the awareness that this self is ultimately a recapitulation of

Table 10.1. "Outside" Associations

Domain-Specific Model	Phase 1	Attributes
Wawilak narrative	Externalization	Sisters leave home, name totemic species, kill totemic species, bear sons. Yurlunggur as father and generic male.
Marriage arrangements	Incest prohibition	Initial "wrong" unions; moiety exogamy; brothers and sisters separate.
Initiation ceremonies	Djungguan	Boys separated from mothers; sisters separate from brothers; foreskins removed; Yurlunggur as separator.
General cultural schema of social reproduction	Understanding as differentiation	Emergence of primary distinctions; externalization; "outside knowledge"; categories; erection of boundaries; comprehension of parts at the cost of an original unity.

other selves of one's clan. It is about reclaiming self and loss of self at the same time. It is about the eventual attainment of *maraiin* (sacred) status.

Tables 10.1, 10.2, and 10.3 set out the associations among the three forms of social reproduction among the Murngin that we have examined in some detail. In each table, one phase of the general dialectical schema is worked out for each of the domain-specific models we have considered: (1) the Wawilak narrative, (2) marriage arrangements, and (3) initiation ceremonies. In addition, the tables link each phase to the general foundational schema which underlies them all. I have called the three phases (1) outside associations, (2) transitional associations, and (3) inside associations, suggesting the Murngin conceptions that the schemas all comprise phases of a journey and that the journey has a kind of epistemological "depth" to it. Though

Table 10.2. Transitional Associations

Domain-Specific Model	Phase 2	Attributes
Wawilak narrative	Incorporation of opposites	Yurlunggur spits out the two sisters (same moiety) but retains their sons (opposite moiety) within him. Yurlunggur as *Gawel* (mother's brother/wife's father).
Marriage arrangements	Mother's-brother's-daughter marriage; short cycles of marriage reciprocity	Children of brother and sister are natural spouses; cycling back in alternating generations and alternating "lines."
Initiation ceremonies	Gunabibi	Sexuality, attraction of opposites, procreation, $1 + 1 = 3$.
General cultural schema of social reproduction	Linkages, rules	Knowledge of complex systems. Sorting out of systematic relations among distinct entities. Knowledge of relationships among distinct things.

Table 10.3. "Inside" Associations

Domain-Specific Model	Phase 3	Attributes
Wawilak narrative	Incomplete; return to journey's starting point for sisters and for totemic species (but not for sons).	Totemic species are cooked and jump back into well; Yurlunggur returns to deep subterranean waters of well; two sisters returned to original country, but sons' journey remains incomplete, calling forth rituals to complete the journey.
Marriage arrangements	Mother's mother's brother's daughter's daughter marriage; mother-in-law bestowal; father's sister's sister's daughter's daughter exchange. Long cycles of reciprocity.	Bestowal arrangements look beyond marriage to distant recapitulations of self; complex long-cycle identifications; reproduction of self through other.
Initiation ceremonies	Ulmark	Entry into innermost core of men's ground and men's knowledge; learning *ki-jin* language (unifying many disparate languages); python as purifying fire; destruction (by fire) revealed as life-renewing; totemic species jump back into well, overcoming their "in-the-world" distinctness.
General cultural schema of social reproduction	Transcendence of opposition; dialectical return (*Aufhebung* effect)	Sacred (inside) knowledge; self-knowledge; finding oneself recapitulated; understanding of how diversity is reconciled in unity; layered knowledge of multivocal symbols; comprehension of metaphorical "depth"; realization of how something may be "all the same but different."

such schematic representations entail inevitable oversimplifications, they have the advantage of illuminating how a single foundational cultural schema underlies three apparently diverse areas of Murngin life.

In Table 10.3, the general schema is only partially realized in the Wawilak narrative. The totemic species and the Wawilak sisters complete their journeys and are returned through the well to where they had begun. But the narrative leaves the journey of the two sons incomplete. The completion of the boys' journey takes place not within the narrative but outside the myth, in the series of initiation rituals that the men prepare to perform at the myth's conclusion.

The narrative is the *foundation* of the ceremonies in two different senses. On the one hand, it establishes a general "track" for the sisters' journey, which the men can follow as they seek to transform their boys into men. In this sense, the rites imitate the myth. On the other hand, the myth narrative describes an incomplete journey, a track that ends too soon and is completed (rather than imitated) by the subsequent age-grading ceremonies.

THE COGNITIVE WORK OF MYTH AND RITUAL

There was a time when anthropologists sought to understand the historical relationship between myth and ritual. Early on, the dominant question was which came first, myths or their associated rites. Such issues no longer trouble anthropologists, who now tend to see myths and rituals as alternative performance modes, the one predominantly language-bound and discursive, the other linked more to the more embodied and presentational discourse of gesture and drama. But in the case of the Murngin, the issues of priority would seem to be important in understanding how these aborigines exploited the resources of these two distinct performance modes.

In this analysis of Murngin myth and ceremony, I have turned away from the unanswerable questions of historical priorities of myth vis-à-vis ritual to ask about the cognitive implications of repeating the same cultural schema in two distinct kinds of code. This is essentially the question of what Levi-Strauss called "the effectiveness of symbols" in ritual (Levi-Strauss, 1967c).

The "effectiveness" that Levi-Strauss attributed to the ritual symbols of curing rites among the Cuna of Panama is at once physiological and psychological. In the Cuna case, a cure for difficult childbirth involves a long incantation chanted by a shaman in the presence of the patient. The chant comprises a mythical journey by a power-being named Muu, who the Cuna believe is responsible for the formation of a fetus (p.182). Levi-Strauss concludes that in the presence of the patient, this myth is transformed into a narrative whose events are localized within the woman's own body and that provide for her a way to externalize, comprehend, and hopefully transform an otherwise inarticulate physiological disorder. The key, says Levi-Strauss, is that the narrative journey proceeds as if in slow motion and reveals a landscape in excruciating detail, suggesting at once geographic and physiological landmarks.

> Everything occurs as though the shaman were trying to induce the sick women—whose contact with reality is no doubt impaired and whose sensitivity is exacerbated—to relive the initial situation through pain, in a very intense and precise way, and to become psychologically aware of its smallest details. Actually this situation sets off a series of events of which the body and internal organs of the sick woman will be the assumed setting. A transition will thus be made from the most prosaic reality to myth, from the physical universe to the physiological universe, from the external world to the internal body. [p. 188]

Levi-Strauss's explanation assumes that the myth narrative permits the patient to cope with a psychophysiological trauma by providing a kind of "objective correlative" for the patient's repressed and otherwise inarticulate experience of bodily suffering. This is made possible by a metaphorically induced parallelism between the myth world and the patient's own experience of her body.

TURNER'S VIEW

Another major contribution to our understanding of the psychological effectiveness of symbols comes from the work of Victor Turner. Though in his classic papers on

Ndembu ritual Turner does not explicitly analyze the relations between myth symbols and ritual, he does take up at length the question of the psychological effectiveness of ritual symbols. Two related concepts of Turner's in particular come to mind: the multivocality of ritual symbols and their bipolar character, linking bodily and social experience.

Multivocality suggests the referential openness and ambiguity of any symbol. Turner suggested, however, that symbols might differ significantly in their potential multivocality:

> Certain dominant or focal symbols conspicuously possess this property of multivocality which allow for the economic representation of key aspects of culture and belief. Each dominant symbol has a "fan" or "spectrum" of referents which are linked by what is usually a simple mode of association, its very simplicity enabling it to interconnect a wide variety of *significata*. [Turner, 1967a:50]

The key word in Turner's description is "interconnect." For symbolic multivocality promotes not only ambiguity about reference but also the possibility of transforming an individual's understanding of things by pointing to the possible relatedness of things that are not normally understood as connected at all. Multivocality is a property of symbols that makes them useful as transformers of consciousness. Not only do such symbols promote associations among diverse public conventions, but the inherent openness of multivocal "fanning" means that conventional understandings will also frequently stream into more private and idiosyncratic associations, giving subjective force to the comprehension of public symbols.[8]

One of Turner's most interesting examples of multivocality occurs in his essay "Paradoxes of Twinship in Ndembu Ritual" from *The Ritual Process*. Here Turner examines an Ndembu ritual that is invoked when twins are born. Twins are considered by the Ndembu to be an anomaly of human procreation. Twins suggest both good fortune and an anxiety-generating surfeit of fruitfulness, more appropriate to animals than to humans. The point of the twinship rites seems to be to transform the consciousness of families with a history of twins, so that the negative associations become transformed into positive ones. This is accomplished largely by a ritual manipulation of multivocal symbols, each of which has a range of meanings that suggest *both* the danger of superabundance and its benefits. The "patients" of the rite are encouraged to experience the transformation of these symbols from negative meaning into positive ones (see Turner, 1969:61, 71).

Symbols are employed as a form of homeopathic intervention, in which the very representations that promote the greatest anxiety may be turned back upon themselves and transformed into the agents of well-being:

> An event, such as twinning, that falls outside the orthodox classifications of society is, paradoxically, made the ritual occasion for an exhibition of values that relate to the community as a whole, as a homogeneous, unstructured unity that transcends its differentiations and contradictions. . . . Every opposition is overcome or transcended in a recovered unity, a unity, moreover, that is reinforced by the very potencies that endanger it. [p. 92]

In the Murngin case, symbolic multivocality provides much of the "depth" that is so evident in the Murngin myth-ritual complex we have explored. While Turner speaks of meaning "fanning out," the Murngin conceive of meanings as moving inward, providing a cumulative accretion of significance to ritual symbols over time. The cumulative layering of diverse meanings throughout the series of initiation rites provides the vehicle for the transformation of the novice's consciousness. This is particularly evident for key symbolic processes such as swallowing, spitting, cooking, and the spilling of vital fluids.

It is not simply that such symbols are inherently multivocal and semantically "open." As we have seen, the initiation process *motivates* a set of transformations in which certain meanings give way to others, often the reverse of the first interpretations. Despite these changes and inversions, new interpretations always retain echoes of earlier meanings, incorporating them as they transcend them. The Murngin conceive of this process of symbolic accretion as moving from outside to inside meanings, a process that shapes the ritual journey of initiation as a whole.

Turner's notion of the bipolarity of ritual symbols is really a specific instance of symbolic multivocality. In many key Ndembu symbols, Turner found that the range of references was not random but tended to move between two poles. Turner refers to the nexus of physiological references as the "orectic pole" and the locus of references to social principles as the "normative pole." Using key Ndembu symbols, Turner shows how ritual symbols work by linking these two poles. Abstract moral norms are thereby infused with the psychological and emotional force of bodily experience. And the most intimate aspects of the body simultaneously become imbued with social value.

In Turner's conception, the effectiveness of ritual symbols is inevitably contingent rather than mechanical and automatic. By using the notion that ritual symbols derived their effectiveness through bipolarity, Turner was among the first anthropologists to stress the importance of "embodied knowledge" as a significant way in which cultural models bridge the gap between personal experience and social convention.

We have seen how the understanding that Murngin men come to have of the sacred Wawilak narrative emerges only gradually from a set of ritual practices, each of which constitutes a distinctive snapshot of the myth rather than a straight enactment of a narrative text. Though *logically* the myth precedes the rites, in *experience* the rituals come first. The understanding made possible by such a myth-ritual complex is inevitably shaped by the dependence of the narrative on the ritual for its ongoing life and its regeneration as narrative. The difference, of course, is that ritual transmission is inevitably "embodied" to a much greater degree than any narrative transmission, with a significant effect on the quality of the resulting understanding.

The general Murngin dialectic, an abstract foundational schema that defines the common track by which society is regenerated, in which the self is reappropriated over time, and which governs the process of knowledge-emergence, is embodied for Murngin in several ways. The idioms that constrain the expressions of the schema are thoroughly suffused with bodily processes. A cursory review of the narrative and the associated initiation rites reveals how completely the schema is grounded in basic physiology. Much of the transformational work that the rites enact upon the narrative is mediated through the bodily experiences of the novices.

MUNN'S INSIGHTS

No one has better clarified this embodied character of ritual knowledge than Nancy Munn. In her penetrating analysis of Murngin myth and ritual, Munn employs an essentially Turnerian model of symbolic process to move well beyond Levi-Strauss's solution to the problem of the psychological effectiveness of ritual symbols. Her analysis offers a crucial insight into the cognitive "work" of such symbols. Munn's intricate exegesis of the Wawilak myth and the Djungguan ritual focuses not on simple parallelism between myth and ritual but on how public codes like ritual symbols *transform* the initiates' prior understandings, concepts that are less articulate and closer to individual subjectivity.

Munn proposes that cultural artifacts like myths, rites, and conventional belief systems vary in their "symbolic distance" from any individual's consciousness. Thus for Murngin, Munn argues, sorcery beliefs and fears are at a "shorter symbolic 'distance' from Ego than the [Wawilak] myth . . . since they refer to activities and relationships directly involving the individual actor in its [sic] everyday existence" (pp.198–199). On the other hand, what she terms "externalized, objectified codes," such as ritual and myth, promote a "symbolic separation of experience from subjectivity" (p. 198).

Specifically, Munn contends that the symbols of the Djungguan ceremony "work on" earlier associations that initiates have of symbols connected with blood and bodily manipulation, associations derived from Murngin sorcery beliefs. Through the manipulation of ritual symbols, these negative associations between sorcery and blood loss and death are converted into positive association of vitality and bodily well being. Sorcery beliefs crystallize for Murngin intimate fears of personal bodily intrusion and destruction by malign agents. Munn argues that such beliefs are inevitably closer to subjective consciousness than are the more abstract conventions of myth and ritual. Thus, because the symbolic transformers (i.e., myth and ritual) are relatively objectified and conventional codes, at a relatively greater symbolic distance from an individual than the prior sorcery beliefs, the psychological transformation they effect is a powerful socializing agent for the initiates, whose most intimate personal fears become subject to what Munn calls "the social, hierarchically regulated forms of the rituals" (p. 199).

Munn's analysis represents a significant advance in our understanding of how myth and ritual "work" upon the consciousness of the individual novice. Her notion of ritual acting not as an enacted version of myth but as a psychosymbolic operator upon the myth symbols is especially illuminating. It is important to consider, however, that Munn's account of Murngin ritual deals only with the first of the initiation ceremonies, Djungguan. She does not treat the "narrative" structure of the entire set of rites, or the effect of the novices' journey through the series—a journey that, if my analysis is right, transforms the novice's consciousness. Moreover, Munn presupposes that the myth and the rite as public, objectified codes are equally available to the novices.

Yet, as we have seen, from the vantage point of the novices, the myth emerges into consciousness only gradually, through the various readings that the rites make upon the myth. Presumably, the Wawilak narrative only emerges as an objectified, public code for a novice quite late in the initiation process. The culturally regulated emergence of knowledge, what I have called epistemogenesis, is both the explicit theme and the implicit result of the work of the initiation rites upon the myth narrative. The emergence of the schema, and resulting transformation in the consciousness of Murngin youth are among the most significant aspects of the entire initiation process.

DREAMTIME LEARNING AND MEMORY

By repeatedly replaying the Wawilak narrative in different "keys" throughout the sequenced age-grading rites, a general foundational "walkabout" schema emerges for the novices as a dimension of their experience. The effectiveness of these rites as agents of this cognitive transformation is dependent upon how the rites exploit different memory systems. To understand the cognitive implications of these rites, we need to review briefly the anatomy of human memory.

Psychologists have long distinguished between *procedural memory* and *episodic memory* as two functionally and anatomically distinct memory systems. Both appear to be present in mammals and birds (Donald, 1991:150; Sherry and Schacter, 1987). Procedural memory is assumed to be the phylogenetically more primitive memory system. Its function is to store and retrieve general schemas of repeated action patterns. Many everyday actions such as walking, throwing a ball, threading a needle, or peeling a potato are constituted in memory as motor schemas and algorithms, coordinating sight, touch, and other sensory modalities.

As Donald suggests, these motor schemas are stored in memory as general procedural programs, necessarily stripped of the specific "episodic" details of any particular instance of the pattern.

> [I]n learning to catch a ball, one must learn the principle of tracking a moving object, no matter what the speed of the object, the starting point, or one's initial posture at the time it is thrown. It would be cumbersome to remember the exact speed, starting point and position of each successful practice catch; a new throw is unlikely to match any specific counterpart in practice. Thus learning a procedure, even on this level, involves setting parameters and forming general rules. Detailed episodic recall would interfere with this process. [Donald, 1991:150]

Human ritual may be thought of as a strategy for inducing shared schemas within a community through repeated action sets often involving rich symbolic content. To the extent that ritual aims at a kind of automaticity or habituation of action, it necessarily exploits procedural memory, or what Connerton calls "habit memory," as a social resource (Connerton, 1989).

By contrast, episodic memory permits the storage and recall of details of specific events in time and space. Whereas procedural memory schematizes events as general programs by deleting contextual information about specific instances, episodic memory stores and makes available for recall precisely these concrete details of actual experiences. It is hardly surprising that with such incompatible functions, procedural and episodic memory would have evolved as anatomically distinct memory systems.

To these two memory systems Donald adds a third, *semantic memory,* which he claims is unique to humans. Semantic memory is less well-defined than procedural memory, but Donald associates it with the evolution of language. Semantic memory involves the capacity to invent signs, the intentional manipulation of symbols, and the attribution of shared meaning to arbitrary or conventional signifiers such as combinations of sound or writing or gesture. Semantic memory goes beyond the ability to associate signs with referents or situations, and involves the invention, storage, retrieval, and intentional manipulation of a vast reservoir of propositions and "facts" about the world (Donald, 1991:152). In this sense, semantic memory is a necessary aspect of what Chomsky called the "generativity" of human language, whereby a limited repertory of signs can be put together in virtually limitless combinations.

The cognitive effectiveness of Murngin rite and myth appear to be linked to the way in which they orchestrate the use of these different memory systems. Levi-Strauss (1966) has discussed in great detail the dialectic by which ritual and myth mediate the human perception of particular events and general semantic structures. In the Murngin case, the general walkabout schema is initially presented to the novices in a narrative format as a retelling of particular events. The initial status of the schema-as-event involves episodic memory in two distinct ways. First, the narrative is presented to the initiates as a repetition of a literal journey made by the two sisters, emphasizing the concrete details of place, action, and personality. Second, the events are conveyed to the novices not as abstract narrative but through specific rites, memorable events performed on the boys at key moments in their lives.

As the rites proceed in time, however, two very different things happen to the episodic character of the walkabout story. First, through repetition and ritualization, these specific events become abstracted and generalized into archetypes. As ritualized performances, the story becomes schematized as a general and foundational set of patterns, with very strong kinesthetic associations. They become "grounded" as an aspect of procedural memory, in some senses a "deeper" and less conscious kind of memory than the episodic memory of particular events.

The second transformation that these episodes undergo exploits semantic memory. The rites work on the narrative by deconstructing the episodes into discrete symbolic units and using them as a kind of general code. These units employ events, agents, objects, or places as language-like symbols. The great python, the rain, the water hole, the two sisters, the acts of naming and killing are examples of the symbolic units of this myth-ritual code. They have the semantic properties of multivocality (i.e., each unit can take on many different meanings) and recombinability (i.e., these units can be used as a kind of code for conveying numerous messages). While they do not approach the flexibility or abstractness of natural language as a code, the myth-ritual code is exploited by the Murngin as a kind of symbolic language for transforming the initiates' understanding of their world and their relations to it.

It would seem then that the cognitive power of dreamtime learning is tied not simply to the symbolic content of the narrative and the rites, but also to the ways in which the myth-ritual complex exploits the various types or "layers" of memory. Beginning as events, accessible through episodic memory, the foundational schema gradually emerges as a form of knowledge through (1) the construction of psychologically primitive motor-schemas, and (2) the simultaneous transformation of the events into a self-conscious and manipulable code for the creation of complex propositions about the world. Moving in opposite directions as a bridge between structure and event, the narrative is translated simultaneously into both procedural and semantic memory. Paraphrasing Marcel Mauss, one might say that the semantic and cognitive power of the walkabout schema is linked to its status as a "total cognitive fact."

CONCLUSION

In this chapter and the last, I have traced out in great detail a single foundational schema for the Murngin as it is transformed in numerous myth and ritual models. These models—various retellings of the Wawilak narrative and three age-grading rites—suggest how dynamic and complex cultural models can be. They represent alternative versions of a foundational schema, but versions whose sequencing is orchestrated so as to transform the consciousness of the initiates about their world and their relationships to it.

I also noted that there are other kinds of variation in Murngin cultural models. Local groups pride themselves in their distinctive versions of traditional myth, songs, paintings, and rites, differences which often serve as boundary markers between groups. Moreover, men's and women's versions of important narratives appear to be different, as one might expect in a society where there is considerable gender segregation of important religious knowledge. All of these variations in cultural models are consistent with a distributive view of culture, a view that understands cultural knowledge as socially distributed in time and space rather than a fixed stock of timeless and fully shared models.

But there is another sort of variation in cultural models that we have not yet considered: the availability to a single individual of alternate or competing versions of a single model. The existence of competing or conflicting models for the same domain of experience presents an interesting challenge to any conception of culture as shared knowledge. Using case studies from my own Samoan fieldwork, Chapters 11 and 12 take up this issue of alternative and competing cultural models and some of the important problems they raise for an adequate theory of culture. Chapter 11 looks at multiple cultural models of space in terms of the important issue of how culture models represent "perspective." Chapter 12 deals with the possibility of direct contradiction between competing cultural models and the implied limitations of cultural models in accounting for human consciousness.

Notes

1. The notion of culture as a set of psychological messages has been developed and extended by Robert Levy. See Levy, 1970, 1973. For a different use of the communication model of culture, see Rappaport, 1968, 1979.

2. See Vygotsky, 1962, 1978, 1987. See also Rogoff, 1990, esp. pp. 35–41; Wertsch, 1978, 1985; Rogoff and Wertsch, 1984; Lave, 1988; Rogoff and Lave, 1984.

3. Detailed accounts of each of the ceremonies are found in Warner (1936/1958), and an even more complete and detailed account of Gunabibi is contained in Berndt's *Kunapipi* (Berndt, 1951). The Narra ceremonies, which will not be considered here, have been analyzed by Berndt (Berndt, 1952) and more recently by Keen (1978). A somewhat different account

of a Djungguan ceremony from Trial Bay is discussed in Morphy 1991 (see especially chaps. 5 and 7). Ian Dunlop has made a film of this ceremony, called *Djungguwan*.

4. It is important to stress that the particular analysis here applies only to the performances Warner saw at Milingimbi in the 1930s. As with all Murngin cultural forms, there is considerable local variation in ritual practice from clan to clan and over time.

5. In the Djungguan at Trial Bay described by Morphy, these posts were replaced by elaborately carved *djuwany* posts, representing both the novices and the Wawilak sisters as well as stringybark trees that were cut down in the sisters' search for wild honey. See Morphy, 1991, chap. 7.

6. For an explicit discussion of the differences between Murngin and Baktaman epistemologies, see Morphy, 1991:92 ff.

7. Morphy refers to the "particularistic meaning" Yolngu paintings come to acquire for individuals participating in ceremonies. Conventional symbols take on added significance for individuals as they associate them with particular events such as deaths of loved ones or the circumcision of one's children (Morphy, 1991:131). This idiosyncratic expansion of meaning of any conventional symbol is inevitably part of the second birth of cultural forms, the creation of mental models out of conventional representations.

8. In language, the multivocality of words means that homonyms and homophones will always open up language to new meaning. The same is no doubt true for gestural signs. Puns are a limiting case of such multivocality. English, however, has no term to distinguish puns, whose various meanings reinforce one another and provide potentially new depth of insight, and those "groaners" where an unfortunate conjunction of sound merely disengages the stream of sound from the stream of meaningful discourse. For more on puns and such, see Shore, 1987.

V
THE PROBLEM OF
MULTIPLE MODELS

11

Tropic Landscapes: Alternative Spatial Models in Samoan Culture

It is fashionable, in this post structuralist era, to attack any binary code as evidence of the imposition of a foreign system on indigenous values; and sometimes, as in the case of *Kypseli*, the complaint seems justifiable. But it does not automatically follow that oppositions such as those between male and female will not be salient for local actors. What must be resisted is the temptation to credit them with coercive power over those actors; for it is the *actors* who use *them*.

—Michael Herzfeld

For the aborigines of Australia, many of their songs, stories, and paintings take the form of maps, abstracted representations of ancestral journeys. The walkabout schema explored in Chapters 9 and 10 exploits the importance and multivocality of spatial models for the aborigines. The aboriginal landscape is understood to quite literally embody sacred history. Features of the landscape are not just symbolic of ancestral creatures and events but are understood to be actual transformations of these *Wongar* beings and events (Morphy, 1991:111).

Cognitive science has also appropriated the notion of landscape as a metaphor for certain kinds of mental models. Since Tolman's early work in learning theory, mental schemas have often been likened to maps, though Tolman's actual model was derived from a rat maze rather than from any kind of human landscape.[1] Because of their importance as basic templates for physical orientation, maps and other spatial models have a unique place among orientational models. As Lakoff and Johnson have shown in their exploration of the structuring of metaphor, spatial models of various kinds have a primacy in cognition because of their link with the human body and its orientations to the world (Johnson, 1987; Lakoff, 1987a; Lakoff and Johnson, 1980).

Although cognitive psychologists have found the notion of mental maps quite useful, they have a more problematical status in anthropology. In his well-known critique of structuralism, Bourdieu cites the appropriation of the map by anthropologists as a way to describe cultural models as evidence of the anthropologist's lamentable penchant for experience-distant representations of human experience:

> It is significant that "culture" is sometimes described as a *map;* it is the analogy which occurs to an outsider who has to find his way around a foreign landscape and who compensates for his lack of practical mastery, the prerogative of the native, by the use of a model of all possible routes. The gulf between this potential, abstract space, devoid of landmarks or any privileged centre—like genealogies, in which the ego is as unreal as the starting point in a Cartesian space—and the practical space of journeys actually made, or rather of journeys actually being made, can be seen from the difficulty we have in recognizing familiar routes on a map or a town-plan until we are able to bring together the axes of the field of potentialities and the "system of axes linked unalterably to our bodies, and carried about us wherever we go," as Poincaré puts it, which structures practical space into right and left, up and down, in front and behind. [Bourdieu, 1977:2]

But Bourdieu's critique is misleading. "Objectivist" knowledge of even familiar spaces is not the province of just social science. It is also an important part of the stock of knowledge of any competent native. Such models are objectivist models and they are cultural resources for orienting outsiders to the immediate environment as well as orienting oneself to new places (such as an unfamiliar city) by comparing the new environment to familiar landscapes or to general conventional models of space.

In other words, while objectivist models might well appear to lack a concrete point of view, they actually embody an important point of view for humans: that of the outsider. As such they are as positioned as any other models, though positioned in a somewhat different way from what Bourdieu has in mind. This is only to confirm from a cognitive perspective the obvious fact that generations of anthropologists have discovered: that communities generally have conventional models of an "outsider role."

In his critique, Bourdieu appears to restrict the notion of map to "sociocentric" models that are not positioned in relation to the subject's own body and point of immediate view. Yet there are several different kinds of map models with quite distinct perceptual and rhetorical potentialities. As cultural models, even sociocentric maps do not usually contain "a model of all possible routes" but rather represent cognitively and culturally salient landmarks.

Moreover, cognitive psychologists recognize the importance of another genre of mental maps, "egocentric maps" that individuals use as cognitive resources for navigating complex landscapes. Egocentric maps do not model, as Bourdieu would have us believe, a "potential, abstract space, devoid of landmarks or any privileged centre." While Bourdieu is right in his critique of the misuse of abstract general models as sufficient representations of an agent's practical knowledge of anything, it is equally misleading to presume that all knowledge is exclusively egocentric in orientation. Even practical reason has need for general and abstract structures. This chapter takes up this problem of the relationship between egocentric and sociocentric models through a close analysis of Samoan cultural models for village space.[2]

The chapter begins in the midst of an admittedly obscure complication of ethnographic description from my own fieldwork in Western Samoa. But its solution addresses some significant theoretical issues about the relationship between cultural symbolism and human perception. The specific problem is to explain the existence of alternative models for village space in Samoan culture, and their distribution as both rhetorical resources and cognitive models.

AN UNFORTUNATE ENCOUNTER

All physical space is also inevitably symbolic space, the most literal aspect of the total semantic environment that Yuri Lotman calls the "semiosphere" (Lotman, 1990, especially pp. 140 ff). That Samoans have long had their own vision of their landscape is suggested by two events, separated by two hundred years. First is the unfortunate encounter between Samoans on Tutuila and the crew of La Pérouse. On December 7, 1787, the French frigates *Boussole* and *Astrolabe,* under the command of Rear Admiral Jean-François Galaup, Comte de La Pérouse, and Captain de Langle, sighted Tutuila at the eastern end of the Samoan archipelago. The ill-fated meeting between La Pérouse's expedition and the Samoans led to de Langle's death on December 10, at the hands of enraged islanders. Here is the account La Pérouse provides of his initial encounter with the Samoans, that I quote at length:

> The same evening, Captain de Langle, embarking with several officers in three armed boats, went to look at a populous village, where he received a very friendly welcome. . . . Everything went well in this first meeting, and the boats returned to the ships.
>
> The next day at sunrise, the natives came on board to trade, exchanging food for ironware and especially for glass beads, which pleased them very much. The longboats went ashore for water, and the two captains followed them in their boats. Relations with the natives were less friendly on this day. Some of the sailors who were ordered to form a cordon around the fresh water at the longboats allowed some women to pass through their line, and a savage who had slipped in behind the longboats hit one of the sailors with a mallet which he had seized. Instead of severely punishing the aggressor, La Pérouse merely had him thrown in the water. He should have acted much more rigorously in order to command the respect of these sturdy, powerful people who exaggerated their physical superiority and derided the slim figures of the strangers. . . .
>
> Nevertheless, La Pérouse and several armed men went to visit the village, which is shaded by groves of fruit trees. *The houses are built around a lovely, circular green,* almost three hundred yards in diameter. Standing in front of the doors of their homes, all the savages, men, women, children, old people—begged La Pérouse to honor them by his visit. He entered several houses. Each has a floor of pebbles selected for the purpose, raised two feet above the ground and covered with well-made mats. . . . This delightful country . . . has the double advantage of soil which is fertile without being cultivated and a climate which does not require any clothing. Breadfruit, coconut, bananas, guava, and oranges, provide the fortunate people with plenty of food. . . . What a picture of paradise this fortunate land presents! But it did not take the French long to discover that this was not the land of innocence. Great wounds, some scars, some still bleeding—betrayed the violent, warlike habits of these savages, and their features expressed the same fierceness.
>
> While the captains were ashore, this aggressiveness was revealed more clearly on board the frigates. Despite the watchfulness of the guards, *some of the savages had slipped onto the deck* and had stolen various articles here and there. Such transgressions

should have been stopped by force, but these herculean fellows ridiculed the short Frenchmen and laughed at their threats. [La Pérouse, 1969:107–108 emphasis added]

In its alternation of horror and admiration for the charming hospitality of the Samoans, this remarkable narrative parallels Melville's account of the Marquesas in his early novel *Typee*. But what strikes me in this account is the geography of the encounter, which is all but ignored by the French narrator. The apparently remarkable juxtaposition of polite hospitality and aggressive villainy, which seem to catch La Pérouse off guard, are mediated by changes in setting. The politeness takes place in and about the circular green, the sacred *malae* of the village. The pilfering is done offshore. This is no coincidence. The apparently contradictory perceptions of Samoan ethos were linked, I think, to a misunderstanding of important dimensions of Samoan spatial models.

THE BACK AREAS OF THE VILLAGE

The second story is closer to home. It concerns my own residence in Western Samoa during my first year as a Peace Corps volunteer in 1969. It had been weeks since I had arrived in the village of Matavai, Safune, a lovely spot at the edge of a fresh-water lake that borders the lagoon. Like Melville in Taipivai Valley on Nukuhiva, I was beginning to feel less and less like an honored guest and increasingly like a prisoner of my own status. I had been given a huge *fale tele*, a chiefly house, for my home. It was right on the *malae*, the central village plaza, so I was in full display of the entire village. I felt like a museum exhibit, and I suppose in a sense I was.

I was constantly accompanied by the children of the family, who would fan my food, carry my toilet paper, fetch my schoolbooks, walk me to the local store, and sleep on mats next to my bed. I was a kind of king, yet I was discouraged from straying too far from my thatched palace. I was discouraged from straying into the "back" areas of the village where the food was cooked or the smaller sleeping houses lay. I was assured that these marginal areas were too dirty or too rocky or too unimportant for a distinguished *palagi* visitor like myself. Yet from these back areas I would hear the delightful peals of laughter and the unrestrained sounds of gossip which broke through the stolid dignity of my house like a cooling rain on a parched desert.

Eventually, I did negotiate the nether regions of the village, and would make the same delicate transition in other villages in which I was to live. But always it took time. I came to realize that my village was a rather complex symbolic landscape. There were all sorts of invisible boundaries, differentiated social spaces that had to be taken into account if ever I were to make myself a home in Samoa.

DIAMETRICALLY OPPOSED

Attempting to map a Samoan village with the help of a local informant drove home the point that a village is organized by a conventional symbolic geography as well as by "objective" physical coordinates. The Samoan physical universe is a world structured by features of village and bush, mountain and sea. My first attempt to clarify how Samoans conceptualize their village space focused on the fact that most modern Samoan villages are strung out in a kind of line along the coast, with a road or path dividing the seaward half of the village from the inland half.

In this linear model, villages are conceived of as having front *(luma)* and back *(tua)* regions. The front of the village is the sea side *(tai),* while the back of the village is the bush side *(uta).* Most modern Samoan villages do in fact conform to this linear organization (Figure 11.1).

The sea-inland model, in which geographic features are used for mapping social, kinesthetic, and moral attributes, appears to be a fundamental orientational framework for Polynesians. A set of concrete geographic features is encoded culturally in binary fashion. The eye is swept back and forth across a diameter that defines opposing sides of a landscape which has at once physical, social, and moral implications. The "back" for Samoans, as for Polynesians more generally, is associated with low rank, and with impulsive rather than socially correct behavior. The "front," by contrast, implies high rank, social authority, and socially visible and hence constrained behavior.

As with front and back, *tai* (shore) and *uta* (bush) are also moral orientations for Samoans. *Tai* suggests not only the sea, but the open coast and areas of intense

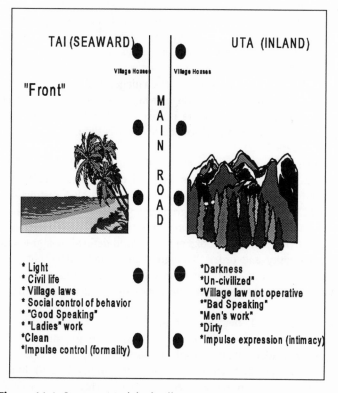

Figure 11.1 Samoan Model of Village Space: Diametric Dualism

social contact. *Tai* suggests organized human life, civility, and the rule of the chiefs and their laws. The "front" of the village faces the sea, and the meanings of *tai* are thus bound up with the notion of *luma* or front. Other symbolic associations link frontness with light and visibility, a complex of features that underlie the Samoan associations between rank, brightness, and physical size, which is to say visual presence. At the front of the village, behavior is on public display, and a suitably dignified front must be maintained.

Uta, the bush, is the back of the village. It represents the realm of darkness associated with *po,* or night. Antisocial behavior is considered more likely to occur here than on the coast, since human affairs are unconstrained by the rules of the chiefs. Relatively unsophisticated Samoans from rural areas are said, by urbanites, to come from "the back" of Samoa. People wishing to escape the insistent etiquette and rigorous restrictions of village life choose to live isolated in the bush. The bush is also linked with male work, while the coastal areas are associated with women's labor. In the distinction between sea and bush, or seaward and landward, there is a general model for a set of analogous attributes of experience.

CENTER-PERIPHERY

The front-back spatial model is in apparent conflict with another cultural model, less explicitly articulated by Samoans, but which seems to be operative in many contexts where behavior is constrained by spatial orientation. This second spatial model has markedly different empirical and logical properties from the first. In this model, the reference points in village orientation are not sea and bush but rather the central *malae* (village green) and the outskirts of the village. The front of the village, in this model, is interior to the back of the village, which is considered the exterior. *'I lumā-fale* (at the front of the houses) refers in this model to the area facing towards the *malae* while *'i tuā fale* (at the back of the houses) is defined as moving away from the *malae* (see Figure 11.2).

The periphery may mean either toward the bush (for houses inland of the main road) or toward the shore (for houses seaward of the main road). Therefore, the model is not fully compatible with that based on the sea-bush distinction. This alternate mapping of the village defines a gradual or *graded relationship* between center and periphery rather than a simple *binary* opposition. It defines a symbolic space in terms of a central viewpoint that looks out at a world defined by a gradually diminishing gradient of dignity and order. Though such a model does not define classical categories, a schematic representation of this model is possible in which village structure is realized as a series of concentric zones radiating out from the heart of the village.

In this second model, the center is implicitly the residential core of a village, and, more precisely, a *malae* or sacred political meeting ground is defined about which the chiefly residences are placed. The *malae* may be compared to a radiant source of dignity and power much like that attributed to royalty and divinity in Southeast Asian kingdoms, often represented as a navel (Errington, 1989:74, 82–84).

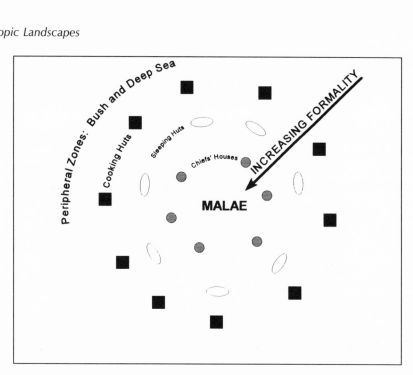

Figure 11.2. Samoan Village Spatial Model: Concentric Dualism

From this viewpoint, we look out through concentric zones of gradually diminishing intensity of power and dignity. Certain features of the landscape mark the gradual transformation: starting with the *malae* itself, *māota* (chiefly meeting/guest houses), then ranging outward to sleeping huts, cook houses, latrines, cultivated gardens or shallow lagoons, the cultivated inland areas or deep sea, and finally to the uncultivated and unknown bushland or the unfished and unknown reaches of the sea.

Samoan behavioral norms are closely tied to this model and its contours shape local moral discourse. Thus, certain acts of aggression which are punishable when done in the village center are tacitly allowed in the bush or at the rear of the village. Traditionally, riding a horse, raising one's arms in an aggressive gesture, or giving a war cry on the *malae* while chiefs were meeting were all considered serious insults to the village, and the offender risked being stoned or worse. The village center and main road were traditionally protected by chiefly edict during the night, when darkness closes in on the village, and even today in many villages, chiefs patrol the central village area to enforce rigid curfews.

Discourse is also keyed to the center-periphery distinction. Centrality of political intercourse is quite literally "grounded" in local geography. Casual discussions may take place in the smaller huts in the peripheral regions of the village. Formal gatherings of chiefs take place in the larger meeting houses on the innermost ring of the village. And when the occasion is one of great sacredness or the utmost seriousness, the village assembles on the *malae* itself. Certain "wrong" acts, acts involving premarital sex and other illicit gratifications of appetites, are understood to have their "proper" expressions in the peripheral areas of the village, such as on the beach or in the bush.

In the most general terms, the center-periphery distinction provides the physical coordinates for relating the sacred *(tapu)* and the profane *(noa)*, where "sacred" means bound or restricted and "profane" implies unbound or free. This concentric model thus does not distinguish sea and inland but rather identifies certain equivalent "outer" areas, whether bush or sea, in terms of their relation to the centers of human political life. In this model, therefore, the shallow lagoon where women collect shellfish is equivalent to the close-in cultivated gardens where men plant and women weed and the deep sea where men fish is equivalent to the inland regions where men work the taro gardens.

EMPIRICAL CORRELATES

While such a concentric schema may be derived from observing variations in Samoan behavior within the village, it is not, linguistically speaking, a well-coded public model for Samoans. There are no terms in Samoan for these zones. Normally, we might conclude that this is an observer's model of space rather than a native model. But the matter is more complex than this. Most Samoan villages appear today to be nucleated hamlets, stretched out along the coastline and divided by a village road. The existence of multiple *malae* in some villages means that the circular arrangement of village space about the focal *malae* is less apparent than the linear organization of space.

Yet there are several villages in Western Samoa that are laid out in a clearly concentric pattern. The most famous is Lepea, home village of the late paramount chief Mataafa. Just outside of Apia, this immaculate village has something of the character of a museum artifact, as if it were intended to represent a prototype of concentrically organized village space. Sale'imoa, along the Airport Road in Western Samoa, is another example of a concentrically laid out village. Moreover, concentric zones are clearly apparent in many villages from the perspective of a *malae* if not from an aerial view.

It is tempting to suggest that an earlier concentric village shape was transformed in modern times into a linear form by the building of coastal roads in Samoa. Yet Roger Green, who has carried out archeological excavations in Samoa, has suggested that the historical "shape" of actual village space in Samoa is linear. He has found no examples of ancient village sites organized in a neat concentric pattern (Roger Green, personal communication). To further complicate matters, however, an early-nineteenth-century lithograph done of a *fono tauati,* a general village meeting of great importance carried out on the village *malae,* clearly shows a concentrically organized village.

Whatever the historical and empirical status of "actual" village space, Samoans appear to have two cultural models for village space. Because it is encoded in a number of linguistic terms, the linear model might be termed an "explicit cultural model." The less articulate but clearly operative concentric model is more of a "tacit cultural model" that is acted upon and represented spatially but not linguistically marked for Samoans. This difference between explicit and tacit cultural models is connected with distinct rhetorical and perceptual contexts.

STRUCTURALIST INTERPRETATIONS OF SPATIAL DUALISM

Readers may recognize the problem of representing dual organization as an example of a structural contradiction that had long ago been addressed by Levi-Strauss. In an important paper called "Do Dual Organizations Exist?" Levi-Strauss described for Bororo and Winnebago villages a very similar structural anomaly between two forms of dual organization (Levi-Strauss, 1967d). In explicating this problem, Levi-Strauss distinguished the two sorts of dualism in formal terms. The binary model suggested by the *tai-uta* distinction Levi-Strauss calls "diametric dualism," while the center-periphery model is distinguished by Levi-Strauss as "concentric dualism." These alternative dual structures, Levi-Strauss argues, have distinct logical and geometric properties, with different implications for their status as symbolic forms.

Diametric dualism is described as static, unable to transcend its own limitations. A logically restricted system, its transformations merely give rise to the same sort of dualism as that from which it rose, binary categories merely generating new binary categories. But concentric dualism is described as logically open and dynamic, containing an implicit triadism.

Both Levi-Strauss and Sahlins (Sahlins, 1976) have explained the coexistence of concentric and diametric dualism as manifesting tensions within the society between restricted and generalized exchange. Restricted exchange, whose classic manifestation in alliance theory is sister exchange, is consistent with symmetrical and egalitarian relationships between allied groups and is spatially linked to diametric dualism. Generalized exchange, on the other hand, is manifested by asymmetry in marriage bestowals, as in matrilateral cross-cousin marriage and by political hierarchy. Such asymmetries in exchange and power are best represented geographically by concentric dualism. Ambiguities or instabilities in these fundamental social orientations, the argument goes, lead to ambiguities in spatial orientation.

RHETORICAL AND PERCEPTUAL ISSUES

While I think that this kind of explanation of spatial organization has something to recommend it, it does not adequately illuminate for me the Samoan case. Though it is easy to transpose onto Samoa the tensions between hierarchy and equality or between asymmetrical and symmetrical exchange modes, these factors did not seem to correlate directly with the variety of ways that these alternative models are used rhetorically by Samoans. Moreover, once I was able to identify the character of this particular representational problem for village space, it quickly became clear to me that parallel contradictions characterized many of the dualistic forms available to Samoans for representing their cultural identity to themselves and others: speech registers, dance styles, diarchic political organization, and so forth.[3] Something even more basic than exchange relations seems to be at issue in these representational anomalies.

In the same essay by Levi-Strauss on dual organization, he suggests that the distinction between the two forms of dualism is equivalent to that between discontinuous and continuous phenomena. Diametric dualism represents the discontinuities of bounded categories, while concentric dualism represents graded relations, continua rather than classical categories. It is helpful to reformulate Levi-Strauss's diametric-concentric distinction, identifying it with the difference between digital and analog structures. In so doing, I want to try to relate the formal qualities of the code with the cultural organization of perception.

DIGITAL AND GRADED CODINGS

Digital distinctions are the precondition for generating categories. Classical categories have been defined in relation to clear boundaries. In terms of communication, their virtue is systematic coherence and clear intersubjective reference. What such digital structures cannot directly represent, however, are the gradations inherent in the individual's sensory and emotional apprehension of the world.[4] Graded structures can better convey the shape of experience, yet they are incapable of formulating the discrete categories through which mutual orientation and reference are made possible.[5] If graded coding underlies the subjective apprehension of experience as continua, so digital coding with its discursive capabilities facilitates intersubjectivity and social coordination.

The graded model of center-periphery manifest in village organization bears a kinship with pictorial or iconic representation in that such a model forms perceptual gestalts not reducible to categories without a basic transformation of structure and perceptual status. But graded models are also different from pictures. They have a generality of reference and a degree of abstraction that actual sensory images do not possess, and they make possible the apprehension of distinct sensory images as equivalent.

This graded model of village space is just one of a large family of related models that share a common foundational schema. As I demonstrated in my 1982 book on Samoa, institutions as variable as brother-sister relations, dance styles, speech styles, and the relations between different kinds of chiefs share a general abstract schema. Despite the obvious differences between chiefs and orators, or different styles of dance, or village orientation, these phenomena all form a class of linked experiences for Samoans because they share this foundational schema. This schema takes the form of what Lakoff and Johnson call a *kinesthetic image-schema* (Johnson, 1987; Lakoff, 1987a). Specifically, the Samoan center-periphery schema appears to be grounded in the experience of a centered body with outward projections (limbs), the kind of somaticized container schemas that commonly structures metaphorical projections from body position to other kinds of social orientation. Such foundational schemas underlie more concrete metaphors and other specific cultural models of which we are more conscious. They have the same relation to concrete human activity that categories have to concrete objects.

BRIDGING SENSORY MODALITIES

While images are normally thought of as visual, these graded, more analogically coded models often bridge sensory modalities synesthetically, incorporating visual, aural, tactile, and even olfactory sensations. For example, the experience of muscle tone and body posture is centrally involved for Samoans in the distinction between center and periphery in numerous contexts, with central experiences associated with muscular tension and postural centering, while peripheral meanings are experienced through muscular relaxation and freeing up of bodily extremities. Sitting posture is one of the earliest ways in which children learn these models. So there are important kinesthetic dimensions underlying this schema, and they provide a powerful sensory confirmation of the more abstract Polynesian distinctions between *tapu* (sacred, tied up) and *noa* (profane, unbound). Thus abstract "metaphorical" knowledge becomes embodied by the knower.

In his discussion of analog and digital communication, Anthony Wilden relates the digital-analog distinction to the difference between information and meaning: "In human communication, translation from the analog to the digital often involves a gain of information (organization) but a loss in meaning. . . . Such translations may generate paradox and contradiction" (Wilden, 1972:168).

This distinction between information and meaning is of great importance here. Digital coding has evolved for the efficient transmission of information but is incapable of directly conveying the kind of patterns or gestalts that humans seem to require for the subjective appropriation of experience as meaningful (compare Chapter 6). Thus, in human life, neither form of coding has ever fully encompassed the other.

If we consider the two models Samoans articulate for the representation of space, there appears to be an attempt to embrace two mutually exclusive but equally basic perspectives. A categorical distinction like front-back or sea-land defines a two-valued system, creating categories that are independent of a particular speaker's point of view. This is why Samoans are able to articulate for outsiders like myself the seaward-landward model but are less likely to convey to an outsider the concentric model, which is more directly linked to the subtle modulations of daily behavior.

Digitally coded models encode easily transmissible information about the environment in general. This advantage entails a corresponding weakness: they cannot directly model the subjective and dynamic shape of an environment for an individual, since such meaning is inherently built from analog perceptions and thus has a gestalt structure rather than a categorical one. The center-periphery model of the environment presumes, on the other hand, the perspective of someone located in a particular place. It is an actor-based model, grounded in human activity. The terms of reference are vectorial or directional rather than fixed points, and they point to dynamic relations rather than to static entities. The use of such graded symbolic forms is appropriate for people who tacitly share the same general perspective, such as members of a common household or village and those whose mutual orientation does not require explicit verbal formulations.

Category models are useful in orienting people who lack such an intimate experiential basis for their knowledge and who require a general, abstract set of references. Because of their status as observers of an alien culture, cultural anthropologists have traditionally been more inclined to such structural models, appropriate for objectifying their fieldwork experience to outsiders. More nuanced inside knowledge is conveyed through anecdote. Structuralist accounts are not thereby false, but they have a more limited epistemological relevance than we might have thought.

THE NEUROPSYCHOLOGY OF SPATIAL PERCEPTION

The two models for village space discussed in this chapter are clearly cultural models, conventional constructs employing culturally constructed coordinates and categories. These models also structure a set of Samoan cultural associations with center and periphery, front and back. Yet cultural models for spatial orientation are inevitably constrained by basic functional requirements of human visual perception. It would appear likely that these alternative egocentric and sociocentric cultural models would have a connection with the neuropsychology of spatial orientation.

Fortunately, the relationship between egocentric and sociocentric cognitive models has been well studied in cognitive psychology in relation to spatial perception. Any viable social organism must be able to navigate in space using two quite different spatial models: an egocentric model, using one's own body as a reference point (left, right, here, there, etc.), and a sociocentric (or referential) model, where sociocentric coordinates (north, south, inland, seaward, etc.) are used. There is some evidence that these complementary kinds of spatial perception are processed by different regions of the brain, some of which are specialized for spatial cognition. Egocentric spatial orientation requires the ongoing integration of diverse sensory information (tactile, visual, proprioceptive, auditory, olfactory). Moreover, this integrated sensory information has to be translated into signals affecting motor control. These navigational aspects of spatial perception appear to be at least partially localized in the brain's posterior parietal cortex (Levinson, 1992:1; Paillard, 1991). Sociocentric spatial models reference absolute locations independent of an individual's location or perspective. They appear to be processed differently from egocentric models. Sociocentric spatial perception seems to be localized in the hippocampus, where cognitive maps of specific places may be stored in specific cells (Levinson, 1992:3; O'Keefe, 1991:273.)

Also relevant to this problem of spatial orientation is the work of psychologist David Marr and his colleagues (Marr, 1982; see also Johnson-Laird, 1983:406 ff). Marr proposed a computational theory of spatial perception that distinguishes three distinct moments in the visual representation of space. The first representation Marr terms a primal sketch. This symbolic representation maps changes in the intensity, reflectance distributions, and local geometric properties of a space. The second representation (the 2½ D sketch) is a viewer centered (what I call egocentric) representation of contours, depth, and the orientation of surfaces. The third representation is a 3D model that is a viewer-independent (objective) fully dimensioned representation of a space or an object in space. Marr's work suggests that distinctive cognitive architectures underlying egocentric and objective perspectives on spatial relations are the universal and irreducible bases of all spatial perception.

Given this neuropsychological basis for two kinds (or phases) of spatial perception, what is the role of cultural models? First of all, cultural models contain specific local resources for mapping the environment, whether from an egocentric or a socio-centric perspective. If the "syntax" of spatial orientation is more or less universal, the "vocabulary" of terms and concepts is not. Cultural models of space are encoded in a great variety of models. Culture-specific vocabularies (lexical models) provide the framework of relevant directional coordinates (downwind, upstream, uptown, in-land, northward, toward the chief's house, on the other side of the gorge, left, right, across the street from the Johnson's, heavenward, etc.). And particular spatial models orient individuals to culture-specific locations. Important examples of conventionally mapped social spaces are shopping malls, with their food courts and hub-and-spoke structures, Samoan village space, American cities (uptown, downtown, east side, west side, inner city, suburbs), and baseball fields.

As Lakoff and Johnson (1980) and Johnson (1987) have argued, everyday speech is saturated with metaphors based on image schemas derived from egocentric spatial representation. These spatial metaphors are grounded in bodily experience. Kinesthetic and postural models (conventional postures associated with specific contexts) index aspects of social relations and personal mood. These are inter-personal spatial models. Bowing, sitting, walking, and styles of interpersonal prox-imity are all commonly based on highly conventional kinesthetic models whose power to shape experience is linked to the fact that they are preverbal, preobjective, and only tacitly understood (Csordas, 1994b).

PARADOXES OF REPRESENTATION

Thus far I have suggested that the simplest way to understand the coexistence of two alternative models of the Samoan village is to link the back-front model and its "digital" representation with an objective, system-oriented perspective based upon categories and to link the center-periphery model and its "analog" representation with a subjective, actor-oriented perspective based on a gradient of experience. Invoking one or the other of these models is a rhetorical strategy for Samoans who can thereby represent their immediate world *either* by simple, concrete categories, easily objecti-fied, *or* by reference to a more intimate gradient of experience more emotionally real but less easily objectified.

Of course, this explanation of these alternative models is itself based on the generation of crisp categorical differences. As such, it manifests Wilden's paradox of translation, conveying the relationship between objectivity and subjectivity nicely in an objectivist manner common in analytical discourse. But a little reflection on this relationship suggests that none of us actually experiences a pure distinction be-tween the digital and analog or the objectively real and the subjectively real. In fact, these two perspectives are easily tangled—with public categories generating private gradients of experience and intimate experiences being re-formed into simple catego-ries for public transmission or conceptual manipulation.

Thus submitting this very analysis to my own critique forces us to push a bit further. When we look closely at how our two models are used, they are not so easy to keep apart as my neat dichotomy suggests. Manifesting themselves in the context of real activity, where the demands of meaning integration and social coordination are both present, each model tends to generate a paradox of representation.

Neither model can be described adequately as purely directional (analog) or purely locational (digital). For example, *tai* and *uta* (or front and back) are often transformed from locations into shifters, indicating direction from a speaker, by the simple addition of a directional particle. *'I tai* indicates the position of something near or in the sea. Using the directional particle *i* (toward) instead of the locative particle *'i* (at) transforms the reference into a direction toward the sea or seaward, while the parallel form *i uta* suggests toward the mountain or bush. *Uta* itself is the uncultivated forest or bushland. Thus, alone or with the locative particle, *tai* and *uta* are fixed locations, features of the landscape viewed "objectively." They form a binary system and hence a set of objectifiable social categories. The addition of the directional particle *i* transforms these terms into vectorial or directional references—that is, references that use an objective feature of a landscape to make a statement about a personal position or direction of movement from the speaker's point of view.

Such variation in use of these terms is very common. So the experiential perspective of the speaker is introduced into the model by a simple syntactic strategy, and a digital structure is realized as a gradient. And of course, the reverse transformation from analog to digital is as readily available to Samoan speakers, thus changing a dynamic, experience-based statement into a static, objective reference.

With "shifters" such as pronouns or directional references, the opposition between subjective and objective perspectives is bridged by creating a set of transformations between location and direction (Hanks, 1990, especially pp. 141 ff; Jakobson, 1971; Silverstein, 1976). A little reflection should clarify why the analog-digital distinction (itself an apparent binary opposition) should be realized in such a graded way. Were the world divided simply between private but tacit experience and public categories, perhaps we would not find such a messy confluence of analog and digital representations. Indeed, there would be no linguistic model possible for the analog, since it would merely be our term for something that had no categorical expression. So the kind of *zone model* of the Samoan village I described above is in fact a set of categories generated from a continuum and thus is actually a digital representation of an analogic form. Human experience is not exhausted by the simple private-public dichotomy but has a full range of moments distinguishing degrees of group intimacy and the proximity of the other to the self. The mutual permeability of these two models of the village permits Samoans to express not only their relation to the world but also their fluid relations to one another in terms of shadings of intimacy and distance.[6]

ALTERNATIVE NAVIGATIONAL STRATEGIES

One of the reasons egocentric and sociocentric spatial models are sometimes hard to distinguish is that, from a cognitive perspective, complex navigation often requires a kind of tacking back and forth between an egocentric representation of an environment and a sociocentric "god's eye view." A classic example of this use of alternate spatial models in navigation comes from the fascinating literature on the mental models used by Micronesian and Polynesian sailors for long-distance canoe navigation without the aid of modern navigation instruments (Finney, 1994; Gladwin, 1970; Hutchins, 1983; Lewis, 1972). In working with a Micronesian navigator named Hipour, David Lewis was struck by the fact that his Micronesian counterpart did not readily understand his attempt to represent from a god's-eye perspective the intersection of two reference bearings (called *etaks*) used by the Micronesian sailors in navigation between Ololuk and Ponape islands. "On his telling me what they were, I drew a diagram to illustrate that Ngatik [island] must necessarily lie where these ETAK bearings intersected. . . . Hipour could not grasp this idea at all. His concept is a wholly dynamic one of moving islands" (Lewis, 1972:142).

Commenting on this apparent gap between Lewis's and Hipour's mental maps, Edwin Hutchins notes both the cultural and universal implications of the coexistence of differently positioned spatial representations for navigation:

> The technique Lewis used. . . contains some very powerful assumptions about the relation of the problem solver to the space in which the problem is being solved. First it requires a global representation of the locations of the various pieces of land relative to each other. In addition, it requires a point of view on the space which we might call the "bird's eye" view. . . . This strategy, then, involves at least creating an abstract representation of a space and then assuming an imaginary point of view relative to the abstract representation. We can guess that Lewis did this because it is for him a natural framework in which to pose questions and solve problems having to do with the relative location of objects in a two dimensional space. . . .
>
> Western navigators make incessant use of this change in point of view. When the navigator takes a compass bearing on a landmark from the bridge of a boat he has a real point of view on a real space, but as soon as he leans over his chart, he is no longer conceptually on the boat, he is over the sea surface looking down on the position of his craft in a representation of the real local space. . . . Regardless of problems of orientation, the change of point of view is manifest in the reconciliation of the map to the terrain. [Hutchins, 1983:206-207]

Hutchins suggests that the representational anomaly had to do with the fact that Micronesian navigators employ a dynamic, graded and egocentric map, using "bearings which radiate out from the navigator" (p. 207). For the Micronesian sailors, Hutchins claims, it was literally inconceivable that the bearings might intersect at a point anywhere but at the navigator's own immediate location.

Yet as Hutchins notes, another Micronesian navigator, Beiong, who was present at these discussions with Lewis, was actually able—though with difficulty—to schematize an alternative mental model roughly parallel to Lewis's own representation in that it employed a bird's eye representation of the islands. In Lewis's words; "He eventually succeeded in achieving the mental tour de force of visualizing himself sailing simultaneously from Oroluk to Ponape and from Ponape to Oroluk and picturing the ETAK bearings at the start of both voyages" (Lewis, 1972:143).

In a more recent account of instrumentless navigation, Ben Finney describes the apprenticeship of a young Hawaiian navigator to a seasoned Micronesian sailor. Finney relates how young Nainoa Thompson gradually devised his own navigating methods, rather than simply appropriating his mentor's navigation techniques wholesale, employing a combination of dead-reckoning, and complex mental maps of stars, solar movements, ocean swells, and bird movements. Significant for our purposes is the fact that Thompson's mental maps alternated between a gradually changing sequence of fixed, chart-like representations of the canoe's position relative to other islands, and a dynamic egocentric mapping similar to that employed by his Micronesian mentor (Finney, 1994:75–88). Thus while cultural representations may privilege either sociocentric or egocentric models of spatial movement, the human mind is capable of schematizing and sometimes must employ both kinds of models, though often for different purposes.

Samoan terrestrial navigators moving through village space make use of both sociocentric and egocentric models of their terrain. These Samoan models exploit the same kind of alternative navigation strategies that sailors use. Yet more than physical space is at issue in the Samoan case. Though Samoans do indeed use these different models to represent alternative readings of their village environment, the distinction between egocentric and sociocentric models goes well beyond the representation of physical space, and maps for a Samoan a more abstract, social terrain marked by distinctions in formality and intimacy in social relationships.

While the symbolic management of intimacy and distance is a universal feature of primate communication, it is especially highly developed in hierarchical societies like Samoa's. Discourse with "outsiders" is marked by elaborate dualism of the binary sort, and such pronouncements sound characteristically simplistic and are rarely empirically accurate. Samoa is good *(lelei)*, America is Bad *(leaga)*. Savai'i people speak in the t-dialect ("good speaking"), Upolu people speak in the k-dialect of Samoan ("bad speaking"). Good girls are chaste, bad girls are promiscuous. There are high chiefs *(ali'i)* and talking chiefs *(tulāfale)*. The social world is composed of commoners *(tūfanua)* and nobility *(tamaali'i)*. Everywhere in this most public model of their own culture, Samoans erect simple categories and clear boundaries. In their representation of their lived-out world as simple categories, Samoans become their own structuralists. Discourse with "insiders," however, employs codings that, by their very analog nature, are less easily objectified and more dependent on a shared experiential basis.

INTIMATELY SPEAKING

A linguistic example might help here. When I first arrived in Samoa after three months of Peace Corps training in Hawaii, I thought I had a rudimentary competence in spoken Samoan. But once I got off the plane in Samoa, I found I could not understand anything that I heard spoken around me. True, Samoans addressed me in a comprehensible version of Samoan, but they seemed to speak to one another in a different language. What I later discovered was that spoken Samoan has two phonological registers—what Samoans call good speaking and bad speaking. Good speaking, which is characterized by "n" and "t" (as in *tatou nu'u*), constitutes a very small percentage of Samoan talk—mainly that with outsiders like myself and with representatives of Western-introduced institutions like the church, schools, and so forth. In contrast, bad-speaking is a kind of colloquial pronunciation in which "t" and "n" undergo lateral shifts, becoming respectively "k" and "ng" (as in *kakou ngu'u*). This colloquial speech register is a Samoan version literally and figuratively of backsliding—relaxed, familiar, intimate, impulsive, and very personal discourse used in most intimate and indigenous Samoan situations including indigenous formal oratory.

Samoans characterize their language publicly as having two forms—*tautala lelei* (good speaking) and *tautala leaga* (bad speaking). But in action, these two categories are actually realized as a full gradient of styles in which there is a subtle and gradual lateralization of consonants and a deepening of vowel quality. Such subtle variation in styles signal important qualities of relationship, identity, and context, among other things, in ways immediately meaningful to Samoan speakers but not easily formulated in a public model of speech interaction. Thus what is *publicly* characterized as a two-valued front-back distinction in the vocal tract is *in practice* realized as a set of polarities with a full gradient of realizations. Both of these realizations of speech registers are models, the one more sociocentric and explicit, the other more egocentric and tacit.

Normally, Samoans insist that there are only two pronunciation styles. Yet when I imitated a sequence of these graded pronunciation styles for Samoans, they could immediately describe hypothetical situations for each style. And they were amused by the public revelation of a tacit "insider's" experience of speech in this way. While lacking an explicit model for this continuum of speech styles, Samoans clearly had a tacit model on which they operated and which they could immediately recognize.

APPARENT CONTRADICTION

Samoans often seem to act in a very different way from what their public claims would lead one to expect. This apparent contradiction was in fact behind the well-publicized debates in the early 1980s about Samoan aggression and Samoan premarital sexuality. In Samoa, public claims represent a very different kind of discourse than everyday behavior. The failure of observers of Samoa to properly contextualize Samoan statements and actions has led to perennial confusion and debate in Samoan ethnology, most notoriously, of course, the attempt by Derek Freeman to demonstrate that Margaret Mead had somehow gotten Samoa backwards (Freeman, 1983). As one can imagine, the failure to distinguish explicit from tacit models and to relate them functionally as alternate kinds of discourse has led to a celebrated muddle in Samoan studies.

Dualism is inherent in many Samoan cultural models. At its most abstract level, the Samoan worldview models interdependent relationships between the dignity of the eternal forms and the necessary power of the mutable events. Both aspects of reality are given conventional representation in linked, complementary units. In other words, Samoans have managed to accord recognition to both the dynamic flow of experience and the power of static structure. History is acknowledged and then encompassed by an ideology of unchanging cultural form.

Such a worldview has been elaborately worked out in Samoan thinking, and a world has been constituted upon it. The accommodation of two apparently contradictory perspectives in a coherent worldview has been accomplished in a complex way.

First and most simply, the world has been realized as a set of linked, complementary phenomena: brothers and sisters, orators and high chiefs, land and sea, intimate and formal pronunciations, and so on. By dissociating the paradoxical elements into mutually exclusive categories of person, movement, sound, or whatever, the world is built up as a set of radical opposites linked to each other by difference and interdependence (Shore, 1982, appendix).

The duality between structure and action evident in complementary relations, such as those between "front" and "back" in village spatial symbolism, is repeated at a level more abstract than that of linked institutions. In key models elaborated in Samoan thought—models for orienting oneself to the world, *two representations of each model are possible*. One version represents this relationship between event and structure as digital, categorical, and static. The other version represents the same relationship in a way that is analogic, graded, and dynamic.

Attention to the relationship between coding and culture thus enables us to more clearly trace the dialectic by which "embodied knowledge" is linked to discursive knowledge. Within each particular model—be it in dance, body posture, spatial orientation, temporal orientation, or speech—there are two "sides," each a part or aspect of a totality. Samoans are also given a choice of two ways of expressing the relationship between these two sides, one requiring categories, the other a gradient of degrees.

If the ceremonial life of Samoans projects a structuralist vision of their world, Samoan political wrangling deals with the implications of unstable and graded categories. Accusations of incestuous liaisons involve disagreements about degree of relatedness, reflecting the hazards—in a society that reckons of kinship ties through all possible connections, whether maternal, paternal or adoptive—of trying to maintain in practice the categorical distinction between potential wives and potential sisters.

The formal distinction between commoners and noblemen is invoked only in structuralist public discourse. Insiders know that, as one wise man put it, "In Samoa there are chiefs and there are chiefs and you should never confuse the two." Therefore, how far out from the *malae* a particular chief has built his house is the kind of issue by which political structure is at once realized and recreated in practice.

Such subtle gradations in kin relations or in chiefly rank are the stuff that make for historical changes in Samoa. But they are not what Samoans mean by their culture—their *aganu'u*. Culture for Samoans comprises the explicit sets of categories that generate consensus and that are presented to outsiders or on occasions requiring public affirmation of common Samoan identity. Thus, when some Samoans have insisted that Margaret Mead lied about premarital sex in their society, I suspect they mean that Mead claimed she was studying Samoan culture when, in fact, she was studying aspects of sexual behavior. Sexual behavior is not, in the Samoan view of things, a description of their culture.

If my analysis of Samoa is right, the structuralist impulse is not confined to structuralist scholars. It would appear to be a cognitive precondition of culture, making possible some degree of intersubjective coordination and providing what Husserl called a common horizon of expectations for a population. What is illuminating in the Samoan case is that this structuralist bias contains its own internal critique, which is so deftly overcome within the culture by a set of alternative models. Just as Samoan culture by its explicit models presents a structuralist vision of the world, it provides in its tacit models equal recognition to the openness and dynamism of human experience in all its forms. That anthropologists have sometimes found themselves confused by this paradox is a source of some pleasure and much amusement to many Samoans.

Notes

1. See Tolman, 1948.

2. On cultural and historical variations in the symbolism of spatial orientation, see Lotman, 1990, especially chap. 12; Hanks, 1990; Reichel-Dolmatoff, 1971; Eliade, 1959, 1965; Bachnik and Quinn, 1994.

3. In his analysis of the complex life of symbols of Greek identity, Herzfeld uses the term "disemia" as a more generalized notion of symbolic registers than the linguistic term "diglossia." In contrast to the linguist's focus on the implications of distinctive speech forms within a community for the negotiation of ethnic identity, the concept of disemia "is the expressive play of opposition that subsists in all the varied codes through which the collective self-display and self-recognition can be balanced against each other" (Herzfeld, 1987:114).

4. Lotman has proposed that spatial models are unique among cultural models in that

> they are constructed not on a verbal, discrete basis but on an iconic continuum. Their foundation are [sic] visually visible iconic texts and verbalization of them is secondary. This image of the universe can better be danced than told, better drawn, sculpted or built than logically explicated. The work of the right hemisphere of the brain here is primary. But the first attempts at self-description of this structure inevitably involve the verbal level with the attendant semantic tension between the continual and the discrete semiotic pictures of the world. (Lotman, 1990:203)

Yet this Samoan example suggests that while the continuous aspects of space may be primary in sensory experience, they may be secondary dimensions of the public cultural representations of space.

5. The distinction I am making between perceptual modes and their symbolic forms recalls Susanne Langer's famous distinction between discursive and presentational symbolisms (Langer, 1957).

6. See Herzfeld, 1987 (pp. 111 ff), for an interesting discussion of how Greeks use their own symbolic resources to convey a sliding scale of intimate and formal relations. As in the Samoan case, a complex code that appears to outsiders as a set of binary oppositions is employed by individuals more as a gradient of possibilities for the negotiation of identity in a contextually nuanced fashion. The Greek construct associates intimacy with "inside" relations rather than with "periphery," as in the Samoan case. In the Greek case, the private domain of the household appears to be a key association with "inside," whereas in the Samoan case, "inside" or "center" suggest the public and formal life of the *malae*.

12

When Models Collide:
Cultural Origins of Ambivalence

The defense lawyers in the Menendez case are clearly hoping to make the either-or approach work for them. The television movie, and there will be one, and soon, will have to purify or demonize the victims for the sake of plot. And Lyle and Erik will become in the script either tormented, abused child-men, or cold-blooded climbers in Porsches. Not both. Never both.

—Anna Quindlen, *New York Times,* November. 15, 1993

The last chapter considered a case of multiple cultural models for the same domain, in this case village space. Two Samoan spatial models, formally characterized as concentric and diametric dualism, provide for Samoans alternative ways to orient themselves within village settings. Though given conventional cultural form in Samoa, these alternative models are probably related to the basic differences between ego-centric and sociocentric spatial perception in all humans.

Not all cases of multiple models can be neatly explained by this sort of appeal to contextual dissociation. *Alternative models,* like those discussed in the preceding chapter, are usually allocated to different social contexts and become part of the complex rhetoric of cultural communication. But sometimes cultural models simply collide and are not rescued by context in the way alternative models are (D'Andrade and Strauss, 1992). In this chapter I want to look at what happens when cultural models come into direct conflict. As in the preceding chapter, the cases to be discussed are taken from my own Samoan fieldwork. Each of the four case studies illustrates a kind of "pathology" of cultural models. In three of the cases, several *incompatible* cultural models exist for the same domain of behavior. In the remaining case, a cultural model conflicts with and blocks the expression of deep personal needs, needs that normally remain culturally unformulated but that come to the surface under unusual circumstances.

RELATIVIZING RELATIVITY

Conflicting models are thus different from alternative models or metamodels. In the case of alternative cultural models, conflict is normally avoided because the models are realized in distinct contexts. The alternative cultural models of village space discussed in Chapter 11 are a fine example of how different models can coexist in complementary perceptual and social contexts. Multiple models become contradictory, however, in situations where significantly incompatible models are simultaneously invoked. The result of such incompatible models is often conflict of various kinds and a high degree of ambivalence. While the term "ambivalence" is generally understood as a feature of individual psyches, Robert Merton has focused on ways in which ambivalence is linked to contradictions built into particular social roles and role relations (Merton, 1976).[1]

I have left these cases of models in conflict to the final ethnographic chapter of the volume. As extreme examples, what we might consider "pathologies of cultural models," they help clarify both the normal place of cultural models in human experience and their problematical relation to lived experience. To anticipate the conclusion of the chapter, if cultural models are the anthropologist's argument for relativizing human experience, then the ambivalence and anxiety generated by conflicting models have the effect of relativizing this relativity. Such conflicted experience forces us to acknowledge that cultural models do not construct reality for people but only the *publicly articulated* part of reality. This chapter uses case studies of models in conflict to point to that less articulate part of reality that is often left out of cultural accounts of meaning. The chapter is about people struggling to make meaning in the context of ethical dilemmas.

ETHICAL RELATIVISM

The cases all deal with ethical dilemmas posed by conflicting cultural models in Samoan culture. I have chosen these cases because they pose the questions about cultural relativism in terms of the specific and troubling issue of ethical relativism. Though ethical relativism is arguably just a special case of cultural relativism, it is an especially provocative case.[2] Geertz (1984:276) has rightly hailed the humanizing effects of cultural relativism, what he called "the repositioning of horizons and the decentering of perspectives" afforded by a confrontation with exotic world views and diverse cultural symbolisms.

For most of us, however, it is alarming to contemplate the irreducible relativity of moral reasoning. Geertz's assurances that such expanded horizons will actually enlarge our moral sensibilities do not finally allay the suspicion that such an enterprise might uproot the very foundations of moral discourse.

The possibility that ethical discourse is just that, a discourse, rooted in a particular time and place, is disconcerting—making relative the foundations of our moral judgment. Of course, the question of whether ethical relativism is desirable has no bearing on whether it is true. Whether we find the prospect of an irreducible multiplicity of moral horizons invigorating or alarming cannot be allowed to shape our perceptions of what is or is not out there. The wish for a transcendent grounding of values does not make it so.

Yet such a desire does point to an important if unspoken motive in cultural anthropology: the possibility that the otherness of those we study might eventually transform the way we understand ourselves, yielding unsuspected congruences as well as the anticipated differences between remote human communities. This possibility is anticipated in the enterprise of ethnography in the act of what Roy Wagner (1975) has called the "bridging" of cultures that inevitably underlies the creation of sensitive ethnography. Such bridging presupposes an intellectual or moral footing in both the observer's culture and that of the observed, as well as a link between them.

This view of anthropology as enlarging human understanding sees ethnography as more than a dispassionate catalogue of various exotic species of human practices and diverse moral fictions. To the extent that the comparative study of ethics is a philosophical as well as a scientific enterprise, it has as its proper goal not only the pursuit of information but also the refinement of our ethical sensibilities: something akin to the pursuit of wisdom.

MAXIMAL CONTRAST

In time, and when we manage to participate in the life-world of others, it is sometimes possible to find our footing on what seems impossibly slippery terrain. These experiences point to a way out of the simplistic dichotomy between the ethnocentric rigidity of moral absolutism and the dizzying free fall of radical relativism. Since neither of these positions strikes me as either empirically defensible or desirable, we need to seek a way out of this impasse.

There is a way out, though it leads us into other, less compliant dilemmas. Ethics involves the evaluation of actions on some moral scale. As such, ethics presupposes some system of moral values. The putative differences among ethical systems assume value differences between cultures. The elucidation of *contrasting values* has been a specialty of cultural anthropologists. The comparativist perspective with its attraction to maximal contrast lies behind much ethnography, though often it is only an implicit bias.

Societies seem to reveal their value systems most clearly to outsiders when these values are represented as coherent models that contrast maximally with the ethical models of another society. As we saw in the last chapter, outsiders' models are often full of neat categorical oppositions. As Melville Herskovitz, one of the more ardent defenders of cultural relativism, once argued: "The very core of cultural relativism is the social discipline that comes with respect for differences—or mutual respect. Emphasis on the worth of many ways of life, not one, is an affirmation of the values of each culture" (Herskovitz, 1972, quoted in Hatch, 1983:64).

The consequence of this dependence on contrastive analysis of alternative models has been the frequent flattening of our renderings of the cultures we describe and the acceptance of a homogenized conception of what a value or value system is that we would not accept as intuitively real for ourselves.[3] Such stereotypic characterizations are useful analytical strategies when we want to delineate differences in emphasis *between* societies. Yet cultural contrasts can also mask empirical complexity and variation, existing not only within a given culture but also within an individual. This is because, at the level of lived experience, ethics is often realized as a dilemma rather than as a simple or automatic mobilization of a cultural model.

CONFLICTING MODELS

In certain cases, both horns of a dilemma are given cultural form as alternative and potentially conflicting cultural models. Each model legitimizes one reading of a situation, and the simultaneous mobilization of multiple models produces both social conflict between groups and ambivalence on the part of individuals. In Chapter 4, we explored the consequences of this kind of collision of models in sports, where it was called "frame violation." Frame violation occurs in any situation where normally contextually distinct models come to overlap one another.

In the case of tennis star Don Budge at Wimbledon, the frame violation involved embedded but mutually exclusive performance frames. A championship tennis match was momentarily upstaged (for everyone but Budge) by the ritual greeting for entering royalty, within which the game at Wimbledon was embedded.

In this chapter, the models in conflict all deal with fundamental Samoan orientational models that govern key social relations. Four examples of such model confusion will be presented. The first three have a tragic cast, while the fourth case suggests the relationship between cultural models and comedic irony.

CASE I: FILIAL PIETY

During my stay in a large village, my host, a distinguished senior chief of the village, was shot to death by another village chief following an argument over a card game (Shore, 1982). Any such violent event would normally create extreme tension within a village, but given the status of the two men involved and the prominence of their respective families in village politics, this murder threatened to unravel the fabric of the village and to precipitate a chain of increasing violence that, once begun, would be hard to stop. Both the village chiefs and the local pastors played important roles in trying to minimize the threat to village peace. Appeals were made to both traditional Samoan and Christian ideals of harmony, patience, and forgiveness. One such appeal that I heard was in the form of a homily delivered by a local pastor to the eldest son of the murder victim the day after the shooting. The pastor counseled forbearance to the young man and recommended that, in the spirit of Christian love, he turn the other cheek to this assault on his father and on his family.

The message was conveyed both explicitly in the content and implicitly through several rhetorical devices. First, the homily was delivered in a polite and formal phonological register which Samoans call "good speaking."[4] "Good speaking" is normally associated with church, school, and other Western-introduced institutions and is linked for Samoans with delicacy of subject matter, personal reserve, social distance, and subordination of personal impulses to social propriety. The other rhetorical strategy was the frequent use of the first-person-plural "inclusive" pronoun *tatou* ("all of us, including you"), a form of verbal co-opting in which potential rifts in an assembly are verbally masked and the organic unity of the assembly is stressed.

This kind of advice from the pastor to the distraught young man was to be expected under the circumstances. What is more surprising is the private conversation I witnessed between them later the same day. Here the pastor, in hushed tones, told the youth "If you don't avenge the death of your father, you are not your father's son." The pastor's advice this time was conveyed to the lad in the colloquial phonological register, in which the phonemes /t/ and /n/ are realized as the sounds [k] and [ng]. This register is linked for Samoans to both traditional fully Samoan institutions (such as traditional oratory) and also to the expression of aggressive or angry impulses.

A day later, the boy attacked his father's murderer with a machete while the prisoner was being escorted through the village by a local constable. While the prisoner survived the attack, he was badly wounded and had to be rushed to a hospital.

How do we make sense of the apparently contradictory advice of the pastor to the distraught youth? Is he simply a hypocrite? Or perhaps he did not *really* mean what he said in one of the conversations? Perhaps Samoans are confused or amoral. What I think was going on in this case was the invocation of alternative Samoan ethical norms in a way that only exacerbated the youth's obvious pain. Each norm, that of revenge and that of Christian love and forgiveness, is usually relegated to a distinct set of contexts in Samoan discourse, contexts that serve to mask their ultimate incompatibility.

In this case, however, there was no easy way out for the dead chief's son. Caught between the demands of incompatible norms, contextual dissociation could not provide for him an escape from what must have been experienced as a double bind. The fact that the youth opted to play out the vengeance scenario rather than the forgiveness one is not predictable from the cultural perspective alone. The son's attack on his father's murderer was a ferocious public display of filial piety. Yet it fell short of lethal revenge. Far from the simple manifestation of cultural value, this violent act can only be understood as the unpredictable product of fundamentally incompatible cultural models for behavior combined with profound personal grief and anger over his father's murder. The youth was caught in an ethical dilemma and did what his heart told him he had to do.

DISSOCIATED REACTIONS

No simple account of cultural norms can explain why the son did what he did. What cultural models can account for in this case is the cultural orchestration of a son's personal dilemma. Samoans do have alternative cultural models for behavior in situations like the one in which the youth found himself. Under normal circumstances, these alternative models are allocated to distinct contexts. But in this case, they met head on. There is an explicit set of Samoan values emphasizing cooperation, harmony, deference to authority, and the subordination of antisocial impulses to the needs of the group. Yet there is another set of Samoan values emphasizing personal heroism, boldness, competitiveness, fierce loyalty to one's own group at the expense of social harmony, and personal touchiness at perceived attacks on personal or family honor.[5]

Several observers of Samoa have noted these contradictory tendencies in the Samoan ethos. Felix and Marie Keesing observed that in the anthropological literature on Samoa there has been an emphasis on " 'security', 'conformity', and 'group responsibility' and the symmetrical balancing of social structures on the one hand . . . [and] 'divisiveness,' 'deviousness,' 'turbulence,' and the potential of 'violence' on the other" (Keesing and Keesing, 1956:8).

Margaret Mead, whose understanding of the complex Samoan ethos tended to stress its cooperative aspects, also noted these two tendencies in terms of Samoan social organization, stressing the

> tendency to place each individual, each household, each village, even (in Western Samoa) each district in a hierarchy, wherein each is dignified only by its relationship to the whole, each performs tasks which contribute the honor and well-being of the whole, and competition is completely impossible. The other tendency, the rebellion of units against subordination to a plan and their use of a place within the component unit to foment trouble and rivalry with other units, while not so strong, is always present. [Mead, 1965:262]

Freeman has characterized the Samoan ethos in terms of "a susceptibility to dissociated reactions" of a sort in which "the emotionally impulsive is split off from the socially acceptable," leading to considerable ambivalence about authority (Freeman, 1983:223).

Though it is true that one dimension of Samoan ethos is associated with the socially acceptable, it is misleading to understand this dichotomy as opposing the ethical to the unethical. As the case study described above suggests, both sides of Samoan ethos have ethical implications, suggesting, in different contexts, appropriate kinds of action. Thus Samoan children are taught publicly by parents to value submission to authority, while at the same time they are often encouraged to defend their honor and that of their family even at the expense of social harmony and hierarchy.

Both heroic assertiveness in the interest of personal or local group status and deference to an encompassing social order are legitimate Samoan values, and both are embodied in a variety of Samoan cultural models. The fact that they often conflict means that Samoan ethical discourse involves competing and mutually exclusive claims. The existence in Samoa of such unresolved competing models for behavior accounts for much of the nervous "edge" one senses in Samoan behavior, and the tendency for either violence or ironic humor to appear just under the surfaces of Samoan politeness and formality.

CASE II: ATTACHMENT DILEMMAS IN ADOPTION

Like other Polynesians, Samoans frequently adopt or foster others' children.[6] While most adoptions are made with close kin, adoptions between unrelated families are also known in Samoa as a way of cementing relationships among families or for other political reasons (Shore, 1976a). An adopted child is called a "made child" *(tama fai),* and adoption is understood to involve the creation and maintenance of a kinship link through feeding and other kinds of nurturance, behaviors that Samoans see as aspects of *alofa* (love/empathy).

Adoption and fosterage in Samoa are extremely common, approaching 40 percent of all children in a village I surveyed in 1972 (Shore, 1976a). Researchers have proposed several different kinds of explanations for adoption. Many have stressed that adoption is consistent with the general flexibility of Polynesian social arrangements (i.e., bilateral reckoning of descent, flexible norms of postmarital residence). Such flexibility has the adaptive advantage of permitting the population to be easily redistributed among land resources on small and vulnerable island habitats.

Robert Levy, on the other hand, has interpreted Tahitian adoption as a potent psychological message, a cultural model of the fragility and contingency of all social ties (Levy, 1973). Phrased more positively, adoption can be understood to be an institution that models an idea of diffuse and generalized social attachments rather than exclusive attachments. Other institutions, such as the common Polynesian pattern whereby older siblings are primary caregivers of young children, would also model the same kind of diffuseness of attachment (Ritchie and Ritchie, 1989).

Early in my stay in Samoa, I had naively assumed that Samoan social values underlying *alofa* were created in a rather direct and uncomplicated way by this kind of modeling. Then I met a young American psychiatrist who was living in Samoa temporarily and had established a practice in Apia. I asked him what sorts of problems his patients came to see him about. He replied that the most common problem he dealt with was the culturally inexpressible guilt and mourning of mothers forced by convention to cheerfully give up their babies to their kin. These patients often came with a variety of other complaints and eventually found a way to talk about their repressed feelings of anger, sadness, and guilt associated with the adoptions.

Does this mean that they did not feel genuine *alofa* for their often childless sisters or brothers to whom their babies went? Not at all. But it does suggest that cultural models do not operate in a psychological or social vacuum. The achievement of a proper attitude of *alofa* exacts a psychic toll on Samoans, albeit one that is often masked.[7] The experience of the adoption model cannot be accounted for in terms of the model alone but must take into account the complex tensions between the cultural model and a mother's attachment to her infant and the personal models that she has constructed as compromise formations in the attempt to reconcile the cultural expectations with her own thwarted desires.

CASE III: A COMEDY OF EROS

The third case was discussed at great length in my doctoral dissertation and can only be summarized here (Shore, 1977). It involved a case of multiple spirit possession in which several young Samoans in their early twenties, all from the town of Apia, were simultaneously possessed by *āitu,* or spirits, while visiting a village on the island of Savai'i as part of an outing of Catholic Sunday school teachers.[8] The seven possessed individuals were brought back to Apia, where they were housed together for several days until the Samoan bishop was called in to treat them.

I was able to study one case of possession quite closely. The victim was a friend of mine and allowed me to interview him at length during and after his possession. I also noted that a young woman from the group was possessed by the ghost of Tui Fiti, a notorious *āitu* who was linked with the history of the village the group was visiting. The spirit speaking through the young woman addressed my friend with extraordinary anger and vehemence. It appeared that I was witnessing a kind of surrogate fight between the boy and girl, waged through the ghostly intermediaries.

When I interviewed the young man after the possession had ended, he claimed no knowledge of what had transpired during the possession. Initially, he also denied that there was any problem between himself and the girl who had confronted him in the persona of Tui Fiti. When I got him to talk about the trip to Savai'i, however, he eventually related a complex and fascinating tale.

The girl, it turns out, had been a sweetheart of his. As is usually the case in Samoa, the relationship was secret. Moreover, the group of Sunday School teachers had decided that each person would consider the others as "brothers and sisters" for the duration of the outing. The boy and girl decided that they would become like siblings and put aside any other feelings for each other.

The brother-sister model of relationships is perhaps the most important kin relation in Samoa (Ortner, 1981; Schoeffel, 1978; Shore, 1981). It is one of the paradigmatic models for nurturant affection *(alofa)* and specifically carries nonerotic associations. Brother-sister relationships do not just characterize actual siblings but define an explicit Samoan relationship type that is used to structure all sorts of relationships even between unrelated boys and girls. Among such brothers and sisters, any suggestion of eroticism in the relationship, including discussions of intimate matters, is proscribed.

In Savai'i, it appears that the boy began to flirt with one of the girls of the host village. Their relationship did not go unnoticed by the boy's hometown sweetheart, who was struggling with her own inexpressible feelings of jealousy. It was in this context that she became possessed by Tui Fiti. Tui Fiti, it appears, was not enjoined, as she had been, from expressing outrage at the adventures of her unfaithful friend.

This case involves the complex models by which Samoans map relationships. Specifically, it involved a kind of frame violation in which an erotically charged relationship, between lovers became confounded with a brother-sister relationship, which barred any hint of erotic intimacy. The specter of incest, what Samoans call *mata 'i fale* (literally, looking into [one's own] house), haunts many relationships between young Samoans, since incest prohibitions forbid any intimate relationship between people known to be related as kin in any way.

In a small island society, where descent reckoning is done through both mothers and fathers, kin relationships proliferate widely. So it is not uncommon for young lovers to discover (or for someone to inform them) that they are distant "brothers and sisters." The potential confounding of a sibling relationship with that of lovers adds a distinctive quality to Samoan romantic ties. This is one of the reasons why simple generalizations about love in Samoa never seem to capture the tense and conflicted quality of courtship in this particular part of Polynesia.

In terms of cultural models, the conflict is not just between two different models

of boy-girl relationships. It is a peculiarity of Samoan society that relationships between the sexes are normatively defined in categorical terms. One is either a sister
or a lover, a brother or a lover. These relationship types permit no middle ground,
either intellectually or emotionally. Yet the cognatic descent system operates in such
a way as to render all boys and girls potential relatives of differing degrees (Shore
1976b, 1981).

These incompatible cultural models for social relationships make romance in
Samoa a thing of peculiar ambivalence that outsiders have struggled to understand.[9]
I suspect that the psychological complexities of making erotic attachments under such
conditions has something to do with the reported practice among some Samoan youth
of initiating a sexual relationship with a girl, after a period of flirtation, by an act of
violence, which consists of a punch in the solar plexus to knock her breathless.

Several Samoan youths have also reported to me that they have the need to get
drunk in order to overcome their initial shyness of a girl. While this is only anecdotal
evidence, it is conceivable that both alcohol and violence may serve to eroticize a
relationship whose outward form has been characterized by reserve and shyness appropriate for a brother-sister relationship.

CASE IV: PARADOXES OF POWER: COMIC DIMENSIONS

Each of the three cases described thus far illustrates the psychological and social
costs of conflicted cultural models. Yet this sort of conflict in Samoa also has a more
cheerful face. It accounts, I think, for much of Samoan humor. Of all the important
aspects of Samoan character, perhaps the most frequently overlooked is the wonderful Samoan sense of irony, which often expresses itself in teasing, mockery, and
what is often quite sophisticated political satire.[10] Irony is contradiction's sweetest
fruit, and in Samoa, it is fueled by the unresolved tensions between contradictory
cultural models of authority relations.

On the face of it, Samoan political life is characterized by an intense concern
with rank, title-status, and honor. Like their neighbors in Tonga, Samoans have a
dual conception of status, in which rank comes alternately through genealogical and
kinship relations and through the possession of titles. Titles form families, which
have genealogical and rank relations among themselves, just as people do. Indeed,
in polite Samoan discourse, one may refer to a titled person as "you-two" *('oulua)*,
acknowledging both the sanctity of the person and that of the title.

The classic descriptions of chiefly authority in Samoa have sometimes portrayed
an aristocratic ideal where chiefs wield enormous power, have total responsibility for
their families' welfare, and command unquestioned deference from the untitled. For
example, Gilson describes the Samoan chief *(matai) as* "a man whose authority extends to all members in their performance of domestic tasks, in the maintenance of
orderly relations among them, and in the regulation of their relations with other
village households" (Gilson, 1970:15). Gilson relates the authority of a Samoan chief
to the seniority of the chief's title in a stable local hierarchy:

> The rank of village titles, however determined and justified, is rigorously institu-
> tionalized in several ways, the most important of which centre in the *fono,* or council

meeting, and the *fa'alupega,* the village's honorific phrases of address. The governing body of the village is the council of chiefs who, when they convene, must observe certain fixed formalities which denote their rank. . . . This multiple recapitulation of village political structure occurs every few days, and in addition, special feasts and ceremonies proceed in similar fashion as far as the formalities go. *No one in the village, therefore, can have any doubt about the relative status, rank and privileges of the titled heads of the various households.* [Gilson, 1970:20–21; emphasis added]

This clear-cut portrait view of Samoan chiefly rank and power seems all the more convincing because it is also the public ideal that many Samoans espouse in describing their chiefs. For instance, Margaret Mead recorded a description by a young Samoan chief of his own sense of the seriousness and dignity associated with the role of *matai:*

I have been a chief only four years and look, my hair is grey, although in Samoa grey hair comes very slowly. . . . But always, I must act as if I were old. I must walk gravely and with measured step. I may not dance except upon most solemn occasions, neither may I play games with the young men. Old men of sixty are my companions and watch my every word, lest I make a mistake. Thirty-one people live in my household. For them I must plan, I must find them food and clothing, settle their disputes, arrange their marriages. There is no one in my whole family who dares to scold me or even to address me familiarly by my first name. It is hard to be so young and yet be a chief. [Mead, 1928:26–37]

In his critique of Mead's Samoan work, Derek Freeman accuses Mead of seriously understating the degree of actual power and sanctity of Samoan chiefs. He attacks Mead's "ignorance of the traditional political life of Samoa," asserting that she was "mistaken in asserting that 'the sanctity surrounding chiefs in Samoa was minimal for the Polynesian area' " (Freeman, 1983:133). Freeman cites the traditional deference accorded the Tui Manu'a as evidence for the extreme sanctity of Samoan chiefs:

The ritual prohibitions surrounding the Tui Manu'a were (as Mead herself noted in 1936) of a most elaborate kind. Similar prohibitions and extreme marks of respect to high-ranking ali'i were also observed throughout the Samoan archipelago. As Thomas Nightengale noted in 1834, no one dared pass in front of the chiefly residence of the paramount chief of western Samoa "under penalty of the severest punishment"; or as Hood observed in 1862, during a meeting of a fono attended by the Tui Atua, any canoe passing by was, as a mark of respect to the Tui Atua, vacated and pushed across the lagoon, its occupants wading up to their shoulders in the water. The sanctity surrounding Samoan chiefs of high rank was almost certainly not "minimal for the Polynesian area." [Freeman, 1983:133–134]

Like Gilson, Freeman's account of Samoan politics emphasizes the extraordinary power of a ranking chief's pronouncement. For Freeman, decision making in a *fono* follows strict precedence of rank, with the actual decision in the hands of the highest-ranking *ali'i,* who is called the *sa'o* (the right or true one) of his village:

In a local polity, while the titular chiefs commonly consult with one another when a judgment on any major issue is being formed, the actual making of this judgment and its announcement to the fono is the prerogative of the ali'i of highest rank . . . . The judgment, in fono, of a paramount chief is also called a tonu, meaning an exact decision. The pronouncement of a tonu by a high-ranking ali'i is usually accomplished with few words and with what Robert Louis Stevenson called "that quiescence of manner which is thought becoming of the great." This aristocratic demeanor may, however, be accompanied by an imposing flourish. [Freeman, 1983:132]

While Freeman accurately stresses that decision making within the Samoan *fono* is constrained by matters of rank and the inequality of voices within the council, his account of chiefly decision making surely does not bring out the pervasive ambiguities in Samoan ranking. It reflects neither my own observations of the prevailing ethos within which decisions are negotiated nor the numerous accounts of Samoan politics that emphasize the relative openness of rank to challenge and the pervasive instability in power relations.

My own experience in Samoa suggests that the vision of the Samoan polity as a clear linear hierarchy, with a "paramount chief" at the top delivering an order to his colleagues in the *fono,* is an oversimplification of a more ambiguous state of affairs. Many council meetings do not have a "paramount chief" present. Some titles are certainly recognized as senior, but I have attended few meetings in which there was a single individual making the decisions.

More convincing are accounts of Samoan politics that stress the instability and openness of authority to challenge. Although Freeman quotes Robert Louis Stevenson to support his contention that ranking Samoan chiefs wielded great autocratic decision-making power, Stevenson's actual understanding of the authority of Samoan chiefs was far more qualified, and interesting:

> Men like us, full of memories of feudalism . . . leap at once to the conclusion that [the title of a high chief] is hereditary and absolute. Hereditary he is: born of a great family, he must always be a man of mark: but yet his office is elective and . . . held on good behaviour: born of the great ones of his clan, he was sometimes appointed its chief officer and conventional father; he was loved and respected and served and fed and died for implicitly . . . and yet, if he sufficiently outraged clan sentiment, he was liable to deposition. As to authority, the parallel is not so close. Doubtless the Samoan chief, if he be popular, wields a great influence, but it is limited. Important matters are debated in *fono* . . . debated I say—not decided; for even a small minority will often strike a clan or province impotent. In the midst of these ineffective councils, the chief sits usually silent: a kind of gagged audience for village orators. The absolute chiefs of Tahiti and Hawaii were addressed as plain John and Thomas; *the chiefs of Samoa are surfeited with lip honour, but the seat and extent of their actual authority is hard to find.* [Stevenson, 1892:3–4, quoted in Meleisea, 1987:16; emphasis added]

Freeman uses the Tui Manu'a as an example of the great sanctity of Samoan ranking chiefs. Yet in his regional analysis of variations in Polynesian status systems, Goldman stresses "the main divergences between status systems of Western Samoa and of Manu'a.

> This experience was the historical event, the energy factor, so to speak, that broke an older traditional pattern and split the head (Manu'a) from its body . . . .Manu'a severed from the body, evolved in isolation. The head, as was its traditional role, continued to develop along the lines of status formalism. Having lost its body, it had lost much of its efficacy, its mana, so that much of the older religious awesomeness once associated with Tagaroa-descended Tui Manu'a drained away. [Goldman, 1970:250–251][11]

Goldman cites Samoa as the clearest example of what he calls an "open society" type polity. Political power in Samoa is inherently dualistic. Samoans developed a bipolar status system in which "the special combination of organic and 'made' features . . . gives to the status system a dual character" (Goldman, 1970:251). Early on, Mead had detected in Samoa, correctly I think, a tension between the political institutions that convey a strong sense of fixity of form with its orderliness of rank to which individuals seem to subordinate themselves, and what she called "the rebellion of the individuals within the units against this subordination" (Mead, 1968:249).

PERVASIVE CONTRADICTORY IMPRESSIONS

This tension that Mead detected is reflected in the pervasive contradictory impressions ethnographies of Samoa leave us with concerning the basic Samoan ethos. For instance, Freeman's account gives the impression that what he terms *tonu* or "exact decisions" within the *fono* are the result of decisions made unilaterally by the highest-ranking chief or chiefs. Another account, this time by a ranking Samoan chief, presents a more populist view of the *fono:* "A real *fono* . . . involved real discussions, and is full of dissenting voices. Consensus is the ideal only when face to face with outsiders" (Larkin, 1972:220).

Thus the view that Freeman provides of Samoan rank, with its unquestioned sanctity, is not exactly wrong, but it represents one kind of model, a public ideology, which presents a highly structured and consensual political order. This kind of model is commonly used rhetorically to convey a picture of Samoa for *outsiders* or for any other occasion when a dignified front is appropriate. Not surprisingly, this categorical model bears only a shadow relationship to what actually occurs in the give and take of Samoan political life.

The Samoan novelist and poet Albert Wendt has characterized this chiefly model of political relations as *tū fa'atamalli'i,* "the way of the chiefs." It is what he calls Samoa's "public face":

> Our public face is nearly always placid, obedient, courtly, orderly, generous, hospitable, considerate, impassive. Freeman knows this face well. It is the *tu fa'atamali'i,* the way of the true aristocrat, the ideal on which all human behaviour must be modelled. . . .
> There is also the opposite way, the way of the *tu-fanua,* he who transgresses, who does not behave like a *tamali'i,* and brings shame to his *'aiga,* village, country. Extreme anti-*faatamali'i* behaviour is described as *tu-faamanu,* the way of the beast. [Wendt, 1983:14]

While these idioms propose a clear-cut distinction between a chiefly ethos and that of a commoner, they actually reflect tensions and ambiguities built right into the chiefly institutions themselves. Chiefly authority in Samoa is a complex fusion of aristocratic and populist ideologies that are the basis of contradictory cultural models of power in Samoa.[12]

Samoan political values are not understood simply by laying out a set of abstract principles. To understand the ethical dimensions of these contradictory models of authority, we need also to examine how conflicting moral or ethical claims are resolved in practice. Thus, ethical discourse is not just the enunciation of moral values but commonly involves a rhetorical struggle to legitimize one course of action and depreciate an alternative, even though both possibilities exist as ethical alternatives.

FALE AITU: SAMOA POLITICAL SATIRE

I suggested above that the contradictory models for authority in Samoa underlie the Samoan predilection for irony and satire. Samoans have a traditional comedy genre called *fale āitu* in which political contradictions are translated into hilarity. Here we have a kind of ludic or performance model that formulates for Samoans a vision of their own paradoxes. Elsewhere, these comedy skits have been analyzed in considerable detail [Shore, 1977, 1993; Sinavaiana, 1992]. Here we can look at only one example of the genre, to appreciate its satirical spirit and understand its role in aesthetically resolving an otherwise irresolvable tension in Samoan political life.

The skit is performed by Petelo and his straight-man Ta'ai, a team that was famous two decades ago in Western Samoa and among communities of Samoans overseas. The skit is called "The Visit of the Prince" and is perhaps Petelo and Ta'ai's most famous skit. Like many of their pieces, it is a political satire based on a real event. In 1970, Great Britain's Prince Philip paid a visit to Samoa, an event that stirred up a good deal of excitement among Samoans, who love any sort of aristocratic show. But the prince portrayed by Ta'ai is not the dignified and charismatic figure the Samoans honored. He is played as a bumbling, inarticulate fool who speaks not the Queen's English but rather a parody of Samoan English as it would be spoken by someone who was pretending to have a mastery over a language he or she actually hardly knew.

Petelo plays the part of Lavea, a well-known radio announcer in Samoa, who broadcasts the arrival of the prince at the Apia wharf. On hand are numerous local dignitaries, including the head of state, the prime minister, and their wives. Petelo deftly impersonates each of these dignitaries and then, taking the role of Lavea, describes for the radio audience the motorcade that makes its way from the wharf to the reclaimed area for the official reception ceremonies. Petelo mimics the sounds of the cars making their way to the reclaimed area.

The performances are very difficult to hear over the shrieks of laughter from Petelo's audience. Up to this point, Petelo maintains a relatively "straight" take on the proceedings, and his tone is one of mock respect. Here and there, however, Petelo interjects a word or phrase that is totally out of character for the occasion. For instance: "It is certainly wonderful to see His Highness the Prince, as the old boy extends his arms and waves, an action that is then copied by his chauffeur" (laughter). It is as if an "offstage" voice were beginning to interfere with the official public voice of the announcer.

The party arrives at the stage which has been erected for the formal reception, and the announcer tells us, "At this time we shall hear the speech which His Royal Highness the Prince will deliver to the nation in respect of his journey to our country." The prince then speaks, in English double-talk, while Lavea provides a Samoan "translation" for the radio audience. The rest of the sketch is reproduced below, in translation:

> *The Prince:* Ladies and Gentlemen.
>
> *Lavea* (translating): His Royal Highness the Prince says that he would like to express his deepest thanks to His Highness the Respected Head of State, to His Excellency, the Prime Minister, as well as to the Honorable Cabinet Ministers, and to their Highnesses, the Royal Consorts, as well as to the honorable and respected people throughout our nation.
>
> *The Prince* (English): All de people of Samoa and come and to see to de people to be able out to see, you see de people. Okay?
>
> *Lavea* (translating): And the Royal Highness the Prince is extending his thanks to His Highness and Head of State, as well as to the Prime Minister and to the dignified and honorable Members of the Cabinet, to their Highnesses, the Royal Consorts, as well as to the dignity and honor of the people at large.
>
> *The Prince:* All de people of Samoa, and come and see to de people. You see? Okay?
>
> *Lavea:* I have a feeling that my translation has been slightly off. It is becoming apparent to me that His Royal Highness the Prince has journeyed to us from somewhere called People. [Laughter.] In my estimation, it appears that His Highness The Prince has already mentioned the name "people" nine times, and so I have come to conclude that he must be here as a representative of the Government of [the country] People. Yes, indeed! And thus he expresses the pride he feels in his heart upon arriving here in our country, a most splendid country, a most humble country, a country of people who know how to get things done. Yes! And therefore I say to you that it is simply none of your business, Prince, know what I mean?! It's simply none of your business whether we are humble or arrogant. Just leave all that to the Government of Samoa! Just look at the dignified and honorable country over there. Look at his bald head! [Laughter.] Why you, Prince, you're no different from me.
>
> *The Prince:* Okay. And again, our my people sailing to Samoa and I come here my people. [Laughter.]
>
> *Lavea:* In the words of the Royal Prince, his heart is filled with pride and joy at having left his wife behind—which, as we all know, he was never really able to find, as well as his dear royal children—which, despite all his frantic attempts to produce, he was never really able to have. [Laughter.] And thus it is that the royal heart of His Royal Highness, the Prince, is filled with pride and joy because he had arrived here in our country while at home his dear—non-existent—wife and their royal—non-existent—children are still in good health.
>
> *The Prince:* And my people who come to see my wife and also Samoa, many people have come.
>
> *Lavea:* And now I feel anger rising as he keeps repeating "people" again and again. There are many reasons why I feel this anger, you know, Prince! Do you know Samoa or not? Look here, buddy, you'd better not try to be nasty inside of this nation, because this nation happens to be the land-of-the-stone-throwers. [Laughter.] So just look you here, Prince, no matter how dignified you may be, no matter how exalted in that great nation of People over there, you can still get your head smashed in over here! [Laughter.] I'm just about to give you a smash in the head myself. Hope you don't mind, but not long from now you're going to find yourself flat on your face! [Laughter.]

The Prince (uncomprehending and therefore oblivious to Lavea's comments): Many people see de journey of my wife . . .

Lavea: He says that his wife's name is Jenny [Journey], but I can tell you here and now that in fact his wife is non-existent, and as for his dear children, well he's tried and tried but never managed to produce any! [Laughter.] For that reason, honorable listeners, look at the hysterical laughter we have over there. And now, honorable and dignified listeners of our nation, I shall return home, for I suspect that His Royal Highness, The Prince, wishes to have a rest, perhaps at the Sunset Club. Therefore the dignitaries of our Government will also return home now, and His Royal Highness The Prince will also depart. Thus the procession of cars is now on its way [imitates the roar of the vehicles]. And the motorcycles are in the lead, driven by the police escorts [imitates the roar of the cycles]. Reupena [?] is riding up ahead while the policeman Jackie is in the rear. And thus we come to our final dance, with your kind permission.

The style of this skit imitates the characteristic progression of the Samoan dance party *(fiafia)*. The opening is controlled and played straight, but this order gradually breaks down as the dignity falls away, revealing a hilarious release from the restraints of formal discourse. An offstage voice takes over from the public persona of the announcer, using the idiom of translating as the pretext for a comic commentary on the proceedings. Then, dignity and calm are restored as the skit concludes. The translation, overtly between Samoan and English, is in fact between two conflicting political models.

The translation by Petelo/Lavea of the grotesque pseudo-English double-talk of Ta'ai/Prince into the elegant and poetic idiom of Samoan oratory defies adequate translation and is one of the high points of the *fale aitu* genre. Moreover, the use of the Samoan language by Lavea to insult the unsuspecting prince and his family creates a comic tension between the polite and restrained discourse of the public Samoan persona and the irreverent populist private sentiments that often mark private and intimate discourse.

In this skit, an intimate voice (an informal Samoan voice) expresses antielitist sentiments, while pretending to convey the elite discourse of a visiting prince. The humor involves a denial of formal deference to rank at the very moment when that rank appears to be acknowledged. In the Samoan setting, rank is not only elite status but European colonial authority. In real life, of course, such a confounding of public and private voices would be completely unacceptable. Here it is merely hilarious.

There are a number of important features common to Samoan satirical skits.

- Most involve status degradation and the humiliation of high-ranking individuals: royalty, fathers, pastors, and European teachers.
- Most of the satires are aimed not at specific individuals but at general social types, such as fathers, elderly pastors, and so forth. There is a degree of abstractness about these satires that gives them a universal appeal in Samoa and also prevents individuals satirized from taking offense.
- A common persona for the comedian is the transvestite *(fa'afafine)*. The speech patterns of many of the *fale āitu* mimic the effeminate style of the transvestite, as does the female dancing style that the performers sometimes adopt. As a marginal individual, the transvestite serves as a kind of privileged

commentator on society and is permitted to make the kind of outrageous comments that would be offensive coming from others.

- All of the skits employ a variety of speech registers: Samoan/English, mock English, formal oratory, and formal (t) and intimate (k) pronunciation. The switching between registers is the major way in which Samoans suggest a split between "onstage" and "offstage" discourse and signal an alternation between contradictory models. The humor in all of the skits is tied to the privileged expression of status resentments that are not normally expressible in public discourse. They represent an undercurrent of status resentment that is represented in public only by the juxtaposition of alternate speech registers.
- *Fale āitu* derive much of their effectiveness from the fact that they take conflicting models of authority, which are experienced as ambivalent but are represented in public culture as clear-cut, and expose their complexity and ambiguities in a public forum for all to experience together. In *fale āitu* these ambivalences are dissociated and represented in comically juxtaposed onstage and offstage voices.
- *Fale āitu* derive much of their comic power from deliberate frame violation. Actors will occasionally step out of their stage roles and comment directly to the audience about what is happening, providing their own choreic commentary. This periodic denial of the performance frame is a very important part of the skit's effectiveness. To the extent that the satires reflect real but "offstage" sentiments of many Samoans, they are really about failed performances. The frame violation reveals, in a way that nothing else can, the performative nature of everyday Samoan life, and its ultimate fragility. It also points to the highly contextual nature of rank and status in Samoa.

PSYCHOLOGICAL IMPLICATIONS

The comic energy of the *fale āitu* proceeds from an unresolved tension between actor and persona, and between an actor and a kind of backstage reality that has few other legitimate public expressions in Samoan life. Samoan humor is often a kind of comically masked status degradation. Yet these comic expressions of resentment against authority are not quite a reversal of the normal attitudes toward elites but rather a manifestation of both the structural ambiguity of many elite roles in the Samoan polity and the ambivalence of many Samoans toward elites. While we have explored the roots of the structural ambiguities in rank and status systems, we need to address more directly the psychological dimensions of Samoan ambivalence.

While no direct study of the psychic ambivalence underlying Samoan politics has been carried out, the literature on Samoan ethos and character is very illuminating. Much of it, in fact, is contradictory. A German resident of Samoa, writing in the first decade of the twentieth century, characterized Samoans as "the most polite people in the South Seas. . . . His politeness is often the cause of what one calls lies" (Neffgen, n.d., quoted in Shore, 1982:151).

The earliest scientific work on Samoan character was Mead's, and it is precisely her characterization of Samoan ethos that has persistently raised questions about the accuracy of her portrait of Samoa. As is well known, Mead's view of Samoan character stressed the absence of strong attachment either to individuals or to personal goals. She characterized the emotional tone of Samoa as "moderate, less charged with strain and violence. It never exerts sufficient repression to call forth a significant rebellion from the individual" (Mead, 1928:494).

Holmes et al. undertook a review of the personality assessments that had been done of Samoan subjects and concluded that "the picture that all these studies present is essentially similar, and there is consistency through time" (Holmes et al., 1970:470). Specifically, the personality profile emerging from their synthesis stressed order, social cooperation, conformity, conservatism, tenacity, and a disinclination to accept leadership roles. Furthermore, Samoans were found to devalue personal autonomy, personal achievement, or behavior that placed them at the center of attention. "They are not," the researchers concluded, an aggressive people, nor are they particularly sensual or creative, and, just to throw in one man's opinion, they are extremely extroverted" (p. 470). In other words, Holmes and his students found that the psychological profile of Samoans revealed by the various tests administered to them largely confirmed Mead's characterization of Samoan ethos.

It was precisely against these sorts of characterizations that Freeman directed his critique of Mead's Samoan writing (Freeman, 1983). Freeman went to great lengths to document what he termed "the rivalrous aggression that is so characteristic of Samoan society" (p. 161). He characterized Samoans as "particularly susceptible to dissociated reactions" (p. 223). The frequent use of corporal punishment creates a climate "in which children are forced to assume an outward demeanor totally at variance with their actual feelings" (p. 223). And this, in turn, creates "states of marked ambivalence, particularly toward those in authority" (p. 223).

Numerous observers of Samoan society have commented on the aggressive side of Samoan personality. The most interesting of these are psychodynamic in character, in that they tend to understand the tendencies to aggression and self-asserting theatricality as a compensation for the dominant cultural emphasis on outward conformity and obedience.

In a comparative study of cultural patterns of alcohol consumption in Samoa, Tahiti, and the Cook Islands, Lemert characterized Samoan personality as manifesting "a deep substratum of aggression . . . which readily comes to the surface with intoxication" (Lemert, 1972:230). Lemert found that this aggression was "in part culturally inculcated . . . [and] encouraged in certain kinds of structured situations" (p. 230). He traces most of the aggression to young, untitled men and argues that chiefs permit and even encourage aggressive behavior in this group as a kind of release from the normal stresses of being under the authority of their titled elders most of the time.

Lemert also suggests that this undercurrent of aggression may be a compensation for the high cultural values placed on deference and social passivity and the cultural emphasis on "conformity, acceptance of group decisions, ceremonial compliance and politeness in interpersonal interactions" (p. 230). Alcohol-related aggression in Samoa is, for Lemert, an indirect expression of fundamental Samoan values, but "it is much more conspicuously a mechanism or device through which individuals in group setting find release for a variety of unintegrated feelings and impulses" (p. 225).

As we have noted, even Mead, though her stress was always on the passive side of Samoan personality, acknowledged that the underside to the dominant Samoan stress on hierarchy and social conformity was the "rebellion of individuals within the units against this subordination" (Mead, 1968:263; see also Feinberg, 1988).

I undertook an analysis of the implicit ideology of personhood and behavior and concluded that many of these observations of outsiders were paralleled by Samoans' own understanding of the dissociation between social conduct and personal impulse (Shore, 1982, especially chap. 9). This study documented considerable Samoan ambivalence about issues of social control and public morality, in which a kind of "public persona" was sharply dissociated from a private "inner persona":

> What is distinctive and interesting [in the Samoan case], is the degree to which this ambivalence is formalized in Samoan thinking. My informants readily and quite unself-consciously expressed this opposition between a strong commitment to public control over others' behavior and a desire to be free themselves of such constraints. There was no sense in their accounts of self-contradiction, since the two kinds of statements seem to have been radically dissociated from each other. [Shore, 1982:186]

It seems likely that the developmental roots of this ambivalence can be traced to aspects of socialization in Samoa. Freeman's claims about the effects of severe corporal punishment are probably on target, though the hypothesis needs close empirical study. Samoan socialization also communicates conflicting messages to children about the very issues of obedience, conformity, and aggression. In a perceptive study of Samoan socialization, and the Samoan conception of the *loto,* the seat of the emotions, Mageo proposes a revision of our understanding of what socialization in any setting produces: "[S]ocialization produces unmanageable and unforeseen byproducts that continue to interfere with compliance for most members of society" [Mageo, 1991:405].

Mageo's thesis is that one of the key elements of Samoan child rearing is the sudden withdrawal of parental affection that characterizes parents' relations with infants.[13] Rather than passively accepting this distancing, Samoan children react by throwing tantrums. This continues until they are encouraged to deal with their affiliative needs by showing *alofa* for others rather than by demanding love.[14]

Mageo's analysis is especially pertinent to this chapter because she links socialization to the larger context of social and political relations. She notes that there are domestic contexts, like treatment of younger siblings or abuse of dogs, where a child's willfulness and aggression are tacitly permitted and even encouraged. Like other observers, she notes the emphasis placed on obedience, attention to hierarchy, deference, and politeness but recognizes a constant subtext of resistance as well (Mageo, 1991:405):

> If the *'āiga* preaches *fa'aaloalo* [respect], in practice it resists the static notion of stratification that *fa'aaloalo* implies. Rather than accepting a fixed position within the village or the district, the *'āiga* continually manipulates and controverts the ranking of titles. Although ranking among families and villages is supposedly established by history, oral history is flexible; talking chiefs may tell it differently from one ceremony to the next, subtly depressing the importance of one title or elevating another. [p. 410]

Samoan conceptions of *alofa* (love or empathy) are embodied for Samoans in hierarchical rather than egalitarian models. More specifically, the prototypical social models for *alofa* typically are directed *upward* from status inferiors to status superiors. Gerber has argued that Samoans frequently associate *alofa* with a scenario of a young person feeling compassion for an older person who needs help (Gerber, 1985:145). The other prototypical model is the feelings of a brother for a sister. Rather than embodying conceptions of obedience upward, or of authority downward, *alofa* seems to suggest a kind of situational transformation of feelings of deference, hostility, or shyness into identification and compassion (see Shore, in press). *Alofa* represents both a positive feeling of compassion and identification and a defense against the hostile feelings commonly associated with deferential relations.

In contrast to the relatively flat characterization of traditional personality inventories, the psychodynamic approaches employed in relation to Samoan personality by Gerber, Mageo, and myself characterize personality in terms of internal tensions and ambivalent motivations. This approach to motivational issues is also consistent with a political system constituted by structural ambiguities. That is, the cultural manifestation of such pervasive ambivalence is a set of contradictory cultural models: role models, speech styles, kinesthetic models, and so forth.

It would appear that the pervasive contradictions in the accounts of both Samoan personality and social organization have been generated by the complexities and anomalies of Samoa itself, and are unlikely to be resolved by simple disconfirmations of the sort that Freeman attempted in relation to Mead's Samoan research. What is called for are better (more subtle, more encompassing) models of both culture and personality and closer attention to the problems of contradictory models as a normal part of cultural life.

ETHICAL RELATIVISM

These Samoan case studies of conflicted cultural models point to an obvious but often overlooked aspect of ethics. Ethical situations are highly charged for us, not so much because they involve choices between right and wrong courses of action but rather because they involve us in "Sophie's choice," dilemmas of competing virtues or evils. In fact, it is difficult to conceive of an ethical choice that does not have as its subtext a competing value that it must override. Such is the nature of ethical discourse. Even the renunciation of incest, as Freud and Levi-Strauss have reminded us, is a deeply ambivalent virtue and derives its moral power from that ambivalence. Wherever there appears to be an ethical problem phrased as a conflict between good and evil, I would suggest that we look just beyond the explicit, public dilemma to a more powerful if shadowy conflict between competing virtues or vices.

Such a perspective on ethics has enabled me to understand my own discomfort with flattened accounts of cultural models. I have found myself insisting that Samoans value community over the individual, or that Samoan women give up their children for adoption without psychological distress, because of a value system that placed emphasis on diffuse family ties rather than on exclusive attachments. While statements like these contain some truth, they also squeeze the life out of the reality of a people by treating human action as if it proceeded from a simple activation of unilateral cultural models. Instead, as we have seen, real life often involves the problematical and always partial resolution of dilemmas proposed by the existence of competing models, or models that are incompatible with key experiences.

In this vein, it is interesting to consider the conclusions reached by psychologist Leonard Carmichael, who argues for a transcultural ethics and recommends great literature as a model for proper values:

> The truly great literature of civilization has provided some people in many generations of men and women with the sort of wisdom that is needed in the subtle selection of proper courses of action in solving the often truly novel problems that arise in each life. . . . The formal study of such writers as Homer, Dante, Moliere, Milton, and Goethe is one tested way that may be used in establishing such self-accepted standards. [Carmichael, 1961:14–15]

Yet something is wrong with this formulation. Dante, Shakespeare, or Milton are not great because they present us with morality tales, with good and evil nicely juxtaposed for our edification. What value exactly do we appropriate from Hamlet, torn as he is between the demands of filial piety and the horror of committing murder? What comfort do we take from Lear's conflict between his public duties as a king and his private needs as a father? Or from Cordelia's dilemma of filial versus wifely duties, to say nothing of her need to have a self? What is the easy lesson to be gleaned from Eve's choice between ignorance and disobedience in Genesis? What are we to make of Milton's God, who is tediously prosaic, while Satan (like Milton himself) plays the seductive poet? Great literature is great because it is truer to life than any morality play could be, presenting us with vivid and compelling evocations of moral paradox.

The same goes for myth and fairy tale. The Big Bad Wolf or Jack's giant may appear to be simple representations of evil for young children, but to adults, at least, their power over our imagination may involve the ambivalence of jealous (and absent) fathers, or the tradeoffs involved in the hard-won autonomy of sons from fathers and family. When we experience great literature or myth as transcending historical or cultural boundaries, is it not in part because such creations present us with a crystallization of human dilemmas rather than with conventional morality?

Comedy and tragedy both derive their depth from types of incongruity. Comedy affects us by juxtaposing incompatible and unexpected perceptions of a situation in a way we find amusing. In tragedy, the incongruities are often moral. If comedy is less directly translatable between cultures than is tragedy, it is probably because the comic mode uses universal forms—formal contradictions and discontinuities—but very local contents. The same cannot be said for tragedy, where essentially human dilemmas are played out. In theory, ethics deals with absolute values. Yet in practice, ethics proceeds from problematics rather than from simple values.

In reformulating ethics from the realm of value propositions to that of contradictions, have I really transcended the dilemma of ethical relativism? In part, I have. For many of the contradictions that generate ethical discourse in human life are themselves transcultural in origin and emerge from contradictions inherent in the human condition. The Samoan mother is caught in a dilemma in which the attachment of mother and infant and all of the moral associations of nurturing one's offspring are incompatible with the social virtues of sharing. Both positions are represented, though unequally, in Samoan ethical discourse.

We can recognize the pastor's appeals to the twin virtues of filial piety and community harmony as based on moral imperatives that have become mutually exclusive in a particular context. Moreover, neither of these values is a Samoan invention, and both are understandable as potential human values. What is Samoan, however, is the particular handling of the dilemma, by dissociating the imperatives and assigning the one to a very personal linguistic register and the other to a more fully socialized and sublimated form of discourse.

What accounts for the cultural variability of ethical systems? If, as I suggest, the hidden agenda of ethical discourse is not a choice between good and evil but one between competing virtues or competing vices, then ethical discourse must be experienced as saturated with considerable anxiety and ambivalence. In this view, ethical discourse would suggest the polyphony of contradictory voices. Yet with the exception of philosophers and other specialists in subtle reasoning, most ethical discourse requires some help in reducing complex and inconclusive evaluations to clear terms and simple choices.

Culture provides us with rhetorical strategies for making such choices in the form of clichés, proverbs, heroic models in myth, and other such cultural resources that help provide partial and temporary resolutions to what may be ultimately irresolvable predicaments. In this view, cultural systems do not invent values so much as they orchestrate rhetorical strategies, organizing the perception of value-laden situations with standardized and culturally acceptable formulations—what we call cultural models.

At their most extreme, cultural models can render certain moral positions shadowy and hard to articulate, as in the cases of the Samoan apprehension of the natural feelings of the mother for her own child or the American understanding of the irreducible moral status of certain forms of personal subordination and dependency. Such inchoate positions remain potentially problematic areas, for individuals may experience them privately, since these conflicts are not always given public articulation. Here, ethical relativism characterizes differences in ethical emphasis *between* cultures.

In other instances contradictions are rationalized by contextual dissociation. Culture can orchestrate alternative justifications for contradictory positions to be invoked by competing interest groups or by a single group on different occasions. Thus the irreducible value of the individual life is invoked by some American groups to attack abortion on ethical grounds, yet many of the same individuals would not choose to invoke this same value in relation to capital punishment, shifting instead to an alternative emphasis on the right of society to exact vengeance or to deter future crimes. In these cases ethical relativism may be said to exist *within* a culture, mediated by competing ethical models.

The cultural variability of ethical systems is linked to the very conditions that generate coherent ethical systems. We have noted that the anxiety surrounding ethically relevant situations is related to the fact that underlying ethical principles are often conflicting virtues (or vices) where tough decisions have to be made. To perceive such dilemmas clearly, to see all sides of an issue all the time, would make action difficult at best. Hamlet's near paralysis in the face of such an ethical dilemma illustrates well the weakness of the philosopher-king. In normal circumstances, cultural models *partly* resolve such dilemmas for us by reducing ambiguity and rendering certain choices cognitively more salient and emotionally more acceptable than others.

Yet the relationship between cultural models of and for experience and the lived experience of real people is never simple or fully determinate. Cultural models such as the baseball games, aboriginal myth models, Kwakiutl dramatic models, and any of the others we have encountered in the course of this book exercise a profound degree of constraint on the everyday thinking, feeling, and motivation of those individuals for whom such instututed models are mental models. Yet the case studies encountered in this chapter suggest that such cultural models never determine our experiences in a simple and direct way. They enter into complex relationships with experiences, with needs and feelings, and with other models, all of which can compromise the effectiveness of the models in producing conceptual clarity and motivational force. Instead, conflicted models generate ambivalence and irony. This is why ethical situations are so emotionally provocative. Not only do cultures fail to eliminate completely the anxiety inherent in ethical dilemmas, but, as we have seen, this ambivalence is frequently linked to the fact that ethical systems themselves usually contain principles that are bound to collide in any given situation.

There is also a control function latent in this very confusion. Sometimes, perfectly ordinary virtues, like filial piety or attachment to life, can turn into vices when taken too far. This is, of course, the frequent stuff of tragedy. We have seen in the Samoan case discussed above, as well as in Hamlet, the bloody possibilities inherent in filial piety. In the Samoan instance, who knows what restraining effect the pastor's hortatory invocation of the value of communal harmony may have had at the moment the near-fatal blow was struck on the murderer's neck by the son of the victim. Ambivalence may paralyze, but, properly orchestrated, it can simply temper behavior, inspire caution, and even engender sufficient guilt to attenuate an extreme response.

We might profitably examine the variety of ethical systems in the world through the analysis of cultural models of normative behavior.This kind of analysis considers the role of models in the fragile resolutions of ultimately irresolvable human dilemmas. Such tentative resolutions are effected by conventional models that serve to reduce the perception of moral ambiguity and make decisive moral action possible. Such conventional ethical models, drawing on a local fund of historical and mythical precedents, proverbs, and clichés, are inevitably only partially and contextually successful at resolving ethical dilemmas. Many of these dilemmas have no final resolution.

Moreover, the analysis of local ethical systems would profit from a look at how specific cultural systems recognize the possibility of alternative and even contradictory "correct" resolutions to ethical problems. The strategies available within a culture for reducing ethical ambiguity are a fascinating though little analyzed aspect of cultural knowledge.

This view of the relationship between ethical knowledge, local culture, and the human condition suggests that we must never mistake the public expression of ethical discourse with the private and subjective experience of a morally problematic situation. While the private experience is apt to be experienced as ambivalent and ambiguous, the public representation is more likely to be framed as categorical and absolute. To confound these two perspectives misstates what is only a partial fit between cultural knowledge and personal experience.

Notes

1. For a South Indian case study of sociological ambivalence, see Nuckolls, 1993. For other significant cross-cultural studies of sociological contradictions and their psychological consequences, see Fortes, 1969; Turner, 1957; Kelly, 1977; Shore, 1978; Knauft, 1985.

2. For an interesting discussion of the issue of cultural relativism in the context of cognitive psychology, see Bruner, 1990; especially pp. 24–30. See also Fiske, 1990; Fernandez, 1990; Hatch, 1983; Hanson, 1975 (especially chap. 2); Lakoff, 1987a; and Shore 1989, 1990a.

3. The most famous paradigm for this kind of contrastive model of cultures is Benedict's *Patterns of Culture*. The explicit model for cultural configuration or what came to be known as "ethos" was the gestalt concept from the psychology of perception then in some vogue. Since the hallmark of this configurationist model of culture was internal coherence, contradiction or contrast came to characterize differences between cultures or else the gap between deviant individuals and the larger pattern. It was only in *The Chrysanthemum and the Sword* that Benedict came to recognize the importance of patterned contradiction within a cultural configuration.

4. On Samoan speech styles, see Shore, 1977, 1982; Ochs, 1986; Duranti, 1981:165–169; see also Chapter 11 in this volume.

5. These apparently contradictory aspects of Samoan ethos were a central factor in the notorious controversy over Margaret Mead's early characterization of Samoa (Mead, 1928, 1930, 1968) provoked by the publication of Derek Freeman's *Margaret Mead and Samoa: The Making and Unmaking of An Anthropological Myth* (1983). Freeman's "refutation" of Mead's characterization focused, among other things, on the stress Mead placed on the casualness of Samoan ethos, and the emphasis on gentleness and cooperation. Freeman takes issue with the characterization, arguing in almost every instance that Mead got it virtually backwards. In his chapter "Cooperation and Competition," Freeman documents the highly competitive and aggressive Samoan ethos, manifesting what Freeman calls, quoting an early European observer of Samoa, "ungovernable pride." (Freeman, 1983:151, see also chap. 11, "Aggressive Behavior and Warfare").

What is to me most striking in this controversy is not so much the differences between Mead's and Freeman's readings of Samoan ethos and values but rather their similarity. Both anthropologists mute the apparent contradictions in Samoan culture in favor of a self-consistent and one-dimensional portrait. Focusing on complementary aspects of a complex culture and downplaying the dualisms that pervade Samoans' own understanding of their ethos (Shore, 1982), both Freeman and Mead present partial visions as if they constituted the whole.

6. On Polynesian adoption, see Brady (ed.), 1976; Carroll (ed.), 1970; Levy, 1970, 1973.

7. See Wikan, 1991, for a powerful evocation of a similar case in Bali.

8. On Samoan spirit possession, see Cain, 1971; Shore, 1977, 1978; Goodman, 1971.

9. This complexity lies behind the famous and apparently irresolvable debate over Mead's early and notorious characterization of the love life of Samoan youth (Mead, 1928; Freeman, 1983).

10. On Samoan humor, see Sinavaiana, 1992; Shore, 1977, 1995; and Mageo, in press.

11. Even the history of succession to the Tui Manu'a title suggests that political cunning could prove as important as pedigree. For an interesting Manu'an story about rivalry between brothers for the Manu'an crown, which was identified more with the tapa headpiece than with the blood of the possessor, see Mead, 1936; Shore, 1982:69; Marcus, 1989:176–177).

12. On chiefly versus populist ideologies in Polynesia, see Marcus, 1989.

13. On the importance of this withdrawal of parental affection as a component of social-

ization in other parts of Polynesia, see Levy, 1973, and Ritchie and Ritchie, 1989. I would add that this withdrawal of close parental affection is accompanied by the development of a network of more diffused social attachments. Contra Levy, I would suggest that the psychological message here is not simply that all relationships are tentative and fragile. Equally, the message is one about generalized emotional and social support rather than exclusive attachments. Rather than being simply a psychological liability, as is sometimes suggested, this shift in attachment modalities is the basis of the diffuse warmth that Mageo suggests characterizes Samoan social relations and which is part of the Polynesian stereotype.

14. I would add to this analysis the often noted replacement for children of specific attachments with a kind of generalized attachment, which is the basis of the affection that Mageo suggests characterizes Samoan social relations.

VI

CULTURE IN MIND

13

Culture and the Problem of Meaning

The deeper the experience of an absence of meaning—in other words, of absurdity—the more energetically is meaning sought.

—Václav Havel

The charm, one might say the genius of memory, is that it is choosy, chancy and temperamental; it rejects the edifying cathedral and indelibly photographs the small boy outside, chewing a hunk of melon in the dust.

—Elizabeth Bowen

Recapitulation: Reasoning from Cases

Over the course of the last twelve chapters, I have sketched a complex portrait of the cognitive life of culture and the cultural life of the mind. Beginning with the ecological brain, and an attempt to untangle the psychic unity muddle, I have tried to define culture as a dimension of the mind as well as a part of social reality. In outlining an ethnographic view of mind, I have used a series of cultural case studies as a rhetorical strategy to underscore the importance of specific cultural models in everyday thinking and feeling. Yet one of the the important goals of this book is to describe the cognitive "architecture" of cultural knowledge and its production. We are not quite there yet. The remaining job is to delineate a more explicitly psychological picture of culture processes.

Because we have traversed a varied and complex landscape in the ethnographic sections of the book, it would be useful here, in anticipation of turning our attention more directly to cognitive psychology, to retrace the major steps we have already taken up to this point. Let us recall the important issues raised by the ethnographic case studies.

The book began with a historical overview of what I call "the psychic unity muddle." The psychic unity doctrine, which has gone largely unchallenged and unexamined by mainstream anthropologists, asserts that all humans, *independent of culture,* share the same basic psychological characteristics. Grounded in an unfortunate confusion between the brain and the mind, this psychic unity doctrine has effectively blocked a rigorous meeting of the minds between cognitive psychologists and cultural anthropologists. By presuming both cultural heterogeneity and psychic unity, cultural difference could be linked to mind only superficially.

My own position is that *the choice between characterizing humankind in terms of psychic unity or psychic diversity is based on a false dichotomy and an overly essentialistic biology*. Developments in cognitive psychology, evolutionary biology, and neuroscience all support the idea that humans possess an eco-logical brain, finely designed for cognitive adaptation to diverse and changeable environments. Properly understood, the common architecture of the human nervous system accounts for important local differences in cognition, just as it accounts for universals of human cognition. Psychic unity and psychic diversity turn out to be two sides of a common coin.

The second major point is that culture is usefully conceived as a collection of models of great diversity. *Cultural knowledge is distributed in many different kinds of models.* The notion of cultural models has been borrowed from schema theory in psychology. But cultural models have many distinct attributes not reducible to mental models. Chapter 2 outlines many of these distinctions and proposes a general typology of genres of cultural model. One of the most important distinctions among different kinds of cultural models is that between a special purpose model and a foundational schema. *Different cultural models may share a family resemblance because they are organized in relation to common foundational schemas.* The distinction between a foundational schema and a cultural model is really extrinsic, since any model can serve to schematize lower-level models. But foundational schemas tend to be more abstract than models and not as committed to a particular form or genre. The value of the distinction between model and schema is clear from the great number of different American cultural models connected through the modularity schema, as outlined in Chapters 5 and 6. The same was true for the walkabout schema of the Murngin, discussed in Chapters 9 and 10, and the Samoan center-periphery schema, described in Chapter 11.

A second crucial distinction was proposed between instituted models and mental models. *Instituted models are the external or public aspect of culture and represent common source domains by which individuals schematize conventional mental models.* Games and other cultural performances are especially useful for demonstrating the complex relations between the external structures of rules and norms and the personal experiences that these make possible (Chapters 3 and 4). The movement between instituted and mental models goes in both directions. Instituted models are made by people and are the objectification over time of someone's inner experiences. The internalization of instituted models and the externalization of mental models usually occur on quite different time scales, but taken together they comprise the basic dialectic of cultural life (Berger and Luckmann, 1966).

Though cultural knowledge is, by definition, shared, the nature of this sharing is a complex matter. *Cultural knowledge is best thought of as a distributed system of models.* Cultural models are *socially distributed* in that not all members of a community will share all models or will have the same variant of a model. An adequate description of cultural models necessarily includes an account of which, or whose, perspective is being modeled. A player's model of baseball is not that of a spectator, and viewing a game through a television tube will engage yet another model of the game (Chapter 3). These models would all be expected to share important properties, however—properties motivated by the framework of constitutive rules and strategies that underlie all play.

Cultural models may also be be *contextually distributed,* such that different versions of a model represent different functional or rhetorical perspectives. A good example of contextual variation in models is the study of egocentric and sociocentric spatial models of Samoan village space (Chapter 11). These cultural models mapped both cultural distinctions in perspective and more universal psychobiological distinctions in spatial perception.

In Chapter 3, where American baseball was the cultural model of choice, cultural knowledge was also understood to be distributed for any spectator among different sorts of knowing. *This suggests that the mind is best thought of as having a polyphonic structure, and that knowledge of cultural models is always layered as different kinds of knowledge, at different degrees of distance from focal awareness.* In Chapter 4, we turned from the perspective of the viewer to that of the players, and took an amusing tour through the marginal zones of various sports in developing a conception of marginal play. Making sense of play in this way required a hierarchical view of how games are regulated. *Constitutive forms (like spatial arrangements), rules of engagement, strategies (including rules for breaking the rules), and the flow of events each occupies a different layer of awareness in any game or performance.* So accounts of strategizing do not necessarily undercut the applicability of structural analysis in any social situation. The tacit integration of deeper levels into our experience of the game makes possible the focal attention to levels of play closer to the surface. Periodically, these levels of organization can interfere with each other, producing paradoxes of play and action—what I have called "marginal play."

In Chapters 5 through 8, I marshaled a set of case studies, drawn from contemporary American culture and from the Kwakiutl of the American coastal northwest, to reflect on the long-standing puzzle about the relationship between culture and rationality. *In assessing the reasonableness of diverse modes of thought, Western notions of rationality have used both inconsistent and overly narrow conceptions of rationality.* Totemism and magic became problems for those anxious to reduce all reasonable thought to what I call "logical rationality." Yet this is only one type among numerous kinds of rationality, and its dominance is itself the product of a certain kind of techologically oriented society. Even the more "illogical" aspects of totemism can be understood as empirically reasonable ways of thinking about such issues as reproduction, origins, organic evolution, and the food chain. Lévy-Bruhl's concept of "participation" is an attempt to represent symbolically the complex interdependencies and exchanges among different modes of life. In contemporary Western popular culture, a high-tech form of totemism, which I call techno-totemism, reproduces many of the paradoxes of classical totemism. Techno-totemism's attraction for us is that it plays on the ambiguities in contemporary experience of human-machine relationships. Their blendings in cyborg images propose (but also, inevitably, undercut) the categorical distinction between the human and nonhuman.

The idea that even we in the West have come to recognize the empirical basis for the apparently unreasonable mythic mixtures that dominate totemic symbolism inspires a new look at the concept of "participation" made (in)famous early in the twentieth century by the French philosopher and speculative anthropologist Lucien Lévy-Bruhl. Because his work has unfortunately been discarded by most modern anthropologists and psychologists, I have deliberately focused considerable attention on Lévy-Bruhl and the potential significance of his ideas for a modern cognitively oriented anthropology. *Lévy-Bruhl's notion of "participation" suggests that certain cultural models (rather than certain mental endowments) promote the perception of powerful identifications between disparate phenomena.* While Western analysts have frequently rejected the "prelogical" notion of participation, they have in fact resurrected Lévy-Bruhl's idea in terms of a theory of tropes. Both metaphor and metonymy represent distinct forms of identification that are important modes of meaning construction. In Chapter 14, we review a set of cognitive processes (prototype matching, schema induction, analogical transfer, connectist models of thinking) central to meaning construction—processes that are consistent with Lévy-Bruhl's notion of "participation".

A cognitive view of cultural symbolism inevitably focuses attention on meaning as meaning *for* someone. In Chapter 8, this concern led to a discussion of the complex life of cultural signs and the various kinds of "motivation" they bear. *Cultural signs have many different kinds of relationship to both the external world and the inner world of personal experience.* Understanding how culture underwrites meaning construction requires us to recognize the implication of these many different kinds of symbolic motivation. This chapter again takes up this issue as we look at why cultural anthropology has failed to develop a cognitively adequate conception of meaning. To anticipate, I will propose that arbitrary (unmotivated) symbols have been emphasized in modern information-processing models of meaning.

In Chapter 8, I suggested that we reconsider the issue of symbolic motivation by recognizing how signs can land at many different places along a spectrum defined by *empirical motivation* and *psychogenic motivation*. Paul Friedrich's notion of *polytropes* was also invoked to recognize the important ambiguities by which certain signs function as both metaphors and metonyns. Both Kwakiutl and Murngin totemism (Chapters 7 to 10) demonstrate the use of such ambiguous metonym-metaphor polytropes to represent complex relations between the importance of animals in the social reproduction of groups and in a food chain. These relations involve both the material incorporation of animal forms and abstract classifications accomplished through the use of animal forms as emblems.

Chapter 10, which looked at the way in which Murngin myth is reconstituted for novices as age-grading rites, takes up the issue of the contingent relations between public, instituted models and personal, mental models. *One of the central problems for cognitive anthropology is to account for how instituted models become internalized as mental models.* Research has focused on how cultural models are embedded in numerous primary social experiences of children, so that the internalization of cultural models takes place within what Vygotsky called the "zone of proximal development" for a child.

The analysis of "epistemogenesis" for Murngin males suggests that this zone of proximal development is transferred from mothers to elder males at an early age. In the hands of the male ritual specialists, the boys' social development takes place under the tight constraints of age-grading rites. A "walkabout" schema is internalized, not by direct transfer of a narrative model to novices but by the translation of the narrative into a sequence of kinesthetic experiences and performances. These symbolic acts do not so much recount the model of knowledge creation in the myth as actually enact the model in the very forms of knowledge transfer. The rites comprise a *culturally motivated process of knowledge transformation.* I call this process *epistemogensis.* In this way the translation of instituted models into personal experience involves the embodiment and transformation of the novice's primary understandings of experience.

Chapters 11 and 12 use Samoan ethnographic case studies to illustrate several important kinds of variation among cultural models for a single domain of experience. Chapter 11 considers alternative models of space as representing different perspectives of the same individual. *Cultural models can be shown to organize not only an individual's experience but also alternative versions of an experience from different points of view.* As illustrated by Samoan cultural models of village space, these alternative perspectives can become conventional models for a community.

Chapter 12 considers alternative models in direct conflict with each other. The possibility of individuals experiencing simultaneously inconsistent cultural models illuminates an interesting kind of relativism within a single cultural community. *Moreover, these case studies suggest that cultural models are not the only way in which people experience the world.* The view that cultural models "construct" reality has dominated cultural anthropology. But a closer look at what happens in the case of conflicting models suggests that the experiences of confusion, ambivalence, and irony, which often accompany serious conflict in models, do not support the strong version of the constructivist view.

Cultural models are better understood as one kind of necessary resource by which people make meaning in their lives. From a cognitive point of view, cultural models are salience-enhancing templates. They render certain kinds of experience perceptually significant and readily communicable within a community. But people may also have powerful experiences not directly predictable from any cultural model. And in the absence of a credible cultural model for making sense of a situation, individuals have the resources for schematizing their own models on the fly. Any powerful theory of cultural knowledge must clarify not just the power of culture to explain how we make meaning but also the limits of culture as an explanatory device.

ON THE NEED FOR A THEORY OF
MEANING CONSTRUCTION

In the attempt to link culture and mind, our emphasis so far has been on culture. Conceiving of culture as models has provided a fruitful way to describe cultural knowledge from a cognitive point of view. What remains for the last two chapters is to provide an explicitly psychological foundation for understanding the internalization of cultural models and their transformation into mental models. To do this, we need first to consider one of the most difficult issues linking psychology and anthropology—the problem of meaning. Specifically, I want to prepare the way for a theory of meaning construction by exploring some of the reasons why anthropology has failed to account for the meaning-making function of culture.

Like the notion of culture itself, the idea of "meaning" is at once intuitively obvious and frustratingly difficult to pin down. Almost forty years ago, the philosopher and logician Susanne Langer proclaimed that Western philosophy had been recast in a new "key." "The problem of observation," she announced, "is all but eclipsed by the problem of meaning" (Langer, 1957:21). Langer was referring to philosophy's retreat from questions of ontology and metaphysics and its turning to the problem of symbolic representation and its relation to meaning and truth.

In recasting their discipline in terms of issues of symbolism and meaning, philosophers were not alone. As structural-functionalism began to exhaust itself in anthropology, the role of culture as a dimension of meaning emerged, starting in the 1960s, as a central concern of American cultural anthropology. While both structuralism and symbolic anthropology developed powerful conceptions of cultural symbolism, the emphasis on disembodied symbolic systems, with no sentient agent for whom the symbols were meaningful, meant that anthropological approaches to meaning were limited to logical meaning ("meaning of . . .") and all but ignored psychological meaning ("meaning for . . ."). What anthropology needed to complement its sociological conception of symbolism was an adequate theory of mind and a conception of meaning making as a *psychocultural process*. Anthropology has long needed a theory not just of symbols or sign systems but of *symbol formation*.

To make matters worse, in recent years the culture concept has been so thoroughly deconstructed by anthropologists that it seems to have lost its power over the anthropological imagination. As questions of agency, personal experience, resistance to hegemonic social forms, and images of cultural heterogeneity have moved from the margins into the center of ethnography, the role of cultural forms in the creation of meaning for people has remained elusive. With our new reflexive sensibility so highly attuned to the moral and epistemological problems of ethnographic writing, we seem to have become smarter about the making of ethnography by anthropologists but more ignorant about the making of meaning by ordinary people.

FROM ETHNOSCIENCE TO ETHNOPSYCHOLOGY

What happened to cognitive anthropology that it has failed to address adequately this problem of meaning? In the 1960s and 1970s, the field of ethnoscience was anthropology's strongest link with cognitive science. But by the 1980s, the formalistic models and methods of ethnoscience had lost their appeal to mainstream anthropology. Ethnoscience was out of tune with the growing poststructuralist and relativistic mood of the field. Psychological anthropologists turned from ethnoscience to what became known as "ethnopsychology," detailed descriptions of local folk psychologies.[1]

Though ethnoscience had focused on cultural variations in the coding of distinct domains like kinship, color terms, or disease classifications, its program was closely tied to the generalizing spirit of cognitive psychology. Ethnopsychology was different. Inspired in part by the realization that not only were classifications culturally variable but that the basic dimensions of classification might vary from culture to culture, ethnopsychologists tended to reject the goal of scientific generalization in favor of culturally specific descriptions of local theories of the person. There was a subtle but critical shift in the significance of "ethno-" from ethnoscience to ethnopsychology. The issue was no longer the study of cultural variability in basic human cognitive processes but the use of that variability to deconstruct and undermine the generalizing enterprise of scientific psychology itself. The effect was to throw into question the relevance of the categories of academic psychology for other cultures. Anthropology and psychology went their separate ways.[2] The lack of a theoretical foundation for integrating symbolic and cognitive anthropology was acknowledged in the editors' introduction to the 1980 special issue on symbolism and cognition of the *American Ethnologist* (Colby, et al., 1981). The editors predicted an imminent convergence of psychological and symbolic anthropology, but this has not yet happened. This book has been written with the conviction that such an integrated perspective is both desirable and within reach.

In these final two chapters, I bring several decades of important research in cognitive psychology and cognitive science into line with the insights derived by research on cultural models. This theoretical framework is not offered to undercut the important insights emerging from recent deconstructions of the culture concept. In fact, it is intended to affirm the importance of cultural cognition, taking into account the place of human agency and historical contingency in the process of meaning construction. Anthropology is ripe for an integrative moment, most especially an integration of its insights with those of cognitive psychology. The way is clear for taking culture back to mind, where it has always belonged. But this is only another way of saying that cognitive anthropologists and psychologists must also be prepared to take cultural models seriously, by locating a key dimension of the human mind in its natural habitat: the midway of social life.

The rest of this chapter will develop a conception of meaning equally at home with cultural models and mental processes. The argument is made is six steps. (1) First, I deal with the relations between *logical* and *psychological* notions of "meaning." (2) Then I propose a crucial distinction between *meaning construction* and *information processing*. (3) Using Plato's *Meno* as an instructive text, I go on to characterize meaning construction in relation to memory. (4) Then I evaluate several competing traditions that have figured significantly in anthropological approaches to meaning. These are simplified somewhat into a distinction between *realist* and *nominalist* approaches to meaning, with Frege and Saussure, respectively, taken as influential representatives of each approach. (5) In considering a way to overcome the false dichotomy of realism versus nominalism, we turn to George Lakoff and Mark Johnson's *experiential realism* as a viable theoretical basis for a culturally mediated conception of meaning construction. (6) Finally, I draw the distinction between *analytical* and *nonanalytical* approaches to concept formation, which is an important (if somewhat technical) issue that has significant implications for cognitive science in how higher levels of representations, such as cultural models, are coded as lower-level mental representations.

MEANING—LOGICAL AND PSYCHOLOGICAL

The text model of interpretation tended to focus on meaning as inherent in the organization of some kind of "text." Here interpretation becomes *Auslegung,* the exegesis of meanings inherent in textlike objects (discourse, gestures, games, artifacts, and so on). By contrast, experientialist interpretive strategies have stressed the role of *Verstehen,* "the recognition of what a foreign subject means or intends on the basis of all kinds of signs in which psychic life expresses itself" (Ricoeur, 1971/1979:73).

Both kinds of meaning, logical and psychological, are real and both are important aspects of cultural cognition. As we noted in Chapter 8, in reference to Kwakiutl animal symbols, each kind of meaning is defined by its own sort of motivation, empirical on the one hand and psychogenic on the other. Yet anthropology has not adequately demonstrated how these two kinds of meaning are related. Psychological meaning (i.e., meaning *for* someone) has been disconnected from logical meaning (i.e., the meaning *of* something).[3] Cultural models research has tended to leave the nature of this linkage ambiguous, and anthropology has remained innocent of any well-formed theoretical link with cognitive psychology.

We need a conceptual bridge between instituted models (Ricoeur's or Geertz's "texts") and mental models. These mechanisms are the mediating processes by which meaning-in-the-world becomes personal experience. In Chapters 9 and 10 the connection between text meaning and personal meaning of a Murngin walkabout schema was made by showing how myth symbols were systematically manipulated and transformed in the course of an extended set of initiation rites. What we have yet to develop is a notion of the cognitive processes by means of which the translation between instituted and mental model takes place.

MEANING CONSTRUCTION VERSUS INFORMATION PROCESSING

Recently, I heard on National Public Radio a program about several remarkable individuals, each of whom is classified as an "idiot savant." These unusual individuals represent a variety of cognitive types: so-called human calculators, musical geniuses, and calendrical savants. I was particularly struck by the disconcerting but amazing memory of one of these men who had a remarkable way with dates. He could instantly and infallibly identify on what day of the week any conceivable date fell within a two thousand year period. While some of these "calendrical savants" seem to calculate the dates on the basis of a perception of complex but repeating patterns or some general algorithm, this particular man had actually committed to memory and to instantly recall several thousand years worth of monthly calendars. His mind was a perfect recording device whose memory banks were not subject to the normal sort of decay most of us know—forgetting experiences that are not important or perceptually salient for us. For this man, the memory for facts did not seem to involve any of the selectivity that normally characterizes episodic memory. His mind absorbed random facts like a sponge. And whatever it absorbed, it refused to forget.

As part of their study, researchers took this man to a Japanese restaurant for dinner. When they returned from the restaurant, they asked him for his impressions of his dinner. His response was to list in fine detail an inventory of ingredients, plates, glasses, cutlery, furniture, and other items that he saw in the restaurant. But when pressed for his general evaluation of the dining experience, he was unable to come up with any kind of coherent judgment or overall impression of the eating experience or the environment. This "idiot savant" was a kind of information virtuoso, with an apparently limitless capacity to store and retrieve discrete data. What was missing however was the ability to construct salient patterns out of these primitive data, or to organize the information according to communicable models other than flat lists. What was missing was the vital human capacity for meaning construction.

Meaning construction involves the perpetual encounter of a meaning-seeking subject and a historically and culturally orchestrated world of artifacts. Meaning construction is a kind of learning, but it is not by itself a complete account of how we learn. Specifically, meaning construction is a Piagetian "assimilation" process whereby people employ old cognitive models as resources for making sense out of novel experiences. This notion of meaning construction comes close to Churchland's cognitively grounded idea of *explanatory understanding*. In his words,

> Explanatory understanding consists in the activation of a specific prototype vector in a well-trained network. It consists in the apprehension of the problematic case as an instance of a general type, a type for which the creature has a detailed and well-informed representation. Such a representation allows the creature to anticipate aspects of the case so far unperceived, and to deploy practical techniques appropriate to the case at hand. [Churchland, 1989:210, quoted in Bechtel and Abrahamsen, 1991:292; emphasis in original]

Cultural meaning construction is a specific kind of assimilation, requiring two distinct cognitive processes. First, a conventional form of a cognitive model is derived from instituted models present in the social environment. Second, a novel experience is organized for an individual in relation to this conventional cognitive model, providing a significant degree of sharing in the way individuals within a community experience the world. Cultural cognition is a special kind of meaning-seeking activity closely related to more general processes of meaning construction.

It is important to distinguish these processes of meaning construction from the information-processing models of mind that are popular among researchers in artificial intelligence research. Meaning making appears to be a distinctively human process and thus is characteristic of what we might call "natural intelligence." As we shall see in the next chapter, the the impulse to make meaning from experience exploits analog rather than digital processing and distinguishes human from machine-intelligence. The growing sophistication of artificial intelligence research has contributed to the tendency to view the human mind as an information processor. These machine-based models of thinking have become so common that cognitive science has tended to bracket the question of meaning in favor of language-based information-processing models of thinking.[4] D'Andrade has rightly stressed that humans are insatiable and opportunistic information processors (1990:804), but they are also avid and opportunistic meaning constructors. And this is not quite the same thing.

MIMETIC REPRESENTATION AND ANALOGIC PROCESSING

Merlin Donald has proposed that the crucial divide between humans and other primates is actually prelinguistic and involves the evolution in the hominid line of what he calls "mimetic culture" regulated by a "central mimetic controller" (Donald, 1991:186). Before early hominids had language, Donald argues, they had the capacity to create and communicate cultural forms, like tools, through mimetic representations. "The mimetic level of representation," says Donald, "underlies all modern cultures and forms the most basic medium of human communication" (1991:186). Memetic representation is distinct from literal mimicry or simple imitation in that "it involves the invention of *intentional* representations" (1991:167, emphasis in original). Rather than simple copies, mimetic representations are *recreations* of perceptual models through analogical schematization.

Donald cites the cognitive competence of deaf-mutes or certain aphasics as evidence that human conceptual abilities are not completely dependent upon language. Humans appear to possess a crucial level of cognitive competence that is not dependent on language and that presumably preceded the evolution of full linguistic competence. This is not to minimize the importance of language for humans, but to propose that distinctly human cognition has multiple roots, some of which antedate the evolution of fully discursive language. The earliest cultural inventions were probably dependent upon mimetic schematization for both their invention and their dissemination in populations with little or no linguistic ability.

Mimetic representation remains an important aspect of human culture despite the evolution of language, and its importance is perhaps clearly evident in the ubiquity of plastic and performance arts in human communities. Mimetic representations are inherently cross-modal and permit representations to move freely among distinct sensory and motor modalities. Human aesthetic qualities such as the feeling for rhythm are supramodal and "once a rhythm is established it may be played out with any motor modality, including the hands, feet, head, mouth, or the whole body" (Donald 1991:186). Indeed this modal "slipperiness" of rhythm goes beyond different motor modalities and includes the ability to perceive analogous rhythm in physical motion, in sound, and in visual representations. The supramodal character of mimetic representation suggests to Donald the existence in the brain of "a central mimetic controller that can track various movement modalities *simultaneously* and in parallel" (1991:186, emphasis in original). Even in the face of mounting evidence for the modular nature of mind in its various specific modes, this mimetic controller would likely have evolved as an unencapsulated central system, a kind of association area, integrating perceptions from numerous sensory and motor modalities.

Though Donald does not discuss the relation between mimetic representation and what I have termed "meaning construction," it seems that there is a strong relation between the two. I propose that the cognitive process underlying both is "analogic processing." The capacity for analogical transfer is a central aspect of hominid cognition. Indeed the proposed antiquity of mimetic representation and the possibility that it predates the evolution of language in humans suggests that cognitive foundations of meaning construction are at least as old as (and perhaps older than) the kind of information processing that is stressed in most linguistically based models of human cognition.

The notion of information processing is used in many different ways, and the term lacks precision when applied to theories of the mind. In contrasting information processing models of thought with meaning construction, I limit the notion of information processing to models of thought that are (1) linear, (2) symbolic, and (3) compositional. By "linear" I mean that thinking is conceived of as the generation of strings of propositions, as is common in "languages" such as symbolic logic, natural language, or computer programs. "Symbolic" refers to the understanding of thought as the manipulation of a stock of elementary pattern units. Typically, whether in linguistics or in artificial intelligence, these symbols are taken to be more or less arbitrary, though nonarbitrary symbols are also recognized. "Compositional" refers to the combinability of elementary units into higher-level symbols according to rules of syntax. Information-processing models of thought are central to what we have commonly assumed to be the nature of logic and, by extension, rational thought.

It is useful to recall at this point that the "rationality debate" (Chapters 7 and 8) inspired by early ethnographic accounts of "primitive thinking" centered on the adequacy of information-processing models of thought in accounting for the diverse kinds of thinking reported in ethnographic accounts of totemism and other cultural practices. Lévy-Bruhl posed his notion of "participation" as a "prelogical" alternative model of thinking to information processing.

The compositional nature of thought is the basis of language's "productivity," its ability to generate a virtually unlimited set of propositions from a limited stock of symbols. There is a strongly rational character to these models, both in the specific sense of stressing internal coherence and rule-dependence and in the more general sense of assuming an innate rational faculty that processes incoming stimuli. While philosophers from Hobbes and Leibnitz to early Wittgenstein proposed such information-processing models of thought, the most ardent contemporary proponents of information-processing models of thought are linguists like Noam Chomsky and Jerry Fodor (Chomsky, 1957, 1965, 1968; Fodor, 1975, 1983; Bechtel and Abrahamsen, 1991, especially in chap. 7).

As we noted in the case of the calendrical savant, there is an atomistic flavor to the idea of "information" or "data." From a purely formal perspective, information is based on the digitalization of signals. Information is, in Gregory Bateson's memorable phrase, "a difference that makes a difference" (Bateson, 1972). In this sense, information processing is closely related to elementary kinds of categorization. We obtain information from the environment by a "chunking" of continuous signals or stimuli into discrete units, which can be organized in many combinations, linked through syntactic operations, and built up through hierarchical nesting into increasingly complex representations. Cognitive scientists and structuralists are not the only people to have recognized the importance of this chunking of experience into comprehensible units. As we have seen for the Murngin, Kwakiutl, and Samoans, the division of the world into communicable chunks is celebrated in origin myths, religious rites, and cultural models of space. Local epistemologies as well as information science commonly acknowledge the sanctity of information and the processes that produce it.

In the terms of information science, any perceptible distinction produces the potential for information. The elementary form of information systems is a "set-theoretic model" based on a simple binary code that employs elementary symbols plus rules of combination capable of generating increasingly complex sequences. Some important implications of binary codes were discussed in Chapters 5 and 6, where I noted their emergence as a dominant and self-conscious feature of contemporary modular design strategies.

MACHINE MODELS OF THOUGHT

An information-processing model of cognition represents complex perceptual and conceptual patterns by breaking them down into their component parts (such as features of categories or dimensions of perceptual patterns). These elementary components can then be arranged in chains connected by operators that link the components into a set. Information-processing models represent mental processes analytically.[5] Sometimes these models are diagrammatic, depicting relations among components of a model in flowcharts or decision trees. Alternatively, they are modeled as discursive "programs" in which symbolic primitives are explicitly related syntactically. The resulting representations are based on what Lakoff (1987a) calls the "mind as machine paradigm," with the digital computer as the current machine of choice.

The analytical character of information-processing models based on this paradigm becomes clearer if we look at an example of the genre. It comes from the literature on mental models. In this case, the authors attempt to produce mental models of simple machines that approximate the simulation of the machine in "the mind's eye" (De Kleer and Brown, 1983:160). Here is how the authors describe their own model:

> We have developed a language of primitives for expressing and defining the structure of a machine. A machine consists of constituents. Some of these constituents themselves consist of parts which themselves can be viewed as smaller machines (e.g., resistors, valves, boilers). Other constituents represent connections (e.g., pipes, wires, cables) through which the pipes communicate by transmitting information. These connections can be thought of as conduits through which "stuff" flows, its flow captured by conduit laws . . . . We call the representation of the machine in these terms its *device topology*. [pp. 161–162]

> We assume that the behavior of the objects in the conduits can be summarized as a collection of attributes (e.g., pressure, velocity, current, voltage, volume) . . . . Each component is modeled by rules that monitor the attribute values in some of the conduits to it and, which can change the state of the component accordingly, thereby affecting other conduits connected to it. These behavioral rules form the essence of a component model. [p. 163]

The authors distinguish between "component models" and "causal models." A component model "characterizes all the potential behaviors that the component can manifest" (De Kleer and Brown, 1983:163). A causal model represents the cause-and-effect relations between known attribute values and unknown values. It distinguishes the inputs and outputs from each component and "identifies which attributes cause component behavior and which attributes are caused by component rules" (De Kleer and Brown, 1983:165).

Component models are a schematic inventory of a device's attributes but do not model specific relationships between one attribute and another. The behavior of any component of a simple machine is divided into a number of relatively simple alternative states or regions, such as "on" or "off." Each state is described in terms of a *definition* and *a transition part*. De Kleer and Brown define the definition part as "a collection of qualitative equations on attribute values which define what it means to be in that state" (1983:165). The transition part "describes how attribute values of the connecting conduits can change the state of behavior of the component (1983:165). The construction of mental models of physical devices is assumed to involve an "envisioning process" which employs the definition part of a model to infer new values of the attributes in some of the connecting conduits in determining the behavior of a particular component.

De Kleer and Brown (1983:164) provide the following general form for their component model:

> *component*: *state 1*:
> *definition-part*,
> *transition-part*.
> *state 2*:
> *definition-part*,
> *transition-part*.
> . . .

The definition part comprises the following sequence:

$$\text{attribute} \Leftarrow \text{value or attribute} \Leftrightarrow \text{attribute}.$$

The transition part is a sequence of the following general kind:

> *If attribute test* CAUSES *transition*.

This general component model is applied to the simple buzzer device consisting of a clapper, a coil, and a buzzer wired together. The following component model is in the form of a symbolic "program." A single attribute of "field strength" is represented as "F" while wires are represented in relation to the single attribute of "current flow" which is represented in the program as "I."

CLAPPER : OPEN :
$$I1 \Leftarrow 0, I2 \Leftarrow 0$$
IF $F1 = 0$ CAUSES: CLAPPER will become
CLOSED.
    CLOSED:
$$I1 \Leftarrow 1, I2 \Leftarrow 1$$
If $F1 = 1$ CAUSES: clapper will become OPEN.

COIL: ON:

    $$F1 \Leftarrow 1$$
    IF I2 = 0 CAUSES: coil will become OFF.
    IF I3 = 0 CAUSES: coil will become OFF.

OFF:

    $$F1 \Leftarrow 0$$
    IF I2 = 1 CAUSES: coil will become ON.
    IF I3 = 1 CAUSES: coil will become ON.

BATTERY: I1 $\Leftrightarrow$ I3.

It is important to remember that DeKleer and Brown are setting out to represent not the machine itself but people's *mental models* of how machines work. They aim to account for an individual's "mind's-eye representation" of the mechanisms. These sophisticated models take the form of computable programs using a symbolic model. De Kleer and Brown term these models "mechanistic models" without noting the irony in the label. Their models are mechanistic in two different senses. They are models *of* mechanisms, which is what the authors intend. But they are also mechanistic in form. In other words, the form of these general mental models appears to have been derived analogically from their subject matter, though the role of analogy is masked by the very analytic character of the model.

The same paradox characterizes much of the work in artificial intelligence that models human thought on computers in two different ways. The machine is the means of representation but also provides the forms (i.e., the source domain) of (metaphorical) representation. The tools employed in the analysis, digital computers, have transformed the object of analysis into their own image. Such is the power of our tools that they alter not only the world but also the conceptual system of who uses them. This is another dimension of the use of machine worlds to model human worlds, a process that I term techno-totemism (Chapter 6). Techno-totemism produced the currently fashionable mind-as-machine paradigm. Jerome Bruner has pointed out that, working within this paradigm, the criterion for a good model of human thought has come to be the "computability" of the model, the ability to successfully "run" the model (understood as a "program") on a computer (Bruner, 1990:4).

Such analytic models of thought are consistent with the modularity schema that, as we have seen in Chapters 5 and 6, has had such a profound impact on modern thought and modern institutions of all sorts. As scientific models, they attempt to describe objectively the way the mind works. But as expressions of cultural models, these descriptions illuminate a conception of mind quite different (and far more culturally and historically mediated) than the one they intend to reveal.

Information-processing models are based on an understanding of cognition that Lakoff calls "computational realism" (Lakoff, 1987a:339–340). This position assumes the separation of body and mind. Thinking is presumed to be inherently distinct from feeling or any other somatic experiences. It also stresses the algorithmic character of mental representations. The mind is a manipulator of symbols and a generator of logical chains. Thinking becomes the mobilization of general and abstract algorithms. In such a view of cognition, for instance, mental imagery is a kind of illusion bearing no direct relation to the algorithms that are presumed to be the actual mental representations of images (Pylyshyn, 1973, 1981).

While no anthropologist has taken the algorithmic conception of mental representations as far as some psychologists, anthropologists have employed a variety of information-processing models in their representations of cultural knowledge. The most common examples of informational models of culture are the ubiquitous kinship diagrams that purport to represent descent and marriage norms in the extensive literature of social anthropology. Another informational model of cultural knowledge is the taxonomic model of knowledge structures that characterized much of ethnoscience and componential analysis in the 1960s and 1970s. A third informational model of cultural knowledge is the highly rational decision-tree model that purports to represent how people actually make decisions in specific domains.

In each of these cases, cultural knowledge is represented through analytical codes which break down cultural patterns into primitive features which can be assembled in a variety of arrangements. Kinship studies do not generally make explicit claims that their genealogical models are psychologically real for the natives, though they are sometimes presumed to be "real" in this way. Both ethnoscience and decision-making models, however, do make at least implicit claims of psychological adequacy, since their models purport to represent cognitive maps ("emic models") of knowledge domains.

I am not suggesting that analytical models are irrelevant to human cognition. Far from it. Many cultural models are themselves in the form of complex programs that have an internal syntax characteristic of informational models. Moreover, these sorts of cultural models probably proliferate under conditions where language is written and practices are rationalized into sets of procedures and formalized recipes. One would also expect them to proliferate in highly industrialized settings where machines mediate human relations. More generally, whenever people are forced to "work out" their models and communicate them in verbal terms, all cultural models are transformable into such propositional models. Indeed, a hallmark of human language is that it possesses the potential of a universal transducer of human experiences into informational terms.

The extent to which such analytical models accurately reflect the way the mind really works is hotly debated among linguists, philosophers, and cognitive scientists. As we shall see in Chapter 14, these debates have split cognitive science into opposing camps, pitting the proponents of more traditional symbolic models of thought against the new "connectionists," whose models employ radically different assumptions about the architecture of mental representations.

Whatever the eventual outcome of these debates, it is clear that, for an anthropologist, something basic is left out by an exclusive focus on analytical models of cognition. Lévy-Bruhl long ago tried to clarify what was missing when he proposed his famous principle of participation. A contemporary version of what Lévy-Bruhl was getting at is suggested by psychologist Robert Haskell: "Main-stream cognitive psychology is half out of its mind. Still largely dominated by a simplistic conception of the brain and nervous system as an information-processing computer, cognitive psychology has refused to compute other than easily controllable mental functions" (Haskell, 1987b:86).

Haskell characterizes the absent half of the mind as "hot cognition," by which he means the emotional aspect of cognition, which is certainly missing from the kinds of informational models discussed above. Haskell's inclusion of feeling as an aspect of thinking is an important post-Cartesian corrective to "cold" and relatively disembodied theories of cognition. I prefer to characterize the crucial missing dimension of mind as its orientation to *meaning construction*.[6]

MENO'S PARADOX: MEANING CONSTRUCTION AS REMEMBERING

In Paul Churchland's view, explanatory understanding is a process of recognition mediated by prototype models. This view suggests that meaning construction is really a kind of remembering. This is an interesting way to think about meaning. Paul Connerton has pointed out that memory can also be understood as a property of communities. In this way, the work of culture in meaning construction may be understood to involve the use of shared models to produce a kind of collective memory (Connerton, 1989). As Bartlett proposed long ago, memory involves storing experience by means of cognitive models (Bartlett, 1932).

So memory is a necessary part of meaning construction, which inevitably involves model-mediated memory processes. In a looser sense, remembering is also a useful metaphor for meaning construction, since the experience of something new becoming meaningful is *similar to* the experience of remembering something long forgotten but recovered in memory.

This similarity between meaning construction and memory is suggested by Plato in his fascinating Socratic dialogue *Meno*, a treatise on learning. Though Plato's conception of learning is not exactly the same as what I call meaning construction, *Meno* effectively suggests the *experiential* similarity between certain kinds of learning and memory. On the face of it, *Meno* is about the meaning of virtue. Ironically, it also turns out to be a commentary on the virtue of meaning. At the outset of the dialogue, Meno tries to define human virtue in general terms. But under Socrates's relentless interrogation, Meno's bid to discover a general definition for virtue falls apart. The dialogue turns from this specific question to a more general issue of how we can ever know anything. More particularly, Socrates raises the troubling question of whether one can ever learn anything new. A moral issue has become an epistemological quandary.

The trouble starts when Meno is able to define virtue only in terms of some of its specific manifestations, such as justice, temperance, and piety. "For every act, and every time of life, with reference to each separate function," says Meno, "there is a virtue for each one of us, and similarly, I should say, a vice" (Plato, 1961:355). Socrates demurs, claiming that Meno cannot define the whole—virtue in general— only in terms of some of its parts. Defining virtue is not the same as a listing of virtues. The meaning of a general concept is not the same as an enumeration of particular examples. "Stop making many out of one . . ." Socrates admonishes Meno. "Just leave virtue whole and sound and tell me what it is as in the examples

I have given you" (p. 360). "Does anyone know what a part of virtue is, without knowing the whole?" (p. 362).[7]

Meno's dilemma prefigures what will become "Meno's paradox." He can name specific virtues but cannot define virtue in general. Yet his command of the particulars suggests that he must already know what he says he does not know—the meaning of virtue in general. Understanding a piece of something points to a prior knowledge of the whole. Conversely, a knowledge of the whole is made manifest through the knowledge of particulars. In this context Meno stumbles upon the famous paradox associated with his name. "But how will you look for something," he queries Socrates, "when you don't in the least know what it is? How on earth are you going to set up something you don't know as the object of your search? To put it another way, even if you come right up against it, how will you know that what you have found is the thing that you didn't know?" (p. 363).[8]

Socrates's solution is the Platonic doctrine of recollections, the claim that all genuine learning is actually a form of memory, since our souls have lived before and merely reexperience life each time. So genuine learning is nothing but remembering. But Plato does not mean remembering in the passive sense of a sudden and involuntary seizure of recollection that takes us by surprise. Plato's notion of recollection is in Greek *anamnesis*—a deliberate calling up to mind of what had been buried. It is not so much a passive recollection of knowledge as an active re-collection of what has already been experienced.

Experiencing something by recollection is another way of describing what I have called meaning construction. To say that humans are opportunistic constructors of meaning is to recognize in humans a desire for wholeness in the face of partial information and coherence in the face of anomaly. Meaning construction is an activity of the mind directed at resurrecting and continually recreating previously incorporated forms of knowledge, knowledge forms that we have characterized through schema theory.

This link between meaning construction and memory is more than just a philosophical speculation. In *How Societies Remember,* Paul Connerton discusses how civic ritual in European history has been used to promote the forced remembering or forgetting of historical events (Connerton, 1989). In this context, it is interesting to consider how the Murngin, in their complex initiation rites for boys and young men, use their narrative and ritual models to manipulate the boys' memory processes. The Wawilak myth, which underwrites the initiation rites by supplying its stock of symbols, characters, and actions, treats the transfer of power from women to men in terms of changes in memory. At the end of the story, the Dua men suddenly remember things that they never directly experienced. They now know what their clan sisters once knew. Conversely, the sisters' loss of their powers—the powers to create by naming, to hunt like men, to perform ritual songs and dances, and to grow their sons into men—is represented in the story as a kind of forgetting. The Wawilak sisters return to where they started their fabulous journey, having forgotten what transpired on their way. The myth thus lays out a conception of power that is closely tied to memory acquisition and memory loss. In the age-grading rites, the initiates undergo a gradual transformation of their experience of themselve through the long ritual sequence. The same events and symbols are replayed again and again for the initiates over a period of years. Old forms take on new meanings as the boys are grown into men through the model-mediated manipulation of their memories.

REALIST AND NOMINALIST APPROACHES
TO CONCEPT FORMATION

Despite the great significance of meaning construction in the cognitive work of culture, it is striking that the psychocultural processes that underlie the flow of meanings from conventional objects to mental models have been so little studied either in psychology or anthropology. To understand why meaning construction has not figured prominently in modern cognitive research, it is important to understand the intellectual context in which modern thinking about mental representations has proceeded. To simplify greatly, modern views of mental representation have tended to fall into two theoretical camps: realist and nominalist. Cognitive realists trace their lineage back to Plato, for whom human understanding was at best a defective apprehension of "real" truths, ideal forms toward whose apprehension the wise aspired.[9] The most influential modern statement of the realist position was made by Frege, whose understanding of mental representation invoked a tripartite distinction among its reference *(Bedeutung)*, its sense *(Sinn)*, and what he called the idea associated with the sign (Frege, 1892/1952).

Frege's theory of meaning is based on the belief that human understanding is constrained by a real object world. Forms of thought are internal representations of the properties of external reality. The reference of any mental representation is thus its analogue in the world. People living in a common world of referents share a stock of "senses" of that world, by which Frege meant their sensory representations of that world's forms. Individual differences in understanding arise because people have distinct "ideas" associated with these senses. Here is how Frege put it:

> If the reference of a sign is an object perceivable by the senses, my idea of it is an internal image, arising from memories of sensory impressions which I have had and acts, both internal and external, which I have performed. Such an idea is often saturated with feeling; the clarity of its separate parts varies and oscillates. The same sense is not always connected, even in the same man, with the same idea. The idea is subjective: one man's idea is not that of another. There results, as a matter of course, a variety of differences in the ideas associated with the same sense. A painter, a horseman, and a zoologist will probably connect different ideas with the name Bucephalus. This constitutes an essential distinction between the idea and a sign's sense, which may be the common property of many and therefore is not a part of the individual mind. For one can hardly deny that mankind has a common store of thoughts which is translated from one generation to another. [Frege, 1982, quoted in Johnson-Laird, 1983:182]

In the Fregean view of meaning, referents undergo two quite different transformations in the mind. First, they are recorded as sensory analogues into forms that are intersubjectively shared by members of a community. Secondly, these shared senses are idiosyncratically attached to a variety of contingent ideas which can differ not only between people but within any single individual in different contexts. What distinguishes the Fregean position as "realist" is its grounding of sensory representation in real-world constraints.

THE NOMINALIST ALTERNATIVE: SAUSSURE

The modern version of the nominalist alternative to realism was worked out in its classic form by the Swiss linguist Ferdinand de Saussure in his characterization of linguistic signs. Saussure defined the sign as a relationship between a "signifier" (an objective sound or visual form) and a "concept." This position is nominalist rather than realist in that it omits reference to an object world as a component of a sign. Because Saussure's conception of the sign is as subtle as it is influential in culture theory, we need to look at Saussure's ideas in some detail.[10]

At first glance, Saussure's synthetic notion of a sign as a relationship presumed some kind of inner linkage between signifier and signified in the mind of the interpreter. Linguistic signs constitute, for Saussure, a "two sided-psychological entity" (Saussure, 1959:66), which unites a concept and an acoustic image. It is interesting that Saussure's preliminary characterization of this union was psychological: "both terms involved in the linguistic sign are psychological and are united in the brain by an associative bond. This point must be emphasized" (pp. 65–66). The concept and the acoustic image are, for Saussure, "intimately united, and each recalls the other" (p. 66). Linguistics, Saussure suggested, deals with "the borderland where the elements of sound and thought combine" (p. 113).

Though Saussure stressed the importance of this psychologically mediated inner connection between signifier and signified, he placed an even greater stress on what he termed the arbitrary nature of linguistic signs, without noting the apparent irony.

> The bond between the signifier and the signified is arbitrary. Since I mean by sign the whole that results from the associating of the signifier with the signified, I can simply say: the linguistic sign is arbitrary. . . . No one disputes the principle of the arbitrary nature of the sign but it is often easier to discover a truth than to assign it to its proper place. [The arbitrariness principle] dominates all the linguistics of language; its consequences are numberless. [Saussure, 1959:67–68]

By "arbitrary" Saussure meant that linguistic signs were unmotivated by any objective qualities of either the sound-shape or the phenomenon named. He cites by way of example the word "sister" (in French, *soeur*). The concept or idea of "sister," he says, "is not linked by any inner relationship to the succession of sounds s-ö-r which serve as its signifier in French; that it could be represented equally by just any other sequence is proved by the differences among languages and by the very existence of different languages" (p. 68).

Saussure recognized that the phenomenon of onomatopoeia undercuts his stress on arbitrariness (p. 69). But he discounts onomatopoeia as a significant linguistic fact because of its relative rarity in language and because "onomatopoeic formations are never organic elements of a linguistic system" (p. 69). Phonemes, in Saussure's view, have "value" *(valeur)* not positively by virtue of their sonic qualities but negatively "simply by the fact that they are distinct. Phonemes, are above all else, opposing, relative, and negative entities . . . language requires only that the sound be different and not, as one might imagine, that it have an invariable quality" (p. 119).

In terms of symbolic motivation, Saussure is arguing that the power of linguistic signs lies in the relative lack of what I have called "empirical motivation." But he is not ready to dismiss the concept of motivation altogether. Indeed, he invokes the notion of motivation in distinguishing between absolute and relative arbitrariness (pp. 131 ff). Here he qualifies in an important way his earlier characterization of signs as radically arbitrary:

> The fundamental principle of the arbitrariness of the sign does not prevent our singling out in each language what is radically arbitrary, i.e., unmotivated, and what is only relatively arbitrary. Some signs are absolutely arbitrary, in others we note, not its complete absence, but the presence of degrees of arbitrariness: *the sign may be relatively motivated*. [p. 131]

It is important, however, to note that Saussure's notion of relative motivation does not suggest either "empirical motivation" (sign-world relations) or "psychogenic motivation" (sign-experience relations). Instead, signs become relatively motivated (1) through their relation to other signs in a sign system (contextual motivation) and (2) by social convention (conventional motivation). In a famous example of contextual motivation, picked up by Levi-Strauss and recycled in *The Savage Mind,* Saussure suggests that "both *vingt* (twenty) and *dix-neuf* (nineteen) are unmotivated in French but not in the same degree, for *dix-neuf* suggests its own terms and other terms associated with it (e.g., *dix,* ten; *neuf,* nine; *vingt-neuf,* twenty nine; *dix-huit,* eighteen; *soixante-dix* seventy; etc.). This kind of contextual motivation of some linguistic units suggests for Saussure certain kinds of "solidarities that bind them; they are associative and syntagmatic, and they are what limits arbitrariness. *Dix-neuf* is supported associatively by *dix-huit, soixante dix,* etc. and syntagmatically by its elements *dix* and *neuf*" (p. 133).

Let us examine closely what Saussure has done. He began by arguing for an important "psychological" association, uniting signifier and signified, but then went on, in an apparent contradiction, to characterize that relationship as "arbitrary." There appear to be two quite different kinds of arbitrariness in Saussure's formulation: what we might term *systematic arbitrariness* and *psychological arbitrariness*. Systematic arbitrariness is a feature of "logical meaning" and suggests that the internal structure of a sign system does not require that a sign have any empirical motivation whatsoever. As with phonemes, its value is determined internally by its several kinds of relations to other signs *within the system*. The notion that the meaning of signs for Saussure derives from internal relations of opposition and alternation (i.e., syntagmatic and paradigmatic relations) suggests the degree to which Saussure was proposing an information-processing model of linguistic value.

The issue of psychological arbitrariness is more complex and relates to what I have called "psychological meaning." Saussure clearly recognized in some way the paradoxical character of linguistic signs. Though arbitrary in relation to an external world, signs were subject to being motivated both contextually and also in relation to the psychological association of sound and sense in the brain of the speaker. Despite his recognition of this experiential link, Saussure downplayed the significance of sound symbolism because it seemed relatively unimportant to language viewed as an objective system. He never considered the possible importance of such symbolism in understanding the way in which the human mind worked to overcome experientially the very arbitrariness of signs viewed historically, systematically, and empirically. In attempting to characterize *langue* as social fact, Saussure turned his back on the psychological motivation of signs that he had at once acknowledged and largely ignored. The fact that linguistic signs were, for Saussure, "radically arbitrary" followed directly from his assumption that linguistic "value" was conventional, imposed by a kind of social contract on otherwise empty forms. The notion of arbitrariness at the heart of language forced Saussure into an extreme contextualism. Linguistic meaning could be exclusively accounted for by appealing to structural relations internal to language and to social relations external to language use. Language creates its own hermeneutic circles of significance but can only achieve reference to a world by a thoroughgoing artificiality.

This is a problematic conception of linguistic meaning, to be sure. Arbitrariness entails a kind of a nonrelation. By contrast, the very notion of meaning implies connection. How can a sign whose objective character is arbitrariness of reference become an agent of psychological meaning? Despite his acknowledgment of the psychological character of signs, Saussure seems to have proposed a logical or structural rather than a psychological grounding for the meaning of signs. The meaning of signs is held to be a function of the complex relations they bear both to alternatives in an utterance (with which it shares paradigmatic relations) and to neighbors to which they are linked by syntactic operations (or syntagmatic relations).

This contextualist notion of meaning has been influential in modern anthropology and provided much of the theoretical framework for structuralism. It has also dominated information-processing models of artificial intelligence (Bechtel and Abrahamsen, 1991:124 ff).[11] Yet it leaves two important issues unresolved. First, there is no place in this theory for the relations between a sign and the external world—what I have called empirical motivation. This is in part due to Saussure's stress on synchronic rather than historical or ontogenetic dimensions of language. The effect of Saussure's argument was to disconnect the mind from the world by making the relations that constitute the sign arbitrary. Saussure's response to the classical debate between viewing the origin of language as a matter of convention (*nomos*) or of nature (*physus*) was to come down strongly on the side of *nomos* or convention.

There is in Saussure's work no developed theory of either empirical or psychogenic motivation that might account for a sign's empirical and psychological force. Motivation, in his view, is provided only by relations internal to language. This is a serious omission. As Johnson-Laird has aptly put it, "unless a theory relates language to the world, or to a model of it, it is not a complete theory of meaning" (Johnson-Laird, 1983:230).

Saussure's extreme nominalism, disconnecting, as it does, the mind and the world, leads to the second problem. As Jakobson, Benveniste, and others have noted, Saussure failed to account for the fact that what may be objectively or historically arbitrary is *experienced* by the user as natural and therefore as fully motivated.[12] There appears to be a gap between the logical status of signs and their psychological character. However conventional they are in fact, cultural signs, like words, are far from arbitrary in feel.

This experiential naturalness of signs is generally the case not just for children but also for mature adults. We do not experience language as an object or a program. Phenomenologically, normal speech does not take place *in* language. Rather, linguistic forms are normally transparent to experience, so that we seem to speak *through* language. Were linguistic signs experienced as arbitrary forms, people would apprehend language shapes as having a life disconnected from their referents.[13]

Saussure's theory of signs accounts for their objective or code-defined properties. The stress on the natural semantic emptiness of signifiers has the advantage of freeing them from concrete ostensive functions to make possible abstract concepts. But this view of signs cannot account for their psychological meaningfulness, what Yuri Lotman calls their status as "meaning-generating mechanisms" (Lotman, 1990).[14]

Linguistic meaning, like other forms of sign-mediated meaning construction, implies two important kinds of association. The first association is what I have termed the *empirical motivation* of signs, their connections to forms in the world. The second association is what Susanne Langer calls "the application of a term to its object," a construction of inner association between signifier and signified. This second association accounts for the *psychogenic motivation* of signs, a second aspect of meaning construction. This internal (cognitive) construction of a nonarbitrary link between signifier and signified undermines the historical contingency by which the two came together in the first place. A third kind of motivation, *conventional motivation,* links a signifier to a conventional concept. Finally, *contextual motivation* endows signs with meaning by virtue of their various relationships to other elements internal to a sign system. It was both conventional motivation and contextual motivation that Saussure stressed in his discussion of the relative motivation of "signs."

We need a theory of cultural cognition that can account for the relations among all four sorts of motivations that constitute human meaning making. Table 13.1 summarizes these four kinds of motivation in relation to Saussure's work.

LAKOFF AND JOHNSON'S EXPERIENTIAL REALISM

Culture theory has been beset by a false choice between nominalist and realist theories of meaning. Extreme forms of realism reduce cultural systems to their real-world adaptive functions and stress the ultimate referential character (and thus the empirical motivation) of cultural symbolism. Extreme nominalism, by contrast, emphasizes the relative freedom of cultural forms from real-world constraints and the conventional and contextual motivations of cultural symbols. Neither approach deals in any significant way with psychogenic motivation, with culture as a property of a particular mind.

In 1980, with the publication of their influential book *Metaphors We Live By,* George Lakoff and Mark Johnson outlined an approach to the study of thinking that sought to reconcile the extreme conventionalism of the nominalist position with the realist's empirical orientation. They would eventually call their view "experiential realism" in an attempt to capture the bull (to use a metaphor) by both its horns. Seven years later, Lakoff elaborated this vision to a full-blown theory of mental representations in his monumental treatise on human classification entitled, *Women, Fire and Dangerous Things* (1987a). Lakoff proposed a typology of various kinds of

Table 13.1. Saussure's Treatment of Four Types of Symbolic Motivation

Type of Motivation	Example	Accounted for by Saussure?
Empirical	Onomatopoeia	No
Psychogenic	Personal experience of signs as "natural"	No (?)
Conventional	S-ö-r = "sister"	Yes
Contextual	Relative motivation of *dix-neuf* from *dix* and *neuf*	Yes

mental models (he calls them idealized cognitive models, or ICMs). While *Metaphors We Live By* focused on tropes—metaphor and metonym models—*Women, Fire and Dangerous Things* was far more ambitious. In addition to trope models, it analyzed the structure of three additional kinds of ICM—propositional models, kinesthetic image schemas, and symbolic models.[15]

Readers are directed to Lakoff's and Johnson's books for a detailed exposition of this theory (Lakoff, 1987a,b; Johnson 1987). For our purposes, I want to summarize what I take to be the most important assumptions of experiential realism as an approach to human cognition.

- The real world exists beyond the mind (the realist part of the theory).
- The world imposes constraints on what can be represented by the mind and how those representations will appear (another realist tenet).
- The world is accessible to thought only through (1) basic-level direct perception and (2) idealized knowledge models.
- Mental representations are not simple sensory recordings of the world, but are transformed by the knower (experientialism).
- Knowledge is hierarchically ordered such that more abstract knowledge is grounded in concrete experiences, most significantly in bodily experiences (a position that straddles the realist-nominalist divide).
- The world's effect on the mind is a function of the relationship of the knower to that world. Concepts do not have referential or objective properties but rather *interactional properties* that index the position of the knower.[16] There is no God's-eye view of reality for human beings.
- Knowledge is mediated by idealized cognitive models (ICMs), which may be grouped into five general kinds of ICM: propositional models, kinesthetic image schemas, metaphors and metonyms, and symbolic models.
- These ICMs are often empirically motivated in one way or another and in different degrees by either basic-level (gestalt) perception or structures of bodily experience (kinesthetic image schemas).
- Many ICMs evidence "prototype effects" in that they make possible categorization in terms of relative goodness of fit rather than absolute identification. Such prototype effects can be produced by metonymy (e.g., focal colors representing a wider class of colors), by graded categories with maximum-degree examples serving as best cases, by radial categories in which a central model constitutes an unmarked best case, and by cultural stereotypes or ex-

emplars. Prototype effects such as these account for the "fuzzy" nature of much classification.

- The mind does not work strictly as an information processor manipulating abstract algorithms. Propositional ICMs such as taxonomies, feature bundles, and radial categories have such an analytical structure, with elementary units being linked by internal structures. Other kinds of ICMs are organized non-propositionally.

- Finally, to quote Lakoff, "Human reason is not an instantiation of transcendental reason; it grows out of the nature of the organism and all that contributes to its individual and collective experience: its genetic inheritance, the nature of the environment it lives in, the way it functions in the environment, the nature of its social functions, and the like" (Lakoff, 1987a:xv).

Experiential realism is a promising theory on which to base an understanding of cultural cognition. It captures what seems to be most true about both realism and nominalism without falling into the excesses of either position. George Lakoff and Mark Johnson have laid a theoretical foundation that is particularly hospitable to the incorporation of cultural models as a central component of mind.

While Lakoff and Johnson's experiential realism provides an excellent foundation for a theory of cultural meaning construction, there are several significant issues for cultural cognition still left unclarified in their work. I formulate these issues as questions.

How basic is basic perception? Both Lakoff and Johnson are anxious to "ground" human thought in basic facts of somatic experience and perception. Yet they are not always clear as to whether their basic level of experience is universally basic or culturally basic. Thus Lakoff sometimes defines basic-level perception as determined by innate human perceptual universals, and sometimes he acknowledges that social experience determines what is basic-level perception.

Are ICMs in the mind or in the world? The concept of ICM is illustrated in tremendous detail in both Johnson's and Lakoff's work. Still, the term suffers from a certain conceptual vagueness. Lakoff and Johnson do not distinguish mental models (in the mind) from instituted models (in the world), a failure that is a serious impediment to an adequate theory of *cultural* cognition. In Chapter 2, I suggested why we need to distinguish instituted models from mental models.

What happened to the individual? More idiosyncratic personal cognitive models are never really distinguished from conventional cognitive models in Lakoff and Johnson's work, presumably because Lakoff and Johnson think they are structurally identical. Still, there tends to be an unanalyzed assumption of uniformity in ICMs between different individuals that needs to be addressed.

Why the exclusive stress in linguistic models? Finally, though Lakoff and Johnson acknowledge the diversity of ICMs, their examples focus on linguistic models. Any culturally oriented theory of ICMs must redress this bias and characterize the full range of sensory modalities employed by cultural models.

While Lakoff and Johnson's approach is not sufficiently elaborated for the purposes of accounting for cultural cognition, it has extraordinary potential as the basis for a robust theory of cultural meaning construction within the tradition of schema theory.[17]

THE CRITIQUE OF ANALYTICAL MODELS OF
CONCEPT FORMATION

Lakoff's work is aimed directly against the "mind-as-machine" paradigm and its focus on analytical models of concept formation. Though Lakoff recognizes, in his elaborate typology of propositional ICMs, an important role for analytical concept formation, he is anxious to underscore the ways in which the privileging of analytical models of mental representations distorts our view of human thinking. In analytical concept formation (what above I have called information-processing models), complex concepts are built up by concatenations of primitive features linked by rules of combination. Concepts are represented as the emergent outcome of discrete logical procedures. Perhaps the best-studied analytical concept is the classical category, which for many years was thought to be the basis of human concept formation.[18]

Classical categories—for example "chair"—were taken to be concatenations of all the necessary and sufficient features or semantic components that distinguished a chair from contrasting classes. Such essential and distinctive features of a "chair" would include: [+4 legs] (i.e., not = "stool"); [+back support] (i.e., not = "bench"); [+single seat] (i.e., not = "couch" or "loveseat"). Secondary (nonessential) features would distinguish particular chairs or might define a subclass of chair. Thus [+pink] or [+shiny] are nonessential features distinguishing particular chairs. For most American speakers, these features would not define a recognizable subclass of chair. On the other hand [+arms] or [+reclining back] are nonessential features of "chair" but necessary features for two recognized subclasses of chair, namely armchairs and reclining chairs.[19]

In the late 1970s, numerous objections began to be raised about the adequacy of this classical model of concept formation. Most obvious was the fact that many categories did not fit the classical model, since there were no necessary and sufficient conditions that covered all uses of the term. Probably the most cited example of this kind of messy category was the concept of "bachelor" studied by Charles Fillmore (Fillmore, 1982; see also Lakoff, 1987a:70–71, 85–86). No necessary and sufficient collection of features could decide whether the term applied to such anomalous cases as the pope, a widower, or a divorced male. Such nonclassical categories were treated as "graded concepts" (Barsalou, 1987) or "fuzzy sets" (Zadeh, 1965).

Another kind of criticism of classical categories was the overreliance on analytic models of concept formation. In the introduction to their influential volume on classification, Eleanor Rosch and Barbara Lloyd suggested that this bias toward rational processing might well be a view of concept formation at once too narrow and too ethnocentric:

> As with questions about real-world stimuli and categories that were not examined because attention was directed elsewhere, questions about the nature of the processor have been bypassed. The processor was assumed to be rational, and attention was directed to the logical nature of problem-solving strategies. The "mature Western mind" was presumed to be one that, in abstracting knowledge from the idiosyncrasies of particular everyday experiences, employed Aristotelian laws of logic. When applied to categories this meant that to know a category was to have abstracted clear-cut, necessary and sufficient criteria for category membership. If other thought processes such as imag-

ery, ostensive definition, reasoning by analogy to particular instances, or the use of metaphors were considered at all, they were usually relegated to lesser beings such as women, children, primitive people, or even to non-humans. [Rosch and Lloyd, 1978:2]

Experimental methods used to test classification tend to assume (and thereby invoke) a rational, feature-sorting processor appropriate for carrying out artificial and self-conscious categorization tasks. Researchers generally did not consider whether the sort of naive and un-self-conscious classification that people employ in everyday life would necessarily invoke these same informational processes (Brooks, 1987: 169 ff).

NONANALYTICAL CONCEPT FORMATION

Gestalt psychologists had long ago objected to this analytical notion of concept formation, arguing for a nonanalytical or holistic mode of apprehending concepts. Thus, in 1932, K. L. Smoke suggested that experience argued against an analytical understanding of a concept like "dog." "As one learns more and more about dogs, his concept of 'dog' becomes increasingly rich," Smoke wrote, "not a closer approximation to some bare element. . . . No learner of 'dog' ever found a 'common element' running through the stimulus patterns through which he learned" (Smoke, 1932:5, quoted in Johnson-Laird, 1983:186). The alternative to analytical concept formation has been variously termed integral processing, holistic perception, gestalt perception or, simply, nonanalytical concept formation. There is in cognitive psychology a long history of debate about the viability of nonanalytical concept formation.[20] Perhaps the most famous recent version of this controversy was over image perception, and whether images were processed analytically as discursive programs or holistically as gestalts in the brain.

THE IMAGERY DEBATE

Steven Kosslyn is probably the best-known advocate of the nonanalytical approach to image representation (Kosslyn, 1978, 1980). The question was whether the intuition that images were nonpropositional representations was a perceptual illusion masking an underlying analytical computational model. Kosslyn argued that image perception was analogical all the way down, and that computational models of mental imagery could not account for the properties of mental imagery.

Specifically, he defined two distinct kinds of image representations, a surface image and a deep representation. The surface representation was "a configuration of points in a matrix while an actual picture is generated by selectively filling in the cells of the matrix. Mental images are not uniformly visualized. Rather there is a central region that is most sharply in focus, with the image tapering off in detail toward its edges" (Kosslyn, 1978:242). The deep representation is equivalent to what I termed a foundational schema. It takes the form of what Kosslyn calls a "global shape" or "skeletal image" that is stored in a kind of image file in long-term memory.

Kosslyn describes these skeletal images as "low-resolution representations of the general appearance which may be embellished at will if ancillary files are available" (p. 242).

In addition to this primary image model, Kosslyn proposes a secondary model of information about the image (names, parts, properties, locations, etc.). This secondary model is hypothesized to be stored in propositional rather than imagistic form. The image models exert prototype effects in the classification of specific images. It is interesting to note that Kosslyn's account of the more detailed image schema having a central area of focus and detail with fuzzier boundaries conforms to the logic of fuzzy or graded classes rather than to the classical image of a well-formed category.

The counterargument about mental imagery came from Zenon Pylyshyn, who argued that the nonanalytical qualities of mental imagery were epiphenomenal, emergent properties of high-level cognitive processes (Pylyshyn, 1973, 1981). He maintained that the low-level representations of mental imagery would inevitably turn out to be in the form of computational models characteristic of digital processing. Pylyshyn argued that complex images (such as two objects next to one another) inevitably employed propositional predicates such as "to the right of" or "to the left of," and that the mental manipulation of such images necessarily entailed a kind of propositional program and not simply an image schema (Pylyshyn, 1973; see also Johnson-Laird, 1983, chap. 7).

In an ecumenical spirit, Johnson-Laird has proposed three irreducible kinds of mental representation, which he calls propositional models, images, and mental models. The first is based on analytical logic. The other two are based on analogical representations and are nonanalytical models. Propositional models are "strings of symbols that correspond to natural language." Mental models are "structural analogs of the world." And images are the "perceptual correlates of models from a particular point of view" (Johnson-Laird, 1983:165).

These debates about how to best model the cognition of imagery may appear to take us quite far from issues of culture and mind. Yet they point to fundamental questions about how equivalent representations at very different levels of coding are related to each other. And this issue is at the heart of the problem of how cultural forms come to be aspects of mind.

At the relatively high level of cultural modeling, the analysis of Samoan spatial models has suggested that cultural models may have both propositional and analogical representations. In the Samoan categorical model of spatial relations discussed in Chapter 11, propositional representations are employed in self-conscious or detailed manipulation of a model. This kind of information-processing model is likely to be invoked in artificial testing situations which promote a high degree of self-conscious manipulation of concepts. It may also be employed in communicating knowledge to outsiders or in trying to work out problematic relations between stored schemas and novel experiences that do not map easily onto them.

Thus, at the level of representation at which these models become relevant to anthropologists, it seems clear that at least some cultural models may be encoded in both their public forms (instituted models) and in their cognitive forms (mental models) as nonanalytical concepts. Many key cultural models appear not to be reducible to programs coded in propositional logic without violating many of their semiotic and cognitive properties. Moreover, the cross-mappings between instituted models and cognitive models appear to involve pattern recognition (analogy formation) that may not employ analytical reasoning (see next chapter).

A CONCEPTUAL LADDER

If we can show ethnographically that alternative cultural models having propositional and integral structures exist for spatial representations, does this mean that both kinds of coding must also operate at the level of mental representations? Not necessarily. Moving between levels of explanation is a very tricky matter. As we have noted in the discussion of how to model mental imagery, many of the most heated debates in cognitive science involve disagreements about the nature of mappings between models at different levels of reality.

To effectively move between cultural and psychological levels of analysis, we need to deal with the question of how models at different levels of analysis (cultural, psychological, neurological) are related to each other. Chapter 14 begins with a consideration of the problem of how to relate cognate models at different levels of organization. If I am right that meaning construction involves concept formation understood as pattern recognition and manipulation, then we need to understand how patterns at relatively high levels of coding (such as instituted models) map onto lower-level coding such as mental constructs and (even lower) neural networks.

While cognitive science is quite far from being able to provide detailed accounts of the relations between higher-level codings and brain organization, advances in connectionism suggest transitional architectures that may well enable us to understand, someday, how cultural models are neurally inscribed. From a phenomenological perspective (higher-level codings), pattern mappings are better treated in terms of the psychology of analogy formation. Anthropology enters the picture in terms of a theory of tropes and their role in modeling cultural practices.

While considerable research has been done within both disciplines, much less attention as been paid to the relations between the psychology of analogy formation and the characteristics of these higher-level conventional models. Analogy formation has been well studied by psychologists and metaphors have been extensively studied by philosophers and anthropologists. Much less attention has been paid in any discipline to the role of "analogical transfer" in cultural cognition.[21]

Accounting for how cultural models underwrite meaning construction presupposes that we have a well-developed conception of meaning. This is not a simple matter, obviously, and is especially difficult in anthropology, where a concern with symbols has not been matched by an equal concern with symbol formation and meaning construction as psychocultural processes. Before moving on to consider the role of analogical transfer in meaning construction, let us take a look at where we have come in this chapter.

- Psychological meaning for people is not exactly the same as logical meaning of things.
- Psychologically, meaning is closely related to memory or recollection (anemnesis). Cultural meaning is linked to conventionally constrained acts of recognition.

- Theories of meaning have tended to polarize along realist and nominalist lines, the one underplaying the extent to which meaning is a human construct, the other underplaying the extent to which real-world constraints enter into that construct. This problem has been analyzed in some detail by Lakoff and Johnson as the false dichotomy between objectivism and subjectivism (Lakoff and Johnson, 1980).
- Saussure's influential theory of signification laid the groundwork for the nominalist view of meaning. In so doing, it failed to provide an adequate notion of this psychological motivation of signs.
- Lakoff and Johnson's notion of *experiential realism* overcomes the realist-nominalist split and suggests a powerful theoretical basis for understanding cultural cognition.
- The human drive toward meaning is an attempt to overcome the historical or objective arbitrariness of signs by a process of *meaning construction.*
- Meaning construction involves the apprehension of novel experience as a kind of memory, through the active mapping of new experiences onto ready-made models.
- There is an important but underappreciated distinction between information processing and meaning construction. Information processing is associated with analytical models, employing strings of manipulable symbols. The test of a good information-processing model of thought is whether it is computable. Such models are influential in artificial intelligence research, which uses the digital computer as a way to model the working of the mind. Information processing models of thought use the mind-as-machine metaphor.
- Meaning construction is associated with nonanalytical models of thought. From a cognitive perspective, meaning construction employs analog rather than digital processes. To understand how cultural models operate, we need to look closely at research on analogy formation and analogic transfer between models.

To make the case for culture in mind we need to turn to these diverse bodies of research in anthropology and psychology on metaphor and on the psychology of analogy formation. And then we need to bring these traditions into a fruitful relationship.

Cognition is often assumed to be stratified hierarchically into higher- and lower-level processes. Higher-level processes, such as cultural models, are usually assumed to be closer to conscious awareness than lower-level processes such as neurological mappings. The following chapter will consider pattern-recognition and analogy formation at three different "levels" of cognition.

First, at the "low" level of microcognition, we shall consider the relevance of connectionist theory and more particularly models informed by parallel distributed processing (PDP) for a neurologically grounded theory of cultural cognition. Second, we turn to analogy formation at a middle level of cognition—concept formation—and to the implications of studies that examine how individuals form and use analogies. Finally, we consider a relatively high level of modeling in examining various kinds of mappings among cultural models. The general aim is to clarify a set of cognitive processes that relate instituted models (in the world) and cognitive models (in the mind). In other words, we will be seeking a conceptual ladder by which we can begin to traverse the conceptual gap between brain, mind, and culture.

Notes

1. Early forerunners of ethnopsychology include Jean Briggs's account of Inuit emotions (Briggs, 1966), Clifford Geertz's classic article "Person, Time and Conduct in Bali" (Geertz, 1973e), and Robert Levy's ethnography of Tahitian personhood (Levy, 1973). For other contributions to ethnopsychology, see Shore, 1982; Heelas and Lock, 1981; White and Kirkpatrick, 1985; Lutz, 1988; Lutz and Abu-Lughod, 1990; Shweder and Levine, 1984.

2. For classic accounts of dimensions of variability in folk classifications and the implications for the generalizability of theory in anthropology, see Conklin, 1955, 1969; Burling, 1969; Schneider, 1968, 1969a, 1969b; Wallace, 1969. Tyler's 1969 collection of essays on ethnoscience is the best general source for early work on ethnoscience (Tyler, 1969).

3. Lakoff refers to these two kinds of meaning as "sentence meaning" and "speaker meaning." He suggests that the dominant "objectivist" paradigm in psychology and linguistics acknowledges only the former kind of meaning (Lakoff, 1987a:171)

4. On the difference between meaning-making and information-processing models, see Bruner, 1990:4ff.

5. Lakoff calls these propositional models. "Propositional models specify elements, their properties, and the relations holding among them. Much of our knowledge structure is in the form of propositional models" (1987a:113).

6. Lotman views this heterogeneity of cognition in terms of the distinction between "two types of text generator":

> In both cases we observe a generally analogous structure: within one consciousness there are as it were two consciousnesses. The one operates as a discrete system of coding and forms texts which come together like linear chains of linked segments. . . .
> In the second system, the text is primary, being the bearer of the basic meaning. This text is not discrete but continuous. Its meaning is organized neither in a linear nor in a temporal sequence, but is "washed over" the n-dimension semantic space of the given text (the canvas of a picture, the space of a stage, of a screen, a ritual, of social behaviour or of a dream). [Lotman, 1990:36]

7. Ironically, Socrates too must communicate the whole (the general point he wishes to make) via the part ("examples I have given you").

8. Meno's paradox is the Platonic version of a classic philosophical conundrum that would later become notorious as the problem of the "hermeneutic circle." This perennial philosophical problem involves the "circular relation between a whole and its parts; the anticipated meaning of a whole is understood through the parts, but it is in light of the whole that the parts take on their illuminating function" (Gadamer, 1975:66 ff; cf. Heidegger, 1962:153; Ricoeur, 1971/1979:91). What for Plato was resolved by an appeal to a notion of transmigration of souls (a transformation of preknowledge to prior experience), became the central problematic for the philosophy of interpretation from Schleiermacher to Gadamer to Geertz. The interpretivist's problem involves simultaneously the twin issues of (a) how one can possibly enter an exotic circle of understanding and (b) how one can possibly transcend one's own domestic *Lebenswelt* in encountering another. These problems are inherent to any form of extreme contextualist epistemology.

9. Cognitive realism bears some similarity to a position that George Lakoff and Mark Johnson have called "objectivism," which they claim has dominated Western thinking about the mind for two thousand years (Lakoff and Johnson, 1980, Lakoff, 1987a; Johnson, 1987).

10. The 1959 English translation of Saussure's *Course in General Linguistics by* Wade Baskin (Saussure, 1959) is actually a compilation of the notes of seven of Saussure's students

who were variously present during his three series of lectures at University of Geneva between 1906 and 1911. Saussure himself never published any of his own lectures. A three-volume critical edition of Saussure's lectures, edited by Rudolph Engler, reproducing three French versions of his lectures, was published in Germany in 1967 (Saussure, 1967).

11. "The main problem that the causal/symbolic approach faces in explaining intentionality is that its basic symbols are treated as *atomic and arbitrary*. As a result there is nothing about the symbol itself that determines its referent. At most, the contact with the external referent is handled by a transduction medium which is capable of generating tokens of the appropriate symbol in the cognizer when the relevant external referent is present. This transduction process is not involved in the mechanisms for symbol processing that figure once the token of the symbol is produced in the system. The cognitive system still seems to *pass over* the world" (Bechtel and Abrahamsen, 1991:125, emphasis in original).

12. For critical discussions of Saussure's emphasis on the arbitrariness of the linguistic sign, see Jakobson, 1971; Benveniste, 1966; Friedrich, 1979; Shore 1987, 1990b; and Lotman, 1990:17–18.

13. In fact, we do experience such a disruption with much annoyance when someone violates the transparency of discourse with a bad pun and draws attention to sound at the expense of sense. The same disconcerting experience with language is shared by people struggling to make themselves understood in a poorly known foreign tongue. In both of these instances language loses its normal transparency and becomes experiences as a rather dense medium within which thought is constructed.

14. Yuri Lotman's semiotics recognizes the psychogenic motivation of texts as a kind of "autocommunication," an "I-I" language that entails "an increase in communication, its transformation, reformulation and . . . the introduction not of new messages but of new codes" (Lotman, 1990:29). For Lotman, such internal meaning generation involves the interaction between a primary code (natural language) and what he terms a "supplementary code" which is in tension with the primary code, and which produces a novel and often idiosyncratic interpretation. In Lotman's view, such autocommunication "has the tendency to build up individual meanings and to take on the function of organizing the disordered associations which accumulate in the individual consciousness. It reorganizes the personality who engages in autocommunication" (Lotman, 1990:28–29). Lotman's notion of the creative role of autocommunication has much in common with Max Black's well-known interactive theory of metaphor (Black, 1962, 1977).

15. Lakoff's elaborate typology of ICMs is rendered somewhat confusing by his tendency to use the same term for two distinct levels of classification (like "New York" being used to designate both a state and a city within that state). Metaphors are assumed to be a distinct kind of ICM, but most all ICMs are said to be structured by metaphorical mapping (Lakoff, 1987:271 ff). Similarly, kinesthetic image schemas are held to be both a distinct category of ICM and the underlying structure of virtually all ICMs (Lakoff, 1987a:283).

16. The notion that things in the world have interactional properties that take into account the relation of the knower and actor to the world gives Lakoff's theory a strongly ecological flavor. The concept of interactional properties bears a strong resemblance to Gibson's notion of "affordances" which govern the relations between people and the environments to which their perceptions are adapted (Gibson, 1966; Neisser, 1976, 1983, 1987; Norman, 1988; Bechtel and Abrahamsen, 1991).

17. Naomi Quinn has criticized Lakoff for ignoring the central role of cultural models in cognition (Quinn, 1991). Quinn is right in the sense that Lakoff does not focus his work explicitly on cultural models. Though his model of the mind would seem to be largely about cultural cognition, Lakoff does not adequately distinguish cultural models from cognitive models.

18. On classical category formation, see Rosch and Mervis, 1975; Rosch et al., 1976;

Rosch and Lloyd, 1978; Barsalou, 1987; Harnad, 1987; Neisser, 1987; Douglas, 1966; Smith and Medin, 1981; Smith, 1990; Berlin et al., 1966; Johnson-Laird, 1983; Lakoff 1987a.

19. The notion of a "distinctive feature" as opposed to just a "feature" is central to classical categories. Chairs have a potentially unlimited number of features, depending on one's perspective. If a class were composed of just features, one might define a chair using features such as [+ object], or [+ extension] or [+ mass], all of which are true of all chairs.

All classical categories enter into taxonomic relations with other categories. These taxonomic relations include contrast (horizontal relations) and class inclusion (vertical relations). Chairs are thus defined classically in relation to other taxa such as "furniture" or "high-chairs" (class inclusion), in relation to which they are a basic-level category. In relation to "sofas" or "tables," chairs form contrast sets.

The fact that "pink chairs" or "shiny chairs" are not recognizable subclasses of "chair" for most Americans, while "easy chair" or "armchair" are subclasses seems to be in part a function of local conventions about which features are definitive and which are not. While research into basic-level categories suggests that intrinsic perceptual and pragmatic constraints may motivate basic-level categorization, what are considered distinctive features for any classification will normally admit of a great range of local variation.

The fact that classical categories are constructed by such contingent distinctive features implies that even classical categories are defined by what Lakoff terms "interactional properties" rather than objective properties (Lakoff, 1987a:51). Categories are products of intentional worlds rather than objective environments.

20. In the literature on category formation, the distinction between analytical and nonanalytical processing has been used to distinguish basic-level categories from other levels of classification. Among the characteristic cognitive properties of basic-level categories is that they are readily perceived as gestalts rather than as concatenations of distinctive features. This is not the case for superordinate or subordinate level categories (Rosch et al., 1976; Lakoff, 1987a:48).

21. A notable exception is Haskell (1987, 1987a–d, 1989).

14

Analogical Transfer and the Work of Culture

> And I cherish more than anything else the Analogies, my most trustworthy masters. They know all the secrets of Nature.
>
> —Johannes Kepler

> O Nature, and O soul of man! how far beyond all utterance are your linked analogies! not the smallest atom stirs or lives on matter, but has not its cunning duplicates in mind.
>
> —Herman Melville

THE QUESTION OF LEVELS

To study the place of culture in mind requires more than just a coordination of concepts from different disciplines. It also means relating models at very different levels of abstraction and organization. The notion that phenomena are ordered at different levels is a common assumption in all the sciences. To study the behavior of an object in motion is different from studying that object's constituent molecules. Likewise, the study of animal behavior is not normally assumed to be reducible to the study of its cell behavior. The various disciplines and subdisciplines in the sciences are usually defined in terms of such distinctive levels of analysis, each with emergent properties (Polanyi, 1966).

Advances in science often require a bracketing of the consideration of how phenomena at one level of analysis (like neural networks) are related to phenomena at a higher level (concepts, for example) or a lower level (such as cells). McCauley has argued persuasively that advances in science frequently occur because of the refinement of models *within* levels or fields rather than because of the influence of models *between* levels or fields (McCauley, 1986). Yet other kinds of important breakthroughs in science require attention to what McCauley terms "inter-theoretic relations," concepts or models that demonstrate important relations between different levels of analysis. Interdisciplinary fields like anthropology or cognitive science will always deal, explicitly or otherwise, with the problem of relating phenomena at different analytical levels. Many disagreements in these fields are really about how to bridge different levels of analysis without doing violence to any of them (Shore, 1988b).

As we saw in Chapter 2, schema theory, when applied to specifically cultural cognition, involves related phenomena at quite different levels of organization. Instituted models (social constructs), mental models (psychological constructs), and neural networks (biological constructs) are all examples of distinct levels at which cognate models exist that are relevant to cognitive science.

One of the central puzzles in cognitive science is whether to assume that mental representations must have the same general design features at all levels relevant to cognitive functioning. The nature of the relations between mental and neural constructs has been a controversial issue in cognitive science, particularly since the development of connectionism. Almost never discussed among cognitive scientists, however, is the relation between instituted (cultural) models and the other (lower) levels of cognition. It is this culture-mind relationship that has been the central problem of this book.

The relevance of the architecture of models at one level to the architecture at another level is one of the thorniest problems in cognitive science. For instance, if a cultural model such as the Samoan dinner invitation script is instituted in a scriptlike format, does this mean that the cognitive model of this script must also have a scriptlike architecture? If so, then we can say there is a *homologous* relationship between models at different levels. Just how far down does this script structure go in the mind? Would a neurological account of this model also have a homologous scriptlike format? Or might it be encoded in a different way? Since we cannot directly observe either mental or neural models, we appear to be quite far from a clear answer to these questions. Yet the implications for cognitive science of how this question is answered could hardly be more important (see Bechtel and Abrahamsen, 1991; especially chaps. 7 and 8).

We have already encountered the issue of how to understand relations between models at different levels in the discussions involving analog and digital coding (Chapters 5, 6, and 11). The assumption in these earlier chapters was that if instituted models (such as spatial layouts or educational curricula) could be demonstrated to be organized in a modular format, then this format somehow shaped the experience of people who regularly used it. In other words, modular social institutions produced modularized mental representations, and these representations left their mark on people's "modular experience" of the world. Conversely, continuously coded institutions (like the concentric model of Samoan village space, or analogically reproduced music) structured experience in a fundamentally different way.

Though retaining the overall form of their empirical analogues in the environment, mental models are often simpler and more "schematic." "Schematization" is an appropriate term for describing the construction of more abstract representations based on relatively concrete source models. My mental model of a baseball park has been abstracted, or schematized, from my experiences with all of the various parks I have seen. The mental model has filtered out many of the particular landmarks and peculiarities of specific parks, leaving behind an abstracted and generalized model that I use to orient myself when I find myself visiting a new park. In the process of schematization, the model loses much of the detail of its analogue but retains salient features of its form, whether that form is imagistic, scriptlike, or kinesthetic.

Models also contain idiosyncratic features that are a function of a particular individual's prior experiences and expectations. Salience normally changes over time and as context or circumstances vary. In addition to individual variations in models over time, these kinds of changes are sometimes culturally standardized. This is the case with Murngin age-grading rites, in which the salience of key symbols within a set of traditional models is altered over time. Fredrik Barth has shown this process of culturally controlled modification of salience structures of models in Baktamen initiation ritual, which in many ways is similar to the Murngin case (Barth, 1975).

Mental models are dynamic, subject to what Piagetians term "adaptive equilibration." Laughlin et al. describe these feedback loops as "empirical modification cycles" in which mental models are constantly being updated and modified based on feedback from the environment (1990:59–60).

I would support this formulation of these dynamic but basically analogical relations between "internal" and "external" models so long as we limit the discussions to models directly accessible to human experience. In this chapter I attempt to outline a more satisfactory account of how such translations between inner and outer experiential models occur through a process I call "analogical schematization." But once we try to describe how models are coded beyond any ordinary experience (as when we try to conceive of a neural representation of the radial schema that informs spatial models like shopping malls or airports), we can no longer be sure that basic similarity in architecture applies to models at different levels. The coding of a model is subject to significant transformation as it is translated between widely separated levels of organization. The architecture of high-level codings, like Samoan postural models for displaying deference to those of high rank or authority, may bear little resemblance to the structure of lower-level codings like neural networks.

For example, an analogical or continuous coding at the level of a cultural model (as in the Samoan concentric model of village space) might be represented neurologically as complex digital codings (neuron firing or inhibition in elaborate patterns). Conversely, what may be culturally represented as a set of discrete categories may turn out to be neurologically coded in terms of a continuous network of neural activation. Direct analogical transfer may well not account for the relations between the architecture of high-level codings like instituted models and low-level codings like neural networks. It is reasonable to expect that any account of modeling at a low level of coding should include consideration of the translation issue—how this coding is translatable or mappable onto higher-level representations.

LOW-LEVEL MODELS: CONNECTIONISM AND PDP MODELS

In this light, some anthropologists interested in cultural models have been drawn in recent years to connectionist models of cognition (for example, D'Andrade, 1992:29; Quinn and Strauss, 1993; Strauss, 1992:11–12). The appeal of connectionism is not that it directly reproduces in any way the architecture of cultural models (in may ways, the opposite is true). What connectionism does suggest is an approach to modeling thought at a relatively low level of coding (neuronlike units) that *can account for* some of the more important characteristics of the behavior of cultural models.

Especially important in illuminating the role of cultural models in meaning construction is the ability of connectionist models to account for pattern recognition and transformation as a central feature of concept formation. To understand why connectionism has proven so appealing for cognitive anthropologists, we need to look more closely at the way that connectionists model the architecture of thinking.

Modern connectionism in cognitive science grew out of early interest in the behavior of networks of neuronlike units that could be activated or inhibited serially.[1] The foundation was laid for connectionist architecture in 1943, when McCulloch and Pitts published a paper proposing a simple network model for performing logical operations (McCulloch and Pitts, 1943). This precursor to connectionist models comprised a network of neuronlike processing units, which could be either activated when the sum of excitatory inputs reached a certain threshold or inhibited. The authors demonstrated that sequences of serial activation of these units could perform logical operations like NOT, AND, and OR (Bechtel and Abrahamsen, 1991:3). Early research into such processing networks demonstrated their capacity for redundancy of coding and for pattern recognition.

Frank Rosenblatt extended these models by conceiving of networks with several layers (Rosenblatt, 1958). Each layer was modeled to receive inputs (excitations or inhibitions) from lower layers and pass them on to higher layers of units. Transmission could also be modeled as occurring in both directions, involving feedback and feedforward networks. Rosenblatt also introduced the fundamental innovation of modeling connections that could vary continuously rather than in binary fashion. These networks, which Rosenblatt called "perceptrons," could mimic learning, since the relative weights of connections and inhibitions could be "trained" to vary under different conditions. Other researchers later assigned specific interpretations to the neuronlike units, permitting the modeling of specific sensory patterning, like the perception of letters of sounds.

These early networks came under criticism from proponents of what I have called information-processing models of thought, who held that logic required a linear system of discrete symbols manipulated in strings by logical operators, as in classic predicate calculus. Noam Chomsky's early assault on behavioristic models of language acquisition argued that the *generativity* of natural languages (i.e., the capacity of language to produce an unlimited set of utterances from a limited set of linguistic primitives) implied the existence of logical operators immanent in the mind (Chomsky, 1959, 1968). Reasoning, he felt, could not be accounted for by a learning system alone. And networks, clever as they were, were at heart pure learning systems.

The most influential early critique of network models appeared in 1969 in Marvin Minsky and Seymour Papert's book *Perceptrons*, which presented sophisticated mathematical arguments to demonstrate that elementary two-layered perceptrons (Rosenblatt's original model) were incapable of performing certain basic logical operations (Minsky and Papert, 1969). Bechtel and Abrahamsen argue that these objections to early network theory really pointed to an even more basic issue:

> The inability of networks to solve problems was, for many investigators, only symptomatic of a more general problem. For them, the fundamental problem was that the only kind of cognitive processes of which networks seemed capable were those involving associations. Within limits, a network could be trained to produce a desired output. Associationism was exactly what many founders of modern cognitivism were crusading against. Chomsky contended, for example, that finite automata or simply association mechanisms were inadequate to generate all the well-formed sentences of a

language. One needed a more powerful automaton capable of performing recursive operations. [Bechtel and Abrahamsen, 1991:15–16]

For a decade, network theory languished under the burden of these critiques. But in the early 1980s, a group of researchers began to produce far more sophisticated network models that addressed many of these early objections. By the end of the decade, this newly invigorated connectionism had begun to win over many converts among cognitive scientists.

While it is beyond the scope of this book to explore these new connectionist models in great detail, it is important to understand what connectionist models have been able to accomplish. The field has spawned a great variety of network architectures far more complex than the early perceptron models. Rumelhart (1990:136–137), specified the following seven basic design features common to any connectionist model:

1. Sets of neuronlike *processing units*
2. *States of activation and inhibition* over the array of units
3. An *output function* for each unit, translating its state of activation into an output
4. An *activation rule* producing new levels of activation from combinations of a unit's current activation state and new inputs
5. A *pattern of connectivity* among units defining the network
6. *Learning rules,* by which patterns of connectivity change over repeated cycles in response to experience
7. An *environment* within which a network operates

The early two-layered networks have been replaced by models using many layers. In addition to input and output layers, which interact directly with an external environment, connectionists have added "hidden layers" having no direct connections outside the network. These hidden layers often contain arrays of microfeatures, which can be activated in many ways to produce a large number of higher-level units. Thus networks for modeling the perception of letters encode low-level features of letters (e.g., line segment primitives) in hidden layers, contributing to the productivity of the system (i.e., a relatively few hidden units can produce a large number of letter patterns).[2]

Many connectionist networks model cognition through parallel distributed processing (PDP) rather than serial processing. Such PDP networks do not function in a linear fashion like traditional predicate calculus. Patterns may involve the simultaneous excitation and inhibition of multiple units. Parallel processing allows for much faster and more efficient processing than is the case for units operating in serial fashion, as in traditional computers or computer-inspired information-processing models of thought. In this way PDP models are neurally inspired rather than computer-inspired representations.

Distributed networks (as opposed to local ones) encode a single concept across a variety of different units rather than locally in a single unit. In distributed networks, there is not a one-to-one relationship between a single unit and a single concept. This is one way in which PDP models do not *directly* map concepts. The distribution of a concept across multiple units gives these models a high degree of redundancy. Even partial activations of such distributed networks can produce correct approximations of patterns (or concepts). The distribution of a single concept among an extensive array of units, and the ability to infer the concept from an incomplete activation of the array, is what connectionists term "coarse coding" (Bechtel and Abrahamsen, 1991:54–55). This characteristic of distributed networks would account for the common phenomenon of people being able to generalize correctly perceptual patterns from incomplete or partially erroneous input. This property of networks in approximating correct responses even in the face of impaired input is termed *graceful degradation*.

Another relevant general characteristic of connectionist models is that they can learn. Connectionist models have been designed to modify themselves over many run cycles based on both internal and environmental feedback. As Rumelhart has argued: "A key advantage of the connectionist systems is the fact that simple but powerful learning procedures can be defined that allow the systems to adapt to their environment" (p.148). Networks have been designed to learn by the development of what is termed a *generalized delta rule,* which takes the forms of a two-stage process. To get the basic idea of how connectionists have simulated learning in networks, I quote Rumelhart at length:

> First an input is applied to the network; then after the system has processed for some time, certain units of the network are informed of the values they ought to have at this time. If they have attained the desired values, the weights are unchanged. If they differ from the target values, then the weights are changed according to the difference between the actual value the units have attained and the target for those units. This difference becomes an error signal. This error signal must then be sent back to those units that impinge on the output units. Each such unit receives an error measure that is equal to the error measure in all of the units to which it connects times the weight connecting it to the output unit. Then, based on the error, the weights into these "second-layer" units are modified, after which the error is passed back another layer. This process continues until the error signal reaches the input units or until it has been passed back for a fixed number of times. The new input pattern is presented and the process repeats. [pp.151–152]

Connectionist models have had impressive success in demonstrating the ability of networks to self-modify over many cycles (or what connectionists call *training epochs*).[3] This ability of networks to "learn" addresses one of the basic weaknesses of traditional information-processing models of intelligence designed as computable programs. This is what is called their *fragility,* their inability to adapt appropriately to novel situations. By contrast, connectionist models have an ecological character, modifying themselves in response to changing conditions.

PATTERN RECOGNITION

Connectionist networks define mobile patterns that have the ability to recognize and adapt to other patterns in the environment. Pattern recognition is the cognitive task for which networks appear to be best adapted. Bechtel and Abrahamsen (1991:106) distinguish several kinds of pattern mappings that apply to the behavior of networks: (1) pattern recognition, (2) pattern completion, (3) pattern transformation, and (4) pattern association. In defining networks as effective pattern-recognition devices, they present experimental evidence that all forms of reasoning, from categorization to logical inference, can be understood as forms of pattern recognition and hence be modeled as networks rather than as symbolic propositions (Bechtel and Abrahamsen, 1991: chap. 4). They conclude: "Any system that allocates a fundamental role to pattern recognition, including but not limited to connectionist systems, has the potential to account for what philosophers have sometimes construed as the distinctive feature of mental life: that is, the *intentionality* of mental states" (p. 123, emphasis in original).

By *intentionality,* Bechtel and Abrahamsen imply something similar to what I call *meaning.* Because they map and respond to changes in states of the external world, connectionist models stress the outside-in character of human understanding. They define processing states that are continuous with external processes and which reproduce and transform those processes as mental constructs. Thus, Bechtel and Abrahamsen argue:

> Connectionism does not propose a gap between symbol processing and other kinds of causal processes (such as those involved in sensation and perception). Thus it provides hope of *situating cognitive processes in the world* and so begins to elucidate what Heidegger may have had in mind when he emphasized that our cognitive system exists enmeshed in the world in which we do things, where we have skills and social practices that facilitate our interactions with objects. [p. 126; emphasis added]

Unlike traditional information-processing programs, which rely on the manipulation of arbitrary and a priori symbols, connectionist models are *continuously motivated* both internally by their own current states and externally by changing inputs from the world.

As pattern generators and transformers, connectionist models are compatible with the operation of exemplar models in classification (Bechtel and Abrahamsen, 1991:135 ff; Medin and Barsalou, 1987; Medin and Schaffer, 1978) and with the notion of prototype effects in classification. Because of their ability to extract patterns from the environment and transform those patterns in relation to changing input, connectionist models of analogy formation have suggested a powerful low-level, neurologically inspired model for analogical schematization (Rumelhart and Abrahamsen, 1973).

THE RELEVANCE OF CONNECTIONISM FOR CULTURAL MODELS

In comparison with the kinds of models anthropologists usually deal with, connectionist models represent a low-level coding at several degrees of remove from social experience. Thus we would not expect such models to look like the kinds of things anthropologists study. Probably, no network resembles a baseball game, a Micronesian star chart, an aboriginal walkabout, an arara parakeet, or a modular furniture design. Yet if these instituted models are to be understood as components of mind as well as of the social environment, we need a theoretical bridge between such overt, patterned sensory experiences and cognitive processes at a much lower level of coding.

Connectionist models of the sort discussed here provide a promising avenue for making the case for culture in mind because they have a number of characteristics of great significance for a theory of cultural cognition:

- They are neurally inspired and provide an important basis for linking concept formation and neurological functioning (i.e., they are connectionist in more than one sense).
- They map continuous relations between the mind and the world and account for the role of analogical schematization in outside-inside mappings.
- They have the capacity to learn and thus to modify themselves.
- They provide a way to understand how models can be both shared within a community and idiosyncratically modified through experience.
- They are excellent ways of modeling pattern recognition, completion, transformation, and association. By basing concept formation on a theory of pattern formation, connectionism can account cognitively for intentionality and meaning in human life.
- They can easily model the role of exemplars and prototype effects in classification.
- They exhibit graceful degradation, permitting intelligent inference even in the face of incomplete or otherwise defective information input.
- They exhibit characteristics of both digital (discontinuous) and analogic (continuous) processing and can account theoretically for intermediate forms of processing such as coarse coding.

Clearly, one of the more appealing aspects of connectionist models of thinking is that they bear some resemblance to neural networks and thus suggest a conceptual bridge between psychological and neurological levels. Enthusiasts of PDP models sometimes use this argument to support the connectionist approach to modeling thought and to counter the claims of symbolic models of thought common in artificial intelligence research and in certain kinds of linguistics (Nadel et al. 1989). Ironically, however, this very architecture that ties connectionist models closely to neurological models also separates them from higher-level phenomena such as speech forms, conscious experience, and instituted models.

While connectionist models do indeed suggest some *abstract* dimensions of these higher-level models, symbolic models in the form of scripts or programs more clearly mimic in some important ways the appearance of higher-level models, a fact which probably contributes to their attractiveness for certain philosophers and linguists. Indeed, connectionists have often found themselves borrowing such languagelike units for their own models. This is in part because information-processing models employ symbols and formal relationships which bear a comforting resemblance to the structure of ordinary speech.

Connectionist models make no such claims. In fact, connectionists like to represent experientially discrete categories as distributed properties of networks rather than as atomic symbols. In this way it is the *lack of direct resemblance* between natural language forms and connectionist models that are stressed. This is what I meant when I claimed that connectionist networks represent a *transduction* or *translation* of experience from one level to another rather than a simple reproduction of models between levels. Similarly, a single feature of a concept might be "coarsely coded," its mental representation distributed among a large number of units in a network, not all of which must fire every time in order for that feature to be activated. Coarse coding, if it turns out to be an accurate model of mental representations, represents a kind of coding intermediate between discrete and continuous, but its formal properties are not directly evident in the experience of perceptions.[4] In a similar vein, I noted in Chapter 6 that digital computers can, with enough speed, simulate the *experience* of continuous signals without actually employing continuous coding. The same might well be true for codings of linked models at different levels.

These very complex issues of interlevel relations present a formidable challenge to any serious attempt to relate cultural forms to mental representations. This is why I have limited my arguments for analogical mapping between levels to issues of *meaning construction*—that is, issues about consciousness and intentionality relevant to models of human experience. The notion that cultural models are brought to mind through an analogical transfer must be qualified, therefore, as a theory of how different levels of *experience* are mediated. Models that are presumed to operate beyond experience must bear some formal and functional relations to these experiences, but these relations are bound to involve transformation and transduction in addition to analogical properties.

The power of connectionist models is that they provide a model of thought that has one sort of analogical relation to the phenomena modeled (in terms of levels of activation) and a quite different sort of analogical relation to lower-level neural networks. But from the perspective of the phenomenon being modeled, the neurally inspired properties (layers, networks, activations, inhibitions) are better thought of as a transformation of experience rather than as an analog of experience. Connectionist models *bridge* higher and lower levels rather than simply replicating the same architecture at different levels.

As to the question of the ultimate form cultural models take in cognitive processing, it may be of little consequence to anthropology whether these low-level representations turn out to be coded analytically or nonanalytically at the neurological level. The integral and nonanalytic character of many cultural models may one day be shown to be an emergent property of mind rather than brain.[5] This discovery will be of little importance to anthropology (though of great importance to neuroscience). Even if the integral character of such cultural models proves to be an epiphenominal illusion, it is still an illusion that provides the authentic shape of human experience.

MIDDLE-LEVEL MODELS: ANALOGICAL REASONING AND ANALOGY FORMATION

In this section we move from low-level, neurally inspired models to psychological models of pattern formation that use more direct experiential data about how individuals form and use analogies in test situations and in everyday thinking. Though the terms "analogy," "analog," and "analogic processing" are obviously related, they are not quite synonymous. In Chapters 5, 6, and 11, I noted how the most common alternative to digital processing is understood to be analog processing. Because of their similar names, it is easy to assume that analog processing and analogy formation are the same thing. But this identification is misleading. Indeed, as we will see, it is very important to distinguish between *analog processing* and *analogy formation*.

Analog processing (as in analog computers) is inevitably based on nonanalytic "direct" mappings between domains. But analogy formation, the mental construction of analogies, has been viewed as a fundamental aspect of both analytic and nonanalytic concept formation. To the extent that analogy formation turns out to be based on a set of discrete analytical mental operations (a kind of program for solving analogy problems), it supports Pylyshyn's view of the ubiquity of analytical processes in cognition. Thus it is important to look more closely at the evidence for both analytical and nonanalytical analogy formation.

ANALOGY FORMATION AS A KIND
OF ANALYTICAL THINKING

Not surprisingly, there is an extensive literature in cognitive psychology on analogy formation.[6] The ability to abstract relations from one stimulus set and apply them to another has long been a hallmark of Western conceptions of intelligence. This is why analogies figure so prominently in most intelligence testing. Piaget defined the mainstream view of analogy formation by identifying competence in analogical reasoning with the attainment of formal operational logic, a stage most children reach by ages 11 to 13 (Piaget et al., 1977; Goswami, 1992:4). In this view, and somewhat paradoxically, analogical cognition is a distilled form of analytical reasoning.

Goswami generally concurs with the view of analogy formation as an analytical, information-sorting process. Yet she argues that experimental data suggest that very young children and even infants can reason analogically so long as they have sufficient background knowledge of the relationships that link the terms of an analogy. Following Gentner, Goswami proposes that a developmental shift takes place in analogical reasoning, such that very young children draw direct perceptual analogies between terms of an analogy, while older children draw higher-level analogies *between the relations* implied by the terms (Goswami, 1992:91).

In her research on children's interpretations of metaphorical imagery in stories, Gentner found that five-year-olds explained metaphors by the matching of direct perceptual attributes (Gentner, 1989; see also Gentner, 1983). A cloud is like a sponge because they are both "soft" and "fluffy." Nine-year-olds, by contrast, use what Gentner calls "relational similarity" to account for metaphorical similarities. Clouds and sponges were held to be similar because they both stored up water and gave it back later on.

Direct perceptual analogies are a kind of *primary analogy formation*. Analogies based on relational similarity are *second-order analogies*. I would argue that while second-order analogies may be based on serial analytical mappings feature to feature, primary analogy probably employs a kind of nonanalytical concept formation that Lakoff termed "basic-level perception."

STERNBERG'S MODEL

The most elaborate model of analogy as analytical reasoning is Sternberg's (Sternberg, 1977). Sternberg views analogical reasoning as a chain of discrete information processes that together constitute a procedural program for solving analogy problems. Using the analogy problem Red:Stop :: Green : (A. Go, B. Halt), Sternberg examines several closely related models of analogical reasoning that employ in slightly different ways the following processes:

1. Encoding of the terms of the analogy by scanning the problem.
2. Inferring a single relationship between a feature of the source stimulus and a feature of the target stimulus ("Red signals Stop"). This constitutes a theory of a relevant relation. In complex analogies, several mappings are possible, and each theory is tested in step 4.
3. A general mapping of the relationship between the specified features of the source domain (Red and Green are different members of the set of color signals in a traffic light).
4. The application in turn of the inferred relationship in step 2 to the second half of the analogy, for each of the choices for completing the analogy (Green signals [Go] / [Halt]).
5. A response.

All theories of analogical reasoning share the encoding, inference, and response segments of the process. They differ in the relative importance of the roles for the inference, mapping, and application steps. In testing the several models theorized for analogy formation, Sternberg found mapping to be a significant parameter in all experiments (1977:375–376). Moreover two different modeling strategies in analogy formation were hypothesized. In the "alternating strategy," the scanning of attributes alternates successively between different possible predicates ("Green signals Going"; "Green *prevents Going"). In the "sequential strategy," individuals scan all possible attributes of one predicate ("Green signals Going"; "Green signals Halt") before going on to scan all attributes of a second (in this case incorrect) option (e.g., "Green *prevents Going"; "Green *prevents Halting"). Experimental data strongly support the alternating model as the preferred strategy for problem solvers faced *with forced-choice analogies.*

SCHEMA INDUCTION

In an important series of experiments, Gick and Holyoak found that the recognition of analogies is facilitated by two cognitive processes: (1) the discovery of what they term "semantic retrieval clues" and (2) the induction of a general schema from the concrete analogs (Gick and Holyoak, 1983). *Schema induction* turns out to be the most important aid to what they call "analogical transfer." They cite both experimental and computational evidence for a close relationship between the processing of concrete analogs and general schemas (p. 2; Schustack and Anderson, 1979; Winston, 1980).

Schema induction involves what Gick and Holyoak call "eliminative induction" from several concrete exemplars. Eliminative induction is a process that involves deleting the differences between the analogs while preserving their commonalities (Gick and Holyoak, 1983:8). The resulting schema, induced from the particulars,

then has the potential status of an abstract category "that the individual analogs instantiate in different ways." These different concrete instantiations of the general
schema are termed structure-preserving differences between the two analogs.

The authors make a number of other useful distinctions. The use of analogs in
reasoning does not require an explicit schema independent of the analogs. Reasoning
may occur directly between two or more analogs at the same level of abstraction.
This sort of analogical reasoning is called "reasoning from an analog" (p. 9). This is
how new schemas are constructed "on the fly"—by reasoning directly from cases
where no prior general schema exists. Presumably, reasoning from analogs requires
the cognitive construction of a "convergence schema" linking the two. Alternatively,
analogies between two phenomena may be mediated by a common general schema
that has already been stored in long-term memory. This is "reasoning from a schema"
(p. 10).[7]

The thrust of Gick and Holyoak's experiments is to compare the relative efficacy
of these two strategies. What their experiments point to is the clear superiority of
analogic reasoning from prior schemas over direct reasoning from two concrete analogs. "An independent schema," they conclude, "will therefore facilitate the retrieval
and noticing of an analogy" (p. 10).

This research is significant because it suggests the importance of prestored general schema for the ongoing construction of novel analogies. While the authors undoubtedly have in mind individual schemas in personal knowledge, the advantages
of a stored stock of ready-made schemas suggest the great advantage of conventional
schemas that are the property of a community rather than of individuals.

Gick and Holyoak underscore the creative and constructive nature of analogical
reasoning. Much of the research on analogies presumes that analogies are just discovery procedures for identifying preexisting features or relationships. Indeed, this assumption underwrites the use of forced analogy in intelligence testing, where subjects
are expected to discover the "right" answers. But analogies are not simply passive
discoveries. They are also actively constructed by the intentional creation of similarities, as anyone knows who has failed an analogy problem by discovering the "wrong"
analogy, even though the "incorrect" answer made perfect sense to the test taker.

Gick and Holyoak propose that "the interpretation of metaphor . . . seems
to begin with detection of salient initial correspondences, followed by the construction of others" (p. 6, fn). Though many simple analogy problems are sufficiently
empirically motivated to appear to be simple discovery procedures, higher level
analogical, metonymic, and metaphorical cognition are important aspects of human creativity. Thus the very same cognitive processes that underlie conventional
analogy have the potential to undermine the very conventions they are supposed
to reinforce.

ANALOGY FORMATION AS A KIND OF INTEGRAL
(NONANALYTICAL) PERCEPTION

We have already encountered examples of primary sensory analogies that do not fit
well the analytical or informational model of analogical reasoning. If high-level rela-

tional similarities can be represented by analytical models that detail feature-to-feature structure-mapping procedures, what kind of perception accounts for more direct analogies between sensory features like "softness" or "fluffiness?" Until the emergence of prototype theory, primary analogy would probably have been modeled by propositional models that stress feature sorting and mapping, much like the models used for second-order analogies. Today, many cognitive psychologists are more prepared to recognize in processes like direct prototype matching important forms of nonanalytical concept formation.

In 1978, Eleanor Rosch went so far as the identify analogical reasoning exclusively with nonpropositional models:

> Analog representations are now seen to be those that contain no relational elements—i.e., nonpropositional representations. In such cases, the properties of individual represented objects are modeled by properties of individual representations, and relationships among sets of represented objects are modeled by properties of individual representations, and relationships among sets of represented objects are modeled by relationships among sets of corresponding representing objects. These relations is [sic] inherent and therefore determines completely the kind of represented relations they can model. [Rosch and Lloyd, 1978:297]

This statement may overstate the degree to which analog models are constrained by real-world contours and does not acknowledge sufficiently the active part of the knower in constructing analogies. Nonanalytic concepts possess what Rosch and Lloyd call "integral attributes," which are perceived as "unitary wholes" rather than concatenations of separable attributes. The kind of model one can use for concept formation is constrained by whether the phenomenon being represented has separable or integral attributes. "For example, if stimulus dimensions are integral and selective attention to a single dimension is not possible, then the extreme form of a critical attribute model . . . which specifies the categories in terms of a list of necessary and sufficient features conjoined by ands, is not tenable" (Rosch and Lloyd, 1978: 74)

The importance of nonanalytical concepts has been masked in cognitive psychology not only by the overreliance on information-processing models of thought but also by the kind of experimental tasks that typically provide cognitive psychologists with their data on analogies. Research on the processing of forced analogies is of limited use in the understanding of the kinds of analogical reasoning people use in ordinary, un-self-conscious contexts. In his discussion of nonanalytic concept formation, Brooks suggests that experimental designs have typically "induced subjects to concentrate on the extraction of generalities rather than on drawing analogies to individuals" (1987:169).

Brooks's own experiments tested whether subjects could learn grammatical patterns better by consciously studying strings of patterned letters or by rapid scanning of the patterns. Without exception, direct pattern recognition proved more effective in this sorting task than any analytical procedure (pp. 174 ff.). Brooks also found that, contrary to what many would assume, direct scanning appears to become a more effective strategy for classifying as the complexity of the stimulus is increased. Typical laboratory cognitive tasks on cognition are far simpler than real-life classification. It is precisely this simplicity, Brooks suggests, that makes the laboratory test material especially susceptible to verbal and analytical modeling (p. 177).

Garner, writing about aspects of perceptual stimuli, distinguishes between "features," "dimensions," and "configurations." Configurations are stimuli whose properties are what he terms "holistic" and thus not analyzable into component parts. Configural properties such as the perception of symmetry, balance, or repetition are emergent properties of perception. Neurologically, Garner suggests that the kind of integral perception of configural properties may result from parallel rather than serial processing. Garner's work stresses the importance of a cognitive process whereby an initial holistic stimulus under certain conditions becomes divided into its constituent dimensions and is processed serially. He argues that certain tasks promote this decomposition of holistic stimuli more than others.

For our purposes, the most significant aspect of Garner's work is his notion that perception of both integral and separable stimuli be divided into "primary" and "derived" processes. For the two kinds of stimuli, the relationships between primary and derived processing are reversed. Integral stimuli are processed through pattern similarity (or analogy). For integral stimuli, dimensional structure is perceived only as an artifact of secondary processing. The relation is reversed in the case of stimuli with separable components, where analytical models are primary and pattern structure is achieved only through secondary processing (Garner, 1978:146).

Integral stimuli, like the attribute features of children's analogies studied by Gentner, are perceived at an earlier age by children than are separable stimuli. They also are inherently easier to process by both children and adults. This is why young children unable to perform classifications at the superordinate level of classification (e.g., pig, dog, and horse as instances of "animals") have no problem making basic-level classifications (e.g., different particular breeds of dog as "dogs"). While superordinate- and subordinate-level classification employs analytical concept formation, basic-level classification appears to use only gestalt perception (Rosch et al., 1976).

Garner cites the experimental research of Posner and his associates for comparing the perception of integral and separable stimuli. Subjects were given letter-matching tasks, with some pairs (A/A) characterized by stimulus similarity, others (C/c) by analogy, and still other pairs (A/a) by conceptual (but not perceptual) equivalence. Reaction times were predictably fastest for the identical pairs, intermediate for the analogue pairs, and slowest for the conceptually equivalent pairings. "According to this theory," Garner concludes, "the physical stimulus undergoes a series of transformations, with deeper levels of processing becoming more conceptual in nature" (p. 147).

MICROANALOGY: THE HIDDEN FACE OF MEANING CONSTRUCTION

Meaning construction that engages cultural models uses analogical mapping of a fairly high order. But the most elementary forms of meaning construction use much more basic kinds of analogical schematization. These elementary forms of analogical transfer are what might be labeled "microanalogy." The most basic kind of microanalogy is synesthesia, otherwise known as cross-modal perception.

In discussing Saussure's view of symbolic motivation, I noted that his emphasis on the arbitrariness of the linguistic sign all but ignored the role of psychogenic motivation. For native speakers, the *experience of linguistic signs* is transformed from one of historical arbitrariness to one of virtual psychological identity. Whatever linguists tell us about the arbitrariness of our words, any native speaker knows better. In our experience, our words do not *represent* concepts: they *present* them in a wholly transparent way. This is what I meant when I noted that native speakers do not normally speak *in* their language, but *through* it.

Through use, words come to be perceived by users as natural rather than as conventions. This virtual identification of signified and signifier, overcoming the contingencies of their historical tie, has been noted in chants, spells, prayers, and other forms of word magic; in the ritual or sacred use of words; and in what Freud called the omnipotence of words in children's thought. Yet, oddly enough, much less has been made of the fact that this very same psychological identification of word and concept is essential to everyday language use. Without it, language would cease to be a transparent medium for feeling and thought. People will kill over words, as if they were things. Most of us will take serious offense at anyone wantonly playing with our names, just as if the name had become an extension of our person. Yet how does this sort of banal word magic happen?

Onomatopoeia and other forms of sound-symbolic schematization provide an important clue. As Saussure and other have pointed out, it is true that overt sound symbolism is a relatively minor part of language use. Yet I think that they were too quick to dismiss the importance of such sound-symbolic modeling. As we will see, there is evidence that onomatopoeia is, so to speak, merely the visible tip of the iceberg. In terms of the analytical distinctions developed in Chapter 2, we might hypothesize that onomatopoeia is an instituted model of relatively limited distribution in most languages.[8] But the cognitive processes that produce this kind of sound-symbolic modeling at the surface of language are probably operating in the ongoing construction of cognitive models of words that approximate onomatopoeia. They do this at the level of personal cognitive models rather than as conventional models. Such sound symbolism is neither publicly visible as instituted models nor conventionally shared. If this is the case, then synesthesia represents the most elementary cognitive process underlying meaning construction.

SYNESTHESIA

Fortunately, synesthesia has been quite well studied by cognitive psychologists, and their research allows us to consider the role of synesthetic cognition in both mental and cultural models.[9] Research on such cross-modal sensory equivalences by Marks and Bornstein (Marks and Bornstein, 1987) views synesthesia as one of a variety of kinds of sensory equivalence that make possible stable perceptions despite the flux of actual physical sensation. In cross-modal perceptual identifications, physically different stimuli are received by different sensory systems but yield the same perception.

Marks and Bornstein provide an example of such classic synesthesia. They use two line drawings. One globular, rounded form is seen as matched to the nonsense word "maluma," while another, straight-edged and pointed, is matched to the name "takete." About 10 percent of the population recognizes synesthetic perception as a common and conscious experience (Marks et al., 1987:3). Synesthesia is reported among children far more commonly than it is among adults in any population. But the fact that individuals do not report an awareness of synesthetic perception does not mean that it is not operative for them in preconscious processes of meaning construction.

Cross-modal perception has been observed for infants. Such early synesthetic experiences are probably the product of both sensory entrainment and innate perceptual processes. Neurologically, a possible basis for such cross-modal identifications has been found in higher primates. Cortical neurons have been located that seem to respond similarly to a given visual stimulus from anywhere within the neuron's receptive field. This would provide a basis for the perception of object constancy, although neural mechanisms linking different sensory modalities have not yet to my knowledge been identified.

Year-old infants have been shown to match visual and auditory stimuli on the axis of up-down directionality, while loudness and brightness equivalence have been identified for infants as young as three weeks. Marks and Bornstein hypothesize that several primitive cross-modal equivalences are hard-wired into human sensory systems through polysensory neurons. These primitive sensory equivalences might provide a scaffolding from which other, more attenuated and socially directed kinds of equivalences may develop.

More complex perceptual associations work through relations of contiguity or what psychologists call association. Technically speaking, they are sensory metonymies rather than metaphors. Examples cited of sensory metonymies are pitch-size associations, or the association of colors with temperatures—cool and hot colors. Experimental evidence cited by Marks and Bornstein suggests that while metaphorical equivalences are likely to employ innate processes of synesthesia, sensory metonymies appear to develop much later and to be far more conventionally mediated than sensory metaphors.

Yet I think this kind of rigid distinction between metaphorical processes of natural equivalence and metonymic processes of conventional identification can be overstated. It ignores the less visible processes of an inner structuralization by which conventional associations become experienced as natural, such that color-temperature linkages may eventually approximate to consciousness the kind of direct equivalence of sensory metaphors. For instance, certain forms of metonymy, namely synecdoche, where part-whole identifications are effected, must employ both metonymic associations and metaphorical identifications to work psychologically. In synesthesia, culturally derived secondary or tertiary equivalence structures as pitch-size, or color-temperature or even social caste-cleanliness or caste-color associations are probably experienced by natives as "naturally" as the primary synesthetic linkages.

CONVENTIONALIZED SYNESTHESIA: PHONESTHEMES

The kind of sound symbolism Marks and Bornstein discover in nonsense words is clearly more idiosyncratic than the conventional forms of onomatopoeia that are routinely dismissed by linguists as theoretically insignificant in language. But it does have a bearing on a class of protoconventions in language that Dwight Bolinger calls "phonesthemes" (Bolinger, 1989:284). They are important because they represent a kind of modeling somewhere between purely public instituted models and purely cognitive mental models.

Phonesthemes are families of words whose overt articulatory patterns mimic in an abstract way some sensory-based semantic component shared by the word group. Bolinger characterizes these associations as frequently depending on "partial accidental clustering in the lexicon" (p. 284) and cites the familiar example of the "visual" implications of the "gl" in words like "glitter", "glisten", "gleam", and "glow". Yet it is an open question how accidental the family resemblance is of words like "hinge" (hang + inge), "fringe" (fray + inge?), "tinge" (tint + inge?), "singe" (sear + inge?), and "impinge" (impose + inge). The articulation of the common phonestheme "inge" mimics the "gradually fading boundaries" of the shared semantic associations. The same goes for "udge-" words like "fudge", "trudge", "budge", "sludge", "grudge", whose phonestheme mimics a kind of "heavy stickiness."

Such phonesthetically linked word families are relatively rare in language. But they provide an interesting example of microanalogy that combines the purely idiosyncratic fusions of sound and sense of personal cognitive models and fully conventional constructs. Phonesthemes, like many forms of sound play in language, may reflect in partially conventional forms the same synesthetic processes by which all signs are rendered idiosyncratically meaningful to subjects. Such deeply embedded "obscure symbolisms" and "unconscious formal feelings" in linguistic sound patterns, anticipated so long ago by Sapir (1921/1949:29), point to as yet unexplained dimensions of symbolic motivation in human sign systems that are central to any theory of meaning construction.

HIGH-LEVEL MODELS: INSTITUTED MODELS AND ANALOGICAL SCHEMATIZATION

Synesthesia and phonesthemes both point to fundamental cognitive processes of nonanalytical concept formation. Both are based on primary analogy. And both suggest a cognitive orientation toward the unification of the senses through cross-sensory analogical transfer. These nonanalytical processes are good candidates for elementary forms of meaning construction by which the mind constructs nodes of resistance to the arbitrariness of signs and provides a sensory basis for their psychogenic motivation. At even lower levels of coding, connectionists have begun to demonstrate how such analogies may be modeled in terms of PDP networks (Rumelhart and Abrahamsen, 1973). The remaining problem is how to connect these low-level microprocesses of meaning construction with the high-level representations we recognize as cultural models.

WERNER AND KAPLAN'S *SYMBOL FORMATION*

What experimental evidence is there for the mind's resistance to the arbitrariness of signs in its use of primary analogical schematization? The brilliant but frequently overlooked experimental research on the psychology of symbol formation by Heinz Werner and Bernard Kaplan provides just such a link between low- and high-level meaning construction. In their 1963 book *Symbol Formation,* Werner and Kaplan present a view of symbolization which they call "an organismic and developmental approach to language and the expression of thought."[10] Werner and Kaplan explicitly reject the prevailing view of the arbitrariness of linguistic forms by making a distinction similar to that drawn by Benveniste in his criticism of Saussure:

> [W]ith the exception perhaps of onomatopoeic word-forms, one can see no external similarity between the properties of objects to which reference is made and the properties of the forms used to refer to these objects. However, when one considers the view that perceptual objects as well as symbolic vehicles are established in terms of organismic schematizing, one may entertain the possibility that an *inner similarity between the vehicle and referent may occur without this similarity being apparent to an observer* who regards solely the external, geometric-technical properties of the word-form and object. [Werner and Kaplan, 1963:26; emphasis added]

This account of symbolizing stresses *the experience* of symbols rather than their formal properties. The authors trace the process by which symbols are infused with psychogenic motivation. They propose that the inner relationship between a symbol and its referent is quite different from any observable external relationship (or nonrelation). This inner relationship rests, they claim, on "an organismic process of schematization" in which "the sign-vehicle becomes transformed into the overt face of a symbolic vehicle and the referent into a connotatively defined referent (significate)" (pp. 29–30). Their hypothesis is that "the bond established between the vehicle and the significate—both structured by a schematizing process—is one of inner similarity."

This schematizing process studied by Werner and Kaplan is, in a sense, the converse of classical (i.e., information-processing) models of logic. Classical logic begins with the principle of noncontradiction, whereby something cannot be both itself and something else at the same time. The result is a category unit that can carry information. Conversely, schematizing has the effect of uniting two perceptual entities that were initially discrete. Its mode is what Lévy-Bruhl called "participation"; its effect is what we normally call "meaning."

As I noted in Chapters 7 and 8, the rationality debate in anthropology and philosophy over the nature of "primitive thought" focused on just such questions of classificatory logic as manifested in totemism. Careful attention to ethnographic accounts of totemic thinking revealed that the "classificatory moment" of totemism only made sense in relation to its converse formulation, a kind of literal and spiritual "participation" between diverse but interdependent species. The kind of psychological "participation" proposed by Lévy-Bruhl suggested Kwakiutl and Murngin understandings of complex identifications between humans and animals. But rather than seeing "participation" as a form of "prelogical" thought limited to traditional cultures, analogical schematization allows us to recognize the meaning-constructing aspect of thought that Lévy-Bruhl called "participation."

Werner and Kaplan cite negative evidence for this schematizing activity by which symbols and their associated referents come to dwell in their knowers. This is the common experience of a momentary lapse of meaning that occurs when a familiar name or word is repeated too many times. The sudden loss of the inner-connectedness of the word and its referent approximates the experience of what language would be like if it were genuinely apprehended as a system of arbitrary signs. What is lost is the inner schematization, what Peirce called the sign's *interpretant*— a mental construction that holds the word together as a psychological whole and connects it to a range of preconscious sensory experiences.

The schematizing activity by means of which symbols come to have psychological meaning is neither fully arbitrary nor fully motivated. The key process in this schematizing activity is the construction of primary idiosyncratic analogies exploiting a range of synesthetic cross-modal mappings. This schematizing process suggests that meaning construction involves the recollection *(anemnesis)* of the subject's physical experience of the world in the mental representation of conventional sign-forms.

The Wernerian model is developmental, so that this activity in children is far more direct and naturalistic than that employed by adults:

> [T]here is, in the course of development, a progressive differentiation or distancing between the inner form of a symbol (the connotational dynamics) and the external form (the phonic or written vehicle). At primordial levels the inner form is fused with the external form and hence is visibly and auditorily carried by the vehicle. With the progression towards the use of conventional forms, the inner form of the symbol (the connotational dynamics) becomes more and more covert in character—carried by "inner gestures," "imagery," "postural affective sets," "feelings," etc. [p. 238]

While there is thus a progression from natural symbolism to conventional symbolism, Werner and Kaplan do not use the term "arbitrary." The inner connection has been established early in development, and becomes simply more covert with maturity. Rather than distinguishing motivated and arbitrary symbolism, the authors differentiate conventional symbols from the "physiognomic shaping" of patterns, which is the primitive and basic mode of constructing symbolic relations. This physiognomic shaping of symbolic patterns is a particularly important kind of analogical schematization that uses bodily experience as a basis for schema construction. This notion of physiognomic shaping of symbolic patterns is closely related to Lakoff and Johnson's understanding of kinesthetic image schemas (e.g., center-periphery, verticality, containment, goal-driven trajectory and front-back), which they claim structure virtually all cognitive models and provide a bridge between the body and the mind.

EMBODIMENT

Physiognomic is used to describe the elementary internal transformation of the relations between signifiers and signifieds into a single experience as signs. Werner and

Kaplan maintain that, at the most primitive level of symbol formation, sensorimotor experience is employed as a mediator between sign vehicles and abstract referents. Our elementary concepts derive their experiential force through embodiment. This role of embodiment in concept formation, prefigured in Piaget's grounding of thought in sensorimotor schemas, has in recent years gained some prominence in anthropology through the work of Michael Polanyi (1966, 1969; Polanyi and Prosch, 1975), Thomas Csordas (1994a,b) Drew Leder (1990), Brenda Beck (1987), Robert Plant Armstrong (1981), George Lakoff and Mark Johnson (Johnson, 1987; Lakoff and Johnson, 1980), among others. The notion of embodiment provides one important foundation for a theory of psychological motivation in cultural symbolism.

This mediation of sign-meaning by reference to one's own body is perhaps the most elementary way in which meaning construction works by a kind of integration of novel stimuli with prior experience. Werner and Kaplan maintain that individual development manifests a movement from physiognomic to conventional apprehension of symbols. But this transformation is never complete. Though there is a "change in the degree to which the dynamic processes of formation and articulation are realized outwardly" (p. 207), the dynamic restructuring of symbols continues in a less obvious way. The result of the complete loss of such restructuring would be a permanent experience of "lapse of meaning." Thus, in Peirce's terms, iconicity is at the heart of all human symbol formation, even where the sign appears objectively to be arbitrary.[11]

Initially, external stimuli become meaningful by being reconstituted (recollected) through primitive sensorimotor patterns. We can still experience these sensorimotor schemas when we use our bodies (i.e., tapping our fingers, nodding our heads, clicking our teeth, etc.) to keep time to music or to keep count or even in performing elementary multiplication problems. Eventually, more attenuated and conventional meaning constructions take place by the metaphorical interaction between these elementary concepts and complex conventional forms.

PROVERBIAL KNOWLEDGE: ANALOGICAL SCHEMATIZATION AT WORK

It is one thing to demonstrate analogical schematization at work in the micro-analogies implicit in relatively low-level symbolic forms like sound symbolism and synesthesia. It is something else again to claim that this same cognitive process underwrites the transfer between complex cultural and cognitive models. While cultural anthropology has a tradition of describing such complex cultural models, there is much less empirical research on the cognitive processes involved in the mappings between instituted models and cognitive models.

Fortunately, there has been solid research done on the cognition involved in one important kind of cultural model: proverbs. This important research supports the contention that analogical schematization is a key cognitive process underlying the translation of instituted models into forms of personal knowledge. Honeck et al., have carried out an interesting series of studies on the cognitive processing of traditional proverbs. The study clearly illustrates the second birth of a publicly available cultural model (the proverb) as a particular set of mental representations (the interpretation of the proverb). Proverbs are a stock of specific cultural models organized around a limited set of general schema, what is sometimes referred to as the proverbs' "conceptual bases" (Honeck et al., 1987:109). The authors were interested in the way that people understand and use this common stock of models.

> Under certain conditions, namely those that lead an observer to recognize that the literal meaning of a proverb is inappropriate and that a nonliteral meaning must be sought, the observer transforms the literal proverb information and whatever contextual information is relevant. *The transformation process often involves analogy formation, which serves as a framework for constructing a figurative meaning.* This meaning serves as the glue for a complex category whose name is the proverb itself and whose range and kind of instantiation is mediated by this meaning. The meaning is the black hole of a category universe, since events are assimilated into (and rejected from) the category via the meaning. . . . *Since a large number of events from different sensory modalities can enjoy the same categorical fate, it is clear that the meaning is generative and amodal.* [pp. 109–110; emphasis added]

The important role of analogical schematization in the comprehension of proverbs is particularly notable. Proverbs are cultural models whose linguistic form might suggest the appropriateness of analytic rather than analogical processing. Yet, as the authors stress, proverbs are special in that they represent a form of figurative rather than literal language. Lakoff and Johnson's analyses of the ubiquitous work of metaphor in all aspects of language renders questionable this simple distinction between literal and figurative language. Nonetheless, the framing of a speech form as explicitly poetic or figurative appears to trigger integral analogical processing more quickly than would be the case if the proverbs were framed as literal propositions. This is what is implied by the general impression that proverbs are somehow more "poetic" than ordinary language. What is true of these linguistic forms is probably all the more true for nonlinguistic cultural models, such as the Kwakiutl Hamatsa dance; the centered and contained body posture that Samoans call *fātai,* and which they associate with deferential and polite self-presentation; or the perception of the atomized imagery one gets by channel surfing on contemporary TV. No researcher has experimentally documented the processes by which these public models are analogically transformed into mental models by those who experience them. Yet the research on proverb perception makes a strong case for the important role of analogical schematization in the translation process by which many cultural models are brought to mind.

CULTURALLY MEDIATED SCHEMATIZING

Meaning construction employs analogical schematizing. Both literary metaphor and scientific theory are grounded in complex forms of analogical transfer. "Human history," Robert Plant Armstrong reminds us, "has been the exploitation of the potentialities of spatial and temporal analogics. . . . The analogic is a primal necessity to being" (Armstrong, 1981:24–25). We have seen how microanalogy (e.g., synesthesia, onomatopoeia, phonesthemes) makes possible a primitive kind of sensory concept. *Such sensory concepts fuse in consciousness signifiers and signifieds, thereby overcoming the initial contingency of their relationship.* These low-level schematizing processes have psychologically primitive manifestations, by which individuals actively construct personal signs. The research on proverb cognition suggests that they have more socially mediated cultural manifestations, by which such analogies are motivated by cultural conventions.

In this book we have had occasion to come across all sorts of culture models, some in exotic locales and others just down the street. We have witnessed the work of culture in forms as variable as proverbs, linguistic metaphors, baseball fields, shopping malls, village spatial configurations, totemic birds, techno-totemic cyborgs, Murngin mythic pythons ingesting boys and spitting out women, and Kwakiutl cannibal dancers swallowing and vomiting up whole tribes. These models are products of the human imagination in its ongoing dialogue with the constraining forces of both our animal being and the physical world.

Cultural models like those discussed in this book have a major role to play in the cognitive work of culture. They act for members of a community as shared and ready-made source domains for analogical schematization. They are the stuff on which the cultural imagination feeds. Such models and the more abstract schemas on which they are often based motivate a high degree of shared analogical schematizing for members of a common community. Through analogical schematizing, powerful equivalences (what we usually call "meanings") can be constructed and reconstructed, formed and reformed. Connectionism has demonstrated how low-level neurally inspired networks can account for the world-openness of cultural models.

In meaning construction, there is a two-way movement between the particular and general. Particular cases can be grounded in relation to prior, encompassing schemas. Alternately, general convergence schemas can be generated "on the fly" out of the experience of novel cases. Foundational schemas make possible the construction of equivalences between different specific models. Thus, as we have seen for modular structures in contemporary America, for the swallowing symbolisms in the Kwakiutl winter ceremony, and for the dialectical walkabout motif in Australia, foundational schemas make possible powerful cross-contextual coherences that contribute to a distinctive worldview. Analogical schematization also makes possible the more idiosyncratic equivalences between public models and aspects of an individual's personal experience. These individual schematizations, much harder to document because they are private and often preconscious, make possible the investing of conventional models with personal psychic force. They are how biography gets tied up with cultural forms.

Through conventional models, communities come to share general cognitive orientations. Though normally conceived in consciousness as a unitary experience, cultural meaning thus has a double birth: once through convention, once through idiosyncratic construction. The underlying cognitive processes of meaning construction should be the same whether subjective or intersubjective meaning is at issue. Without this kind of linkage between meaning construction as an individual activity and the social construction of meaning through cultural models, it is hard to understand how conventional representations could come to have psychological force and powerfully shape human motivation (D'Andrade and Strauss, 1992).

Though I have focused on the role of analogical schematizing in cultural cognition, the thrust of this study is not to reduce the work of culture to exclusively nonanalytical processing. Cultural models, as we noted in the last chapter, come packaged in many forms. As Lakoff has suggested, metonymy may be as important a source of cognitive models as metaphor. Moreover, propositional models appear to have great significance for thought. Many cultural models—like scripts, recipes, and a whole host of other task models—commonly take the form of programs or procedures and are probably modeled analytically in many of their uses. It is also probable that the feature-sorting processes of classical categorization accurately represent certain kinds of taxonomic knowledge.

Moreover, any cultural model is subject to analytical manipulation (or may have an analytical "version") in situations when individuals are forced to transform tacit models into explicitly verbalized "explain-to-me" models. I noted this analogic-to-analytical shift in the two alternative models Samoans have for village spatial orientation, discussed in Chapter 11. Analytical models permit individuals to consciously manipulate and communicate their understandings. The evolution of language has provided us with a way to analytically re-present virtually any aspect of our experience. But the fact that a model *can be* represented as a set of analytical procedures does not mean that this is its normal status as a cognitive model for those who use it. That is an empirical question.

FOUR LEVELS OF ANALOGY FORMATION

Analogical schematizing occurs at several different levels of cognition, ranging from the behavior of networks of a neural type, to microanalogy employing synesthetic perception to quite elaborate macroprocesses of schematizing. These differences were clear in the review of the psychological literature on analogy formation. Some "analogies" seemed relatively direct and integral cognitive acts, while others appeared to be highly structured and procedurally complex.

Earlier I distinguished primary analogy from second-order analogy. Now we are ready to make even more refined distinctions among different "levels" of analogy formation. Let us distinguish four levels at which analogy formation takes place.

Most basic is *analogy 1*. These low-level primary analogies are the pattern-seeking and recognition behavior of connectionist networks. To the extent that they correctly model the way in which neural networks learn analogically, analogy 1 provides a neurologically relevant scaffolding for other kinds of analogy formation.

Analogy 2 is produced by basic sensorimotor cross-modal associations that Gentner identified as attribute similarity. Analogy 2 underlies such microanalogies as synesthesia, phonesthemes, iconicities in serial music and other art forms, as well as the physiognomic apprehension of symbols studied by Werner and Kaplan.

Analogy 3 describes more attenuated and self-conscious associations among relationships rather than among primitive features. Most forced analogy tests are testing for the ability to schematize this third type of analogy.

Analogy 4 is what Haskell calls "structural metaphor." Structural metaphor schematizes the relationships between more complex and elaborate models:

> Structural metaphor . . . is a subliteral action mode that is equivalent or isomorphic to the content or thought being expressed. This praxis mode can be semantic where

a writer uses words that have associated meaning; it can be phonetic where the sound of the words used are equivalent to the literal content, as in puns; it can be structured in . . . the form or style or structure of what is being written or spoken about. In short it is isomorphic to the given content of an interaction. [Haskell, 1987c:252]

Analogy 4 as a form of cultural meaning construction is based on cultural schemas of great generality. Such general schemas have the ability to schematize a great number of different cultural models, lending an ineffable sense of familiarity that members of a community take for granted and that few could account for explicitly. These general organizations of experience are foundational schemas. They are commonly found in myth and ritual models of religious traditions, such as we noted for the Kwakiutl in Chapter 8 and for the Murngin in Chapters 9 and 10. The operation of these foundational schemas underlies the intuition that cultures have distinctive worldviews.

Any of these analogies may be modeled analytically as procedural programs under conditions (like artificial testing, or explaining one's culture to an anthropologist) calling for a high degree of conscious control and strategic manipulation. On the other hand, we have reviewed experimental evidence suggesting that the least complex analogies (analogy 2) and some of the more complex analogies (analogy 4) may normally be perceived nonanalytically through integral or gestalt perception. This would make sense of the fact that many models and schemas are not easily accessible to verbal articulation by the people who "know" them most intimately.

MANY TYPES OF SCHEMATIZING

Cultural models exploit the human capacity for meaning-making through analogical schematizing at a high level, usually analogy 4. Cultural models employ analogical schematizing in a number of different ways. Most commonly, meaning construction draws upon a store of previously learned foundational schemas in relation to which novel information can be analogically mapped. More rarely, cognitive models may be constructed opportunistically as a way to resolve otherwise incoherent experiences for which no prior schema exists. Some of these novel models may become conventionalized for a community, though most will probably remain relatively poorly cognized aspects of private experience.

Behavior is structured at three different levels of abstraction. At the greatest level of particularity are (1) *specific cases,* concrete experiences which provide the most direct basis for general reasoning. More abstract and institutionalized are (2) *instituted models,* which are the behavioral equivalent of conventional "categories" for experience. Instituted models are usually labeled or otherwise explicitly coded by members of a community, so that they are easily recognized forms of institutionalized experience. Most abstract are (3) *foundational schemas.* Foundational schemas are very general models which work across empirically heterogeneous domains of experience and underlie a community's worldview. Foundational schemas are usually only tacitly known and not explicitly cognized by members of a community. Few people are able spontaneously to describe their operative foundational schemas.

In relation to the modular schema discussed in Chapters 5 and 6, the abstract "modular design strategy" is such a foundational schema. Each of these specific institutional domains organized by the schema—domains such as shopping malls, educational curricula, and music videos—are specific instituted models sharing a common cultural schema. Any specific experience of shopping or television watching or educational planning would be a case, which might or might not conform to the instituted model and its encompassing foundational schema.

Using this framework, we can understand the complexity of the actual schematizing relations that involve these three levels of organization. Figure 14.1 represents six possible kinds of schematizing that relate these levels. The first three types of analogical schematization are examples of the cognitive process that Piaget identified as "assimilation" (Piaget, 1962). By assimilation, Piaget meant the organization of novel experiences in relation to preexisting schemas.

Type I mappings are those in which specific personal experiences are organized

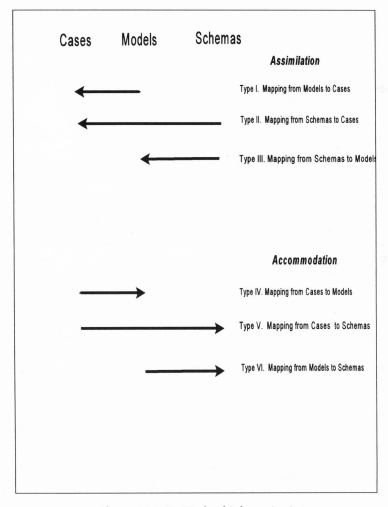

Figure 14.1 Six Kinds of Schematization

by being mapped onto specific instituted models. This is the standard form of the "cultural construction of experience" that is a commonplace of anthropological analysis. Whenever we treat an experience as an instance of some conventional "type" of experience within a cultural setting, we are employing type I schematizations, mappings from case to model. For example, this process is clearly evident in Murngin marriages, where "wrong" marriages are brought into line with the accepted cultural models of marriage through a variety of imaginative "remappings" of kin relations.

In type II schematizations, specific experiences are mapped directly onto very general foundational schemas. This is a much rarer form of cultural schematization than type I, because most of our experiences are mediated by specific cultural models rather than modeled directly by general schemas. However, type II schematizations would occur where a novel event had no clear "home" in any specific instituted model. This would be the case, for instance, in cross-cultural experience, where an individual attempted to make sense of an experience that had no specific institutional analogue in his new cultural setting. Recent Samoan immigrants to the United States, residing in typical American neighborhoods and superficially adopting an American lifestyle, may still employ Samoan foundational schemas for formal and intimate spatial and social relations in situations where there is little or no institutional overlap with their traditional instituted models. One can infer here an attempt to invoke as a guide to action a general foundational schema that governs formality and intimacy rather than any domain-specific instituted models.

Type III schematizations are analogical mappings from foundational schemas to specific instituted models. Not all instituted models have an encompassing foundational schema that links them to other models of the same general type. Take, for instance, "jokes," a common genre of ludic models. Some jokes have a unique narrative format and are not instantly recognizable as jokes. Others, however, such as "knock-knock jokes," "playing the dozens," or the ethnic joke ("How many x's does it take. . .") share a general schema and readily engage participants in a well-defined play frame.[12]

Frequently, people remain unaware of the degree to which diverse instituted models share a common foundational schema. Though I have suggested that many different Murngin institutions are organized by a common "walkabout" schema, it is unlikely that most natives would spontaneously make these cross-model associations. The same goes for the foundational schema that relates time and space asymmetrically, organizes many aspects of baseball, and makes baseball lingo appropriate for modeling courtship (Chapter 3) . This does not mean that the schema-to-model mappings are completely unconscious. Instead, they tend to be tacitly known and usually evoke immediate recognition from people when these connections are pointed out to them. This suggests that self-conscious schema-to-model mappings would usually occur only in very special circumstances of heightened cultural awareness or intercultural conflict.

In types IV to VI, schematizations represent a cognitive process that Piaget called "accommodation." Here the schemas themselves are transformed (or even created) by their encounter with novel experiences. These are cases where one can see forms of cultural knowledge being created, transformed, and negotiated on the fly. Anomalous experiences can alter old cultural models or even create new ones (type IV case-to-model mappings).

I once participated in such a cultural innovation in Western Samoa, when I was the "leader" of a research expedition that spent two months in a village studying aging. When we prepared to bid farewell to the village, we improvised a ceremonial response to the Samoan presentation of fine mats as gifts. Instead of fine mats (which are called *'ie* or "cloth"), our group had brought along a bolt of fine printed cloth several hundred feet long. Everyone present in the group "wrapped" the house in which our farewell ceremony was taking place in the proffered cloth by unraveling the entire bolt in a long procession around the house and then piling the material at the house's center. Amid the delighted oohs! and ahs! from the assembled women of the village, we heard comments to the effect that we had created a fine new tradition of "mat" presentation that would forever be remembered in the village.

It is important to note that one of the reasons this new "model" of gift giving was such a hit was that it conformed to several instituted models, such as "wrapping" and "piling up gifts ostentatiously." Moreover, the cloth we offered was probably analogically schematized as a good equivalent of traditional mats. Such is the peripatetic life of cultural models.

It is much less common for a foundational schema to be transformed or created through a single instituted model. Foundational schemas are inherently conservative and thus resistant to such change. Rarely are schemas transformed or created quickly enough to be clearly visible to members of a community. It is possible to document, however, the gradual transformation or emergence of a foundational schema over a long period through the influence of novel cultural models.

For instance, Peter Lawrence's classic study of the fate of a cargo cult in New Guinea, *Road Belong Cargo,* traces the gradual transformation of an indigenous schema for making sense of relationships between the living and their ancestors. Here, particular events (cases) associated with World War II gradually and progressively altered a variety of local cultural models. Eventually the foundational schema employed to bring these events into line with traditional understandings of wealth and of the relations between the living and the dead was rendered incapable of making sense of the world and set the local populations on a search for new schemas to explain the new conditions of their lives (Lawrence, 1964). In this case, schematizations of both types V and VI took place, as cataclysmic events altered specific models of religion and social relations; eventually these altered models transformed the foundational cultural schema that had underwritten many traditional cultural models in the Madang region of New Guinea.

Closer to home, we are ourselves experiencing the emergence of relatively new foundational schemas for organizing many of our experiences. Chapters 5 and 6 documented how numerous technological and social changes are contributing to the creation of a distinctively postmodern "technologic." Yet characteristically, it is very difficult to track such emerging model-to-schema mappings while one is caught in the flow of the transformation.

Note that I used the verb "mapping" in preference to the noun "maps" in order to stress the active and intentional nature of meaning construction. Clearly, this typology of schematizations does not imply that real meaning construction falls neatly and uniquely into such simple categories. In the real world, cultural meaning construction exploits several different types of schematizing simultaneously or as alternative strategies. Because the mind is an opportunistic meaning-constructor, the actual life of culture is best understood as a set of contingent resources to be used in a whole variety of ways by people as they seek to transform the unsteady flow of their lives into pockets of significance. What is predictable, however, is the general use of analogical schematization to underwrite the continuing sense that we live in a world of comprehensible and adjustable experiences.[13]

This chapter has presented a considerable body of evidence about the processes involved in and the importance of many kinds of analogy formation. It would be useful at this point to summarize the key points made in this chapter.

- Connecting culture and mind inevitably involves linking concepts at different levels of organization.
- Analogical schematization as a linking process presupposes that there are fundamental similarities among the architectures of models at different levels of organization (neural, cognitive, social).
- This kind of structural parallelism has important limits, since it does not account for the possible transformations and transductions that occur between very low level models like neural networks and very high level models such as cultural models.
- The strongest case for analogical schematization as a linking process involves highly cognized experiential models (i.e., instituted models and concepts) at a relatively high level of organization. Thus, structural parallelism may or may not turn out to characterize how cultural models are inscribed neurologically. This is a matter of considerable debate within cognitive science.
- The PDP connectionist models do show promise in demonstrating a direct bridge between low-level and high-level models. This is because connectionist models are largely "indexical" models, designed to respond analogically to changing inputs. Because connectionist models are particularly good at indexing and mapping dynamic pattern relations, they provide an attractive theoretical bridge between the lowest and highest levels of modeling.
- Schema induction represents an important mid-level modeling process that is central to cultural cognition. .
- Analogies may also be constructed analytically, through complex sorting and matching processes. The conditions under which such analytical models of analogy formation apply need to be studied relative to those situations in which analogies are produced through integral processing.
- The degree of complexity of a source domain may affect which strategy of analogy formation is employed. Experimental research has suggested that both the simplest and most complex source domains encourage nonanalytical and integral processing, while those at intermediate levels of complexity encourage analytical strategies.
- Analytical strategies are also common for highly self-conscious analogy tasks like constructing forced-choice analogies or explaining an analogy to others. Analytical strategies are basically information-processing models and are cognitively quite different from more holistic strategies of analogy formation.
- Analogy formation may be described at at least four different levels of organization, ranging from primitive neurological pattern seeking to high-level concepts like structural metaphors and foundational schemas.

- Werner and Kaplan have described a kind of primary analogical schematization that accompanies symbol formation and underwrites the psychological meaningfulness of symbols. Its effect is to undercut the perception of arbitrariness.

- High-level processes of analogy formation are central to the work of culture. Analogical schematization can be seen in a great variety of ways in which specific cases, cultural models, and foundational schemas interact. The significance of analogical schematization is suggested in terms of six possible kinds of mappings among cases, models, and schemas. Examples were given of each kind of mapping, though they are not equally common. These diverse mappings suggest the complex ways in which analogy formation governs the relations between specific experiences, cultural forms, and mental representations.

- To the extent that conventional models are used as source domains for analogical schematization, meaning construction is a cultural and social process.

- But analogical schematization is not a passive mapping process. It is an intentional activity by a meaning-seeking agent. Analogies are constructed, not discovered. The manner in which conventional models are brought to mind is best thought of as a creative and contingent activity rather than as a determinate and passive replication process.

CONCLUSIONS: ANALOGICAL SCHEMATIZATION IN THE WORK OF CULTURE

By now it should be clear that cultural knowledge is not accurately characterized as a timeless and fixed stock of received models. The instituted models, which are the public forms of culture, and the cognitive models, which are their instantiations in the mind, are both historically contingent artifacts. Though they are often perceived as timeless and ahistoric forms (by natives as well as anthropologists), cognitive models and foundational schemas are always subject to continual renegotiation in their performance or nonperformance. As forms of life, they are born, run their course, and (for the most part) die. At any given time in the life of a community, however, the stock of models is usually sufficiently stable to produce among its members the sense of living in a "natural" universe with a shared stock of common resources for making sense out of things.

This shared stock of instituted models and conventional cognitive models does not produce shared meaning in the direct and simple sense that was once the received wisdom in anthropology. Instituted models do not automatically generate meaning. As tools for meaning construction, models are a common fund of conventional resources for the ongoing construction of meaning by people. Though normally encountered as a unified tissue of experience, every model has two distinct moments of birth, one public and conventional and the other a subjective appropriation and integration of a conventional form by a particular person. The links between public models and personal knowledge are contingent relations. The analogical schematizing processes by which cultural models are brought to mind are activities of an active, intentional, and opportunistic intelligence, not a passive recording device.

The relationship between instituted models and conventional cognitive models is mediated by analogical schematization. Instituted models are inevitably recreated as they are internalized. Thus, they are endowed with psychic as well as social force. Because it is always an active construction by an intentional, sentient, and creative mind, analogical schematization introduces a gap, a crucial lifegiving contingency, between the conventional forms of cultural life and their inner representations in consciousness. This gap guarantees the ongoing regeneration of conventions through practice just as it makes possible intersubjective meaning.

Thus, to recognize the importance of cultural models and schemas in cognition does not entail viewing cultural cognition as either monolithic or ahistorical. For the dual creation—the two births—of cultural signs guarantees their double character as at once conventional and idiosyncratic constructs. Cultural models are shared and conventional representations, but only in a limited sense. Culturally constituted meaning points not to closed systems but only to a probability of a significant overlap within a community in how novel experiences will be reconstituted as memory.

Notes

1. There is a large and growing literature on connectionism in cognitive science. For general accounts of connectionism and its more recent incarnation as parallel distributed processing (PDP) models, see Rumelhart et al., 1986; Rumelhart, 1990; Smolensky, 1987, 1988; and Bechtel and Abrahamsen, 1991.

2. The assignment of a qualitative value or interpretation to specific units raises a number of difficult questions about network architecture. There seems to be nothing in the architecture of these systems that can account for the qualitative distinctions between different values or interpretations. Activation values seem to differ only as varying quantities of energy. Unless these qualities are accounted for compositionally in terms of even more primitive units or even "dots," the qualitative differences in interpretation of units would have to be accounted for as an emergent property of activation levels and patterns. Until we have an adequate account of this emergent property of units, connectionists are open to the accusation that they have slipped into their models something that looks suspiciously like qualitative symbols, albeit symbols that do not always act like symbols in information-processing accounts.

3. For detailed examples of such training of networks, see Bechtel and Abrahamsen, 1991, chap. 3.

4. On coarse coding, see Bechtel and Abrahamsen, 1991. I am grateful to Robert McCauley for pointing out that phenomena like coarse coding soften the hard distinction I was making between analog and digital codings.

5. Gregory Bateson took a great interest in this debate about analytic versus nonanalytic cognition. For the most part Bateson stressed the digital nature of information processing and argued that "the description of the brain has to start from the all-or-nothing characteristic of the neuron [whereby] . . . the neuron either fires or does not fire" (Bateson, 1979:111). Yet Bateson also recognized that the functioning of the brain, with its extraordinary combinations of neural firings, suggested a resolution of the old debate about whether brain functioning was primarily analogical or digital.

> [I]t is possible to make systems out of digital neurons that will have the *appearance* of being analogic systems. This is done by the simple device of multiplying the pathways so that a given cluster of pathways might consist of hundreds of neurons, of which a certain percentage would be firing and a certain other percentage would be quiet, thus giving an apparently graded response. In addition, the individual neuron is modified by

hormonal and other environmental conditions around it that may alter its threshold in a truly quantitative manner. [Bateson, 1979:111]

In this early statement of "coarse coding," Bateson suggests how lowlevel digital processing can produce analogical representations at higher levels of cognition.

6. For important works on analogical cognition, see Beck, 1987; Billow et al., 1987; Barth, 1975; Bolinger, 1980; Gentner, 1983, 1989; Gentner and Stevens, 1983; Shore, 1990b; Gibbs, 1987; Gick and Holyoak, 1983; Goswami, 1992; Haskell, 1987, 1987a–d, 1989; Hoffman and Honeck, 1987, Honeck et al., 1987; Keane, 1988; Levi-Strauss, 1967d; Lotman, 1990; Newport and Bellugi, 1978; Ortony, 1979; Shustak and Anderson, 1979; Sternberg, 1977; Tversky, 1977; Vosniadu and Ortony, 1989; Winner, Cicchetti and Gardner, 1981; Kosslyn, 1980; Piaget, Montangero, and Billeter, 1977; Winston, 1980; and Wilden, 1972.

7. Schema induction is the best candidate for a cognitive process that can account for the psychological reality of foundational schemas, the global and abstract cognitive models that I argued in Chapter 2 provided a common foundation for a related family of specific mental models.

8. Just how limited sound-symbolic modeling is in language is unclear. In a famous formulation, Edward Sapir proposed that language was saturated with hidden sound patterning of which most speakers were unaware (Sapir, 1921). Whorf was interested in synesthesia as an important dimension of language structure (Whorf, 1956). Other linguists who have underscored the role of sound-symbolic modeling in language are Benveniste (1966), Jakobson (1971), Bolinger (1980, 1986, 1989), Friedrich (1979), and J. Nuckolls (1992, 1996).

9. For important research on synesthesia, see D'Andrade and Egan, 1974; Gick and Holyoak, 1983; Haskell, 1989; Johnson et al., 1986; Kieffer, 1974; Marks et al., 1987; Marks and Bornstein, 1987; Spelke, 1976; Lewkowicz and Turkewitz, 1980; Winner et al., 1981; and Godfried et al., 1977.

10. Werner and Kaplan are not only unfamiliar to most anthropologists but they have also been marginalized within their own discipline. This is probably due to their uncritical use of the once popular assumption of significant parallelism between the mental life of children, "primitive" people, and psychotics. As with other significant thinkers who shared these equations, it is perfectly possible to look beyond the unfortunate implications of this position and cull what is important from their work.

11. Iconicity in human communication seems to serve a variety of "meaning-related" functions. For example, Bateson proposed that communication employing iconic signs continues to serve for interacting humans the primitive mammalian function of providing continuous feedback on the "quality" and credibility of the relationship rather than on the content of a message. He suggests that faced with a contradiction between the iconically based contours of paralinguistic communication (gesture, intonation, etc.) and the explicit content of a message, humans will almost always ignore the content message in favor of the relationship message (Bateson, 1972).

Consistent with Bateson's speculations are Dwight Bolinger's fascinating studies of intonation patterns (Bolinger, 1983, 1986, 1989). Bolinger contrasts the "relative arbitrariness and unintelligibility of the words and structures of a language one does not know" (Bolinger, 1989:1) with "the fundamental iconic nature of intonation" (p. viii). He argues for the existence of a universal code in intonation which, though often colored by convention, is never arbitrary and indeed may transcend the human species (p. viii). Such iconic forms are aptly suited for conveying the speaker's emotional stance toward the discourse situation.

12. Of course a joke that was too predictably an instance of its schema would probably not be very funny. Many jokes derive their humor precisely from their unexpected deviations from type.

13. For a suggestive account of cultural models within a single region of New Guinea being reformed on the fly, see Barth, 1987.

Epilogue:
The Ethnographic Mind

That the tragic events of a moment could be convincingly illuminated as a cultural mystery, and that this mystery could be resolved through the lens of Samoan culture is, for the moment, solution enough. The fact, however, that we could make intelligible the patterns that shape Samoan lives and even, perhaps, glimpse in them something of our own lives, points beyond Samoa to something else. But that is another, deeper, mystery.

—Bradd Shore, *Sala'ilua: A Samoan Mystery*

I want to end this book with a story. It is an old story, about people struggling to make meaning in the face of chaos. I have told it before, yet time has had its way with my memories.[1] The tragic events into which I stumbled back in 1973 look a little different to me now. I remember that it was about six o'clock in the evening and I was jogging my way back home, through a patch of rain forest that separated the small villages just south of my village, Sala'ilua. I don't believe I had a watch on. But I recall that the dogs were already starting to claim the road, as they did every night. I was running hard, breathing hard in the heavy air of a Samoan afternoon. Now and then the dirt road would turn out from the forest, and I'd find myself running along the rugged, lava-strewn coast of western Savai'i. The waves thundered on the reef far offshore. Mercifully, the sun had sunk low in the sky. It cast a warm light across the grassy *malae* at the heart of each village I passed through.

As I entered a village, the pattern of human activities told me it was *afiafi*—"fire time." The heat of the day had broken and was already giving way to the gentler evening air. The acrid smell of the cooking fires filled my nostrils. In every cook house large pots were cooking up the evening *saka*—boiled taro. I came upon a boy astride an old horse, returning from the gardens. I could hear the water from the pipes at the rear of the houses: the sound of cold showers washing away the accumulated sweat and dirt of the day, before family prayers. Unconsciously I increased my pace, knowing that the church bells would soon be ringing to clear the public areas of the village. Even a *pālagi* visitor to the islands was expected to observe the village curfew, returning home for prayers, or, failing that, simply ducking into any pastor's house.

Now and then, someone would call out to me from a house as I passed by. *Po'o fea le mea e te susu i ai, lau susuga le faia'oga?* "Where are you heading, honorable teacher?" It was always thus, even when they knew exactly where I was heading. Sometimes I made the appropriate response; at other times I was short of breath, and my manners failed me as I pretended not to hear. They knew I was pretending, I was sure, but mostly *they* pretended not to notice my rudeness. At other times I would acknowledge the greetings silently, merely raising my eyebrows and quickly flicking back my head in response.

DEATH IN THE AIR

Approaching my own village, I gradually became uneasy. The houses at the outskirts of the settlement were usually filled with kids calling out to me, *"Palagi! Palagi!"* Sometimes they ran out to the road to try and touch the light-skinned stranger who had moved into their district several months earlier. But tonight the houses were empty. The silence was eerie. As I made my way into the heart of my village, I saw a crowd of people gathered outside my family's main house, a hundred yards down the road. At first dimly, but then unmistakably, a terrible sound could be heard coming from the house. It was a wail, an agonizing moan, arching upward toward a scream. I knew now that there was death in the air, and it was very close to home.

The voice was Elena's. Elena was the wife of my Samoan "father," Tuatō. This kind of wailing could only mean death. It was a ritual form I recognized at every Samoan funeral I attended. And yet it was unmistakably Elena's agony, unlike any other cry I have ever heard. It was all unreal. With no warning, on a perfectly ordinary afternoon, Tuatō was dead, shot in the chest by a young schoolteacher, following an argument at the primary school building over a card game. They had all been drinking. Accusations began to fly about cheating at poker. Old rivalries, wounds long ago buried, began to surface. Tuatō's lifeless body had been rushed by truck to the small hospital several villages over, but by the time they arrived, it was clear that there was no hope. Tuatō Fatu, one of the two ranking chiefs of the village, had been murdered.[2] Making his way home from the schoolhouse, he had been ambushed by a rifle shot fired by the son of the village's other leading chief.

I stood, listening to the news as if it were a dream. The words seemed to bounce off me, as they had when my mother had, four years earlier, called me at home from work to tell me that my father had just died of a heart attack. Though I am embarrassed to admit this even now, I found myself thinking that I was an anthropologist studying conflict resolution in Samoa and that I had better start getting all of this down. I felt the desire to start recording and writing, as if recounting the murder would make the pain and confusion go away. But I did not start writing for several hours.

All over the village, people were doing their own recollecting, recounting their stories, again and again, compulsively telling what they had seen or heard, where they had been when the shot rang out, how the man with the rifle had locked himself in his father's house. Gradually, from out of these stories would come a "line"—the seed of some kind of coherent "take" on the murder. In some cases, it was the drink that figured in the story, alcohol, which everyone knew brought out the devils in people. Other accounts stressed old histories of conflict between the men. Still others framed the murder in relation to the two prominent families, ancient and sometimes bitter rivals in the village. There was much talk of sin, of the breakdown in tradition. Some even wondered if something at the heart of this village might be wrong. The talk went on like this for weeks following the murder.

Within a couple of hours, the district constable had arrested the young teacher and had tried to take him away to the district police headquarters. But Tuatō's son got to him first, attacking the young chief with a machete while he was being escorted out of the village. Publicly, people shook their heads and clucked in dismay at the attack, but privately no one really blamed the son for attacking his father's killer. Vengeance in cases like this was the least a son could do for his family's honor.[3] Everyone knew the vengeance scenario: a good son would never let his father's murderer live the night. There had been other cases just like this that the events brought to mind. Instead of ending up in prison, the murderer was taken to the island's main hospital at Tuasivi, where local surgeons managed to save his life.

By midnight, a disconcerting quiet came over the village. Tuatō's body had been brought from the hospital back to his own house, where it lay at the center of the house, surrounded by his wife and kids, alternately sobbing and wailing, and chatting amiably with the dozens of relatives and neighbors that had gathered there. Just outside the house, something I had never seen before was taking place. Several elders from the family of the murderer had seated themselves on the ground, facing the house, their legs folded in the dignified *fātai* position, several huge fine mats thrown over their heads. This was an *ifoga*, a ceremonial humiliation, by which one family sought to avoid war by publicly apologizing on behalf of one of their own and by offering up valuable mats as a kind of blood payment. They sat, heads down and perfectly still, for most of the night.

"THE HEAVENS ARE BROKEN"

Over the course of the next week, there were many ways in which the villagers tried to make sense of what had happened. "The Heavens are broken, the moon has fallen," intoned an old orator at the funeral. He was speaking in the high-blown, poetic style by which Samoans frame any weighty occasion. Tuatō's was no ordinary funeral but a *lagi*, a kind of state funeral for a ranking chief. A *sā*—a sacred period of mourning—was declared. The lagoons and the gardens had been closed off to normal activities by official edict. Tuatō's relatives had come in from all over the islands, bringing pigs, huge metal crates of *masi* biscuits, large cans of *pisupo* (canned corned beef). Entering the village, each visitor would be greeted by a member of Tuatō's family. The visitor would state the "path" (i.e., social connection) which brought him or her to the funeral. Then the visitor would recite the *fa'alupega*, the traditional roll call of village titles and families, acknowledging and honoring the hierarchy of the village as they entered it.

The visitors all brought treasured *'ie toga* in Tuatō's honor, the large finely woven pandanus mats that were exchanged at weddings, title ceremonies, and funerals. A person's life could be traced in such exchanges, as the various sides or parts of a person's identity were each proclaimed in the giving of mats and the accompanying high words of praise and commemoration. Tuatō, the brother, was honored by mats brought by his elder sisters. Tuatō, the teacher, was acknowledged by the mats given by his colleagues from the school he had headed. His mother's family had one part of him, his father's family another. From American Samoa came Elena's brothers with mats on behalf of their sister. Their mats asserted claims on the couple's children, and, breaking the marriage bond, claimed back their sister as their own. And since the dead man had several chiefly titles, there would be mats from those sides of his "family" too. As the mats piled up, and the speeches went on into the night, a person's life and dignity were proclaimed in the language of woven pandanus.

The village pastors had a big part to play in making sense of what had happened in the village. Their sermons stressed patience, love, and forgiveness in the face of adversity. Parables of Christian love were summoned; biblical quotes about forgiveness and forbearance were marshaled. The very speech forms adopted by the pastors modeled gentleness and harmony. The pastors spoke in the refined "good pronunciation," expected of them. But now their t's seemed especially delicate and proper, almost schoolmarmish.[4] Their talk was laden with words like *alofa* (compassion) and with the inclusive pronoun form *tatou* ("our"), as in "our village," "our chief," and "our love," as they worked to refocus attention on harmony rather than division. Many Samoans are highly skilled in this kind of linguistic manipulation of a difficult situation, having at their disposal an elaborate stock of conventional rhetorical devices by which they try to contain and transform a volatile or awkward emotional atmosphere.

FINDING A CAUSE

After the funeral, the village chiefs assembled inside a large meetinghouse to discuss the murder among themselves. The *fono* (meeting) was long and emotional. Every important political faction in the village would have its say. The meeting began and ended with elaborate speeches, ritually constrained oratory. But in between, the talk was looser, more highly charged, redolent with anger and recrimination. Strikingly, there was no talk about the individuals involved in the murder. The events of that tragic day had no explicit part to play in these talks, nor did any discussion of motives, feelings, or personal relationships. Instead, the chiefs spoke about the political structure of the village and its role in the murder. Where, it was asked, was the dignity of the high chiefs in this village that such a shocking thing as the murder of a senior chief could have come to pass? Where was the balance between the power of the orators *(tulāfale)*, who controlled this particular village, and that of the noble high chiefs *(ali'i)*, whose power here seemed strangely diminished? In this context, the murder began to take on new and unforeseen meanings, ones that an anthropologist would find of special interest.

The meeting ended with the decision to banish the murderer's father and his family from the village forever (which, it turned out, meant about six years). The young untitled men of the village would carry out the order, by destroying all the crops of the offending family and seeing to it that they left the village in good time. This was done not simply as an act of punishment, but to expeditiously remove the offending family from the village, and with them the motive for violent revenge.

The decision of the chiefs was announced outdoors, in public, at a *fono tauati,* a rare general assembly of a village. As a sign of its importance, this meeting took place outside, on the *malae* itself, rather than inside a meeting house. The *malae* became like the floor of a great house. And each house that encircled the village green became like one of the house posts that framed the meetinghouse and at which chiefs usually took up their stations. The village gathered, in its various sectors, one political group to each house. The chiefly representatives of each family stood outside their house shouting their speeches across the *malae*. In one house, representatives of Tuatō's political family sat, while the senior chief among them spoke on behalf of the family. Across the *malae,* in another house, the killer's uncle spoke on behalf of his family. The tone was suitably elevated. Each side honored the ranks and dignities of the other, and formal apologies were made for all to hear. Then, in lofty chiefly language, the senior orator of the village announced the banishment order. A collective shudder seemed to pulse through the crowd as the implications of the order became apparent.

MAKING MEANING IN THE FACE OF DEATH

As I argued in my 1982 monograph, there is no final meaning to be found in shocking events such as these. There is only the ceaseless flow of meaning making, as people use whatever resources they can summon to make sense of senseless acts. Periodically they stop up the flow, in a temporary holding action—we usually call it "an explanation."

My own act of meaning construction involved writing an ethnography—a conventional narrative genre by which anthropologists transform a skein of personalities and events into a coherent story. This account cast the events as a murder mystery and then recast this mystery as a cultural mystery, to be explained in terms of a combination of Samoan folk theories about human behavior and our own scientific theories about the work of culture. Like the others who found themselves caught up in the tragic events of a Samoan afternoon, I started telling stories almost as soon as I heard about the murder. Now, twenty-two years later, I am still caught up in this narrative, telling it yet again. But now it has taken on new meaning for me, as I have begun to understand the extent to which Samoans marshaled a wide variety of cultural models in their efforts to make sense of murder in high places.

In one sense, my Samoan friends and neighbors were fortunate in having a large stock of ready-made instituted models at their disposal. Like many aristocratic peoples, Samoans are formalists, masters of etiquette, with a rich tradition of ceremony, oratory and other cultural forms on which they can draw. When chaos threatens, as it did on that afternoon, Samoans are very skilled manipulators of their social environment, using their cultural forms in an effort to *teu*—to reign in—disorder and reorient themselves. Some of these models, such as the polite forms of oratory, the chiefly funeral with its mat exchanges, or the spatial schema which framed the choice of meeting sites, were more or less taken from everyday life and adapted to the crisis at hand. Other models—the ceremonial humiliation of the *ifoga,* or the outdoor meeting on the *malae*—I had never seen before. These were relatively rare institutions— special-purpose models—kept in reserve for occasions like this.

For individual Samoans, there were models that engaged their private feelings more directly. Elena's wailing comes to mind, an act in which intensely personal and highly conventional forms of grief came together. The same might be said for the narratives that made their way around the village and eventually through the islands, as people sought to construct a coherent account of the murder and its surrounding events. The stories were all personal fictions, made on the fly, but they were neither entirely personal nor completely fictional. Such storytelling necessarily exploits a limited range of conventional narrative models, even as it is experienced as a freewheeling account of what "really" happened. In this way, meaning construction is always at once a personal and conventional process.

As the Murngin Wawilak story reminds us, the making of a meaningful world engages a set of preexisting forms, but only in relation to a set of personal dispositions of a particular knower. The emergent world is a coming-into-knowledge of another world that already exists. This is the Murngin version of culture's twice-born character, the ceaseless flow of semiosis, inside-out and outside-in, linking culture in the world and culture in the mind.

TAKING CULTURAL DIVERSITY SERIOUSLY

Difference is at the heart of all anthropology, and so is the question of human nature. My first words to students in "Anthro 101" is that anthropology is the study of human nature *through* the study of human difference. To understand the *nature* of the human primate is, I think, to place that primate's extraordinary capacity for *historical and cultural variability* at the heart of any definition. Of course, this way of putting the matter produces a kind of essentialist-existentialist paradox. Generalizations about human nature emerge most powerfully and convincingly when they are in a dialogue with history and culture, two things that, at first glance, one might expect to undermine any viable conception of human nature. Yet the two perspectives—psychic unity and psychic diversity—are not, in fact, mutually exclusive.

In this book, I have tried to show how attention to cultural particulars, properly orchestrated, can contribute to a set of powerful generalizations about mind at the same time as they draw attention to the local character of specific mental representations. This approach is an ethnographic view of mind, in that it recognizes the profound degree to which cultural models are implicated in our mental life, *all the way in,* and in our social life, *all the way out.*

We hear much about the need to focus attention on cultural diversity these days. Multiculturalism has become something of an academic fad. Yet it is notable that so many of the voices from within anthropology that call for a greater attention to cultural difference in a curriculum are profoundly uncomfortable with taking the idea of difference really seriously *as a cognitive phenomenon* as well as in matters of history, social discourse, and politics. Back in Chapter 1, we explored some of the reasons for this discomfort, and why anthropologists have been reluctant to take cultural difference indoors, so to speak, as a constituting dimension of mind. Yet it is inconsistent with current thinking about either culture or about mind to ground a pluralist conception of culture in an essentialist conception of mind. Taking culture seriously as a dimension of mind is in no sense an impediment to a unified and scientifically robust understanding of brain and mind. A genuinely scientific general study of mind and brain can (indeed must) coexist fruitfully with an appreciation of historical and cultural consciousness.

To that end, this book has fused two quite different rhetorical traditions: an interpretive approach to culture, drawn from a humanistic tradition of scholarship, and a more generalizing, explanatory approach to mind, drawn from the positivistic tradition of experimental science. Though the voices of these two very different traditions are inevitably in some tension throughout this book, they are directed at a single coherent enterprise: making a credible case for culture in mind to psychologists and anthropologists alike. Indeed, to ignore the particulars of culture in the general study of mind is to refuse to take into account what is empirically obvious to any anthropologist: culture, as models, is as real as any other component of the mind.

This way of reconciling psychic unity and psychic diversity does not entail a reversion to the errors of psychic developmentalism—the primitive mentality fallacy—discussed at length in Chapters 7 and 8. To acknowledge and explore the multiple modalities of human thought and feeling that are common cognitive resources for all humans—and their openness to different orchestrations of mind in different cultural, historical, or social contexts—does not entail that we adopt any version of the primitive mentality myth. The ethnographic mind is not the primitive mind except in the very restricted sense that it reflects Geertz's fundamental insight: that the nervous system of modern humans evolved under the selective pressures of a hominid line increasingly given over to *cultural adaptations*. The ethnographic mind, at once dependent for its functioning on extrinsic models, and opportunistically creative in producing those models, is an essential feature of a culture-bearing and meaning-making primate.

CONCLUSION: TAKING THE BLACK BOX OUT OF DOORS

The ethnographic approach to mind is about culture's contribution to meaning construction. So it is as much a study of the human imagination as it is an account of the physical and ecological constraints on human understanding. It is fitting, therefore, that I should give over the final words of this book to a great champion of the life of the imagination, the poet Wallace Stevens. No writer in our century has better evoked the importance of meaning construction as a human vocation. Stevens's words have served as a blaze throughout this volume. They serve to, quite literally, re-mind us, to help us recall the mind's work in the ongoing construction of meaning.

In Stevens's vision, the human mind is to be found at the intersection of our general imaginative sensibilities and the particular odds and ends of the local worlds in which we happen to find ourselves. From this vantage point, we might observe that the mind is better evoked through the image of a blackbird than a black box. ✘

Thirteen Ways of Looking at a Blackbird
Wallace Stevens

I

Among twenty snowy mountains,
The only moving thing
Was the eye of a blackbird.

II

I was of three minds,
Like a tree
In which there are three blackbirds.

III

The blackbird whirled in the autumn winds.
It was a small part of the pantomime.

IV

A Man and a woman
Are one.
A man and a woman and a blackbird
Are one.

V

I do not know which to prefer,
The beauty of inflections
Or the beauty of innuendoes,
The blackbird whistling
Or just after.

VI

Icicles filled the long window
With barbaric glass.
The shadow of the blackbird
Crossed it, to and fro.
The mood
Traced in the shadow
An indecipherable cause.

VII

O thin men of Haddam,
Why do you imagine golden birds?
Do you not see how the blackbird
Walks around the feet
Of the women about you?

VIII

I know noble accents
And lucid, inescapable rhythms;
But I know, too, that the blackbird is involved
In what I know.

IX

When the blackbird flew out of sight,
It marked the edge
Of one of many circles.

X

At the sight of blackbirds
Flying in a green light,
Even the bawds of euphony
Would cry out sharply.

XI

He rode over Connecticut
In a glass coach.
Once, a fear pierced him.
In that he mistook
The shadow of his equipage
For blackbirds.

XII

The river is moving.
The blackbird must be flying.

XIIII

It was evening all afternoon.
It was snowing
And it was going to snow.
The blackbird sat
In the cedar-limbs.

Notes

1. Shore 1982, Chapter 1.

2. As in the original account, the orator title, Tuatō, is accurate, but the personal names of the chief and his wife have been changed.

3. See Chapter 12 for a discussion of this incident.

4. For more on these pronunciation styles see Chapters 11 and 12.

Bibliography

Abrahams, Roger D., and Richard Bauman
   1978   Ranges of Festival Behavior. In *The Reversible World: Symbolic Inversion in Art and Society,* pp. 193–208. Barbara A. Babcock, ed. Ithaca, NY: Cornell University Press.
Abu-Lughod, Lila
   1986   *Veiled Sentiments: Honor and Poetry in a Bedouin Society.* Berkeley, CA: University of California Press.
Allen, Louis A.
   1975   *Time Before Morning: Art and Myth of the Australian Aborigines.* New York: Crowell.
Anderson, Lawrence B.
   1966   *Module, Proportion, Symmetry, Rhythm, New York Module: Measure, Structure, Growth and Function,.* pp. 102–127. Gyorgy Kepes, ed. New York: George Braziller.
Angell, Roger
   1972   *The Summer Game.* New York: The Viking Press.
   1977   *Five Seasons.* New York: Simon & Schuster.
Armstrong, Robert P.
   1981   *The Powers of Presence: Conscious Myth and Affecting Presence.* Philadelphia: University of Pennsylvania Press.
Asad, Talal
   1983   Anthropological conceptions of religion: Reflections on Geertz. *Man* 18 (2):237–259.
Ashley, Kathleen, ed.
   1990   *Victor Turner and the Construction of Cultural Criticism.* Bloomington, IN: Indiana University Press.
Asinof, Eliot
   1963   *Eight Men Out.* New York: Holt, Rinehart and Winston.
Austin, John L.
   1962   *How to Do Things with Words.* Cambridge, MA: Harvard University Press.
Axelrod, Joseph, Joseph Kate, Mervin Friedman, Winslow Hatch and Nevitt Sanford
   1969   *Search for Relevance: The Campus in Crisis.* San Francisco: Jossey-Bass, Inc.

Babcock, Barbara A, ed.
   1978   *The Reversible World: Symbolic Inversion in Art and Society.* Ithaca, NY: Cornell
         University Press.
Bachnik, Jane M., and Charles J. Quinn, Jr., eds.
   1994   *Situated Meaning: Inside and Outside in Japanese Self, Society and Language.*
         Princeton, NJ: Princeton University Press.
Bakhtin, Mikhail
   1981   *The Dialogic Imagination.* Michael Holquist, trans. Austin, TX: University of
         Texas Press.
Bandura, Albert
   1974   Behavior theory and the models of man. *American Psychologist* 29:859–869.
Barsalou, Lawrence W.
   1987   The stability of graded structure: Implications for the nature of concepts. In *Con-
         cepts and Conceptual Development: Ecological and Intellectual Factors in Cat-
         egorization,* P.101–140. Ulrich Neisser, ed. Cambridge, England: Cambridge
         University Press.
Barth, Fredrik
   1975   *Ritual and Knowledge Among the Baktamen of New Guinea.* New Haven, CT:
         Yale University Press.
   1987   *Cosmologies in the Making: A Generative Approach to Cultural Variation in Inner
         New Guinea.* New York: Cambridge University Press.
Bartlett, F. C.
   1932   *Remembering.* Cambridge, England: Cambridge University Press.
Basso, Ellen B.
   1985   *A Musical View of the Universe.* Philadelphia: University of Pennsylvania Press.
Bateson, Gregory
   1955   A theory of play and fantasy. *Psychiatric Research Reports* 2:138–151.
   1972   *Steps to an Ecology of Mind.* Novato, CA: Chandler Publishing Company.
   1979   *Mind and Nature: A Necessary Unity.* New York: Dutton.
Bateson, Gregory, and Margaret Mead
   1942   *Balinese Character: A Photographic Analysis. Special Publications of the New
         York Academy of Science,* vol. 2. New York: New York Academy of Science.
Baudrillard, Jean
   1981   *Critique of the Political Economy of the Sign.* C. Levin, trans. St. Louis: Telos
         Press.
   1983   The implosion of meaning in the media. In *In the Shadow of the Silent Majorities,
         or the End of the Social.* New York: Semiotext(e).
   1988   *America.* Chris Turner, trans. London: Verso.
   1990   *Cool Memories.* Chris Turner, trans. New York: Verso.
Bechtel, William, and Adele Abrahamsen
   1991   *Connectionism and the Mind: An Introduction to Parallel Processing in Networks.*
         Cambridge, England: Blackwell.
Beck, Brenda E. F.
   1987   Metaphors, cognition and artificial intelligence. In *Cognition and Symbolic Struc-
         tures: The Psychology of Metaphoric Transformation,* pp. 9–30. Robert Has-
         kell, ed. Norwood, NJ: Ablex.
Benamou, Michel, and Charles Caramello
   1977   *Performance in Postmodern Culture.* Madison, WI: University of Wisconsin
         Press.
Benjamin, Walter
   1968   The work of art in the age of mechanical reproduction. In *Illuminations: Essays
         and Reflections,* pp. 217–252. Hannah Arendt, ed. New York: Schocken.

Benveniste, Emile
  1966.   *Problemes de Linguistique Générale.* Paris: Gallimard.
Berger, Peter, and Thomas Luckmann
  1966   *The Social Construction of Reality: A Treatise on the Sociology of Knowledge.*
          Garden City, NY: Doubleday.
Berlin, B., D. Breedlove, and P. H. Raven
  1966   Folk taxonomies and biological classification. *Science* 154:273–275.
  1973   General principles of classification and nomenclature in folk biology. *American
          Anthropologist* 75:214–242.
Berndt, Ronald M.
  1951   *Kunapipi: A Study of an Australian Anboriginal Fertility Cult.* Melbourne:
          Cheshire.
  1953   *Djanggawul: An Aboriginal Religious Cult of North-Eastern Arnhem Land.* New
          York: The Philosophical Society.
  1955   "Murngin" (Wulamba) social organisation. *American Anthropologist* 57(1): 84–
          106.
  1965   Marriage and family in northeastern Arnhem Land. In *Comparative Family Sys-
          tems.* M. F. Nimkoff, ed. Boston: Houghton Mifflin.
  1976   *Love Songs of Arnhem Land.* Chicago: University of Chicago Press.
Berndt, Ronald, and Catherine Berndt
  1970   *Man, Land and Myth in North Australia: The Gunwinggu People.* East Lansing,
          MI: Michigan State University Press.
Bettelheim, Bruno
  1976   *The Uses of Enchantment: The Meaning and Importance of Fairy Tales.* New
          York: Knopf.
Billow Richard, Jefferey Rossman, and Nona Lewis
  1987   Metaphoric communication and miscommunication in schizophrenic and border-
          line states. In *Cognition and Symbolic Structures:The Psychology of Metaphoric
          Transformation,* Robert Haskell, ed. Norwood, NJ: Ablex. pp 141–162.
Black, Max
  1962   Models and metaphors. In *Metaphor.* Ithaca, NY: Cornell University Press.
  1977   More about metaphor. *Dialectica.* 31(3–4):431–457.
Blair, John G.
  1988   *Modular America: Cross-Cultural Perspectives on the Emergence of an American
          Way.* New York: Greenwood Press.
Boas, Franz
  1887a A year among the Eskimo. *Bulletin of the American Geographical Society*
          19:383–402.
  1887b The occurrence of similar inventions in areas widely apart. *Science* 9:485–486.
  1897   *The Social Organization and Secret Societies of the Kwakiutl.* United States Na-
          tional Museum Report for 1895, pp. 311–738.
  1910a Psychological problems in anthropology. *American Journal of Psychology*
          21:371–384.
  1910b Kwakiutl Tales. *Columbia University Contributions to Anthropology,* vol. 2.
          New York: Columbia University Press.
  1911/1938   *The Mind of Primitive Man.* Rev. ed. New York: Free Press.
  1916   The origin of totemism. *American Anthropologist* 18.
  1930   The religion of the Kwakiutl Indian. *Columbia University Contributions to Anthro-
          pology,* vol. 10. New York: Columbia University Press.
  1938   An anthropologist's credo. *The Nation* 147:201–204.
  1966   *Kwakiutl Ethnography.* Helen Codere, ed. Chicago: University of Chicago
          Press.

Bolinger, Dwight
    1980   *The Melody of Language*. Baltimore: Johns Hopkins Press.
    1986   *Intonation and Its Parts: Melody in Spoken English*. Stanford, CA: Stanford University Press.
    1989   *Intonation and Its Uses*. Stanford, CA: Stanford University Press.
Boswell, Thomas
    1984   *Why Time Begins on Opening Day*. Garden City, NY: Doubleday.
Bourdieu, Pierre
    1977   *Outline of a Theory of Practice*. London: Cambridge University Press.
Bowen, Elenore
    1964   *Return to Laughter*. Garden City, NY: Doubleday
Brady, Ivan, ed.
    1976   *Transactions in Kinship: Adoption and Fosterage in Oceania*. Honolulu: University of Hawaii Press.
Briggs, Jean
    1966   *Never in Anger*. Cambridge, MA: Harvard University Press.
Brooks, Lee R.
    1987   Decentralized control of categorization: The role of prior processing episodes. In *Concepts and Conceptual Development: Ecological and Intellectual Factors in Categorization*, p. 141–147. Ulrich Neisser, ed. Cambridge, MA: Cambridge University Press.
Bruner, Jerome
    1990   *Acts of Meaning*. Cambridge, MA: Harvard University Press.
Burling, Robbins
    1969   Cognition and componential analysis: God's truth or hocus-pocus. In *Cognitive Anthropology*. Stephen A. Tyler, ed. p. 419–427. New York: Holt, Rinehart, and Winston.
Caillois, Roger
    1958   *Les Jeux et Les Hommes*. Paris: Gallimard.
Cain, Horst
    1971   The sacred child and the origin of spirits in Samoa. *Anthropos* 66:173–181.
Calhoun, Donald W.
    1987   *Sport, Culture, and Personality*. 2nd ed. Champaign, IL: Human Kinetics Publishers.
Candelaria, Cordelia
    1976   Baseball in American Literature: From Ritual to Fiction. Notre Dame, IN: Doctoral dissertation, University of Notre Dame.
Carmichael, Leonard
    1961   Absolutes, relativism and scientific psychology. In *Relativism and the Scientific Study of Man*. H. Schoek and J. Wiggens, eds. Princeton, NJ: Van Nostrand.
Carroll, Vern ed.
    1970   *Adoption in Eastern Oceania*. Honolulu: University of Hawaii Press.
Casson, Ronald
    1983   Schemata in cognitive anthropology. *Annual Review of Anthropology* 12:429–462.
Changeux, Jean-Pierre
    1983   Concluding remarks: On the "singularity" of nerve cells and its ontogenesis. In *Molecular Interactions Underlying Higher Brain Functions*. J. P. Changeux, ed. *Progress in Brain Research* 58:465–478.
    1986   *Neuronal Man*. New York: Oxford University Press.
Chomsky, Noam
    1957   *Syntactic Structures*. The Hague: Mouton.
    1959   Review of Skinner's *Verbal Behavior*. *Language* 35:26–58.

1965 *Aspects of the Theory of Syntax.* Cambridge, MA: MIT Press.

1968 *Language and Mind.* New York: Harcourt, Brace and World.

Churchland, Paul

1989 On the nature of explanation: A PDP approach. In *A Neurocomputational Perspective: The Nature of Mind and the Structure of Science.* P. M. Churchland, ed., Cambridge, MA: MIT Press/Bradford Books.

Coffin, Tristram P.

1971 *The Old Game: Baseball in Folklore and Fiction.* New York: Herder and Herder.

Colby, Benjamin N., James W. Fernandez, and David B. Kronenfield

1981 Toward a convergence of cognitive and symbolic anthropology. *Symbolism and Cognition.* Special Issue. *American Ethnologist* 8(3):422–450

Cole, Michael, and Silvia Scribner

1974 *Culture and Thought: A Psychological Introduction.* New York: Wiley.

Conklin, Harold

1955 Hanuóo color categories. *Southwestern Journal of Anthropology* 11(4):339–344.

1969 Lexicographical treatment of folk taxonomies. In *Cognitive Anthropology,* p. 41–59. Stephen A. Tyler, ed. New York: Holt, Rinehart and Winston.

Connerton, Paul

1989 *How Societies Remember.* Cambridge, England: Cambridge University Press.

Crapanzano, Vincent

1986 Hermes' dilemma: The masking of subversion in ethnographic description. In *Writing Culture: The Poetics and Politics of Ethnography.* James Clifford and George E. Marcus, eds. Berkeley and Los Angeles: University of California Press.

Crepeau, Richard

1980 *Baseball: America's Diamond Mind, 1919–1941.* Orlando, FL: University of Florida Press.

Crocker, Jon Christopher

1985 My brother the parrot. In *Animal Myths and Metaphors in South America,* pp. 13–47. Gary Urton, ed. Salt Lake City: University of Utah Press.

Crocker, Jon Christopher, and J. David Sapir (eds.)

1977 *The Social Uses of Metaphor.* Philadelphia: University of Pennsylvania Press.

Csicsery-Ronay, Istvan

1991 Cyberpunk and neuro-romanticism, in *Storming the Reality Sudio,* pp. 182–193. Larry McCaffery, ed. Durham, NC: Duke University Press.

Csordas, Thomas, ed.

1994a *Embodiment and Experience: The Existential Ground of Culture and Self.* New York: Cambridge University Press.

1994b *The Sacred Self: A Cultural Phenomenology of Charismatic Healing.* Berkeley: University of California Press.

Da Matta, Robert

1984 *Carnival in Multiple Planes: Rite, Drama, Festival, Spectacle: Rehearsals Toward a Theory of Cultural Performance.* John J. MacAloon, ed. Philadelphia: Institute for the Study of Human Issues (ISHI).

D'Andrade, Roy G.

1987a Cultural meaning systems, In *Culture Theory: Essays on Mind, Self, and Emotion,* pp. 88–119. Richard Shweder and Robert LeVine, eds. Cambridge; England: Cambridge University Press.

1987b A folk model of the mind. In *Cultural Models in Language and Thought.* Dorothy Holland and Naomi Quinn, eds. Cambridge; England: Cambridge University Press.

1990   Cultural cognition. In *Foundations of Cognitive Science,* pp. 795–830. Michael I. Posner, ed. Cambridge; MA: MIT Press.

1992   Schemas and motivation. In *Human Motives and Cultural Models,* pp. 23–44. Roy D'Andrade and Claudia Strauss, eds. Cambridge, England: Cambridge University Press.

1995   *The Development of Cognitive Anthropology.* New York: Combridge

D'Andrade, Roy G., and M. Egan

1974   The colors of emotion. *The American Ethnologist* 1:49–63.

D'Andrade, Roy G., and Claudia Strauss, eds.

1992   *Human Motives and Cultural Models.* Cambridge, England: Cambridge University Press.

Daniel, E. Valentine

1984   *Fluid Signs.* Berkeley, CA: University of California Press.

D'Aquili, Eugene, John McManus, and Charles Laughlin

1979   *The Spectrum of Ritual.* New York: Columbia University Press.

DeKleer, Johan, and John Seely Brown

1983   Assumptions and ambiguities in mechanistic mental models. In *Mental Models,* pp. 155–190. Dedre Gentner and Albert L. Stevens, eds. Hillsdale, NJ: Erlbaum.

Doi, Takeo

1974   *Amae:* A Key Concept for understanding Japanese personality structure. In *Culture and Personality: Contemporary Readings,* pp. 307–314. Robert Levine, ed. Chicago: Aldine.

Donald, Merlin

1991   *Origins of the Modern Mind: Three Stages in the Evolution of Culture and Cognition.* Cambridge: Harvard University Press.

Dougherty, Janet

1978   Salience and relativity in classification. *American Ethnologist* 5:66–80.

Douglas, Mary

1966   *Purity and Danger.* Baltimore: Penguin Books.

Dumont, Louis

1965   The individual in two kinds of society. *Contributions to Indian Sociology* 8:7–61.

1970   *Homo Hierarchicus.* Chicago: University of Chicago Press.

Duranti, Alessandro

1981   *The Samoan Fono: A Sociolinguistic Study.* Pacific Linguistics (Series B) 80. Canberra: Department of Linguistics, The Research School of Pacific Studies, Australian National University.

1994   *From Grammar to Politics: Linguistic Anthropology. In a Western Samoan Village.* Berkeley and Los Angeles: University of California Press

Durkheim, Émile

1915   *The Elementary Forms of the Religious Life.* Joseph Ward Swain, trans. London: Allen and Unwin.

1951   *Suicide: A Study in Sociology.* John A. Spaulding and George Simpson, trans. New York: Free Press

Durkheim, Émile, and Marcel Mauss

1963   *Primitive Classification.* Rodney Needham, ed. London: Cohen and West.

Edwards, Harry

1969   *The Revolt of the Black Athlete.* New York: Free Press.

1973   *The Sociology of Sport,* Homewood, IL: Dorsey Press.

Eliade, Mircea

1959   *The Sacred and the Profane: The Nature of Religion.* New York: Harcourt, Brace.

1965   *The Myth of the Eternal Return or Cosmos and History,* Rev. ed. Princeton, NJ:
       Princeton University Press.

Elkin, A. P.

1933–1934   Studies in Australian totemism: The nature of Australian totemism. *Oceania*
            4(2):113–131.

1950   The complexity of social organization in Arnhem Land. *The Southwestern Journal
       of Anthropology* 6(1):1–210.

Erikson, Erik H.

1977   *Toys and Reasons.* New York: Norton.

Errington, Shelly

1989   *Meaning and Power in a Southeast Asian Realm.* Princeton, NJ: Princeton Univer-
       sity Press.

Evans-Prichard, E. E.

1937   *Witchcraft, Oracles and Magic Among the Azande.* Oxford, England: Clarendon
       Press.

1940   *The Nuer.* Oxford, England: Clarendon Press.

Feinberg, Richard

1988   Margaret Mead and Samoa: *Coming of Age* in fact and fiction. *American Anthro-
       pologist* 90:656–663.

Feld, Steven

1982   *Sound and Sentiment: Birds, Weeping, Poetics and Song in Kaluli Expression.*
       Philadelphia: University of Pennsylvania Press.

Fernandez, James

1974   The mission of metaphor in expressive culture. *Current Anthropology* 15
       (2):119–145.

1990   Tolerance in a repugnant world and other dilemmas in the cultural relativism of
       Melville J. Herskovitz. *Ethos* 19(2):140–164.

Fernandez, James W., ed.

1991   *Beyond Metaphor: The Theory of Tropes in Anthropology.* Palo Alto, CA: Stan-
       ford University Press.

Fillmore, Charles

1982   Towards a descriptive framework for spatial deixis, in *Speech, Place and Action,*
       pp. 31–59. R. Jarvella and W. Klein, eds. London: Wiley.

Fine, Gary A.

1987   *With the Boys: Little League Baseball and Preadolescent Culture.* Chicago: Uni-
       versity of Chicago Press.

Finegan, Edward, and Niko Besnier

1989   *Language: Its Structure and Use.* San Diego, CA: Harcourt Brace Jovanovich.

Finney, Ben

1994   *A Voyage of Discovery: A Cultural Odyssey through Polynesia.* Berkeley and Los
       Angeles: University of California Press.

Fisher, Lawrence M.

1992   The Borland barbarian's new weapon. *New York Times,* July 27, section 3, pp.
       1, 6.

Fiske, Alan P.

1990   Relativity within Moose ("Mossi") culture: Four incommensurable models for so-
       cial relationships. *Ethos* 19(2): 140–164.

Flanigan, C. Clifford

1990   Liminality, carnival and social structure: The case of late medieval biblical drama.
       In *Victor Turner and the Construction of Cultural Criticism,* pp. 42–63. Kath-
       leen Ashley, ed. Bloomington, IN: Indiana University Press.

Fodor, Jerry A.
    1975   *The Language of Thought.* New York: Crowell.
    1983   *The Modularity of Mind: An Essay on Faculty Psychology.* Cambridge, MA:
           MIT Press.
Fodor, J. A., and Z. W. Pylyshyn
    1988   Connectionism and cognitive architecture: A critical analysis. *Cognition* 28:3–71.
Fortes, Meyer
    1969   *The Web of Kinship among the Tallensi; the Second Part of an Analysis of the
           Social Structure of a Trans-Volta Tribe.* Oosterhout, N.B., Netherlands: An-
           thropological Publications.
Fowler, Donald D.
    1972   *In a Sacred Manner We Live.* Barre, MA: Barre Publishing.
Frank, Lawrence
    1983   *Playing Hardball: The Dynamics of Baseball Folk Speech.* New York: Peter
           Lang.
Frazer, Sir. James
    1910   *Totemism and Exogamy.* Vol. 3. London: Macmillan.
    1935   *The Golden Bough: A Study in Magic and Religion,* 3rd ed. New York: Mac-
           millan.
Freeman, J. Derek
    1983   *Margaret Mead and Samoa: The Making and Unmaking of an Anthropological
           Myth.* Cambridge, MA: Harvard University Press.
Frege, Gottlob
    1892/1952   On sense and reference. In *Translations from the Philosophical Writings of
           Gottlob Frege.* P. Geach and M. Black, eds. Oxford, England: Blackwell.
Freud, Sigmund
    1950   *Totem and Taboo.* James Strachey, ed. New York: W.W. Norton.
Friedrich, Paul
    1979   *Language, Context and the Imagination.* Stanford, CA: Stanford University
           Press.
    1991   Polytropy. In *Beyond Metaphor: The Theory of Tropes in Anthropology,* pp 17–
           55. James W. Fernandez, ed. Stanford, CA Stanford University Press.
Frommer, Harvey
    1988   *Primitive Baseball: The First Quarter Century of the National Pastime.* New
           York: Atheneum.
Gadamer, Hans-Georg
    1975   The problem of historical consciousness. *Graduate Faculty Philosophy Journal*
           5(1):1–87.
Gardner, Howard
    1985   *The Mind's New Science: A History of the Cognitive Revolution.* New York: Ba-
           sic Books.
Gardner, P.
    1975   *Nice Guys Finish Last: Sports and American Life.* New York: Universe Books.
Garner, W. R.
    1978   Aspects of a stimulus: Features, dimensions, and configurations. In *Cognition and
           Categorization,* pp. 99–134. Eleanor Rosch and Barbara Lloyd, eds. Hillsdale,
           NJ: Erlbaum.
Garvey, Catherine
    1977   *Play.* Cambridge, MA: Harvard University Press.
Gaskell, George, and Robert Pearton
    1979   Aggression and sport. In *Sports, Games and Play: Social and Psychological View-
           points,* pp 263–296. Jeffrey H. Goldstein, ed. Hillsdale, NJ: Erlbaum.

Geertz, Clifford
    1965   Religion as a cultural system. In *Anthropological Approaches to the Study of Religion*. Michael Banton, ed. London: Tavistock.
    1973a *Interpretation of Cultures*. New York: Basic Books.
    1973b The growth of culture and the evolution of mind. In *Interpretation of Cultures*, pp. 55–86. New York: Basic Books.
    1973c Thick description: Toward an interpretive theory of culture. In *Interpretation of Cultures*, pp. 3–30. New York: Basic Books.
    1973d The impact of the concept of culture on the concept of man. In *Interpretation of Cultures*, pp. 33–54. New York: Basic Books.
    1973e Person, time and conduct in Bali. In *Interpretation of Cultures*, pp. 360–411. New York: Basic Books.
    1973f Deep play: Notes on a Balinese cockfight. In *Interpretation of Cultures*, pp. 412–454. New York: Basic Books.
    1980   *Negara: The Theatre State in Nineteenth-Century Bali*. Princeton, NJ: Princeton University Press.
    1984   From the native's point of view: On the nature of anthropological understanding. In *Culture Theory: Essays on Mind, Self, and Emotion*, pp. 123–136. Richard Shweder and Robert LeVine, eds. Cambridge, England: Cambridge University Press.
Gentner, Deidre
    1983   Structure-mapping: A theoretic framework for analogy. *Cognitive Science* 7:155–570.
    1989   The mechanisms of analogical learning. In *Similarity and Analogy in Reasoning and Learning*. S. Vosniadou and A. Ortony, eds. Cambridge, England: Cambridge University Press.
Gentner, D., and A. L. Stevens, eds.
    1983   *Mental Models*. Hillsdale, NJ: Erlbaum.
Gerber, Eleanor
    1985   Rage and obligation: Samoan emotions in conflict. In *Person, Self and Experience,* G. White and J. Kirkpatrick, eds. pp.121–167. Berkeley, CA: University of California Press.
Giamatti, A. Bartlett
    1977   The green fields of the mind. *Yale Alumni Magazine*. New Haven, CT: Yale University. November.
Gibbs, Raymond W.
    1987   What does it mean to say that a metaphor has been understood? In *Cognition and Symbolic Structures: The Psychology of Metaphoric Transformation*, pp. 31–48. Robert Haskell, ed. Norwood, NJ: Ablex.
Gibson, J. J.
    1966   *The Senses Considered as Conceptual Systems*. Boston: Houghton Mifflin.
Gibson, William
    1984   *Neuromancer*. London: Gollancz.
Gick, Mary L., and Keith J. Holyoak
    1983   Schema induction and analogical transfer. *Cognitive Psychology* 15:1–38.
Giddens, Anthony
    1976   *New Rules of the Sociological Method*. New York: Basic Books.
Gilson, Richard
    1970   *Samoa 1830–1900: The Politics of a Multicultural Community*. Melbourne: Oxford University Press.
Gitlin, Todd
    1980   *The Whole World Is Watching*. Berkeley, CA: University of California Press.

Gladwin, Thomas
    1970   *East is a Big Bird*. Cambridge, MA: Harvard University Press.
Gluckman, Max
    1954   *Rituals of Rebellion in Southeast Africa*. Manchester, England: Manchester University Press.
    1962   *The Ritual of Social Relations*. Manchester, England: Manchester University Press.
Gluckman, Max, and Mary Gluckman
    1983   On drama, and games, and athletic contests. In *Play, Games and Sports in Cultural Context*, pp. 191–209. Janet Harris and Roberta Park, eds: Champaign, IL: Human Kinetics Books.
Goffman, Erving
    1959   *The Presentation of Self in Everyday Life*. New York: Doubleday.
    1967   *Interaction Ritual: Essays on Face-to-Face Behavior*. New York: Doubleday/ Anchor.
Goldenweiser, A.
    1910   Totemism: An analytical study. *Journal of American Folklore* XXIII.
    1918   Form and content in totemism. *American Anthropologist* 20.
Goldman, Irving
    1970   *Ancient Polynesian Society*. Chicago: University of Chicago Press.
    1975   *The Mouth of Heaven: An Introduction to Kwakiutl Religious Thought*. New York: Wiley.
Goldstein, Jeffrey, ed.
    1979   *Sports, games and Play: Social and Psychological Viewpoints*. Hillside, NJ: Erlbaum.
Goodman, Richard
    1971   Some *Aitu* beliefs of modern Samoans. *Journal of the Polynesian Society* 80:463–479.
Goody, Jack
    1977   *The Domestication of the Savage Mind*. Cambridge, England: Cambridge University Press.
    1986   *Literacy in Traditional Societies*. Cambridge, England: Cambridge University Press.
Gordon, Peter H., ed.
    1987   *Diamonds Are Forever: Artists and Writers on Baseball*. San Francisco: Chronicle Books.
Gorer, Geoffrey
    1948/1964   *The American People: A Study in National Chaacter*. New York: Norton.
Goswami, Usha
    1992   *Analogical Reasoning in Children*. Hillsdale, NJ: Erlbaum.
Grice, Paul
    1989   *Studies in the Way of Words*. Cambridge, MA: Harvard University Press.
Grimes, Ronald L.
    1976   *Symbol and Conquest: Public Ritual and Drama in Santa Fe, New Mexico*. Ithaca, NY: Cornell University Press.
    1982   *Beginnings in Ritual Studies*. Washington, DC: University Press of America.
    1985   *Research in Ritual Studies: A Programmatic Essay and Bibliography*. Chicago: American Theological Library Association.
    1990   *Ritual Criticism: Case Studies in Its Practice, Essays on Its Theory*. Studies in Comparative Religion. Columbia, SC: University of South Carolina Press.
Gruneau, Richard
    1982   *Sport, Culture and the Modern State*. Toronto: University of Toronto Press.

Gulick, Walter B.
  1988 Reconnecting Geertz's middle world. *Soundings* 71 (1):113–153.
Guttman, Allen
  1978 *From Ritual to Record.* New York: Columbia University Press.
Haffner, Katie, and John Markoff
  1991 *Cyberpunk: Outlaws and hackers on the computer frontier.* New York: Simon & Schuster.
Hallowell, A. Irving
  1955 The self and its behavioral environment. In *Culture and Experience,* pp. 75–111. Philadelphia: University of Pennsylvania Press.
Handelman, Don, and Bruce Kapferer
  1980 Symbolic types, mediation and the transformation of ritual contexts: Sinhalese demons and Tewa clowns. *Semiotica* 30:41–77.
Hanks, William F.
  1990 *Referential Practice: Language and Lived Space Among the Maya.* Chicago: University of Chicago Press.
Hanson, F. Allan
  1975 *Meaning in Culture.* London: Routledge.
  1982 Female pollution in Polynesia. *Journal of the Polynesian Society* 91:335–381.
Harnad, Stevan, ed.
  1987 *Categorical Perception: The Groundwork of Cognition.* Cambridge, England: Cambridge University Press.
Harris, Janet C.
  1983 Sport and ritual: A macroscopic comparison of form. In *Play, Games and Sports in Cultural Contexts,* pp. 177–189. Janet C. Harris and Roberta J. Park, eds. Champaign, IL: Human Kinetics Books.
Harris, Janet C., and Roberta J. Park, eds.
  1983 *Play, Games and Sports in Cultural Contexts.* Champaign, IL: Human Kinetics Books.
Harris, Mark
  1984 *Bang the Drum Slowly.* Lincoln: University of Nebraska Press.
Hart, Marie
  1972 *Sport in the Socio-Cultural Process.* Dubuque, IA: William C. Brown.
Haskell, Robert E., ed.
  1987 *Cognition and Symbolic Structures: The Psychology of Metaphoric Transformation.* Norwood, NJ: Ablex.
Haskell, Robert E.
  1987a Giambattista Vico and the discovery of metaphoric cognition. In *Cognition and Symbolic Structures: The Psychology of Metaphoric Transformation,* pp. 67–82. Robert E. Haskell, ed. Norwood, NJ: Ablex.
  1987b Cognitive psychology and the problem of symbolic cognition. In *Cognition and Symbolic Structures: The Psychology of Metaphoric Transformation,* pp. 85–102. Robert E. Haskell, ed. Norwood, NJ: Ablex.
  1987c Structural metaphor and cognition. In *Cognition and Symbolic Structures: The Psychology of Metaphoric Transformation,* pp. 241–255. Robert E. Haskell, ed. Norwood, NJ: Ablex.
  1987d A phenomenology of metaphor: A praxis study into metaphor and its cognitive movement through semantic space. In *Cognition and Symbolic Structures: The Psychology of Metaphoric Transformation,* pp. 257–292. Robert E. Haskell, ed. Norwood, NJ: Ablex.
  1989 Analogical transforms: A cognitive theory of the origin and development of equivalence transformations. *Metaphor and Symbolic Activity* 4:247–277.

Hatch, Elvin
    1983   *Culture and Morality: The Relativity of Values in Anthropology.* New York: Co-
           lumbia University Press.
Havelock, E.
    1982   *The Literate Revolution in Greece and Its Cultural Consequences.* Princeton, NJ:
           Princeton University Press.
Haviland, John B.
    1992   Guugu Yimithirr cardinal directions. Unpublished paper delivered at the session
           "Studying Spatial Conceptualization Across Cultures." Annual Meeting of the
           American Anthropological Association, December 12, 1992.
Hearst, Eliot, and Michael Wierzbicki
    1979   Battle royal: Psychology and the chess player. In *Sports, Games and Play: Social
           and Psychological Viewpoints,* pp. 26–64. Jeffrey H. Goldstein, ed. Hillsdale,
           NJ: Erlbaum.
Heelas, Paul, and Andrew Lock, eds.
    1981   *Indigenous Psychologies: The Anthropology of the Self.* London: Academic Press.
Heidegger, Martin
    1962   *Being and Time.* New York: Harper & Row.
    1977   *The Question Concerning Technology and Other Essays.* William Lovitt, trans.
           New York: Harper & Row.
Heim, Michael
    1987   *Electric Language: A Philosophical Study of Word Processing.* New Haven, CT:
           Yale University Press.
Hernandez, Keith, and Mike, Bryan
    1994   *Pure Baseball.* New York: HarperCollins.
Herskovitz, Melville
    1972   *Cultural Relativism: Perspectives in Cultural Pluralism.* New York: Random
           House.
Herzfeld, Michael
    1987   *Anthropology Through the Looking Glass: Critical Ethnography in the Margins of
           Europe.* Cambridge, England: Cambridge University Press.
Hillary, Edmund
    1966   Summit. In *The Realm of Sport,* pp. 528–535. Herbert W. Wind, ed. New York:
           Simon & Schuster.
Hockett, Charles
    1960   The origin of speech. In *Human Communication: Language and Its Psychobiologi-
           cal Base,* pp. 5–12. San Francisco: Freeman.
Hoffman, Robert R., and Richard P. Honeck
    1987   Proverbs, pragmatics and the ecology of abstract categories. In *Cognition and
           Symbolic Structures: The Psychology of Metaphoric Transformation,* pp. 121–
           140. Robert E. Haskell, ed. Norwood, MA: Ablex.
Holland, Dorothy
    1992   How cultural systems become desire: A case study of American romance. *Human
           Motives and Cultural Models,* pp. 61–89. In R. D'Andrade and C. Strauss,
           eds. Cambridge, England: Cambridge University Press.
Holland, Dorothy , and Naomi Quinn, eds.
    1987   *Cultural Models in Language and Thought.* Cambridge, England: Cambridge Uni-
           versity Press.
Hollander, Zandor
    1967   *Baseball Lingo.* New York: Norton.
Holmes, Lowell, Gary Tallman, and Vernon Jantz
    1978   Samoan personality. *Journal of Psychological Anthropology* 1(4): 453–472.

Holyoak, Keith, and P. R. Thagard.
   1989   Analogical mapping by constraint satisfaction. *Cognitive Science* 13:295–355.
Honeck, Richard, Clare Kibler, and Michael J. Firment.
   1987   Figurative language and psychological views of categorization: Two ships in the night? In *Cognition and Symbolic Structures: The Psychology of Metaphoric Transformation.* Robert E. Haskell, ed. pp. 103–120. Norwood, NJ: Ablex.
Huff, Sarah
   1992   Virtual worlds: Redesigning our lives with new realities. *Creative Loafing* 18(7):15–21.
Huizinga, Johan
   1938   *Homo Ludens: A Study of the Play Element in Culture.* London: Temple Smith.
Hutchins, Edwin
   1983   Understanding Micronesian navigation. In *Mental Models,* pp. 191–226. Dedre Gentner and Albert Stevens, eds. Hillsdale, NJ: Erlbaum.
   1989   The technology of team navigation. *In Intellectual Teamwork: The Social and Technical Bases of Cooperative Work,* J. Galegher, R. Kraut, and C. Egedo, eds. Hillsdale, NJ: Erlbaum.
Hymes, Dell
   1975   Breakthrough into performance. In *Folklore: Performance and Communication.* Dan Ben-Amos and K. S. Goldstein, eds. The Hague: Mouton.
Jakobson, Roman
   1971   Quest for the essence of language. In *Selected Writings,* vol. II: *Word and Language,* pp. 345–359. The Hague: Mouton.
   1975   Shifters, verbal categories, and the Russian verb. In *Selected Writings of Roman Jacobson,* vol. 2, pp. 130–147. The Hague: Mouton.
Jakobson, Roman, and Morris Halle
   1956   *Fundamentals of Language.* The Hague: Mouton.
Jhally, Sut
   1987   *The Codes of Advertising: Fetishism and the Political Economy of Meaning in the Consumer Society.* London: Frances Pinter.
Jinkner-Lloyd, Amy
   1993   Heaven in a baseball field. *Creative Loafing,* June 26.
Johnson, A., O. Johnson, and M. Baksh
   1968   The colors of emotions in Machiguenga. *American Anthropologist* 88(3):674–681.
Johnson, Mark
   1987   *The Body in the Mind.* Chicago: University of Chicago Press.
Johnson-Laird, P. N.
   1983   *Mental Models: Towards a Cognitive Science of Language, Inference, and Conciousness.* Cambridge, MA: Harvard University Press.
   1990   Mental models. In *Foundations of Cognitive Science,* pp.469–500. Michael I. Posner, ed. Cambridge, MA: MIT Press.
Jonassen, David H., and Heinz Mandl
   1990   *Designing Hypermedia for Learning. NATO Advanced Science Institute Series,* vol. 67. Berlin: Springer-Verlag.
Kahn, Roger
   1957   Intellectuals and ballplayers. *American Scholar* 26(3):342–249.
Kapferer, Bruce
   1984   The ritual process and the problem of reflexivity in Sinhalese demon exorcisms. In *Rite, Drama, Festival, Spectacle: Rehearsals Toward a Theory of Cultural Performance,* pp. 179–213. John J. MacAloon, ed. Philadelphia: Institute for the Study of Human Issues (ISHI).

Karsten, Rafael
    1926   *The Civilisation of the South American Indians.* London: Kegan Paul.
Keane, M.
    1988   *Analogical Problem Solving.* Chichester, England: Ellis Horwood.
Kearney, Michael
    1984   *World View.* Novato, CA: Chandler and Sharp.
Keen, Ian
    1977   Ambiguity in Yolngu religious language. *Canberra Anthropology* 1:33–50.
    1978   *One Country, One Song.* Doctoral dissertation. Canberra: Department of Anthro-
                pology, Australian National University.
Keesing, Felix, and Marie Keesing
    1956   *Elite Communication in Samoa.* Stanford, CA: Stanford University Press.
Keesing, Roger .
    1987   Anthropology as interpretive quest. *Current Anthropology* 28(2):355–357.
Keil, Frank
    1987   Conceptual development and category structure. In *Concepts and Conceptual
                Development: Ecological and Intellectual Factors in Categorization,* pp.
                175–200. Ulrich Neisser, ed. Cambridge, England: Cambridge University
                Press.
Keil, Frank C., and Michael H. Kelly
    1987   Categorical perception: The groundwork of cognition. In *Developmental Changes
                in Category Structure,* pp. 491–510. Stevan Harnad, ed. Cambridge, England:
                Cambridge University Press.
Kelly, Raymond C.
    1977   *Etoro Social Structure: A Study in Structural Contradiction.* Ann Arbor, MI: Uni-
                versity of Michigan Press.
Kieffer, M.
    1974   *Color and Emotion: Synaesthesia in Tzutujil Mayan and Spanish.* Doctoral disser-
                tation. Irvine, CA: Department of Anthropology, University of California at
                Irvine.
Kluckhohn, Clyde
    1942   Myths and rituals: A general theory. *Harvard Theological Review* 35:45–79.
Knauft, Bruce
    1985   *Good Company and Violence: Sorcery and Social Action in a Lowland New
                Guinea Society.* Berkeley, CA: University of California Press.
Konner, Melvin
    1982   *The Tangled Wing: Biological Constraints on the Human Spirit.* New York: Holt,
                Rinehart and Winston.
Kosslyn, Steven
    1978   Imagery and internal representation. In *Cognition and Categorization.* E. and
                Lloyd, B. Rosch, eds. Hillsdale, NJ: Erlbaum.
    1980   *Image and Mind.* Cambridge, MA: Harvard University Press.
Kroker, Arthur, and David Cook
    1986   *The Postmodern Scene: Excremental Culture and Hyper-Aesthetics.* New York:
                St. Martin's Press.
Kuhn, Thomas
    1970   *The Structure of Scientific Revolutions.* 2nd ed. Chicago: University of Chicago
                Press.
La Pérouse, Jean-Francois Galaup de, comte
    1969   *Voyage and Adventure's of La Pérouse.* Julius S. Gassner, trans. Honolulu: Uni-
                versity of Hawaii Press.

Lakoff, George
    1987a *Women, Fire and Dangerous Things: What Categories Tell Us About the Mind.*
            Chicago: University of Chicago Press.
    1987b Cognitive models and prototype theory. In *Concepts and Conceptual Develop-*
            ment: Ecological and Intellectual Factors in Categorization, pp.63–100. Ulrich
            Neisser, ed. Emory Cognition Project Symposium No. 1. Cambridge, England:
            Cambridge University Press.

Lakoff, George, and Mark Johnson
    1980 *Metaphors We Live By.* Chicago: University of Chicago Press.

Laney, Al
    1966 The mystery of Wimbledon. In *The Realm of Sport,* pp. 605–611. Herbert W.
            Wind, ed. New York: Simon & Schuster.

Langacker, Ronald W.
    1987 *Foundations of Cognitive Grammar.* Stanford, CA: Stanford University Press.

Langer, Susanne
    1957 *Philosophy in a New Key.* 3rd ed. Cambridge, MA: Harvard University Press.
    1967 *Mind: An Essay on Human Feeling.* 2 vols. Baltimore: Johns Hopkins University
            Press.

Larkin, Fanaafi Ma'ia'i
    1972 Review of the second edition of Mead's *The Social Organization of Manu'a. Jour-*
            nal of Pacific History 7:219–222.

Laughlin, Charles, John McManus, and Eugene D'Aquili
    1990 *Brain, Symbol & Experience: Towards a Neurophenomenology of Human Con-*
            sciousness. New York: Columbia University Press.

Lave, Jean
    1990 The culture of acquisition and the practice of understanding. In *Cultural Psychol-*
            ogy: The Chicago Symposia on Culture and Development, pp. 309–327. J.
            Stigler, R. Shweder, and G. Herdt, eds. New York: Cambridge University
            Press.

Lawrence, Peter
    1964 *Road Belong Cargo: A Study of the Cargo Movement in the Southern Madang*
            District, New Guinea. Manchester, England: Manchester University Press.

Leach, Edmund R.
    1968 Ritual. *International Encyclopedia of the Social Sciences.* New York: Macmillan.

Leder, Drew
    1990 *The Absent Body.* Chicago: University of Chicago Press.

Lee, Dorothy
    1959 Lineal and non-lineal codings of reality. In *Culture and Freedom.* Englewood
            Cliffs, NJ: Prentice-Hall.

Lemert, Edwin
    1972 Forms and pathology of drinking in three Polynesian societies. In *Human Devi-*
            ance, Social Problems and Social Control. Edwin Lemert, ed. Englewood
            Cliffs, NJ: Prentice-Hall.

LeRoy Ladurie, Emmanuel
    1979 *Carnival in Romans.* Mary Feeney, trans. New York: Braziller.

Levinson, Richard
    1993 Studying Spatial Conceptualization Across Cultures: The Cognitive Science Back-
            ground. Unpublished ms. Delivered at the Meetings of the American Anthropo-
            logical Association, December 1992.

Levi-Strauss, Claude .
    1963 *Totemism.* Rodney Needham, trans. Boston: Beacon Press.

1966 *The Savage Mind.* Chicago: University of Chicago Press.

1967a *Structural Anthropology.* New York: Doubleday/Anchor.

1967b Do dual organizations exist. In *Structural Anthropology.* New York: Doubleday/ Anchor.

1967c The effectiveness of symbols. In *Structural Anthropology.* New York: Double-day/Anchor.

1967d The sorcerer and his magic. In *Structural Anthropology.* New York: Doubleday/ Anchor.

1969 *The Elementary Structures of Kinship.* Boston: Beacon Press.

1979 *Myth and Meaning.* New York: Schocken Books.

1982 *The Way of the Masks.* Sylvania Modelsky, trans. Seattle, WA: University of Washington Press.

Levy, Robert I.

1970 Tahitian adoption as a psychological message. In *Adoption in Eastern Oceania,* Vern Carroll, ed. Honolulu: University of Hawaii Press.

1973 *Tahitians: Mind and Experience in the Society Islands.* Chicago: University of Chicago Press.

1984 Emotion, knowing, and culture. In *Culture Theory: Essays on Mind, Self, and Emotion,* pp. 214–237. Richard Shweder and Robert LeVine, eds. Cambridge, England: Cambridge University Press.

Lévy-Bruhl, Lucien

1926 *How Natives Think.* New York: Knopf.

1975 *The Notebooks on Primitive Mentality.* Peter Riviere, trans. Oxford: Blackwell.

Lewis, David

1972 *We the Navigators.* Honolulu: University of Hawaii Press.

Lewkowicz, D. J., and G. Turkewitz

1980 Cross-modal equivalence in early infancy: Auditory-visual intensity matching. *Developmental Psychology* 16(6):597–607.

Lipsky, Richard

1983 Toward a political theory of American sports symbolism. In *Play, Games and Sports in Cultural Contexts,* pp. 79–92. Janet C. and Roberta J. Park Harris, eds. Pp. 79–92. Champaign, IL: Human Kinetics Books.

Littleton, C. Scott

1985 Lucien Levy-Bruhl and the concept of cognitive relativity. In *How Natives Think,* pp. v-xlvii. Princeton, NJ: Princeton University Press.

Lotman, Yuri

1990 *Universe of the Mind: A Semiotic Theory of Culture,* Ann Shukman, trans. Bloomington, IN: University of Indiana Press.

Lounesbury, Floyd

1964 The structural anlaysis of kinship semantics. In *Proceedings of the Ninth Annual Congress of Linguists,* pp. 1073–1090. Horace B. Lunt, ed. The Hague: Mouton.

Lowe, Benjamin

1977 *The Beauty of Sport.* Englewood Cliffs, NJ: Prentice-Hall.

Luhrmann, Tanya

1989 *Persuasions of the Witch's Craft: Ritual Magic in Contemporary England.* Cambridge, England: Harvard University Press.

Lutz, Catherine

1988 *Unnatural Emotions: Everyday Sentiments on a Micronesian Atoll and their Challenge to Western Theory.* Chicago: University of Chicago Press.

Lutz, C. and L. Abu-Lughod, eds.
   1990   *Language and the Politics of Emotion.* Cambridge, England: Cambridge Univer-
          sity Press.
MacAloon, John J.
   1984   Olympic Games and the theory of spectacle in modern society. In *Rite, Drama,
          Festival Spectacle: Rehearsals Toward a Theory of Cultural Performance,* pp.
          241–280. J. MacAloon, ed. Philadelphia: Institute for the Study of Human
          Issues (ISHI).
MacAloon, John J., ed.
   1984   *Rite, Drama, Festival Spectacle: Rehearsals Toward a Theory of Cultural Perfor-
          mance.* Philadelphia: Institute for the Study of Human Issues (ISHI).
Mageo, Jeanette M.
   1991   Samoan moral discourse and the *Loto. American Anthropologist* 93(2):405–420.
   1995   Validating and reversing hierarchies: The cultural function of spirits in Samoa. In
          Pacific Spirits in Culture and in Mind. A. Howard and J. Mageo, eds., New
          York: Routledge.
Malinowski, Bronislaw
   1954   *Magic, Science and Religion, and Other Essays.* Garden City, NY: Doubleday.
Mander, Jerry
   1978   *Four Arguments for the Elimination of Television.* New York: Quill.
Mangler, Jean, ed.
   1984   *Stories, Scripts and Scenes: Aspects of Schema Theory.* Hillsdale, NJ: Erlbaum.
Marcus, George
   1989   Chieftainship. In *Developments in Polynesian Ethnology,* pp. 175–211. A. How-
          ard and R. Borofsky, eds. Honolulu: University of Hawaii Press.
Markoff, John
   1992   Though illegal, copied software is now common. *New York Times* CXLI(49040),
          July 27, p. 1.
Marks, Lawrence E., and Marc H. Bornstein
   1987   Sensory similarities: Classes, characteristics, and cognitive consequences. In *Cog-
          nition and Symbolic Structures: The Psychology of Metaphoric Transformation,*
          pp. 49–65. Robert Haskell, ed. Norwood, NJ: Ablex.
Marks, Lawrence, R. J. Hammeal, and M. Bornstein
   1987   *Perceiving Similarity and Comprehending Metaphor. Monographs for the Society
          for Research in Child Development.* v. 52(1), Serial no. 215.
Marr, David
   1982   *Vision: A Computational Investigation in the Human Representation of Visual In-
          formation.* San Francisco: Freeman.
Mays, Terry, Tony Anderson, and Mike Kibby
   1990   Learning about learning from text. In *Designing Hypermedia for Learning.* David
          Jonassen and Heinz Mandl, eds. NATO Advanced Science Institute Series 67.
          Berlin: Springer-Verlag.
McCauley, Robert N.
   1986   Intertheoretic relations and the future of psychology. *Philosophy of Science*
          53:179–199.
McCulloch, W., and W. S. Pitts
   1943   A logical calculus of the ideas imminent in nervous capacity. *Bulletin of Mathe-
          matical Biophysics* 5:115–133.
McKnight, C. , A. Dillon, and J. Richardson, eds.
   1991   *Hypertext in Context.* Cambridge, England: Cambridge University Press.

McLennan, John F.
   1869–1870   The worship of animals and plants. *Fortnightly Review* 6–7:407–427; 194–216.
McPhee, Colin
   1966   *Music in Bali: A Study in Form and Instrumental Organization in Balinese Orchestral Music.* New Haven, CT: Yale University Press.
Mead, Margaret
   1928   *The Coming of Age in Samoa.* New York: Morrow.
   1930   *The Social Organization of Manu'a. Bulletin of the Bernice P. Bishop Museum* 76. Honolulu: Bishop Museum Press.
   1968   The Samoans. In *Peoples and Cultures of the Pacific,* pp. 244–273. Andrew Vayda, ed. New York: Natural History Press.
Medin, Douglas, and Lawrence Barsalou
   1987   Categorization processes and categorical perception. In *Categorical Perception: The Groundwork of Cognition,* pp. 455–490. Stevan Harnad, ed. Cambridge, England: Cambridge University Press.
Medin, Douglas, and M. Schaffer
   1978   A context theory of classification learning. *Psychological Review* 85:207–238.
Medin, Douglas, and William D. Wattinmaker
   1987   Category cohesiveness, theories, and cognitive archeology. In *Concepts and Conceptual Development: Intellectual Factors in Categorization,* pp. 25–62. Ulrich Neisser, ed. Cambridge, England: Cambridge University Press.
Meleisea, Malama
   1987   *The Making of Modern Samoa: Traditional Authority and Colonial Administration in the Modern History of Western Samoa.* Suva, Fiji: Institute of Pacific Studies of the University of the South Pacific.
Merton Robert
   1976   *Sociological Ambivalence.* New York: Free Press.
Mervis, Carolyn B.
   1987   Child-basic object categories and early lexical development. In *Concepts and Conceptual Development: Intellectual Factors in Categorization,* pp. 201–233. Ulrich Neisser, ed. Cambridge, England: Cambridge University Press.
Mindell, David A.
   1989   Dealing with a digital world. *Byte* 14(8), August: 246–256.
Minsky, Marvin, and Seymour Papert
   1969   *Perceptrons.* Cambridge, MA: MIT Press.
Mischel, Walter
   1968   *Personality and Assessment.* New York: Wiley.
Moffatt, Michael
   1989   *Coming of Age in New Jersey: College and American Culture.* New Brunswick, NJ: Rutgers University Press.
Mooney, James
   1890/1983   The Cherokee play ball. In *Play, Games and Sports in Cultural Contexts,* pp. 259–282. Janet C. Harris and Roberta J. Park, eds. Champaign, Il: Human Kinetics Books.
Morgan, Sophia
   1984   Borges's "Immortal": Metaritual, metaliterature, metaperformance. In *Rite, Drama, Festival Spectacle: Rehearsals Toward a Theory of Cultural Performance,* pp. 79–101. J. MacAloon, ed. Philadelphia: Institute for the Study of Human Issues (ISHI).

Morphy, Howard
  1978 Rights in paintings and rights in women: A consideration of some of the basic problems posed by the asymmetry of the "Murngin system." *Mankind* 11:208–219.
  1991 *Ancestral Connections: Art and an Aboriginal System of Knowledge.* Chicago: University of Chicago Press.
Morrison, Kevin
  n.d. Triple Play: Three Perspectives on the Game. Unpublished ms.
Morrison, Philip
  1966 Module, proportion, symmetry, rhythm. In *The Modularity of Knowing,* pp. 1–19. Gyogry Kepes, ed. New York: Brazilier.
Munn, Nancy
  1966 Visual categories: An approach to the study of representational systems. *American Anthropologist* 68:936–950.
  1969 The effectiveness of symbols in Murngin myth and rite. In *Forms of Symbolic Action.* Robert Spencer, ed. Seattle, WA: University of Washington Press.
  1973 *Walbiri Iconography.* Ithaca, NY: Cornell University Press.
Murray, David
  1977 Ritual communication: Some considerations regarding meaning in Navajo ceremonials. In *Symbolic Anthropology: A Reader in the Study of Symbols and Meanings,* pp. 195–220. Janet Dolgin, David Kemnitzer, and David M. Schneider, eds. New York: Columbia University Press.
Nadel L., L., Cooper, P. Culicover, and R. M. Harnish
  1989 *Neural Connections, Mental Computation.* Cambridge, MA: MIT Press/Bradford Books.
Nakane, Chie
  1970 *Japanese Society.* Berkeley, CA: University of California Press.
Neisser, Ulrich
  1976 *Cognition and Reality: Principles and Implications of Cognitive Psychology.* San Francisco: Freeman.
  1983 Toward a skillful psychology. In *The Acquisition of Symbolic Skills.* D. R. Rogers and J. A. Sloboda, eds., New York: Plenum Press.
Neisser, Ulrich, ed
  1987 *Concepts and Conceptual Development: Ecological and Intellectual Factors in Categorization.* Emory Symposia in Cognition, vol. 1. Cambridge, England: Cambridge University Press.
Newport, Elissa, and Ursula Bellugi
  1978 Linguistic expression of category levels in a visual-gestural language: A flower is a flower is a flower. In *Cognition and Categorization,* pp. 49–71. E. Rosch and B. Lloyd, eds. Hillsdale, NJ: Erlbaum.
Norman, Donald A.
  1988 *The Psychology of Everyday Things.* New York: Basic Books.
Novack, Michael .
  1976 *The Joy of Sports: End Zones, Bases, Baskets, Balls, and the Consecration of the American Spirit.* New York: Basic Books.
Nuckolls, Charles W.
  1993 Sibling myths in a South Asian fishing village: A case study in sociological ambivalence. In *Siblings in South Asia,* pp. 191–217. C. W. Nuckolls, ed. New York: Guilford.

Nuckolls, Janice
    1992   Sound symbolic involvement. *Journal of Linguistic Anthropology* 2(1):51–80.
    1996   *Sounds Like Life: Sound-Symbolic Grammar, Performance, and Cognition in Pas-
            taza Quechua*. New York: Oxford University Press.
O'Keefe, J.
    1991   The hippocampal cognitive map and navigational strategies. In *Brain and Space*,
            pp. 38–76. J. Paillard, ed. Oxford, England: Oxford University Press.
Obeyesekere, Gananath
    1981   *Medusa's Hair: An Essay on Personal Symbols and Religious Experience*. Chi-
            cago: University of Chicago Press.
    1990   *The Work of Culture*. Chicago: University of Chicago Press.
Ochs, Elinor
    1986   *Culture and Language Acquisition: Acquiring Communication Competence in a
            Western Samoan Village*. Cambridge, England: Cambridge University Press.
    1988   *Culture and Language Development: Language Acquisition and Language De-
            velopment in a Samoan Village*. Cambridge, England: Cambridge University
            Press.
Ochs, Elinor, and Bambi Schieffelin, eds.
    1979   *Developmental Pragmatics*. New York: Academic Press.
Ochs, Elinor, and Bambi Scieffelin
    1984   Language acquisition and socialization: Three developmental stories and their im-
            plications. In *Culture Theory: Culture and Its Acquisition*. R. Shweder and R.
            LeVine, eds. Chicago: University of Chicago Press.
Oh, Sadaharu, and David Falkner
    1984   *Sadaharu Oh: The Zen Way of Baseball*. New York: New York Times Books.
Olsen, Jack
    1969   *The Black Athlete: A Shameful Story*. Boston: Little Brown.
Ong, Walter J.
    1967   *The Presence of the Word: Some Prolegomena for Cultural and Religious History*.
            New Haven, CT: Yale University Press.
    1971   *Rhetoric, Romance and Technology: Studies in the Interaction of Expression and
            Culture*. Ithaca, NY: Cornell University Press.
    1977   *Interfaces of the Word: Studies in the Evolution of Consciousness*. Ithaca: Cornell
            University Press.
    1982   *Orality and Literacy: The Technologizing of the Word*. London: Methuen.
Ortony, Andrew ed.
    1979   *Metaphor and Thought*. Cambridge, England: Cambridge University Press.
Ortner, Sherry
    1981   Gender and sexuality in hierarchical societies. In *Sexual Meanings: The Cultural
            Construction of Gender and Sexuality*. Sherry Ortner and Harriet Whitehead,
            eds. Cambridge, England: Cambridge University Press.
Paillard, J., ed.
    1991   *Brain and Space*. Oxford, England: Oxford University Press.
Passingham, Richard E.
    1982   *The Human Primate*. Oxford, England: Freeman.
Paul, Robert A.
    1977   The first speech events: "Genesis" as the nursery for the consciousness. *Psychocul-
            tural Review*, Spring, pp. 179–194.
Peirce, Charles S.
    1932   *The Collected Papers of Charles S. Peirce*. Cambridge, MA: Harvard University
            Press.

Pepper, Stephen C.
 1942 *World Hypotheses: A Study in Evidence.* Berkeley, CA: University of California Press.
Piaget, Jean
 1932 *The Development of Moral Reasoning in Children.* M. Gabain, ed. New York: Free Press.
 1962 *Play, Dreams and Imitation.* New York: Norton.
Piaget, Jean, J. Montanegro and J. Billeter
 1971 *Biology and Knowledge.* Chicago: University of Chicago Press.
 1977 Les correlats. In *L'Abstraction Réfléchissante.* J. Piaget, ed. Paris: Presses Universitaires de France.
Plato
 1961 *Plato: The Collected Dialogues.* Edith Hamilton and Huntington Cairns, eds. Princeton, NJ: Princeton University Press.
Polanyi, Michael
 1966 *The Tacit Dimension.* New York: Doubleday.
 1969 *Knowing and Being.* London: Routledge.
Polanyi, Michael, and Harry Prosch
 1975 *Meaning.* Chicago: University of Chicago Press.
Pylyshyn, Zenon
 1973 What the mind's eye tells the mind's brain: A critique of mental imagery. *Psychological Bulletin* 80:1–24.
 1981 The imagery debate: Analogue media versus tacit knowledge. In *Imagery.* N. Block, ed. Cambridge, MA: MIT Press.
Quinn, Naomi
 1987 Convergent evidence for a cultural model of American marriage. In D. Holland and N. Quinn, eds. *Cultural Models in Language and Thought.* pp. 173–192. Cambridge, England: Cambridge University Press.
 1991 The cultural basis of metaphor. In *Beyond Metaphor: The Theory of Tropes in Anthropology,* pp. 56–93. James W. Fernandez, ed. Palo Alto, CA: Stanford University Press.
 1992 The motivational force of self-understanding: Evidence from wives' conflicts. In *Human Motives and Cultural Models,* pp. 90–126. R. D'Andrade and Claudia Strauss, eds. Cambridge, England: Cambridge University Press.
Quinn, Naomi, and Dorothy Holland
 1987 Culture and cognition. In *Cultural Models in Language and Thought,* pp. 3–401. Dorothy Holland and Naomi Quinn, eds. Cambridge, England: Cambridge University Press.
Radcliffe-Brown, A. A.
 1951 Murngin social organization. *American Anthropologist* 53(1):37–55.
Radin, Paul
 1927 *Primitive Man as a Philosopher.* New York: Appleton.
Rappaport, Roy
 1968 *Pigs for the Ancestors.* New Haven, CT: Yale University Press.
 1979 *Ecology, Meaning, and Religion.* Berkeley, CA: North Atlantic Press.
Reichard, Gladys
 1974 *Navaho Symbolism: A Study in Meaning.* Princeton, NJ: Princeton University Press.
Reichel-Dolmatoff, Gerardo
 1971 *Amazonian Cosmos: The Sexual and Religious Symbolism of the Tukano Indians.* Chicago: University of Chicago Press.

Reisman, David, Joseph Gussfield, and Zelda Gamson
    1970 *American Values and Mass Education*. Garden City, New York: Doubleday.
Reiss, Steven
    1980 *Touching Base: Professional Baseball and American Culture in the Progressive Era*. Contributions in American Studies 48. Westport, CT: Greenwood Press.
Ricoeur, Paul
    1971/1979 The model of the text: Meaningful action considered as text. In *Interpretive Social Science: A Reader*. pp. 73–101. Paul Rabinow, and William M. Sullivan, eds. Berkeley and Los Angeles: University of California Press.
Ritchie, James, and Jean Ritchie
    1989 Socialization and character development. In *Developments in Polynesian Ethnology*. pp. 95–136. Alan Howard and Robert Borofsky, eds. Honolulu: University of Hawaii Press.
Rivers, William H. R.
    1916/1926a *Psychology and Ethnology*. New York: Harcourt, Brace.
    1916/1926b Sociology and psychology. In *Psychology and Ethnology*, pp. 3–20. New York: Harcourt, Brace.
Rogoff, Barbara
    1990 *Apprenticeship in Thinking: Cognitive Development in Social Context*. Oxford, England: Oxford University Press.
Rogoff, Barbara, and Jean Lave, eds.
    1984 *Everyday Cognition: Its Development in Social Contexts*. Cambridge, MA: Harvard University Press.
Rogoff, Barbara, and J. V. Wertsch, eds.
    1984 *Childrens Learning in the "Zone of Proximal Development."* San Francisco: Jossey Bass.
Roheim, Geza
    1945 *The Eternal Ones of the Dream: A Psychoanalytic Interpretation of Australian Myth and Ritual*. New York: International Universities Press.
    1988 *Children of the Desert*. University of Sydney: Oceania Publications.
Rosaldo, Michelle
    1984 Toward an anthropology of self and feeling. In *Culture Theory: Essays on Mind, Self, and Emotion*, pp. 137–156. Richard Shweder and Roy D'Andrade, eds. Cambridge, England: Cambridge University Press.
Rosaldo, Renato
    1980 *Ilongot Headhunting 1993–1974: A Study in Society and History*. Palo Alto, CA: Stanford University Press.
Rosch, Eleanor
    1978 Fundamental aspects of cognitive representations. *In Cognition and Categorization*. Eleanor Rosch and Carolyn Mervis, eds. Hillsdale, NJ: Erlbaum.
Rosch, Eleanor, and Barbara Lloyd, eds.
    1978 *Cognition and Categorization*. Hillsdale, NJ: Erlbaum.
Rosch, Eleanor, and Carolyn B. Mervis
    1975 Family resemblances: Studies in the internal structure of categories. *Cognitive Psychology* 7:573–605.
Rosch, Eleanor, C. Mervis, and W. D. Johnson
    1976 Basic objects in natural categories. *Cognitive Psychology* 8:382–439.
Roseberry, William
    1982 Balinese cockfights and the seduction of anthropology. *Social Research* 49:1013–1028.

Rosenblatt, Frank
  1958 The perceptron: a probabilistic model for information storage and organization in the brain. *Psychological Review* 65:368–408.
Rosenzweig, Mark R., David Krech, Edward L. Bennet, and James F. Zolman
  1962 Effects of environmental complexity and training on brain chemistry and anatomy: A replication and extension. *Journal of Comparative and Physiological Psychology* 55:429–437.
  1972 Brain changes in response to experience. *Scientific American,* March, 22–29.
Rozin, Paul, and Carol Nemeroff
  1989 The laws of sympathetic magic: A psychological analysis of similarity and contagion. In *Cultural Psychology: Essays on Comparative Human Development,* pp. 205–232. J. W. Stigler, R. A. Shweder, and G. Herdt, eds. Cambridge, England: Cambridge University Press.
Rumelhart, David
  1990 The architecture of mind: A connectionist approach. In *Foundations of Cognitive Science,* pp. 133–160. Michael Posner, ed. Cambridge, MA: MIT Press.
Rumelhart, David, and Adele A. Abrahamsen
  1973 A model for analogical reasoning. *Cognitive Psychology* 5:1–28.
Rumelhart, David E., McClelland, J. L., and the PDP Research Group
  1986 *Parallel Distributed Processing: Explorations in the Microstructure of Cognition,* vol. 1: *Foundations.* Cambridge, MA: MIT Press/Bradford Books.
Sahlins, Marshall D.
  1963 Poor man, rich man, big man, chief: Political types in Melanesia and Polynesia. *Comparative Studies in History and Society* 5:285–303.
  1976 *Culture and Practical Reason.* Chicago: University of Chicago Press.
  1983 Other times, other customs: The anthropology of history. *American Anthropologist* 85(3):517–544.
Sahlins, Marshall D., Elman Service, and Thomas Harding
  1960 *Evolution and Culture.* Ann Arbor, MI: University of Michigan Press.
Salter, Michael A.
  1983 Meteorological play forms in the eastern woodlands. In *Play, Games and Sports in Cultural Contexts,* pp. 211–223. Janet. C. Harris and Roberta J. Park, eds. Champaign, IL: Human Kinetics Books.
Sapir, Edward
  1921/1949 Language. In *Culture, Language and Personality: Selected Essays,* pp. 1–44. David Mandelbaum, ed. Berkeley and Los Angeles: University of California Press.
  1949 The psychological reality of phonemes. In *Culture, Language and Personality: Selected Essays,* pp. 46–60. David Mandelbaum, ed. Berkeley and Los Angeles: University of California Press.
Saussure, Ferdinand de
  1959 *A Course in General Linguistics.* Charles Bally and Albert Sechehaye, eds. Wade Baskin, trans. New York: Philosophical Library.
  1967 *Cours de linguistique générale,* critical ed. Rudolph Engler, ed. Wiesbaden: Otto Harrassowitz.
Schank, Roger C.
  1991 *The Connoisseur's Guide to the Mind.* New York: Summit Books.
Schank, Roger C., and Robert P. Abelson
  1977 *Scripts, Plans, Goals and Understanding.* Hillsdale, NJ: Erlbaum.
Schechner, Richard
  1977 *Essays on Performance Theory.* New York: Drama Book Specialistis.

1978   Anthropological analysis. *Drama Review* 22(3):23–32.

1985   *Between Theatre and Anthropology*. Philadelphia: University of Pennsylvania Press.

Schechner, Richard, Willa Appel, and Victor Turner

1990   *By Means of Performance: Intercultural Studies of Theatre and Ritual*. New York: Cambridge University Press.

Schieffelin, Bambi

1990   *The Give and Take of Everyday Life*. Cambridge, England: Cambridge University Press.

Schieffelin, Bambi, and Elinor Ochs, eds.

1986   *Language Socialization Across Cultures*. Cambridge, England: Cambridge University Press.

Schieffelin, Edward

1976   *The Sorrow of the Lonely and the Burning of the Dancers*. New York: St. Martins Press.

Schneider, David M.

1968   *American Kinship: A Cultural Account*. Englewood-Cliffs, NJ: Prentice-Hall.

1969a   Componential analysis:A state of the art review. Paper presented at the Wenner-Gren Symposium on Cognitive Studies and Artificial Intelligence Research. University of Chicago Center for Continuing Education.

1969b   American kin terms and terms for kinsmen: A critique of Goodenough's componential analysis of yankee kinship terminology. In *Cognitive Anthropology,* pp. 288–310. Stephen A. Tyler, ed., New York: Holt, Rinehart, and Winston.

Schneiderman, B., and G. Kearsley

1989   *Hypertext Hands-On: An Introduction to a New Way of Organizing and Accessing Information*. Reading, MA: Addison-Wesley.

Schoeffel, Penelope

1978   Gender, status and power in Samoa. *Canberra Anthropology* 1(2):69–81.

Schustak, M., and J. R. Anderson

1979   Effects of analogy to prior knowledge on memory for new information. *Journal of Verbal Learning and Verbal Behavior* 18:565–583.

Scribner, Sylvia, and Michael Cole

1974   *Culture and Thought: An Introduction*. New York: Wiley.

Segal, M, D. Campbell, and M. Herskovitz

1966   *The Influence of Culture on Visual Perception*. Indianopolis, IN: Bobbs-Merrill.

Segal, Robert

1988   Interpreting and explaining religion: Geertz and Durkheim. *Soundings* 71(1):29–52.

Shankman, Paul

1984   The thick and the thin: On the interpretive theoretical program of Clifford Geertz. *Current Anthropology* 25:261–279.

Shapiro, Warren

1968   The exchange of sister' daughters' daughters in northeast Arnhem Land. *South Western Journal of Anthropology* 24:346–353.

1969   Semi-moiety organization and mother-in-law bestowal in northeastern Arnhem Land. *Man* 4:629–640.

1981   *Miwuyt Marriage: The Cultural Anthropology of Affinity in Northeast Arnhem Land*. Philadelphia: Institute for the Study of Human Issues, (ISHI).

Sherry, D.F., and D.L. Schacter

1987   The evolution of multiple memory systems. *Psychological Review* 94:439–454.

Shore, Bradd

1976a   Adoption, alliance and political mobility in Samoa, in *Transactions in Kinship:*

Adoption and Fosterage in Oceania. Ivan Brady, ed. Honolulu: University of Hawaii Press.

1976b Incest prohibitions, and the logic of power in Samoa. *Journal of the Polynesian Society* 85(2):275–296.

1977 *A Samoan Theory of Action: Social Control and Social Order in a Polynesian Paradox.* Disserlation Department of Anthropology, University of Chicago.

1978 Ghosts and government: A structural analysis of alternative institutions for conflict management in Samoa. *Man* ns 13:175–599.

1981 Sexuality and gender in Samoa: Conceptions and missed conceptions. In *Sexual Meanings,* pp.192–215. S. Ortner and H. Whitehead, eds. Cambridge, England: Cambridge University Press.

1982 *Sala'ilua: A Samoan Mystery.* New York: Columbia University Press.

1987 Is language a prisonhouse. *Cultural Anthropology* 2(1):115–536.

1988a An introduction to the work of Clifford Geertz. *Soundings* 71(1):15–27.

1988b Interpretation under fire. *Anthropological Quarterly* 68(4).

1989 Mana and tapu. In *Developments in Polynesian Ethnology,* pp. 137–173. A. Howard and R. Borofsky, eds. Honolulu: University Press of Hawaii.

1990a Human ambivalence and the structuring of moral values. *Ethos* 18(3):165–579.

1990b Twice-born, once conceived: Meaning construction and cultural cognition. *American Anthropologist* 94(4):10–27.

1995 The absurd side of power in Samoa. In *Changing Leadership in the Pacific: Essays in Honour of Sir Raymond Firth.* R. Feinberg and K. Watson-Gegeo, eds. London: LSE Press.

Shustak, M. and J. R. Anderson

1979 Effects on analogy to prior knowledge on memory for new information. *Journal of Verbal Learning and Verbal Behavior* 18:565–583.

Shweder, Richard A.

1984 Anthropology's romantic rebellion against the enlightenment, or there's more to thinking than reason and evidence. In *Culture Theory: Essays on Mind, Self, and Emotion,* pp. 28–66. Richard Shweder and Robert LeVine, eds. Cambridge: England Cambridge University Press.

1989 Cultural psychology: What is it? In *Cultural Psychology: The Chicago Symposia on Culture and Development,* pp. 1–46. J. Stigler, R. Shweder, and G. Herdt, eds. New York: Cambridge University Press.

Shweder, Richard, and Robert Levine, eds.

1984 *Culture Theory: Essays on Mind, Self, and Emotion.* Cambridge, England: Cambridge University Press.

Silverstein, Michael

1976 Shifters, verbal categories and verbal description. In *Meaning in Anthropology,* pp. 11–57. K. Basso and H. Selby, eds. Alburqueque, NM: The School for American Research.

Sinavaiana, Caroline

1992 Where the spirits laugh last: Comic theater in Samoa. In *Clowning as Critical Practice,* pp. 192–219. William E. Mitchell, ed. Pittsburgh: University of Pittsburgh Press.

Slusher, Howard.

1967 *Man, Sport and Existence: A Critical Analysis.* Philadelphia: Lea & Febiger.

Smith, Edward E.

1990 Concepts and induction. In *Foundations of Cognitive Science,* pp. 501–526. Michael Posner, ed. Cambridge, MA: MIT Press.

Smith, Edward E., and Douglas L. Medin

1981 *Categories and Concepts.* Cambridge, MA: Harvard University Press.

Smith, G. Elliott
    1926   *Dr. Rivers and the New Vision in Psychology and Ethnology.* New York: Harcourt, Brace.
Smith, Jonathan Z.
    1972   I am a parrot [red]. *History of Religions* 2(4):391–413.
Smoke, K. L.
    1932   An objective study of concept formation. *Psychological Monographs* 42(191).
Smolensky, P.
    1987   The constituent structure of connectionist mental states: A reply to Fodor and Pylyshyn. *Southern Journal of Philosophy, Supplement,* 26:137–161.
    1988   On the proper treatment of connectionism. *Behavioral and Brain Sciences* 11:1–74.
Spalding, Albert
    1911   *America's National Game.* New York: American Sports Publishing Company.
Spelke, E.
    1976   Infants' intermodal perception of events. *Cognitive Psychology* 8:553–560.
Spencer, Herbert
    1890   *The Principles of Sociology.* New York: Appleton.
Sperber, Dan
    1975   *Rethinking Symbolism.* Alice Morton, trans.. Cambridge, England: Cambridge University Press.
    1985   *On Anthropological Knowledge: Three Essays.* Cambridge, England: Cambridge University Press.
Spradley, James P., ed.
    1972   *Culture and Cognition: Rules, Maps and Plans.* Prospect Heights, IL: Waveland Press.
Stanner, W. E. H.
    1966   *On Aboriginal Religion.* Oceania Monograph No. 11. Sydney: Oceania Publications.
    1976   Some aspects of aboriginal religion. *Colloqiium* 9(1):19–35.
Sternberg, R. J.
    1977   Component processes in analogical reasoning. *Psychological Review* 84:353–378.
Stevenson, Robert Louis
    1892   *A Footnote to History.* New York and London: Cassells.
Stocking, George W.
    1960   Franz Boas and the founding of The American Anthropological Association. *American Anthropologist* 62:1–17.
    1968   *Race, Culture and Evolution: Essays in the History of Anthropology.* New York: Free Press.
    1974   *The Shaping of American Anthropology, 1883–1911: A Franz Boas Reader.* New York: Basic Books.
Stoeltje, Beverly
    1978   Cultural frames and reflections: Ritual, drama, spectacle. *Current Anthropology* 19:450–460.
Stoller, Paul
    1989   *The Taste of Ethnographic Things: The Senses in Anthropology.* Philadelphia: University of Pennsylvania Press.
Strauss, Claudia
    1992   Models and motives. In *Human Motives and Cultural Models,* pp. 1–20. R. D'Andrade and Claudia Strauss, eds. Cambridge, England: Cambridge University Press.

Strauss, Claudia, and Naomi Quinn
   1994   A cognitive/cultural anthropology. In *Assessing Cultural Anthropology*, pp. 284–
          300. R. Borofsky, ed. New York: McGraw, Hill.
Sweetser, Eve E.
   1987   The definition of a lie: An examination of the folk models underlying a semantic
          prototype. In *Cultural Models in Language and Thought*, pp. 43–66. D. Hol-
          land and N. Quinn, eds. Cambridge, England: Cambridge University Press.
Talmy, Leonard
   1978   Figure and ground in complex sentences. In *Universals of Human Language*, Vol.
          4. pp. 625–654. J. Greenberg, Charles Ferguson, and Edith Moravcsik, eds.
          Stanford, CA: Stanford University Press.
   1983   How language structures space. In *Spatial Orientation: Theory, Research and Ap-
          plications*, pp. 225–282. H. L. Pick and L. P. Acredolo, eds., New York:
          Plenum Press.
Tambiah, Stanley J.
   1969   Animals are good to think and good to prohibit. *Ethnology* 8(4):423–459.
Taylor, Charles
   1971/1979   Interpretation and the sciences of man. In *Interpretive Social Science: A
          Reader*, pp. 25–71. Paul Rabinow, and William M. Sullivan, eds. Berkeley,
          CA: University of California Press.
Thorn, J., P. Palmer, and D. Reuther
   1984   *The Hidden Game of Baseball: A Revolutionary Approach to Baseball and Its
          Statistics*. New York: Doublerday.
Tolman, E. C.
   1948   Cognitive maps in rats and men. *Psychological Review* 55:189–208.
Torgovnik, Marianna
   1990   *Gone Primitive: Savage Intellects, Modern Lives*. Chicago: University of Chi-
          cago Press.
Truebetzkoy, N. S.
   1969   *Phonology*. Berkeley, CA: University of California Press.
Turner, Frederick
   1990   "Hyperion to a Satyr": Criticism and anti-structure in the work of Victor Turner.
          In *Victor Turner and the Construction of Cultural Criticism*, pp. 147–162.
          Kathleen M. Ashley, ed. Bloomington, IN: Indiana University Press.
Turner, Terence
   1991   "We are parrots, "Twins Are Birds": Play of tropes as operational structure. In
          Beyond Metaphor: The Theory of Tropes in Anthropology, pp. 121–158. James
          W. Fernandez, ed. Palo Alto: Stanford University Press.
Turner, Victor
   1957   *Schism and Continuity in an African Society: A Study of Ndembu Village Life*.
          Manchester, England: Manchester University Press.
   1967a   Ritual symbolism, morality and social structure among the Ndembu. In *The For-
          est of Symbols*. pp. 48–58. Ithaca, NY: Cornell University Press.
   1967b   *The Forest of Symbols*. Ithaca, NY: Cornell University Press.
   1969   *The Ritual Process*. Ithaca, NY: Cornell University Press.
   1974   *Dramas, Fields and Metaphors: Symbolic Action in Human Society*. Ithaca, NY:
          Cornell University Press.
   1972/1983   Passages, margins and poverty: Religious symbols of communitas. In *Play,
          Games and Sports in Cultural Contexts*. pp. 326–359. Janet C. Harris and Ro-
          berta J. Park, eds. Champaign, IL: Human Kinetics Books.
   1983.   Liminal to liminoid in play, flow, and ritual: An essay in comparative symbology.

In *Play, Games and Sports in Cultural Contexts,* pp. 123–164. Janet C. Harris and Roberta J. Park, eds. Champaign, IL: Human Kinetics Books.

1984   Liminality and the performative genres. In *Rite, Drama, Festival, Spectacle Rehearsals Toward a Theory of Cultural Performance,* pp. 19–41. John J. MacAloon, ed. Philadelphia: Institute for the Study of Human Issues (ISHI).

Turner, Victor, and Richard Schechner

1986   *The Anthropology of Performance.* New York: PAJ Publications.

Tversky, Amos

1977   Features of similarity. *Psychological Review* 84:327–352.

Tversky, Amos, and I. Gati

1978   Studies of similarity. In *Cognition and Categorization,* pp. 79–98. Eleanor Rosch and Barbara Lloyd, eds. Hillsdale, NJ: Erlbaum.

Twitchell, James B.

1992   *Carnival Culture: The Trashing of Taste in America.* New York: Columbia University Press.

Tyler, Stephen A., ed.

1969   *Cognitive Anthropology.* New York: Holt, Rinehart and Winston

Ullman, Stephen

1957   *The Principles of Semantics.* Oxford, England: Basil Blackwell.

Urton, Gary, ed.

1985   *Animal Myths in South America.* Salt Lake City: University of Utah Press.

Valeri, Valerio

1985   *Kingship and Sacrifice: Ritual and Society in Ancient Hawaii.* Chicago: University of Chicago Press.

Van Baaren, Th. P.

1969   Are the Bororo parrots or are we? In *Liber Anicorum: Studies in Honor of Dr. C. J. Bleeker.* Leiden: E. J. Brill

Van Gennap, Arnold

1920   *L'État Actuelle Du Probleme Totemique.* Paris.

Voigt, David Q.

1974   Reflections on diamonds: American baseball and American culture. *Journal of Sports History* 1:3–25.

1976   *America Through Baseball.* Chicago: Nelson Hall.

1983   Myths after baseball: Notes on myths on sports. In *Play, Games and Sports in Cultural Contexts,* pp. 93–106. Janet C. and Roberta J. Park Harris, eds. Champaign, IL: Human Kinetics Books. Pp. 93–106.

Von den Steinen, Karl

1894   *Unter den Natürvolkern Zentral-Brasiliens.* Berlin: Verlagsbuchlandlub Dieter Reimer.

Vosnaidu, S., and A. Ortony, eds.

1989   *Similarity and Analogy in Reasoning and Learning.* Cambridge, England: Cambridge University Press.

Vygotsky, Lev Semenovich

1962   *Thought and Language.* Eugenia Hanfmann and Gertrude Vakar, eds. Cambridge, MA: MIT Press.

1978   *Mind in Society: The Development of Higher Psychological Processes.* Cambridge, MA: Harvard University Press.

1987   *The Collected Works of L. S. Vygotsky* L. Mimick, trans. New York: Plenum Press.

Wagner, Roy

1975   *The Invention of Culture.* Chicago: University of Chicago Press.

Walens, Stanley
    1981   *Feasting With Cannibals.* Princeton, NJ: Princeton University Press.
Wallace, Anthony F. C.
    1969   The problem of the psychological validity of componential analysis. In *Cognitive Anthropology,* pp. 396–418. Stephen A. Tyler, ed., New York: Holt, Rinehart and Winston.
Walters, Ronald G.
    1980   Signs of the times: Clifford Geertz and historians. *Social Research* 47(3):537–556.
Warner, W. Lloyd
    1936/1958   *A Black Civilization.* New York: Harper & Row.
Webb, T. T.
    1933   Tribal organization in eastern Arnhem Land. *Oceania* 3(4):406–417.
Weiss, Paul
    1969   *Sport: A Philosophic Inquiry.* Carbondale, IL: Southern Illinois University Press.
Wendt, Albert
    1983   Three Faces of Samoa: Mead's, Freeman's, and Wendt's. *Pacific Islands Monthly,* April, pp. 10–14.
Werner, Heinz, and Bernard Kaplan
    1963   *Symbol Formation.* New York: Wiley.
Wertsch, James V.
    1978   Adult-child interaction and the roots of metacognition. *Quarterly Newsletter of the Institute for Comparative Human Development,* 2:15–58.
    1985   *Vygotsky and the Social Formation of Mind.* Cambridge, MA: Harvard University Press.
Wertz, S. K.
    1981   The varieties of cheating. *Journel of the Philosophy of Sport* 8:19–40.
White, Geoffrey and John Kirkpatrick, eds.
    1985   *Person, Self and Experience: Exploring Pacific Ethnopsychologies.* Berkeley, CA: University of California Press.
Whiting, Robert
    1977   *The Chrysanthemum and the Bat: Baseball Samurai Style.* New York: Dodd, Mead.
Whorf, Benjamin L.
    1956   *Language, Thought and Reality.* John B. Carroll, ed. Cambridge, MA: MIT Press.
Wikan, Unni
    1991   *Managing Turbulent Hearts.* Chicago: University of Chicago Press.
Wilden, Anthony
    1972   *System and Structure.* London: Tavistock.
Williams, Nancy
    1986   *The Yolngu and Their Land: A System of Land Tenure and Its Fight for Recognition.* Dissertation. Canberra: Australian Institute of Aboriginal Studies.
    1987   *The Yolngu and Their Land.* Stanford, CA: Stanford University Press.
Wilson, Bryan, ed.
    1970   *Rationality.* Oxford, England: Blackwell.
Winner, Ellen, D. Cicchetti, and H. Gardner
    1981   "Metaphorical" mapping in human infants. *Child Development* 52:728–731.
Winston, P. H.
    1980   Learning and reasoning by analogy. *Communications of the ACM* 23:689–703.
Zadeh, Lofti
    1965   Fuzzy sets. *Information and Control* 8:338–353.

Name Index

Abelson, Robert, 43, 52
Abrahamsen, Adele, 346, 348, 349
Abu-Lughod, Lila, 55
Anderson, Lawrence, 130
Angell, Roger, 78–79
Aristotle, 175
Armstrong, Robert Plant, 362, 363
Austin, John L., 199
Axelrod, Joseph, 129

Bandura, Albert, 162n. 13
Barth, Fredrik, 209, 248, 345
Bartlett, F. C., 45, 326
Bastian, Adolph, 20
Bateson, Gregory, 36, 90–91, 111, 114,
    236, 321, 372n. 5, 373n. 11
Baudrillard, Jean, 118, 131, 148, 150, 154,
    155, 161n. 11, 163n. 21
Bechtel, William, 346, 348, 349
Beck, Brenda, 362
Benedict, Ruth, 10, 36, 45, 306n. 3
Benjamin, Walter, 154, 157
Benko, Paul, 113–14
Benveniste, Emile, 331, 360
Berndt, Ronald, 213, 232nn. 2, 7, 8, 233n.
    19, 234n. 25, 239
Black, Max, 191, 341n. 14
Blair, John, 126, 131, 132
Blumenthal, Michael, 87
Boas, Franz, 19–22, 24, 26, 29, 32, 34, 51,
    189, 194, 203n. 1
Bolinger, Dwight, 359, 373n. 11

Bornstein, Mark H., 357, 358, 359
Boswell, Tom, 80, 81
Bourdieu, Pierre, 105, 106, 266
Brooks, Lee R., 355
Brown, John Seely, 323, 324
Bruner, Jerome, 58, 71n. 19, 324
Budge, Don, 112–13, 287
Burke, Kenneth, 112

Caen, Herb, 78
Caillois, Roger, 105, 114
Carmichael, Leonard, 303
Cartwright, Alexander J., Jr., 97–98n. 7
Chadwick, Henry, 80
Changeux, Jean-Pierre, 16–17, 38
Chomsky, Noam, 136–37, 138, 161n. 2,
    259, 321, 346
Churchland, Paul, 319, 326
Conklin, Harold, 54
Connerton, Paul, 48, 258, 326, 327
Cook, David, 124
Cramm, Gottfried von, 112–13
Crick, Francis, 130
Csicsery-Ronay, Istivan, 159

D'Andrade, Roy, 45, 57, 319
Darwin, Charles, 18, 173, 184
De Kleer, Johan, 323, 324
DiMaggio, Joe, 85
Donald, Merlin, 258, 320
Donham, Donald, 51
Doubleday, Abner, 80, 97n. 7

Drysdale, Don, 114
Dumont, Louis, 133
Dunlop, Ian, 261*n*. 3
Durkheim, Émile, 24, 25, 26, 35, 50, 51,
    110, 169, 170, 172, 173, 174, 175,
    178–81, 189, 203*n*. 3, 222

Eliade, Mircea, 104, 105, 228
Eliot, Charles William, 126–27
Erikson, Erik H., 92
Evans-Prichard, E. E., 63, 169

Fillmore, Charles, 335
Finney, Ben, 279
Fodor, Jerry, 130, 151
Foucault, Michel, 8, 161*n*. 2
Frake, Charles, 54
Frazer, James, 168
Freeman, Derek, 281, 289, 293, 294, 295,
    300, 301, 302, 306*n*. 5
Frege, Gottlob, 317, 328
Freud, Sigmund, 168, 302
Friedrich, Paul, 314

Gallego, Mike, 102
Gardner, Howard, 10
Garner, W. R., 356
Garvey, Catherine, 92
Geertz, Clifford, 8, 32–35, 36, 38, 50–51,
    52, 54, 75, 285, 340*n*. 1, 380
Gentner, Deidre, 352, 356
Gerber, Eleanor, 302
Gibson, William, 161*n*. 9, 181–82
Gick, Mary L., 353, 354
Gilson, Richard, 292–93
Gitlin, Todd, 124
Goffman, Erving, 52, 103, 112, 132, 149
Goldenweiser, A., 172, 186*n*. 9
Goldman, Irving, 190, 196, 197, 199, 293
Goodenough, Ward, 34, 50, 51, 54
Gorer, Geoffrey, 124, 131, 132
Gorman, Lou, 102, 103
Goswami, Usha, 352
Graves, Abner, 80
Green, Roger, 272
Guttman, Allen, 84

Haddon, Alfred C., 22
Hall, Donald, 78
Halle, Morris, 137
Hallowell, A. Irving, 61

Hanks, William F., 58
Hanson, F. Allan, 234*n*. 25
Haskell, Robert, 325–26, 365
Havelock, E., 140
Hegel, Georg, 228
Heidegger, Martin, 143–44, 146, 157, 160–
    61, 163*n*. 22
Heim, Michael, 143, 153
Henderson, Allan, 163*n*. 20
Henderson, Robert, 97*n*. 7
Hernandez, Keith, 77
Herskovitz, Melville, 286
Herzfeld, Michael, 283*n*. 3
Hinkle, Lon, 103, 106
Hobbes, Thomas, 321
Hockett, Charles, 130, 140
Holmes, Lowell, 300
Holyoak, Keith J., 353, 354
Honeck, Richard, 362
Horton, Robert, 36
Huizinga, Johan, 99*n*.24, 104
Husserl, Edmund, 157
Hutchins, Edwin, 279
Hutchins, Robert M., 127

Itobe, Inazo, 99*n*.23

Jackson, Michael, 159
Jakobson, Roman, 58, 137, 138, 331
Jhally, Sut, 41*n*. 9
Johnson, Mark, 53, 59, 101, 265, 274, 277,
    317, 332–34, 339, 340*n*. 9, 361, 362,
    363
Johnson-Laird, P. N., 64, 69*n*. 10, 70*n*. 15,
    331, 337

Kahn, Roger, 78
Kant, Immanuel, 19, 44, 174
Kaplan, Bernard, 199, 201, 360, 362, 365,
    371, 373*n*. 10
Kapor, Mitchell D., 155
Kearney, Michael, 70*n*. 14
Keen, Ian, 211, 213, 224, 231*n*. 2, 233*n*.
    10, 234*nn*. 24, 25, 238, 239
Keesing, Felix, 289
Keesing, Marie, 289
Kosslyn, Steven, 336–37
Kroker, Arthur, 124

Lacan, Jacques, 161*n*. 2
Lakoff, George, 53, 58, 59, 69*n*. 11, 101,

265, 274, 277, 317, 322, 324, 332–34, 335, 339, 340nn. 3, 9, 341nn. 15, 17, 342n. 19, 361, 362, 363, 365
Landis, Kennesaw Mountain, 100n. 28
Langacker, Ronald W., 58
Langer, Susanne, 57, 138, 172, 201, 316, 332
La Pérouse, comte de, 267–68
Lawrence, Peter, 369
Leary, Timothy, 161n. 10
Leibnitz, Gottfried, 321
Lemert, Edwin, 300
Levi-Strauss, Claude, 29–32, 34, 54, 65, 89–90, 91, 99n. 24, 137, 169, 170, 171, 172, 173, 174, 175, 176, 177, 178–79, 180, 181, 183, 185–86n. 8, 186n. 12, 187n. 15, 188, 192, 201, 203nn. 1, 7, 204n. 12, 254, 259, 273, 274, 302, 330
Levy, Robert I., 63, 69n. 2, 290, 340n. 1
Lévy-Bruhl, Lucien, 24, 26–29, 31–32, 35, 168, 170, 175, 178, 181, 183, 202, 313, 314, 321, 325, 360–61
Lewis, David, 279
Linnaeus, Carl, 173
Lipsky, Richard, 104
Lloyd, Barbara, 335, 355
Lorenz, Konrad, 88
Lotman, Yuri, 267, 283n. 4, 332, 341n. 14
Lounesbury, Floyd, 54
Lutz, Catherine, 55

Mageo, Jeanette M., 301, 302, 307n. 13
Malinowski, Bronislaw, 168
Mander, Jerry, 125–26, 148
Markoff, John, 154
Marks, Lawrence E., 357, 358, 359
Marr, David, 276
Marx, Karl, 41n. 9
Mary, queen of England, 112–13
Mauss, Marcel, 24, 25, 26, 169, 170, 172, 174, 260
McCauley, Robert, 70n. 12, 343
McCulloch, W., 346
McDougall, William, 22, 23
Mead, George Herbert, 149
Mead, Margaret, 36, 236, 281, 282, 289, 293, 295, 299–300, 301, 306n. 5
Merton, Robert, 285
Meyers, Charles, 22
Mills, Abraham, 80

Mindell, David, 152
Minsky, Marvin, 346
Mischel, Walter, 162n. 13
Moffat, Michael, 127
Morgan, Lewis Henry, 18
Morphy, Howard, 210, 213, 228, 230, 231, 233n. 20, 234nn. 25, 26, 238, 247, 261n. 7
Morrison, Kevin, 93–96
Morrison, Philip, 130
Munn, Nancy, 233nn. 16, 17, 21, 247, 257–58

Neisser, Ulric, 70n. 12
Nemeroff, Carol, 204n. 13
Novak, Michael, 84

Obeyesekere, Gananath, 36, 49
Ochs, Elinor, 237
Ong, Walter, 131, 140, 153
Oppenheimer, Joel, 77

Papert, Seymour, 346
Parsons, Talcott, 32
Peirce, Charles S., 59, 117, 199, 361, 362
Piaget, Jean, 36, 45, 92, 114, 115, 352, 362, 367, 368
Pitts, W. S., 346
Plato, 44, 317, 326, 327, 340n. 8
Polanyi, Michael, 362
Posner, Michael, 336
Pylyshyn, Zenon, 337, 352

Quinn, Naomi, 53, 341n. 17

Reshevsky, Samuel, 113–14
Rivers, William, 22, 23, 24, 25
Rogoff, Barbara, 237
Rosch, Eleanor, 64, 335, 355
Rosenblatt, Frank, 346
Rousseau, Jean-Jacques, 98n. 15, 138
Rozin, Paul, 204n. 13
Rumelhart, David, 347, 348
Ruth, Babe, 87

Sahlins, Marshall, 133, 273
Sapir, Edward, 36, 57, 161n. 4, 373n. 8
Saussure, Ferdinand de, 36, 137, 138, 317, 329–32, 339, 340–41n. 10, 357, 360
Schank, Roger, 43, 48, 52
Schechner, Richard, 92

Schieffelin, Bambi, 237
Schneider, David M., 32, 36, 54
Schutz, Alfred, 157
Scott, Robert, 99n. 27
Shapiro, Warren, 232n. 2, 234n. 24
Showalter, Buck, 102
Shweder, Richard A., 35–39
Slusher, Howard, 104
Smoke, K. L., 336
Socrates, 326, 327
Spalding, Albert, 80, 86
Spencer, Herbert, 18
Sperber, Dan, 31, 184–85n. 4
Stanley, Mike, 102
Stanner, W. E. H., 217
Sternberg, R. J., 352–53
Stevens, Wallace, 380–82
Stevenson, Robert Louis, 294
Stocking, George W., 15, 18
Strauss, Claudia, 52, 69n. 3
Sturdevant, William, 54

Talmy, Leonard, 58
Tambiah, Stanley J., 186n. 13
Toffler, Alvin, 159, 160
Tolman, E. C., 265
Trubetzkoy, N. S., 137
Turner, Terence, 186n. 14

Turner, Victor, 36, 52, 54, 70n. 13, 106,
   180, 254–56
Twitchell, James B., 160
Tylor, Edward, 18, 36

Veeck, Bill, 81, 98n. 9
Vygotsky, Lev Semenovich, 75, 202, 237,
   314

Wagner, Roy, 286
Walens, Stanley, 191–92, 193, 196, 203n. 6
Warner, W. Lloyd, 210, 212, 213, 224,
   231n. 2, 233nn. 10, 11, 14, 22, 234n.
   25, 239, 247
Watson, James, 130
Wayland, Francis, 126–27
Welke, Tim, 102
Wendt, Albert, 295
Werner, Heinz, 36, 199, 201, 360, 361–62,
   365, 371, 373n. 10
Whorf, Benjamin L., 36, 58, 373n. 8
Wikan, Unni, 49
Wilden, Anthony, 275, 277
Williams, Nancy, 221
Wilson, Robert Anton, 145–46
Wittgenstein, Ludwig, 321
Wolfe, Tom, 80
Wundt, Wilhelm, 173

Subject Index

Aborigines. *See* Australian aborigines
Abortion, 304
Action sets, 60
Actors' model, 54–56, 275
Adaptations, cultural, 380
Adoption, 289–90, 302
Age-grading ceremonies, 236–60, 314–15
  examples of, 238–47
  learning and memory in, 258–60
  novice's viewpoint of, 248–49
  ritual disclosure in, 249–53
  ritual transformation in, 247–48
  symbols in, 254–56, 345
Aggression, 194
Air travel, 147–48, 162n. 12
Alcohol consumption, 300
Algorithmic conception, 325
Alien series (films), 158
Alofa concepts, 301–2
Amazon tribes, 24
Ambivalence, 284–306
  case studies about, 287–95
  contrasting values and, 286–87
  ethical relativism and, 285–86
  relativity and, 285
Analog coding, 152–54, 155, 162n. 17, 275, 320–22
Analogical schematization, 357, 359–60, 362–66, 370, 371–72
Analogical transfer, 343–72
  analog processing vs. analog formation, 351–52

  as analytical thinking, 352
  connectionism/PDP models and, 345–48
  embodiment and, 361–62
  instituted models and, 359–60
  levels of, 343–45, 365–66
  microanalogy and, 356–57
  as nonanalytical perception, 354–56
  pattern recognition and, 348–49
  relevance of connectionism for, 349–51
  schema induction for, 353–54
  schematization of, 70, 357, 362–65, 371–72
  Sternberg's model of, 352–53
  symbol formation and, 360–61
  synesthesia and, 357–58, 359
Analogy formation, 345–56, 365–66
Analytic models, 70n. 15, 317, 325, 372n. 5
Animals
  brain growth compared with human, 3
  as crests, 189, 197–99
  as food, 198–99
  names used by humans, 193, 204n. 12
  regenerative cycles of totemic, 197–99
  relationship with humans, 190–91, 192, 193, 204n. 12
  skins used for marriage exchange, 197
  symbolism of, 186nn. 10, 13, 193
  totemic symbols of, 172, 179, 188–202, 212, 203n. 6
Anomalies, narrative, 226–27
Anthropology, 325
  cognitive, 35, 55–56

Anthropology (*continued*)
   concepts about culture, 44
   cultural imagination lacking in, 55
   false dichotomy in, 37–38
   interpretive, 32
   structuralism in, 137
   study of, 7, 8, 9, 17
   symbol formation needs, 316
   Victorian, 17, 18–19, 20
   See also Cultural anthropology
Arbitrariness, 38, 331
Area maps, 61
Arnhem Land, Australia, 209
Asexual reproduction, 196
Asymmetry
   in baseball, 76–77
   in exchange and power, 273
Atomism, 138, 152
   social, 132–34
Australian aborigines
   dreamtime schema of, 54, 107, 144, 207–31
   kin relations of, 63
   totemism and, 208
   walkabout journey of, 84
   See also Dreamtime learning; *specific groups*

Bad speaking, 280–81, 287–88
Baktaman people, 248
Bali
   cockfight as social templates in, 75
   conventional vs. personal model in, 49
   music in, 62
   outside-in culture, 236
Baltimore Orioles, 108
Baseball, 75–97, 312–13
   batter position, 82–83
   commmunitarian vs. individualistic values in, 76
   as cultural performance, 76
   differing views of, 93–96
   emotion model, 97*n*. 4
   fans of, 86–87, 108
   field as social space, 277
   fielder position, 98*n*. 13
   fixed beginnings of, 79–80
   foundational schema in, 368
   free agency in, 100*n*. 30
   game fixing in, 100*n*. 28
   grandstand fielding in, 102–3
   home run in, 87–88

mental aspects of, 78–79
metaphors, 97*n*. 4
metaphors for love and marriage, 88–89, 101–2, 116
normative liminality in, 107–8
origins of, 97*n*. 4
as reality frame, 90–93
rules in, 86–87
as social relations model, 88–89
statistics in, 84–85
umpire position, 86, 100*n*. 27
as walkabout, 84
Baseball space, 54, 80–82, 108
Baseball time, 77–79, 80, 108
Baseball trading cards, 85
Basketball, 112
Behavioral norms, 271
Behavior levels, 366
Bill of Rights, U.S., 133
Biographical models, 62
Biology, study of, 51
Birth imagery, 196
Black Sox scandal (1919), 100*n*. 28
Bladerunner (film), 158
Blood symbolism, 219–21, 224, 233*nn*. 20, 21, 234*n*. 25
Body. *See* Embodiment
Bororo people, 175, 186*n*. 14
Brain
   as central information processor, 7, 36–39, 46
   cultured, 5
   dependence on patterning and activation, 34
   flexibility of, 16–17
   human compared with animal, 3
   mind vs., 312
   as model generator, 46
   organized experience and, 31
   psychic unity and, 16–18, 34
   uniformity of vs. pluralistic culture, 37
   weight at birth, 3
   See also Eco-logical brain
Bricolage, 30, 175
British psychic unity theories, 22–24
Brother-sister relationships
   Hawaiian chiefs, 186*n*. 10
   Samoan, 186*n*. 10, 291–92, 302

Calculating rationality, 169
Calligraphy, 140
Capital punishment, 304

Carpentered environment, 4, 22
Car racing, 112
Caste relations, 187n. 15
Category models, 275–76
Causal models, 322–23, 341n. 11
Causal reason, 169
Center-periphery model, 45, 53, 54, 270–72, 275
Chain stores, 121
Cheating, 113–14
Checklists, 63, 66
Cheering, sports, 99n. 22
Chess, 113–14
Chicago White Sox, 100n. 28
Children
    adoption or fosterage of, 289–90, 302
    baseball card trading by, 85
    cognitive development of, 237
    corporal punishment of, 300
    cross-modal perception in infants, 358
    parental affection withdrawal effects on, 289–90, 301, 306–7nn. 13, 14
    speech of, 71n. 19
    as spirits, 220
    t-ball and, 104
China, written language in, 140
Chirographic culture, 140
Christ reenactments, 92
Chrysanthemum and the Sword, The (Benedict), 306n. 3
Cincinnati Reds, 80
Circumcision rites, 238, 239, 250
Clan
    names, 189
    totem, 185n. 7
Classification
    of animal symbols, 193
    categories of, 335, 342nn. 19, 20
    in logic, 25, 175
    models of, 64
Clockwork Orange, A (film), 158
Cloud symbolism, 225
Cockfight, 75
Coding. See Analog coding; Digital coding
Cognative romanticism, 35–36
Cognition, 339, 340n. 9, 341n. 17
    cultural diversity and, 379–80
    technology and, 156–58
Cognitive models, 338. See also Idealized cognitive models
Cognitive psychology, 4, 10–11, 49
Collective effervescence, 110

Collective representations, 25, 27
Color symbolism, 60
Comedy skits (Samoan), 296–99
Comiskey Park (Chicago), 81
Communicative rationality, 170
Communitas model, 133
Componential analysis. See Ethnoscience
Component models, 322–23
Computers
    software design, 155–56, 162–63n. 19
    for telephone answering, 139
    virtual reality and, 144–48
    for word processing, 141–43
Concentric dualism, 273
Concept formation, 328–40
    analogical transfer and, 343
    analytical models of, 335–36
    experiential realism and, 332–34
    imagery debate and, 336–38
    nonanalytical, 336
    realist/nominalist approaches, 328–32
Conception stages (Murngin), 220
Conceptual models, 64–65
Concrete logic, 175–77
Conflict-resolution strategies, 52
Connectionism, 345–48, 349–51, 370
Conscious reason, 169
Constitution, U.S., 132, 133
Constitutive rules, 103, 105
Constraint, cultural, 39, 41n. 9
Contemplative reason, 169
Context-framing devices, 62
Context markers, 62
Contextual motivation, 332
Contextual rationality, 170
Conventionality, 38
Conventional models, 46–50, 52
Conventional motivation, 332
Cook Islands, 300
Corporal punishment, 300
Corporate modules, 123
Creation, naming as, 173–74
Creation myths
    as externalization, 217–19
    as killing, 221–24
    Kwakiutl, 195–96
    Murngin, 209–31
    as origin of individual's world consciousness, 229
Crests, 189, 197–99
Cross-cultural psychology, 20
Cross-modal perception, 358

Cultural adaptations, 380
Cultural anthropology, 4–5, 15–16, 17, 49
Cultural constraint, 39, 41n. 9
Cultural diversity, 379–80
Cultural models, 6, 10, 44–45, 69n. 10, 312
  ambivalence of, 284–306
  baseball as, 88–89
  case studies, 289–95
  connectionism and, 349–51
  contrastive, 306n. 3
  definitions of, 45–46
  distribution of, 313
  functional distinctions, 61–67
  general representations, 49, 51
  genres, 56–60
  personal model compared with, 46–50,
    379–80
  role of, 277
  television as source for, 160
  See also specific types, e.g., Mental
    models
Cultural psychology, 35–39
Cultural relativism, 36. See also Ethical
  relativism
Cultural symbols, 41n. 9, 51
Cultural templates, 32, 45, 51
Culture
  analogical transfer and, 343–72
  biology compared with, 51
  cognitive theory of, 35, 50
  difficulty defining, 42–43, 44
  diversity of, 15, 16, 17–18
  evolution as basis for, 18, 32, 33–34
  human dependence on, 33
  learning approach, 236–38
  mind contents vs. attributes of, 22
  particularism of, 32
  patterns of, 5, 10
  pluralism of vs. uniformatarian mind, 37
  relativism of, 32
  as semiotic system, 32
  twice-born character of, 379
Cuna people, 254
Cyberpunk, 158, 168, 181–82
Cyberspace, 144
Cyclical models, 62

Dale Carnegie course, 149–50
Dating behavior, baseball terms used for,
  89, 116
Death, clouds as symbol for, 225
Declaration of Independence, U.S., 132

Decolonization process, 9
Decremental models, 62
Department stores, 121–22
Diagnostic models, 63
Diametric dualism, 273
Dictionaries, 57
Diffusionism, 23–24
Digital coding, 152–56, 158, 162n. 17, 274,
  275
Disemia, 283n. 3
Distinctive feature, 342n. 19
Distributed networks, 347
Diversity. See Cultural diversity
Divinity models, 63
Djunggun ceremonies, 238–41, 249–50
Djunkgao sisters' myth, 212, 213, 233n. 19,
  379. See also Wawilak sisters'
  chronicle
DNA model, 130
Dramatic models, 65
Dreamtime concept, 54, 107, 144
Dreamtime learning (inside-out), 207–31
  distributive cultural knowledge and, 209
  epistemology of, 211–13
  Murngin overview and, 209–11
  religious knowledge and, 211
  totemism in, 207–8
  Wawilak myth and, 213–31
Dreamtime learning (outside-in), 236–60
  archtypes in, 247–48
  ceremonies for, 238–47
  culture-as-learning approach, 236–38
  memory and, 258–60
  myth and ritual in, 254
  novice's viewpoint and, 248–49
  ritual disclosure in, 249–53
  symbols in, 254–58
Drive-by shootings, 147
Drugs, theraputic, 150
Dualism
  Murngin, 187n. 16
  Samoan, 281–83, 292
  structuralist interpretations of spatial, 273

Eco-logical brain, 3, 4, 34
Ecological psychology, 4
Education
  experiments, 128–30
  reform, 126–28, 134–35n. 4
Egocentric cognitive models, 276
Egocentric maps, 266
Elevator behavior, 52

Elementargedanke, 20
Embodiment, 361–62
Emotion models, 60, 63
  in baseball, 97*n*. 4
  of Samoans, 5
Empathic engagement, 78, 109–10
Empirical motivation, 200–201, 314, 330, 332
Empirical rationality, 170
Enlightenment, 18, 33, 36
Epistemogensis, 315
Eskimo studies, 19
Espisodic memory, 258–59
Essentialist language, 83
Eternal return, 228
Ethical relativism, 285–86, 302–6
Ethics, 286
Ethnicity, race vs., 21
Ethnographic mind, 10, 37, 75, 76, 379, 380
Ethnopsychology, 65, 316–17, 340*n*. 1
Ethnoscience, 35, 316–17
Ethos, 306*nn*. 3, 5
Etiquette, 43, 45
Event exemplars, 65
Evolution
  anthropological romanticism and, 24–25
  anti-hierarchical views and, 20, 31
  as basis for culture, 18, 32, 33–34
  of brain, 34
  critical point theory of, 33
  cultural differences as stages of, 18
  culture's effect on, 4
  in sense perception, 21
Exchange, restricted and generalized, 273
Exemplar models, 64–65
Experiential domains, 69*n*. 2
Experiential realism, 317, 332–34, 339
Explanatory understanding, 319
Expressive models, 64–65

Face recognition, 157
Fairy tale, 303
Fale aitu skit, 296–99
Family resemblance, 171
Fandom, 86–87, 108
Fast food, 122
Fax view, 52
Federalist Papers, The, 132
Female power and pollution, 234*n*. 25
Fertility rituals, 203*n*. 6, 239
Fielders, baseball, 98*n*. 13

Field of Dreams (film), 84
Filial piety case, 287–89
Folk taxonomies, 57
Folk theories, 65
Forms, general, 44–45. *See also* Schemas
Fosterage, 290
Foundational schema, 45, 53–54, 69–70*n*. 12, 116–34
  for analogical transfer, 366, 368
  corporate modules as, 123
  educational reform and experiments as, 126–30
  furniture and housing as, 118–20
  hamburger technology as, 122
  modularization origins and, 130–32
  in Murngin myths, 222–23
  shopping malls as, 120–22
  social atomism and, 132–34
  television as, 123–26
  as template, 117–18
Frame violations, 112–13
Frankenstein (Shelley), 159
Free agency, 100*n*. 30
French anthropological romanticism, 24–26
Frog symbolism, 203*n*. 6
Functional rationality, 169–70
Funerary rites, 220–21

Game fixing, 100*n*. 28
Games
  empathic engagement in, 109–10
  as ludic model, 75–76, 90
  rituals and, 89–90, 91
  See also specific games, e.g., Baseball
Game space, 104–5
Game time, 105
Generalized exchange, 273
German idealistic worldview, 146
Gestalts, 156, 306*n*. 3
Gestural models, 47
Golf, 103, 106
Good speaking, 280–81, 287–88
Graded coding, 274
Grammatical models, 57–58
Grandstand fielding, 102–3
Great Books curriculum, 127
Greek identity symbols, 283*nn*. 3, 6
Gulf War, 146–47
Gunabibi ceremonies, 239, 241–43, 249–50
Guttenburg revolution, 140–41

Habit memory, 258
Hamburgers, 122

Handwriting, 140–41
Hawaiian chiefs, brother-sister marriages by, 186n. 10
Hierarchical society, 280, 282, 292, 294, 295, 301–2
Hierarchical solidarity, 133
Hockey, 111–12
Home run, baseball, 87–88
Huichol Indians, 107
Human nature, 33, 379. See also Psychic diversity
Humor, 292, 296
Hunting symbolism, 194
Hypermedia, 143
Hypertext, 142–43

ICMs. See Idealized cognitive models
Iconicity, 373n. 11
Iconic signs, 200
Iconographic models, 60, 63
Idealized cognitive models (ICMs), 333–34, 341n. 15
Idiographic writing, 200
Idiosyncratic models, 46
Idiot savant, 318–19
Imagery representation, 336–38
Image schemas, 59
Imagination, 380–82
Impression management, 132, 149
Incest
  brother-sister marriages, 186n. 10
  prohibitions, 291, 302
Incremental models, 62
Indexical relations, 59
Indexical signs, 200
India, Varna system of social roles in, 63
Industrial modularization, 134
Infants. See Children
Information processing, 157, 275, 317, 318–20, 321, 346
Initiation rites, 48, 212, 236–60. See also Age-grading ceremonies
Inning time, 77
Inside knowledge, 217–18, 224–26, 252–53
Inside-outside model, 54, 203n. 5, 250. See also Dreamtime learning
Instituted models, 50–52, 236, 312, 314, 337–38, 344
  analogical schematization and, 359–60, 366, 372
  See also Templates
Intellectual property, 154

Intentionality, 349
Intention displays, 64
Interactive fiction, 143
Interpersonal space, 61–62
Interpretant, 361
Invitation script, 44, 45
Irony, 292
Irrationality, 29–30

Jajmani system, 63
Japan, 99n. 23, 140
Java, 62

Kaluli people (New Guinea), 60
Kava ceremonies, 44
Kinesthetic image-schema, 274, 275, 333
Kinesthetic models, 66–67
Kinesthetic schemas, 59–60
Kin relations, 63
Kinship structures, 195–96
Knockoffs, 154–56
Knowledge
  baseball as, 102
  cultural, 11, 44, 209
  inside, 217–18
  inside to outside, 224–26
  modularity of, 130
  outside, 224–26, 252–53
  personal, 10–11
  regeneration and, 238
  religious, 211
  transformation of, 229–30, 315
Kwakiutl people, 174, 314
  animal symbolism of, 188–202, 203n. 6
  belief in regenerative totems, 197–98
  Hamatsa dance of, 363
  kinship structures in, 195–96
  seasonal symbolism of, 191–93

Laban Notation, 66
Laindjung story, 212
Landscape, as metaphor, 265
Language
  basic unit of, 40n. 1
  conversational templates, 57
  culture-specific, 277
  essentialist, 83
  ethical relativism and, 287–88
  hierarchical, 280–81, 287–88
  learning as socialization, 237
  models of, 56–59, 62, 63, 66, 67, 71n. 19, 136–39, 334

modular, 136–39
multivocality of, 261*n*. 8
oral traditions, 139–40, 193–95
polysynthetic, 161*n*. 4
ritual, 224
of social life, 83
symbols and signs of, 200, 329, 332
vocabulary, 57, 277
written, 67, 139–41, 200
Lexical models, 57, 62, 66
Lifestyles, 148–50, 160
Liminality, 106–9
Linguistics. *See* Language
Lists, as lexical model, 57
Logic, classificatory, 25, 175
Logical meaning, 318
Logical rationality, 169, 313, 317
Love, baseball terms used for, 88–89, 101–
2, 116
Ludic models, 65, 75–76, 90

Mac (as verbal icon), 134*n*. 2
Machine models, 322–26
Magic, 313
Maori women, 234*n*. 25
Maps, 46, 47, 61, 265–66, 268–70, 276–
77, 279–80. *See also* Analogical
schematization
*Margaret Mead and Samoa: The Making
and Unmaking of An Anthropological
Myth* (Freeman), 306*n*. 5
Marginal play, 103, 106–7, 109–10, 112–
13
Marndiella ceremonies, 238
Marriage
animal symbolism in, 197
asymmetries in, 273
baseball terms used for, 88–89, 116
brother-sister, 186*n*. 10
cultural model for, 53
Murngin cultural model of, 368
role in continuity of life, 251
Marxist view of baseball, 99*n*. 21
Mass reproduction, 121
McDonald's Corporation, 122, 134*n*. 2
Meaning, 311–40, 340*n*. 3, 349
case studies in, 311–15, 374–79
concept formation and, 328–40
from ethnoscience to ethnopsychology,
316–17
information vs., 275, 318–20
logical and psychological, 318

mimetic representation and analogic
processing, 320–22
Meaning construction, 52, 157, 158, 315–
16, 319, 378–79
analogical mapping used for, 356–57
human imagination and, 380–82
as remembering, 326–28
Mechanical solidarity, 25
Medical diagnostic models, 63
Melanesia, 22–23
Memory
cognitive schemas and, 45
dreamtime learning and, 258–60
meaning construction as, 326–28
Meno's paradox, 326–28, 340*n*. 3
Menstruation, 233*nn*. 20, 21, 234*n*. 25
Mental baseball, 78–79
Mentality
differences based on social milieu, 27
endowment vs. characteristics, 20–21, 22
primitive, 21, 27–28, 30, 380
racial variation in, 20–21
unitary nature of, 31
Mental maps, 46, 47, 265–66, 279–80
Mental models
general representations, 49
instituted vs., 51–52, 312, 314, 337–38
personal vs. conventional, 46–50, 52
of simple machines, 322–26
variability of, 48
Mental representations, 47
Mental states, 349
Metamodels, 160
Metaphor-metonym scale, 201–2
Metaphor models, 59, 63
in baseball, 88–89, 97*n*. 4, 101–2, 116
Metaphors We Live By (Lakoff and
Johnson), 332, 333
Meteorological models, 63
Metonymic signs, 200, 204*n*. 12
Metonymic totemism, 173
Metonym-metaphor scale, 201–2
Metonym models, 59, 358
Microanalogy, 356–57
Micronesia, 279
Microsoft Windows program, 143
Mimetic models, 66, 320–22
Mind, 312, 313, 335
ethnographic, 10, 37, 75, 76, 379, 380
Wallace Stevens's poetic vision of, 380–
82
See also Brain; Mentality

Models, cultural. *See* Cultural models; Scripts, cultural
Models, kinesthetic, 66–67
Models, linguistic. *See* Language, models of
Models, ludic, 65, 76–76, 90
Models, mental. *See* Mental models
Models, trope. *See* Tropes
Modernity myths, 118
Modularity
  in furniture, 118–19
  in language, 136–39
  organizational features, 151
  orientation, 129
  origins, 130–32
  schema, 54, 117–18, 167
  of self, 148–49
  technology and, 139, 151
  of word processing text, 141
Moiety system, 232*n*. 6
Mortuary rites, 220–21
Motivation
  empirical, 200–201, 314, 330, 332
  psychic unity of, 23
  psychogenic, 200–201, 203–4*n*. 10, 314, 332
  symbolic, 41*n*. 9, 199–202, 203*nn*. 6, 9, 314
Movies, 3D, 145
MTV videos, 160
Müller-Lyer illusion, 22
Multiculturalism, 379–80
Multivocality, 259, 261*n*. 8
Murder. *See* Violence
Murngin people, 209–31, 314
  age-grading rites of, 236–60, 345
  Baktaman people compared with, 248
  cosmology of, 250
  duality concepts of, 187*n*. 16
  epistemology of, 211–13
  inside-outside schema of, 54, 203*n*. 5, 250
  knowledge transformation by, 229–30
  marriage models of, 368
  name origins, 231*n*. 2
  naming as creation act in, 173
  power transfer from women to men by, 327–28
  religious knowledge of, 211
  sacred as separate refuted by, 222
  symbolism of, 255–56
  walkabout schema of, 62, 318, 368

  See also Dreamtime learning; Wawilak sister's chronicle
Music, 50–51, 62
Mysticism, 180
Myth, 238, 254, 303
Mythical thought, 30

Names and naming
  animal used for human, 193, 204*n*. 12
  for asserting ownership, 221
  clan, 189
  as creation act, 173–74
  lists, 57
  personal, 62
Narrative, 58–59, 211–12, 379
  anomalies, 226–29
  exemplars, 65
  oral traditions, 139–40, 193–95
  See also Myth; *specific stories*
Naturalistic theories, 138, 331–32
Navigational models, 61, 278–80
Neoteny, 3
Nervous system, 3, 4, 38
Network architecture, 372*n*. 2
Neural networks, 17, 343
Neurological mappings, 339
Neuromancer (Gibson), 161*n*. 9, 181
Neuromantic mind, 143–44
New York Knickerbockers, 81
New York Yankees, 102
Noetic field, 140
Nominalism, 317, 328–32
Nonanalytical approach, 317
Nonlinguistic models, 59–60
Nonverbal recipes, 66
Nostalgia, 97*n*. 6
Nuer people, 63
Numayma, 189, 193, 195, 197, 203*n*. 1

Oakland A's, 96–97
Object exemplars, 64
Objectivism, 266, 340*n*. 9
Object-oriented programming, 162*n*. 19
Observers' model, 54–56
Olfactory models, 275
Onomatopoeia, 57, 329, 333
Ontological atomism, 152
Open society, 295
Oral traditions, 139–40, 193–95
Organic solidarity, 25
Orientational models, 61–64
Oriole Park (Baltimore), 108

Outside-in model. *See* Dreamtime learning
Outside knowledge, 224–26, 252–53

Pain, 91–92
Pain symbolism, 91
Papua New Guinea, 22–23, 63
Parallel distributed processing (PDP), 339,
    345–48, 359, 370
Participation, law of, 26–29
Pattern, 45, 338
Pattern recognition, 345–46, 348–49
Patterns of Culture (Benedict), 306n. 3
Peace Corps, 42–43, 280–81
Perception, 4, 273–77
    analogy formation and, 354–56
    basic-level, 334
    cross-modal, 358
    See also Visual perception
Perceptual skills, 4
Performance genres, 52, 137. *See also*
    Ritual performance
Persian Gulf War, 146–47
Personality, 148–49
Personal models, 46–50
Personal names. *See* Names and naming
Person exemplars, 64–65
Persuasion models, 66–67
Philippines, 92
Phoneme, 40n. 1, 138, 329–30
Phonesthemes, 57
Phonological speech registers, 57
Physiognomic, 361
Pictorial recipes, 66
Pinocchio (Collodi), 182
Plastic, 119–20
Play frame, 90–91, 92
Politically aware language, 139
Political satire, 296–99
Politics, 9, 132, 306n. 11
    Samoan, 292–96
Polynesians
    flexibility in social arrangements, 290
    gender concepts of, 186n. 10
    navigational strategies of, 279
    visual models of, 60
Polytropes, 314
Power
    asymmetries in, 273
    female, 234n. 25
    Samoan politics and, 292–95
Prague school (linguistics), 137–38
Praxis theory, 92

Prelogical thought, 27, 28
Primary code, 341n. 14
Primitive classification, 25
Primitivism, 25, 26, 168, 175–77
    mentality, 21, 27–28, 30, 380
    totemism and, 178–81
Procedural memory, 258–59
Procedural rules, 103, 105
Programmability, 153
Propositional models, 57, 70nn. 14, 15,
    333, 337
Prototype effects, 64
Prototype theory, 26
Proximal development, 237
Psychic diversity, 7, 312, 379
Psychic unity, 5, 6–7, 16, 168, 311–12
    ambivalence about, 29, 30–31
    British studies, 22–24
    early ideas about, 18–19, 21, 22
    Enlightenment view vs. romantic
        rebellion, 36
    human brain and, 16–18, 34
    of motivation, 23
    mythical thought vs., 30
    reconciled with psychic diversity, 379,
        380
    See also Rationality
Psychocultural process, 316
Psychogenic motivation, 200–201, 203–4n.
    10, 314, 332
Psychological meaning, 317, 318, 330,
    338–39
Psychologism, 50
Psychologizing, 34
Psychology
    cross-cultural, 20
    cultural, 35–39
    of meaning, 317, 318
    of Samoan ambivalence, 299–302
    sociology distinguished from, 26
Public models. *See* Instituted models

Race, vs. ethnicity, 21
Racial groups, 20–21, 23
Radburn development (Fairlawn, N.J.),
    119–20
Rainman (film), 121
Rain symbolism, 225
Rapid fading, 140
Rapid-fire visual change, 160
Rationality, 167–84, 313
    as romance, 24–26

Rationality (*continued*)
  romance vs., 29
  of savage mind, 29–32
  types of, 30, 169–70
Reality, 90–93, 317, 328–29. *See also*
    Experiential realism
Recipe models, 66
Recombination, 130, 138, 259
Regeneration, 197–99, 238
Relativism, 36. *See also* Ethical relativism
Religion
  knowledge of, 211
  mysticism in, 180
  totem as symbol of, 174, 178–81
Remembering. *See* Memory
Restaurant scripts, 48, 52, 66
Restricted exchange, 273
Rhetoric. *See* Language
Rhythmic models, 62
Rites of passage, 47–48. *See also* Age-
    grading ceremonies
Ritual, 63
  models for, 65
  myth and, 238, 254
  as reality frame, 91
  social coordination in, 90
  symbols in, 254–58, 261*n*. 7
  See also specific rituals, e.g., Games
Ritual acting, 257
Ritualized play, 92
Ritual language, 224
Ritual performance, 60, 76, 89–90
Robocop (film), 158
Role-playing, 83
Romanticism
  cognitive, 35–36
  rationality as, 24–26
  rationality vs., 29
Route maps, 61
Rules, 103, 105–6
Rutgers University, 127

Sacred relations, 192
Sacred scripts, 66
St. John's College (Annapolis and Santa
    Fe), 127
St. Louis Browns, 81
Samoa, 5–7, 265–306
  alcohol consumption in, 300
  center-periphery schema in, 53, 54, 270–
    72
  cultural models in, 44, 47

  dualism in, 281–83, 292
  empirical correlates in, 272–73
  etiquette as cultural script in, 43, 45
  explorers' contacts in, 267–68
  kava ceremonies in, 44
  language forms in, 280–81, 287–88
  and making meaning out of chaos, 374–
    79
  Peace Corps training in, 42–43
  perceptual issues in, 273–74
  political satire, 296–99
  politics, 292–96
  spatial models in, 56, 265–83, 337
  symbolic maps of, 268–70
San Francisco earthquake (1989), 96–97
San Francisco Giants, 96–97
Sarah Lawrence College, 128
Satiric skits (Samoan), 296–99
Savage mind, 29–32, 54
Savage Mind, The (Levi-Strauss), 175
Schema
  for analogical transfer, 353–54, 362–65
  center-periphery, 53
  cognitive, 45
  defined, 44–45
  image, 53
  for modularity, 54, 117–18, 167
  related phenomena, 344
  television as model for, 160
  See also specific types, e.g., Foundational
    schema
Schema theory, 44–45
Schematization, 47, 344, 362–65, 366–71
Scholarly theories, 65
Science, primitive/modern split, 30
Scientific theories, 65
Scripts, cultural, 43, 52, 57, 66. *See also*
    specific types, e.g., Invitation script
Seal and Sparrow societies, 193
Seasons, 191–93
Self-help programs, 149–50
Semantic memory, 259
Semen symbolism, 219
Semiosis, 117, 231, 379
Semiosphere, 267
Semiotics, 32, 199, 341*n*. 14
Sense perception, evolution of, 21
Sensory experiments, 22
Sensory modalities, 67, 275–76
Sexual relations
  conventional vs. personal model, 49
  male-female distinction and, 180

as Murngin conception stage, 220
oral imagery of, 193–95
in Samoa, 282
symbolism of, 186*n*. 10, 195–96
Shared resources, 50
Shell programs, 143
Shopping malls, 120–22, 277
Signs, 199–200, 331–32
Simulacra, 154, 155
Sister-brother relationship. *See* Brother-sister
relationship
Sisters' myth. *See* Wawilak sisters' chronicle
Skinheads, 111
Snake symbolism, 212–13, 224
Soccer, 110–12
Social atomism, 132–34
Social coordination, 63
Social distinctions, 25–26
Social engineering, 132
Social environment, 49–50
Socialization, 237
Social mind, 26
Social orientation models, 62–63
Social relations, 88–89
Social role sets, 63
Societas model, 133
Sociocentric cognitive models, 276
Sociocentric maps, 266
Sociocultural environments, 4
Sociology, 26
Software design, 155–56, 162–63*n*. 19
Sound
cyclical model, 62
image model, 60
symbolic model, 57, 357, 373*n*. 8
See also Music
Source code, 155
Spatial models, 56, 61–62, 265–83, 283*n*. 4
center-periphery, 270–72
digital/graded codings, 274
dualism of, 273, 281–83
empirical correlates, 272–73
language and, 280–81
navigational strategies and, 278–80
neuropsychology of, 276–77
representation paradoxes, 277–78
rhetorical and perceptual issues, 273–74
of Samoan geography, 268–70, 337
sensory modalities and, 275–76
structuralist interpretations of, 273
Speech. *See* Language
Spirit children, 220

Spirit possession, 290–92
Sports, 101–15
cheating in, 113–14
cheering in, 99*n*. 22
liminality in, 106–9
as ludic model, 75–76
rules in, 103, 105–6
time and space in, 104–5
See also specific sports, e.g., Baseball
Sri Lanka, 49
Statistics, baseball, 84–85
Status system, 292, 295
Storytelling. *See* Narrative
Strategy, 103, 105–6
Structuralism, 32, 56, 92, 273
Structural parallelism, 370
Supplementary code, 341*n*. 14
Surface talk, 137
Swallowing symbolism, 195
Symbol formation, 316, 360–61
Symbolic maps, 268–70, 276
Symbolic motivation, 314, 357
Symbolic space, 267
Symbolic transformation, 219
Symbols
bipolarity of, 256
cultural, 41*n*. 9, 51
emergence of, 224–26
natural, 201
psychological effectiveness of, 254–56
ritual, 254–58, 261*n*. 7
totemic, 171–73, 313–14
Synesthesia, 357–58, 359
Syntax, 138

Tahiti, 290, 300
Task models, 65–67
Taxonomies, 57, 175–76, 200
Technology, 136–61
analog and digital coding, 152–56, 158,
162*n*. 17, 274, 275, 320–22
cognitive consequences of, 156–58
cyberpunk and, 158, 168, 181–82
Greek meaning of, 163*n*. 22
knockoffs as reality, 154–56
language and, 136–38
lifestyle affected by, 148–50
modular aspects of, 139, 151
neuromantic mind and, 143–44
totemic imagery and, 159–61, 181–84
virtual reality and, 144–48, 162*n*. 12
word processing and, 141–43, 161*n*.6

Technology (*continued*)
  writing systems and, 139–41
Techno-totemism, 159–61, 313
Telephones, 139
Television, 123–26, 160
Templates
  conversational, 57
  cultural, 32, 45, 51
  foundational, 117–18
  social, 75
  See also Instituted models
Temporal models, 62
Ten Commandments, 57
Tennis, 112–13
Terminator, The (film), 158
Texts, cultural, 34
Thailand, 49, 186*n*. 13
Theories, 65
3D movies, 145
Time management, 153
Toronto Blue Jays, 102
Torres Strait expedition, 22–23
Totalitarian ambition, 30
Totemic complex, 186*n*. 9
Totemism
  ambiguities of, 201
  analogy formulas, 176–77
  animal classification through oral
    characteristics, 194
  Australian, 208, 212–13
  as center of primitive religion, 178–81
  clan and, 185*n*. 7
  demystification of, 174–75
  identification of, 24
  illusion of, 207–8
  Kwakiutl, 188–202
  naming and, 173–74, 193
  rationality debate and, 167–84, 313
  regenerative animals, 197–98
  religious symbolism of, 174, 178–81
  symbolic motivation and, 199–202
  symbols of, 171–73, 313–14
  technology combined with, 159–61, 181–84
Totemism (Levi-Strauss), 174, 175
Transitional associations, 252
Tropes, 35, 59, 333
Twin symbolism, 255

Ulmark ceremonies, 239, 243–47, 249–50
Umpire, baseball, 86, 100*n*. 27

University of California (Santa Cruz), 128
University of Chicago, 127

Values, 286, 287–95, 302
Varna system, 63
Vengeance, 376
Verbal models, 58, 63, 67. *See also*
  Language
Victorian anthropology, 17, 18–19, 20
Violence
  Samoan, 287–89, 306*n*. 5, 375–78
  in soccer, 110–12
  virtual, 146–47
Virtual cultural models, 160
Virtual reality, 144–48, 162*n*. 12
Virtue, 326–28
Visual perception
  ability types, 3–4
  image models, 60, 67
  in infants, 358
  studies, 22
  television effects on, 160
Vocabulary
  culture-specific, 277
  subsets as lexical models, 57
Völksgedanke, 20

Walkabout schema, 84, 222–23, 235*n*. 31,
  258–60, 314–15, 318
War Games (film), 146
Water symbolism, 219
Wave motion, 77–78
Wawilak sisters' chronicle, 212, 213–17,
  233*n*. 19, 379
  blood bonds in, 219–20
  ceremonies in, 238–47
  creation as killing in, 221–24
  as externalization, 217–19
  myth and ritual in, 238
  narrative anomalies in, 226–29
  novice's viewpoint in, 248–49
  ritual disclosure in, 249–53
  symbolism in, 224–26
  transformation of knowledge in, 229–30
Winter Ceremonies, 194–95
Women, Fire and Dangerous Things
  (Lakoff), 332–33
Word processing, 141–43, 161*n*. 6
Wrestling, 110
Written language, 139–41, 200
Written models, 67

Yolngu. *See* Murngin people